REVOLUTION IN THE HEAD

Ian MacDonald was born in 1948. A writer of many interests, he was Assistant Editor of the *New Musical Express* during 1972-5. He also worked as a songwriter and record producer, and is the author of *The New Shostakovich* (1990), *The People's Music* (2003) and *The Beatles at No.1* (2003). He died in August 2003.

Praise for *Revolution in the Head*

'A pinnacle of popular music criticism . . . In Ian MacDonald,
The Beatles at last have a critic worthy of their oeuvre'
Independent

'What a critique! And what songs! MacDonald analyses
the Fab Four's output beautifully, mixing anecdote with
serious scholarship'
Daily Telegraph

'In a dazzling piece of scholarship, MacDonald unravels
the dynamics and production tricks of The Beatles'
records and music, and shows how the group reflected
and shaped the century's most contentious decade. Best
of all, the book drives you back to the music itself with
fresh ears and understanding'
Observer

'An extraordinary book about an extraordinary pop group.
Elaborate and engrossing, *Revolution in the Head* succeeds
like very few pop culture music books do: it brings you back
to the music.'
Tribune

'After finishing it, I went out and bought a pile of Beatles CDs
and listened to them properly for the first time in my life.'
Nick Hornby

'Combines musical analysis and acute historical awareness
with jaw-dropping facility'
Nicholas Lezard, Paperback of the Week, *Guardian*

IAN MACDONALD

Revolution in the Head

The Beatles' Records and the Sixties

SECOND REVISED EDITION

VINTAGE BOOKS
London

Published by Vintage 2008

10 9

Copyright © The Estate of Ian MacDonald 1994, 1997, 2005

Ian MacDonald has asserted his right under the Copyright, Designs
and Patents Act 1988 to be identified as the author of this work

First published in Great Britain by Fourth Estate, 1994

Pimlico edition 1995

Fully updated version first published by Fourth Estate, 1997

Pimlico edition 1998

Second revised edition first published in Great Britain
by Pimlico 2005

Vintage
Random House, 20 Vauxhall Bridge Road,
London SW1V 2SA

www.vintage-books.co.uk

Addresses for companies within The Random House Group Limited
can be found at: www.randomhouse.co.uk/offices.htm

The Random House Group Limited Reg. No. 954009

A CIP catalogue record for this book
is available from the British Library

ISBN 9780099526797

The Random House Group Limited supports The Forest Stewardship
Council® (FSC®), the leading international forest-certification organisation.
Our books carrying the FSC label are printed on FSC®-certified paper.
FSC is the only forest-certification scheme supported by the leading
environmental organisations, including Greenpeace. Our
paper procurement policy can be found at
www.randomhouse.co.uk/environment

Printed and bound in Great Britain by Clays Ltd, St Ives plc

To
SHE KNOWS WHO

CONTENTS

PUBLISHERS' NOTE

Revolution in the Head was first published, in hardback, by Fourth Estate in 1994 and subsequently, in paperback, by Pimlico in 1995. Fourth Estate published a fully revised and updated edition in 1997, which appeared in Pimlico in 1998.

Before his death in August 2003, Ian MacDonald had prepared this second revised edition.

PREFACE TO THE SECOND REVISED EDITION

As the 21st century advances, no abatement of popular interest has yet occurred in The Beatles, a product of the 1960s. They always figure uniquely high in polls and voting lists, while books on every conceivable aspect of the group continue to pour out annually. This is the more remarkable in that, so far from great lyricists, they were reliant on a method of lyric-writing which, rather than aspire to through-composed verse forms in the traditional style, worked more as chains of phrases, some inspired, some hackneyed, others randomly surreal. If we were to ask average listeners what The Beatles' lyrics mean, they would likely say very little. If, on the other hand, we asked the same listeners what The Beatles mean *to them*, we would get a very different response. Attached to the most original and imaginative popular music of the last fifty years, The Beatles' lyrics enjoy a charmed existence in which their relative inconsequentiality is as nothing beside their association with joy, love, and freedom. An enormous amount is forgiven The Beatles as wordsmiths because of the sheer benignity of their idiom, its suffusion in loving feeling and (especially during the group's psychedelic years) its subversive carnivalism. Compared to the best of, say, the American singer-songwriters of the late 1960s and 1970s, the lyrics of The Beatles were wrought in a collage spirit, line by line. The group rarely thought of them as overall structures, still less as of any real emotional consequence ([86] ELEANOR RIGBY being an untypical example in The Beatles' songbook of a sustained line of thought and expression amounting to a poem). They were, in short, instinctive, rather than rational, as artists – a trait which might be ascribed to their youth and social origin, but which owes most to the fact that they were working musicians rather than composers. All the great songwriting teams to have preceded them were, in that sense, composers rather than performers.

In early 20th-century popular music, composing teams almost invariably wrote for performers. Only a handful of performers ever wrote their own material before The Beatles and Bob Dylan appeared, neither of whom set out on their careers with the explicit intention of supplying themselves with their own songs. Dylan had little idea when he started writing songs that this would become his life; similarly, The

Beatles started writing songs chiefly as a means of preventing other groups from stealing their own purloined material. They discovered that they had a powerful musical gift when Lennon and McCartney began to work 'one on one, eyeball to eyeball' in 1963. Steered by their instant harmonising, the duo's way of composing produced unusual moves that released a flood of catchy melody to which they sang dummy words or pure nonsense. Only later, generally speaking, did they fill in their lyrics – and then mainly phrasally, only bothering about overall concepts in formula terms (e.g., using the second or third person, aiming towards a sort of punch-line, and so on). Rather than tell a story in traditional Tin Pan Alley style, Lennon and McCartney wrote their lyrics to create a mood or a tone, so as not to get in the way of the effect created by the music and the sound. This bred a casual attitude to normal sense which later turned explicitly free-associational. There was always just enough sense in a Beatles lyric for the listener to get the general idea. The rest came from the sum of the parts of the record as a whole. The Beatles rarely thought long about their lyrics.

The Beatles' casual lyrics look slipshod beside the careful verses and refrains of the great composers of popular song before them. Those raised on more traditional standards will listen to late-period Beatle songs and quite legitimately ask 'but what do they mean?' To reply that they mean something more general than traditional lyrics, that they were conceived as records not songs, may or may not explain much. To those who grew up with The Beatles (and those who came after them, whose popular music is fundamentally cast in The Beatles' image), it makes sense to say that the group's lyrics work as general signifiers, the message blending into a newly charged medium rather than composing itself into a coherent whole, detachable as verse. As verse, little of The Beatles word-output coheres, except by way of mood and style. Is this a serious criticism of their work? Yes. Nevertheless, it continues to be enormously popular – and, in the general terms proposed, quite rightly so. All that can ultimately be said about this aspect of The Beatles' output is that it need not have been so; that they could have written lyrics in a more traditional style but that this would have made their songs and records very different from the way they are and, perhaps, far less alive with overall spontaneity. After all, no traditional lyricist could compose music like The Beatles. The comparative vagueness of their lyrics is the price we pay for their main inspiration: their musical originality.

This is not to say that there won't come a time when future listeners will look back on The Beatles and find them lyrically wanting, if not incomprehensible. In a century from now, the lingering aura of

The Beatles will presumably have dispersed enough for the group's work to be looked at more objectively than we are capable of doing less than fifty years after them. Perhaps then the haphazard nature of many of The Beatles' lyrics will be less easy to overlook and The Beatles' nonchalant stories of how these lyrics came to fall into place will have lost their excusing charm. Or perhaps their music will continue to preserve them in a sort of protective aspic. For the fact is that The Beatles' way of doing things changed the way things were done and, in so doing, changed the way we expect things to be done. That the future is partly a consequence of the existence of The Beatles is a measure of their importance.

Speaking of which, the most important thing to have happened in connection with The Beatles since this book was last revised in 1997 is the death of George Harrison on 29th November 2001. Of the songwriting Beatles, Harrison was the one with the most coherent belief system and the one most likely to think his lyrics through. This makes his lyrics perhaps more dogged than Lennon and McCartney's, but at least the listeners of the future have more chance of working out what he was driving at. Arguably more responsible than any other individual for popularising Oriental, and particularly Hindu, thought in the West, Harrison was a countercultural figure in his own right, albeit that his natural modesty would not have allowed him to relish the accolade. Most of his work from [105] WITHIN YOU WITHOUT YOU on *Sgt Pepper* to *Living In The Material World* (1973) is governed by assumptions taken from Indian religious philosophy, in particular the concept of *karma* whereby the soul is said to be bound by its egoistic attachments to a cycle of rebirth into existence. This makes his work more impressive as a sustained effort of mind than much of The Beatles' output. On the other hand, it is not for their intellectual content that the average listener loves and reveres The Beatles, but for their musical inspiration.

When Harrison died, a shiver must have passed through a generation which thereby felt its mortality suddenly that bit more acutely. He was 58, not a great age nowadays, but nonetheless significantly further into life than one's twenties. When the remaining two Beatles are gone, the afterglow of the group's presence in 20th-century popular culture may begin to wane. Or perhaps The Beatles changed history enough to reorder the way we regard things, so that their aura will never henceforth depart from the popular cultural scene. All we can be sure of is that something extraordinary happened in pop music during the 1960s and that the centre of it was the eight or so years of The Beatles' public career. They broke and rewrote the rules. We live partly in the consequences of the resulting renewal (or, according to bias, collapse of traditional values). The Beatles are, in a sense, us. No wonder we find it difficult to see them objectively.

This second revised edition of *Revolution In The Head* contains a number of corrected details made as a result of consulting certain books published since 1997, chief among which are *The Beatles Anthology*, Andy Babiuk's *Beatles Gear*, and Barry Miles's *Paul McCartney: Many Years From Now*. In the latter book, McCartney has a lot to say about The Beatles' records and makes a general claim about his partnership with Lennon which contradicts the impression of it left by Lennon in some of his early post-Beatles interviews. Speaking to *Rolling Stone* in 1970, Lennon described this collaboration as anything from discontinuous to non-existent for most of The Beatles' career. By contrast, McCartney stresses its continuity and professional formality, revealing that, during the run-up to recording a new album, he and Lennon would regularly convene for three-hour 'writing sessions' at the latter's house in Weybridge. In such meetings, they would deploy their new songs, finished or partly written, so that each could 'check' these, suggesting adjustments and helping with sections on which the other had got stuck, such as bridges and middle eights.

McCartney's testimony is a necessary corrective to Lennon's initial version of events, but it should be remembered that the latter revised his story in 1980, conceding that he'd earlier misrepresented the extent to which he and McCartney had co-operated in songwriting.[1] As fundamental as they are for anyone seeking to understand the Lennon–McCartney partnership, McCartney's assertions don't discredit Lennon's claim that 'one on one, eyeball to eyeball' collaborations (or start-to-finish fifty-fifty co-compositions) effectively ceased after the first year or so of their Parlophone contract. Mostly the pair worked by bringing each other songs either two-thirds done, or complete and requiring only fine tuning or the post-factum approval of the other. McCartney, though, goes further than stressing the professionalism of their partnership, claiming a degree of shared input on several songs hitherto generally accepted as solo pieces (e.g., [101] BEING FOR THE BENEFIT OF MR KITE!). The truth may never be established.[2] Each a

---

[1] Sheff and Golson, *The Playboy Interviews with John Lennon and Yoko Ono*, p. 117.
[2] McCartney rightly points out that no one but he and Lennon knew what went on in their collaborations, but this must be set against his freedom to say what he likes in Lennon's absence, and the fact that time can distort memory (as it often did in

self-sufficient writer, McCartney and Lennon saw their working relationship as one of mutually interested (and, at their happiest, mutually enthusiastic) business partners. Beginning as more or less separate writers during 1957–61 (see [23], note), they drifted back into this set-up during the last five years or so of The Beatles' career, a process marked by increasing rivalry which, by 1965, was causing studio ructions.[1] What remained basic to them was each other's input on material otherwise independently conceived and originated. This could range between general comment to additional writing amounting to fifty-fifty co-composition. However, such collaborations were rarely, if ever, comparable with the intensity of work on such early songs as [21] I Want To Hold Your Hand, in which they competed at the same piano to carry the melody or lyric on to its next section.

It is in filling out the revised picture of The Beatles conveyed by McCartney to Miles that this second revised edition differs chiefly from what went before, although there are also many other small details that have been altered as the result of newly acquired information. Apart from that, *Revolution In The Head* is much the same as it was before.

Lennon's case). In Part 7 of the *Anthology* video, McCartney, Harrison, Starr, and Martin each have different recollections of whether Lennon wrote [114] All You Need Is Love specifically for the *Our World* global TV broadcast, while there are moments in the series when each misremembers when albums were recorded or which tracks they contain. As for misrepresentation, Lennon falsely claimed to have written [161] Two Of Us, 'about 70 per cent' of the lyric of [86] Eleanor Rigby, and most of the music for [67] In My Life (Sheff and Golson, pp. 130, 172; *Hit Parader*, April 1972). While there's no evidence of anything similar on McCartney's part, he has blotted his copy-book by disingenuously professing surprise at being described as the instigator of *Magical Mystery Tour* and, according to those who know him, is generally as prone to self-justification as Lennon was (which is not to say that McCartney's revised version isn't closer to the truth).

[1] Norman Smith, the group's engineer during 1962–6, recalls that 'with *Rubber Soul* the clash between John and Paul was becoming obvious' (Salewicz, p. 117).

PREFACE TO THE FIRST REVISED EDITION

Over and above the material already published in the first edition of this book, the present volume contains extra entries, sections, paragraphs, and notes, as well as many minor changes. More significantly, it deals with a large tranche of material issued in 1994–96 in *The Beatles Live at the BBC* and the *Anthology* series, as well as the two 'reunion' singles [187] FREE AS A BIRD and [188] REAL LOVE (looked at, along with the *Anthology* project in general, in Part 4).

Speaking to Barry Miles,[1] Paul McCartney has confirmed The Beatles' creative friction with the main countercultural currents of the Sixties. Some reviewers of *Revolution in the Head* expressed reservations about what they saw as its incongruously 'intellectual' approach to certain areas of the group's discography. McCartney, whose interests have always been omnivorous, is keen to place the later work of The Beatles in precisely this 'intellectual' context, albeit mediated through the group's innately sceptical humour. The influence of the mid-to-late-Sixties English counterculture is clearer in The Beatles' music than in that of any of their rivals. This arose from a conflux of links, beginning with their introduction by Brian Epstein to the film director Richard Lester, continuing with McCartney's friendships with Miles and John Dunbar, and culminating in the meeting of Lennon and Yoko Ono. Through Lester and his associates – who included The Beatles' comedy heroes Spike Milligan and Peter Sellers – the group's consciousness around the time of *Sgt. Pepper* was permeated by the anarchic English fringe theatre, with its penchant for Empire burlesque (e.g., The Alberts, Ivor Cutler, Milligan and Antrobus's *The Bed Sitting Room*). This atmosphere mingled with contemporary strains from English Pop Art and Beat poetry; the 'happenings' and experimental drama of The People Show, Peter Brook's company, and Julian Beck's Living Theatre; the improvised performances of AMM and what later became the Scratch Orchestra; the avant-garde Euro-cinema of Fellini and Antonioni; and the satire at Peter Cook's Establishment club and in his TV show with Dudley Moore, *Not Only . . . But Also* (in which Lennon twice appeared). From the cultural watershed of 1965–6

---

[1] In *Paul McCartney: Many Years From Now* (1997).

onwards, The Beatles' American heroes of the rock-and-roll Fifties gave way to a kaleidoscopic *mélange* of local influences from the English fringe arts and the Anglo-European counterculture as well as from English folk music and music-hall.

Although something akin to this cross-cultural soup existed in San Francisco during 1965–7, it's difficult to imagine an equivalent American pop group of the period – say, The Byrds or The Lovin' Spoonful – opening themselves so hungrily to such highbrow influences. In America, a gulf of distrust exists between 'instinctual' rock and 'intellectual' art, a divide less noticeable in England where there is no equivalent of the discrete (and peripheral) category of art-rock in America. This is largely due to the English institution of art school. The art schools, of which there are specimens in every medium-to-large town throughout the country, originated from a mid-Victorian campaign to improve the languishing standards of British industrial design. Chiefly a legacy of Sir Henry Cole's Great Exhibition of 1851 – and of 'Albertopolis', the cluster of great museums in South Kensington close to the Albert Hall – the art school system proliferated across England as a parallel educational structure, becoming a home from home to the gifted but wayward and often frankly eccentric people with which English life overflows (or used to).[1] John Lennon was a classic case of the art school type: an academic misfit who could more or less draw and was otherwise consumed by a chaotic creativity in need of channelling. (In fact, he did no more serious work at Liverpool Art College than he had at Quarry Bank High School.)

The key to the English art school experience is that it was founded on talent rather than on official qualifications. In such an environment, one might interact with a wide spectrum of people, regardless of class or education, and draw from a multitude of activities often taking place in the same hall, separated only by screens. In addition to this, the quarterly dances – supplemented by more frequent one-nighters as the art schools became incorporated into the UK gig-circuit during the Sixties – provided opportunities for students to hear the top British R&B and jazz-blues groups, as well as visiting bluesmen from America. Already a crucible for creative fusion, art school as a result became the secret ingredient in the most imaginative English pop/rock.[2]

---

[1] Art schools and colleges do exist in North America but bear no resemblance to English ones, being instead institutes of design and technology catering to the needs of industry and commerce. The only notable North American musician of the Sixties to have attended art school (Alberta) is Joni Mitchell.

[2] After the affluent Sixties, English art schools began to follow other parts of the

Though he didn't attend Liverpool Art College, McCartney visited it regularly while Lennon was there, absorbing a diverse range of influences, including an interest in painting which he still pursues.[1] The Rolling Stones' Charlie Watts likewise went to art school (Harrow) and still paints, as does Ron Wood (Ealing). Keith Richards emerged from the same art school (Sidcup) as Phil May and Dick Taylor of The Pretty Things. The Pink Floyd's Syd Barrett went to Camberwell while his colleagues Roger Waters and Nick Mason studied architecture at the Regent Street Polytechnic. Drawn from several London art schools, The Bonzo Dog Doo-Dah Band began their career at the RCA. Other Sixties pop/rock figures who attended art school include The Who's Pete Townshend (Ealing); Ray Davies of The Kinks (Hornsey); Roy Wood of The Move (Moseley); The Yardbirds' Keith Relf and Eric Clapton (both Kingston), Jeff Beck (Wimbledon), and Jimmy Page (Sutton); Eric Burdon and John Steel of The Animals (both Newcastle); Charlie Whitney of Family (Leicester); blues musicians John Mayall (Manchester) and Christine Perfect (Birmingham); folk artists John Renbourn and Sandy Denny (both Kingston); Thunderclap Newman (Ealing); and Cat Stevens (Hammersmith). Adjacent to the art school world were Steve Marriott of The Small Faces, Mitch Mitchell of The Jimi Hendrix Experience, and Davy Jones of The Monkees, all of whom began in theatre, while David Bowie drew from both fringe theatre and the Arts Lab scene, in which areas The Soft Machine were also involved.

The anarchic-individualistic art school ethos has brought unusual invention and articulacy to British pop, ensuring that even when its forms cease evolving it can still ring changes in presentation and interpretation which provide the appearance of something new. With the decline of genuine innovation, this adaptiveness has diverted into more entrepreneurial directions (as with ex-Goldsmiths student Malcolm McLaren) or the informal post-Punk alliance between artists and

---

educational establishment by tightening supervision and examination and moving towards the North American model (see preceding note). Many involved in the Punk/New Wave and early Eighties pop scene began as art students, but the number of art school 'crossovers' has declined markedly since then. The cutting edge of UK pop culture in the mid-Nineties is at the commercial nexus of computer music and computer graphics, a fusion of synthesised sound and design on the cusp between pop and advertising.

[1] Bill Harry, later editor of the fanzine *Mersey Beat* and author of many books on The Beatles, was also at Liverpool Art College, where he introduced Lennon to his friend Stuart Sutcliffe, with whom Harry shared an enthusiasm for Kerouac, the American Beat poets, and Europe's Existentialists.

journalists in the mutually profitable business of conceptualisation.[1] Yet, like almost everything else going on today in pop culture, the roots of these phenomena lie in the Sixties. It was the art school backgrounds of The Beatles, The Who, The Kinks, et al., which allowed them to introduce the concept of 'concept' into pop, along with other postmodern motifs like eclecticism, self-referentiality, parody, and pastiche. More than anything else, though, the art-school/fringe-theatre tradition in English pop represents the English love of fantasy and creative artifice, and the concomitant English boredom with 'authenticity' and 'honesty' in art. Outside the realm of public gossip, English popular culture invariably prefers an imaginative contrivance to almost any kind of truth.

In this way, England differs fundamentally from America. Though English audiences do appreciate soulful realism (particularly in the North, where sensibilities are down-to-earth), they are also more open than American audiences to artifice and aesthetic adventure, as well as to irony and bleakness. Apart from being conceptual in a way which most American pop/rock is not, the pop music made in Britain over the last thirty years, while predominantly gay in the old sense, is also permeated by the wry scepticism of the country's self-deprecating humour. An offshore adjunct to the often-ruined culture of Europe, Britain – more especially England – is cheerfully inured to failure and decline. As such, the native humour is based mainly on pessimism and self-mockery, while the English notoriously derive perverse pleasure from the prospect of disaster. This delight in gloom is intrinsically linked (as one side of a coin to another) to the English love of pretending, dressing-up, and being silly – a basic frivolity that embraces a fascination with fakes and frauds as well as accounting for aspects of English pop music which baffle the more sensible American mind.

The result of this mismatch of sensibilities has been a transatlantic translation problem which has occasioned much amusement on both sides. Just as radio signals bouncing off TV satellites once caused a slight delay between a remark made in London being heard in New York, so a faint pause for interpretation continues to mark exchanges between the users of British English and American English. Not that Americans (as Britons tend to conclude) are without irony – let alone without awareness of the 'translation problem', which up to a point entertains and intrigues them. The drier kind of American employs irony as

---

[1] Damon Albarn of Blur: 'There wouldn't have been a Britpop scene if it hadn't been conceptualised and explained.' (*Observer*, 21st April 1996.)

naturally as the English; indeed, the best American comedians are as ironic as it is possible to be without actually vanishing in a corkscrew twist before their audiences' eyes, and much admired in Britain for this reason. Yet irony, as purveyed in the US media, is always circumscribed; audiences are clearly cued (in inferior TV sitcoms, by a ponderous archness guaranteed to set English teeth on edge) that irony is imminent and self-congratulatory laughter required, while irony is an entirely foreign concept to the weirdly complacent exhibitionists who parade their lives through America's tabloids and their TV equivalents. If the heroic-lachrymose tone of American middlebrow culture ('the shining city on the hill', etc.) is certain to put a pained smile on the straightest English face, then the bogus bluster and penny-dreadful pathos of US evangelism seem, to overseas observers, excruciatingly primitive. Here, the abyss of mutual incomprehension is huge.

The literal-mindedness of Middle America is a legacy of the country's historical youth and pioneer puritanism. Citizens of a can-do culture, Americans by and large remain optimistic in their ideals of self-betterment, sincerity, and trust. In such a mythos, irony is either signposted with billboard enormity or confined to the smart-arse disposition of the intellectual and the outsider. Against those who poke fun, the 'moral majority' may contend that a surfeit of cynical wit goes hand in hand with a dearth of values; that a straightforward attitude gets things done, while an excess of irony is a sign of decadence. There is some truth in this; conceivably too much public irony is socially corrosive. Yet postmodern relativism, which rots away old certainties by the day, makes an ironic outlook not so much *la mode* as part of the air we breathe. (Ideally, the solution would be to balance contemporary scepticism against our forebears' uncomplicated ethic of honest toil and respect for achievement – but, since these are opposed outlooks, such a *rapprochement* seems rather unlikely.)

While the minority of natural ironists in America rarely misreads The Beatles,[1] this is not the case with mainstream American fans, whose innocence of how completely English culture is pervaded by sardonic indirectness often leads them to take literally statements and lyrics by the group which their English audience would instinctively identify as, at most, half-serious. Aside from adducing the more blatant instances of this – the Bible Belt reaction to Lennon's remarks about Jesus and Christianity in 1966 or Manson's fantasies about various lyrics

---

[1] A notable exception is [96] A DAY IN THE LIFE, interpreted too austerely by American critics.

on the 'White Album' – it is hard to summarise a trait which is less an accumulation of cross-purposes than a way of life. To British viewers, for example, the New Age piano links on US TV epitomise the mawkish Middle American state of mind; by contrast, there is nothing the British loathe more than earnestness. Self-solemnity is the primary social *faux-pas* in the UK – and nowhere more than in Northern England, Liverpool being a designated area of outstanding natural sarcasm in this regard. Thus, to take The Beatles too seriously, missing the undertone of irony present even in their moments of ostensible decorum, creates a sentimental misconception. In terms of the transatlantic translation problem, the rustle of laughter which follows [105] WITHIN YOU, WITHOUT YOU is very 'key' indeed. When Harrison visited the hippie capital San Francisco in 1967, he saw not a mass of sincere seekers after enlightenment and social reformation but 'a load of horrible, spotty drop-out kids on drugs'.[1] Serious in his spiritual life, Harrison is nonetheless at heart a sharp-tongued Liverpudlian cynic ('a dry sod', as they say on Merseyside) and, as such, a long-standing debunker of The Beatles' myth. Yet in this he is merely the most overtly ironic ex-Beatle, the seemingly more soft-focused Starr and McCartney echoing his wryness when they deem it necessary.

It is no coincidence that the only American groups of the late Sixties who shared Harrison's derisive view of the US counterculture were steeped in the same highbrow eclecticism as their art school cousins in the UK. Warhol's protégés The Velvet Underground and California's nearest equivalents The Doors (products of the UCLA film school) duly became the most influential bands of their era on post-Sixties English pop/rock, while Frank Zappa's eclectic satire won a fanatical fan-base in Britain from 1967 onwards.[2] Nor is it coincidental that, though immediately taken up in Europe, neither The Mothers of Invention nor The Velvet Underground ever held much appeal for

---

[1] *Anthology* video, Part 7.
[2] A romantic misconception has grown up among the post-1976 generation that The Doors and The Velvet Underground were neglected in their time and only later discovered by the punks of the mid-Seventies. This is totally false so far as the UK is concerned. These groups were identified as excitingly distinctive by both the British underground and the student constituency from the moment their first albums arrived as imports. All the interesting musicians of the time were aware of them and they were formative influences on David Bowie and the artists who went on to form Roxy Music. As such, The Doors and The Velvet Undergound were established classics to the journalistic generation of 1972–5 and figured highly in critical and readership polls in *New Musical Express* at the time. The myth of their romantic neglect which grew up during the Eighties is an historical solecism overdue for debunking.

their home audience. As for The Doors, their American popularity was based less on their 'intellectual' side – their (to English ears, fascinatingly decadent and arty) psychoanalytical and literary allusions[1] – than on their 'instinctual' aspect: Morrison as erotic 'rock god' and modern pseudo-Dionysus. Not that the 'art' echoes in the music of these groups and their UK cousins were in themselves substantial, let alone of any intrinsic integrity; merely that they *worked* in terms of bringing about new forms and neat collisions of old ones. As a result, there is no unambiguous way of judging this 'intellectual' inheritance. Some of what The Beatles said in radio interviews and at press conferences was tosh; confusingly, the rest was often acute and very funny. In the same way, their use of 'random' (borrowed from the fine art avant-garde) veered from the dazzling to the downright daft. Moreover, far from being belatedly unmasked by the disenchanted Eighties, this self-indulgent inconsistency prompted every bit as much backbiting within the Sixties' highbrow-ironic pop/rock élite. Zappa skewered the cod Freudianism of The Doors' 'The End' and satirised The Beatles as industry stooges on *We're Only In It For The Money*. Recoiling from the artifice of his own 1965–6 period, Bob Dylan scoffed at *Sgt. Pepper* as effete ostentation, while Lou Reed and his colleagues in the New York milieu of Andy Warhol's Factory detested everything emanating from San Francisco. Then, as always, originality was a short step from absurdity. What was different about that time was the sense that such distinctions were worth bitching about – that something significant was at stake in what had previously been seen as a trivial and ephemeral idiom.

Such was the intensity of The Beatles' cultural context in 1966–9 that a certain amount of misinterpretation was guaranteed. Part of the aim of this book is to replace gushing hero-worship with a detached, posterity-anticipating tally of what The Beatles did. While this entails some deflation and occasionally a little harsh criticism, the hope is also, by avoiding clichés in favour of close examination in context, to make the group's music as fresh and exciting as it was when it first appeared; better still, to deepen its meaning and impact for those who may have missed the decade which The Beatles dominated. In general, this stricter focus has been approved by British and European readers: it makes sense to people who live in The Beatles' local culture. However, The Beatles are also part of world culture. More specifically, they are

---

[1] Eg., the title 'Not To Touch The Earth, Not To See The Sun', taken from the contents list of the 'Taboo' volume of Sir James Frazer's then fashionable anthropological epic *The Golden Bough*.

loved with special ardour in the USA, where their early music has its roots.

Some of the affection America feels for The Beatles has been expressed in good journalism, although no top Stateside rock writer has ever considered them at book-length, probably because the level of pop contrivance and frivolity in their music makes them hard to assimilate into the more earnest and heroic (and often, to be fair, more adult) American rock culture. Much of this flows from the literary cast of mind of such critics, many of whom originate in, or identify with, the campus/coffee-house folk-blues ethos which, mutated by electricity in 1965, continues to ensoul the US rock idiom. These writers expect lyrics to make a certain sense and, if not to carry significance or responsibility, then at least to have the decency to be authentically rooted in their appropriate sub-cultural contexts. The Beatles, though, like so much English pop/rock, are too given to artifice and effect to be sociologically grounded in this way.[1] Lennon and McCartney moved from thinking hardly at all about words to treating them as collage scraps to be pasted on to their music much as Picasso placed newspaper cuttings into his paintings. Few of their lyrics are comparable in style or ambition with the careful, verse-like constructions of songwriters like Dylan, Lou Reed, Neil Young, Joni Mitchell, Jackson Browne, and others in their inexhaustible line of succession. Aware of the absurdity of solemnly pondering what 'John' and 'Paul' meant by every word they emitted during the course of their hectic career, the smarter American critics have found more suitable subjects for intensive treatment, leaving literal-minded analyses of The Beatles' lyrics to plodders (and their music to instrumental magazines or academics bent on transplanting Lennon and McCartney into the alien environment of the 19th-century art-song). As for the American mainstream audience, in both its published commentaries and fan effusions The Beatles are worshipped and every fragment of their output treated as sacred. Fanatical to a degree that amazes the average British enthusiast, some American 'Beatleologists' sustain lifetime careers based on minute scrutinies of The Work which can produce anything from reports of all harmonic movements in every song,[2] to graphs showing how many times the phrase 'yeah, yeah, yeah' was used in pre-Beatles pop,[3] and

---

[1] Hence the preference, among the more politicised young in Sixties America, for the blues-based – and thus supposedly more 'authentic' (and so supposedly more 'radical') – Rolling Stones.

[2] O'Grady, *The Beatles: A Musical Evolution*.

[3] Kelly, *The Beatles Myth*, p. 99.

biblical concordances of the group's lyrics, syllable by syllable.[1] In as much as *Revolution in the Head* voices some non-congregational opinions, such pietists may deem it blasphemously iconoclastic. This being so, the author would like to reassure his prospective readers that, short of supine adoration, he loves The Beatles' music too.

A study of the contrast between American naturalism and English artifice in pop music (and life in general) would make a fascinating book. A comprehensive history of Sixties culture is likewise long overdue, although that will be a gigantic, not to say multi-skilled, enterprise. Meanwhile there's scope for several 'special area' investigations within this period. For example, we await decent accounts of either the British 'beat group' era or the UK's Sixties counterculture, and lack any histories at all of the English Beat or Mod movements. New tomes to be scribbled (but not by me!).

January 1997

---

[1] Campbell and Murphy, *Things We Said Today*. The authors list words in order of frequency. First is 'the' (1027 instances), with 'love' coming in sixth (485). On the basis of [137] HEY JUDE, 'nah' rates an unexpectedly high twenty-fifth (257 uses). Trees were chopped down to bring you this information.

ACKNOWLEDGEMENTS

For their help, I wish to thank Mark Lewisohn, Sir George Martin, Chris Thomas, Miles, Charles Shaar Murray, Jon Savage, Tony Tyler, Phil Manzanera, Dave Vaughan, Paul Wheeler, Chris Salewicz, John Bauldie, Roy Carr, Sandy Loewenthal, Trevor Smith, Bill MacCormick, Derek King, Annette Carson, my agent Julian Alexander, my Fourth Estate editors Giles O'Bryen, Jane Carr, and Sally Holloway, Will Sulkin at Cape, Murray Chalmers at Parlophone, Jim Meikle at the Kneller Hall Music Library, the staff of Bingham Library, Cirencester, and my parents.

Half of what I say is meaningless
But I say it just to reach you

Introduction: Fabled Foursome, Disappearing Decade

If you want to know about the Sixties, play the music of The Beatles.
Aaron Copland

The young make their own fun whatever time and place they're in, the natural dynamism of youth serving to heighten its surroundings. Excited by their own passing blends of music and fashion, teenagers in every generation since 1955 have believed that theirs was a uniquely special time. Yet the Sixties were special to an age-range far broader than any period before or since. The spirit of that era disseminated itself across generations, suffusing the Western world with a sense of rejuvenating freedom comparable to the joy of being let out of school early on a sunny afternoon. Though ultimately the product of influences deeper than pop, the Sixties' soaring optimism was ideally expressed by it, and nowhere more perfectly than in the music of The Beatles. Certainly those years would have been similar in tone and direction had they not existed; yet so vital was the charge emitted by their music and so vividly did it reflect and illuminate its time that, without it, the irreverently radiant Sixties atmosphere, described by Liverpool poet Brian Patten as like 'a fizzly electrical storm', might hardly have sparked at all.

So obviously dazzling was The Beatles' achievement that few have questioned it. Agreement on them is all but universal: they were far and away the best-ever pop group and their music enriched the lives of millions. Yet while The Beatles have passed into the pantheon of permanent regard, the Sixties, with which they were intimately linked, are now an ideological battleground upon which there is no agreement at all. Seen as everything from the foundation of modern liberty to the primary cause of present chaos, this carefree age – in which nothing was hidden and all caution and modesty were cast to the wind – has become the most obscure period of our century, mythologised into a mirage of contradictions: a disappearing decade. Detached from this revaluation, the records of The Beatles and their contemporaries continue to ring out blithely from radio stations while the period that gave birth to them is fought over in every other niche of the media. But if The Beatles and the Sixties are so closely related, they must surely have reflected each other's ambiguities. And if they did, how can the group's music evade the charges now being made against the times which it so perfectly mirrored?

One of the earliest repudiators of the Sixties was John Lennon. Talking to *Rolling Stone* in 1970, he dismissed the preceding years of social upheaval and countercultural revolt as little more than a clothes show: 'Everyone dressed up but nothing changed.' To Lennon, then rendered austere by Janov's 'primal therapy',[1] both the Sixties and The Beatles seemed to have been divorced from reality: middle-class daydreams funded on unprecedented affluence and fueled by delusive drugs. Now, insisted the therapised and detoxified ex-Beatle, the Dream was Over. Sporting dungarees, plimsolls, and a purposeful crew-cut, he was graphically dressed to clean up the mess. Within a year, he had graduated to revolutionary black leather jacket, beret, and Mao badge. Eighteen months later, he was seen reeling drunk in a Los Angeles restaurant with a sanitary towel on his head. And so the fashion parade – if that was what it was – went on.

The punk rebels of 1976–8 saw the Sixties in much the same way, their stripped-down, furious music echoing the naked truth aesthetic of Lennon's 1970 'primal' album *John Lennon/Plastic Ono Band*. To them, the preceding decade had been a silly self-indulgence followed by a six-year hangover of complacent grandiloquence which had palliated the energy of pop culture. 'Horrid hippies', the self-styled Beautiful People with their vague ideals and LSD-decelerated minds, were the problem; speed, sarcasm, and deliberate ugliness the solution. (Dress-code: spiked hair, ripped T-shirts, safety-pins through the face.) By the early Eighties, the Sixties had declined into a subject of cynical indifference to the denizens of Margaret Thatcher's deregulated anti-society, simultaneously turning into a standard target of left-wing 'alternative' comedy – reviled from both sides. A figure of futility, the burlesque hippie was an unkempt and pathetic dreamer, body unwashed and mind blown by drugs. Yet, at the same time, this object of scorn seemed to be a scapegoat for some obscure sense of loss. It was

---

[1] System created by Dr Arthur Janov of Los Angeles in which adult neurosis is ascribed to repressed 'pain' caused by traumatic incidents in childhood. The unhappiness incurred through these 'primal scenes' is released by a confrontational therapy in which the patient emits the 'primal scream'. *John Lennon/Plastic Ono Band* includes many references to this technique.

considered a truism that the Sixties had been an empty style-display (a concept the Eighties had little trouble grasping); but, if the ambitions of the Sixties generation had really been so irrelevant and impractical, why such resentment at its supposed failure to realise them?

At any rate, the hippies seemed to have got *something* right: during the second half of the Eighties, bored with the mechanical products of so much contemporary pop, a new generation seized on the passionately imaginative music of the Sixties, elevating to cult status the records of Jimi Hendrix, The Doors, The Byrds, Led Zeppelin, and The Velvet Underground. The only comparable Eighties artist, Prince, digressed into a brief Beatles phase with a pastiche of their LSD period in his album *Around the World in a Day*. More than a few of his peers admitted that they not only revered the sounds of the Sixties but approved the ideals associated with them. Persisting into the late Eighties, this style-rehabilitation of the Disappearing Decade was enthusiastically embraced in the Acid House dance idiom of the 'second summer of love' with its psychedelic fashions, LSD-reviving 'raves', and eclectic sampling of Sixties soul classics – a mood-altered mode which has hardly been out of fashion since owing to the omnipresent influence of sense-amplifying drugs like Ecstasy.

At the beginning of the Nineties, however, the 'retro' vogueishness of the Sixties temporarily faded as that era came under attack from a right-wing political culture in search of something to blame for the socio-economic chaos it had created in the Eighties. Far from failing, claimed these critics, the Sixties' revolution had succeeded only too well. The rising rates of assault, rape, robbery, drug-abuse, divorce, and abortion were all the fault of the permissive society supposedly fomented by left-wing subversives in the Sixties. (Likewise the parallel declines in industrial and academic performance, respect for authority, and general attention-span.) In America, young conservatives accused their parental generation – the 'Baby Boomers' born in the late Forties – of creating the Nineties' victim/dependency culture of casual violence, trash consumerism, and semi-literate Political Correctness. Sixties anti-institutionalism had, they claimed, wrecked the nation's education system and plundered its social security coffers, leaving a national deficit which today's young will spend their lives paying off (supposing they can find jobs). As for the Sixties' sexual revolution, it merely produced a flood of pornography and a high divorce/low legitimacy underclass of sullenly unsocialised and unemployable youth. To these critics, everything wrong with modern America was the fault of the irresponsible free-lunch hedonists who 'liberated' the Wood-stock Festival instead of standing dutifully in line for tickets.

Rising to the bait, the Boomers launched a counterattack, claiming *au contraire* that most of the civic breakdown in Britain and America after the early Eighties was caused by the socially ruinous tax-phobia of the Right. Reagan, they pointed out, may not have agreed in so many words with Thatcher's claim that 'There is no such thing as society',[1] but his monetarism said the same in fiscal language. As for Woodstock, it was, in venture capital terms, indubitably a shambles, yet one untypical of the West Coast counterculture, which, during the late Sixties and early Seventies, so successfully operated its own press, merchandising, and distribution networks that right-wing libertarian Frank Zappa felt obliged to remind hippie entrepreneurs that an alternative economy would no more effect structural change than declining to vote. Far from changing the system from within, underground radicals had been disposed to ignore mainstream society altogether, and could hardly be blamed for expensive welfare programmes which not they but the orthodox majority voted for. Nor could Woodstock (ran the case for the defence) be accounted for within the dully materialistic framework of the Nineties. Much of what happened in the Sixties had been spiritual in impulse, the free festivals being expressions of a shared feeling intrinsic to the times in which they took place. Moreover huge sections of society effectively disfranchised before the Sixties had, as a direct result of the decade's widespread change in attitudes, found their voices and – at last – a share of social justice.

The fact that the debate continues to rumble on is in itself a tribute to the momentousness of the Sixties. But if blaming the shameless greed of the Reagan–Thatcher era on the sociable and morally concerned We Generation is transparently silly, it would be just as fatuous to pretend that the Sixties did not harbour its own complement of idiots, demagogues, and outright criminals. Haight-Ashbury, a quiet bohemian haven till the invention of the hippie movement at the Trips Festival in January 1966, lasted barely two more years before degenerating into a methedrine/heroin ghetto. Few hippie communes survived into the Seventies without becoming cults of one kind or another. During the confrontations of 1968–70, almost as many 'freaks' wilfully provoked the police as were gratuitously brutalised by rioting 'pigs'. Much countercultural rhetoric – notably its airy notion of a money-free, share-all society ('post-scarcity anarchism') – was adolescent nonsense. Many underground leaders were either sociopaths in love with disruption for its own sake or self-dramatising opportunists

---

[1] *Woman's Own*, October 1987.

on their way to careers in Wall Street and Madison Avenue. Yet, in spite of all this, the sense then of being on the verge of a breakthrough into a different kind of society was vivid and widely felt. Attitudes formed in this potent atmosphere were lasting, the glimpse of something better, however elusive, permanently changing the outlooks of millions. Why?

To understand the Sixties, two overriding principles need to be considered. First, what went on then was by no means homogeneous. Many separate trends were working in different phases of development at the same time, much of the decade's contradictory character stemming from unexpected interactions between them. Second, the Sixties were a reaction to the Fifties – which is to say that passing judgement on the Sixties without some idea of what provoked them is tantamount to forbidding them a fair trial. While a strong case can be made for tracing today's falling standards to the Sixties' anti-élitism, it would be as prejudicial to contend that this impulse was without cause as to blame it on any one social group at large in that era.

The Fifties may have been relatively snug for the generation which had endured the Second World War, but their teenage children saw the period as a stifling 'drag' against which they felt obliged to kick, in a desultory way, with rock-and-roll. While theirs was at best a flirtation with freedom, their older siblings – for whom the Fifties were a 'nightmare decade'[1] of Cold War paranoia and sinister power without moral legitimacy – posed a more serious challenge to the *status quo*. In Britain, it was the time of the Angry Young Men, in America of the Beat Generation. Isolated rebels against social and intellectual restriction, the Angry Young Men came and went between the Suez fiasco and Macmillan's boom of the late Fifties. The Beats, though, more than mere heretics of the Eisenhower era, were a real foretaste of a revolutionary future.

Often assumed to be a musical reference, the Beat Generation's name in reality referred to a sense of being roughed up by life and flung into the wasteland margins of a materialistic civilisation. Carrying apocalyptic overtones, the Beat 'condition', as defined by its leading voice Jack Kerouac,[2] involved a state of being stripped of social

---

[1] Cook (1974), *passim*.
[2] *On The Road* (1957). Other leading Beats were Allen Ginsberg, Gregory Corso, Lawrence Ferlinghetti, Neil Cassady, Alan Watts, Gary Snyder, and Ken Kesey.

insulation and endowed with epiphanic clarity as a result. The mostly middle-class Beats were visionary hobos alienated from society: 'on the road', both literally and metaphorically. American cousins of the Existentialists – whose enigmatic chic drew Lennon and McCartney to Paris in 1961 and, in the form of Germany's 'Exis', fascinated them in Hamburg – they were less preoccupied with the integrity of the self than with transcending personal limits, reaching out to something beyond the range of everyday experience. Since they did not know precisely where they were going, they defined themselves instead by what they were for and against. They were against soul-numbing materialism ('Moneytheism'); for imagination, self-expression, Zen. Against society's approved depressants (alcohol, barbiturates); for outlawed stimulants like marijuana, amphetamines, and mescaline. Against rationalism, repression, racism; for poetry, free sex, jazz. Seeking self-realisation through 'hipness' and paradox, the Beats were the authentic religious voice of the Atomic Age. As such, they were formatively influential on the Sixties counterculture in California and New York, their sensibility reaching Britain through the freewheeling vernacular verse of the Liverpool poets.[1]

As late products of the spiritual crisis Western civilisation has been undergoing since the inception of the scientific outlook, the Beats were part of a venerable historical succession. The 'death of God', with its concomitant loss of both a moral reference-point and our ancient faith in personal immortality, began percolating down into society from its origins among rationalist scholars around four hundred years ago. As its influence spread, altering every sort of assumption and subtly retuning human relations, science's analytical attitude and technological products came to be perceived as a threat to the realm of the imagination, provoking regular cultural revolts: the late 18th-century *Sturm und Drang* and Gothic movements, the 19th-century Romantics and Impressionists, the Symbolists and Surrealists of the 20th century. At the same time, the loss of a transcendent moral index prompted artists to probe the frontiers of personal ethics, rolling back the limits of acceptable behaviour and stressing the authenticity of individual

---

[1] As elsewhere in this introduction, judgements are made from a general, rather than a specialist or coterie, perspective. The American Beats, for example, began to spawn English Beatniks as early as 1959. This influence, first felt in the fringe 'protest' movement surrounding CND at the beginning of the Sixties, had by mid-1965 (with the Wholly Communion event at the Albert Hall) spread into the expanding counterculture; but it did not reach the awareness of the general public until Penguin published its best-selling anthology of verse by Adrian Henri, Roger McGough, and Brian Patten in 1967.

experience over dogma handed down from the past or the ruling class. Received wisdom, traditional values and structures, everything that had once given life form and stability – all were challenged. The Beats were merely another psychic ripple from the rock of materialism dropped into the placid theocratic pond of the Western mind by the early scientists of the late 16th century – as, indeed, were the Sixties, although 'ripple' hardly does justice to their convulsive cross-currents of inner and outer unrest.

As a rebellion of free essence against the restraints of outmoded form, the Sixties began with a flood of youthful energy bursting through the psychic dam of the Fifties.[1] The driving force of this rebellion resided in The Beatles in their capacity – then suspected by no one, least of all themselves – as 'unacknowledged legislators of populist revolt'.[2] Born in Liverpool in the early Forties, John Lennon, Richard Starkey (Ringo Starr), Paul McCartney, and George Harrison were late arrivals in the first generation of British 'teenagers' (a sociological concept coined around 1930 and later adopted by advertisers in recognition of the then-novel spending-power of the post-war young). In America, a so-called 'generation gap' had been heralded in the early Fifties by J. D. Salinger's *The Catcher in the Rye* and screen stars like Dean and Brando. In Britain, this disjuncture became apparent half-way through the decade with the simultaneous appearances of rock-and-roll, television, *Look Back in Anger*, and the Suez crisis (the first crack in the façade of the establishment since 1945). Any domestic film of the

---

[1] Dividing the seamless flow of history into neat ten-year chapters is less arbitrary than some might claim, if only because the human awareness of what year it is has an effect on human behaviour and hence on history itself. While millennial panics are the simplest examples of this, something similar, if less obviously intense, has followed the ten-year calendar cycle for at least the last two centuries in Europe. The sense of coming into a new decade encourages an expectation of novelty and renewal which partially fulfills itself by the mere fact of being present in people's minds. There is, naturally, disagreement about when the 'metaphorical' Sixties started in the UK, estimates ranging from 1956 (rock-and-roll and Suez) to 1962–3 (The Beatles' advent, coinciding with the onset of a new sexual and political frankness in British public life). The abolition of National Service on the last day of 1960 has a claim, although conscription in itself is unlikely to have held back the psychological forces bottled up by the Fifties. It is interesting to note, too, how the middle of the decade shows an appropriate 'half-wayness': the arrival of the English counterculture at the Wholly Communion event at the Albert Hall in 1965; the appearance on the world stage of LSD and press attacks on 'beat music' in 1966; the onset of very long hair and colourful clothes for men in 1966–7; the cessation around this time of the quaint British ritual of standing to attention in cinemas when the National Anthem was played; and so on.

[2] Beer, *Britain Against Itself*, p. 139.

period will convey the genteel, class-segregated staidness of British society at that time. The braying upper-class voices on newsreels, the odour of unearned privilege in parliament and the courts, the tired nostalgia for the war, all conspired to breed unrest among the young. Lennon, in particular, loathed the Fifties' stiff and pompous soullessness, revelling in the surreal satirical attacks on it by Spike Milligan, Peter Sellers, *et al.*, in BBC radio's *The Goon Show*. For him, as for the other Beatles, the arrival of Elvis Presley turned the key. ('Rock-and-roll was real. Everything else was unreal.') Yet, within three years, the Conservatives had been re-elected on the back of Macmillan's 'never-had-it-so-good' business boom, while the rock-and-roll rebellion had collapsed with most of its leading figures *hors de combat*.[1]

With economic contentment in Britain and America at the turn of the Sixties, there seemed no reason to suppose that the youth disquiet of the mid-Fifties would be resurrected. In the USA, the 'kids' were diverted by cars, beach movies, bobbysox heart-throbs, and surf music. In Britain, cheap Vespas and Lambrettas offered youth transport and prestige symbols, jive-halls and espresso bars catered for surplus adolescent energy, and pop idled by on a turnover of skiffle, trad, and clean-faced 'teen idols' mass-produced in Denmark Street or imported by quota from America. Prosperity had even lulled the fight out of the Angry Young Men, former firebrands John Osborne and Arnold Wesker muttering peevishly that there were 'no great causes left'. Yet appearances were deceptive. Beneath the wiped and polished surface of British culture around 1960 lay a festering mess of sexual ignorance, prejudice, and repression only slightly ameliorated since the 19th century. Erotic experience was mostly confined to the dutiful discontent of marriage, while women were so routinely belittled that they barely noticed it, obediently accepting demeaning fashions and failing to demur with the prevalent male view of rape as something every female secretly wanted.[2] In this slow-thinking world, as yet unaccelerated by television, gentle neighbourliness co-existed with half-conscious prejudices against outsiders – Jews, blacks, 'queers' – and complacently censorious ideas of what was proper and decent. National

---

[1] Little Richard got religion and forswore 'the Devil's music' in 1957. In 1958 Elvis Presley was drafted, staying in the army until 1960. In the same year Jerry Lee Lewis's career dived after he married a 14-year-old girl. In 1959 Buddy Holly, Richie Valens, and The Big Bopper were killed in a plane crash, while Chuck Berry was arrested for transporting a minor across a state line. In 1960 Eddie Cochran died in a car-crash in which Gene Vincent was badly hurt. Within months, Larry Williams was convicted on a drug charge.

[2] See, for example, Ann Jellicoe's *The Knack*, filmed by Richard Lester in 1965.

Service was still in force and conformism was universal. Immensely smug, the condescension of the ruling class was reproduced on each social stratum beneath it, all males below one's own level being addressed by their surnames as if the whole country was in the army. Britain was stiff with a psychic tension which was bound, sooner or later, to explode.

Linked with the deferential quietude that tranquillised the UK at the outset of the Sixties was an embarrassed unco-ordination of mind and body. Even a basic sense of rhythm was rare, as anyone who witnessed TV shows like *Six-Five-Special* and *Juke Box Jury* will recall. (Ninety-five per cent of any audience – which in those days meant whites only – clapped doggedly on the on-beat.) While the heavy-petting and high-fiving of today's sportsmen is barely less mechanical, the rigid inhibition of early Sixties English cricketers, beside the relaxed naturalness of touring players from the West Indies, was positively comic. Much the same was true of the USA. Arriving there in 1964, The Beatles were amazed to discover how 'unhip' young white Americans were. A generation raised on crew-cuts, teeth-braces, hot rods, and coca-cola knew nothing of blues or R&B and had forgotten the rock-and-roll which had excited their elder brothers and sisters only five years earlier.

In this docile context, one of the most powerful currents to animate the Sixties was that of black emancipation. Embodied politically in Africa's drive to independence and the march of the civil rights movement in America, its most immediate impact on white culture was made through music, beginning with the blues, rock-and-roll, and rhythm-and-blues records which, entering Liverpool via its harbour-city import shops and the US airbase at RAF Burtonwood,[1] inspired The Beatles. The influence on them of black singers, instrumentalists, songwriters, and producers was, as they never failed to admit in their interviews, fundamental to their early career. Vocal stylings which white audiences in the USA later heard as foreign, harmonic progressions mistaken by classical critics for Mahler – these were as often as not adapted by Lennon and McCartney from doo-wop discs or Tamla Motown[2] records (notably those written and lead-sung by

---

[1] Otherwise known as Little America. (See Martin, *Summer of Love*, pp. 41–2.)
[2] America's most successful black-owned record company, founded in 1959 by Berry Gordy. Tamla was a separate label, but in Europe the two were amalgamated. Artists included Smokey Robinson and the Miracles, Marvin Gaye, Junior Walker and the All Stars, The Marvelettes, Mary Wells, Martha and the Vandellas, The Supremes, The Velvelettes, The Contours, The Elgins, The Temptations, Stevie

William 'Smokey' Robinson). Reviving the Fifties' rock-and-roll rebellion in the mid-Sixties with cover versions of records by Chuck Berry, Little Richard, Larry Williams, and The Isley Brothers, The Beatles acted as a major conduit of black energy, style, and feeling into white culture, helping to restore it to its undernourished senses and thereby forwarding the 'permissive' revolution in sexual attitudes.

If a black legacy bulked large in The Beatles' heritage, everything that passed through their writing and arranging process was so creatively reshaped that few other artists of any background ever came close to matching them. Though they were embarrassed to perform their rock-and-roll and R&B covers in America (especially in front of black audiences), their hard seasons in Hamburg's dive-bars during 1960–62 put enough toughness and attack into their act to place them on an equal footing with any pop music then performed live in the USA. Moreover they knew exactly how good they were as song-writers, conceding to no one, including their erstwhile American heroes. While their early lyrics were simplistic by the standards of Chuck Berry, Smokey Robinson, Eddie Cochran, Leiber and Stoller, and the teams associated with New York's Brill Building, The Beatles far outstripped their rivals in melodic and harmonic invention, baffling seasoned professionals with their surprising chord sequences.

More than mere novelty, such breezy unorthodoxy was one of the key characteristics of the Sixties. Self-made as musicians, Lennon and McCartney had a wry disregard for education and training, shunning technical knowledge in the fear that it would kill their spontaneity and tame them into sounding like everyone else. In this attitude they were at one with most young British songwriters of the period, the work of Jagger and Richards, Ray Davies, Pete Townshend, Syd Barrett, Roy Wood, and The Incredible String Band being likewise shaped by a cultivated element of self-surprise based on a lack of any ingrained sense of what ought to come next. Like Irving Berlin and Noel Coward, Lennon and McCartney were not only unable to read music, but firmly declined to learn.[1] Writing, to begin with, mainly on guitars, they

---

Wonder, The Four Tops, Jimmy Ruffin, Brenda Holloway, Kim Weston, Tammi Terrell, Gladys Knight and the Pips, The Isley Brothers, The (Detroit) Spinners, Edwin Starr, and The Jackson Five.

[1] Pope's principle that a little learning is a dangerous thing applies especially to pop music, where technical expertise tends to produce either songs of lifeless textbook correctness or *kitsch* exhibitions of decorative pseudo-classicism. Invariably the most original pop songs have been written by artists cleaving to their own private ideas of musico-lyrical design. (A forerunner to The Beatles in this respect was Roy Orbison.) Without a complete technical training – rare in the pop world – pop

brought unpredictable twists to their tunes by shifting chord-positions in unusual and often random ways, and pushing their lines in unexpected directions by harmonising as they went along in fourths and fifths rather than in conventional thirds.[1] In short, they had no preconceptions about the next chord, an openness which they consciously exploited and which played a major role in some of their most commercially successful songs (e.g., [21] I WANT TO HOLD YOUR HAND)[2] Nor was their sense of form any less personal, manifesting in the irregular phrases and unorthodox bar-groups which make even The Beatles' earliest work constantly surprising.[3] Knowing that their music's lack of institutional structure was chiefly what made it so alive and authentic, they kept it from becoming stale by continually investigating new methods and concepts: beginning and ending songs in the 'wrong' key, employing modal, pentatonic, and Indian scales, incorporating studio-effects and exotic instruments, and shuffling rhythms and idioms with a unique versatility. Forever seeking new stimuli, they experimented with everything from tape-loops to drugs and chance procedures borrowed from the intellectual avant-garde. And, as if this were not enough, all three songwriting Beatles had very different ways of composing which, together, lent their output an even greater richness and unpredictability.

While the group's musical unorthodoxy quickly attracted the attention of classical critics, the latter's failure to spot that the

writers usually become trapped between knowing too much to be roughly spontaneous and too little for a smooth transcription of their finer ideas, supposing they have any. (The only outstanding Sixties pop songwriter to have worked from full knowledge without compromising his creativity was Burt Bacharach, who studied under Milhaud, Martinu, and Cowell.)

[1] This trait probably had its origins in a background influence of British and Irish folk music filtered through skiffle. (See, for example, the droning open fifths of the folk-pastiche [37] BABY'S IN BLACK.) Writing in *The Times* on 27th December 1963, classical music critic William Mann observed that it sounded as if Lennon and McCartney 'think simultaneously of harmony and melody, so firmly are the major tonic sevenths and ninths built into their tunes, and the flat-submediant key-switches'.

[2] In the second half of The Beatles' career, Lennon took to composing on keyboards precisely because he knew less about them than the guitar. He confessed to *Rolling Stone* in 1970 that he was aware of only the basic piano chords – 'So I surprise meself.'

[3] Growing up in an atmosphere infused with the 'hip' ideals of the Beats and the Existentialists, Lennon and McCartney were instinctively biased against 'square'ness in everything from philosophy of life to musical form. Hence the prevalence in their songs of syncopation, half-bars, switches in time-signature, sections constructed from odd numbers of bars and, later, non-recurring linear layouts.

Lennon–McCartney partnership contained two separate composers was a revealing blunder, if an understandable one.[1] After all, if the idea that one could write and play one's own music was in itself startling in 1962–3, the notion that a songwriting team might consist, not of a composer and a lyricist, but of two independent writer/performers, was unheard of. (That The Beatles included a *third* writer/performer, capable of what Frank Sinatra has called 'the greatest love-song of the last fifty years', testifies to their rare depth of talent.)[2]

In fact, the differences in musical style between Lennon and McCartney were, from the beginning, quite distinct. Reflecting his sedentary, ironic personality, Lennon's melodies tend to move up and down as little as possible, weaving deviously through their harmonies in chains of repeated notes ([56] HELP!, [77] TOMORROW NEVER KNOWS, [85] I'M ONLY SLEEPING), two-note oscillations on minimal intervals ([26] I SHOULD HAVE KNOWN BETTER, [31] A HARD DAY S NIGHT, [116] I AM THE WALRUS), or reiterated phrases ([45] I FEEL FINE, [81] RAIN, [103] LUCY IN THE SKY WITH DIAMONDS). Basically a realist, he instinctively kept his melodies close to the rhythms and cadences of speech, colouring his lyrics with bluesy tone and harmony rather than creating tunes that made striking shapes of their own. McCartney's lines, by contrast, display his extrovert energy and optimism, ranging freely across the stave in scalar steps and wide intervals, often encompassing more than an octave. His is the expression of a natural melodist, a creator of tunes capable of existing apart from their harmony – whereas Lennon's lines tend to be allusive, moody affairs which make sense only when accompanied (particularly the more chromatic creations of his later style). In other words, while the tunes of both are marked by an unusual incidence of non-chordal notes,

---

[1] See Ned Rorem in the *New York Review of Books* in January 1968 (where he also describes The Beatles as cockneys) and the first edition of *The Penguin Stereo Record Guide*, in which The Beatles, appearing between Bax and Beethoven, receive the credit 'music principally by Paul McCartney; words principally by John Lennon'. The belief that McCartney was the composer and Lennon the lyricist was inherited partly from the set-up of conventional songwriting teams before 1963 and partly from the fact that Lennon published two books of stories and poems. In fact, he wrote more of The Beatles' output than McCartney (about ten more songs' worth – Dowlding, pp. 297–301). Typically the classicists' accounts of The Beatles, while technically precise, miss the spirit of the music or discuss it in inappropriate contexts. (Exhibiting an embarrassing tin ear, Glenn Gould compared The Beatles' songs unfavourably with Tony Hatch's for Petula Clark.)

[2] George Harrison. The song: [170] SOMETHING.

McCartney's method is, in terms of intervals, 'vertical' (melodic, consonant), and Lennon's 'horizontal' (harmonic, dissonant).

In a less narrowly structural sense, the two represented a classic clash between truth and beauty. Seeing music as a vehicle of thought and feeling, Lennon stressed expression at the expense of formal elegance, which held no interest or value for him *per se*. Intuitive, he cared little for technique and nothing for the rules, which he would go out of his way to break. As a result, while sometimes obsessive and crabbed, his music rarely betrays itself and hardly ever strays unintentionally into bad taste. On the other hand, McCartney, by nature drawn to music's formal aspects yet wholly untutored, produced technically 'finished' work almost entirely by instinct, his harmonic judgement based mainly on perfect pitch and an acute pair of ears.[1] However, while his music, at its best, is the very opposite of inexpressive, he could, entranced by his own fluency, all too easily be distracted from meaning, producing glib prettiness, vapid exercises in style, and excruciating lapses of taste.[2]

Brought together by their common love of rock-and-roll, Lennon and McCartney were psychologically cemented by the harsh coincidence of losing their mothers in their early teens. But though they never lost their respect for each other's talent, their temperaments and egos soon caused them to diverge as songwriters, displacing genuine fifty-fifty collaboration. For most of their career, their partnership was a formal arrangement, each writing the lion's share of his own songs before bringing the results to be checked, and where necessary altered or added to, by the other. That said, their close creative proximity generated the electric atmosphere of competitive rivalry which was the secret of The Beatles' extraordinary ability to better themselves; and where they did collaborate on an equal basis the results were nearly

---

[1] As a boy, he picked up a little piano and trumpet from his self-taught father Jim and was always far more widely curious about music than Lennon, enjoying, amongst other things, show tunes, music-hall, traditional jazz, and classical. In Hamburg, aged 19, he was intrigued by Astrid Kirchherr's Stravinsky records and investigated Stockhausen long before Lennon showed any interest in the avant-garde.

[2] Eg., [178] MAXWELL'S SILVER HAMMER. McCartney's sometimes thoughtless flippancy (see Coleman, Vol. 1, p. 199; Salewicz, p. 3) indicates a shallower commitment to feeling than that of his brooding partner. That the shape and surface of life and art interest him more than their depths and contradictions is apparent in his delight in the sound, rather than the meaning, of words – a facet which became more obvious once The Beatles had broken up and Lennon's sarcasm was no longer there to snap him out of it.

always remarkable, ascending on the tension between their contrasting personalities and gifts.

The Beatles' appearance in 1962–3 coincided with the fall of Conservatism in Sixties Britain. Caught between its election pledges and a balance of payments crisis, Harold Wilson's Labour government of 1964 was forced to raise income tax (including the swingeing rates for high earners which George Harrison later railed against in [84] TAXMAN). Fortunately buoyancy in the property market, aided by full employment, quickly created a youth-led consumer boom. Spearheaded by The Beatles, the two-year 'British Invasion' of the American top ten established the UK as the centre of the pop world with a flowering of talent matched nowhere else before or since. As British Pop Art and Op Art became the talk of the gallery world, a new generation of fashion designers, models, and photographers followed Mary Quant's lead in creating the boutique culture of Swinging London to which international film-makers flocked in the hope of siphoning off some of the associated excitement into their pictures. Long-standing class barriers collapsed overnight as northern and cockney accents penetrated the hitherto exclusively Oxbridge domains of television, advertising, and public relations. Hair lengthened, skirts shortened, and the sun came out over a Britain rejuvenated, alert, and determined to have the best of good times.[1]

Yet while change made itself felt across the board, many of its effects were local or ambiguous. The sexual repression of the past all but vanished from the world of the newly classless metropolitan young, but it took another decade to begin to disappear elsewhere; and while censorship was rolled back, homosexuality legalised, and women given the benefit of the pill and abortion on demand, the loosening of over-restrictive divorce laws inevitably created the conditions for the replacement of marriage by 'relationships' in the Seventies and a widespread collapse of the nuclear family during the Eighties. Immediate sexual gratification became the ideal of a society in which church-going was falling in inverse relationship to the rise in television ownership. As tradition became outmoded and a dispirited Christianity forfeited influence, the public focus began to shift from nostalgia and the compensation of a reward in heaven to an eager stress on the

---

[1] For an overview, see Chronology.

present combined with an impatient hope for a social heaven on earth in the near future.

The emphasis on informal and immediate fun that was the hallmark of Swinging Britain during pop's peak years of 1965–7 was less evident abroad, particularly in America, where two other socio-cultural movements were unfolding. Inherited from the Beat Generation of the late Fifties, the first of these took the form of a radical 'counterculture' which, springing up in opposition to the materialism of mainstream society, arose in California with a special concentration in and around San Francisco. Though framed in terms of sexual liberation and scaffolded by religious ideas imported from the Orient, the central shaft of the counterculture was drugs, and one drug above all: d-lysergic acid diethylamide 25, or LSD. Synthesised in 1938 by a Swiss chemist looking for a cure for migraine, LSD is a powerful hallucinogen whose function is temporarily to dismiss the brain's neural *concierge*, leaving the mind to cope as it can with sensory information which meanwhile enters without prior arrangement – an uncensored experience of reality which profoundly alters one's outlook on it. Recruited by Dr Timothy Leary to the existing underground pharmacy of marijuana, mescalin, and magic mushrooms, LSD came to the attention of the mass media in early 1966 when, as state legislatures moved to ban it, Allen Ginsberg urged that all healthy Americans over the age of fourteen should take at least one 'trip' in order to perceive 'the New Wilderness of machine America' as it really was. 'If there be necessary revolution in America,' declared the poet, 'it will come this way.'

The LSD view of life took the form of a smiling non-judgemental-ism which saw 'straight' thinking, including political opinion across the board from extreme Left to far Right, as basically insane. To those enlightened by the drug, all human problems and divisions were issues, not of substance, but of perception. With LSD, humanity could transcend its 'primitive state of neurotic irresponsibility'[1] and, realising the oneness of all creation, proceed directly to utopia. This, however, was not the only utopian prescription on offer. Born from the freedom-rides and marches of the civil rights movement, the American New Left offered an alternative route: a neo-socialist moral rearmament crusade aimed at discrediting the System – the 'power élite' perceived as directing the somnambulistic progress of a media-drugged mainstream 'Amerika' – and, more specifically, its supposed creation the Vietnam

---

[1] A satirical phrase from the script of Jean-Claude Forrest's *Barbarella* as filmed by Roger Vadim in 1967.

war. Centred on Students for a Democratic Society, this coalition was campus-based, youth-orientated, deeply idealistic, and highly self-righteous. As such, it had much in common with the burgeoning student protest movements in France and Germany with their Oedipal revolts against, respectively, the old Communist party and the post-war conspiracy of silence about Nazism. In each case the governing motifs were the 'repressive tolerance' of an unfeeling institutional hierarchy without moral mandate as against everything new, young, unprejudiced, experimental, and irresponsible.

Though they competed with each other, the hyperpolitical New Left and apolitical 'acid' counterculture in America in many ways overlapped. The hippie communes and alternative economy were based partly on the 'parallel structures' ideology of the Student Non-violent Co-ordinating Committee and partly on the philosophy of the Diggers, an LSD-propelled San Francisco anarchist group which took its name and inspiration from a 17th-century English proto-communist movement. At the incessant sit-ins and demonstrations organised in Berkeley during the Sixties, it was often impossible to distinguish between these two cultural streams, although the New Left's agitational/confrontational priorities became significantly less fashionable at the peak of LSD's influence in 1966–7. Whatever else it was, this multifaceted phenomenon was fascinating, tempting hundreds of thousands of young pilgrims to San Francisco to, as Frank Zappa drily put it, 'play their bongos in the dirt'.[1] Recording *Sgt. Pepper* at the time, The Beatles were more affected by this ferment than any other British group, McCartney and Harrison each visiting California to make their own evaluation of what was going on.

That there was indeed something unusual in the air can still be heard from many of the records of the period: a light, joyous optimism with a tangible spiritual aura and a thrillingly fresh informality (McCartney: 'Drugs, basically').[2] For some, though – like the satirist Zappa, the urban-realistic Velvet Underground, and The Doors in their darker songs – this was no more than a fey daydream. Within the ranks of The Beatles, such scepticism was the prerogative of Lennon whose main '1967' songs [114] ALL YOU NEED IS LOVE and [123] ACROSS THE UNIVERSE are unconvincing beside Harrison's philosophical centrepiece

---

[1] 'Flower Punk' (*We're Only In It For The Money*, 1967).
[2] The best example of this is *Sgt. Pepper* itself, though all who were there at the time will have their nominations for records which distill the 'spirit of '67'. For the present writer, another instance would be The Grateful Dead's bubblingly ecstatic 'The Eleven' (from *Live Dead*, 1970).

for *Sgt. Pepper*, [105] WITHIN YOU WITHOUT YOU – and far less authentically personal than the angry [116] I AM THE WALRUS or the tragic-transcendent [96] A DAY IN THE LIFE. 'Paul said "Come and see the show",' Lennon later observed. 'I said "I read the news today, oh boy".' In this respect, he anticipated the shift from 1967, the year of peace and love, to 1968, the 'year of the barricades'. In fact, so aware was he of the growing confrontation between the counterculture and the establishment that he wrote his polemical [125] REVOLUTION months before *les événements* of May '68 whilst in the rarefied air of the Maharishi Mahesh Yogi's Himalayan retreat at Rishikesh.

Had he made the pilgrimage to San Francisco in 1967, Lennon would no doubt have sensed the counterculture's incipient commercialisation and impending decline into hard drugs, and written a perceptive song about it; however, he was too engrossed in psychedelic inner exploration to be bothered. Self-absorbed at one reach of his personality, self-erasingly utopian at the other, he was a typical LSD user only in his willingness to believe that the drug's effects would inevitably do him good. His perilous brush with identity-loss ([77] TOMORROW NEVER KNOWS) was brought about not by a single catastrophic bad trip but through massive over-indulgence. Others were less lucky, suffering permanent, even fatal, damage.[1] Yet for the mass of LSD users (which, during the late Sixties, numbered several millions of the brightest young men and women of their generation) the effects of this potent hallucinogen were more benign, if in the long run nonetheless insidious.

The paradox of the so-called 'love drug' was that the universal empathy it created rarely translated into concrete love for another human being, an effect due to the self-negation of the typical LSD experience in which individuality in itself ceased to seem important. Using it, normal people were able to move directly to the state of 'oceanic consciousness' achieved by a mystic only after years of preparation and many intervening stages of growing self-awareness – as a result of which most of them not unnaturally concluded that reality was a chaos of dancing energies without meaning or purpose. There being no way to evaluate such a phenomenon, all one could do was 'dig' it. Hence at the heart of the counterculture was a moral vacuum: not God, but The Void. Enshrined in the motto of *Rolling Stone* magazine as 'the cosmic giggle', this implied a world view with neither framework nor stability; indeed one contemporary social study notes

---

[1] The LSD used in today's dance scene is up to ten times weaker than the average late Sixties dose.

that Sixties hippies actively revelled in 'ontological insecurity', treating those who sought fixed truths and values with a mischievous irony their victims were hardly aware of and never understood.[1]

Despite this, the hippie outlook, if so heterogeneous a group can be said to have cleaved to one position, was by no means flippant. Theirs was a kaleidoscopically inventive culture, actively devoted to the acquisition of self-knowledge and the promotion of fundamental social change. In rejecting the hippies, the punks of 1976–7 discarded only a caricature, coming nowhere near an adequate grasp of what they imagined they were rebelling against.[2] Hippie communality was real without being ideological, and many of its concerns – the open attitude to sex, the interest in spirituality, the pioneering focus on ecology, the enthusiasm for alternative technology and medicine – were quickly assimilated to the intelligent fringes of the mainstream. Committed hippies, moreover, soon realised the dangers of drugs, instead pursuing their inner quests through Eastern mysticism. (Their respect for tradition – providing it was older than that of the previous generation – contrasted sharply with the sweeping iconoclasm of their New Left rivals, among whom were the punks' own preceptors, the Situationists.) Yet only a small minority of those exposed to LSD went on to follow this life-style. For the majority, self-contemplation became self-regard, and merry detachment degenerated into the sort of nihilistic game-playing epitomised by the sordid Discordian philosophy of the *Illuminatus* trilogy.[3]

Propagated through a haze of drugs and half-baked ideas, what began as a flirtation with indeterminism amongst modern artists (see [144]) entered the mainstream via the pop culture of the late Sixties. The result was what might be called the 'rock mentality': a state of mind (regularly linked in later decades with irrational murders and suicide-pacts) in which urge ousts ethics under the haphazard tutelage of semi-coherent song lyrics.[4] The Beatles made a substantial

---

[1] Willis, *passim*.

[2] Peter Roberts: 'The point of the counterculture is that they were stars at living. The idea of the hippie as an aristocrat.' (Green, *Days in the Life*, p. 188.)

[3] Shea and Wilson (1975). *Illuminatus*, in which all the cryptic cross-references ever to have entranced a drugged mind are melded into one enormous political intrigue, was a passing fancy among survivors of the counterculture during the mid-Seventies. It is interesting to compare its paranoiac conspiracy-theory mentality with that of Charles Manson as documented by Bugliosi and Gentry (1974).

[4] During the late Seventies, the smarter pop stars saw the danger of pandering to this outlook and either stopped striking portentous poses or made sure such posturing was understood as in some way ironic. The slower-witted Heavy Metal idiom, however, preserved the tradition intact, duly encouraging an endless stream of

contribution of their own to amoral meaninglessness with the random lyrics and effects which adorned their later work. Just as this backfired on them in the form of the 'Paul is dead' hysteria (see [144], note) and Lennon's death at the hands of a demented fan in 1980, so the playful relativism of the 'flower power' summer of 1967 produced its own nemesis in 1968–9 in the shape of acid-crazed extremists like the Motherfuckers, the Manson Family, the Molotov Cocktail Party, and the Weathermen. The sad fact was that LSD could turn its users into anything from florally-bedecked peaceniks to gun-brandishing urban guerrillas.

The most explicit link between 'acid' and anarchistic violence was made by the Weathermen. Responsible for thousands of bomb attacks on US institutions during 1969–72, they attempted to forestall FBI/CIA infiltration by convening meetings in which everyone present took LSD on the principle that no secret policeman could maintain his cover whilst tripping. In 1970, this group – renamed the Weather People in deference to its many zealous female members – 'liberated' acid guru Timothy Leary from a minimum security jail, hailing him as a key figure in 'the revolution'. Buckling on a pistol before fleeing to Algeria, the former prophet of love and peace exhorted what remained of his gullible audience to get off their 'pious non-violent asses' and free by force all other incarcerated representatives of the once-benign alternative society. While The Beatles had nothing directly to do with any of this, Lennon, having set out from a position of scepticism, agreed to write [179] COME TOGETHER for Leary's 1969 California election campaign and later found himself composing a paean to White Panther John Sinclair and inviting the risible Jerry Rubin to play bongos in his pseudo-revolutionary New York group. There was, in truth, little of significance that happened in their time, however foolish or disreputable, which did not almost immediately find its way into The Beatles' life and work.

Though the late Sixties' youth rebellion declined into an ugly farce of right-on rhetoric and aimless violence, it would be a gross distortion to pretend that this was not substantially provoked by the stone-faced repressive arrogance of the establishment in those days.[1] As brutal as

sinister or tragic obsessions (and a Christian fundamentalist backlash).
[1] See the epochal trial of the Chicago 8 in 1969 and other comparable juridical travesties in contemporary America and Britain.

the backlash against the civil rights movement, the attack launched on the counterculture by US law enforcement agencies was massive and paramilitary, embracing everything from sabotage and spying to assault and battery. While Abbie Hoffmann's Yippies bear a large share of the blame for the riot at the Chicago Democratic convention in August 1968, the violence of the police (as of the state troopers at People's Park in 1969 and Kent State University, Ohio, in 1970) was wildly disproportionate and guaranteed, if not actually calculated, to generate extremism. Nor was this simply a question of blue-collar impatience with the 'unpatriotic' exhibitionism of a crowd of cosseted middle-class kids. Simultaneously besieged by blazing black ghettos and a swelling clamour against the Vietnam war, the US government saw the social critique advanced by the counterculture as a direct threat to national security. As such, the hippie/New Left amalgam constituted an 'internal enemy' which had to be defeated. Thus what began as an earnest but peaceful conflict between parental conservatism and youthful idealism gradually degenerated into a head-on clash between a repressive past and an ultra-libertarian future.[1]

The axis of this collision was the revolutionary present: the NOW in which all protest demands were ritually required to be met. The chanting of this magic word at demonstrations more than anything else distinguished the Sixties from the Fifties and marks the watershed between the precarious instability of the world we live in today and the hollow rigidity of what it sprang from during 1963–73.[2] The ethos of preceding generations had been one of prudent, orderly accumulation based on budgeting for the future and controlling one's appetite. Essentially an ethic of scarcity, this way of life — sneered at as 'bourgeois' by Sixties revolutionaries, but as firmly espoused by the proletariat — began to seem dated as post-war affluence expanded and youngsters for the first time found themselves with spending money. But while relative wealth may have been the immediate instigator of the 'now' mentality, there was something deeper at work: a reaction against spiritual inertness comparable to that of the Beats and Existentialists in the Fifties. Much of this (as The Beatles noted in [86] ELEANOR RIGBY) stemmed from the failure of the Church to provide

---

[1] See The Jefferson Airplane's 'Crown of Creation', The Doors' 'Five To One', The Mothers of Invention's 'Mom & Dad', The Electric Flag's 'Killing Floor', Chicago Transit Authority's 'Someday (August 29 1968)', MC5's *Kick Out the Jams*, etc.
[2] Cf. the hippie/Oriental maxim 'Be here now', The Doors' 'We want the world and we want it now' ('When The Music's Over'), etc.

anything more than a weekly social focus for local communities. With its promise of personal immortality, Christianity had for centuries focused its congregations' eyes on the happy future rather than on present injustice. By the 1950s, when The Beatles and their audience were growing up, it seemed clear that religion no longer had any supernatural collateral to support its claims. The young deduced that their parents' assumptions were obsolete and that, since this world was the only one they would ever know, postponing pleasurable self-discovery was pointless.

The Beatles' lives and works are prototype models of post-Christian 'nowness'. Entirely lacking the uptown urbanity or proverbial worldly wisdom of pre-1963 popular music, their early lyrics are careless, streetwise, immediate, sensationalistic – the expression of minds without respect for age or experience, interested only in the thrills, desires, and disappointments of the present. Lennon later spoke of this outlook as if it had been derived from LSD, but the imperative 'to live now, this moment'[1] was central to Sixties culture from the outset. Furthermore the feeling was communicable across generations, being felt by many then in their thirties and forties. Indeed, the format of modern pop – its fast turnover, high wastage-rate, and close link with fads and styles – is intrinsically instantaneous. Few of The Beatles' first hundred records last much longer than two minutes and the musical structure of all of them assumes a rapid cycle of repetition absolutely at one with the jerkily busy production-line of the juke box. Compared with the slumberous tranquillity of Fifties crooners like Perry Como and Michael Holliday, Sixties pop was, in the words of The Who's resident cultural analyst Pete Townshend, 'in a flat spin'.

Instantaneity defines the pop life and, as such, saturates The Beatles' music. Their domestic behaviour – filling their drives with multiple Rolls-Royces and their houses with expensive junk they never looked at again – is standard among young pop stars and may appear to be no more than a slight acceleration of the *nouveau riche* syndrome. Yet, as George Martin amusedly observed, the same casually voracious 'nowness' marked everything they did in the studio too. Lennon rarely bothered to learn any instrument properly, always wanting to move straight to expressing himself. More studious than his partner, McCartney nonetheless showed the same impatience, growing testy if any delay occurred in rigging up the new recording effects he and his colleagues constantly demanded. If an arrangement or an unusual

---

[1] Wenner, p. 136. Lennon: 'The whole Beatles message was Be Here Now.' (Sheff and Golson, p. 70.)

instrument or an entire orchestra was needed, The Beatles expected it to be there immediately. Waiting killed the spontaneity they so prized, taking them back into the patient, postponed, *slow* world of their parents. (Even the long hours of improvisation they indulged in during their later studio career were governed by the same present-time mentality, Martin's engineers yawning and glancing glumly at the clock while the group played on and on, lost in their collective perpetual 'now'.)

While The Beatles' faith in instantaneity produced marvellous (if occasionally monstrous) musical results, it worked less reliably when translated into ordinary speech. The irreverent directness of their early interviews was funny and endearing precisely because so obviously uncalculated. Unlike previous pop stars – programmed to recite their future itineraries and favourite colours – The Beatles replied to the press in facetious ad-libs provoked by whatever was going on in the immediate present. Yet, when anything more serious came up, their thought-processes often betrayed themselves as trite and tangled. Lennon's casually incautious remarks about Jesus and McCartney's careless admission that he regularly took LSD brought howls of righteous anger on their heads, while profligate confusion characterised the entire 'philosophy' of their business creation Apple. When Yoko Ono, asked how she would have coped with Hitler, replied that she would have changed his attitude by sleeping with him, the mirth her instant redemptionism provoked among the assembled press stung Lennon into losing his temper, exposing his similarly instant pacifism. The Beatles *felt* their way through life, acting or expressing first, thinking, if at all, only later.

Partly prescribed by the self-mocking Liverpudlian wit which never lets anyone hog the limelight for long, the scattergun style of Beatles press conferences owed most to the simple fact that they were a group. Before them, pop acts had been neatly presented as soloists or well-drilled units each with its clearly identified leader. With their uncanny clone-like similarity and by all talking chattily at once, The Beatles introduced to the cultural lexicon several key Sixties motifs in one go: 'mass'-ness, 'working-class' informality, cheery street scepticism, and – most challenging to the status quo – a *simultaneity* which subverted conventions of precedence in every way. Briefly a buzz-word among Parisian poets and Cubists before 1914, simultaneity was revived in the early Sixties by Marshall McLuhan in texts hailing society's liberation from the 'tyranny' of print by electronic media (of which the most dominant was, and is, television). Deploring linear thought and fixed points of view, which he saw as sources of conflict and tension in the

Western mind, McLuhan welcomed the chaotic 'flow' of media simultaneity, communal exchange, and amplified sensory experience. Little read today, he was a prophet of modern fragmentation – of multi-channel TV, multiculturalism, multimedia, multipolar politics, poly-morphous sexuality, and the extreme critical relativism of Deconstruc-tion. In their characters, collective and individual, The Beatles were perfect McLuhanites. More importantly, their work showed them to be prophets on their own terms: pioneers of a new 'simultaneous' popular art.

Referring loftily to Lennon's *In His Own Write* in the House of Commons in 1964, Charles Curran described its author as existing 'in a pathetic state of near-literacy'. 'He seems,' sneered Curran, 'to have picked up bits of Tennyson, Browning, and Robert Louis Stevenson while listening with one ear to the football results on the wireless'. As it happened – substituting Lewis Carroll for Tennyson and the Goons for the football results – this was a fairly shrewd summary in Lennon's case.[1] Setting a style which later spread throughout the younger generation, The Beatles liked to surround themselves with a continuous low-level media babble of loosely scattered newspapers and magazines and permanently murmuring radios and TVs. Apart from the fact that it amused them to live like this – relishing the coincidences and clashes of high and low style that it entailed – they valued simultaneity for its random cross-references which suggested ideas that might otherwise not have occurred to them. Many Beatles songs stemmed from chance meetings between scraps from the day's papers and half-attentive toying with bars from songs on the radio. Furthermore, as they grew more confident, they increased this random factor by making regular use of accidental occurrences during recording (such as the radio broadcast of *King Lear* fortuitously mixed into the coda of [116] I AM THE WALRUS), or by deliberately setting up chance-generated musical events (of which the most sustained is [127] REVOLUTION 9, an explicit evocation of modernity's saturated simultaneity of awareness).

As records – as distinct from songs – The Beatles' works grew increasingly multi-focal, the conventionally dominant lead vocal vying for the listener's ear with disconcerting harmonies, instrumental countermelodies, backwards tapes, and distracting sound-effects. Using the overdub facilities of multitrack recording, they evolved a new way of making records in which preplanned polyphony was replaced by an

---

[1] His favourite authors were Robert Louis Stevenson (for *Treasure Island*), Edgar Allan Poe, James Thurber, Edward Lear, Richmal Crompton, Kenneth Grahame, and (above all) Lewis Carroll.

unpredictable layering of simultaneous sound-information, transformed by signal-distortion and further modified during the processes of mixing and editing. The same multifocal mentality determined their lyrics, which, starting from barely considered verbal projections of musical moods in their early work, later became largely randomised streams-of-consciousness, cut up and sprinkled into the sensory cauldron of the general sound. Here the literate, crafted, and consequential ethos of such representatives of erstwhile social stability as Ira Gershwin, Cole Porter, Lorenz Hart, Frank Loesser, Oscar Hammerstein, and Noël Coward was superseded by an elusive maelstrom of fragmentary impressions, perceptions, and jokes reflecting the *collage* spirit of an instantaneous, simultaneous, chance-embracing new age.

Not that The Beatles were fans of formlessness; quite the opposite. Lennon and McCartney had a fine nose for weak points and how to strengthen them, bringing to their work a tight, if idiosyncratic, sense of structure, and a high density of musical incident bespeaking a habit of detailed listening. Yet even this attentiveness differed from that of the preceding generation in that its priority was not the song but the folk-technological artefact of *the record*. What thrilled The Beatles about early rock-and-roll and rhythm-and-blues records was the sheer strangeness of the sound they made. And what delighted them (simultaneously cultivating their future creativity), was deciphering how the elements of this – words, melody, voices, instruments, arrangement, production – worked together. Emerging from this multifocal artistic background, Lennon wrote 'to create a sound'. ('The words were almost irrelevant.')[1] And, while McCartney established a kind of continuity with earlier generations with his style-pastiches and narrative lyrics, he did this chiefly to hold his audience's interest by constantly multiplying The Beatles' idiomatic allusions. As their rivals followed suit, pop shifted from a stable medium of social confirmation to a proliferating culture of musical postcards and diary-jottings: a cryptic forum for the exchange of individual impressions of accelerating multifocal change.[2]

---

[1] Bob Dylan – who had likewise begun from an adolescent love of rough and ready blues and R&B discs before moving into the more intellectual folk-protest idiom – urged Lennon to 'listen to the words'. The latter replied that he couldn't be bothered, that he preferred 'the sound of it, the overall thing'. ('Like,' he explained, quoting McLuhan, 'the medium is the message'.)

[2] Roger McGuinn of The Byrds recalls the transatlantic camaraderie between pop artists during the mid-Sixties as 'a sort of international code going back and forth through records'. (Somach and Somach, p. 166.)

Fast-moving and devolved, the pop culture of the Sixties was intrinsically democratic. Its meaning grounded more in feeling than sense, it represented an upsurge of working-class expression into a medium till then mostly handed down to the common man by middle-class professionals with little empathy for street culture. Leading this democratisation of a profession of trained specialists, The Beatles were amused, on entering Abbey Road in 1962, to discover it staffed by boffin-like technicians in white lab-coats. Attached to this curious scene was a 'right' way of doing things which initially thwarted the accommodation of their sound but which, after seven years of destruction-testing in a dozen Beatle albums, had completely changed. (A microcosm of the assault on orthodoxy then going on across the cultural spectrum, The Beatles' revolutionising of the recording studio, prompted by the demands of Lennon's unruly imagination, was masterminded by the more methodically exploratory McCartney in tandem with George Martin and his talented engineers Geoff Emerick and Ken Scott.) The only significant aspect of pop The Beatles failed to change was the business itself. Acquiring possibly the only honest manager in Britain at the time (certainly the only one to vote Labour), they nevertheless ended their career together on the time-honoured killing-field of the contractual dispute. Twenty-five years after them, the commerce in this area continues to move in the traditional direction: into the bank accounts of the money men.

Of all the manifestations of instantaneity in the Sixties, the most obviously hapless was the instant revolution of Euro-Maoism. While change in mid-Sixties Britain might be symbolised by a jeans-clad photographer driving a Rolls-Royce, the democratic impulse elsewhere was less merrily hedonistic, more seriously political. After the social uprising of the first half of the decade, the Vietnam war incited a moral uprising in the second half; but it was not till Mao Tse-tung launched his Cultural Revolution in 1966 that the European Left found a faith to replace the one shattered by Khrushchev's exposure of Stalin in 1956. The attraction of 1966-vintage Maoist revolution in the age of instantaneity was that it eliminated the preparatory phases of Lenin's model, positing a direct leap to the Communist millennium which would expunge all class distinctions at a stroke. This, decided the excited young ideologues of the West, amounted to 'a break with history'. All that remained was to take to the streets and 'tear down the walls'.

In the heady, simultaneous, present-time Sixties atmosphere, enthusiasm for Mao's instant revolution spread rapidly on the campuses of France, Germany, Italy, Spain, and Britain – and again The Beatles found themselves, culturally, in the thick of it. For hinting that baiting the establishment with red flags would only spark a backlash, Lennon's [132] REVOLUTION was vilified in the left-wing press on both sides of the Atlantic (see [125]). The radical film-director Jean-Luc Godard, fresh from a politically correct portrayal of The Rolling Stones, blasted The Beatles for their apoliticism[1] an attack which, while it glanced off Lennon, accurately reflected the mood among Left activists of the time. Egged on by demagogues like Sartre and Foucault calling for 'direct action' (violence) and 'people's justice' (lynch law), extremists hijacked the hopeful energy of the Sixties, turning it into a rolling riot. While the sun still shone on the almost entirely peaceful outdoor rock festivals whose era continued for another five years, 1968 cast a shadow of pessimism which lengthened during the following decade, leading inevitably to the anger of 1976–8 and the cynicism of the Eighties. Student unrest rumbled on in Britain for the rest of the Sixties and was eventually replaced by the violent Situationism of the Angry Brigade. On the continent, Euro-Maoism persisted into the Seventies, crash-helmeted rioters periodically taking to the streets in France and anarchists breaking into gigs and concerts in Germany to 'liberate' them. Finally, turning desperate, it went underground with the kidnappings, bank-robberies, and assassinations of Action Direct, the Red Brigades, and the Red Army Faction.[2]

The student revolts of the late Sixties – not only in Western Europe but in Czechoslovakia, America, and Japan – were surprisingly quickly forgotten. By 1972, the campuses had settled down and 'student revolution time', as The Beach Boys had serenaded it,[3] was so much a thing of the past that it was possible to attend university in the mid-Seventies without knowing it had happened. At its height, this tumult divided America against itself more violently than at any time since the Civil War and came within a whisker of sweeping the French government out of office; yet its actual achievements were meagre: a few curriculum changes and some minor additions to civil rights legislation. Though the revolutionary Left's calls for 'self rule' and

---

[1] *International Times*, 6th September 1968.
[2] Still the doyens of the Left approved. Genet supported the Baader–Meinhof Gang while Sartre continued to condone the violence of the Euro-Maoist young. Some diehards even approved of Pol Pot.
[3] *Surf's Up* (1971).

'participatory democracy' were timely, its venerable class-war ideology was an anachronism even in 1968. Instead the real legacy of the Sixties' democratic impulse was handed down from sources rooted in that era: the civil rights movement (black emancipation and multiculturalism), the hippies (environmental and health pressure groups), and the permissive society (feminism and gay liberation). Essentially populist, the Sixties were also essentially non-ideological – socially reformative rather than politically revolutionary. As such, the events of 1968 were a kind of street theatre acted out by middle-class radicals too addled by theory to see that the real Sixties revolution was taking place, not in the realms of institutional power, but in the minds of ordinary people. The 'masses', whom activists had been taught to regard as inert material to be moulded to their ends, turned out to be impervious to crude attempts to raise their consciousness or pretentious 'happenings' designed to reveal their 'true desires'. They knew their desires quite well already and were getting on with satisfying them.

The true revolution of the Sixties – more powerful and decisive for Western society than any of its external by-products – was an inner one of feeling and assumption: a revolution in the head. Few were unaffected by this and, as a result of it, the world changed more thoroughly than it could ever have done under merely political direction. It was a revolution of *and in* the common man; a revolution (as Aaron Copland, author of the eponymous fanfare, observed), whose manifesto – its vices as much as its virtues, its losses as well as its gains, its confusions together with its lucidities – is readable nowhere more vividly than in The Beatles' records. In effect, the 'generation gap' which opened in the Fifties turned out not to be a quarrel between a particular set of parents and children but an historical chasm between one way of life and another. After the Sixties, references to the generation gap lapsed largely because few were any longer aware of such a thing; indeed, it would have seemed reasonable at the time to have assumed that the lesion had miraculously closed up and healed. Yet what actually happened was that a new way of life so persuasively and pervasively replaced an earlier one that the majority made the mental crossing between them without really noticing it (much as Britain passed from imperial to decimal coinage around the same time).

A transitional period, the Sixties witnessed a shift from a society weakly held together by a decaying faith to a rapidly desocialising mass of groups and individuals united by little more than a wish for quick satisfaction; from a sheltered assumption of consensus, hierarchy, and fixed values to an era of multiplying viewpoints and jealously levelled standards; from a naive world of patient deferral and measurable progress to a greedy simultaneity of sound-bite news and thought-bite politics; from an empty and frustrating moral formality to an underachieving sensationalism. What playwright (and *A Hard Day's Night* scriptwriter) Alun Owen has called the 'divine right of the establishment' was definitively punctured in that decade and, while the establishment itself survived, its grandly complacent delusion of immunity did not. Thirty years later the conservative political culture of the West, democratised from below and harried by a contemptuous media, is riven by factions and rotten with corruption. Yet, ironically, orthodox socialism – the secular faith of humanism – appears equally obsolete in the face of the multifocal chaos of modern selfishness. The truth is that the Sixties inaugurated a *post-religious* age in which neither Jesus nor Marx is of interest to a society now functioning mostly below the level of the rational mind in an emotional/physical dimension of personal appetite and private insecurity.[1]

These contradictions were unresolved in the Sixties, it being chiefly the clash between them which sparked the electricity millions then felt in the air. Symbolised by Bob Dylan and The Rolling Stones, the revolt of youth against institutional authority was at first less obvious in The Beatles because suppressed by Brian Epstein in the interests of popular appeal. Packaged for family consumption, The Beatles nonetheless felt as nonconformist as their colleagues, and after breaking Epstein's benign hold over them in 1966 they began, in uncertain terms, to speak their minds. Lennon and Harrison were the main dissidents, Lennon in particular angry in the belief that The Beatles had

---

[1] While most of the populace in developed countries still believes in the soul and its post-mortem salvation, religion in the old sense – a supramundane outlook standardised by monolithic sacred institutions – has largely been replaced by subjective individual beliefs in a personal God, in angels, or in a general transcendentalism based on near-death experiences. Christianity has fissured into a multiplicity of churches and sects, some of which consist of a handful of people. This tendency is most extreme in America, where polls consistently show a majority claiming some sort of 'Christian' or 'religious' belief. Compared to the religions of the past, these claims are, at best, to a form of convenience-faith – passive, sentimental, often indistinguishable from patriotism, and to be picked up or laid aside according to the awkwardness of the moral predicaments confronting it (a self-excusing relativism formed in the image of the hypocrisy of many American evangelical leaders). By the standards of Islamic fundamentalism, the average American's claim to faith is flimsy while, faced with its own fundamentalists at elections, America as a whole continues to endorse secular values.

become *embourgeois*ed, initially by the conventions of showbiz and later by the fantasy world of LSD. (A temperamental socialist who voted conservative to guard his money, he embodied all the tensions and contradictions inherent in the transitional Sixties and, as such, was a shrewd choice – by Desmond Morris – as 'Man of the Decade'.)

At the point at which The Beatles took control of their destiny – coinciding with the simultaneous appearance of LSD and the counter-culture – right-wing papers began predicting the demise of the 'beat groups' and attacking the alleged worship of youth and novelty among their Fleet Street rivals. In *The Neophiliacs*, the Christian writer Christopher Booker saw what was happening as a mass-hysteria based on a 'vitality fantasy', describing the youth uprising and its leaders The Beatles as a manifestation of 'evil'. Based on an eccentric Spenglerian system of historical cycles, *The Neophiliacs* was written too close to the events it sought to explain to see that, far from fizzling out as its author and most of the upmarket press assumed, they were about to take on a new intensity. As for The Beatles, rather than played out, they were on the verge not only of their best work but of adding to it a philosophical dimension wholly defying Booker's analysis. Since middle-class Christians tend to conceive a 'spiritual crisis' as something which happens only to conscientious individuals and in the best of Anglican good taste (and certainly not to the accompaniment of electric guitars), it was hard for Booker, or Malcolm Muggeridge, or Mary Whitehouse to understand that much of what appeared to be profane in Sixties youth culture was quite the opposite. Writing three years later, a more open-minded Christian, Kenneth Leech, was able to grasp the late Sixties for what they were: a spiritual crisis *en masse*.

Far from appearing out of thin air in the Sixties, as many conservatives now like to believe, the decade's mass-transition from sacred to secular represented a climactic stage in the historical rise of science. Over recent centuries, the Christian glue which once cemented Western society had been progressively weakened by the shocks of scientific discovery (the most catastrophic being the realisations that not only is the earth neither the centre of creation nor four thousand years old but that humanity is physically descended from the apes). With the arrival of the 20th century, the technological spin-offs the scientific outlook became increasingly forceful in their social impact. During the 1914–18 war, the old order was brought close to collapse by the devastating invention of the machinegun, surviving the disillusionment of the Twenties only because their Sixties-like tastes for novelty, promiscuity, and drugs were too much the indulgence of a privileged few to pose a general threat to stability. In the Sixties, however, socially liberating post-war affluence conspired with a cocktail of scientific innovations too potent to resist: TV, satellite communications, affordable private transport, amplified music, chemical contraception, LSD, and the nuclear bomb. For ordinary people – the true movers and shakers of the Sixties – these factors produced a restless sense of urgency headily combined with unprecedented opportunities for individual freedom. Abandoning a Christian world of postponed pleasure for a hungry secularism fed by technological conveniences, they effectively traded a hierarchical social unity in which each 'knew his place' for the personal rewards of a modern meritocracy.

The mass shift to individualistic materialism came into full swing as The Beatles appeared, and the records they made in their early career reflect its mood with unselfconscious elation: 'good time' music, simple in feeling and with the accent on physical excitement. At the same time, as if shadowing the rise of the new secularism, society's intake of consciousness–depressing drugs[1] grew so rapidly that when consciousness–*enhancing* drugs like marijuana and LSD appeared around 1965–6 the contrast was inescapable. Advocated in America by former Beats like Ginsberg and Ken Kesey, psychedelic drugs exposed modernity's spiritual emptiness, challenging the 'unexamined life' of the consumer society. The resulting acid counterculture of the mid-Sixties was both a mass attempt to transcend the self in the absence of God and an echo of the 19th-century Romantics' use of opium to release the imagination from the tiresome constraints of rationalism.[2] Switching from mainstream drugs to countercultural drugs (and, in doing so, rejecting the naive materialism implicit in their early style), The Beatles made quality of awareness the overriding topic of their work from *Revolver* onwards. Writing about this ten years later, Lennon described his own and his generation's 'so-called "drug-abuse"' as a struggle to break out of the straitjacket of the mind – 'to reach "out there"'.[3] For him, the cultural continuity with artistic revolts in earlier periods and with driven individuals like Van Gogh and Dylan Thomas was obvious. (The 'sky' and celestial imagery in songs of this period – Lennon offering one

---

[1] See The Rolling Stones' 'Mother's Little Helper' (1966).
[2] Fashion around 1964–8 borrowed lavishly from both Romanticism and the Hollywood-Oriental opulence of the Twenties, the classic instance of this style being Barbara Hulanicki's Biba.
[3] *Skywriting by Word of Mouth*, pp. 34–6.

notable case-study, Jimi Hendrix another – dramatises this generational yearning for a spiritual life beyond the banality of the material one.)[1]

As the externalised conscience of mainstream society, the counter-culture soon came into conflict with the surviving class-stratified, conservative/religious mentality of the Fifties, vying with it for the soul of consumerdom. Happy to be consumers, ordinary people remained unmoved by this battle, instead getting on with enjoying their new modern world of convenience and independence. During 1967, all they noticed of the Consciousness War being waged over their heads was that certain hippies and pop stars were being made examples of by being 'busted' for possessing drugs, and that The Beatles were, as the Queen quaintly put it, 'getting awfully strange these days'. With the establishment fighting back hard in 1968, another element was provoked into play: the revolutionary anarcho-communism of the New Left. Yet, while riots and bombs were hard to ignore, the great mass of society was no more taken with the student radicals than it had been with the restrained grey Fifties or the multicoloured hippies. Resisting these various pitches for social consensus, the mainstream continued with its acquisitive individualism, buying Beatles records for their tunes and tolerantly ignoring their lyrics. Thus, by a devilish paradox, those who thought they were at the cutting edge of social development in the Sixties – the hippies, the New Left – soon found themselves adrift in the wake of the *real* social avant-garde of the period: ordinary people. The individualism of the Me Decade, as Tom Wolfe dubbed the Seventies, was a creation of the Sixties' mass mainstream, not of the peripheral groups which challenged it. Former hippies and radicals who abandoned the utopian 'we' for rueful self-interest in the Seventies, far from leading public taste, were merely tagging along behind it. As for the punks, their blurt of betrayal in 1976–8 was apprehended by the comfortable, sensible majority of Western society with no more than mystified amusement.

The irony of modern right-wing antipathy to the Sixties is that this much-misunderstood decade was, in all but the most superficial senses, the creation of the very people who voted for Thatcher and Reagan in the Eighties. It is, to put it mildly, curious to hear Thatcherites condemn a decade in which ordinary folk for the first time aspired to individual self-determination and a life of material security within an

---

[1] A parallel impulse was at work in contemporary jazz with the simultaneous/instantaneous free collective improvisation of the New Thing. Sun Ra, John Coltrane, Albert Ayler, and Pharoah Sanders were all transcendental artists searching for pure expression unshackled by the rational intellect.

economy of high employment and low inflation. The social fragmentation of the Nineties which rightly alarms conservatives was created
neither by the hippies (who wanted us to 'be together') nor by the
New Left radicals (all of whom were socialists of some description). So
far as anything in the Sixties can be blamed for the demise of the
compound entity of society it was the natural desire of the 'masses' to
lead easier, pleasanter lives, own their own homes, follow their own
fancies and, as far as possible, move out of the communal collective
completely.[1]

The truth is that, once the obsolete Christian compact of the Fifties
had broken down, there was nothing – apart from, in the last resort,
money – holding Western civilisation together. Indeed the very labour-
saving domestic appliances launched onto the market by the Sixties'
consumer boom speeded the melt-down of communality by allowing
people to function in a private world, segregated from each other by
TVs, telephones, hi-fi systems, washing-machines, and home cookers.
(The popularity in the Eighties of the answering machine – the phone-
call you don't have to reply to – is another sign of ongoing
desocialisation by gadgetry.) It is, in short, no accident that Mrs
Thatcher should have founded her outlook on the conviction that
society does not exist – and no surprise that her favourite Sixties tune is
'Telstar' by The Tornados, a record symbolising the rise of technology-
driven post-war prosperity and mass social emancipation. She and her
radicalised, post-consensus Conservative voters are the true heirs of the
Sixties. *They* changed the world, not the hippies (and certainly not the
New Left). What mass society unconsciously began in the Sixties,
Thatcher and Reagan raised to the level of ideology in the Eighties: the
complete materialistic individualisation – and total fragmentation – of
Western society.

Hoist with its own petard, the New Right now seeks to pin the blame
for the unhappier aspects of the Sixties' social revolution on groups

---

[1] Short of a swing to quasi-fascist populism, the mid-Nineties' clamour for a
moral revival based on 'communitarianism' will remain empty for as long as we
continue to value community less than we value privacy. (The success of CCTV and
'zero tolerance' policing suggests that a major change is on the way – although it is
unclear whether this will lead to a genuine communitarian revival or is merely the
prelude to a segregation of society into 'have' and 'have-not' areas enforced by
vigilante law.)

whose influence on the course of events over the past quarter of a century has been at best peripheral, at worst non-existent. While female, gay, and racial liberation have agitated against the *status quo*, none of these movements is pro-consensus or (except at their extremes) utopian. Pressure groups promoting issues specific to themselves, women, gays, and blacks have been as much at war with the Left as with the Right, having less in common with socialist factionalism than with the upwardly mobile constituency that elected the Conservatives and the Republicans in the Eighties. The logic of their drive for self-determination predicts *less* social unity, not more – as (given the chances of any special interest minority imposing a totalitarian rule on the West) does the otherwise illiberal language of political correctness.

Almost as destructive, the facile 'psychobabble' disseminated via post-Freudian quick-cure therapies stems not from the utopian selflessness of the hippies or New Left, but from the navel-gazing of the Seventies and the shameless self-love of the Eighties. (The right-wing lineage of modern 'empowering' cults from Ayn Rand to Scientology is self-proclaimed, while the most popular brand of Buddhism in the West exhorts its adherents to chant for Porsches.) As for the clearly Leftist philosophy of Deconstruction, its cynical egalitarianism has done great damage to the old cultural consensus of the West, demolishing respect for tradition and authority with nihilistic relish. A malignant rot has spread through the Western mind since the mid-Seventies: the virus of meaninglessness. Yet this infection threatens *all* ideologies, Left or Right, being at root no more than a leveling crusade on behalf of the aesthetically deprived – a Bad Taste Liberation Front. The reason why cultural relativism has caught on is not because ordinary people read Derrida but because the trickle-down essence of Deconstruction suits both the trash aesthetic of media-hounds and the philistinism of Essex Man.

The same goes for the wider post-Sixties social effects recently lamented by politicians on the look-out for votes. The slackening of parental control and educational standards – and the associated decline in areas of achievement less concrete than the pursuits of wealth, health, physical beauty, and sporting excellence – are too pervasive and run too deep in the modern world to be blamed on a conspiracy of utopian Baby Boomers. Leaving aside the philistine nature of contemporary conservatism, the 'anti-élitism' of the Sixties, far from restricted to the counterculture, was intrinsic to the democratic spirit of the age. As such, the popular rebellion against authority was well under way before the arrival, in 1966, of its would-be hippie/anarchist leaders. Persisting in the background while the flower children and Maoists enjoyed their

Warholian fifteen minutes of fame, the Sixties' anti-authoritarian mood of cheeky undeceivability continued to make way for the quiet inner revolution of attitude and assumption within whose consequences, propitious and otherwise, we live today.

Again, most of the work of this revolution was inspired and facilitated by the productions of science. It is, for example, difficult to contemplate a labour-saving device without thinking somewhat less of traditional virtues like application and persistence. A culture of convenience is inevitably a culture of laziness – and, in this respect, the role of television in turning humanity into a passive audience has been much agonised over by social analysts of all persuasions. Yet the passivity of the TV experience is precisely what we enjoy about it; indeed television, with its in-built sensationalistic bias and bathetic discontinuities ('And now for something completely different . . .') has been more influential in advancing the post-Sixties revolution in the head than any other technological innovation. (Another culturally symbolic gadget from the Eighties is the TV remote-control which allows us to watch in a simultaneous state of mind, 'channel-hopping' so as to preclude sequential thought whilst decreasing emotional purchase on the material thus idly scanned.) Pop music, too, has played a role in reinforcing the manifest relaxation of goals and standards since the Sixties. Aside from the inescapable fact that this relaxation was to various degrees willed by the majority, pop and its shatteringly sensationalistic cousins rock, disco, and 'rave' music have been as much colonised by technology as any other area of modern life. Its once flexible human rhythms replaced by the mass-production regularity of the drum-machine, its structures corporatised by the factory ethic of the sequencer, its vitality digitised to death and buried in multi-layered syntheticism, pop is now little more than a soundtrack for physical jerks.[1]

While the instantaneous/simultaneous mentality introduced by the Sixties suited new idioms like pop and television (mainly because substantially created by them), it had a less benign effect on older established forms. Classical music, once an art of expression, became a pseudo-scientific, quasi-architectural craft of technique whose principles of design, opaque to the ear, were appreciable only by examining

[1] Interviewed about his reading habits, a leading pop dissident of the Eighties, Mark E. Smith, castigated the illiterate shallowness of much of his audience: 'Kids' brains nowadays are like sludge. It's the machines. I've seen it change in ten years. They're not thinking or listening any more. Obsessed with technology. Video games? It's just an elaborate fruit machine.' (*Independent*, 6th May 1993.)

the 'blueprint' of the score. Similarly the rapid succession of conceptual *coups* in the world of painting and sculpture, so novel at the time, turned out to be merely the end of modernism and, as such, the dying fall of Western art. Overtaken by the 'artistic discourse' of postmodernism, art became as literary as post-Webernian classical music was visual, producing the arid paradox of paintings to listen to and music to look at. Shorn of their content, art, music, and literature degenerated by increasingly inconsequential stages from art about art, to jokes about art about art, and finally to jokes about jokes about art about art.[1] Pure surface, the screen-prints (instant paintings) of Warhol gave way, as if by design, to the empty, 'hyper-realist', air-brushed perfection of the Seventies' ad-mass graphics style. Equally pure surface, the 'minimalism' (organised underachievement) of Philip Glass and Steve Reich moved smoothly from avant-garde status in the Sixties to soundtrack big business in the Eighties, while jazz fled the smouldering multifocal wreckage of the instantaneous/simultaneous New Thing to commercial sanctuary in the machine art of 'jazz-funk', there to tick over as efficiently as any other assembly-line.

The crucial thing that died with the rise of the instantaneous/simultaneous outlook was *development*: development of theme and idea, of feeling and thought, of story and character. Just as post-religious life has seen a rapid dwindling of interest in the process of growing older and wiser, so art has drifted up to the surface, forsaking progress for process, consequence for multifocal chaos, meaning for maximum impact. Thus, paralleling the general expectation of multiple orgasms instilled by the proliferating sex industry, the cinema has created the multiclimactic film in which narrative sense and dramatic structure are sacrificed to a sequence of sensationalistic shocks – a soullessly carnal genre appealing to the lowest common denominators in human nature: erotic titillation and the childish love of being thrilled or horrified. (Where linear development lingers on in the film world, it does so mainly in limply ironic form, typified by the designedly meaningless drift of the 'road movie'.)

The root of contemporary intellectual scorn for narrative – apart from the enjoyment of despising precisely what ordinary people enjoy most: a good story – is post-religious egoism. Confessedly self-centred, Lennon mocked McCartney's 'novelist' songs [102], contending that artistic authenticity could be achieved only by writing about oneself. If,

---

[1] The shift, during the Sixties, from a convergent literate/narrative moral culture to a divergent visual/structural relativism can be discerned in the various elements of the Chronology, below.

as lyrico-musical unities, his songs clearly cut deeper than McCartney's, they are ultimately as idiosyncratic as those of Dylan. Shallow as much of his work is, McCartney, facing candidly out into the world, repeatedly achieves the trick of matching popular appeal with quality of expression. If the difference between talent and genius in tune-writing lies in the degree to which a melody, more than merely catching the ear, tells an emotional story, he is beyond doubt an intermittent musical genius. By the same token, the depressing decline in his melodic gift since the break-up of The Beatles is the product of a deflation of feeling once his life outside the group lapsed into comfortable normality. Losing their expressive force, his tunes, while as crafted as ever, have become emotionally bland, while his music as a whole has lost the crucial element of habit-transcending surprise. This, though, has happened sooner or later to every artist working in pop. (Lennon, whose music was always more expressive than tuneful, managed to sustain his creative vitality only a little longer than his partner.) The ultimate root of this degenerative trait lies in the psychological change introduced into Western life during 1963–73: the revolution in the head which The Beatles played a large part in advancing and whose manifesto runs willy-nilly through their work, rendering it not only an outstanding repository of popular art but a cultural document of permanent significance.

The destabilising social and psychological evolution witnessed since the Sixties stems chiefly from the success of affluence and technology in realising the desires of ordinary people. The countercultural elements usually blamed for this were in fact resisting an endemic process of disintegration with its roots in scientific materialism. Far from adding to this fragmentation, they aimed to replace it with a new social order based on either love-and-peace or a vague anarchistic European version of revolutionary Maoism. When contemporary right-wing pundits attack the Sixties, they identify a momentous overall development but ascribe it to the very forces who most strongly reacted against it. The counterculture was less an agent of chaos than a marginal commentary, a passing attempt to propose alternatives to a waning civilisation.

Ironically the harshest critics of the Sixties are its most direct beneficiaries: the political voices of materialistic individualism. Their recent contribution to the accelerated social breakdown inaugurated around 1963 – economic Darwinism wrapped in self-contradictory socio-cultural prejudices – hasn't helped matters, yet even the New

Right can't be held responsible for the multifocal and fragmented techno-decadence into which the First World is currently sinking as if into a babbling, twinkling, microelectronically pulsing quicksand. During the Nineties, the fashion was to reprove others for our own faults; yet even if we take the blame for ignoring our limitations and eroding our own norms over the last thirty years, it is hard to imagine much, short of Fascism or a Second Coming, that will put Humpty back together again.

The Sixties seem like a golden age to us because, relative to now, they were. At their heart, the countercultural revolt against acquisitive selfishness – and, in particular, the hippies' unfashionable perception that we can change the world only by changing ourselves – looks in retrospect like a last gasp of the Western soul. Now radically disunited, we live dominated by and addicted to gadgets, our *raison d'être* and sense of community unfixably broken. While remnants of our once-stable core of religious faith survive, few are very edifying. Till hard drugs are legalised, the old world will retain some moral hold on us; but when they are, as the dictates of vulgar pragmatism predict, the last ties will be cut with our former way of life, far away from us on the other side of the sun-flooded chasm of the Sixties – where, courtesy of scientific technology, The Beatles can still be heard singing their buoyant, poignant, hopeful, love-advocating songs.

October 1993/January 1997

THE BEATLES' RECORDS

Note on the cataloguing system

The following account of The Beatles' official EMI discography treats their records in order of recording – that is, in the order in which issued tracks were commenced in the studio. Original songs by The Beatles released in the primary Parlophone/Apple discography of 1962–70 are catalogued from [1] (LOVE ME DO) to [186] (I ME MINE). Within this discography, non-original songs (titles recorded, but not written by, The Beatles) are indicated by numbers (signifying their place in the sequence) and letters (signifying their status as non-originals). Hence ANNA (GO TO HIM), recorded after [9] HOLD ME TIGHT, is listed as [9b], while BOYS, made after ANNA, becomes [9c].

The classification [U] indicates 'Unreleased', i.e., records not issued as part of the primary Parlophone/Apple discography. For example, IF YOU'VE GOT TROUBLE is catalogued as [U54], indicating that it was unreleased, but that, if issued, it would have been [54] in the overall sequence (between [53] YOU'VE GOT TO HIDE YOUR LOVE AWAY and [54] TELL ME WHAT YOU SEE). Again, unreleased songs not written by The Beatles are distinguished by numbers (indicating their place in the overall sequence) and letters (indicating their status as non-originals). Hence, LEAVE MY KITTEN ALONE, made after [38] I'M A LOSER and [38b] MR MOONLIGHT, becomes [U38c].

The classification [E] indicates 'Early', i.e., tracks and records taped before the first release [1] in the Parlophone/Apple discography. The same method of distinguishing originals from non-originals applies here. (Hence, MY BONNIE, made after [E3] CAYENNE, becomes [E3b].)

Although the primary Parlophone/Apple discography is discussed in full, a complete commentary on the Beatles' recordings issued by Apple/EMI between 1994 and 1996 has not been attempted, partly on the grounds that this would be pedantic and repetitious, but mainly because much of this material is of interest only to completists.

References to the tracks released on *Live At The BBC* and the *Baby It's You* single are, with one or two exceptions, confined to footnotes. Wherever mentioned, such tracks are given catalogue numbers, *although these references do not always imply corresponding entries in the main text, being intended only to indicate place in sequence.* Tracks issued on the three *Anthology* collections are dealt with more thoroughly, albeit without mechanical consistency. An extra section covers The Beatles' post-Lennon singles of 1995–6 and the *Anthology* project in general. There is also a complete compact discography.

Part 1
Going Up

- Where are we going, fellas?
- To the top, Jimmy.
- And where's that?
- Why, the toppermost of the poppermost!

John Lennon and Paul McCartney met on 6th July 1957 at a Saturday evening fête in St Peter's Church, Woolton, in Liverpool, where the 16-year-old Lennon's skiffle group, The Quarry Men, was performing. McCartney, nearly two years his future partner's junior, impressed him with his knowledge of chords, obscure rock-and-roll lyrics, and the correct way of tuning a guitar. Quickly enrolled into The Quarry Men, McCartney showed Lennon his early efforts at songwriting, startling him into trying his own hand at composition. Their songbook grew steadily over the next five years.

Consisting mainly of Lennon's school cronies, The Quarry Men were amateurish, perpetually losing and gaining members, and winning fewer and fewer engagements during 1958 and 1959. The only notable event of this period was the recruitment, in March 1958, of the 15-year-old George Harrison, who – along with Lennon, McCartney, John Lowe (piano), and Colin Hanton (drums) – appears on The Quarry Men's sole surviving artefact: a ten-inch shellac 78 made, during the summer of that year, at Phillips Sound Recording Service, Liverpool, for the sum of seventeen-and-sixpence (87.5p). Lennon sings lead on both tracks – a version of Buddy Holly's 'That'll Be The Day' (a UK hit from late 1957) and a McCartney–Harrison composition [E1] IN SPITE OF ALL THE DANGER,[1] both available on *Anthology 1*. The latter, a dreary doo-wop pastiche, has little to recommend it, but [E1b] THAT'LL BE THE DAY offers some reasonably nifty lead guitar (whether by Harrison or McCartney is unclear).

By the end of 1959, The Quarry Men existed chiefly as a name, the only survivors being Lennon, McCartney, and Harrison. As if to celebrate the new decade, March 1960 saw the birth of 'The Beatals', as Stuart Sutcliffe, Lennon's best friend and their reluctant new bass-player, rechristened them. For the moment drummerless and therefore

---

[1] A McCartney song for which Harrison was given equal credit because he played the solo.

largely gigless, they kept things going by rehearsing and recording rough home demos, three of which appear on *Anthology 1*: a McCartney rendition of Eddie Cochran's version of [E1c] HALLELUJAH, I LOVE HER SO, a McCartney–Lennon spoof of The Ink Spots entitled [E2] YOU'LL BE MINE, and a McCartney instrumental called [E3] CAYENNE, which, again, features some capable Shadows-style lead guitar.

[E3b] MY BONNIE *(trad. arr. Sheridan)*

> **Tony Sheridan** lead vocal, lead guitar; **Harrison** lead guitar,
> backing vocal; **Lennon** rhythm guitar, backing vocal;
> **McCartney** bass,[1] backing vocal; **Pete Best** drums
> Recorded: 22nd June 1961, Friedrich-Ebert-Halle, Hamburg.
> Producer: Bert Kaempfert. Engineer: Karl Hinze.
> UK release: 21st November 1995 (2-CD: *Anthology 1*)[2]
> US release: 21st November 1995 (2-CD: *Anthology 1*)

Joined in August 1960 by Pete Best on drums, The Beatles toiled through two years of poorly-paid and physically demanding gigs in Liverpool and Hamburg, gradually putting on musical muscle. Three tracks dating from their three-month stint at Hamburg's Top Ten Club in summer 1961[3] appear on *Anthology 1*. Taped in the assembly hall of a local infants' school, they come from a batch of seven The Beatles made for Polydor as a backing group for Tony Sheridan.[4] The latter, then regarded as the 'guvnor' of British rock-and-roll, was a useful guitarist and The Beatles were happy to grab the chance of occupying a stage with him at the Top Ten. Sharing a similar humour and thirst for German beer, they reputedly played hard together and some say that it was during this season of their Hamburg apprenticeship that the group acquired their rock-and-roll 'chops' (and general life experience) most intensively.[5]

---

[1] Stuart Sutcliffe left The Beatles in November 1960. McCartney took over bass a month later.

[2] This refers to the track's incorporation in the official Apple/EMI discography. As with the following two tracks, MY BONNIE has long been available on Polydor, having originally been issued in the UK on 23rd April 1962 (c/w 'The Saints'), credited to Tony Sheridan and The Beat Brothers.

[3] See Chronology.

[4] Tracks omitted by Apple/EMI are 'When The Saints Go Marching In', 'Why (Can't You Love Me Again'), 'Nobody's Child', and 'Take Out Some Insurance On Me, Baby'.

[5] Pete Best's believable account of this pill-popping, boozy, prostitute-populated period in *Beatle!, The Pete Best Story*, usefully fills in a section of The Beatles' story discreetly skipped over in the *Anthology* video and crudely caricatured in the feature

Sheridan and The Beatles were jamming together one night when the former's German publisher Albert Schacht dropped in to arrange a recording date for him. Enthused by what he heard, Schacht prevailed upon his friend composer/producer Bert Kaempfert to sign The Beatles on a short-term contract to enable them to back Sheridan on the session. (Because of this, they were still contracted to Kaempfert in April 1962 when Brian Epstein was hustling the deal with Parlophone. As his condition for an early contractual release, Kaempfert stipulated a second date – fulfilled somewhere between 23rd and 27th April 1962 in an unknown Hamburg venue – at which The Beatles recorded versions of 'Sweet Georgia Brown' and 'Swanee River'.)

MY BONNIE was selected because of incessant requests for it from drunken sailors. (The Beatles kept it in their set for the same reason.) A Scottish 3/4 ballad grotesquely unsuited to rock-and-roll treatment, the song required a fundamental adaption. Sheridan's characteristically full-tilt answer was to strum an A major verse in waltz-time before jumping randomly into a fast Twist-beat in C, his frenetic two-chorus guitar solo driving a performance entertaining enough to have penetrated the local German top five. The late-teen Beatles – energy hopeful, background vocals scrupulously rehearsed – are clearly aware that, here, opportunity (of a sort) knocks.

[E3c] AIN'T SHE SWEET *(Ager–Yellen)*

Lennon lead vocal, rhythm guitar; **Harrison** lead guitar;
  McCartney bass; **Pete Best** drums
Recorded: 22nd June 1961, Friedrich-Ebert-Halle, Hamburg.
Producer: Bert Kaempfert. Engineer: Karl Hinze.
UK release: 21st November 1995 (2-CD: *Anthology 1*)
US release: 21st November 1995 (2-CD: *Anthology 1*)

In the last hour of the Tony Sheridan session, The Beatles – presumably on a *quid pro quo* basis – had the opportunity to record a couple of numbers of their own. Considering that this was a chance to gain exposure as songwriters, it's odd that they didn't choose to record one of their originals – say, McCartney's [E5] LIKE DREAMERS DO or Lennon's [E6] HELLO LITTLE GIRL.[1] Instead, Lennon stepped up to

---

film *Backbeat* (1994).
[1] According to Harrison (*Anthology* video, Part 1), the group had misunderstood the conditions of the recording date. Having discovered that they were to play second fiddle to Sheridan, they may have decided not to throw away any stronger material on a self-negotiated year's contract.

take the vocal on another incongruous Twist-beat arrangement of an undistinguished standard. Written in 1927 by Milton Ager and Jack Yellen, AIN'T SHE SWEET was originally recorded by The New York Syncopators, although The Beatles would have known it from Gene Vincent's version made in 1956.[1] While it presumably went down well with the raucous clientèle of the Top Ten Club, it made little sense as a choice for The Beatles' first professional recording and fails to reward attention in hindsight.

[E4] CRY FOR A SHADOW *(Harrison–Lennon)*

Harrison lead guitar; **Lennon** rhythm guitar; **McCartney** bass;
  Pete Best drums
Recorded: 22nd June 1961, Friedrich-Ebert-Halle, Hamburg.
Producer: Bert Kaempfert. Engineer: Karl Hinze.
UK release: 21st November 1995 (2-CD: *Anthology 1*)
US release: 21st November 1995 (2-CD: *Anthology 1*)

The Beatles' first professionally produced original composition is an instrumental roughly in the style of The Shadows. Dating from their three-month stint at the Top Ten Club in Hamburg in summer 1961, it was taped in the assembly hall of a Hamburg infants' school in the last hour of the session during which they backed Tony Sheridan on five tracks made for Polydor.[2]

With Stuart Sutcliffe and probably Astrid Kirchherr present in the hall. The Beatles chose to record two tracks: the Lennon-led 'Ain't She Sweet' and CRY FOR A SHADOW. A Simple C major affair built on the most basic guitar changes, the only musical point of interest in CRY FOR A SHADOW is Lennon's recurrent strumming between B diminished and F major seventh, holding the low F with his thumb – a performance accomplished on a thru-pickup Rickenbacker 325 bought in Hamburg in 1960 (his sole electric guitar until 1964). McCartney plays his later famous Hofner 500/1 violin bass, purchased in Hamburg at the beginning of 1961. Using a twin-pickup Gretsch Duo Jet, the eighteen-year-old Harrison does a passable Hank Marvin impersonation

---

[1] The song was in their act continuously from 1957 to 1962. A different version of AIN'T SHE SWEET, sung in ragtime style by a sore-throated Lennon, was ad-libbed on 24th July 1969 during a session otherwise devoted to [181] SUN KING *(Anthology 3)*.

[2] 'My Bonnie Lies Over the Ocean', 'When The Saints Go Marching In', 'Why (Can't You Love Me Again)', 'Nobody's Child', and 'Take out Some Insurance On Me, Baby'. 'By Bonnie' and 'The Saints' *(sic)* were released as a single credited to Tony Sheridan and the Beat Brothers, selling a reputed 100,000.

on the middle eight;[1] apart from that, his only idea is to play the tune an octave down on the third chorus. Roughhouse teenage fun.

[E5] LIKE DREAMERS DO *(McCartney–Lennon)*[2]

McCartney lead vocal, bass; **Lennon** rhythm guitar; **Harrison** lead guitar; **Pete Best** drums
Recorded: 1st January 1962, Decca Studios, London.
Producer: Mike Smith. Engineer: Unknown.
UK release: 21st November 1995 (2-CD: *Anthology 1*)[3]
US release: 21st November 1995 (2-CD: *Anthology 1*)

Their seasons in Hamburg built The Beatles into what their then-drummer Pete Best describes as 'a charismatic powerhouse' – something wild at the fringe of British pop, uninhibited by the fixed ideas and anaemic politeness of the dominant London scene. Unfortunately, their manager Brian Epstein, a mere month in the job, misguidedly tried to court this outmoded convention by making his 'boys' play a versatility-demonstrating showbiz set at their audition for Decca in January 1962.[4] The strategy backfired. Forced by the Decca engineers

---

[1] Harrison was far more interested in guitars than Lennon and McCartney and picked up more than a dozen during his Beatles career. He acquired the Duo Jet, the first of several Gretsch models he used, from a 'Cunard Yank' (Liverpool liner seaman) who had brought it back from America in 1961; it replaced his Futurama, a fake Fender Stratocaster imported by Selmer from Czechoslovakia. (Careful to distinguish themselves from The Shadows, The Beatles steered clear of Fenders until 1965.)

[2] This was the writing credit on the first Beatles issues. The familiar 'Lennon–Mc-Cartney' became standard only with the release of the group's fourth single [12] SHE LOVES YOU.

[3] This refers to the track's incorporation into the official Apple-approved discography. As with the following four tracks, LIKE DREAMERS DO has long been available on Decca.

[4] Epstein, son of an upper middle-class Jewish businessman, ran NEMS (North End Music Stores), the leading record outlet in the North-west. Shy, sensitive, temperamental, and charming, he knew record retail and ran an efficient operation. Beyond that, he was something of an innocent abroad – a lonely rich boy looking for a reason. Discovering this in The Beatles, he believed fiercely in them and, lacking family commitments, worked round the clock for them; yet management was new territory for him and, unversed in the customs of the music business, he was taken for many rides to begin with. (As late as the 1964 American tour, he was still naively giving away merchandising concessions to anyone who asked for them.) Sincere as he was, Epstein made many friends in this new milieu and, despite initially trying too hard to clean up The Beatles' image and music, his efforts at remoulding them paid off in opening up the crucial London end of the business both for them and for his other NEMS acts. His approach was based on the old showbiz ethic in which a gentleman's handshake was his co-signature. (So disgusted was he with the crass exploitativeness of the standard pop contract that he drew up his own.) The showbiz

to use the studio equipment rather than their own battered Vox amps, The Beatles were unable to reproduce the energy and dirty, overdriven sound which made their stage-act so exciting. Nor were they helped by a recording regime which budgeted for one take per song and no overdubs. Unbewitched by the group's facetious manner, and refusing in any case to believe that a Liverpool act could appeal to a national audience, Decca turned them down.

LIKE DREAMERS DO, written by McCartney in 1957, kicked off the ill-fated Decca session with its ear-catching intro, in which unison guitars play an ascending chromatic scale from C sharp minor to A major before reaching a verse which disrupts a standard doo-wop sequence (I-vi-IV-V) by adding jazzy sixths in the bass. Sadly, this devious originality isn't matched by the unctuous melody and lyric, which are entirely of their Brylcreemed era. In June 1964, when everything Beatleoid was bankable, The Applejacks invested in a version of this number, but ran out of credit at No. 20.

[E5b] THE SHEIK OF ARABY *(Smith–Wheeler–Snyder)*

Harrison lead vocal, lead guitar; **Lennon** rhythm guitar, backing
vocal; **McCartney** bass, backing vocal; **Pete Best** drums
Recorded: 1st January 1962, Decca Studios, London.
Producer: Mike Smith. Engineer: Unknown.
UK release: 21st November 1995 (2-CD: *Anthology 1*)
US release: 21st November 1995 (2-CD: *Anthology 1*)

Passing swiftly on via versions of [13c] MONEY and [13e] TILL THERE WAS YOU, The Beatles tried the cheeky chappie approach with this vaudeville song written in 1922 by Irving Berlin's New York sidekick Ted Snyder. THE SHEIK OF ARABY was a typical banjo/ukelele novelty number which wouldn't have been out of place in the mouth of Harrison's cult-fancy of the 1930s–40s, George Formby.[1] During the

---

background gave him a broader view than that of the wide-boys who were his main rivals, allowing him to associate The Beatles with the smarter side of the entertainment industry: playwright Alun Owen, film director Richard Lester, and many top British character actors. Driven and obsessive, Epstein got emotionally involved with his acts, devoting all of himself to them and loving The Beatles almost to the point of adoration. At a lower temperature and to varying degrees, they reciprocated this, albeit masking it under their usual barbed mickey-taking.

[1] In fact, Harrison had copped it from a version by Formby's Sixties successors, Joe Brown and The Bruvvers. One of Britain's original Fifties rock-and-rollers, Brown invented his own brand of cockney music-hall in the Sixties, probably under the influence of Lionel Bart's East End musicals *Fings Ain't Wot They Used To Be* and

Fifties, English parents still sang music-hall songs to their children and this tradition consequently permeated English pop throughout the Sixties, peaking with *Sgt. Pepper's Lonely Hearts Club Band*, the 'East End soul' of The Small Faces, the pastiches of The Bonzo Dog Doo-Dah Band, and the 1966–9 output of The Kinks (the only group to rival The Beatles for variety of form and style).[1] By 1970, this tradition was dying and, despite a limp attempt to revive it by Cockney Rebel, played little part in the theatrical 'glam rock' era of 1971–3. During the late Seventies, the London groups Madness and Ian Dury and the Blockheads resuscitated the music-hall theme and echoes of it can be heard in the Nineties output of Blur. However, this style, like folk music, is no longer an organic part of English popular culture, much to the latter's detriment.

Sadly, the present track is a poor example. A dull song finds Harrison frequently off-key, the pseudo-cockney interjections of Lennon and McCartney grate, and Best is forced to trundle out his only snare 'fill' (a press roll) half a dozen times too often.

[E6] HELLO LITTLE GIRL *(McCartney–Lennon)*

> **Lennon** lead vocal, rhythm guitar; **McCartney** bass, harmony
> vocal; **Harrison** lead guitar; **Pete Best** drums
> Recorded: 1st January 1962, Decca Studios, London.
> Producer: Mike Smith. Engineer: Unknown.
> UK release: 21st November 1995 (2-CD: *Anthology 1*)
> US release: 21st November 1995 (2-CD: *Anthology 1*)

Sweating to impress the Decca executives, The Beatles followed THE SHEIK OF ARABY with versions of The Teddy Bears' 'To Know Her Is To Love Her', Bobby Vee's 'Take Good Care Of My Baby', Chuck Berry's [U13s] MEMPHIS, TENNESSEE, and Carl Perkins' [U11c] SURE TO FALL (IN LOVE WITH YOU). They then turned to this, Lennon's first original song, written in 1957 as a response to his partner's early efforts

---

Oliver! Harrison, who became, and remains, good friends with Brown, sang four of the latter's repertoire songs with The Beatles during 1960–2: 'Darktown Strutters Ball', 'What A Crazy World We're Living In', 'A Picture Of You', and 'I'm Henry the Eighth I Am'.

[1] The Small Faces: *Ogden's Nut Gone Flake* (1968). The Bonzo Dog Doo-Dah Band: *Gorilla* (1967), *The Doughnut in Granny's Greenhouse* (1968), *Tadpoles* (1969), *Keynsham* (1969). The Kinks: *Something Else* (1967), *Village Green Preservation Society* (1968). See also The Blossom Toes' *We Are Ever So Clean* (1968).

at composition. As with [E5] Like Dreamers Do, Hello Little Girl is in A major, a consciously 'pop' creation based on the obvious chords and lacking Lennon's trademark blue notes.[1] Then the most blatantly commercial thing in their repertoire, it's sung with hardly a trace of the group's Northern tang, presumably to suggest to Decca's A&R men that The Beatles could, if required, fit into the prevailing Southern pop ethos.[2]

[E6b] THREE COOL CATS *(Leiber–Stoller)*

Harrison lead vocal, lead guitar; Lennon rhythm guitar, backing vocal; McCartney bass, backing vocal; Pete Best drums
Recorded: 1st January 1962, Decca Studios, London.
Producer: Mike Smith. Engineer: Unknown.
UK release: 21st November 1995 (2-CD: *Anthology 1*)
US release: 21st November 1995 (2-CD: *Anthology 1*)

Having dashed off Buddy Holly's [U13m] Crying, Waiting, Hoping, McCartney's 'Love Of The Loved', Dinah Washington's 'September In The Rain', and a version of [E6d] Besame Mucho, The Beatles concluded proceedings with two numbers written for The Coasters by the New York partnership of Jerry Leiber and Mike Stoller. Harrison does better with Three Cool Cats than with [E5b] The Sheik of Araby, but this is far from Leiber–Stoller's finest hour and his exertions are palpably in vain.

[E6c] SEARCHIN' *(Leiber–Stoller)*

McCartney bass, lead vocal; Lennon rhythm guitar, backing vocal; Harrison lead guitar, backing vocal; Pete Best drums
Recorded: 1st January 1962, Decca Studios, London.
Producer: Mike Smith. Engineer: Unknown.
UK release: 21st November 1995 (2-CD: *Anthology 1*)
US release: 21st November 1995 (2-CD: *Anthology 1*)

McCartney gives it his all on The Coasters' American top 5 hit of 1957,[3] but the song soon wears thin and Best's limitations as a drummer are nakedly apparent. All in all, Decca's coolness about The

---

[1]. The only musical point of interest is the swift chromatic descent at the end, paralleling the equally swift chromatic ascents in [E5] Like Dreamers Do.
[2]. In October 1963, The Beatles' NEMS stablemates The Fourmost took their cover of Hello Little Girl to No. 9 in the UK singles chart.
[3]. The Beatles also performed the B-side of Searchin': [U11b] Young Blood (*Live At The BBC*).

Beatles in January 1962 is quite understandable. Though Mike Smith, the producer who oversaw the audition, had seen the group in action at The Cavern, there was no precedent for signing an act merely because they could whip up their home crowd. The first prerequisite for an early Sixties recording contract was presentability: potential 'artistes' had to be 'professional', i.e., musically competent, groomable, and acquiescent to the demands of their producers who, it was assumed, would select their songs for them from batches circulated by writing teams through the normal channels. Loud, long-haired, and seemingly incapable of desisting from laughter, The Beatles did not meet these requirements. Nor, at this stage, did they have much going for them as songwriters. It didn't help that, while there was nothing wrong with his managerial instincts, Brian Epstein lacked musical judgement. Left to his own devices, he would have been at a loss to develop the group's creativity. Doing that would require someone highly qualified yet unhampered by the hidebound UK studio scene of 1962. By a coincidence so unlikely as to be positively mind-boggling, The Beatles were about to encounter such a man.

[E6d] BESAME MUCHO *(Velazquez–Skylar)*

McCartney vocal, bass; **Lennon** rhythm guitar; **Harrison** lead
   guitar; **Pete Best** drums
Recorded: 6th June 1962, Abbey Road 2/3?
Producers: Ron Richards/George Martin. Engineer: Norman Smith.
UK release: 21st November 1995 (2-CD: *Anthology 1*)
US release: 21st November 1995 (2-CD: *Anthology 1*)

On 9th May 1962, The Beatles were in the middle of their third residency in a Hamburg 'beat cellar' (seven weeks at the Star-Club) when a telegram arrived from Brian Epstein in London. He was delighted to inform them that he'd secured a recording contract and an initial studio date with an EMI subsidiary called Parlophone. This was a canny lie. The agreement, brokered with Parlophone's chief producer George Martin, was actually for nothing more than a try-out. After the flop of the Decca audition four months earlier, Epstein seems to have wanted his 'boys' to go into the Parlophone session with no qualms, and was perfectly happy for them to turn up at Abbey Road under the false impression that this was to be a full-blown recording session.

At this point, The Beatles had been playing as a four-piece with Pete Best in the drum seat for nearly eighteen months – by far their most enduring line-up prior to Ringo Starr's recruitment three months later. When, on the afternoon of Wednesday 6th June, they pulled into the Abbey Road car park in their rusty white van, they were only four days off the plane from Hamburg: tired but sharp. Having rehearsed for two evenings before heading south on Tuesday, they carried with them a neatly-typed set list, presumably drawn up by Epstein and apparently conceived on the assumption that the Parlophone staff would wish to be entertained by their entire club repertoire. No one knows how far they got with this before the engineers intervened to point out that McCartney's spluttering vox amp needed looking at if any actual recording was to take place.[1] Since there was no time for repairs, a vast Tannoy had to be wheeled up from the echo chamber downstairs and hooked to a Leak in Studio 2. By the time the tape was ready to roll, George Martin had departed to the canteen, leaving his specialist rock-and-roll assistant Ron Richards at the desk with engineers Norman Smith and Chris Neal in attendance.

The Beatles began their first Parlophone recording session at 7pm with Besame Mucho, a typically blowsy rumba ballad of the 1940s. Written by Consuelo Valazquez for the Mediterranean/Latin American audience, the song had 'crossed over' to the Anglo-American market in 1944 courtesy of Sunny Skylar's bilingual lyric and its appearance in the all-star revue film *Follow the Boys*, subsequently becoming one of the big hits of the end of the Second World War in a swing arrangement by Jimmy Dorsey's Orchestra sung by Bob Eberly and Helen O'Connell. Rated a standard during the Fifties, Besame Mucho was recorded by many 'artistes', and McCartney confesses himself unable to recall which version, if any, he based his arrangement on.[2]

Like other, similar material foreign to The Beatles' basic R&B/rock-and-roll style – e.g., [66b] A Taste of Honey, [13e] Till There Was You, Stephen Foster's 'Beautiful Dreamer', Marlene Dietrich's 'Falling In Love Again', and (especially) Cole Porter's 'Begin the Beguine' – Besame Mucho was adopted by The Beatles, or at any rate by McCartney, as not entirely serious showcase for his winsome versatility. During the group's Hamburg sets, the song was reserved for the early mornings when a grinning McCartney would step forward and deliver it with parodic gusto while the others shrank from him,

---

[1] To judge by the 6th June take of [1] Love Me Do (*Anthology 1*), the break-up in the signal from McCartney's bass seems not to have been fixed.

[2] It was certainly not The Coasters' very different attempt, a miss for them in 1960. Possibly The Beatles' arrangement was based on (or at least suggested by) others than in circulation on the UK beat scene. Jet Harris, for example, hastened to record an instrumental version after leaving The Shadows in early 1962, a single which peaked at No. 22 in the *Record Retailer* chart a week before the Beatles' 6th June session at Abbey Road.

miming excruciated embarrassment. Such fooling around was vital in venues like the Star-Club, as much for the sake of the band's sanity as to keep their clientèle of inebriated seamen and bored whores satisfied. (The others both had similarly anomalous 'features': Lennon and 'My Bonnie Lies Over the Ocean', Harrison with his imponderable predilection for the novelty cockney songs of Joe Brown and The Bruvvers.) Why BESAME MUCHO was promoted for the Decca and EMI auditions is unclear; probably Epstein engineered it.[1]

In G minor, the song contains descending chromatic changes – picked up in interjections from Harrison's guitar – of the kind that crop up often in the later Lennon–McCartney canon. The arrangement, such as it is, consists of (a) McCartney shouting 'Cha-cha *boom!*' in apparent homage to Xavier Cugat, and (b) cramming both guiatars low over rumbling semiquavers from Best's tom-toms before breaking into a straight Twist-beat on the chorus. The group plays fast in the wan hope of generating some excitement, but the hackneyed cabaret breast-beating of the lyric obstinately obtrudes through McCartney's winking braggadocio, while his decision to drop the passing G at the end of each chorus ('Make all my drea-*eams* come true') – possibly a shot at bringing the song into line with 1962 Northern vernacular – merely sounds clumsy.[2]

[E7] LOVE ME DO *(McCartney–Lennon)* [audition version]

Lennon vocal, rhythm guitar, harmonica; **McCartney** vocal, bass;
   Harrison lead guitar; **Pete Best** drums
Recorded: 6th June 1962, Abbey Road 2/3?
Producers: Ron Richards/George Martin. Engineer: Norman Smith.
UK release: 21st November 1995 (2-CD: *Anthology 1*)
US release: 21st November 1995 (2-CD: *Anthology 1*)

If BESAME MUCHO failed to impress the Parlophone crew, the next track The Beatles recorded prompted engineer Norman Smith to send tape-op Chris Neal to the canteen to fetch George Martin. The reason is clear from the audition tape, issued on A*nthology 1*. Here, suddenly, was something utterly fresh and original. Intrigued, Martin supervised a take which caught the cold Northern breeze of a very unusual sound.

At the same time, this audition version shows one of the reasons

---

[1] BESAME MUCHO entered The Beatles' set in 1961 but was dropped after 1962.
[2] The Beatles briefly returned to BESAME MUCHO at the end of an aimless day during the 'Get Back' sessions at Apple on 29th January 1969.

why Pete Best was sacked: in moving to the ride cymbal for the first middle eight, he slows down and the group falters. (On the other hand, his switch to Twist-beat for the second – instrumental – middle eight is effective, suggesting that this is how The Beatles may then have played the song live, whipping up the audience with a mini-crescendo.)

Two more originals followed: [2] P.S. I LOVE YOU and [4] ASK ME WHY, neither of which survive today in their 6th June versions. After the session ended at 10.00pm, the now-wary group entered the control room and lounged with studied cool while Martin explained to them in great detail where they were going wrong. When he had finished, he sat back, genially inviting them to say whether there was anything *they* didn't like. 'Well, for a start,' drawled the lugubrious Harrison, 'I don't like your tie.' Fortunately Martin elected to see the funny side of this and, the ice thus broken, The Beatles thereupon slipped gratefully into comedy mode. By the time they left twenty minutes later, the Parlophone team were literally crying with laughter, a factor which, more than anything else, seems to have induced Martin to sign the group.[1]

[E7b] HOW DO YOU DO IT? *(Murray)*

Lennon vocal, rhythm guitar; **McCartney** vocal, bass; **Harrison**
  backing vocal, lead guitar; **Starr** drums
Recorded: 4th September 1962, Abbey Road 2.
Producer: George Martin. Engineer: Norman Smith.
UK release: 21st November 1995 (2-CD: *Anthology 1*)
US release: 21st November 1995 (2-CD: *Anthology 1*)

Despite inking the contract, George Martin was far from convinced by The Beatles' provisional pretensions to songwriting and immediately began casting around for a third-party hit for them. Learning of this, his deputy Ron Richards fished out a demo of the present ditty by its writer Mitch Murray, arguing that a 'beat' arrangement of it was

[1] The contract was backdated to 4th June so as to secure copyright to the 6th June session, for which The Beatles were paid the standard fee of 7 each. At this stage, The Beatles had recorded many tracks on various occasions, none of outstanding quality. Their earliest recordings, with and without Tony Sheridan, have been issued complete by Polydor; three of these ([E3b], [E3c], [E4]) are available on *Anthology 1*. Other early material has been assembled by Decca. Including live tapes from the Star-Club, there are 53 such tracks in all. (For a detailed discussion see Russell, *The Beatles: Album File and Complete Discography*, pp. 4–28.) A further 56 tracks made for BBC radio during 1963–5 were issued by Apple/EMI in December 1994 *(Live at the BBC)*. Some of these are discussed in the following text.

virtually guaranteed to find its way up the charts. An acetate of How Do You Do It? was accordingly despatched to Liverpool, where The Beatles – certain that if they recorded the song they'd never be able to show their faces in the city again – glumly set about rearranging it in readiness for their first full recording date at Abbey Road.

They began this session with Murray's number, quickly getting shot of it so as to spend as much time as possible on their own [1] Love Me Do. In the contemporary Tin Pan Alley spirit of keeping-it-simple-for-the-kids, How Do You Do It? revolves around a shamelessly bright, breezy, and childish G major tune.[1] Anxious not to get saddled with it, The Beatles saw no percentage in working too hard on a vocal arrangement and came up with the most obvious possible harmony: a string of facile thirds. Their performance, captured in an unknown number of takes, ingeniously combines obliging efficiency with affable indifference. Only Harrison bothers to have a little fun with his semi-snappy, semi-sloppy guitar solo.

More than ever persuaded of the song's commercial potential, Martin was doubtless impressed, if mildly miffed, by The Beatles' steadfast disinclination to have anything to do with it. How Do You Do It, with its 'toe-tapping' Twist-beat and faceless catchiness, was an obvious hit for someone, but stylistically *passé*. (It might have suited Cliff Richard and The Shadows, the major force in British pop during 1960–2.) For a while, though, it was touch-and-go as to whether Love Me Do would win the contest, both tracks being mastered in readiness for cutting. Eventually, to The Beatles's relief, Martin capitulated, offering their version of How Do You Do It? to fellow NEMS[2] signings Gerry and The Pacemakers. Sensibly dropping the ghastly harmony but retaining the rest of the arrangement, Gerry Marsden and his colleagues took the song to No. 1 in April 1963, displacing Cliff Richard's 'Summer Holiday' and being themselves dethroned three weeks later by the Beatles' [10] From Me To You.

---

[1] This lowest common denominator strategy paid off. Murray achieved two No. 1's with Gerry and The Pacemakers (How Do You Do It? and 'I Like It') and two near-misses for the top spot with Freddie and The Dreamers ('I'm Telling You Now' and 'You Were Made For Me'). All are in the same cunningly brainless vein.
[2] See [E5], note.

[1] LOVE ME DO *(McCartney–Lennon)*

McCartney vocal, bass; **Lennon** vocal, harmonica, rhythm guitar
(?); **Harrison** acoustic rhythm guitar, backing vocal; **Starr** drums
(version 1); tambourine (version 2); **Andy White** drums (version
2)
Recorded: 6th June; 4th, 11th September 1962, Abbey Road 2.
Producer: George Martin. Engineer: Norman Smith.
UK release: 5th October 1962 (A single/P.S. I LOVE YOU)
US release: 22nd July 1963 (LP: *Introducing The Beatles*)

Made up while 'sagging off' (playing truant) from the Liverpool
Institute in 1958, LOVE ME DO was one of 16-year-old Paul
McCartney's earliest songs.[1] Unsure of how to finish it, he showed it
to his friend John Lennon, who may have contributed the rudimentary
middle eight.[2] The lyric is perfunctory and, where pop numbers of
this period classically revolved around three common chords, LOVE ME
DO mostly makes do with two (G and C).

One of half a dozen songs rehearsed during the afternoon of 4th
September 1962 in Abbey Road's Studio 3, LOVE ME DO had to wait
on Parlophone's preferred choice [E7b] HOW DO YOU DO IT? before
being attempted by an understandably jittery group. (Unused to
headphones, they were stiff with nerves and took fifteen takes to get it
right.) Both songs were considered for release as The Beatles' debut
single but, during the two hours it had taken to make, Martin had
formed a hunch about LOVE ME DO. Its vernacular title, dockside
harmonica, and open harmonies had a freshness that suited the group
and seemed intriguingly hard to categorise. Texan singer Bruce
Channel's plaintive 'Hey! Baby', a hit in Britain that spring, had
featured similar harmonica[3] but, apart from that, nothing else on the
market sounded anything like it.

There was still, though, something bothering him about LOVE ME
DO: Starr's drumming. (The legend is that he was unsteady, hurrying
into the choruses.) According to Abbey Road's general manager Ken

---

[1] The first was 'I Lost My Little Girl', closely followed by [94] WHEN I'M SIXTY-
FOUR. According to Pete Best (p. 155), LOVE ME DO was 'conceived' during The
Beatles' third Hamburg season in April–May 1962. It started life, he insists, as 'Love,
Love Me Do', becoming shortened soon afterwards. Possibly he misunderstood that
it was an old song being tried out in the band's set for the first time.
[2] McCartney recalls the song as 50-50 between him and Lennon (Miles, *Paul
McCartney: Many Years From Now*, p. 36).
[3] Played by Delbert McClinton, whose style Lennon imitated. (The Beatles
shared a bill with Channel and McClinton at the Tower Ballroom, Wallasey, on 21st
June 1962.)

Townsend, McCartney was as dissatisfied as George Martin with Starr's approach, though when questioned by Mark Lewisohn twenty-five years later the song's author put a different spin on it.[1] Martin, he recalled, decided that LOVE ME DO needed remaking with a session drummer because Starr had failed to 'lock in' his bass-drum with the bass guitar. This convention of the polite studio style of the early Sixties was about to vanish under the impact of loose-swinging drummers like Starr and The Rolling Stones' Charlie Watts (to reappear around 1980 under the automated auspices of the drum-machine). However in 1962 Starr's virtue as an intuitive time-keeper had yet to be recognised and consequently the group trooped back into Studio 2 a week later to record LOVE ME DO all over again. Andy White, a regular player on EMI sessions, 'sat in' on drums while a disenchanted Starr tapped a superfluous reinforcement to the snare on tambourine. In the event, both versions of LOVE ME DO were issued: the first (mixed bottom-light to disguise Starr's bass-drum) went out as the A-side of The Beatles' first single; the second was issued on later versions of the single and as the opening track on Side 2 of the group's debut album *Please Please Me*.

Written in what the group thought of as a 'bluesy' style, LOVE ME DO was extraordinarily raw by the standards of its time, standing out from the tame fare offered on the Light Programme and Radio Luxembourg like a bare brick wall in a suburban sitting-room. Indeed, next to the standard pop output then strolling blandly up and down the 'hit parade' on Alan Freeman's *Pick of the Pops* every Sunday, its modal gauntness seemed almost primitive. As such, the public were puzzled by it and sales were cautious. While the record's erratic progress to its highest position at No. 17 in December was followed with excitement by Beatle fans in Liverpool, many thought it a poor advertisement for the energy the group generated live. Purists claimed, too, that the arrangement had been messed about with. George Martin had changed the solo vocal line crossing into the harmonica break, giving it to McCartney instead of Lennon on the grounds that, due to an overlap between the last word and the first harmonica note, the latter had been singing 'Love me *waahh!*', which was deemed uncommercial. (According to McCartney, they hadn't rehearsed with the harmonica and had to alter the arrangement on the spot under Martin's direction.)[2]

Simple as it is, LOVE ME DO was quite a cunning record, serving to

---

[1] Lewisohn, *Sessions*, pp. 6, 18.
[2] In the 6th June version, Lennon sings against his overdubbed harmonica.

introduce The Beatles to the English public in several ways at once. As rearranged under Martin's direction, it offered two features for the leaders (Lennon's harmonica riff, McCartney's unaccompanied title-phrase) as well as its playground-appeal 'hook' (the drone-harmonised 'Ple-e-e-ease') and a little character spot for Starr (his po-faced cymbal crash at the end of Lennon's solo). Only Harrison stayed in the background, strumming diffidently. But the subtlest effect was the record's air of unvarnished honesty. Though the stark, open-fifth vocal harmony was bathed in reverb, the rest of the production was startlingly 'dry' compared with the echo-saturated sound of UK pop during the preceding four years. The result was a candour which perfectly complemented the group's forthright image, setting them apart from everything else on offer.

If one element of the record can be said to have counted above all others it was Lennon's wailing harmonica. Played with passionate overblowing and no 'bent' notes, it had little in common with any of the American blues styles,[1] instead suggesting to British audiences the blunt vitality of working-class Northernness as introduced around 1960 in the soundtracks to films like *Room At The Top*, *Saturday Night and Sunday Morning*, and *A Taste Of Honey*.

Many UK pop musicians have since recalled sensing something epochal in LOVE ME DO when it first appeared. Crude as it was compared to The Beatles' later achievements, it blew a stimulating autumn breeze through an enervated pop scene, heralding a change in the tone of post-war British life matched by the contemporary appearances of the first James Bond film, *Dr No*, and BBC TV's live satirical programme *That Was The Week That Was*. From now on, social influence in Britain was to swing away from the old class-based order of deference to 'elders and betters' and succumb to the frank and fearless energy of 'the younger generation'. The first faint chime of a revolutionary bell, LOVE ME DO represented far more than the sum of

---

[1] In a 'life-lines' feature for *New Musical Express* in 1963, Lennon nominated as his favourite player the North Carolina country blues harmonica virtuoso Sonny Terry, but their styles bear no resemblance. Meeting Lennon around this time in the Crawdaddy Club in Richmond, The Rolling Stones' Brian Jones asked him whether he'd used 'a harmonica or a blues harp' on LOVE ME DO (Coleman, Vol. 1, p. 186). Jones was differentiating between the one-key diatonic harmonica employed in blues and the chromatic harmonica played by more sophisticated musicians such as Stevie Wonder. Lennon told him he'd used 'a harmonica with a button', meaning a chromatic, which is actually played with a slide-bar. (LOVE ME DO is playable on a diatonic, but the solo involves some tricky 'bent' notes.)

its simple parts. A new spirit was abroad: artless yet unabashed – and awed by nothing.[1]

[2] **P.S. I LOVE YOU** *(McCartney–Lennon)*

> **McCartney** vocal, bass; **Lennon** backing vocal, acoustic rhythm guitar; **Harrison** backing vocal, lead guitar; **Starr** maracas; **Andy White** drums
> Recorded: 11th September 1962, Abbey Road 2.
> Producer: Ron Richards. Engineer: Norman Smith.
> UK release: 5th October 1962 (B single/Love Me Do)
> US release: 22nd July 1963 (LP: *Introducing The Beatles*)

Written in Hamburg in 1961 by McCartney,[2] this song became a staple of The Beatles' act during 1962–3, being especially popular with the group's girl fans. Because of this, it was one of the four songs they chose to demo at their EMI audition on 6th June, following which it was taped after the remake of [1] LOVE ME DO a week later. Andy White, brought in to play drums on [1], also played on P.S. I LOVE YOU, adding Latin rim-shots to what is basically a brisk cha-cha. A contribution to the sub-genre of pop 'letter' songs, P.S. I LOVE YOU deploys a simple, derivative lyric draped, with smooth feminine rhymes, around the contours of a tune in D whose main surprise is a dark sidestep to B flat on the chorus ('P.S. I love *you* . . .').[3]

McCartney's gift as a melodist is obvious in the bold range of his line. Whereas Lennon's lazy irony is reflected in his inclination towards the minimal intervals of everyday speech, McCartney's sentimental optimism emerges in the wide rise and fall of his tunes and bass lines. P.S. I LOVE YOU, for instance, covers more than an octave – yet, in its middle eight, which doubles as its intro, Lennon obstinately harmonises on one note. (This is, in fact, one of the few Beatles records in which the vocal harmonies, including some unusually low-lying parts, aren't entirely convincing – particularly McCartney's line in the second and third middle eights.)

Many of the group's early originals show an eagerness to fit existing

---

[1] None of this meant anything in America, where a mystified Capitol Records declined to issue the record. Finally released on Tollie in 1964, it displaced Mary Wells's Motown classic 'My Guy' (written by Smokey Robinson) at the top of the US singles chart in the first week of June 1964.

[2] The 'you' of the title is usually said to have been McCartney's girlfriend Dot Rohne. He, however, denies this, recalling it as simply an exercise in the 'letter song' idiom (Miles, op. cit., p. 38).

[3] The model was The Shirelles' 'Soldier Boy', an American No. 1 in May 1962.

showbiz categories, and P.S. I LOVE YOU sounds like a hopeful 'standard' to be offered to established performers. Unlike Lennon, who managed to place only three nondescript numbers with other artists ([7] DO YOU WANT TO KNOW A SECRET, recorded by Billy J. Kramer and The Dakotas, and [E6] HELLO LITTLE GIRL and 'I'm In Love', both recorded by The Fourmost), McCartney sold a dozen titles during The Beatles' career, including three of his most harmonically ambitious songs – 'Loved Of The Loved', 'It's For You', and the remarkable [U146] STEP INSIDE LOVE (all for Cilla Black). One of his first efforts in this vein, P.S. I LOVE YOU, despite its naivety, survives on the strength of its expressive verse/chorus.

[3] PLEASE PLEASE ME *(McCartney–Lennon)*

> **Lennon** vocal, rhythm guitar, harmonica; **McCartney** vocal, bass
>   guitar; **Harrison** harmony vocal, lead guitar; **Starr** drums
> Recorded: 11th September; 26th November 1962, Abbey Road 2.
> Producer: George Martin. Engineer: Norman Smith.
> UK release: 11th January 1963 (A single/ASK ME WHY)
> US release: 25th February 1963 (A single/ASK ME WHY)

John Lennon wrote PLEASE PLEASE ME at his Aunt Mimi's house, taking the first line of Bing Crosby's Thirties hit 'Please' as a starting-point for a mid-tempo solo ballad in the doomily climactic style of Roy Orbison.[1] Tried out at the end of the final session for [1] LOVE ME DO, it intrigued George Martin without seeming to him to be finished. Still sceptical of Lennon and McCartney's songwriting capacities, he suggested that they speed it up, rearranging it for harmonised voices.

With the threat of [E7b] HOW DO YOU DO IT still hanging over them, The Beatles worked hard on the rewrite and, nine weeks later, with LOVE ME DO dithering in the UK chart, they returned to Abbey Road with what they knew had to be an all-out success. The redraft, including a new hook played by Harrison, retained, in its octave-leaping chorus, Orbison's characteristic rise from sepulchral chest-register to moaning falsetto. However, the main influence was now that of The Everly Brothers' 1960 No. 1 'Cathy's Clown'. (Lennon and McCartney were practised Everlys impersonators, 'Cathy's Clown' being a special favourite.) Restricting the verse virtually to one chord, the group had gone all out for impact, with Lennon singing the melody

---

[1] According to Lennon, the inspiration was Orbison's 1960 hit 'Only The Lonely' ('or something').

(the low 'Don Everly' part) while McCartney (Phil Everly) held a repeated high root E mirrored in the bass. Tension mounted graphically through a syncopated bridge of call-and-response between Lennon and a powerfully harmonised McCartney and Harrison, before exploding in three parts on the chorus. In truth, it was contrived and, in relation to the lyric, more than a little hysterical – yet contrived hysteria only fails if the material is weak and The Beatles had done a thorough job of covering every crack in the façade.[1] (McCartney, in particular, demonstrates his perfectionist attention to detail with his counter-melody bass line through the bridge and the backing vocals for the middle eight, where a hint of Buddy Holly is discernible in the interjected 'i-un my heart'.[2])

Apart from requesting a harmonica overdub doubling Harrison's guitar riff, a delighted George Martin had little to add. 'Congratulations, gentlemen,' he said, pressing the control room intercom button after the final take. 'You've just made your first Number One.'[3] That he was right is less remarkable than that someone of his age and background should have understood music as new and rough-hewn as The Beatles' well enough to see that emphasising its quirks would improve it. Martin has painstakingly refuted the notion, floated by classical critics, that he was the real genius behind The Beatles. ('I was purely an interpreter. The genius was theirs, no doubt about that.') Nevertheless, it's almost certainly true that there was no other producer on either side of the Atlantic then capable of handling The Beatles without damaging them – let alone of cultivating and catering to them with the gracious, open-minded adeptness for which George Martin is universally respected in the British pop industry.

PLEASE PLEASE ME pinned back many ears in the UK music business. On the strength of this record, publisher Dick James approached Brian Epstein to found Northern Songs, the group's own copyright company. Meanwhile engineer Norman Smith sent an

---

[1] Another possible influence is that of the outline (and contrived hysteria) of Burt Bacharach's 'Tower Of Strength', a UK No. 1 for Frankie Vaughan a year earlier [9e].

[2] This is absent from the harmonica-less take of PLEASE PLEASE ME issued on *Anthology 1* as the 11th September version. (In fact, this is an early take from the eighteen compiled during the actual recording of PLEASE PLEASE ME on 26th November. At this stage, it seems, there was no vocal arrangement for the middle eight. Presumably George Martin asked the group to create one on the spot.)

[3] Lennon's Aunt Mimi, who had sniffed that if her nephew thought he was going to make his fortune with LOVE ME DO he had another think coming, observed, on hearing PLEASE PLEASE ME: 'That's more like it. That should do well.'

uncredited tape of PLEASE PLEASE ME to Dick Rowe, the legendary 'man at Decca' who had turned The Beatles down, hoping to trick him into rejecting them twice. (He failed to fall for it.) With excited reviews in the British pop press and extensive airplay, the record was selling so well by its third week of release that Martin advised Epstein to call the group in from their spot on Helen Shapiro's UK tour to record an album. The Beatles were accordingly booked for three three-hour sessions on 11th February 1963 in Studio 2 (making their debut LP *Please Please Me* with only an hour's overspill and going back out on the road the following day!). Two weeks later PLEASE PLEASE ME arrived at the top of the UK singles chart, fulfilling George Martin's prediction.[1]

As with [1] LOVE ME DO, there was a transatlantic translation problem. EMI's American outlet, Capitol, could make no sense of PLEASE PLEASE ME and refused to release it, believing it to be a purely British phenomenon. (Part of the problem for American ears was the production – too raw and raucous for a white group. Another difficulty was the lyric, widely interpreted as an exhortation to fellatio.) Epstein swiftly licensed the disc to the Chicago label Vee Jay, which issued it to nil reaction in February 1963. Not until it was reissued in January 1964 in the dam-busting wake of [21] I WANT TO HOLD YOUR HAND did PLEASE PLEASE ME win American recognition, climbing into the US top five fifteen months after being released in Britain.

[4] ASK ME WHY (McCartney–Lennon)

Lennon vocal, rhythm guitar; McCartney backing vocal, bass;
  Harrison lead guitar; Starr drums
Recorded: 6th June; 26th November 1962, Abbey Road 2.
Producer: George Martin. Engineer: Norman Smith.
UK release: 11th January 1963 (B single/PLEASE PLEASE ME)
US release: 25th February 1963 (B single/PLEASE PLEASE ME)

Mainly by Lennon, ASK ME WHY is the first of his exercises in the style of Smokey Robinson, lead singer and songwriter for Tamla Motown harmony group The Miracles.[2] Demoed at the EMI audition on 6th

---

[1] There being no standardised chart, PLEASE PLEASE ME made No. 1 only in *Melody Maker*, *New Musical Express*, *Disc*, and on the BBC's *Pick of the Pops*, other sources registering its highest position as No. 2 (to Frank Ifield's 'Wayward Wind').
[2] The guitar figure derives from The Miracles' 'What's So Good About Goodbye', issued in 1961. Other Robinson trademarks include the falsetto verse-endings and the characteristic doo-wop triplets in the 'I . . . I-I-I' and 'You . . . oo-

June, ASK ME WHY was recorded in six takes during the same session as [3] PLEASE PLEASE ME, for which it became the B-side.[1] Though awkward, its lyric shows personal traces, suggesting that Lennon might have had his wife Cynthia in mind. Unfortunately, owing to a mid-compositional lurch into protective irony, the music fails to match the intensity of his words, offering pastiche without substance and fumbling the conventions of early Sixties pop in a clumsy transition to the middle eight. Part of the trouble is that the song is played too fast, but at this stage The Beatles' production budget was too tight to allow for second thoughts. Even 'dropping in' to erase small mistakes (such as the guitar fluff at 1:26) was deemed a luxury for a B-side knocked off at the end of a strict three-hour session.

[5] THERE'S A PLACE *(McCartney–Lennon)*

Lennon vocal, harmonica, rhythm guitar; **McCartney** vocal, bass;
   Harrison backing vocal, lead guitar; **Starr** drums
Recorded: 11th February 1963, Abbey Road 2.
Producer: George Martin. Engineer: Norman Smith.
UK release: 22nd March 1963 (LP: *Please Please Me*)
US release: 22nd July 1963 (LP: *Introducing The Beatles*)

Nothing better demonstrates the speed at which The Beatles found themselves as songwriters than this stirring period piece, the first title to be taped during the ten-hour session for their debut LP, *Please Please Me*. Borrowed from Leonard Bernstein's 'There's A Place For Us', the lyric is a young man's declaration of independence – an assertion of self-sufficient defiance which, matched by music of pride and poignancy, marks a minor milestone in the emergence of the new youth culture. The strength of feeling in this record is inescapable and, arriving at No. 2 in the US singles chart in April 1964,[2] it duly transfixed American adolescents used to the bland commercialisation of their lives in 'beach movies' and 'teen music'.

Some of the forcefulness of THERE'S A PLACE may have derived from Lennon's original intent to emulate what he referred to as the 'Motown, black thing', though little of this survives in the finished song. (He was presumably thinking of The Isley Brothers, then signed

---

oo-oo' phrases.
[1] Another McCartney–Lennon song, 'Tip Of My Tongue', was considered for this slot but rejected by George Martin on the grounds of a poor arrangement.
[2] As the B-side of [9f] TWIST AND SHOUT on the Tollie label.

to the Wand label [9f].) Recorded in thirteen takes, it's a rough-house performance whose two-part harmony in fourths and fifths shows, if nothing else, that Lennon had a heavy cold; yet the passion of his and McCartney's singing cuts through, while the band's drive is fiercely urgent. Lennon supplies the low harmony for McCartney, stepping forward only on the first and third lines of the middle eight and dropping back again to an octave unison for the aerial answering phrases.[1]

Taking into account the taming effects of compression and the then-standard UK studio practice of damping the bass to stop the stylus jumping on domestic record decks, this is the authentic contemporary sound of The Beatles live – the singers miked in front of their backline of amps, unsegregated by baffles. With the studio clock ticking implacably and a near-impossible schedule to keep, the immediacy of the take was everything and no concession to tidiness could be afforded. Pitches wobble, microphones 'pop', drums stumble, larynxes tear: 1:47 of the real thing.

[6] I SAW HER STANDING THERE *(McCartney–Lennon)*

McCartney vocal, bass, handclaps; **Lennon** backing vocal, rhythm
  guitar, handclaps; **Harrison** lead guitar, handclaps; **Starr** drums,
  handclaps
Recorded: 11th February 1963, Abbey Road 2.
Producer: George Martin. Engineer: Norman Smith.
UK release: 22nd March 1963 (LP: *Please Please Me*)
US release: 22nd July 1963 (LP: *Introducing The Beatles*)

Written in late 1962, this explosive rocker is often ascribed to its singer McCartney; indeed, Lennon himself recalled little involvement with it. Interviewed by Mark Lewisohn in 1988, however, McCartney remembered writing it with Lennon in the 'front parlour' of his house at 20, Forthlin Road, Allerton.[2] What seems to have happened is that

---

[1] According to Miles (op. cit., p. 95), the song is a co-composition 'but with a bias towards being Paul's original idea' since he owned a copy of Bernstein's *West Side Story* in which 'There's A Place For Us' appears.

[2] *Sessions*, p. 9. McCartney indicates that the song was written, like [1] LOVE ME DO, while 'sagging off' school. However, he adds that they were '18, 19, whatever' at the time – well past school age; indeed, if McCartney was 19 when he wrote it, this would put the song's origin in 1961. Coleman prints a Mike McCartney photograph of Lennon and McCartney working on I SAW HER STANDING THERE in the front room at Forthlin Road, dated September 1962. Going by its style, this is a fair guess.

he presented a lyric plus a start on the music, at which point the two sat down and wrote the rest of the song on guitars (with, as McCartney remembers, 'a little bit on the piano that I had there').[1] Exactly what Lennon contributed is unknown, though according to McCartney his partner scoffed at the George Formby-style opening lines 'She was just seventeen/Never been a beauty queen', replacing them with the streetwise 'She was just seventeen/You know what I mean'. As 'Seventeen', the song became part of The Beatles' live act in 1962 and was still listed under that title when, following [5] THERE'S A PLACE, they devoted the rest of the morning session of 11th February to it.

Now rated a rock-and-roll standard, I SAW HER STANDING THERE is reckoned by those who knew The Beatles in their early days to be one of the two most representative Liverpool club songs, the other being The Big Three's version of [U11e] SOME OTHER GUY, which The Beatles, too, played live. Lennon, in particular, was haunted by the latter, originally recorded in 1962 by Ritchie Barrett and written by Barrett with Jerry Leiber and Mike Stoller. In an interview given to *Rolling Stone* in 1968, he mentioned it twice as a record he wanted somehow to emulate. I SAW HER STANDING THERE may have been The Beatles' first attempt at writing something 'off' SOME OTHER GUY.[2]

Both songs were influenced by the prototype English rock-and-roller Tony Sheridan, whom The Beatles backed at Hamburg's Top Ten Club in 1960 and whose Eddie Cochran guitar style suggested the bluesy sevenths which litter their early output [E3b]. Hoping to capture some of the excitement of this 'jive-hall' ambience, George Martin considered recording *Please Please Me* in front of the group's home audience, and it was probably this unfulfilled plan which prompted him to retain McCartney's introductory 'count off', so evocative of The Beatles' gigs at The Cavern and The Casbah.

In performance, I SAW HER STANDING THERE would stretch out for up to ten minutes, punctuated by multiple guitar solos. For the recording, precision and the strictly curtailed demands of radio-play

---

[1] According to McCartney, the bass line was taken from Chuck Berry's 'I'm Talking About You' (Miles, op. cit., p. 94).

[2] A live take of 'Some Other Guy', made for *Pop Go The Beatles* in the Playhouse Theatre, London, on 19th June 1963 *(Live At The BBC)*, is disappointing – swung sloppily rather than rocking hard. This may have been the result of a mismatch between The Beatles' original version and a different approach Starr brought with him from Rory Storm and The Hurricanes. (The *Anthology* video performance filmed at The Cavern for Granada TV on 22nd August 1962, less than a week after Starr had replaced Pete Best, failed to satisfy at least one male fan who, as the song ended, shouted 'We want Pete!')

called for something more concise and the group were obliged to confine themselves to the basic structure, giving Harrison a modified sixteen-bar verse/chorus break in which to get his reverbed Gretsch Duo Jet into action. His first solo on a Beatles record, it might have been reeled off with more authority under less finger-trembling conditions. That apart, this is an electrifying performance and proof that the 'charismatic powerhouse'[1] which shook the Liverpool clubs during 1961–2 was no myth.

Built on blues changes and the group's trademark abrasive vocal harmonies in open fourths and fifths, I SAW HER STANDING THERE sent a shock of earthy rawness through a British pop scene whose harmonic ethos had been shaped largely by the sophistication of Broadway. Lyrically, too, it called the bluff of the chintz-merchants of Denmark Street with their moody, misunderstood 'Johnnies' and adoring 'angels' of sweet sixteen (the legal age of consent). By contrast, The Beatles' heroine was *seventeen*, a deliberate upping of the ante which, aided by Lennon's innuendo in the second line, suggested something rather more exciting than merely holding hands. But the clincher for the teenage audience was the song's straight-from-the-shoulder vernacular. Its hero's heart didn't 'sing' or 'take wing' when he beheld his lady love; this guy's heart 'went boom' when he 'crossed that room' – a directness of metaphor and movement which socked avid young radio-listeners deliciously in the solar plexus. With the authentic voice of youth back on the airwaves, the rock-and-roll rebellion, quiescent since 1960, had resumed.[2]

---

[1] Pete Best quoted in Somach and Somach, p. 74. Liverpool promoter Sam Leach saw The Beatles at Hambleton Hall in Huyton on 25th January 1961: 'I can still feel those numbers vibrating through me. It was an absolute knock-out: I couldn't believe the dynamism and the charisma.' (Salewicz, p. 105.)

[2] Since 1994, three other versions of I SAW HER STANDING THERE have been added to The Beatles' compact discography. The earliest – from the 11th February 1963 session and issued on the [187] FREE AS A BIRD single – is the most revealing. This is take 9 (the last), which provided the count-in for take 1, chosen as the master. In stereo and without EQ, it highlights the vocal harmony and exposes some poor tuning and the odd wrong chord. It also proves that McCartney's bass sound *was* captured during recording (and presumably progressively reduced in the mix and cut). With this bass level, his high C below the chorus ('Woo!') is as startling in its E major key-context as it was in 1963. The second version (*Live at the BBC*) is a boomy mono recording for *Easy Beat* made on 16th October 1963. Faster than usual, it features Harrison's most organised recorded solo on this number. Another live recording for radio (*Anthology 1*), made eight days later in Stockholm, has less drive and seems to have been taped using an omnidirectional overhead microphone,

[6b] A TASTE OF HONEY *(Scott–Marlow)*

> **McCartney** double-tracked lead vocal, bass; **Lennon** backing vocal,
>   rhythm guitar; **Harrison** backing vocal, lead guitar; **Starr** drums
> Recorded: 11th September 1962, Abbey Road 2.
> Producer: George Martin. Engineer: Norman Smith.
> UK release: 22nd March 1963 (LP: *Please Please Me*)
> US release: 22nd July 1963 (LP: *Introducing The Beatles*)

Filmed by Tony Richardson in 1961, Shelagh Delaney's play *A Taste Of Honey* was among the lighter products of the Northern new wave of English cinema at the start of the Sixties. Starring Liverpudlian actress Rita Tushingham, whose wide-eyed, plain-spoken persona briefly became a fixture of the UK screen industry, the film's wry vision of sentimental self-sufficiency appealed strongly to McCartney [115]. Its theme-tune, previously recorded in several instrumental versions, had been a small hit in autumn 1962 for Lenny Welch, whose arrangement McCartney adopted with minor modifications to the chorus lyric. When Acker Bilk had a hit with it while the group were planning *Please Please Me*, the song voted itself onto the album; yet, like McCartney's other mainstream fancies of the period ([E6d] BESAME MUCHO, [13e] TILL THERE WAS YOU), it had little to do with The Beatles, and its ponderous time-changes and general earnestness must have tested the patience of the others. Starr gamely gets out his brushes and Lennon and Harrison keep straight faces for their chorus responses, but McCartney's weighty approach drags the tempo and a portentous Picardy third fails to redeem a trying two minutes.

[7] DO YOU WANT TO KNOW A SECRET
(McCartney–Lennon)

> **Harrison** vocal, lead guitar; **Lennon** backing vocal, rhythm guitar;
>   **McCartney** backing vocal, bass; **Starr** drums
> Recorded: 11th February 1963, Abbey Road 2.
> Producer: George Martin. Engineer: Norman Smith.
> UK release: 22nd March 1963 (LP: *Please Please Me*)
> US release: 22nd July 1963 (LP: *Introducing The Beatles*)

At just under two minutes, DO YOU WANT TO KNOW A SECRET is the first Beatles original to outstay its welcome. Written by Lennon to give Harrison a solo-spot,[1] it was, according to its author, based on a tune

---

somewhat frazzled by Starr's open hi-hat.
[1] 'I thought it would be a good vehicle for him because it only had three notes and he wasn't the best singer in the world.'

from a Disney film sung to him by his mother when he was a toddler ('I'm Wishing' from *Snow White and the Seven Dwarfs*). The middle eight, on the other hand, is pure Buddy Holly, while the three descending major sevenths of the verse are borrowed from McCartney's arrangement of [13e] TILL THERE WAS YOU.[1] Recorded in eight takes, the song clearly wasn't treated very seriously. The accompaniment is perfunctory, production is limited to echoed drumstick-clicks on the middle eight, Harrison's weak singing goes uncorrected, and the engineers ignominiously fail to clean up his vocal track properly (1:29).

Lennon taped a demo of this twee ditty for fellow NEMS artist Billy J. Kramer while sitting in a lavatory in a Hamburg nightclub – following which he pulled the chain. (He later claimed that this was the only place in which he could find sufficient quiet to record it.) An unenthusiastic Kramer and his group The Dakotas surprised themselves by taking it to the top of the UK charts in June 1963. Issued in the USA by Vee Jay at the height of American Beatlemania (backed by [11] THANK YOU GIRL), The Beatles' own version bluffed its way to No. 2 in May 1964.

[8] MISERY *(McCartney–Lennon)*

Lennon vocal, rhythm guitar; **McCartney** vocal, bass; **Harrison**
   lead guitar; **Starr** drums; **George Martin** piano
Recorded: 11th February 1963, Abbey Road 2; 20th February
   1963, Abbey Road 1.
Producer: George Martin. Engineers: Norman Smith/Stuart Eltham.
UK release: 22nd March 1963 (LP: *Please Please Me*)
US release: 22nd July 1963 (LP: *Introducing The Beatles*)

With this song, Lennon and McCartney achieved eight writing credits for The Beatles' first LP – an unprecedented achievement for a pop act in 1963. For an 'artist' (or artiste, as they were then referred to) to try to write anything at all in those days of dependence on professional songwriters was considered positively eccentric. Even vaunted originals like Chuck Berry, Buddy Holly, and Roy Orbison looked to other songwriters to help them out. The sudden arrival of a group which wrote most of its own material was a small revolution in itself, and it is a recurring testimony of later songwriters that it was the do-it-yourself

---

[1] McCartney remembers DO YOU WANT TO KNOW A SECRET as a 50-50 co-composition (Miles, op. cit., p. 95). Harrison cites The Stereos' 1961 R&B hit 'I Really Love You' as an influence on the song (*Musician*, November 1987).

example of The Beatles which impelled them to form bands of their own.

Lennon and McCartney wrote MISERY during the Helen Shapiro tour in late January,[1] hoping to sell it to the headliner herself who, having just had two No. 1's in the UK, was hot property. When, despite Lennon's warm relationship with Shapiro, this scheme came to nothing, the singer/actor Kenny Lynch smartly staked a claim to it – the first Beatles song to be recorded by another performer.

A droll portrait of adolescent self-pity, MISERY was taken no more seriously by the group than its predecessor [7] DO YOU WANT TO KNOW A SECRET. Bashed out at the end of the afternoon, it runs its po-faced course with neither dynamic variation nor punctuating drum-fills, neatly complementing the lyric's deliberate bathos.[2] Lennon and McCartney sing in a louche unison whose humour is echoed in the scalar fall and comic 'solitary' Gs on piano which Martin added to the middle eight nine days later.[3] Though Harrison's discreet guitar-work is standard Chuck Berry and Lennon's departing 'la-la-la-la' alludes to the daftness of early doo-wop, MISERY is essentially English in its self-mockery. As such, it compounded Capitol's bemusement, providing further proof that *Please Please Me* would never sell in America.

[9] HOLD ME TIGHT *(Lennon–McCartney)*

McCartney vocal, bass, handclaps; Lennon backing vocal, rhythm
   guitar, handclaps; Harrison backing vocal, lead guitar, handclaps;
   Starr drums, handclaps
Recorded: 11th February; 12th September 1963, Abbey Road 2.
Producer: George Martin. Engineer: Norman Smith.
UK release: 22nd November 1963 (LP: *With The Beatles*)
US release: 20th January 1964 (LP: *Meet The Beatles!*)

Written largely by McCartney and part of The Beatles' act from 1961 to 1963, HOLD ME TIGHT was an ill-fated song which neither he nor Lennon rated in retrospect. The Beatles wasted the early part of the

---

[1] Kelly (*The Beatle Myth*, p. 89) bizarrely claims that MISERY was written by an American team for an obscure US group called The Dynamics.

[2] Letting off steam after a sequence of false starts, Starr tried some boisterous fills on Take 6, but this received a thumbs-down. (The high number of takes The Beatles sometimes accumulated was due mainly to mistakes over their lyrics. Since the multitrack was left running, even the briefest of false starts had to be counted as a take for indexing purposes. Thus the multitrack for MISERY shows them running through takes 2–5 in four minutes, none of these attempts lasting longer than thirty seconds.)

[3] This line was originally played, unsteadily and with varying phrasings, by Harrison.

evening session for *Please Please Me* trying to record it, the track sheet showing thirteen takes, a uniquely protracted failure for a number so familiar to them ('a work song', as McCartney later put it). A finishing edit was planned, but it wasn't needed and HOLD ME TIGHT was shelved for seven months before being exhumed during the fourth session for the band's next album. Junking the first version, they recommenced at take 20 (skipping the intervening seven for luck) and finally got what they wanted by joining takes 26 and 29.

Unloved by The Beatles, HOLD ME TIGHT has done no better by the critics, who have called it aimless and half-finished, its bass inaudible, and McCartney's singing out of tune. Certainly the bass end is light, though not exceptionally so for a Beatles track of this period. Apart from that, its bad press hardly seems fair.

Beginning with the last bars of its middle eight, HOLD ME TIGHT mounts via augmentation on a syncopated call-and-response bridge to an unexpected falsetto tag. (Note how the lyric here overlaps into the middle eight, the ruefulness of 'You don't know . . .' supported in the downturning harmony.) Displaying McCartney's characteristic vertical design, the octave-doubled boogie bass/guitar line powers the song relentlessly along in the style of [9f] TWIST AND SHOUT, until it grinds to a unique *ritardando* stop. The arrangement, driven by over-dubbed clapping, is equally effective, Starr switching to tom-toms as the hanging chords of the middle eight plunge dramatically into minor darkness before re-emerging in the triumphant light of the major.[1] The lyrics may be trite, but no more than those of other early Beatles songs. Play it loud with the bass boosted, and you have an overwhelming motoric rocker strongly redolent of the band's live sound.

[9b] ANNA (GO TO HIM) *(Alexander)*

> **Lennon** vocal, acoustic rhythm guitar; **McCartney** backing vocal,
>   bass; **Harrison** backing vocal, lead guitar; **Starr** drums
> Recorded: 11th February 1963, Abbey Road 2.
> Producer: George Martin. Engineer: Norman Smith.
> UK release: 22nd March 1963 (LP: *Please Please Me*)
> US release: 22nd July 1963 (LP: *Introducing The Beatles*)

Having wasted the first hour of the evening on [9] HOLD ME TIGHT, The Beatles had to accelerate. The plan was to record a set of 'covers' from their regular act – songs they played often enough to be able to

---

[1] The song sounds in F but was recorded in E and varispeeded up.

knock them out quickly. They began with ANNA by Arthur Alexander, a black singer from Alabama with a reputation among English R&B fans for numbers like 'You Better Move On', later covered by The Rolling Stones, and [U15d] A SHOT OF RHYTHM AND BLUES, then a club standard.[1] Alexander's moody romantic resignation held obvious appeal for the rebel in Lennon, but the discreet display of sensitivity in the lyric – the singer attempting to melt Anna's heart by assuring her that he cares more for her happiness than his own – found no echo in Lennon's dealings with women at the time. The result is a slightly callow performance, lacking the depth of Alexander's delivery and the sophistication of his Muscle Shoals arrangement (a key feature of which is a yearning string line).

Lennon loses the weight of the song by transposing it up three keys, partly to let Harrison pick the original record's Floyd Cramer piano figure in D – allowing its plangent F sharps to ring – and partly to give his own voice an extra edge of passion on the pleading middle sixteen. This works inasmuch as the words at this point ('All of my life I've been searching . . .') carried personal meaning for him. Yet, singing outside his usual range on the verse – he sounds uncannily like Harrison – and negotiating wider intervals than he would have written for himself, Lennon encounters pitching problems which compromise his performance. Though he and Alexander were the same age (22), the effect is of a passionate youth grappling with a man's song.

[9c] BOYS *(Dixon–Farrell)*

Starr vocal, drums; **Lennon** backing vocal, rhythm guitar;
   Harrison backing vocal, lead guitar; **McCartney** backing vocal,
   bass
Recorded: 11th February 1963, Abbey Road 2.
Producer: George Martin. Engineer: Norman Smith.
UK release: 22nd March 1963 (LP: *Please Please Me*)
US release: 22nd July 1963 (LP: *Introducing The Beatles*)

An up-tempo twelve-bar written by Luther Dixon and Wes Farrell for the original American 'girl group' The Shirelles, BOYS[2] stood service in 1961–4 as The Beatles' main 'drummer's number', Starr inheriting it

---

[1] Released on the Dot label in September 1962, ANNA was too recent to have been long in The Beatles' repertoire and took three takes to record. The group played [U15d] A SHOT OF RHYTHM AND BLUES during 1962 (*Live At The BBC*), Lennon taking lead vocal. They also sang Alexander's [U13b] SOLDIER OF LOVE on *Pop Go The Beatles* on 16th July 1963.
[2] The B-side of the first of their two US No. 1's on Scepter, 'Will You Still Love Me Tomorrow', which rose to No. 4 in the UK charts during spring 1961.

from Pete Best. As such, it needed (and deserved) only one take. Hurled out with happy abandon, it works well enough as a glimpse of the group's contemporary act, Starr bellowing his vocal with sturdy good humour and Harrison tossing off a pastiche Chet Atkins solo.[1]

[9d] CHAINS *(Goffin–King)*

Harrison vocal, lead guitar; **McCartney** harmony vocal, bass;
   Lennon harmony vocal, rhythm guitar, harmonica; **Starr** drums
Recorded: 11th February 1963, Abbey Road 2.
Producer: George Martin. Engineer: Norman Smith.
UK release: 22nd March 1963 (LP: *Please Please Me*)
US release: 22nd July 1963 (LP: *Introducing The Beatles*)

A minor 1962 hit on the Dimension label for Little Eva's backing singers The Cookies, CHAINS was a short-stay guest in The Beatles' live set, and it shows. The performance, slightly out of tune, is low on spontaneity, freshened only by Lennon's 'Northern' harmonica. Offered as Harrison's second feature on *Please Please Me* [7], it muffs the very aspect which presumably drew the group to it in the first place: The Cookies' skirling three-part harmony. The decision to lower the key to accommodate Harrison's limited range forfeits the original's swagger and is, in any case, defeated by pushing him in the mix so as to hide the harmony and reveal the thinness of his voice.

Like another contemporary Gerry Goffin and Carole King number, the notorious 'He Hit Me (And It Felt Like A Kiss)' – recorded by The Crystals in 1961 and withdrawn under pressure, becoming the only single issued on Phil Spector's Philles label not to be a hit – CHAINS flirts coyly with sado-masochism; yet it's a good enough period pop song to have deserved better from The Beatles.[2] No one sounds committed and the fade shows the group heading for a full close later edited out – either because in retrospect it seemed corny or because they messed it up.

---

[1] A more convincing live version recorded on 19th April 1964 is available on *Anthology 1*.
[2] According to a contemporary report in *New Musical Express*, The Beatles taped another Goffin and King number on 11th February – Lennon's version of [U4b] KEEP YOUR HANDS OFF MY BABY (*Live At The BBC*), a minor hit for Little Eva a few weeks before; however, the song does not appear on the track sheet for this session. It is also rumoured to have been tried during the recording of *Help!*

[9e] BABY IT'S YOU *(David–Williams–Bacharach)*

Lennon vocal, rhythm guitar; **McCartney** backing vocal, bass; **Harrison** backing vocal, lead guitar; **Starr** drums; **George Martin** celesta
Recorded: 11th February 1963, Abbey Road 2; 20th February 1963, Abbey Road 1.
Producer: George Martin. Engineers: Norman Smith/Stuart Eltham.
UK release: 22nd March 1963 (LP: *Please Please Me*)
US release: 22nd July 1963 (LP: *Introducing The Beatles*)

The Shirelles must have been surprised to find two of their songs covered on one LP by an English male group, let alone by the soon-to-be-godlike Beatles. Unlike the raunchy [9c] BOYS, this mid-tempo ballad is ethereal *kitsch* brought down to earth only by its quietly vicious lyric ('Cheat! Cheat!').[1] The Beatles, who played the song during 1962–3, embrace its genre clichés with gusto, Lennon's full-tilt vocal coming close to turning it from a curio into something of substance.

[9f] TWIST AND SHOUT *(Medley–Russell)*[2]

Lennon vocal, rhythm guitar; **McCartney** backing vocal, bass;
  Harrison backing vocal, lead guitar; **Starr** drums
Recorded: 11th February 1963, Abbey Road 2.
Producer: George Martin. Engineer: Norman Smith.
UK release: 22nd March 1963 (LP: *Please Please Me*)
US release: 22nd July 1963 (LP: *Introducing The Beatles*)

With [9e] BABY IT'S YOU in the can, the clock in Studio 2 showed 10pm. The Beatles had been recording for twelve hours and time was officially up. George Martin, though, needed one more number – something to send the album out with a bang. Accordingly he and his team retired with the group to the Abbey Road canteen for a last cup

---

[1] This provocative mismatch came about as a result of second thoughts. Originally entitled 'I'll Cherish You', the song was selected by The Shirelles' producer Luther Dixon on condition that Burt Bacharach altered its anodyne lyric. Distinguished by its swimmy sound and cheap plastic organ solo, The Shirelles' version, a US hit in 1961, is in fact Bacharach's original home demo with the girls' voices dubbed on top.
[2] Pseudonym of New York songwriter Bert Berns, composer of several Sixties pop standards (including 'Here Comes The Night', 'Hang On Sloopy', and 'Piece Of My Heart').

of coffee (or, in Lennon's case, warm milk for his ragged throat). They knew what they had to do – the wildest thing in The Beatles' act: TWIST AND SHOUT, their cover of a 1962 US hit by black Cincinnati family act The Isley Brothers. An out-and-out screamer, it was always demanding. That night it was a very tall order indeed.

Back in Studio 2, the group knew they had at most two chances to get this arduous song on tape before Lennon lost his voice. At around 10.30pm, with him stripped to the waist and the others 'hyping' themselves by treating the control room staff as their audience, they went for it. The eruptive performance that ensued stunned the listening technicians and exhilarated the group (as can be heard in McCartney's triumphant '*Hey!*' at the end). Trying for a second take, Lennon found he had nothing left and the session stopped there and then – but the atmosphere was still crackling. Nothing of this intensity had ever been recorded in a British pop studio.

As in their version of The Shirelles' [9c] BOYS, The Beatles' arrangement of TWIST AND SHOUT makes the original bass line more explicit by formalising it into a riff and doubling it with Harrison's lead guitar. Starr's tremendous hammering drums – his best playing on the album – are crucial to what is, in effect, a prototype of the 'heavy metal' idiom, the group self-transformed into a great battering machine. On The Isley Brothers' version, the bass is looser and the conception more spontaneously chaotic, with saxes and trumpets joining in on what is basically a party record with Latin overtones.[1] Transposing the key down, Lennon moves away from the demented airborne shriek of Ronald Isley's extraordinary performance towards something less sensual, more devilishly challenging. With his hoarse 'C'mon, c'mon, c'mon, c'mon, *baby*, now!', he shrewdly adapts the song to a white female audience for whom such primal abandon was frenziedly thrilling in 1963.

Those who knew the group in their club days maintain that George Martin never captured their live sound. To the extent that this is true, it was largely due to the inability of contemporary British studios to cope with the bass amplitudes essential to rock-and-roll. On TWIST AND SHOUT, he goes some way to rectifying this by turning up the drums and pushing the gain to get more ambience, but even so the band's

---

[1] A variation on 'La Bamba', TWIST AND SHOUT was an attempt to revive The Isleys' chart career by marrying something from their 1959 hit 'Shout' with the Twist dance craze launched by Hank Ballard and Chubby Checker in late 1960.

authentic powerhouse sound, achieved through overdriving the Top Boost tone of their Vox AC30 amps,[1] is only partly conveyed. Yet the result is remarkable for its time: raw to a degree unmatched by other white artists – and far too wild to be acceptable to the older generation. As such, it became a symbolic fixture of the group's act during Beatlemania: the song where parents, however liberal, feared to tread.[2]

[10] FROM ME TO YOU *(McCartney–Lennon)*

Lennon vocal, rhythm guitar, harmonica; **McCartney** vocal, bass;
  Harrison harmony vocal, lead guitar; **Starr** drums
Recorded: 5th March 1963, Abbey Road 2.
Producer: George Martin. Engineer: Norman Smith.
UK release: 11th April 1963 (A single/THANK YOU GIRL)
US release: 27th May 1963 (A single/THANK YOU GIRL)

Though Lennon and McCartney wrote a substantial number of songs between 1957 and 1962,[3] their confidence in all but a few of them was low. The majority of the group's pre-1963 act consisted of other people's material with only an apologetic leavening of Lennon–McCartney originals.[4] Realising the weakness of his protégés' existing

---

[1] As a result of demand from Nineties bands wanting to reproduce the early Sixties 'beat group' sound, the 1963-spec Vox AC30/6 TB went back into production in 1994.

[2] Energised by the occasion, The Beatles' performance of TWIST AND SHOUT at the Royal Command Performance on 4th November 1963 *(Anthology 1)* gives an idea of the power they could generate live.

[3] Some sources claim up to two hundred – but since no list of titles has ever been published, it's impossible to verify this. Mark Lewisohn *(Chronicle*, pp. 361-5) refers to twenty early Lennon–McCartney titles, including half a dozen that survived to be recorded by The Beatles. Many early Beatle songs were lost when Jane Asher threw out a lot of apparent scrap paper while spring-cleaning in 1965.

[4] Seven very early songs, dating from 1957, were played by The Quarry Men until 1959: 'Just Fun', 'That's My Woman', 'Thinking Of Linking', 'Keep Looking That Way', 'Too Bad About Sorrows', 'Years Roll Along', and 'I Lost My Little Girl'. The last two were McCartney compositions. ('I Lost My Little Girl' was the first original song he showed Lennon at their meeting on 6th July 1957.) [E1] IN SPITE OF ALL THE DANGER, a unique McCartney–Harrison collaboration, featured in The Quarry Men's set between 1958 and 1959. From the same period, Lennon's [E6] HELLO LITTLE GIRL was a regular fixture in the group's act between 1957 and 1962. Another early Lennon song, [U12/167] ONE AFTER 909 featured live from 1957 to 1962, as did McCartney's [E5] LIKE DREAMERS DO. Other early songs to be recorded by The Beatles were [1] LOVE ME DO, [46] I'LL FOLLOW THE SUN, and [94] WHEN I'M SIXTY-FOUR – all written before 1960, all by McCartney, and all part of the group's act until 1962. Two more live songs from this period, both by McCartney, were 'Love Of The Loved' (a minor hit for Cilla Black in November 1963) and [U13] I'LL BE ON MY WAY. McCartney's [9] HOLD ME TIGHT was a

catalogue, George Martin advised them to come up with more hits without delay, a plea repeated with added urgency when [3] PLEASE PLEASE ME began to move in large quantities. They wasted little time. Based on the letters page of *New Musical Express* ('From You To Us'), FROM ME TO YOU was written on the Helen Shapiro tour bus on 28th February 1963 – the group's first custom-built Beatles song as Parlophone artists.

Dismissed in most accounts of their career as a transitional time-marker between PLEASE PLEASE ME and [12] SHE LOVES YOU, FROM ME TO YOU was actually a brilliant consolidation of the emerging Beatles sound,[1] holding the No. 1 position for seven weeks (the longest occupation of this place by any of their eighteen British No. 1 singles apart from [120] HELLO, GOODBYE and [160] GET BACK).[2] That it was specifically designed to accomplish this testifies to the canny practicality of the group's songwriting duo. Like most of Lennon and McCartney's few recorded full fifty-fifty collaborations, FROM ME TO YOU proceeds in the two-bar phrases a pair of writers typically adopt when tentatively ad-libbing at each other. The usual result of such a synthetic process, in which neither contributor is free to develop the melody-line in his normal way, is a competition to produce surprising developments of the initial idea. As in [21] I WANT TO HOLD YOUR HAND, the variation surprise in FROM ME TO YOU consists of a sudden falsetto octave leap, a motif first tried on the chorus of [3] PLEASE PLEASE ME (itself rewritten in this to-and-fro fashion).[3]

Bluesily horizontal in its intervals, FROM ME TO YOU clearly grew from an original Lennon phrase, perhaps passing to McCartney for the vertical second phrase (delivered by Lennon with a rasping upward slide into falsetto, harmonised by his partner a pleading third below). The New York quartet The Four Seasons, then climbing the UK charts with 'Big Girls Don't Cry', employed similar falsetto and almost

---

staple of The Beatles' act between 1961 and 1963. Three new songs played live in 1962 were never returned to: 'I Fancy Me Chances', 'Pinwheel Twist', and 'Tip Of My Tongue', the last two by McCartney. ('Tip Of My Tongue' was tried out at the session for [3] PLEASE PLEASE ME, and later recorded by Tommy Quickly.) According to Lennon (*Hit Parader*, April 1972), McCartney's 'A World Without Love', a No. 1 for Peter and Gordon in 1964, was written around 1958–9. (See also [119] FLYING, note.)

[1] Observing 'this was our real start', McCartney describes FROM ME TO YOU as 'a pivotal song . . . very much co-written' (Miles, op. cit., p. 149).

[2] The source used for Beatles singles data in the UK is *Record Retailer/ Music Week*.

[3] The coda pushes this 'surprise' idea further, taking the augmentations from the middle eight and, using ambiguous vocal harmonies, bypassing a full close to finish on the root of the relative minor.

certainly influenced The Beatles in this respect.[1] Yet where the Americans built falsetto into their four-part harmony, The Beatles wielded it as an isolated device, and it was mainly these sudden hair-raising wails that made their early records so rivetingly strange.[2] Far from a clever novelty, however, FROM ME TO YOU has a distinctive mood of its own, Lennon's abrasive voice – the trademark of the group's 'Beatlemania' phase – turning a trite lyric into something mordantly sardonic. His harmonica, insisted on by George Martin, maintains continuity with the group's first two singles, adding to the wildness so crucial to The Beatles' early impact. (At the peak of the second middle eight, the brew bubbles over as McCartney's ascending harmony meets Lennon's octave-jumping lead above an augmented seventh and a typically idiosyncratic 'backwards' fill from Starr.)[3]

FROM ME TO YOU demonstrates The Beatles' pop professionalism, only the functionality of McCartney's bass part betraying that less than a week had elapsed between writing and recording it.[4] Echoing the wit they were displaying in their TV and radio interviews, their deftness and adaptability in the studio was already far beyond the reach of their immediate competitors.

By now, it was clear that something unprecedented and unpredictable was happening and, as the song raced to the top of the UK singles chart during the summer of 1963, a change could be felt in the atmosphere of English life. With sex newly an acceptable social topic courtesy of Vassall, Ward, Keeler, and James Bond, the frank physicality of The Beatles' music – epitomised by Lennon's mocking leer, lazy strum, and open-legged stance at the microphone – had arrived at

---

[1] In October 1964, Vee Jay wrung the last drops out of their licensed Beatles material by combining them with a side of songs by The Four Seasons in a hybrid LP entitled *The Beatles vs. The Four Seasons*.

[2] Sometimes (e.g., [3] PLEASE PLEASE ME and the present number) the trick was done merely by momentarily jumping the melody an octave. In other examples, the falsetto 'Ooo!' was intensified by being combined with an unexpected chord change, such as the swerve to the parallel minor in the chorus of [6] I SAW HER STANDING THERE.

[3] A left-hander playing a right-handed kit, Starr would, during fills, come off the snare onto the tom-toms with his left hand leading so that he could only progress 'backwards' from floor tom to small tom or from small tom to snare (e.g., his second fill on the coda of [11] and the second fill on the fade of [5] THERE'S A PLACE [1:41–2]). His droll variations on this, including rolling off the hi-hat, delighted orthodox drummers and added to the newness of The Beatles' sound.

[4] They were still adding to it as they recorded it, e.g., the semi-instrumental verse/chorus with vocal interjections and the half-bar vi chord (Am) between the first two verse/choruses. On every take, McCartney, apparently worried that the tempo was too slow, tried to gee things up with his count-in.

exactly the right time.[1] As the nation's centre of gravity slid from upper lip to lower hip, a degree of Dionysiac abandon was only to be expected, yet the shrill gales of ululation which began to greet the announcement of the group's names before their live appearances took even The Beatles by surprise. Girls had been squirming about and screaming at their pop idols since Presley first pumped his pelvis at them in 1956, but what was happening now was mass hysteria. Jess Conrad, a typical 'teen idol' of the period, recalls appearing with the group on a pop show around this time: 'I did my record and the girls went crazy as usual – but when The Beatles went on the place exploded! I thought "These boys really have it".'[2] This orgiastic release of erotic energy dammed up during the repressive Fifties – a ceaseless avian shrilling so loud that the bands, standing only yards away from their amplifiers, could barely hear what they were playing – was soon greeting every 'beat' group to bob up in The Beatles' wake.

[11] THANK YOU GIRL (*McCartney–Lennon*)

Lennon double tracked vocal, rhythm guitar, harmonica;
  McCartney harmony vocal, bass; **Harrison** lead guitar; **Starr** drums
Recorded: 5th, 13th March 1963, Abbey Road 2.
Producer: George Martin. Engineer: Norman Smith.
UK release: 11th April 1963 (B single/FROM ME TO YOU)
US release: 27th May 1963 (B single/FROM ME TO YOU)

Until [10] FROM ME TO YOU turned up, THANK YOU GIRL had been scheduled as The Beatles' third single. It was recorded in the same afternoon session as FROM ME TO YOU, the group's only free day for weeks. That evening, they made a rejected version of [U11] ONE AFTER 909 and abandoned a try at [72] WHAT GOES ON. Next day, they returned to their hectic life of crisscrossing Britain from gig to gig, Lennon briefly dropping out of the tour a week later to overdub his harmonica on the present track.

Like [10] FROM ME TO YOU, THANK YOU GIRL was written 'head to head' by Lennon and McCartney. Again, the pattern of alternation between the two writers is clear, Lennon in the three-chord verse and

---

[1] The cliché that, compared to The Rolling Stones, The Beatles were asexual 'family entertainers' developed later. Their initial impact was very different, while the Stones, with what seemed then like positively Neanderthal animality, didn't begin to figure as rivals until the end of 1963.
[2] Leigh, p. 23.

McCartney in the chorus and its related middle eight. The same seems to have gone for the lyrics, Lennon initiating things with the down-to-earth first line and McCartney replying with the Tin Pan Alley tone and slick internal rhyme of the second. (Like any pop act, they were looking for variations on their previous hit, the descending scalar crotchets of THANK YOU GIRL's middle eight being recycled from the verse of [3] PLEASE PLEASE ME.)

Entitled 'Thank You, Little Girl' when it was recorded, the lyric shows Lennon and McCartney cultivating their audience by encouraging each of their female fans to hear it as gratitude for her part in The Beatles' success. Lennon was typically ambivalent about the group's fans, hating their juvenility but acknowledging their loyalty and grimly recognising their ordinariness, a psychological lifeline to him in a world of showbiz unreality. (When fans mobbed his Rolls-Royce one night in 1963, he told his chauffeur not to worry: 'They bought the car. They've got a right to smash it up.') Despite this hard-nosed calculation, THANK YOU GIRL emerges as an engaging rocker, and the closing reprises of its key-concealing opening bars, with Starr offering his version of a Sandy Nelson/Tony Meehan drum break, are as quirky as the group's next B-side [13] I'LL GET YOU.[1] Yet, beside FROM ME TO YOU, the track's weaknesses are obvious. Its rock-and-roll rhythm, later alchemised into The Beatles' first American hit [21] I WANT TO HOLD YOUR HAND, is here hamstrung by a bass line that smacks of studio make-do, suggesting that McCartney hadn't had time to work out anything more fluent;[2] and while it shares FROM ME TO YOU's lay-out of solo and harmonised lines (not to mention the leaping falsetto of its chorus), the track lacks a life of its own, sounding like a stepping-stone to the style achieved in the later song.

---

[1] The multitrack shows the group uncertain how to focus the song, much of the final effect deriving from Starr's drum part being beefed up, presumably on George Martin's suggestion. The seven short edit-pieces described by Mark Lewisohn as being for 'the guitar flourish at the end' (*Sessions*, p. 28) were actually for Starr's closing fills, which Lennon felt weren't 'on the beat'.

[2] Three months later, he had found an alternative: a fortuitous anticipation of the 'In The Midnight Hour' riff, preserved in a live tape made at the Playhouse Theatre on 19th June 1963 (*Live At The BBC*).

[U12] ONE AFTER 909 *(Lennon–McCartney)*

Lennon lead vocal, rhythm guitar, harmonica; **McCartney**
   harmony vocal, bass; **Harrison** lead guitar; **Starr** drums
Recorded: 5th March 1963, Abbey Road 2.
Producer: George Martin. Engineer: Norman Smith.
UK release: 21st November 1995 (2-CD: *Anthology 1*)
US release: 21st November 1995 (2-CD: *Anthology 1*)

This abortive try at an early number resuscitated six years later [166]
reveals The Beatles in comic disarray. Most of the trouble stemmed
from the fact that no one was sure of the lay-out of the song. On take
2, McCartney was ready for another middle sixteen after the guitar
break;[1] on take 4, Lennon came in two-thirds of the way through
Harrison's solo – a revealing error, suggesting that he was counting bars
instead of following the sequence.[2] Take 3, presented on *Anthology 1*,
breaks down when, unable to sustain his monotonous high B without
the aid of a plectrum, McCartney busks a botched boogiewoogie line.
'What are yer *doin*'?' demands an exasperated Lennon. (In fact,
McCartney's idea was, as usual, a good one which merely needed
working out.)

[U13] I'LL BE ON MY WAY *(Lennon–McCartney)*

Lennon lead vocal, acoustic guitar; **McCartney** harmony vocal,
   bass; **Harrison** lead guitar; **Starr** drums
Recorded: 4th April 1963, BBC Paris Theatre, London.
Producer: Bryant Marriott. Engineer: Unknown.
UK release: 30th November 1994 (2-CD: *Live At The BBC*)
US release: 5th December 1994 (2-CD: *Live At The BBC*)

Taped for the Light Programme series *Side By Side* and broadcast on
24th June 1963, I'LL BE ON MY WAY was donated to – if not written
for – Billy J. Kramer and the Dakotas, who placed it on the B-side of
their debut single (their hit version of [7] DO YOU WANT TO KNOW A
SECRET). Lyric and music alike are almost derisively naive. Played a little
faster, the song reveals its debt to Buddy Holly's simple three-chord
schemes. (Imagine each chorus finishing 'I'll be on my way ah-hey-
hey'.)

---

[1] Typically, Harrison began interestingly, playing with minor and major
inversions, but lost his way, tripping over his fingers. At the end of the take, Lennon
asked incredulously 'What kind of a solo was *that*?'
[2] This blunder was fixed with an edit-piece (Take 5) going from Harrison's solo
to the end.

[12] SHE LOVES YOU (Lennon–McCartney)

Lennon vocal, rhythm guitar; **McCartney** vocal, bass; **Harrison**
harmony vocal, lead guitar; **Starr** drums
Recorded: 1st July 1963, Abbey Road 2.
Producer: George Martin. Engineer: Norman Smith.
UK release: 23rd August 1963 (A single/I'LL GET YOU)
US release: 16th September 1963 (A single/I'LL GET YOU)

Lennon and McCartney wrote SHE LOVES YOU in a Newcastle hotel
room after a gig at the Majestic Ballroom on 26th June 1963. The
initial idea (from McCartney) consisted of using the third person rather
than their usual first and second.[1] To judge from the expressive link
between the song's words and melody, a roughed-out lyric must have
come next, after which the pair presumably fell into the phrase-
swapping mode familiar from [10] FROM ME TO YOU.

The opening lines follow speech inflections and stay within the
compass of their chords – obviously Lennon's work. What changes
them, making a straightforward sequence surprising, is McCartney's
harmony. Already maturing, the partnership's writing formula can be
heard here as the dual expression of Lennon's downbeat cynicism and
McCartney's get-up-and-go optimism [2]. Much of the pair's musical
originality derived from their self-taught willingness to let their fingers
discover chord-sequences by exploring the architecture of their guitars
rather than following orthodox progressions. Yet these choices were
driven by the harmonies they used – and these arguably reflected the
contrast of their temperaments. Even at this stage their relationship
could be acerbic and they were capable of bickering vitriolically in
public,[2] though under this lay an enduring emotional bond and a
steady respect for each other's talent and intelligence which overrode
their disagreements. Like all lasting music, The Beatles' best work is as
much the expression of a state of mind as a construction in sound, and
in SHE LOVES YOU Lennon and McCartney can be heard fusing their
different outlooks in musical form. The result is an authentic distillation
of the atmosphere of that time, and one of the most explosive pop
records ever made.

Five days after writing the song, they were in Studio 2 at Abbey
Road, giving it final shape. Beyond the basic words and music lay the
vital work of arranging, at which juncture The Beatles became not a

---

[1] McCartney recalls some musical influence from Bobby Rydell whose 'Forget
Him' was then in the UK charts (Miles, op. cit., p. 149).
[2] See Coleman, Vol. 1, pp. 199–200.

duo but a quartet. The contribution of Starr and Harrison to SHE LOVES YOU demonstrates the group's acute cohesion. The drums on the chorus – which, reputedly on George Martin's advice, begins the song, delaying arrival at the tonic (G major) – are intrinsic to the track's dynamics, creating tension by replacing the offbeat with tom-tom quavers before blazing into the thrashed open hi-hat of Starr's classic Beatlemania style.[1] Steering the arrangement's changes with his gruff seven-note riff and gleaming Gretsch arpeggios, Harrison completes his contribution by adding a jazz sixth to the final 'Yeah' of the chorus. No record of the takes involved in making SHE LOVES YOU survives and it is impossible to know how much of its final form was evolved during the five-hour session in which it and its B-side, [13] I'LL GET YOU, were recorded. The Beatles were known for their agility in making adjustments from take to take, and Johnny Dean, editor of *The Beatles Book*, who was at the session, recalls that the song seemed to him to have altered quite dramatically by the time it reached the form preserved on record.[2] If so, that only serves as further testament to the tightness of The Beatles as an operating unit. There were no passengers in this group and, when a situation warranted it, their drive to achieve was unanimous.

Issued in Britain in August 1963, SHE LOVES YOU was an enormous hit and remains their biggest-selling UK single. Prodigally original yet instantly communicative, it owed much of its success to the naturalness of the match between its music and the everyday language of its lyric. The contour of the melodic line fits the feeling and rhythm of the words perfectly – and, where it doesn't, the singers make a virtue out of it by altering their inflection (e.g., the cajoling emphasis of 'apologise to her'). Indeed, so much were Lennon and McCartney led by their lyric conception here that there was no room for their usual middle eight, the space being usurped by an outrageous eight-bar bridge which, via a violent push, lands on C minor.[3] Beyond doubt, though, the record's hottest attraction was its notorious 'Yeah, yeah, yeah' refrain, from which the group became known throughout Europe as The Yeah-Yeahs. (Almost as celebrated were their falsetto 'ooo's, stolen from The Isley Brothers' [9f] TWIST AND SHOUT and grafted onto SHE LOVES

---

[1] The punctuating snare flams suggest McCartney's influence (cf. [47] TICKET TO RIDE).

[2] Lennon: 'We stuck in everything – thinking when Elvis did "All Shook Up", that was the first time I heard "Uh huh", "Oh yeah", and "Yeah, yeah" all in the same song.' (Coleman, Vol. 1, p. 286.)

[3] Note, too, the dissonant minor seventh in bar 2 of the verse ('You think you've lost your *love*').

You, along with the visual hook of McCartney and Harrison shaking their mop-top hair-dos as they delivered them. When The Beatles first showed this to their colleagues on tour, it was greeted with hilarity. Lennon, though, insisted that it would work, and was proved correct. Whenever the head-shaking 'ooo's came round, the level of the audiences' delirium would leap.)

Claiming the British showbiz throne with their appearance on ITV's *Sunday Night At The London Palladium* on 13th October, the group brought their set to a climax with SHE LOVES YOU. For the first time, a pop phenomenon which thrilled the country's youngsters became ruefully acknowledged by their parents.[1] Overnight, Britain took The Beatles to its heart. (And enter the calculatingly offensive Rolling Stones.) Meanwhile America remained immune, Capitol again refusing a release. When Vee Jay too backed out, a desperate Epstein licensed SHE LOVES YOU to Swan Records of Philadelphia, yet the compilers of US radio playlists showed no interest. Not until Jack Paar screened film[2] of The Beatles performing the song on his show in January 1964 was the US public exposed to Beatlemania. As in Europe, the 'Yeah, yeah, yeah' refrain caught on instantly, but Swan Records held off from reissuing SHE LOVES YOU until Capitol released [21] I WANT TO HOLD YOUR HAND. On 21st March 1964, the record finally arrived at the top of the US chart, where it stayed for a fortnight before being dislodged by [23] CAN'T BUY ME LOVE.

[13] I'LL GET YOU *(Lennon–McCartney)*

> **Lennon** vocal, rhythm guitar, harmonica; **McCartney** vocal, bass;
> **Harrison** harmony vocal, lead guitar; **Starr** drums
> Recorded: 1st July 1963, Abbey Road 2.
> Producer: George Martin. Engineer: Norman Smith.
> UK release: 23rd August 1963 (B single/SHE LOVES YOU)
> US release: 16th September 1963 (B single/SHE LOVES YOU)

Squeezed in at the end of the [12] SHE LOVES YOU session, 'Get You In The End', as it was then called, was tossed off in confidently casual style. Only the uncorrected vocal fluffs (0:56; 1:14; 1:16) prove that

---

[1] Most commentators, including The Beatles' press secretary Tony Barrow, date the start of Beatlemania to this event, marked as it was by crowd disturbances outside the venue which made the front pages of the national press. In fact, although the term was coined by newspapers during the following weeks, the phenomenon itself had been building since the beginning of 1963 and was in full swing when [10] FROM ME TO YOU arrived at No. 1 during the summer. (Lewisohn, *Chronicle*, pp. 88–135.)

[2] Footage from Don Haworth's BBC TV documentary *The Mersey Sound*, shot in August 1963.

what little time was left afterwards had to be devoted to Lennon's harmonica overdub. One of the group's most delightful throwaways, I'll Get You works its audience so brazenly that it's hard not to laugh at its cheek. Lennon and McCartney play up their Liverpool accents for all they're worth, drawling their way through a mock-naive love lyric framed by sardonic 'Oh yeahs' that echo the refrain of the track's A-side.[1] To judge by its melodic directness and the climactic seventh in its middle eight, I'll Get You was written in late 1962, fifty-fifty by McCartney, who probably started it, and Lennon, who may have provided the chorus and the jeering middle section with its reiterated phrases over a shifting harmony. To be a true Beatles fan during the early Sixties entailed a fanatical devotion to the group's B-sides, and, with its plumply rounded bass sound and air of dry self-sendup, I'll Get You is one of the best.[2]

[U13d] SOLDIER OF LOVE (LAY DOWN YOUR ARMS)
(*Cason–Moon*)

Lennon lead vocal, rhythm guitar; **McCartney** backing vocal, bass;
  Harrison backing vocal, lead guitar; **Starr** drums
Recorded: 2nd July 1963, BBC Maida Vale Studios, London.
Producer: Unknown. Engineer: Unknown.
UK release: 30th November 1994 (2-CD: *Live At The BBC*)
US release: 5th December 1994 (2-CD: *Live At The BBC*)

SOLDIER OF LOVE was the third of five songs to be taped for the fifth edition of *Pop Go The Beatles*.[3] This dramatic number, written by

---

[1] The Scouse the group adopted for publicity purposes annoyed those who knew them in Liverpool, especially their middle-class relations (Starr being the only working-class member of the group).
[2] A charming document of Beatlemania exists in the live take of I'll Get You (*Anthology 1*), taped at the group's career-clinching appearance on *Sunday Night At The London Palladium* on 13th October 1963. What clapping can be heard is, typically, on the on-beat, but the screams which regularly greet the song's unorthodox lift from D major to A minor – which McCartney recalls as 'nicked from a song called "All My Trials" which is on an album I had by Joan Baez' (Miles, op. cit., p. 151) – show how instinctively The Beatles' fans identified what they liked about their music. (For more Beatlemania, see the live version of [37] BABY'S IN BLACK taped at the Hollywood Bowl in August 1965 and issued on the [188] REAL LOVE single.)
[3] The others were a competent McCartney cover of Presley's [U.13b] THAT'S ALL RIGHT (MAMA) (*Live At The BBC*), a sloppy version of Chuck Berry's [U.13c] CAROL sung by Lennon (*Live At The BBC*), a worthy shot at Carl Perkins' [U.13e] LEND ME YOUR COMB (*Anthology 1*), and a functional McCartney screamer, The Jodimars' [U.13f] Clarabella (*Live At The BBC*). (Had SOLDIER OF LOVE been issued,

Buzz Cason and Tony Moon and recorded by Arthur Alexander in 1962, was an ideal vehicle for Lennon and, played slower and with more soul, would have been an irresistible contender for *With The Beatles* − were it not that Lennon decided instead to pinch the song's moody vi-I motion and (very 'Lennonish') augmented change to write [14] IT WON'T BE LONG, [18] ALL I'VE GOT TO DO, and [19] NOT A SECOND TIME.

[13b] YOU REALLY GOT A HOLD ON ME *(Robinson)*

Lennon vocal, rhythm guitar; **Harrison** vocal, lead guitar; **McCartney** harmony vocal, bass; **Starr** drums; **George Martin** piano
Recorded: 18th July, 17th October 1963, Abbey Road 2.
Producer: George Martin. Engineer: Norman Smith.
UK release: 22nd November 1963 (LP: *With The Beatles*)
US release: 10th April 1964 (LP: *The Beatles' Second Album*)

A fortnight after recording their fourth single [12], The Beatles slipped out of their manic touring schedule to begin their second album. Not yet ready with new songs, they reversed the procedure adopted for *Please Please Me* by beginning with non-original filler material,[1] choosing to start with YOU REALLY GOT A HOLD ON ME, a US Top 10 hit for Smokey Robinson and The Miracles during the previous winter.[2] Apart from Arthur Alexander's [9b] ANNA, Robinson's serpentine 6/8 ballad with its emotionally complex lyric was the most challenging song The Beatles ever tried to cover − and, again, it was Lennon's choice. Its stop-time structure was a test even for The Miracles' superb Motown session musicians, but The Beatles had been playing their version since the first import copies arrived in Liverpool and were able to attack it with confidence.[3] Even so, the basic track took them seven takes to get right, plus two edits for the *echt*-Motown instrumental coda (not on the original).[4]

---

it would have become [13b], predating YOU REALLY GOT A HOLD ON ME.)
[1] They may simply have been in the mood for recording non-originals, having taped thirty-six such titles for the BBC between 2nd and 16th July, sixteen of which are available on *Live At The BBC*.
[2] YOU REALLY GOT A HOLD ON ME was (unsuccessfully) released in Britain on the Oriole label.
[3] They first recorded YOU REALLY GOT A HOLD ON ME on 24th May 1963 for *Pop Goes The Beatles*. The alternative take on *Live At The BBC* is the second of three further versions made for the BBC.
[4] Unsatisfied with their recording, they tried unsuccessfully to make another, four-track version in October.

Though EMI's production is characteristically bass-light beside Motown's, despite being pitched a minor third below it, the performance is more seamless and sure-footed. Lacking the original's sax section, The Beatles rephrase the arrangement very effectively for guitars, George Martin 'comping' low in the mix on electric piano. Starr's splashy open hi-hat shows little finesse, but his bold second fill on the middle eight beats anything on The Miracles' recording. Closely harmonised by Harrison, Lennon offers a passionate lead vocal which makes up in power what it wants for nuance beside the exquisite fragility of Smokey Robinson. If the final score is a draw, that is remarkable tribute to The Beatles' versatility as interpreters.

[13c] MONEY (THAT'S WHAT I WANT) *(Bradford–Gordy)*

Lennon vocal, rhythm guitar; **McCartney** backing vocal, bass;
   Harrison backing vocal, lead guitar; **Starr** drums; **George
   Martin** piano
Recorded: 18th, 30th July 1963, Abbey Road 2.
Producer: George Martin. Engineer: Norman Smith.
UK release: 22nd November 1963 (LP: *With The Beatles*)
US release: 10th April 1964 (LP: *The Beatles' Second Album*)

If The Beatles' version of [13b] YOU REALLY GOT A HOLD ON ME does not actually surpass The Miracles' original, their redraft of another (very early) Motown hit, Money, comprehensively demolishes Barrett Strong's 1959 recording.[1] A pounding rock-and-roll twelve-bar with a bluesy riff and a blowsy lyric, MONEY suited Lennon's persona and the group's live requirements so well that they featured it regularly between 1960 and 1964. Their recording, made immediately after YOU REALLY GOT A HOLD ON ME on the evening of Thursday 18th July,[2] distills the essence of The Beatles' contemporary act – an aural snapshot of a phenomenon then provoking a huge boom in 'beat music', galvanising thousands of youths to form similar groups and opening up hundreds of new venues to accommodate them.

Strong's original is a loose-to-messy affair, swung warmly with handclaps and a tambourine. The Beatles' version is tight, impatient, and driven by harshly clanging guitars: early Sixties beat music

---

[1] Berry Gordy's first success, MONEY predates Motown, being issued on his Anna label. Licensed to London-American in the UK, it made no appearance in the British charts. An inferior earlier version of MONEY from The Beatles' audition of 1st January 1962 has been issued by Decca.
[2] George Martin overdubbed his piano twelve days later.

personified. While, within a few years, any number of groups would be able to produce a fair facsimile of the instrumental energy in this recording, no British act has ever matched the intensity of the vocal performances captured here. On MONEY, two of the finest rock-and-roll voices outside America are heard together at full throttle: McCartney raving away as the top half of the backing harmony, Lennon roaring the lead with a guttural ferocity special even for him.

Myth-spinning American critics have claimed that The Beatles were politically subversive in confronting their mass-audience with this brazen paean to avarice – yet while Lennon's performance brims with his usual irony, he and the others embodied the go-getting spirit of their time well enough to be clear that they *did* want money and plenty of it. Cash was very much to the point for four young misfits on the make who, as they admitted in interviews, were working on the assumption that, like earlier pop crazes, they had at most three years of prime earning-time ahead of them. When, on the closing choruses of MONEY, Lennon screams 'I wanna be free!', he isn't subverting the lyric's greed or venting some kind of rock-and-roll existentialism, but merely saying what he expects money to do for him. (His 'professional ambition', confided to *New Musical Express* around this time, was 'to be rich and famous'.) Though never the sole motivation, possessions were part of the package of success – a fact which he and the other Beatles found it harder to come to terms with, if less burdensome to put up with, as the decade proceeded.

[13d] DEVIL IN HER HEART *(Drapkin)*

> **Harrison** double-tracked vocal, lead guitar; **McCartney** backing
> vocal, bass; **Lennon** backing vocal, rhythm guitar; **Starr** drums,
> maracas
> Recorded: 18th July 1963, Abbey Road 2.
> Producer: George Martin. Engineer: Norman Smith.
> UK release: 22nd November 1963 (LP: *With The Beatles*)
> US release: 10th April 1964 (LP: *The Beatles' Second Album*)

The third number taped on the evening of 18th July was this Harrison feature, a drooping scoop of candyfloss originally perpetrated by obscure American girl group The Donays on the Oriole label in 1962. What with [7] DO YOU WANT TO KNOW A SECRET, Harrison was clearly being groomed as the doo-wop little-boy-lost of the group. The Beatles get through the song faster than The Donays but, that apart, the only redeeming feature of their version is Lennon's deliberately absurd nagging in the backing vocals.

[13e] TILL THERE WAS YOU *(Willson)*

McCartney vocal, bass; **Harrison** acoustic lead guitar; **Lennon**
    acoustic rhythm guitar; **Starr** bongos
Recorded: 18th, 30th July 1963, Abbey Road 2.
Producer: George Martin. Engineer: Norman Smith.
UK release: 22nd November 1963 (LP: *With The Beatles*)
US release: 20th January 1964 (LP: *Meet The Beatles!*)

The Beatles' relationship with the literate, crafted Broadway tradition
which preceded them was wryly respectful. Feeling obliged to push
their own writing standards as high as possible in order to become 'the
best', Lennon and McCartney worked hard on their songs, composing
against a background of show music instilled in them as children. In the
case of the organised and attentive McCartney, his self-taught musician
father Jim was an overt persuader. Lennon's mother Julia exerted a
comparable influence on her son, although the strains of Broadway and
Hollywood permeated his awareness more indirectly, reflecting his less
disciplined approach to life. The sort of kitsch McCartney adored left
Lennon in two minds, stuck between its sentimentality, which he
loathed, and its dreaminess, which he rather enjoyed. (The sequence
[133] CRY BABY CRY, [127] REVOLUTION 9, and [130] GOODNIGHT on
The Beatles offers an insight into this contradictory state of mind.)[1]

TILL THERE WAS YOU, a song from Meredith Willson's 1957
Broadway hit show *The Music Man*, came to McCartney's ears via a
slower Latin version made in 1958 by one of his favourite artists, Peggy
Lee. Skillfully rearranged by him, the song stayed in The Beatles'
repertoire from 1961 to 1964, being wheeled out at strategic moments
– such as the Royal Command Performance in November 1963 and
The Ed Sullivan Show in February 1964 – when they needed to court a
wider audience. TILL THERE WAS YOU was the last number to be
attempted during the first session for *With The Beatles* and went to three
takes before being held over and remade in a further eight takes a
fortnight later (the snag being that the harmonically complex acoustic

---

[1] Lennon's 'personal ambition' in 1963, according to *New Musical Express*, was to
write a musical. He and McCartney spoke of vague plans for a show based on the
idea of Jesus 'coming back as an ordinary person', a six-year anticipation of Pete
Townshend's mod-messianic 'rock opera' for The Who, *Tommy*. (One of Lennon's
showbiz friends was Lionel Bart, creator of *Lock Up Your Daughters!*, *Fings Ain't What
They Used To Be*, *Oliver!*, *Blitz*, and *Maggie May*, the last using a Liverpool
background.)

arrangement exposed the slightest mistake). The only unconvincing element is Starr's at best hopeful bongo-playing. Harrison's much-practised Spanish guitar solo is despatched with smooth aplomb, while McCartney's winsomely 'sincere' vocal plays astutely on its plain Englishness, sung without softening the 't' of 'at all' into the transatlantic 'd' usually considered essential to a pop singer's microphone technique.

[13f] PLEASE MR POSTMAN
(Holland–Bateman–Garrett–Dobbins–Gorman)

Lennon double-tracked vocal, rhythm guitar; **McCartney** backing
   vocal, bass; **Harrison** backing vocal, lead guitar; **Starr** drums
Recorded: 30th July 1963, Abbey Road 2.
Producer: George Martin. Engineer: Norman Smith.
UK release: 22nd November 1963 (LP: *With The Beatles*)
US release: 10th April 1964 (LP: *The Beatles' Second Album*)

The second session for *With The Beatles* started with a cover of The Marvelettes' PLEASE MR POSTMAN, an ascending four-chord vamp which had given Motown its first American No. 1 in December 1961. The Beatles played it frequently during 1962, but it had lapsed from their act by 1963 and required some time to get right in the studio. Lacking the loose-limbed playfulness of the original, their version steamrollers the song, turning it into a wall of sound that quickly weighs on the ear. The decision to double-track Lennon for impact only increases the general airlessness, ruling out the tonal and enunciatory idiosyncrasies that make Gladys Horton's original vocal so charming.

[14] IT WON'T BE LONG *(Lennon–McCartney)*

Lennon double-tracked vocal, rhythm guitar; **McCartney** backing
   vocal, bass; **Harrison** backing vocal, lead guitar; **Starr** drums
Recorded: 30th July 1963, Abbey Road 2.
Producer: George Martin. Engineer: Norman Smith.
UK release: 22nd November 1963 (LP: *With The Beatles*)
US release: 20th January 1964 (LP: *Meet The Beatles*)

The first Lennon–McCartney original to be recorded for *With The Beatles*, IT WON'T BE LONG became the opening track. Confidently identifying the 'yeah yeah' choruses of the unreleased [12] SHE LOVES YOU as an exploitable trademark, the song wastes no time in setting up an appropriate call-and-response pattern. Yet its layout is unusual, kicking off on a minor chorus, moving to a short major verse, back to the chorus, and then straight into the long chromatically descending phrase of the middle eight with its intricate vocal arrangement. Based on three chords, IT WON'T BE LONG says 'Lennon' in every bar (especially the one brusquely dropped from the verse to make it go faster).[1] Everything revolves around lazy semitones, the middle eight pursuing these with the augmentations and sixths typical of its author's later style. (Typical, too, is his play on 'be long' and 'belong', puns being the verbal equivalent of his close intervals.)

Taped in two sessions on 30th July, between which The Beatles dashed out to the Playhouse Theatre to record two shows for the BBC, IT WON'T BE LONG ran to twenty-three takes before it could be fitted together to the group's satisfaction. Even so the mix is poor – bass-light and with Harrison's guitar fills too detached from the rest of the sound. (There is also a dreadful edit at 1:08, slicing off an impatient flourish from Lennon's Rickenbacker.) Never part of their live set, the song shows signs of hasty arranging, and McCartney's bass line, aside from his doubling of Harrison's figure at the end of each chorus, is unusually cautious. That aside, the performance has characteristic guts and drive, grabbing the attention with its punchy irregularities, graphic mood-changes, and sudden crescendo turnarounds. Piling surprise on surprise, the track veers from strident 'Twist-beat' roughness to smooth Miracles-style sophistication in its middle eight, ending cheesily on one of the group's favourite barber-shop major sevenths. The Beatles' early philosophy of recording was to pack it tight without a single dull second, 'needle-time' being precious. The hungry urgency of that period is loud and clear here.

[14b] ROLL OVER BEETHOVEN *(Berry)*

Harrison double-tracked vocal, lead guitar, handclaps; **Lennon** rhythm guitar, handclaps; **McCartney** bass, handclaps; **Starr** drums, handclaps
Recorded: 30th July 1963, Abbey Road 2.
Producer: George Martin. Engineer: Norman Smith.
UK release: 22nd November 1963 (LP: *With The Beatles*)
US release: 10th April 1964 (LP: *The Beatles' Second Album*)

The second number taped during the evening session of 30th July was Chuck Berry's ROLL OVER BEETHOVEN, originally issued in America on the Chess label in 1956. The most influential performer/songwriter of

---

[1] McCartney recalls it as a co-composition from an original idea by Lennon (Miles, op. cit., p. 152).

the Fifties, Berry effectively created the genre of rock-and-roll by the simple stratagem of constantly invoking it in his clever, quickfire lyrics. Between 1957 and 1966, The Beatles performed more songs written by him than by any other artist.[1]

With its references to 'these rhythm-and-blues', ROLL OVER BEETHOVEN was one of its author's earliest attempts to mythologise his market category. As a performance, his version hints at the transition between the thumping crotchet swing of R&B and the hammering quavers of rock-and-roll, travelling from the former to a preview of the latter within the span of nine choruses. By contrast, The Beatles approach the song from the vantage of later Berry songs like [U22c] JOHNNY B GOODE and [U13c] CAROL, slowing it down, lowering its key, and giving it the rolling rhythm of boogiewoogie. Harrison, who took over the vocal from Lennon in 1961, sings it genially, replacing the angry hornet of Berry's early staccato guitar with a pastiche of his mellower later style. Though hardly a dazzling performance,[2] the point lies in its generation-defining lyric: 'Beethoven and Tchaikovsky were yesterday; *this* is the sound of today.' With ROLL OVER BEETHOVEN, The Beatles struck a chord for their audience – especially in America where their version appeared on the singles chart during the initial rush of Beatlemania in 1964.

---

[1] This excludes songs sung (though not written by) Lennon's greatest hero Elvis Presley, of which The Beatles performed about thirty between 1957 and 1962, recording only three of them: [U13b] THAT'S ALL RIGHT (MAMA), [U13k] I'M GONNA SIT RIGHT DOWN AND CRY, and [U31c] I FORGOT TO REMEMBER TO FORGET – all on *Live At The BBC*. Nearly all of their Chuck Berry originals were sung by Lennon, the most frequent (apart from ROLL OVER BEETHOVEN) being [U22c] JOHNNY B. GOODE *(Live At The BBC)* and [46c] ROCK AND ROLL MUSIC. Others included [U13g] SWEET LITTLE SIXTEEN *(Live At The BBC)*, 'Maybellene', 'Almost Grown', [U13c] CAROL *(Live At The BBC)*, [U13s] MEMPHIS, TENNESSEE *(Live At The BBC)*, 'Reelin' and Rockin'', [U15e] TOO MUCH MONKEY BUSINESS *(Live At The BBC)*, 'I'm Talking About You', [U11d] I GOT TO FIND MY BABY *(Live At The BBC)*, 'Thirty Days', and 'Vacation Time'. McCartney sang 'Little Queenie'.
[2] The live recording made in Sweden on 24th October 1963 *(Anthology 1)* is better.

[15] ALL MY LOVING (*Lennon–McCartney*)

McCartney double-tracked vocal, bass; **Lennon** backing vocal,
   rhythm guitar; **Harrison** backing vocal, lead guitar; **Starr** drums
Recorded: 30th July 1963, Abbey Road 2.
Producer: George Martin. Engineer: Norman Smith.
UK release: 22nd November 1963 (LP: *With The Beatles*)
US release: 20th January 1964 (LP: *Meet the Beatles!*)

Written two months earlier by McCartney during the Roy Orbison
tour, ALL MY LOVING was unusual in originating as a lyric. This he
evolved one afternoon on the tour bus, later finding a piano at the
venue and using it to work out the music. A light-hearted 'letter song',
its metre creates the melody, marching triumphantly up and down the
scale of E major with typical McCartneyesque harmonic brio and
abundance. Like so many of his happiest moments (e.g., [44b] KANSAS
CITY/HEY, HEY, HEY, HEY), the arrangement features a wide-flung
walking bass, spiced up by fast rhythm-guitar triplets stolen by Lennon
from The Crystals' 'Da Doo Ron Ron' (then at the height of its success
in the UK singles chart). ALL MY LOVING was made in thirteen takes at
the end of the evening of 30th July and is one of the best-recorded
songs on *With The Beatles*, benefiting from an open, spontaneous sound
and minimal overdubs. Despite some wobbly pitching, McCartney's
vocal is as irresistibly joyous as Harrison's Carl Perkins-style guitar break
and the brightly lolloping beat of the track as a whole.

The innocence of early Sixties British pop is perfectly distilled in
the eloquent simplicity of this number. Though never considered for a
single, it drew so much radio-play and audience response that, in
February 1964, EMI issued it as the title track of a best-selling EP. Part
of The Beatles' act during 1963 and 1964, it was performed during the
group's first appearance on *The Ed Sullivan Show* on 9th February 1964.
Contemporary interviews show that at this stage McCartney regarded
Lennon as the leader of the group, a feeling more or less echoed by the
record-buying public. WITH ALL MY LOVING, he began to be seen as
more of an equal with his partner. Meanwhile, The Beatles' rivals
looked on amazed as songs of this commercial appeal were casually
thrown away on LPs.

[16] I WANNA BE YOUR MAN *(Lennon–McCartney)*

Starr double-tracked vocal, drums, maracas; **McCartney** backing
vocal, bass; **Lennon** backing vocal, rhythm guitar; **Harrison** lead
guitar; **George Martin** Hammond organ
Recorded: 11th–12th, 30th September, 3rd, 23rd October 1963,
Abbey Road 2.
Producer: George Martin. Engineer: Norman Smith.
UK release: 22nd November 1963 (LP: *With The Beatles*)
US release: 20th January 1964 (LP: *Meet the Beatles!*)

Reminiscing about this rudimentary rocker in 1980, Lennon recalled it
as mainly by McCartney. However, Ron King, who drove the coach
on the group's 1963 UK tour, claims that Lennon, an inveterate media
scanner who often found lines and ideas in newspapers or TV
programmes, noted down this title earlier that year.[1] Invited, on the
spur of the moment, by The Rolling Stones' manager Andrew Loog
Oldham, Lennon and McCartney turned up at the Studio 51 Club in
Great Newport Street with a half-chewed idea of McCartney's ('We
weren't going to give them anything *great*, were we?').[2] Mick Jagger
and Keith Richards, with whom they were on comradely terms, agreed
that what there was of it was compatible with their style. Repairing to a
corner, the two Beatles thereupon finished the song (it being at this
point that Lennon may have tendered the phrase 'I wanna be your
man', of which the chorus consists of four repetitions).[3] Though the
result was very far from a masterpiece, Jagger and Richards were so
impressed that a song could be slung together in a few minutes that
they resolved from then on to write their own material, soon becoming
The Beatles' only plausible rivals in UK pop songwriting of the 1963–6
period.

The recording of *With The Beatles*, suspended in August to
accommodate a seven-week tour, resumed the day after I WANNA BE
YOUR MAN was written. Chosen as Starr's solo spot for the new album
(presumably replacing LITTLE CHILD), it was begun in a native Beatles

---

[1] Coleman, Vol. 1, p. 195.
[2] In *Many Years From Now* (pp. 153-4), McCartney recollects the song as originally
written for Starr and later offered to the Stones. Other witnesses, however, are sure
that the song was finished on the spot in front of the Stones.
[3] He may also have added the bluesy down-turn at the end of the chorus,
reminiscent of [U11e] SOME OTHER GUY, a song with which he was obsessed (see
[6], note). McCartney, however, recalls the source as 'Fortune Teller' by New
Orleans R&B singer Benny Spellman (Miles, op. cit., p. 153). The song,
coincidentally, had been the B-side for the Stones cancelled second single, 'Poison
Ivy'.

version immediately – yet, for such a palaeolithically simple song, it caused them a lot of trouble, being laid aside twice and finished only during the last day of recording. Faster than the Stones' version and with a hint of Bo Diddley courtesy of the *vibrato* setting on Lennon's Vox amp, it's an undistinguished effort, sung by Starr with a cordial lack of conviction and lashed on to little effect by increasingly bogus yells from the others.[1]

[17] LITTLE CHILD *(Lennon–McCartney)*

> **Lennon** vocal, rhythm guitar, harmonica; **McCartney** vocal, bass, piano; **Harrison** lead guitar; **Starr** drums
> Recorded: 11th–12th September, 3rd October 1963, Abbey Road 2.
> Producer: George Martin. Engineer: Norman Smith.
> UK release: 22nd November 1963 (LP: *With The Beatles*)
> US release: 20th January 1964 (LP: *Meet the Beatles!*)

A fifty-fifty collaboration between Lennon and McCartney, LITTLE CHILD was originally written for Starr to sing.[2] It was never part of The Beatles' act and, including overdubs, took over twenty takes and three sessions to get right. The result is nonetheless spontaneous, albeit that the harmonica playing is sloppy and the vocals (credited to Lennon and McCartney, but more like the former double-tracked) are poorly synchronised. Typical early Beatles, its sly match of words and melody allows for some modestly theatrical variations of tone. Mock-coy, cajoling, bragging, suggestive – LITTLE CHILD's rapid manoeuvring conjures the sexual street banter of Liverpudlian youth. Even in a roughneck potboiler, Lennon and McCartney could rise above the norm by virtue of keen observation.

---

[1] A snappier version with a smart guitar solo was recorded for Rediffusion's *Around The Beatles* TV special on 19th April 1964 (see *Anthology 1*).

[2] Miles, op. cit., p. 153. McCartney adds that part of the melody is stolen from a song by folk balladeer Elton Hayes.

[18] ALL I'VE GOT TO DO *(Lennon–McCartney)*

> **Lennon** vocal, rhythm guitar; **McCartney** backing vocal, bass;
>   **Harrison** backing vocal, lead guitar; **Starr** drums
> Recorded: 11th September 1963, Abbey Road 2.
> Producer: George Martin. Engineer: Norman Smith.
> UK release: 22nd November 1963 (LP: *With The Beatles*)
> US release: 20th January 1964 (LP: *Meet the Beatles!*)

Another song never taken into the group's live repertoire, ALL I'VE GOT TO DO was recorded during the afternoon session in which [16] I WANNA BE YOUR MAN and [17] LITTLE CHILD were begun. Eight of its fourteen takes petered out in the kind of mistakes inevitable with an under-rehearsed number, but the group were pleased with its downbeat atmosphere and the hurt, halting mood of its nervy rhythmic interplay of damped guitar chords and sparse hi-hat strokes.[1] By Lennon, the song shows his then well-guarded serious side. Plain and even clichéd in parts, the lyric revolves on an assurance of comfort against the loneliness evoked in the stark suspended fourth which begins the track (a device probably borrowed from Smokey Robinson and The Miracles' 'You Can Depend On Me' which may also have suggested the general line of Lennon's lyric). Rising in intensity, Miracles-style, through the middle eight, the song reaches its release in block harmony, dissolving on a pensive fade suggesting a frustrating emotional impasse. Only the superfluous addition of some trademark 'yeah's cheapens the effect.

[19] NOT A SECOND TIME *(Lennon–McCartney)*

> **Lennon** double-tracked vocal, acoustic guitar; **McCartney** bass;
>   **Harrison** acoustic guitar; **Starr** drums; **George Martin** piano
> Recorded: 11th September 1963, Abbey Road 2.
> Producer: George Martin. Engineer: Norman Smith.
> UK release: 22nd November 1963 (LP: *With The Beatles*)
> US release: 20th January 1964 (LP: *Meet the Beatles!*)

The last of Lennon's three non-collaborative contributions to *With The Beatles* (see [14], [18]), NOT A SECOND TIME is a rambling affair composed of an irregular fourteen-bar verse joined to a ten-bar chorus

---

[1] [14] IT WON'T BE LONG uses the same clash of E major against C sharp minor, although here, owing to the rarity of the dominant, it is more fundamental, rendering much of the song 'homeless' in key terms. Compare McCartney's sweeter use of this chord/key relationship in [15] ALL MY LOVING.

which sounds more like a middle eight. McCartney obviously had no hand in this and some sources deny his presence during the recording, despite the fact that his bass can be heard low in the mix. The bitter lyric, too, is typical of Lennon, though ill-matched to his lachrymose Miracles-influenced melody. Struck by the song's self-taught unorthodoxies, the classical critic of *The Times* drew attention to its author's use of Aeolian cadences. 'To this day,' Lennon admitted to *Playboy* in 1980, 'I have no idea what they are. They sound like exotic birds.'

[20] DON'T BOTHER ME (Harrison)

Harrison double-tracked vocal, lead guitar; **Lennon** rhythm guitar,
    tambourine; **McCartney** bass, claves; **Starr** drums, bongos
Recorded: 11th–12th September 1963, Abbey Road 2.
Producer: George Martin. Engineer: Norman Smith.
UK release: 22nd November 1963 (LP: *With The Beatles*)
US release: 20th January 1964 (LP: *Meet the Beatles!*)

Written while ill in bed in a Bournemouth hotel during The Beatles' residency at the local Gaumont in August 1963, George Harrison's first original song is dourly resentful in tone. (He claims it was because he felt low and wanted to be left alone. Liverpudlian journalist Bill Harry insists it was because he had badgered Harrison into writing it, having enjoyed the guitarist's early Shadows pastiche [E4] CRY FOR A SHADOW.) DON'T BOTHER ME has never had a good press, even its author doubting its right to be called a song, yet its shadowy atmosphere and plangent modal flavour remain distinctive. An authentic expression of Harrison's deep-seated need for privacy, it adds a haunting, if erratically pitched, new voice to The Beatles' repertoire, miscalculating only by prolonging its depressive minor mood a chorus too far.[1]

Recorded not much more than a fortnight after it was written, the song set the group problems which they failed to solve during the evening session of 11th September. Accordingly, they began it again the following afternoon (after the remake of [9] HOLD ME TIGHT), this time evolving a Latin rhythm in which the accent fell, oddly, on the on-beat. Steered deftly around its stop-time structure by an enthusiastic Starr, the performance, with its ominous bass triplets and fierce guitar solo, was unlike anything the group had done before.

---

[1] This would turn out to be a recurring trait of Harrison's writing. [66] IF I NEEDED SOMEONE is also over-extended and [136] WHILE MY GUITAR GENTLY WEEPS originally had an extra verse (*Anthology 3*). Once on one of his hobby-horses, say friends, it is often difficult to get him to stop talking.

[21] I WANT TO HOLD YOUR HAND *(Lennon–McCartney)*

Lennon vocal, rhythm guitar, handclaps; **McCartney** vocal, bass, handclaps; **Harrison** harmony vocal, lead guitar, handclaps; **Starr** drums, handclaps

Recorded: 17th October 1963, Abbey Road 2.

Producer: George Martin. Engineer: Norman Smith.

UK release: 29th November 1963 (A single/THIS BOY)

US release: 26th December 1963 (A single/I SAW HER STANDING THERE)

With [12] SHE LOVES YOU at No. 1 in the UK throughout September, The Beatles took their second holiday since signing with EMI, returning to Britain early in October. During this break Lennon and McCartney wrote the two sides of their next single, the first Beatles songs for nearly a year not to have been dashed off while touring. Capitol's refusal to issue the band's product in the USA was by now an impediment to their career and a major worry to Brian Epstein who advised the pair to write with America in mind. Knowing they were on their mettle induced a tension tangible in the introduction of the song they came up with: I WANT TO HOLD YOUR HAND.[1]

Written ('one on one, eyeball to eyeball', according to Lennon) in the basement of Jane Asher's parents' house in Wimpole Street, I WANT TO HOLD YOUR HAND displays the traits of the early Lennon–McCartney collaborative style (see [10]). Going above all for impact, it makes no attempt at sustained melody, moving instead in half-bar phrases governed by its fourth-dominated harmony, the result of two writers competing with each other side by side at the same piano. As with [3] PLEASE PLEASE ME and [10] FROM ME TO YOU, the method depended on surprise; indeed, the song is so dense with incident that McCartney's octave jump to falsetto at the end of the verse is pre-empted by another shock four bars earlier: a plunge from the home key of G major onto an unstable B minor.[2] Such blatant

---

[1] In Part 2 of the *Anthology* video series, George Martin questions the idea that I WANT TO HOLD YOUR HAND was made with America in mind. While this may not have been announced as such at the session, it was certainly a priority for Epstein. The Beatles had refused to go to the States without already having a US hit single, yet their February 1964 mini-tour of New York, Washington, and Miami was set up within days of making I WANT TO HOLD YOUR HAND, suggesting that they'd decided to gamble on getting this record into the US charts by the time the American dates were due.

[2] Lennon remembered this as the chord that 'made' the song. When McCartney found it – to judge by the movement of the melody line, he was sitting on the left, voicing the chord-sequence in descending inversions – Lennon shouted 'That's *it*! Do that again!' (Sheff and Golson, p. 117.) Left to their own devices, Lennon and

contrivance mattered no more than it had in PLEASE PLEASE ME. It was exciting, unexpected, irreverent – and in practice made to seem natural by the beatific vitality with which the group belted it out.

Brought into the studio four days after the press had announced the onset of Beatlemania following the group's appearance on *Sunday Night At The London Palladium*, I WANT TO HOLD YOUR HAND was thoroughly prearranged and rehearsed, only the eleven-bar middle section being altered on take 2, dropping Lennon's rock-and-roll rhythm figure for the contrast of quiet arpeggios. The introduction postponed arrival at the tonic by starting with the last bars of the middle section. This time, though, the device was intensified with hammering repetition and a 'pushed' beat which created ambiguity in the rhythm, compounded by having the vocals enter two beats ahead of the verse ('*Oh yeah*, I . . .'). To complete this barrage of dazzling effects, the group brought the performance to a breathless full close on two bars of hard-braking 3/8. Apart from ending with the studio exploding, they could scarcely have hit their prospective American audience with more in two-and-a-half minutes.[1]

In the UK, I WANT TO HOLD YOUR HAND was The Beatles' first Christmas hit, entering the shops in late November with advance orders of more than a million. In the USA, release came too late for the festive season which, in any case, had been dampened by the recent assassination of President Kennedy. When Capitol finally capitulated to Epstein's pressure and issued I WANT TO HOLD YOUR HAND, the record's joyous energy and invention lifted America out of its gloom, following which, high on gratitude, the country cast itself at The Beatles' feet. Their TV performance on *The Ed Sullivan Show* on 9th

---

McCartney were generally less liable to make ostentatious chord selections (e.g., the mostly separately-written songs on *A Hard Day's Night*, where an interest in key relationships leads to more integrated designs).

[1] Because they were performers as well as songwriters, Lennon and McCartney had to find convincing ways of concluding their songs onstage. (Their main rivals – American studio artists and writer-producer teams – worked under no such constraints and so inclined to the unresolved expedient of the fade-out.) Almost all of The Beatles' 1962–5 records finish with varieties of close, including covers of records by other artists which fade out in the originals. The extent of their craftmanslike preference for 'proper endings' is manifest in albums like *A Hard Day's Night* and *Help!*, where they were free to use fade-outs but instead composed scrupulous intros and closes to almost all of the tracks. *A Hard Day's Night*, for example, employs fade-outs on only four of its thirteen tracks, three of which are faded for specific dramatic effect: [31] A HARD DAY'S NIGHT, [35] THINGS WE SAID TODAY, [33] I'LL BE BACK. During the second half of their recording career (1966–70), they mildly relaxed this embargo on fades, but closes still predominated while most of their rivals continued to favour fade endings.

February, claimed by many US commentators to be the pivotal event in American post-war culture, sealed the deal and, by April, their back catalogue was flooding the US charts.[1]

I WANT TO HOLD YOUR HAND electrified American pop. More schooled in technique than their British cousins, aspiring American players and writers listened to The Beatles' free-spirited unorthodoxies in excited disbelief. Just as Lennon, McCartney, and Harrison had studied the licks, changes, and production-effects used in the rock-and-roll and R&B records they had once bought at Liverpool import shops, so now American youths crouched by their dansettes with guitars trying to work out what The Beatles were doing. Most of the North American groups of the late Sixties acknowledged the inspiration of The Beatles and their role in breaking the grip of showbiz convention on the US pop industry. In fact every American artist, black or white, asked about I WANT TO HOLD YOUR HAND has said much the same: it altered everything, ushering in a new era and changing their lives.[2] That The Beatles represented something transmitting at a higher creative frequency was clear even to many outside the pop audience. The poet Allen Ginsberg, for example, amazed his intellectual *confrères* by getting up and dancing delightedly to I WANT TO HOLD YOUR HAND when he first heard it in a New York night club. Bob Dylan, too, was able to see past the song's naivety to the epoch-making spirit animating it. (Fascinated by The Beatles' unorthodox chords and harmonies, he decided they must have been chemically assisted, mishearing the line 'I can't hide' as 'I get high'.)

Not that The Beatles were uniformly welcomed in the USA. The up-market press was notably sniffy, finding the group's music barbarous and their lyrics illiterate, while the existing pop industry naturally resented the prospect of overnight obsolescence. (In moves to avoid this, many established artists made floundering attempts to adjust their styles to meet the 'British Invasion' of lesser UK acts that soon poured in following The Beatles' breakthrough.)[3] Some of the adverse

---

[1] In the first week of April 1964, The Beatles held the first five positions in the American Top 10: 1. [23] CAN'T BUY ME LOVE; 2. [9f] TWIST AND SHOUT; 3. [12] SHE LOVES YOU; 4. [21] I WANT TO HOLD YOUR HAND; and 5. [3] PLEASE PLEASE ME A week later, they occupied *fourteen* positions in the Hot 100, a record exceedingly unlikely to be approached again.

[2] Somach and Somach, *passim*; Dowlding, pp. 60–61.

[3] The 'British Invasion' was more symbolic than actual – the high-profile appearance of a new dynamism rather than a literal occupation of the American charts. The 'invasion' was, in any case, highly heterogeneous, including acts as far from the 'beat group' format as Petula Clark and The Bachelors. For a while

reaction was justified. Tommy James, a pop star with an interest in production, thought much of the early Beatles repertoire poorly recorded – which, by US standards, it was. While I WANT TO HOLD YOUR HAND (the first Beatles song to be made in true stereo on Abbey Road's new four-track desk) sounded better than most of the group's previous discs, it was primitive compared with the product of American studios, lacking bass response and offering raw vocal sound.[1] What it did have, apart from power and originality, was an instinct for dynamic contrast and a brilliant grasp of construction.

Primarily a hit *record*, I WANT TO HOLD YOUR HAND makes less sense considered as a song. So much of its melody line is disguised harmony that singing it without chordal support makes for comic results, while its lyrics are embarrassingly perfunctory. In America, the words to I WANT TO HOLD YOUR HAND were heard as a token of the group's social acceptability. Where The Rolling Stones dealt in sex, The Beatles supposedly respected propriety, knowing how far a young man should go with a young woman and hence how far a pop group could trespass without causing offence. This was true to the extent that Brian Epstein had carefully sweetened The Beatles' image for public consumption (much to the rebellious Lennon's annoyance).

Yet the real reason for the group's lyric blandness at this stage was that they didn't much care what words they sang as long as they fitted the overall sound.[2] It was the record, rather than the song, that interested them. Haunted by the often imponderably strange productions that emerged from US studios during the Fifties – 'Give Me Love' by Rosie and The Originals being one of their favourites – McCartney and (particularly) Lennon were more devoted to spirit than form. To them, the sound and feel of a record mattered more than what it literally said; hence, the first requirement of a lyric was not to get in the

engrossed in vain attempts to come up with an answer to The Beatles, US acts remained, if only numerically, ascendant on the American scene. Nor did British style-dominance last long, the main impact of the 'Invasion' registering in the year after I WANT TO HOLD YOUR HAND. Yet its effect was marked, with half of the new US artists who would normally have arrived in 1964 displaced by UK acts. (Kelly, *The Beatle Myth*, p. 155.) Moreover, the chart placings of the British invaders were disproportionately high. Before I WANT TO HOLD YOUR HAND there had been only two British No. 1 hits in America – Acker Bilk's 'Stranger on the Shore' and The Tornados' 'Telstar' – together holding the top spot for a total of four weeks. During 1964–5, British acts occupied the US No. 1 position for no less than fifty-two weeks!

[1] Lennon, for whom the song held significance, considered remaking it after The Beatles broke up.

[2] Lennon and McCartney worked by singing random phrases while feeling around for chords. The title of the present track, for example, was probably a variation on 'I wanna be your man'.

way of the general effect. The Beatles sang of 'diamond rings' in their early songs ([23], [45], [64]) not because they wished to identify themselves with the marital conventions of the silent majority, but because it then seemed to them that clichés were less distracting than anything more original.

The epochal change that American listeners sensed in I WANT TO HOLD YOUR HAND was, in fact, nothing less than a resumption, at higher intensity, of the carefree sensationalism of Fifties rock-and-roll. Since Little Richard's crazed clarion call of 'Awopbopaloomop, alopbamboom!', pop had strayed only timidly from the straight and narrow of civilised 'good sense'. Indeed, the American folk-protest movement had thrust plain-speaking so obtrusively into the pop domain that every transient youth idol was then routinely interrogated concerning his or her 'message' to humanity. If it has any message at all, that of I WANT TO HOLD YOUR HAND is 'Let go – *feel how good it is*'. This though (as conservative commentators knew very well) implied a fundamental break with the Christian bourgeois status quo. Harbouring no conscious subversive intent, The Beatles, with this potent record, perpetrated a culturally revolutionary act. As the decade wore on and they began to realise the position they were in, they began to do the same thing more deliberately.

[22] THIS BOY *(Lennon–McCartney)*

Lennon vocal, acoustic guitar; **McCartney** vocal, bass; **Harrison** vocal, lead guitar; **Starr** drums
Recorded: 17th October 1963, Abbey Road 2.
Producer: George Martin. Engineer: Norman Smith.
UK release: 29th November 1963 (B single/I WANT TO HOLD YOUR HAND)
US release: 20th January 1964 (LP: *Meet The Beatles!*)

Like its British A-side, THIS BOY is a mood piece of little meaning. (Lennon admitted there was 'nothing in the lyrics – just a sound and a harmony'.) The allusion is, again, to doo-wop (see [8], [50]), with special reference to the early records of Smokey Robinson and the Miracles, whose characteristic 'sobbing' climaxes are echoed in the melodramatic middle eight. With its warm major sevenths, THIS BOY adapted a traditional Fifties pop model[1] and became a feature of The Beatles' act during 1964 owing to the three-part close harmony which

---

[1] The circular doo-wop sequence I-vi-ii-V, a variation of the more usual I-vi-IV-V (still being milked today, e.g., Whitney Houston's 1992–3 No. 1 hit 'I Will Always Love You').

brought Lennon, McCartney, and Harrison to the microphone as a unit.[1] But if the gentle reproach of the song's falling major second (a doo-wop hallmark) acquits it of the charge of unadulterated *kitsch*, the overall effect is of tweeness unrelieved by a formulaic 'teen' lyric.

Using drums only in the middle eight, the arrangement takes its slightly unsteady 12/8 pulse from a blend of pattering hi-hat and acoustic guitar, recorded with faint repeat-echo, on the left channel. This leaves the voices crammed onto the right channel, their heavy reverb leaking into the centre of the sound-picture. Lennon's solo spot in the middle eight is, moreover, brutally cut off in the edit. (An amusing excerpt from the session for this song, with Harrison and McCartney continually mixing up their 'this boy's and 'that boy's, was issued with [187] FREE AS A BIRD.)

[23] CAN'T BUY ME LOVE (Lennon–McCartney)

McCartney double-tracked vocal, bass; **Lennon** acoustic rhythm
   guitar; **Harrison** double-tracked lead guitar; **Starr** drums
Recorded: 29th January 1964, EMI Pathé Marconi, Paris; 25th
   February 1964, Abbey Road 2.
Producer: George Martin. Engineer: Norman Smith.
UK release: 20th March 1964 (A single/YOU CAN'T DO THAT)
US release: 16th March 1964 (A single/YOU CAN'T DO THAT)

The Beatles' January 1964 residency at the Paris Olympia was a chore, their audiences finding the new British pop idiom hard to grasp and the French press loftily insulting the group as 'juvenile delinquents' and 'has-beens'. While their spirits were raised by hearing that [21] I WANT TO HOLD YOUR HAND had vaulted in virtually one bound to the top of the American charts, more drudgery had to be faced on 29th January when they reluctantly attended EMI France's Paris studio to tape German-language versions of it and [12] SHE LOVES YOU.[2] These

---

[1] McCartney, who co-wrote the song with Lennon, recalls that it was evolved as a close two-part harmony, later adding the third part for Harrison (Miles, op. cit., p. 155). According to him, the group first learned to sing three-part harmony by copying The Teddy Bears' 1959 hit 'To Know Him Is To Love Him'. (See *Live At The BBC*).

[2] I WANT TO HOLD YOUR HAND ('Komm, Gib Mir Deine Hand') was made first, using a two-track mixdown of the original backing track over which new vocals were sung. (Newly anxious to exploit every last scrap of Beatles product, Capitol issued this version on the American compilation LP *Something New* in June 1964.) SHE LOVES YOU ('Sie Liebt Dich') was entirely remade in fourteen takes – thirteen for the backing track, one for the vocals. (The German rewrite didn't go as far as insisting on 'ja, ja, ja'.) Since the Swan label still held the US rights to SHE LOVES YOU, it issued the German version as a single in America, backed with [13] I'LL GET

done, they used the last hour of the session to record a number McCartney had written only days before.[1] Originally conceived with the rolling backbeat and bluesy delivery later used in [44] SHE'S A WOMAN, CAN'T BUY ME LOVE was altered on the spot, turning into a bouncily commercial pop song – a redraft accomplished in four takes. The fact that George Martin had to tell the group to start with the chorus rather than the verse shows how little they'd considered the song before recording it (the change being so obvious that they would have made it themselves had they tried the tune out earlier).[2]

Among the simplest of the group's hits, CAN'T BUY ME LOVE consists of a jazzy blues in minor chords with a straight-up eight-bar major chorus. As such, it spoke a musical language the parental generation could relate to, and it was almost logical that Ella Fitzgerald recorded a cover version as soon as she heard it.[3] The only incongruity lay in McCartney's artless lyric which, despite some smart syllabics in the second line of its second verse, stands no comparison with the work of the professional lyricists to whom Fitzgerald was accustomed. The most effective aspect of the words to CAN'T BUY ME LOVE was largely accidental: its author's decision to replace the conventional 'my dear/ my love' with the bluff, asexual 'my friend'. Though McCartney was merely recycling a throwaway rhyme from the little-known [13] I'LL GET YOU, the effect was arresting, seeming to define the casual etiquette of a coolly unromantic new age.[4]

Partly by luck, partly by intuition, The Beatles managed time and

---

YOU, in May 1964. The custom of recording special versions for foreign markets, standard practice at the time, was never afterwards bothered with by The Beatles and consequently fell into disuse. The resulting promotion of the English language around the world is one of their most substantial, and least documented, achievements.
[1] Many of the songs for *A Hard Day's Night* were written, or begun, while Lennon and McCartney were in Paris where they had a grand piano installed in their suite at the Hotel George V.
[2] The arrangement initially featured a superfluous lead guitar figure on the chorus and interjected backing vocals from Lennon and Harrison on the verse.
[3] Apart from its many melodic blue-notes, CAN'T BUY ME LOVE emulates the swing style with its 'big band' stop-time breaks ('I don't care too' [beat] 'much for money') and the rich jazz turnaround chords at the end of each chorus ('Can't buy me lo-' [Dm11] '-o-' [G13] '-ove' [C]). McCartney may have dropped into this idiom – that of Sinatra and Peggy Lee – after hearing Helen Shapiro's version of Lee's 'Fever', then climbing the UK singles chart. Lee was one of his favourite singers [13e].
[4] The sentiment of the lyric, McCartney later noted (Miles, op. cit., p. 162), seemed contradicted by the group's life-style of the time, wherein their attraction allowed them access to almost any young women they wanted. McCartney: 'It should have been "Can Buy Me Love", actually.'

again with such simple strokes to place themselves in a subtly futuristic context. As the decade advanced and they continued to bring off variations on this trick, a sense grew among their audience that the group 'knew what was going on' and were somehow poised above events, guiding them through their music. Yet The Beatles wooed convention with an equally intuitive touch, establishing their cross-generational viability in America with CAN'T BUY ME LOVE in the aftermath of the youthquake impact of I WANT TO HOLD YOUR HAND. Where the latter threatened something almost too vigorous to be contained, the idiomatic familiarity of CAN'T BUY ME LOVE, delivered with old-fashioned showbiz 'oomph' by the wholesome McCartney, offered canny reassurance – a sly conquest soon consolidated by the cheeky wit of *A Hard Day's Night*.

The Beatles' ability to be two contradictory things at once – comfortably safe and exhilaratingly strange – has been displayed by no other pop act. A by-product of the creative tension between the group's two dominant personalities, this effect increased as Lennon and McCartney drew apart as writers, and it is significant that, with CAN'T BUY ME LOVE, their 'one on one, eyeball to eyeball' collaborations more or less came to an end. So far as records are concerned, the pair's golden age of full fifty-fifty co-composition was 1963, with a sustained run of such numbers ([10], [11], [12], [13], [16], [17], [21]). Only one such occurred in 1964 [37] and the same was true in 1965 [61]. During The Beatles' last four years, Lennon and McCartney stopped working together like this, though they continued to meet formally to 'check' each other's new songs in three-hour writing sessions[1] held mostly at Lennon's house in Weybridge. Here, they would show each other their new material, fixing details and often helping with unfinished or unwritten sections, such as middle eights. Several of their best tracks resulted from semi-collaborations begun after one of them had written part of a number and needed help from the other with finishing it (e.g., [68], [74], [96], [110], [158]). So far as songwriting was concerned, Lennon and McCartney saw themselves as business partners and took a disciplined professional attitude to their work. Yet the truth was that each was a self-sufficient entity with an egotistic eye on his own career and a different conception of the group.[2] Similar enough to allow

---

[1] These, notionally, matched the three-hour recording sessions then standard, owing to Musicians' Union rules, at Abbey Road.

[2] A list of early Beatles songs sent by Brian Epstein to George Martin on 6th June 1962 shows Lennon and McCartney's 'original compositions' under their respective authors rather than as the product of a partnership. (McCartney: [1] LOVE ME DO, [2] P.S. I LOVE YOU, [E5] LIKE DREAMERS DO, 'Love Of The Loved'; Lennon: [4] ASK

fruitful interaction in the later stages of composition, their tastes in music, as they grew up, diverged too much to accommodate much fullscale start-to-finish collaboration. Theirs was a classic attraction of opposites, and one which worked increasingly at a distance after CAN'T BUY ME LOVE, the first Beatles single to feature only one singer. (See [24].)

With its bobbing beat and light acoustic rhythm, CAN'T BUY ME LOVE prefaced the second phase of The Beatles career: that of global recognition and 'standard' status. Its effortless rightness – from McCartney's boisterous vocal (beginning three beats before the rest join in) to Harrison's first wholly memorable guitar solo – bespeaks a band of talents on top of their world. Their teenage ambition to displace Elvis Presley from the ruling summit of pop is achieved here.

[24] YOU CAN'T DO THAT *(Lennon–McCartney)*

> **Lennon** vocal, lead guitar; **McCartney** backing vocal, bass, cowbell; **Harrison** backing vocal, rhythm guitar; **Starr** drums, conga
> Recorded: 25th February, 22nd May 1964, Abbey Road 2.[1]
> Producer: George Martin. Engineer: Norman Smith.
> UK release: 20th March 1964 (B single/CAN'T BUY ME LOVE)
> US release: 16th March 1964 (B single/CAN'T BUY ME LOVE)

Returning to London a week after recording [23] CAN'T BUY ME LOVE, The Beatles paused for a day before flying to New York for a brief round of TV and concert engagements to consolidate the success of [21] I WANT TO HOLD YOUR HAND. Back a fortnight later, with their first feature film due to start shooting in five days, they dashed into Abbey Road to do a B-side for their sixth single, finishing it in four takes. Like its A-side, YOU CAN'T DO THAT is a blues with a contrasting eight-bar section, this time given a bitter pentatonic twist. Written by Lennon, the song is punchily aggressive, leaning towards outright dissonance in its arpeggio guitar riff and equipped with frankly autobiographical lyrics. (He later recalled it as written under the influence of Wilson Pickett. Pickett, though, was then an obscure singer of 6/8 'talking' ballads a year away from his first hit, 'In The Midnight Hour', which is presumably what Lennon was referring to.) As a performance, it's among The Beatles' best from this period, with McCartney and Harrison yelling one of their most exciting backing vocal arrangements and tension tightening at the guitar solo before

ME WHY, [E6] HELLO LITTLE GIRL.)
[1] The second date consisted of an unused piano overdub by George Martin.

relapsing on a sullen lead-bass unison at the end. Not surprisingly, it was taken into The Beatles' act during 1964.

The paranoid possessiveness of YOU CAN'T DO THAT marks it 'personal' in more ways than one. After the head-to-head collaboration of I WANT TO HOLD YOUR HAND, McCartney and Lennon had rebounded into competitive solo writing, McCartney pushing himself with the optimistic CAN'T BUY ME LOVE, Lennon covering his partner's move with some self-promotion of his own in the present track. This divergence was to become emphatic with *A Hard Day's Night*. In the first phase of The Beatles' career (up to and including I WANT TO HOLD YOUR HAND), Lennon and McCartney had been equal in their output of solo and collaborative songs, Lennon stealing fractionally ahead of McCartney on *With The Beatles*. During *A Hard Day's Night*, Lennon began to work very hard on his songwriting, contributing over half of the group's originals by himself. Rivalry was always hot between them and McCartney's gesture of A-side independence with CAN'T BUY ME LOVE must have jolted Lennon who, till then, had regarded himself as undisputed leader. Coinciding with McCartney's newfound concentration on the actress Jane Asher, Lennon's sudden burst of work allowed him to dominate the band's composing for almost a year. In this light, the imperious YOU CAN'T DO THAT, title and all, sounds very much like the first blow in a deliberate campaign of reconquest.

[25] AND I LOVE HER *(Lennon–McCartney)*

McCartney vocal, bass; **Lennon** acoustic rhythm guitar; **Harrison** acoustic lead guitar; **Starr** bongos, claves
Recorded: 25th–27th February 1964, Abbey Road 2.
Producer: George Martin. Engineer: Norman Smith.
UK release: 10th July 1964 (LP: *A Hard Day's Night*)
US release: 26th June 1964 (LP: *A Hard Day's Night*)

Having recorded [23] YOU CAN'T DO THAT in the morning, the group returned in the afternoon to attempt this limpid ballad, subsequently to become one of their most covered numbers. McCartney began writing the song (which concerns Jane Asher) with the verse and its brief chorus. Rising and falling across the span of an eleventh with no repeated adjacent notes, it's a characteristic line of starkly simple beauty.[1] By contrast, the three G sharps which start the middle eight

---

[1] Note the similarity between the guitar figure and the one from the middle eight of [U13o] THE HONEYMOON SONG *(Live At The BBC)*.

are Lennon's horizontal hallmark, as is the fact that what follows is a crablike manoeuvring around a single chord.[1] The lyric, with its simple metaphors of bright stars and dark sky, succeeds in capturing a moment in a private emotional location where only two can meet – or at least it does in the version the group finally arrived at, for they started out with their full electric line-up and drums. (This version, disfigured by an awful staccato arpeggio, can be heard on *Anthology 1*.) On the second day, the present arrangement was evolved, though, as with [13e] TILL THERE WAS YOU, the delicacy of the sound exposed every fluff, and most of the sixteen takes were breakdowns. At last, on the second take of day three, they got what they wanted: a performance of such calm lucidity that the semitonal key-change for Harrison's solo (swooping suddenly to G minor) seems like a revelation and the closing Picardy third almost celestial – effects maximised by George Martin's spacious use of echo.

[26] I SHOULD HAVE KNOWN BETTER *(Lennon–McCartney)*

Lennon double-tracked vocal, acoustic rhythm guitar, harmonica;
  McCartney bass; **Harrison** lead guitar; **Starr** drums
Recorded: 25th–26th February 1964, Abbey Road 2.
Producer: George Martin. Engineer: Norman Smith.
UK release: 10th July 1964 (LP: *A Hard Day's Night*)
US release: 26th June 1964 (LP: *A Hard Day's Night*)

Written during the preceding month and begun as a recording in the same afternoon session as [25] AND I LOVE HER, Lennon's I SHOULD HAVE KNOWN BETTER is a cheery potboiler based on an imitation of Bob Dylan's huffing harmonica style and developed into a melody composed largely of one note. (The Beatles had become infatuated with Dylan after Harrison bought *Freewheelin'* in Paris in January.) The words, as their author later conceded, mean nothing, and several of the twenty-two takes it took to record broke down when he became

---

[1] The *A Hard Day's Night* material shows an interest in tonal ambiguity which contrasts markedly with earlier Beatles' key-schemes. (Around half of their previous originals are in straight E major, the blues guitarist's first-choice key.) [25] AND I LOVE HER veers indeterminately between C sharp minor and its relative major (E). The only previous Beatle song to embrace such ambiguity is [18] ALL I'VE GOT TO DO, which uses the same major/minor relatives. See also [29] I'M HAPPY JUST TO DANCE WITH YOU (C sharp minor/E major again); the parallel major/minor schemes of [33] I'LL BE BACK and [35] THINGS WE SAID TODAY; the major/minor fade of [31] A HARD DAY'S NIGHT; etc.

helpless with laughter. With its bitty minor middle sixteen, this is one of the least distinguished Beatles songs of the period and its inclusion on the *A Hard Day's Night* soundtrack in preference to the subtler music on the LP's second side can only have been due to production deadlines. Lennon strums a Gibson Jumbo J-160E, The Beatles' then-standard electro-acoustic 6-string while Harrison plays his new Ricken-backer 360 Deluxe electric 12-string, an instrument whose chiming overtones (as in the sustained chords of the middle sixteen) colour much of the album.[1]

[27] TELL ME WHY *(Lennon–McCartney)*

Lennon vocal, rhythm guitar; **McCartney** harmony vocal, bass;
   Harrison harmony vocal, lead guitar; **Starr** drums
Recorded: 27th February 1964, Abbey Road 2.
Producer: George Martin. Engineer: Norman Smith.
UK release: 10th July 1964 (LP: *A Hard Day's Night*)
US release: 26th June 1964 (LP: *A Hard Day's Night*)

Like the previous song, this was knocked off by Lennon, in Paris or New York, as a filler for *A Hard Day's Night*. (Both verse and chorus employ the standard doo-wop ballad changes.) Of no more conse-quence than [26] I SHOULD HAVE KNOWN BETTER, TELL ME WHY creates an illusion of sincerity through its sheer attack, though its unhappy sentiments are undermined by the *fortissimo* zest of the band's block harmonies.[2] Finished in eight takes during the morning on which [25] AND I LOVE HER was completed, this track is interesting for its walking bass and triplet swing, unusual for Lennon and proof of The Beatles' matchless capacity for rhythmic variety.

---

[1] First produced at the end of 1963, the 360/12 concealed its second set of machine heads behind the first – thus looking, from a distance, like an ordinary 6-string. Harrison's, acquired in New York in February 1964, was only the second of these instruments to be made; he first used it on [23] CAN'T BUY ME LOVE, though it is more audible in the arpeggios of [24] YOU CAN'T DO THAT. The Rickenbacker 12-string was later taken up by Roger McGuinn, becoming the trademark sound of The Byrds. (The Beatles' fellow Liverpudlians The Searchers, who had half a dozen hits during 1963–4, also used the Rickenbacker 12-string and sang close harmony very similar to that later adopted by The Byrds.)

[2] Attracted by these, The Beach Boys covered the song on their 1965 album *Beach Boys Party!*

[28] IF I FELL *(Lennon–McCartney)*

Lennon vocal, acoustic rhythm guitar; **McCartney** vocal, bass;
  Harrison lead guitar; **Starr** drums
Recorded: 27th February 1964, Abbey Road 2.
Producer: George Martin. Engineer: Norman Smith.
UK release: 10th July 1964 (LP: *A Hard Day's Night*)
US release: 26th June 1964 (LP: *A Hard Day's Night*)

The suspicion that, in some songs on *A Hard Day's Night*, The Beatles
were exploiting the theme of adolescent naivety to appeal to their
young public is strong in the nursery-rhyme prelude to IF I FELL.[1]
Lennon, though, later recalled this as his first shot at a ballad, comparing
it harmonically with [67] IN MY LIFE and hinting at similar personal
content. This casts a different light on the song, in particular the plea in
its second line which anticipates the more desperate [56] HELP! by over
a year. But if the young Lennon's fear of seeming 'soft' fits the pained
hesitance of IF I FELL, its almost demure embarrassment is too immature
for a man of 23 with five orgiastic years on the road behind him. In
fact, as with [17] LITTLE CHILD, Lennon and McCartney are here
writing as observers, allowing their past to inform their work.
(McCartney takes the high-lying melody to Lennon's low harmony,
possibly a matter of vocal horses for courses.)[2]

In view of McCartney's credentials as a melodist, it's worth noting
that three of The Beatles' most romantic early songs ([22], [28], [50])
were substantially, though by no means entirely, by Lennon. It's
significant that all are close-harmony numbers, confirming that his
melodism was more linked to his choice of chords than was
McCartney's. While one can imagine McCartney arriving at many of
his tunes independently, only afterwards going to a guitar or piano to
work out the chords, Lennon's melodies feel their way through their
harmonies in the style of a sleepwalker, evolving the unconventional
sequences and metrically broken phrasing typical of him. (George
Martin recalls that he conceived of writing songs as 'doing little bits
which you then join up'.) *A Hard Day's Night*, an LP written largely by
Lennon, offers the richest harvest of implied harmonies of any single
Beatles collection, while IF I FELL is the most chord-intensive song The
Beatles had so far recorded, its changes moving with nearly every note
of the tune. Taken on its own merits, the song's melody is attractive

---

[1] While striking, the modulation (D flat major resolving to D major) is abrupt and
somewhat artless.
[2] McCartney recalls the song as co-written 'but with the emphasis on John'
(Miles, op. cit., p. 162).

and unusual for Lennon in ranging over an octave. (Indeed, the *tessitura* tests McCartney's pitching, causing cracks in the second middle eight which he attempted to cover up by tracking himself.) Recorded in fifteen takes during an afternoon session, the song made the US Top 20 as the B-side of [25] AND I LOVE HER in August 1964.

[29] I'M HAPPY JUST TO DANCE WITH YOU
(Lennon–McCartney)

Harrison vocal, lead guitar; **Lennon** backing vocal, rhythm guitar;
   McCartney backing vocal, bass; **Starr** drums, African drum
Recorded: 1st March 1964, Abbey Road 2.
Producer: George Martin. Engineer: Norman Smith.
UK release: 10th July 1964 (LP: *A Hard Day's Night*)
US release: 26th June 1964 (LP: *A Hard Day's Night*)

Starting with a key-disguising foretaste of its middle eight, I'M HAPPY JUST TO DANCE WITH YOU was co-written by Lennon and McCartney for Harrison, the repeated notes of its verse being there to accommodate the latter's limited range. (Harrison's sardonic gloom is amusingly caught in the chorus line, where his declaration of happiness coincides with a doleful shift to the relative minor.) Adopting the 'kid brother' tone of [7] DO YOU WANT TO KNOW A SECRET, the song shares the adolescent quality of [26] I SHOULD HAVE KNOWN BETTER and [28] IF I FELL, displaying little care in its lyric. Made during the morning of the group's first Sunday session, it was recorded as a backing track with a busy counter-melody bass line, plus overdubbed vocals. Starr's additional thumps on the first and fourth quaver of each verse bar are derived from the 'pushes' in the minor-key middle eight (given contrast by extra reverb). The Bo Diddley rhythm guitar pattern was probably suggested by The Rolling Stones' 'Not Fade Away', a new entry to the UK Top 40 two days before.

[29b] LONG TALL SALLY *(Johnson–Penniman–Blackwell)*

McCartney vocal, bass; **Lennon** rhythm guitar; **Harrison** lead
   guitar; **Starr** drums; **George Martin** piano
Recorded: 1st March 1964, Abbey Road 2.
Producer: George Martin. Engineer: Norman Smith.
UK release: 19th June 1964 (EP: *Long Tall Sally*)
US release: 10th April 1964 (LP: *The Beatles' Second Album*)

The Beatles' love of Little Richard's high-energy camp led to the inclusion in their act of many of his raging rock-and-roll hits of the Fifties. Most were sung by McCartney who, unlike Lennon, could pull off an authentic impression of the singer's ranting delivery, for which their version of LONG TALL SALLY became a showcase.[1] Originally titled 'Bald Headed Sally', the lyric, like that of Little Richard's famously impenetrable first hit 'Tutti Frutti', supposedly consists of gay sexual code, a fact immaterial to The Beatles who turned it into a straightforward raver.[2] As such, it featured throughout their career from 1957 to their last live appearance at Candlestick Park, San Francisco in 1966 – the longest run of any number they performed. Documents from the sessions for *A Hard Day's Night* suggest that the song was originally intended for the film's soundtrack, presumably in its capacity as the band's standard finale.

Captured in a single take around 11am on 1st March 1964, LONG TALL SALLY enjoys a reputation among Beatle fans comparable to that of Lennon's similar one-take *tour-de-force* [9f] TWIST AND SHOUT. Next to Little Richard's original, a 1956 hit for the Specialty label, The Beatles' version is more manic, being pitched a tone higher and projected at greater velocity. It's also more climactically arranged, taking in two nicely sloppy Harrison solos – the second prepared by a bridge of ascending chords in $3/8$[3] – before reaching a crescendo with Starr pummelling his kit in continuous rolling triplets. Little Richard's record offers a richer bass-end and a more organic rhythm based on his boogiewoogie piano and the R&B swing of his band, The Upsetters. By contrast, McCartney's walking bass clashes with Martin's chords (voiced too high and in mechanical straight eights). Where The Beatles score is with McCartney's mock-hysterical vocal which, despite garbling the words,[4] drives the track with blistering power. The difference between the two versions is that between deep joy and wild

---

[1] Apart from LONG TALL SALLY, McCartney handled 'Tutti Frutti', [U15f] LUCILLE *(Live At The BBC)*, 'Miss Ann', 'Good Golly Miss Molly', [U15b] OOH! MY SOUL *(Live At The BBC)*, and [44b] KANSAS CITY/HEY, HEY, HEY, HEY. Lennon sang 'Slippin' and Slidin'', [U164b] RIP IT UP *(Anthology 3)*, 'Ready Teddy', and 'Send Me Some Lovin''. LUCILLE, another powerful vehicle for McCartney, would have been a better choice for the group's main sequence discography than, say, Larry Williams' [56c] BAD BOY. (A version of LUCILLE is said to have been taped by The Beatles in late 1962.)

[2] Richard himself insists that songs like LONG TALL SALLY and 'Good Golly Miss Molly' concerned people known to the Penniman family during his teenage years in Macon, Georgia.

[3] Seemingly added for the recording, this passage is curiously absent from the live version taped for *Around The Beatles* just under three weeks later on 19th April 1964 *(Anthology 1)*, but was back in place for the European leg of The Beatles' June 1964 overseas tour (see Part 3 of the *Anthology* video).

[4] At 0:52: 'Well, Long Tall Sally, she's built for speed . . .'

excitement. Arguably McCartney's later Little Richard cover [44b] KANSAS CITY/HEY, HEY, HEY, HEY has greater style and soul.

[30] I CALL YOUR NAME (Lennon–McCartney)

Lennon vocal, rhythm guitar; **Harrison** lead guitar; **McCartney**
  bass; **Starr** drums, cowbell
Recorded: 1st March 1964, Abbey Road 2.
Producer: George Martin. Engineer: Norman Smith.
UK release: 19th June 1964 (EP: *Long Tall Sally*)
US release: 10th April 1964 (LP: *The Beatles' Second Album*)

One of Lennon's earliest songs, I CALL YOUR NAME was updated with a new middle eight for Billy J. Kramer and The Dakotas during summer 1963. Evidence of the distance between its composer's crude first efforts and the onset of his mature style, this curious song incorporates a third hybrid element during its guitar solo, when the group drop into the bone-shaking rhythm of Ska, a fusion of R&B and calypso then little known outside the shanty towns of Kingston.[1]

Lyrically a mess, I CALL YOUR NAME becomes compelling only during its harmonically tortuous middle eight. The looseness of the performance – Harrison muffing his double-time figures on the first middle eight, McCartney casually shifting up an octave at the end of the fade – suggests that the group weren't trying very hard, probably because they knew that the song wasn't up to scratch. With its clomping four-in-the-bar cowbell, I CALL YOUR NAME resembled [24] YOU CAN'T DO THAT too closely to be allowed on the *A Hard Day's Night* album and was thus diverted into The Beatles' first non-compilatory EP, along with [31b] MATCHBOX, [32b] SLOW DOWN, and the title track [29b] LONG TALL SALLY.[2]

---

[1] Millie's 'My Boy Lollipop', a ska song and a big hit in the UK during April–June, entered the Top 40 three weeks after I CALL YOUR NAME was made. Possibly The Beatles heard an advanced copy.

[2] Released in June 1964, *Long Tall Sally* stayed at the top of Britain's EP chart for seven weeks. Of The Beatles' fourteen EPs, only three were not compilations from LPs: *Long Tall Sally* and the double-EP pack *Magical Mystery Tour*, issued in December 1967.

[31] A HARD DAY'S NIGHT *(Lennon–McCartney)*

Lennon double-tracked vocal, electric and acoustic rhythm guitars;
   McCartney double-tracked vocal, bass; **Harrison** lead guitar;
   Starr drums, bongos; **George Martin** piano
Recorded: 16th April 1964, Abbey Road 2.
Producer: George Martin. Engineer: Norman Smith.
UK release: 10th July 1964 (A single/THINGS WE SAID TODAY)
US release: 26th June 1964 (LP: *A Hard Day's Night*)

The mighty opening chord of A HARD DAY'S NIGHT (G eleventh suspended fourth) has a significance in Beatles lore matched only by the concluding E major of [96] A DAY IN THE LIFE, the two opening and closing the group's middle period of peak creativity. Their rivals must have heard this portentous sound with awe. Apart from Bob Dylan, none could match such an impression of panoramic sweep and power.

Seven weeks of shooting for *A Hard Day's Night* intervened between this and the group's previous session, and they went straight back to location work in London after it. The title had been uttered by Starr after an exhausting day's filming on 19th March.[1] Bandied about as a priceless witticism during the next three weeks, it was officially adopted for the film in mid-April, at which point Lennon hurried home to ensure that it was he and not McCartney who wrote the song.[2] ([23] CAN'T BUY ME LOVE, with which McCartney had stolen a march on him, was then at No. 1 on both sides of the Atlantic.) A typically horizontal modal melody, it was soon finished, whereupon Lennon convened the group and it was recorded the following day – the shortest interval between writing and recording of any Beatles song not made up in the studio.

Taped in mono, the backing track was achieved on the fifth of nine takes. Following this, Lennon and McCartney did their vocals, tracking them before adding bongos, extra percussion, and another acoustic guitar.[3] Harrison's solo, doubled on piano by Martin, was taped at

---

[1] Lennon used the same phrase in *In His Own Write*, published three days later. He, though, accepted it as a coincidence – a typical 'Ringoism'.

[2] Bootleg tapes show that, in the early stages of the A HARD DAY'S NIGHT session, McCartney, unfamiliar with the changes, was busking uncertainly to and fro between root and fifth.

[3] Lewisohn (*Sessions*, p. 43) reports that only Lennon sang on track 2. However, McCartney also seems to be double-tracked through the middle eight, so he must have sung on track 2 as well. (McCartney's harmony vocal in the verses could have gone on either track 2 or track 3.) The strange custom of recording voices and instruments on the same track, rather than keeping them separate and 'bouncing down' onto a spare track (as in any modern studio), continued to be The

Beatles' half-speed, as was the jangling arpeggiated fade.[1] The latter, so influential on The Byrds, consists of a ticktocking swing between a fifthless Am7 and F major, each contained within the song's opening chord (neither major nor minor). Acting coincidentally as a musical pointer to the major/minor structures used throughout the album, it was part of the concept from the first take, presumably envisaged by Lennon as a transition from the film's main titles to the first scene. With this powerful, bluesy song – a performance made incandescent by Starr's excited contribution – The Beatles completed the seven titles required for the soundtrack.

[31b] MATCHBOX *(Perkins)*

Starr double-tracked vocals, drums; **Lennon** rhythm guitar;
   Harrison lead guitar; **McCartney** bass; **George Martin** piano
Recorded: 1st June 1964, Abbey Road 2.
Producer: George Martin. Engineer: Norman Smith.
UK release: 19th June 1964 (EP: *Long Tall Sally*)
US release: 20th July 1964 (LP: *Something New*)

Back from a month's holiday after finishing filming on *A Hard Day's Night,* The Beatles set about the second side of the album. Two tracks ([29b] and [30]) were available. A third, [24] YOU CAN'T DO THAT, had already been issued as the B-side of [23] CAN'T BUY ME LOVE, but since the latter was on the album, there was no reason to omit the former. Vague about the rest, the group recommenced with what they assumed would be Starr's feature, a song their former drummer Pete Best had sung and which Lennon had taken over after Best was sacked. MATCHBOX was by Carl Perkins, a pioneer rock-and-roller who might have been more famous if Elvis Presley hadn't stolen his hit 'Blue Suede Shoes' while its author was recovering from a car-crash in 1956. The Beatles elected Perkins one of their US icons and played a dozen of his songs between 1957 and 1962.[2] None were left in their act by 1964,

---

standard practice as late as *Sgt. Pepper,* largely due to EMI's bizarre disinclination to invest in an eight-track desk.
[1] Leigh, p. 37. The guitar break originally took the form of a variation on the verse melody.
[2] Apart from MATCHBOX, Lennon sang 'Tennessee', 'Bopping' The Blues', [U164d] BLUE SUEDE SHOES (revived in 1969 for The Plastic Ono Band's *Live Peace In Toronto),* and its original B-side [46e] HONEY DON'T, recorded by The Beatles with Starr singing in 1964. McCartney sang the country-and-western [U11c] SURE TO FALL *(Live At The BBC)* and dueted with Lennon on [U13e] LEND ME YOUR COMB *(Anthology 1).* Harrison sang 'Your True Love', [U13q] GLAD ALL OVER *(Live At The BBC),* and [46b] EVERYBODY'S TRYING TO BE MY BABY. The group also did a version of Perkins' third single 'Gone, Gone, Gone'.

but since Perkins was in London at the end of a tour, they asked him to the session, MATCHBOX being the result.

A routine rockabilly twelve-bar based on a blues by Blind Lemon Jefferson, Perkins' original derives its charm from his wincing, shrugging vocal and his rhythm section's eagerly swinging string-bass and brushed snare. By contrast, The Beatles are flat-footed, McCartney adopting a foursquare style and Starr managing to do little more than holler the words in the right places. Only Harrison – who idolised Perkins so earnestly that, during the era of The Silver Beatles in 1960, he rechristened himself Carl – finds any motivation, faithfully reproducing his mentor's ragged lines.[1] Much messy double-tracking abounds in an authentically reverb-drenched production.

[32] I'LL CRY INSTEAD *(Lennon–McCartney)*

Lennon double-tracked vocal,[2] acoustic rhythm guitar;
  McCartney bass; **Harrison** lead guitar; **Starr** drums,
    tambourine[3]
Recorded: 1st June 1964, Abbey Road 2.
Producer: George Martin. Engineer: Norman Smith.
UK release: 10th July 1964 (LP: *A Hard Day's Night*)
US release: 26th June 1964 (LP: *A Hard Day's Night*)

The slightest composition on *A Hard Day's Night*, I'LL CRY INSTEAD was written by Lennon for the film's 'break-out' sequence; hence its brevity.[4] Richard Lester, though, preferred [23] CAN'T BUY ME LOVE for its energy and because the sour autobiographical lyric of Lennon's song was unsuitable. Recorded in two edit-sections after [31b] MATCHBOX, I'LL CRY INSTEAD is a country-and-western pastiche featuring an idiomatic turnaround in its middle eight which Lennon remained pleased with sixteen years later.[5] Released as a single in USA in July 1964, it peaked at No. 25.

---

[1] Rumour has it that the low boogie riff was in fact played by Perkins himself.
[2] Tony Barrow's note for *A Hard Day's Night* wrongly calls this a Lennon and McCartney duet.
[3] Some sources ascribe the tambourine to Lennon, but this is unlikely in view of his notoriously poor sense of rhythm and the arcane subtleties of decent tambourine playing.
[4] A longer edit of the song was issued on the American version of the album. The 1982 reissue of the film *A Hard Day's Night* prefaces the title-sequence with a collage of stills accompanied by this track.
[5] Country and western was popular in Liverpool during the Fifties and Lennon grew up listening to it before he heard rock-and-roll.

[32b] SLOW DOWN *(Williams)*

Lennon double-tracked vocal, lead guitar; **McCartney** bass;
  Harrison rhythm guitar; **Starr** drums; **George Martin** piano
Recorded: 1st, 4th June 1964, Abbey Road 2.
Producer: George Martin. Engineer: Norman Smith.
UK release: 19th June 1964 (EP: *Long Tall Sally*)
US release: 20th July 1964 (LP: *Something New*)

Though overshadowed by Little Richard, Larry Williams wrote and
recorded a sequence of rock-and-roll standards during the late Fifties,
two of which, 'Bony Moronie' and 'Short Fat Fanny', were hits on
both sides of the Atlantic. Lennon, an enthusiast of Williams' sighing
screams and surreal vocal mannerisms, sang both of his hits with The
Beatles during 1957–61, plus at least four others, three of which he
recorded with the group: SLOW DOWN, [56b] DIZZY MISS LIZZY, and
[56c] BAD BOY. (The fourth was 'Peaches and Cream'.) Part of The
Beatles' act from 1960 to 1962, SLOW DOWN had been in mothballs for
well over a year by the time Lennon decided to record it, which
probably accounts for the feebleness of the result. Having taped a
backing track, the others stood down for Lennon to add a double-
tracked vocal, following which George Martin dubbed on the piano
three days later. How much subsequently got lost in the mix is hard to
tell, although McCartney is unlikely to have forgotten to turn up his
bass. Beside Williams's original, released on Specialty in 1958, The
Beatles' version lacks bottom, drive, and basic cohesion. The guitar solo
is embarrassing and the sound balance a shambles. (At one point – 1:14
– George Martin's lightweight vamping cuts out completely.) While
the only thing that shows any semblance of soul is Lennon's vocal, next
to Larry Williams he lacks *savoir faire*. One of the band's least successful
rock-and-roll covers.[1]

---

[1] A better version, recorded live at the BBC Paris Theatre, London, on 16th July
1963, can be found on *Live At The BBC*.

[33] I'LL BE BACK *(Lennon–McCartney)*

Lennon double-tracked vocal, acoustic rhythm guitar; **McCartney**
  harmony vocal, bass, acoustic guitar; **Harrison** harmony vocal (?),
  lead acoustic guitar; **Starr** drums
Recorded: 1st June 1964, Abbey Road 2.
Producer: George Martin. Engineer: Norman Smith.
UK release: 10th July 1964 (LP: *A Hard Day's Night*)
US release: 15th December 1964 (LP: *Beatles '65*)

This fascinating Lennon song, probably written during his holiday in
May, occupied the evening session of 1st June.[1] A personal favourite
of his, it was based on the descending chords of Del Shannon's 1961
No. 1 'Runaway', though loosely enough to be unnoticeable except to
other guitarists. Starting, as it ends, with an irresolute swing from A
major to A minor (a triplet plus a dislocating push which recurs in both
the bridge and the middle section), I'LL BE BACK is a melancholy essay
in major/minor uncertainty mirrored in the emotional instability of its
lyric. The most unorthodox thing Lennon had yet written, it has no
real chorus, being constructed as a twelve-bar verse in two equal
sections (shortened to six bars in its final reprise), a six-and-a-half bar
bridge, and a nine-and-a-half bar middle featuring a characteristic
chromatic descent.[2] Despite all this, and as so often with Lennon's
more bewildering constructions, the whole rings totally true, being his
deepest emotional expression to date.

 With its warmly resonant acoustic backing track, I'LL BE BACK is
driven by a swinging beat loosened by a cross-rhythm of flamenco-style
half-time triplets.[3] Lennon is harmonised by McCartney in shifting
major and minor thirds, resolving on a Picardy third at the end of the
first and second verses. (Someone – McCartney or Harrison – holds the
upper E of the harmony throughout.) The singing could have been
subtler and the harmony is at points sufficiently recondite that
McCartney's pitching wobbles, but as a whole this is one of the most

---

[1] McCartney recalls the song as 'co-written, but largely John's idea' (Miles, op.
cit., p. 163).
[2] Some describe the song as having 'two different bridges' or 'two different middle
eights'. (On *Anthology 1*, take 3 is faded on a repeat of the last two bars of the second
bridge.)
[3] An experiment in 6/8 was tried on take 2, but got no further than the bridge
before Lennon broke down, unable to sing it. In his notes to *Anthology 1*, Mark
Lewisohn takes this to indicate that Lennon conceived the song as a waltz, claiming
that take 3, with the group back in 4/4, offers an example of how quickly they could
alter arrangements. However, I'LL BE BACK was clearly composed in common time,
the anomaly being the experimental 6/8 version (perhaps suggested by McCartney or
Martin).

concise and integrated songs The Beatles had so far created. Fading away in tonal ambiguity at the end of *A Hard Day's Night*, it was a surprisingly downbeat farewell and a token of coming maturity.

[34] ANY TIME AT ALL (*Lennon–McCartney*)

Lennon vocal, acoustic rhythm guitar; **McCartney** harmony vocal,
bass, piano; **Harrison** lead guitar; **Starr** drums
Recorded: 2nd June 1964, Abbey Road 2.
Producer: George Martin. Engineer: Norman Smith.
UK release: 10th July 1964 (LP: *A Hard Day's Night*)
US release: 20th July 1964 (LP: *Something New*)

The first song to be tried on the last day of recording for *A Hard Day's Night*, Lennon's ANY TIME AT ALL was so new that it had no middle eight. Accordingly, the group taped a backing track of the verse/chorus structure in the afternoon and left it while they addressed [35] and [36], returning to the incomplete ANY TIME AT ALL late in the evening, whereupon they added a powerful ten-bar instrumental crescendo on the dominant. (This passage may have been worked out by McCartney, who leads it on piano.) In effect, the song fuses the music of [14] IT WON'T BE LONG with the lyric of [18] ALL I'VE GOT TO DO, trading their depth for an outpouring of energetic exhilaration captured in the decisive slam of Starr's snare at the end of each verse. One of The Beatles' most buoyant rockers, ANY TIME AT ALL features a classic 'shouting' vocal from Lennon, overlapping in double-track around the six-bar sections of the verse with aid from McCartney on the high answering phrase of the chorus. Harrison's guitar-fills anticipate his increasingly central work on *Help!* and *Rubber Soul*, while Starr, in his element, propels the track with vigour.

[35] THINGS WE SAID TODAY (*Lennon–McCartney*)

McCartney double-tracked vocal, bass; **Lennon** acoustic rhythm
guitar, piano; **Harrison** lead guitar; **Starr** drums, tambourine
Recorded: 2nd June 1964, Abbey Road 2.
Producer: George Martin. Engineer: Norman Smith.
UK release: 10th July 1964 (B single/A Hard Day's Night)
US release: 20th July 1964 (LP: *Something New*)

Written by McCartney on holiday in the Bahamas with Jane Asher in May 1964, THINGS WE SAID TODAY is uncharacteristic in its ominous mood and the obsessive horizontal pull to the tonic in its melody. (Lennon, whose style it resembles more than McCartney's, particularly liked this song.) The sombre lyric – provoked by the frustrating interruptions of a relationship between two career people – matches the lowering gloom of the music.[1] Similar to that of Harrison's [20] DON T BOTHER ME, this stormy atmosphere is made more compelling by the relentless agitation of Lennon's whipcrack guitar against Starr's crisp snare. To this driving performance – the first complete take, preceded by a single false start – was added a second McCartney vocal (part unison, part harmony), plus tambourine and piano on the middle eight.[2]

Its mixture of ease and effectiveness ensured that the song became part of the group's act during 1964. With its modal A minor verse firming on an obstinate tonic to A major for the tough, bluesy middle section, THINGS WE SAID TODAY established a model of strident dramatic contrasts which The Beatles would exploit on their next LP in tracks like [37] BABY'S IN BLACK, [39] EVERY LITTLE THING, [40] I DON'T WANT TO SPOIL THE PARTY, and [42] NO REPLY. The idea of a melody in offbeats was similarly developed by Harrison in [66] IF I NEEDED SOMEONE on *Rubber Soul*.

[36] WHEN I GET HOME (Lennon–McCartney)

Lennon vocal, rhythm guitar; **McCartney** harmony vocal, bass;
 Harrison harmony vocal, lead guitar; **Starr** drums
Recorded: 2nd June 1964, Abbey Road 2.
Producer: George Martin. Engineer: Norman Smith.
UK release: 10th July 1964 (LP: *A Hard Day's Night*)
US release: 20th July 1964 (LP: *Something New*)

The last song for *A Hard Day's Night*, WHEN I GET HOME is a burden-lifting rocker featuring some of Lennon's most rantingly pugnacious lyrics and a vicious push in the chorus that several times defeats Starr's cymbal crash. A round-the-changes tour between the keys of A[3] and C, the song bristles with bluesy sevenths and repeated falling major

---

[1] This is reinforced by a chilly shift to B flat and back to A minor at the end of the verse/chorus ('not a *lot to say*') and likewise at the end of the middle eight – a flat II, or Neapolitan sixth, derived from a Lennon-like chromatic descent (cf. the middle seven of [55] YOU'RE GOING TO LOSE THAT GIRL).

[2] According to Mark Lewisohn (*Sessions*, p.44), the piano was omitted from the final mix but left traces on the other tracks through leakage during recording. It's hard to see how this can have happened, since the piano and the main backing track were recorded in different takes.

[3] In fact, A major–minor, thus completing a trilogy of A major–minor songs on *A Hard Day's Night* (the others being [33] I'LL BE BACK and [35] THINGS WE SAID TODAY). In terms of A minor and C major, WHEN I GET HOME is also part of a parallel major/minor triad on the same LP (the others being [25] AND I LOVE HER and [29] I'M HAPPY JUST TO DANCE WITH YOU).

seconds, its origin in soul music clear in McCartney's shift into boogie mode for its ten-bar middle section.[1] Made in eleven takes, it exudes relief at finishing an album begun over three months earlier – the first Beatles LP to consist entirely of original compositions (and the only one ever to be made solely of Lennon–McCartney songs). Since few artists wrote any of their own material in 1964, this was a considerable coup, placing the group in a category they shared only with Bob Dylan.

[U37] YOU KNOW WHAT TO DO *(Harrison)*

Harrison vocal, rhythm guitar, bass, tambourine (?)
Recorded: 3rd June 1964, Abbey Road 2/3?
Producer: George Martin. Engineer: Norman Smith.
UK release: 21st November 1995 (2-CD: *Anthology 1*)
US release: 21st November 1995 (2-CD: *Anthology 1*)

According to Lewisohn, this session was booked to record the fourteenth song for *A Hard Day's Night* – leading to the intriguing question: which song had The Beatles intended to record? In the event, Starr was taken ill that morning and the others had to spend part of the day rehearsing with stand-in drummer Jimmy Nicol for their forthcoming overseas tour. They also recorded three demos: 'It's For You', a McCartney number written for Cilla Black; a version of Lennon's [42] NO REPLY, announced as intended for NEMS artist Tommy Quickly; and this palely nondescript effort from Harrison, his second completely self-penned song (see [20]). Since YOU KNOW WHAT TO DO was taken no further, and because nothing on the surviving demo was unplayable for the song's writer, it seems fair to assume that he was the sole participant.

[37] BABY'S IN BLACK *(Lennon–McCartney)*

Lennon vocal, acoustic rhythm guitar; **McCartney** vocal, bass;
  Harrison lead guitar; **Starr** drums
Recorded: 11th August 1964, Abbey Road 2.
Producer: George Martin. Engineer: Norman Smith.
UK release: 4th December 1964 (LP: *Beatles For Sale*)
US release: 15th December 1964 (LP: *Beatles '65*)

Scarcely had the sessions for *A Hard Day's Night* finished than The Beatles set off on an ambitious sequence of foreign tours (see Chronology). It was during this exhausting itinerary that Lennon and

---

[1] Lennon claimed Wilson Pickett as inspiration, but see [24] YOU CAN'T DO THAT.

McCartney wrote most of the unusually despondent songs that make up the bulk of the group's fourth album, *Beatles For Sale*. Scheduled for Christmas, the LP was begun in August, a mere week after *A Hard Day's Night* had topped the album charts on both sides of the Atlantic.

The songs for the second side of *A Hard Day's Night* had explored a more introspective manner and, along with other influences, this injection of novelty spread to affect the technical range of Lennon and McCartney's writing. Written in a hotel room, BABY'S IN BLACK bears just such signs of conscious experiment. Probably they began by joking around with sea shanties and nursery rhymes before arriving at a variation of 'Johnny's So Long At The Fair' (which also supplied the song's 6/8 time-signature). Harmonised in plangent country-and-western thirds and revolving on three major triads, the song is a simple compromise between its creators' traits, highlighted by a dramatic shift to the relative minor in its four-bar middle section.[1] Lyrically, though, the effect is spoiled by the inane rhyme of 'only a whim' with 'she thinks of him', a miscalculation that shows how little Lennon and McCartney considered the words they were then using. (This may have been a careless carry-over from the ear-catching lyric of [36] WHEN I GET HOME, with its ostentatious blend of articulacy – the rhyme 'trivialities' – and vernacular cliché: 'till the cows come home'.[2])

Recorded in fourteen disorganised takes, BABY'S IN BLACK took an entire evening, largely because of trouble with Harrison's guitar part (uncharacteristic in its dissonant angularity and hence probably worked out by one of the others, presumably McCartney). Though the group seem to have been cool about the result, the performance, courtesy of Starr, swings infectiously, and the song's folk-ballad overtones charmed their fans enough to keep it in The Beatles' act for the next three years.

---

[1] So closely co-written is this song that, as McCartney points out, it's hard to determine harmony from melody (Miles, op. cit., p. 175).

[2] Perhaps borrowed from The Searchers' 'Farmer John' (issued on *Meet The Searchers* in August 1963) which includes the line 'I'm gonna love her till the cows come home'.

[38] I'M A LOSER *(Lennon–McCartney)*

Lennon vocal, acoustic rhythm guitar, harmonica; **McCartney**
harmony vocal, bass; **Harrison** lead guitar; **Starr** drums,
tambourine
Recorded: 14th August 1964, Abbey Road 2.
Producer: George Martin. Engineer: Norman Smith.
UK release: 4th December 1964 (LP: *Beatles For Sale*)
US release: 15th December 1964 (LP: *Beatles '65*)

Written during summer 1964 – though not, as often claimed, during
the group's first American tour[1] – I'M A LOSER was acknowledged by
Lennon as the first fruit of his 'Dylan period'. The only figure to have
matched The Beatles' influence on popular culture since 1945, Bob
Dylan had yet to escape his media categorisation as a 'protest singer'.
The feral energy of his first album (*Bob Dylan*, 1962), too raw to reach a
broad audience, had electrified folk circles in America and Britain,
while its successors, *Freewheelin'* and *The Times They Are A-Changin'*,
spread his reputation among the pop cognoscenti. Then unique in
being prolific enough to fill complete LPs with their own material,
Dylan and The Beatles were bound eventually to collide and react.

Harrison was the first Beatle to discover Dylan and remains a
faithful fan.[2] Transfixed by his untamed quality – 'some vital energy, a
voice crying out somewhere, toiling in the darkness', as he put it – he
urged *Freewheelin'* on Lennon, who passed the summer of 1964
exploring Dylan's output in his own special way, absorbing its sound,
mood, and tone without paying particular attention to the words.[3]
Indeed, it was Dylan's general style, rather than his standing as a folk-
poet, which so commended him to the burgeoning British pop
aristocracy. Typifying this, the Newcastle group The Animals made
their chart debut in mid-1964 with covers of two songs from his first
album ('Baby Let Me Take You Home' and 'House Of The Rising
Sun', the latter a No. 1 on both sides of the Atlantic). At this period

---

[1] Jackie DeShannon's recollection (*Rolling Stone*, 16th February 1984) that
Lennon wrote I'M A LOSER on the tour plane is irreconcilable with the song's
recording date. (The tour began on 19th August 1964.)
[2] One of Harrison's finest songs, 'I'd Have You Anytime', was co-written with
Dylan in 1970. In the late Eighties, they joined other pop luminaries (including Roy
Orbison) in forming The Traveling Wilburys. Harrison introduced Dylan at the 30th
anniversary of his New York debut in November 1992.
[3] Or, at least, affecting not to. Dylan's lyrics of this period were so brilliant that
rival songwriters could have 'ignored' them only out of jealousy or sheer terror.
Listeners who, having grown up since the Sixties, are unacquainted with Dylan's best
work are urged to familiarise themselves with his first six official albums (up to and
including *Blonde On Blonde*, 1966) and the 'Basement Tapes' (1966–7).

Lennon was spending much of his time night-clubbing with The Animals' Eric Burdon and The Rolling Stones' Mick Jagger (another Dylan fan), and his idea of Dylan was formed through their shared enthusiasm for folk-blues[1] and R&B. In the event, I'M A LOSER is more country-and-western than a folk/protest pastiche. Lazily intuitive, and determined not to be overawed, Lennon here merely adopts a tone. A touch of rough harmonica, some strummed acoustic guitar, a slightly more thoughtful and hard-bitten lyric – this was the extent of his 'Dylan influence' when the song was recorded, just before The Beatles left on their second trip to America.

Ten days later, after a concert at Forest Hills, The Beatles met Dylan in Manhattan's Hotel Delmonico. During their career, they had, like other British acts, fuelled their touring energy with alcohol and amphetamines, a cocktail unconducive to dignified behaviour, let alone deep thought. When Dylan offered to roll a joint, the group were embarrassed to admit that marijuana was beyond their ken. The result was a revelation. McCartney, who seems to have had an out-of-body experience,[2] declared that he was *really* thinking' for the first time and ordered road manager Mal Evans to write down everything he said. (The 'meaning of life' as dutifully transcribed by Evans was *There are seven levels.*)

28th August 1964 was a watershed for The Beatles. 'Till then,' McCartney recalls, 'we'd been hard scotch and coke men. It sort of changed that evening.'[3] From now on, the superficial states of mind induced by drink and 'speed'[4] gave way to the introspective and

---

[1] An East Coast form (distinct from the 'country blues' of Texas and the Delta) in which blues tapers away into ragtime, gospel, and the narrative ballads and fingerpicking styles of white Anglo-Celtic folk music. The leading black figures in this genre included Leadbelly, Big Bill Broonzy, Mississippi John Hurt, Sleepy John Estes, Jesse Fuller, Reverend Gary Davis, and Sonny Terry and Brownie McGhee. Black folk-blues artists – together with Delta one-offs like Robert Johnson, Skip James, Blind Willie McTell, Mance Lipscomb, Bukka White, and Snooks Eaglin – had a major influence on the white urban American folk scene of the early-to-mid Sixties. The most significant product of this fusion of black and white sensibilities was Dylan himself. Others so influenced were Dave Van Ronk, Rambling Jack Elliott, Phil Ochs, John Fahey, John Hammond Jnr., Tom Paxton, Tom Rush, Tim Hardin, Spider John Koerner, Stefan Grossman, The Holy Modal Rounders, Leo Kottke, and Ry Cooder.
[2] Grabbing publicist Derek Taylor by the arm, he exclaimed 'It's as if we're up there' – pointing at the ceiling – 'Up there, looking down on us!' (Taylor, p. 91.) This reflects the group's often reported sense of psychic collectivity: McCartney seems to have felt that the others were up by the ceiling, too.
[3] *Mojo*, November 1993.
[4] Amphetamines. Needing a stimulant to see them through exhausting touring

sensual moods associated with cannabis and later LSD. As for Dylan, The Beatles' musical vitality prompted his return to the rock-and-roll that had motivated him as a teenager, the result being *Bringing It All Back Home*, one of the decade's most influential albums.

I'M A LOSER consists of a four-line verse with chorus, the lack of a middle eight being its nod to the plainer conventions of folk balladry, albeit that its flat sevenths are blues-derived. Made in eight takes, it sports a Carl Perkins solo from Harrison and swings engagingly (especially in the chorus which, with its double-time walking bass, suggests the composing hand of McCartney). The pained lyric is autobiographical, masked by a smile. Lennon later saw this as a built-in ambivalence – 'Part of me suspects I'm a loser and part of me thinks I'm God almighty' – but the tune of the verse, with its comic drop of a fifth into the bottom of his range, can only be voiced tongue in cheek, and the humour of the words must have followed accordingly.[1] With its graphic match of melody and meaning, I'M A LOSER, like [8] MISERY (which sports a similar mock-declamatory introduction), is an expression of rueful self-ridicule, this time with a hint of genuine confession.[2] Lennon was pleased with it and, like [43] EIGHT DAYS A WEEK, the song was earmarked as a possible single.

---

schedules, pop groups used these extensively in the early Sixties, as did 'mod' audiences in all-night jazz-blues and ska clubs, the main brands being 'purple hearts' (drinamyl) and 'dexies' (dexedrine). The Beatles used speed ('prellies' or preludin) during their Hamburg seasons. In 1965–8, speed was replaced as the youth drug of choice by cannabis and LSD, returning in the form of intravenous methedrine in San Francisco and New York around 1968–9. During the Seventies and Eighties, cocaine took over from amphetamine, though the latter made a comeback in the late Eighties as an ingredient of Ecstasy.

[1] In a version recorded on 26th May 1965 for the Light Programme, Lennon sings 'Beneath this wig, I am wearing a tie'. The genesis of the song is unknown and he may have started, folk style, with the first lines of the lyric. However, the last verse, with its unmetrical scansion on the word 'before', suggests that he soon began to concentrate on the music, leaving the remainder of the lyric till later.

[2] On bootlegs of the multitrack, take 1, which opens abruptly (and fades) with the unadorned first line of the chorus, finishes with McCartney perceptively observing 'There's a frayed edge for you'.

[38b] MR MOONLIGHT *(Johnson)*

> **Lennon** vocal, acoustic rhythm guitar; **McCartney** harmony vocals,
> bass, Hammond organ; **Harrison** harmony vocals, lead guitar,
> African drum; **Starr** percussion (?)
> Recorded: 14th August, 18th October 1964, Abbey Road 2.
> Producer: George Martin. Engineer: Norman Smith.
> UK release: 4th December 1964 (LP: *Beatles For Sale*)
> US release: 15th December 1964 (LP: *Beatles '65*)

Begun after [38] I'M A LOSER, this gross quasi-calypso[1] got as far as
four takes before being junked and remade two months later. Bolstered
by massive double-tracked harmonies, Lennon's berserk delivery blasts
away much of the song's gaudy chintz, only for this to be reinstated in
all its gold lamé ghastliness by McCartney's Hammond organ solo.
(How much of this is a joke is hard to say, The Beatles being by no
means immune to bad taste.[2]) The percussion track remains a minor
curiosity in that, while Harrison's wallops on an African drum are
beyond rational dispute, Starr's alleged bongos suggest instead the
slapped packing-case which Derek Taylor's sleeve-note ascribes to his
part in the similarly excruciating [46d] WORDS OF LOVE.

[U38c] LEAVE MY KITTEN ALONE *(John–Turner–McDougal)*

> **Lennon** double-tracked vocal; **Harrison** double-tracked lead guitar;
> **McCartney** bass, piano; **Starr** drums, tambourine
> Recorded: 14th August 1964, Abbey Road 2.
> Producer: George Martin. Engineer: Norman Smith.
> UK release: 21st November 1995 (2-CD: *Anthology 1*)
> US release: 21st November 1995 (2-CD: *Anthology 1*)

LEAVE MY KITTEN ALONE was taped at the end of the second day of
recording for *Beatles For Sale*, following which The Beatles left for their
first full tour of the United States. An orthodox rock-and-roll 12-bar
with a stop-time break and accent variations on its later choruses, the
song had originally been recorded in 1959 by the stormy Arkansas
prodigy Little Willie John, though Lennon learned it from Johnny
Preston's 1961 version (a failed try at revising the latter's drooping
career after the death of his mentor The Big Bopper).

---

[1] The original was the B-side of a club R&B hit 'Dr Feelgood', released on the
Okeh label in 1962 by Dr Feelgood and The Interns (a pseudonym for Georgia
singer-pianist Piano Red and his band).
[2] The solo was originally played on comically quivering slide guitar by Harrison
(*Anthology 1*).

The Beatles hadn't played the song for two years and needed five tries at it before shutting down for the night. While the generally bolshy tone of the track was ostensibly tailor-made for Lennon at this stage of his life, he found it hard to let loose until he laid his guitar aside on take 3. By take 5, he was on blistering form. Polished off with rough overdubs and marked as a contender, this version was later ditched, probably because the LP needed a Harrison vocal ([46b] EVERYBODY'S TRYING TO BE MY BABY). A boisterously raw and noisy performance, LEAVE MY KITTEN ALONE would have made a far more convincing closing track.

[39] EVERY LITTLE THING *(Lennon–McCartney)*

Lennon double-tracked vocal, acoustic rhythm guitar; **McCartney** harmony vocal, bass, piano; **Harrison** double-tracked lead guitar; **Starr** drums, timpani
Recorded: 29th–30th September 1964, Abbey Road 2.
Producer: George Martin. Engineer: Norman Smith.
UK release: 4th December 1964 (LP: *Beatles For Sale*)
US release: 14th June 1965 (LP: *Beatles VI*)

EVERY LITTLE THING is lead-sung by Lennon and shows more of his melodic touch than his partner's. From its desperate passion alone, one would deduce it to be Lennon's, particularly at this stage of The Beatles' career. Yet it was written by McCartney in his bedroom at Wimpole Street as an attempt at the band's next single (after [31] A HARD DAY'S NIGHT). Superseded by more commercial songs, it ended up as a 'filler' on Side 2 of *Beatles For Sale*, only lowly regarded by its composer. The puzzle is that EVERY LITTLE THING is one of the most emotional tracks on the album.

In the age of Political Correctness, a song where every little thing a woman does is done for her man is bound to be regarded with suspicion. In fact, the lyric makes it clear that the man is devoted to the woman because taken by emotional surprise – indeed overwhelmed – by the extent of her care for him, a revelation of self-worth brought about by the love of someone he respects. Nor is there any hint of male supremacy in the mood of the music, which, being genuinely moved, is genuinely moving. If this is a love-song to Jane Asher, it corrects the impression of disharmony given in other numbers (e.g., [41]) and confirms the depth of feeling displayed in [35] THINGS WE SAID TODAY. The caricature of McCartney as an emotional lightweight – gainsaid by [68] WE CAN WORK IT OUT and later non-Beatles songs like 'Maybe I'm Amazed' and 'Dear Friend' – is here confirmed as a misleading oversimplification. (McCartney's biographer Chris Salewicz is not alone in describing him as the most complex of The Beatles.)

Creating a potent charge from simple harmonic material, EVERY LITTLE THING supports a similarly direct lyric so perfectly that the release of a middle eight would have fatally slackened its tension. Lennon's influence is felt in the major seconds of the chorus ('me-e, yea-eah') and in the general intensity of mood and feeling. More clearly McCartneyesque are the wide intervals of the fifth and sixth bars of the verse and the first and fifth bars of the chorus. (His opening line for IN MY LIFE is comparably difficult.) Like several other songs on *Beatles For Sale*, EVERY LITTLE THING holds onto the tonic for the contrasting section (in this case, the chorus) before falling soulfully into the arms of the flat VII in a surrender shadowed by Starr's timpani. With its classically understated guitar solo, this haunting track required nine takes, spread over two days.

[40] I DON'T WANT TO SPOIL THE PARTY
(Lennon–McCartney)

Lennon vocal, acoustic rhythm guitar; **Harrison** vocal, lead guitar;
   McCartney harmony vocal, bass; **Starr** drums, tambourine
Recorded: 29th September 1964, Abbey Road 2.
Producer: George Martin. Engineer: Norman Smith.
UK release: 4th December 1964 (LP: *Beatles For Sale*)
US release: 15th February 1965 (B single/Eight Days A Week)

If [38] I'M A LOSER is an update of [8] MISERY, I DON'T WANT TO SPOIL THE PARTY is a revision of [32] I'LL CRY INSTEAD and a preview of [53] YOU'VE GOT TO HIDE YOUR LOVE AWAY. With its doleful minor third harmony, high snare tuning, and Carl Perkins-style guitar solo,[1] this is Lennon and McCartney's most overt exercise in country-and-western on an album dominated by the idiom, the secret being that they originally wrote it for Starr.[2] Again, like I'M A LOSER, confession

---

[1] Harrison played this on a Gretsch Tennessean, which replaced the Gretsch Country Gentleman first used on [12] SHE LOVES YOU. Generally speaking, he liked to change his main guitar for each LP. Thus the Country Gentleman shares duty on *With The Beatles* with a single-pickup Rickenbacker 425 bought in America in September 1963, *A Hard Day's Night* features the Rickenbacker 12-string, and much of *Beatles For Sale* (e.g., [38] I'M A LOSER, [46e] HONEY DON'T) is coloured by the Tennessean.
[2] Miles, op. cit., p. 175. Contrary to McCartney's recollection, Starr did not sing on the song. (McCartney estimates the song as '80-20' to Lennon.)

is given a protective shell of pastiche, Lennon hiding his confessedly 'very personal' feelings in genre cliché. (In G major, the song's undertow of loneliness emerges in the subtle dip to the flat VII in the final line of each verse.) As in other numbers written around this time (see [35]), a climactic outburst occurs in the middle section with a delayed shift to the parallel key (in this case the minor) in which the melodic peak of the song is reached. The mood of the verse/chorus is intensified by an initial shift to a high inversion of the tonic, a reinforcement of the home key used to similar effect in [37] BABY S IN BLACK, [39] EVERY LITTLE THING, and [42] NO REPLY.[1]

[41] WHAT YOU'RE DOING (Lennon–McCartney)

> McCartney vocal, bass; Lennon harmony vocal, acoustic rhythm
> guitar; Harrison harmony vocal, lead guitar; Starr drums;
> George Martin piano
> Recorded: 29th–30th September, 26th October 1964, Abbey Road
> 2.
> Producer: George Martin. Engineer: Norman Smith.
> UK release: 4th December 1964 (LP: *Beatles For Sale*)
> US release: 14th June 1965 (LP: *Beatles VI*)

Mainly by McCartney, this simple three-chord number caused the group unexpected problems, being started after [40] I DON'T WANT TO SPOIL THE PARTY, continued the following evening, and then abandoned and remade a month later. Mark Lewisohn's description of the state of the track by the end of the second day[2] suggests that this may have been because the song was evolved in the studio. Getting Starr and Harrison to play the song the way its author wanted may have caused resentment and taken up time, as it often did during the group's later career. The drum-pattern that begins and ends the track sounds like a McCartney part, as do the overdriven riff and guitar solo which anticipate the treble distortion effects used on *Help!* (McCartney learned to play drums on his brother Mike's kit as a teenager.)

With its 'drop in' barrelhouse piano and resonant bass end (faded to a rumble for the verse/choruses) this is something of an experimental recording, though whether this was the first time The Beatles played

---

[1] After the key-change structures on *A Hard Day's Night*, it's possible that Lennon and McCartney were experimenting with writing 'no change' middle eights which began on the tonic (much as they later experimented with writing songs on one chord or on 'one note').

[2] *Sessions*, p. 49.

tricks with the mixing desk and with orthodox ideas of arrangement and texture can only be determined by comparing the first version with the remake (taped a week after [45] I Feel Fine, usually cited as the group's first sound experiment); unfortunately, the first version of What You're Doing was omitted from *Anthology 1*.[1] With its indignant tone and angry emphases, this song is ostensibly untypical of McCartney, although at one with other stormy songs inspired by his relationship with Jane Asher (e.g., [35] and [70]; see also [68], note).[2]

[42] No Reply *(Lennon–McCartney)*

> **Lennon** double-tracked vocal, acoustic rhythm guitar, handclaps; **McCartney** harmony vocal, bass, handclaps; **Harrison** acoustic rhythm guitar, handclaps; **Starr** drums, handclaps; **George Martin** piano
> Recorded: 30th September 1964, Abbey Road 2.
> Producer: George Martin. Engineer: Norman Smith.
> UK release: 4th December 1964 (LP: *Beatles For Sale*)
> US release: 15th December 1964 (LP: *Beatles '65*)

Probably written on holiday in May 1964, No Reply was recorded as a demo for Tommy Quickly on 3rd June.[3] Featuring the bossa nova beat introduced to the world beyond Brazil by Carlos Jobim, Stan Getz, and Charlie Byrd, the song was lyrically inspired by 'Silhouettes', a Top 5 American hit for New York R&B quartet The Rays in late 1957. In terms of Lennon's own music, it is a development of [36] When I Get Home, with which it shares the same 'pushed' phrase ('Woh-oh-woh *I* . . .'; 'I saw the *light*').[4]

Recorded in an evening session, No Reply required eight takes. The final mix shows The Beatles starting to master the studio, using tracking and echo to create depth and space. As in [33] I'll Be Back, a cushion of acoustic guitars provides the basic timbre, with George Martin's piano paradoxically producing a larger sound by being reduced to a darkly reverbed presence rather than a voice in its own right.

---

[1] More interested in production than the others, McCartney developed a taste for 'defeating' the desk by deliberate over-recording, the only way unusual sounds could be obtained at that stage of technology.

[2] Lacking a clear recollection of this song, McCartney now estimates it as a 50-50 co-composition (Miles, op. cit., pp. 175-6).

[3] This demo – actually no more than Lennon, McCartney, and Harrison (and Jimmy Nicol?) fooling around in rock-and-roll rhythm – shows that Lennon hadn't finished the song. Instead of the poignant vi–iii–IV7–iii sequence in bars 9–12, he makes do with a perfunctory two bars of A minor.

[4] McCartney recalls the song as partly co-written but mainly by Lennon (Miles, op. cit., p. 176).

Massively haloed in echo and set 'big' against the backing, the double-tracked vocals generate a stunning power in the climactic middle sixteen with its surprising feint to A major from the tonic C. So strong was this section that the group tried repeating it and its following verse, adding a full minute to the track. Wisely – and in the less-is-more spirit now governing their arrangement and production ideas – they decided against this, leaving the central bars of NO REPLY, with their steep dynamic and driving drums and claps, as among the most exciting thirty seconds in their output.

Chosen as an entieingly downbeat opener for the album, NO REPLY is one of Lennon's most affecting songs of this period, its lyric matching the sad succinctness of its melody. Almost nothing is said, but the story is complete, the sighing added ninth of the final C major accepting the bad news: there's no reply and never will be.

[43] EIGHT DAYS A WEEK *(Lennon–McCartney)*

Lennon vocal, acoustic rhythm guitar, handclaps; **McCartney**
  vocal, bass, handclaps; **Harrison** vocal, lead guitar, handclaps;
  Starr drums, handclaps
Recorded: 6th, 18th October 1964, Abbey Road 2.
Producer: George Martin. Engineer: Norman Smith.
UK release: 4th December 1964 (LP: *Beatles For Sale*)
US release: 15th February 1965 (A single/I DON'T WANT TO SPOIL
  THE PARTY)

Supposedly written as a title-track for The Beatles' second film, scheduled to start shooting five months later, EIGHT DAYS A WEEK was brought into the studio by Lennon and McCartney in an unfinished state. (The title was taken from a remark made by a chaffeur who drove McCartney out to Lennon's Kenwood house for one of their writing sessions.[1]) Once in the studio, they wrote a middle eight and worked out a harmonised introduction which they toyed with in several ways before dropping it on take six. The track was finished in seven more takes, during which the melody of the title-phrase was changed.[2] Edit-sections for the intro and ending were added during the album's penultimate session twelve days later.

With a classic McCartney walking bass, EIGHT DAYS A WEEK

---

[1] When The Byrds' Roger McGuinn wrote 'Eight Miles High' in 1965, he intended to call it 'Six Miles High', which more accurately measured the cruising height of an airliner. His colleague Gene Clark, however, persuaded him to alter it on the grounds that 'eight', as in The Beatles' EIGHT DAYS A WEEK, had a more 'poetic ring' to it. (Somach and Somach, p. 165.)
[2] See *Anthology 1*.

swaggers up and down the scale of D major much like [15] ALL MY
LOVING in E. Again like ALL MY LOVING, it shows signs of having been
worked out on a piano (particularly the four-bar bridge – 'Hold me,
love me' – with its harmony in perfect fourths and concluding
diminished G sharp). Nothing in the throwaway lyric would have been
out of place in the group's 1963 output and the brilliant simplicity of
the whole thing has 'hit single' written all over it. In fact, Lennon was
about to produce the basis of [45] I FEEL FINE – the riff from which he
insisted on doodling between takes – and EIGHT DAYS A WEEK had to
wait until March 1965 to lodge for two weeks at No. 1 in America,
where it was issued after I FEEL FINE had held the same position for
three weeks in January.

Lennon later thought little of this song, implying that it was
superficial – yet no such attitude can be detected in his vocal, which is
sung in brassy unison with McCartney with all the excitement of the
creative moment.[1] On any list of pop records that capture the soaring
sunshine optimism of the mid-Sixties, EIGHT DAYS A WEEK would be
near the top, along with [21] I WANT TO HOLD YOUR HAND and [95]
PENNY LANE. Musically less involving than either of them, it holds its
place with its sheer verve and the embracing warmth of its sound,
whose texture of carillon electric lead and chiming acoustics was so
influential on the nascent American folk-rock scene.

[44] SHE'S A WOMAN *(Lennon–McCartney)*

McCartney vocal, bass, piano, lead guitar(?)[2]; **Lennon** rhythm
  guitar; **Harrison** lead guitar(?); **Starr** drums, chocalho
Recorded: 8th October 1964, Abbey Road 2.
Producer: George Martin. Engineer: Norman Smith.
UK release: 27th November 1964 (B single/I FEEL FINE)
US release: 23rd November 1964 (B single/I FEEL FINE)

Written by McCartney (some say on the spot in the studio),[3] SHE'S A
WOMAN is a wire-taut 24-bar blues in A with two brief four-bar
excursions to C sharp minor. The most extreme sound The Beatles had

---

[1] The out-takes on *Anthology 1* show that McCartney began by harmonising on
the bridge; this was dropped for the recording.
[2] Since there's no evidence of Harrison on the surviving tapes of this session
(space being left for the solo), it seems probable, especially on the basis of sound and
style, that McCartney played lead guitar.
[3] Before the radio version recorded on 17th November 1964 for *Top Gear* (see
Live At The BBC), Lennon told Brian Matthew that, on the morning of the Abbey
Road session, they had 'about one verse and we had to finish it off rather quickly'.
Presumably this means he helped McCartney with the lyric.

manufactured to date, it's propelled entirely by the rolling *legato* rhythm of the bass (recorded so high for 1964 that the engineers nervously duck it in the mix each time it leaves the home triad). The structural centrepiece of the track – without it, the other elements in this stark arrangement would make no sense – it's the first of McCartney's high profile bass lines. From now on, he'd be striving to get his instrument 'up' in volume, tone, and octave.

Starting, jokingly, on the on-beat, a harshly overdriven and tightly gated rhythm guitar shifts to the offbeat as the song gets under way, chopping out a reggae accent of surprising violence.[1] With the snare-drum's normal timekeeping role usurped by the rise and fall of the bass, Starr's kit is squashed almost inaudibly into the left channel, offering no bass-drum and breaking out only to double his chugging chocalho with blows to the bell of his ride cymbal. Echoing [41] WHAT YOU'RE DOING, the piano arrives as texture from nowhere, landing in the right channel on the second chorus without prior notice. McCartney's voice, too, is at the edge, squeezed to the upper limit of his chest register and threatening to crack at any moment. In short, everything here is pushed out of its normal place. (Even the guitar solo sets itself in arch quotation marks.)

In all respects an experimental recording, SHE'S A WOMAN is driven by its author's cannabis-cultivated curiosity to pursue every 'what if?' he could think of. At the same time, the overriding priority was to rock hard – a token of a group which, until 1966, continued to think of themselves as 'just a little R&B band'. (The song's powerful swinging beat drew the hard-won approval of America's session men, the Sir Douglas Quintet's 1965 single 'She's About A Mover' being an explicit homage.) Knowingly functional in keeping with the genre, the lyric is notable for the phrase 'turns me on', inserted on Lennon's insistence as a clue to the group's conversion to marijuana – and to give Bob Dylan a *real* drug reference to spot (see [21]).

---

[1] Lennon played this and McCartney gives him the credit for the idea (Miles, op. cit., p. 173). Bootlegged out-takes show Lennon muffing the changes. Take 7 develops into an extended jam in which he thrashes his Rickenbacker almost at random.

[44b] KANSAS CITY/HEY, HEY, HEY, HEY
(Leiber-Stoller/Penniman)

McCartney lead vocal, bass; **Lennon** backing vocal, rhythm guitar;
Harrison backing vocal, lead guitar; **Starr** drums; **George Martin** piano
Recorded: 18th October 1964, Abbey Road 2.
Producer: George Martin. Engineer: Norman Smith.
UK release: 4th December 1964 (LP: *Beatles For Sale*)
US release: 14th June 1965 (LP: *Beatles VI*)

The day after making [44] SHE'S A WOMAN, The Beatles set out on yet
another hectic tour of the UK. With a third of *Beatles For Sale* still to be
made, they would now have to work on their rest days, 18th October
being set aside for a blitz of fast recording. Starting this nine-hour
Sunday session with edits for [43] EIGHT DAYS A WEEK, they then
plunged into KANSAS CITY/HEY, HEY, HEY, HEY, a Little Richard
medley from 1959. They'd heard him perform the sequence and used it
in their own act, though it didn't survive into 1963.[1] Two years later,
they dusted it off for the penultimate date of their first American tour in
Kansas City itself on 17th September 1964, a month before this
recording. The reaction it drew ensured its place on the LP.

Tired of fiddling about with EIGHT DAYS A WEEK, Lennon urged
McCartney to go all out, and the result went down in one take.[2] With
its uncomfortable shuffle beat, Little Richard's is not one of his
strongest recordings, although the timbre of his voice is delicious. The
Beatles simplify the original's dotted rhythm with a walking bass and
triplet piano chords, imparting a sassy swing to a performance let down
only by its lightweight mono mix. McCartney throws the lyric around
to great effect, standing off the mike to belt it from the back of his
throat. After Harrison's solo, Starr marks the segue with a droll hi-hat/

---

[1] They played as Little Richard's support in 1962: at the Tower Ballroom,
Wallasey (12th October), at the Empire Theatre, Liverpool (28th October), and at
the Star-Club, Hamburg (1st–14th November) where McCartney got to know
Richard, who taught him the secret of his scream. (They remain friends, Richard
describing McCartney as his 'blood brother'.) The Beatles had previously recorded
the sequence as The Beat Brothers, backing Tony Sheridan on an unissued Polydor
session in Hamburg in 1961 (not to be confused with Wilbert Harrison's gentler
1959 version of the song, also in The Beatles' repertoire and revived by them during
the 'Get Back' sessions in 1969).
[2] An only slightly less successful second take (without Martin's overdubbed piano)
is available on *Anthology 1*. KANSAS CITY seems to have consistently brought out the
best in The Beatles. The version on *Live At The BBC*, recorded on 16th July 1963 at
the BBC Paris Theatre, is one of the highlights of this generally mediocre collection,
featuring a strong McCartney vocal and an attacking Harrison solo.

bass-drum thump and the track rocks confidently through to its coda, Lennon's sarcastic nasal tone in the backing harmony returning the favour McCartney did him on [13c] MONEY. One of The Beatles' best covers.

[45] I FEEL FINE *(Lennon–McCartney)*

Lennon double-tracked vocal, lead/rhythm guitar; **McCartney** harmony vocal, bass; **Harrison** harmony vocal, lead/rhythm guitar; **Starr** drums
Recorded: 18th October 1964, Abbey Road 2.
Producer: George Martin. Engineer: Norman Smith.
UK release: 27th November 1964 (A single/SHE's A WOMAN)
US release: 23rd November 1964 (A single/SHE's A WOMAN)

Following [44b] KANSAS CITY and the remake of [38b] MR MOONLIGHT, the group turned to new song I FEEL FINE, begun 'at a recording session'[1] and now intended as the next single. ([43] EIGHT DAYS A WEEK had been first choice as recently as six days earlier, with [38] I'M A LOSER and [42] NO REPLY as other contenders.) Lennon had the original idea for the song – the riff and most of the melody – but it was otherwise co-written.[2] Like [44] SHE's A WOMAN, I FEEL FINE is a mutated blues (making this pairing the second Beatles single to be based on blues changes);[3] but there's nothing depressive about the song, which takes its effervescent mood, as well as its form, from the difficult guitar riff which Lennon and Harrison play, often in unison, more or less throughout.[4]

The track opens with a sustained low A on bass as a foundation for feedback from Lennon's Rickenbacker (obtained by striking the note with the volume switch down and then turning up while pointing the pickups towards his amp). He was inordinately proud of this in later years – 'The first time feedback was used on record' – and the effect is often cited as The Beatles' first recording experiment. However, McCartney can claim precedence in three cases, all (like I FEEL FINE) recorded in the first flush of the group's encounter with marijuana: the

---

[1] Sheff and Golson, p. 147. The session in question was probably the one for [43] EIGHT DAYS A WEEK.
[2] Miles, op. cit., p. 172.
[3] The first was [23] CAN'T BUY ME LOVE/[24] YOU CAN'T DO THAT.
[4] The riff (derived from 'Watch Your Step' by Bobby Parker) was too hard for Lennon to play and sing at the same time, so the song was taped as a backing track to which he then added his vocal – the first Beatles track to be thus recorded.

overdriven guitar and drop-in piano of [41] WHAT YOU'RE DOING, the pioneering fade-in to [43] EIGHT DAYS A WEEK, and the generally *outré* [44] SHE'S A WOMAN. As for the origin of Lennon's feedback inspiration, he later conceded that 'everyone' then playing live was using it. For electric guitarists, feedback is a hazard of amplification, to be either avoided or incorporated into their sound in a controlled way. The only local guitarist using feedback as pure noise in 1964 was Pete Townshend, soon to manipulate the effect spectacularly in The Who's outrageous second single 'Anyway Anyhow Anywhere'. A couple of days after recording [38] I'M A LOSER, The Beatles shared a Blackpool bill with The High Numbers (a few weeks before they became The Who). Did Lennon – as he had after hearing harmonica-player Delbert McClinton at the Tower Ballroom, New Brighton two years earlier – mark, learn, and inwardly digest?[1]

Recorded in nine takes, I FEEL FINE, far from a brand new number, sounds like something the group had been playing for years. The lack of a conventional rhythm guitar opens the sound out, allowing the syncopations in the riff to spark and jump. Responding to this, Starr turns in a buoyant performance, playing Latin-style on the ride-cymbal with conga accents on the high tom-tom. Considering that it's mostly his energy that lifts the track – for instance, coming out of the middle eights (0:54, 1:50) – it's unfortunate that the production parks him far left in the stereo spectrum rather than in the middle.[2] Harrison's four-bar guitar break similarly distills the overall feel of the track: not so much a solo as a pithy summary of its bluesy mood and form. Though not an outstanding song, I FEEL FINE went straight to No. 1 in the UK where it resided for six weeks. In America, its stay at the top was shorter, though its B-side, SHE'S A WOMAN, climbed to No. 4 on the strength of point-of-sale requests.

---

[1] A few months later, when asked what sort of music The Beatles were listening to, McCartney admitted 'Dylan and The Who are two great influences'.

[2] Stereo would not become standard for another three years, obliging mixes to be designed for monophonic radio play and the 'compatible' styluses then used in most domestic gramophones.

[46] I'll Follow The Sun *(Lennon–McCartney)*

McCartney vocal, acoustic lead guitar; **Lennon** harmony vocal, acoustic rhythm guitar; **Harrison** lead guitar; **Starr** percussion (?)[1]
Recorded: 18th October 1964, Abbey Road 2.
Producer: George Martin. Engineer: Norman Smith.
UK release: 4th December 1964 (LP: *Beatles For Sale*)
US release: 15th December 1964 (LP: *Beatles '65*)

The descending sevenths of the introduction to [44] SHE's A WOMAN may have reminded McCartney of this very early song of his. (Or, alternatively, trying I'll Follow The Sun on electric guitar might have given him the idea for SHE's A WOMAN.) Written during the summer of 1960 in Hamburg, it's a regretful if ultimately rather callous ditty composed, like [94] When I'm Sixty-four, as a diversion from nights of noisy rock-and-roll. According to former Beatles drummer Pete Best, the 18-year-old McCartney would play it on a piano between sets at The Kaiserkeller, announcing cheerily to anyone in earshot 'I've written a song'.[2] He had, in fact, already written dozens of songs, having begun doing so at least two years earlier. Made in eight takes after [45] I Feel Fine, I'll Follow The Sun featured an acoustic guitar solo (presumably by McCartney) until the last take, when a simple statement of the melody on electric guitar was substituted. Despite the song's tactful brevity, its unresolved stepwise sequence soon palls.

---

[1] The personnel listing is conjectural. McCartney is usually said to be double-tracking himself on the verse, but the second voice sounds more like Harrison. Starr is slapping something, but what it is is unclear (the top of an acoustic guitar?).
[2] At this juncture, McCartney had temporarily become The Beatles' pianist, his cheap Rosetti Solid 7 guitar having rapidly succumbed to the rigours of knockabout performances in sweaty fleapits and fallen to pieces. When, within weeks, Lennon bought his Rickenbacker 325 (see [E4]), he gave McCartney the single pickup Hofner Club 40 he'd acquired in Hamburg a few months earlier.

[46b] EVERYBODY'S TRYING TO BE MY BABY *(Perkins)*

Harrison vocal, lead guitar; **Lennon** acoustic rhythm guitar,
tambourine; **McCartney** bass; **Starr** drums
Recorded: 18th October 1964, Abbey Road 2.
Producer: George Martin. Engineer: Norman Smith.
UK release: 4th December 1964 (LP: *Beatles For Sale*)
US release: 15th December 1964 (LP: *Beatles '65*)

Contrary to PR claims that Lennon and McCartney had a fund of top-class original compositions with which to stock their albums till well into the Seventies, new songs were in short supply, as the inclusion of [46] I'LL FOLLOW THE SUN proved. Repeating the all-original *A Hard Day's Night* was out of the question. The trouble was that, since The Beatles' concerts now consisted almost entirely of their own material, they'd given little thought to their old repertoire of songs by other artists. As a result, the selection of these marshalled on *Beatles For Sale* was highly erratic.

The first of three covers knocked out in the last hour of the Sunday session, EVERYBODY'S TRYING TO BE MY BABY was a rockabilly blues from Carl Perkins' 1958 Sun album *Teen Beat*. It had featured occasionally in The Beatles' act during 1961–4 and, as a result of this recording, returned to their set in 1965. More or less identical to the original, their arrangement adds a jokey false ending and an odd mistake in the introduction, where Harrison's voice and Lennon's guitar are two beats out of synch. (Lennon often had trouble keeping time and was notorious for confusing on-beats and off-beats.) Recorded in one take, the track makes a lame finale to *Beatles For Sale*. Harrison's guitar work consists chiefly of a single fill, while his vocal, overloaded with echo and unnecessary double-tracking, fails to emulate the modest wit of Perkins' original.[1]

---

[1] Harrison's retiring dislike of the false and ego-inflating is amusingly caught in the live version of EVERYBODY'S TRYING TO BE MY BABY in Part 4 of the *Anthology* video. When he sings 'They took some honey from a tree/Dressed it up and they called it me', he barely voices the last word.

[46c] ROCK AND ROLL MUSIC *(Berry)*

Lennon vocal, rhythm guitar; **McCartney** bass; **Harrison** acoustic
    guitar; **Starr** drums; **George Martin** piano
Recorded: 18th October 1964, Abbey Road 2.
Producer: George Martin. Engineer: Norman Smith.
UK release: 4th December 1964 (LP: *Beatles For Sale*)
US release: 15th December 1964 (LP: *Beatles '65*)

Uniquely fast on their feet, The Beatles moved from the disappointing
[46b] EVERYBODY'S TRYING TO BE MY BABY to a wonderfully
spontaneous single-take version of ROCK AND ROLL MUSIC, one of
Chuck Berry's myth-making hits of the mid-Fifties [14b]. Half the
secret of this thunderous performance is that the song was continuously
in their act between 1959 and 1966. Lennon's urgency is nonetheless
remarkable after over eight hours in the studio, almost certainly
prompted by his anxiety to do justice to a song he clearly regarded as
virtual holy writ. No hint of irony intrudes as he roars through Berry's
verses, creating a wave of tearful elation that sweeps George Martin
into his most convincing rock-and-roll playing. Pitched a fifth higher
than Berry's record, The Beatles' cover of ROCK AND ROLL MUSIC has
greater energy than the original and is in every respect worthy of
comparison with it.

[46d] WORDS OF LOVE *(Holly)*

McCartney vocal, bass; **Lennon** vocal, rhythm guitar; **Harrison**
    lead guitar; **Starr** drums, suitcase
Recorded: 18th October 1964, Abbey Road 2.
Producer: George Martin. Engineer: Norman Smith.
UK release: 4th December 1964 (LP: *Beatles For Sale*)
US release: 14th June 1965 (LP: *Beatles VI*)

The last song to be taped on the marathon session of 18th October
1964 was a belated tribute to one of the group's formative influences:
Buddy Holly. Before his death in a plane crash in 1959, this young
Texan singer-songwriter-guitarist-producer had been a prototype
modern pop star. His March 1958 tour of Britain with The Crickets
was a major influence on the subsequent UK 'beat boom' and the
teenage Beatles idolised him, performing a dozen of his songs.[1] A miss

---

[1] These included [E1b] THAT'LL BE THE DAY, 'Peggy Sue', 'Everyday', 'It's So
Easy', 'Maybe Baby', 'Think It Over', 'Raining In My Heart', and [U13m] CRYING,
WAITING, HOPING *(Live At The BBC)*. The Beatles supposedly arrived at their name
as a variation on Buddy Holly's backing group, The Crickets (though see Davies, p.
58). The 18-year-old Lennon was very shaken by Holly's death, while McCartney

in 1957, WORDS OF LOVE was adopted by them in 1958 but, like their other Holly material, left their act in 1962. Showing its author's pioneering interest in recording techniques, the original features the first known double-tracked pop vocal: Holly harmonising with himself in the style of The Everly Brothers. Lennon and Harrison sang the song live but the credits for this track show Harrison replaced by McCartney (though the actual sound suggests otherwise). Made in two takes with a vocal overdub, the group's version of this rather sickly number sticks close to Holly's while avoiding his feyness and stressing the upper harmony. Harrison turns up the treble on his Gretsch Tennessean while Starr slaps a packing case with a loose fastening, a noise resembling out-of-time clapping (see [38b]).

[46e] HONEY DON'T *(Perkins)*

> **Starr** vocal, drums; **McCartney** bass; **Lennon** acoustic rhythm
> guitar; **Harrison** lead guitar
> Recorded: 26th October 1964, Abbey Road 2.
> Producer: George Martin. Engineer: Norman Smith.
> UK release: 4th December 1964 (LP: *Beatles For Sale*)
> US release: 15th December 1964 (LP: *Beatles '65*)

From the last day's recording for *Beatles For Sale*, HONEY DON'T required five takes, following which the group concluded with a remake of [41] WHAT YOU'RE DOING. The B-side of Carl Perkins' original [U164d] BLUE SUEDE SHOES (see [31b]), the song had been in their act since 1962, sung by Lennon.[1] Starr took it over for the purposes of this recording, retaining it until 1965, after which it was dropped. The group's version lacks the essential Perkins bounce, while Starr's doleful vocal, punctuated by desperate attempts to gee things up, offers only a rapidly dwindling fund of hopeless charm. The Beatles were understandably exhausted – yet next day they were back on the treadmill of their UK tour, with no real break until December.

---

was so devoted to the singer's work that he later bought the copyrights to his catalogue.
[1] See *Live At The BBC*.

[47] TICKET TO RIDE *(Lennon–McCartney)*

Lennon double-tracked vocal, rhythm guitar; McCartney harmony
vocal, bass, lead guitar; Harrison harmony vocal, rhythm guitar;
Starr drums, tambourine, handclaps
Recorded: 15th February 1965, Abbey Road 2.
Producer: George Martin. Engineer: Norman Smith.
UK release: 9th April 1965 (A single/YES IT IS)
US release: 19th April 1965 (A single/YES IT IS)

Following their UK tour at the end of 1964 and another long
Christmas season, the group took a month off before starting work on
the second of their films. At this stage entitled *Eight Arms To Hold
You*[1] the project was ill-conceived, swiftly degenerating into a
whimsical working holiday in the Bahamas and Austria. In the week
before they flew to Nassau, The Beatles met at Abbey Road to start
work on the soundtrack album, returning to Studio 2 on the day that
[43] EIGHT DAYS A WEEK arrived at No. 1 in America. They began
with their new single, a co-composition mainly by Lennon.[2]

A bitter, dissonant mid-tempo song with a dragging beat, TICKET
TO RIDE[3] was hardly an obvious choice for a Beatles single and there
was said to be disagreement about it behind the scenes. In the run-up to
its UK issue, the pop press trailed it as a new departure for the group:
something unusual, even uncommercial.[4] In the event, while British
record buyers kept it at No. 1 for three weeks, America was less
impressed, purchasing enough copies to haul it laboriously to the top
for one week before it was deposed by The Beach Boys' cheery 'Help
Me Rhonda'. With its melancholy B-side [50] YES IT IS, TICKET TO
RIDE was psychologically deeper than anything The Beatles had
recorded before and a sharp anomaly in a pop scene where doomy
melodramas from balladeers like Gene Pitney and P. J. Proby stood in
for real feeling.

---

[1] The title appears on the first pressings of both [47] and [56]. *Help!* was supposed
to be the second of a three-film contract between The Beatles and United Artists.
Plans for a third film (rumoured to have been based on Richard Condon's novel *A
Talent for Loving*) were subsequently shelved.
[2] Claiming the harmony parts, McCartney estimates the work as 60-40 to Lennon
(Miles, op. cit., p. 193).
[3] The title arose from a pun on Ryde, the ferry port in the north of the Isle of
Wight. Lennon and McCartney took a daytrip ferry from Portsmouth to Ryde to
visit friends (possibly on 8th April 1963).
[4] This ploy was not original. The Animals' 'House of the Rising Sun' was
promoted by playing up its 'uncommercial' length (four minutes, almost twice as
long as the average pop single).

Yet there was more to the record than unusual emotional depth. As sheer sound, TICKET TO RIDE is extraordinary for its time – massive with chiming electric guitars, weighty rhythm, and rumbling floor tom-toms. Among the first attempts to convey on record the impact achievable live by an amplified group, it was later recalled by Lennon as 'one of the earliest heavy metal records'. As such, he may have been going for the effect he'd heard The Who produce seven months earlier (see [45]), though it must be said that interest in the possibilities of amplified sound was very much in the air around this time. Apart from The Who's as-yet unrecorded ventures in pure noise, Jeff Beck, a master of controlled feedback, was about to replace bluesman Eric Clapton as lead guitarist with one of Britain's most exciting live groups, The Yardbirds. A tougher sound had also entered the UK singles chart towards the end of 1964 with The Animals' 'I'm Crying', The Kinks' 'You Really Got Me', Them's 'Baby Please Don't Go', and Keith Richards' ferocious minimalist solo in The Rolling Stones' 'It's All Over Now'. Having played acoustic guitar throughout most of *A Hard Day's Night* and *Beatles For Sale*, Lennon returned to electric guitar[1] in [45] I FEEL FINE and TICKET TO RIDE with an energy drawn partly from the air of adventure then abroad on the UK scene. But there was perhaps a more potent reason for his renewed absorption in the texture of high amplification.

Some time early in 1965 – the exact date is unknown but it may have been in January or February, before The Beatles went abroad to film *Help!* – Lennon and Harrison encountered LSD.[2] 'Spiked' by a foolish acquaintance who slipped it into their coffee after dinner, they found themselves careering through late-night London, dazzled and near-hysterical as the powerful hallucinogen took effect. Lennon later admitted that the experience had stunned him, revealing a mode of perception which marijuana had barely hinted at. Whether TICKET TO RIDE was his first creative response to LSD is, on current evidence, impossible to say. Its heavy rhythm and immersion in electric sound may have been a spin-off from the cannabis inspiration audible in the later work for *Beatles For Sale*. On the other hand, the track is far more

---

[1] He plays a Jetglo Rickenbacker 325 12-string presented to him in America in mid-1964. Harrison is probably using his Rickenbacker 360/12 (although for the TICKET TO RIDE promo film he sported a recently-acquired Gibson ES345 stereo). McCartney's lead lines in the fade-out are performed on his new Epiphone Casino, a semi-acoustic modelled on the Gibson ES330 which he bought in late 1964.

[2] According to Peter Brown (p. 149) it was during the filming of *Help!*, i.e., after the end of March 1965. Goldman, whose account (pp. 195–7) is the most detailed, claims it took place 'back in 1964'.

intense than anything The Beatles made in late 1964, pointing forward to 1966 and such frankly psychedelic records as [81] RAIN, which shares its gong-like clangour of saturated guitar tone, and [77] TOMORROW NEVER KNOWS, which emulates its high-lying one-note bass line and broken drum pattern. (It also shows signs of 1966-style varispeeding, being pitched in the gap between G sharp and A.) TICKET TO RIDE is even more unusual for The Beatles in clinging, entranced, to its opening chord for six long bars (ten, including the introduction). Like the middle eight experiments on *Beatles For Sale*, this was clearly deliberate and may, in this case, have been suggested by Martha and the Vandellas' similarly obsessional 'one-chord' hits for Motown towards the end of 1964: 'Dancing in the Street' and 'Wild One'. Again anticipating 1966, Lennon's melody rises and falls in mesmeric *raga*-style – A, C sharp, D, E, G – making McCartney's harmony in bluesy fourths and thirds seem shockingly harsh.[1]

Though it had appeared in half a dozen Beatle songs, the word 'sad' here carries a weight graphically embodied in the track's oppressive pedal tonality and deliberately cumbersome drums. There is, too, a narcotic passivity about Lennon's lyric: though the girl is leaving him, he makes no attempt to stop or threaten her as he would have done in earlier songs; all he does – in the ruminative, monochordal middle eight – is mutter bitterly while she 'rides high', absorbed in herself (a self whose chief characteristic is that of not caring). By 1966, according to Lennon, he was 'eating' LSD, taking 'thousands' of trips and lapsing into introspective states for days on end. This self-centred, addictive outlook, which eventually led him to heroin, is vividly prefigured in the droning sound and lethargic mood of TICKET TO RIDE. The first Beatles recording to break the three-minute barrier,[2] it is an extraordinary precognition of their next stage of development, commenced fifteen months later with [77] TOMORROW NEVER KNOWS.

---

[1] Lennon's formal introduction to Indian classical music took place six months later [63]. Although probably derived from Motown, the sustained tonic at the beginning of TICKET TO RIDE is equivalent to the static Indian drone foundation. Hence, perhaps, the *raga*-like melodic results.

[2] At 2:58, YOU REALLY GOT A HOLD ON ME is the longest Beatles track before SHE'S A WOMAN (2:59) in October 1964. Leaving aside [75] YOU WON'T SEE ME (3:17), The Beatles' time-scale only began to expand significantly on *Sgt. Pepper*.

[48] ANOTHER GIRL *(Lennon–McCartney)*

McCartney double-tracked vocal, bass, lead guitar; **Lennon**
harmony vocal, acoustic rhythm guitar; **Harrison** harmony vocal,
electric rhythm guitar; **Starr** drums
Recorded: 15th–16th February 1965, Abbey Road 2.
Producer: George Martin. Engineer: Norman Smith.
UK release: 6th August 1965 (LP: *Help!*)
US release: 13th August 1965 (LP: *Help!*)

Made in the evening after [47] TICKET TO RIDE, this McCartney
number revamps, in softer style, the swinging, guitar-off-beat design of
[44] SHE'S A WOMAN. A casual three-chord throwaway, it works off
the metre of its lyric, its melody emerging from a harmonic game with
A major and A minor, modulating to a surprising C major in the
middle eight. Harrison had a lead guitar idea, but McCartney replaced
this next day with a bullish country-and-western counterpoint to his
vocal played on an Epiphone semi-acoustic. As a recording, ANOTHER
GIRL is distinguished by its dark shading, McCartney singing at the low
end of his very wide range. Lyrically, it may be another reflection on
his relationship with Jane Asher, throughout which he maintained a
secret flat in London for assignations with many another girl (see [68],
note).

[49] I NEED YOU *(Harrison)*

Harrison double-tracked vocal, lead guitar; **Lennon** harmony
vocal, acoustic rhythm guitar; **McCartney** harmony vocal, bass;
Starr drums, cowbell
Recorded: 15th–16th February 1965, Abbey Road 2.
Producer: George Martin. Engineer: Norman Smith.
UK release: 6th August 1965 (LP: *Help!*)
US release: 13th August 1965 (LP: *Help!*)

This characteristically melancholy number was allegedly written for
Patti Boyd, a young model Harrison met in March 1964 while filming
A Hard Day's Night. Legend has it that, separated from her during
filming for *Help!* in the Bahamas, he poured out his heart to her in this
song. In fact it was taped a week before the Bahamas shoot began. The
feeling is real enough, though, and emphasised by a volume swell-pedal
which gives his chordal riff a choked, tearful quality. (The same gadget
was used the following evening on Lennon's similarly emotional [50]
YES IT IS.[1]) Harrison's second number for The Beatles (see [20]), I

---

[1] The first notable use of this device (by session guitarist Big Jim Sullivan)

NEED YOU, while effective in the first eight bars of its verse/chorus structure, is let down by an harmonically banal bridge. A sketchy arrangement and murky recording suggest that he got little help with it.

[50] YES IT IS *(Lennon–McCartney)*

Lennon double-tracked vocal, acoustic rhythm guitar; **McCartney** harmony vocal, bass; **Harrison** harmony vocal, lead guitar; **Starr** drums, tambourine (?)
Recorded: 16th February 1965, Abbey Road 2.
Producer: George Martin. Engineer: Norman Smith.
UK release: 9th April 1965 (B single/TICKET TO RIDE)
US release: 19th April 1965 (B single/TICKET TO RIDE)

Though Lennon was often brusquely unfeeling with women, his behaviour hid an idealist who believed in destiny and the One True Love. His most yearningly romantic song,[1] YES IT IS is positively 19th century in its haunted feverishness, its Poe-like invocation of the colour scarlet, and its hint that the lost lover of its lyric is dead. The fantasy-figure conjured here is probably a transmutation of Lennon's dead, red-haired mother, Julia [156]. The heroine of Yes It Is has something in common with the mysterious women in Dylan songs like 'Love Minus Zero/No Limit' and 'Sad-Eyed Lady of the Lowlands', and those who obsessed Jimi Hendrix in what Charles Shaar Murray calls the 'Angel cycle'.[2] In folk convention, these love/death figures traditionally dwell in a twilight borderland of the male psyche where masculine identity dissolves. In their different ways, Dylan, Hendrix, and Lennon all surrendered to this Belle Dame archetype (the latter two most obviously in their greedy submission to the unpredictable whims of the goddess LSD). In YES IT IS, the essential masochism of this fixation appears in the song's Gothic overtones and the self-flagellatory outburst of its ten-bar middle section. The 'pride' Lennon curses stems from his attachment to this feminine ideal, Herself arguably a reflection of the personal uniqueness he had felt since childhood. (What prevents him loving the ordinary woman to whom the song is addressed is pride in his singularity, personified by his mirror-image Ideal. The song's title can thus be heard as an acknowledgement of this obsession, by which its author, on his own admission, felt both exalted and bound.)

occurred on Dave Berry's 'The Crying Game', a UK Top 10 hit six months earlier.
[1] McCartney recalls helping on this song at Lennon's Kenwood house (Miles, op. cit., p. 176).
[2] Murray, *Crosstown Traffic* (Faber, 1989), pp. 74–79.

Lennon later recalled YES IT IS as a failed rewrite of [22] THIS BOY. Yet, while formally alike – both are in 12/8, employ an intricate three-part major seventh harmony, and work off the standard four-chord doo-wop verse sequence – the two songs have little else in common, THIS BOY being merely a well-wrought genre product of The Beatles' adolescence compared to the moodily expressive YES IT IS with its rich and unusual harmonic motion. Moreover, though impatient with attempts to foist inappropriate significance on his work, Lennon read critical analyses with interest and acknowledged his capacity for unconscious self-revelation.[1] Written in the shadow of [47] TICKET TO RIDE, YES IT IS may have lost its resonance for him in retrospect. It is also possible that he wrote it overnight after hearing Harrison use the volume-pedal on [49] I NEED YOU, and that the words rushed out without much consideration.[2] More probably the song's expression of emotional bondage to a tragic past became finished business for him once he had found fulfilment with Yoko Ono.

[51] THE NIGHT BEFORE *(Lennon–McCartney)*

McCartney double-tracked vocal, bass, lead guitar; **Lennon**
  harmony vocal, electric piano; **Harrison** harmony vocal, guitar;
  Starr drums, tambourine (?)
Recorded: 17th February 1965, Abbey Road 2.
Producer: George Martin. Engineer: Norman Smith.
UK release: 6th August 1965 (LP: *Help!*)
US release: 13th August 1965 (LP: *Help!*)

Like [48] ANOTHER GIRL, this slight McCartney number contains faint echoes of [44] SHE'S A WOMAN, here disguised by replacing the original reggae inflection with Lennon's enthusiastic comping on electric piano. Nothing surprising happens in the harmony, the lyrics are weak, and the track as a whole is only fair mainstream pop of its period. Even McCartney's voice sounds tired. Doubled at the octave, the guitar solo is its most notable ingredient – pithily predictive of the more integrated lead work the group would favour from now on. Usually credited to Harrison, it sounds tonally more like McCartney.[3] The percussion

---

[1] Interview with Jonathan Cott, *Rolling Stone*, 1968.
[2] Take 1, issued on *Anthology 2*, shows that the song was new enough for him not to have written a close. Presumably McCartney and Harrison worked out the coda with its unexpected G sharp.
[3] Miles confirms that the solo is by McCartney (op. cit., p. 195).

instrument with which Starr shakes up the middle eight is unidentified. (The same sound appears on [50] YES IT IS.)

[52] YOU LIKE ME TOO MUCH *(Harrison)*

> **Harrison** double-tracked vocal, lead guitar; **McCartney** bass, piano (with **George Martin**); **Lennon** acoustic rhythm guitar, electric piano; **Starr** drums, tambourine
> Recorded: 17th February 1965, Abbey Road 2.
> Producer: George Martin. Engineer: Norman Smith.
> UK release: 6th August 1965 (LP: *Help!*)
> US release: 14th June 1965 (LP: *Beatles VI*)

Harrison's third song to be recorded by The Beatles (see [20], [49]), YOU LIKE ME TOO MUCH replaces the melancholy of its predecessors with a gawky grin and an ungainly verse that collapses breathlessly at the end of each line. The blandly happy lyric, probably about his affair with Patti Boyd [49], offers self-deprecation in lieu of depth, a wryness picked up in a drop-in four-hand barrelhouse piano. As on the previous track, Lennon plays Hohner electric piano (Pianet), this time with reverb.

[53] YOU'VE GOT TO HIDE YOUR LOVE AWAY
(Lennon–McCartney)

> **Lennon** vocal, acoustic rhythm guitar; **McCartney** acoustic rhythm guitar; **Harrison** acoustic lead guitar; **Starr** tambourine, shaker, maracas; **Johnnie Scott** tenor/alto flutes
> Recorded: 18th February 1965, Abbey Road 2.
> Producer: George Martin. Engineer: Norman Smith.
> UK release: 6th August 1965 (LP: *Help!*)
> US release: 13th August 1965 (LP: *Help!*)

Taped fast in an afternoon session, this was the first all-acoustic Beatles track, a format inspired by their Dylan fad. Ironically, at exactly the same time as The Beatles were laying aside their electric guitars and drums under the influence of Dylan's *Another Side*, he was in a New York studio recording his first amplified set, *Bringing It All Back Home* – a move he had made after hearing and meeting The Beatles. Featuring Lennon's first vocal for two years not to be double-tracked, YOU'VE GOT TO HIDE YOUR LOVE AWAY is a sort of sequel to his earlier 'Dylan' number, [38] I'M A LOSER. In fact, the stylistic resemblance in both cases is superficial, being limited mainly to a downbeat starkness of sound and delivery. (A more direct steal from Dylan can be heard in the recurring 'Aaahs' of [47] TICKET TO RIDE.) Musically, the debt is to the strummed major triads of the Anglo-American folk style, the only anomaly being a poetic coda for flutes, written and played by EMI arranger Johnnie Scott. Singer and gay rights champion Tom Robinson has suggested that the lyric refers to homosexuality and concerns Lennon's relationship with Brian Epstein, but it is a mistake to imagine that a singer-songwriter always works autobiographically, and in this case Lennon clearly adopts a persona.

[U54] IF YOU'VE GOT TROUBLE *(Lennon-McCartney)*

Starr double-tracked vocal, drums; **Lennon** backing vocal, rhythm
    guitar; **McCartney** backing vocal, bass; **Harrison** backing vocal,
    lead guitar
Recorded: 18th February 1965, Abbey Road 2.
Producer: George Martin. Engineer: Norman Smith.
UK release: 18th March 1996 (CD: *Anthology 2*)
US release: 18th March 1996 (CD: *Anthology 2*)

The only unmitigated disaster in the Lennon–McCartney catalogue, IF YOU'VE GOT TROUBLE was churned out as a vehicle for Starr in the middle of the *Help!* sessions. Whenever they were dozing as lyricists, The Beatles tended to burble about diamonds, rings, and money, and so it goes here. A tone of patronising offhandedness taints a truly terrible text, apparently designed to exploit Starr's image as the amiable beringed twit of the group. If the lyric is preposterous, the tune does Ringo no favours either, requiring him to sing in triple time whilst driving a 4/4 rock-and-roll thrash. So dire that no further attempts were made on it after the first take, this track has no claim on posterity's attention other than its hint that the 'comedy song' concept mooted a few months later (see [63]) had been in the air for some while.

[54] TELL ME WHAT YOU SEE *(Lennon–McCartney)*

McCartney vocal, bass, electric piano, guiro; **Lennon** harmony
    vocal, rhythm guitar; **Harrison** lead guitar; **Starr** drums,
    tambourine, claves
Recorded: 18th February 1965, Abbey Road 2.
Producer: George Martin. Engineer: Norman Smith.
UK release: 6th August 1965 (LP: *Help!*)
US release: 14th June 1965 (LP: *Beatles VI*)

The melody of this almost childishly simple song, gravitating throughout to G major, suggests that it dates from early in McCartney's career, but it was, in fact, a contemporary composition about which he

recollects little.[1] Recorded immediately after the failed attempt at IF
YOU'VE GOT TROUBLE, TELL ME WHAT YOU SEE is notable mainly for
its arrangement/production of compressed drums, Latin percussion, and
electric piano (the latter 'dropped in' in the manner established in [41]
WHAT YOU'RE DOING). The shallowness of this and other tracks on
Help! contrasts with the depressive depth of much of *Beatles For Sale*,
and it is possible that the group had made a decision to lighten their
approach. On the other hand, their giggling behaviour while filming
Help! suggests a simple over-indulgence in cannabis.

[55] YOU'RE GOING TO LOSE THAT GIRL
(Lennon–McCartney)

Lennon double-tracked vocal, acoustic rhythm guitar; **McCartney**
    backing vocal, bass, piano; **Harrison** backing vocal, lead guitar;
    Starr drums, bongos
Recorded: 19th February 1965, Abbey Road 2.
Producer: George Martin. Engineer: Norman Smith.
UK release: 6th August 1965 (LP: *Help!*)
US release: 13th August 1965 (LP: *Help!*)

Recorded in an afternoon session – the last track for *Help!* before the
group flew to the Bahamas to start filming – YOU'RE GOING TO LOSE
THAT GIRL is more substantial than most of the album, if no less of a
filler. Lennon's hardbitten lyric suits the music and is very well sung –
particularly the falsetto A that ties the song's basic E major to the jeering
G major of its middle eight.[2] The explosive release here sparks the
others into a powerful performance, Starr battering somewhat chaoti-
cally on bongos as McCartney and Harrison belt out their ringing
response-pattern backing vocals. With the best vocal sound on a Beatles
record of this period, YOU'RE GOING TO LOSE THAT GIRL, unlike most
of the *Help!* material, stands the test of time.[3]

---

[1] Miles, op. cit., p. 200.
[2] McCartney estimates the writing as 60–40 to Lennon (Miles, op. cit., p. 195).
[3] Harrison's guitar solo features the first use of his new Sonic Blue Fender
Stratocaster. Given to him during the 1965 American tour (Lennon got one too), this
became one of his favourite instruments, being the vehicle of the slide ('bottleneck')
sound for which he still uses it (see [187]).

[U56] THAT MEANS A LOT (Lennon–McCartney)

McCartney vocal, bass, piano; **Lennon** backing vocal, rhythm
guitar, maracas; **Harrison** backing vocal, lead guitar, maracas;
Starr drums
Recorded: 20th February, 30th March 1965, Abbey Road 2.
Producer: George Martin. Engineer: Norman Smith.
UK release: 18th March 1996 (CD: *Anthology 2*)
US release: 18th March 1996 (CD: *Anthology 2*)

Two days after failing with the facetious [U54] IF YOU'VE GOT
TROUBLE, The Beatles found themselves failing again with this track – a
meaningful coincidence which, like much about the *Help!* album,
indicates that they had begun to overdo the drugs.[1] Described by
Lennon as a ballad which he and McCartney wrote for the *Help!* film,
THAT MEANS A LOT went through two very different versions during
the pair of sessions the group devoted to it. Beginning with a loud,
heavily overdubbed take on 20th February, they returned to the song
after five weeks on location, trying for a lighter, faster remake in four
increasingly chaotic attempts. Finally admitting themselves stumped,
they donated the song to American histrionicist P. J. Proby, whose
single version duly vanished into oblivion some months later.

Judging from the first version (*Anthology 2*), THAT MEANS A LOT
was an attempt by McCartney to rewrite Lennon's [47] TICKET TO
RIDE, recorded five days earlier. Apart from being fascinated by the
sheer massiveness of the sound achieved in TICKET TO RIDE (to which
take 1 of THAT MEANS A LOT bears a blatant resemblance), McCartney
presumably wanted to try a minor harmony in the second bar of
Lennon's verse where the latter stays in the major, clinging to an
unyielding tonic ('I think I'm gonna be *sad* . . .'; 'Your friend says that
your *love* . . .'). Given that the songs are a fourth apart, the transition
from the verse (to the chorus on TICKET TO RIDE, to a four-bar bridge
on THAT MEANS A LOT) is identical (IV–V). Moreover, the diminished
seventh in the sixth bar of the chorus of TICKET TO RIDE also occurs in
THAT MEANS A LOT (the final chord of the middle eight). Here the
shift to the relative minor is natural, while logic also dictates the
dissonant progression whereby C sharp minor explodes back into E
major via an added seventh ('Love can *be* suicide'). Despite this, the
structure sounds wrong and, at worst, seems completely arbitrary.

---

[1] The group's intoxicant of the time was cannabis, although it's possible that
Lennon and Harrison had recently also become acquainted with LSD (see [47]
TICKET TO RIDE).

This is partly a question of secondary inspiration supplemented by analysis. TICKET TO RIDE isn't 'thought out'; on the contrary, it bears the Lennonian hallmarks of having been torn spontaneously from an aggrieved heart. Yet if THAT MEANS A LOT was indeed mostly written by McCartney,[1] it remains of interest in showing him creatively incapable of operating in Lennon's *outré* harmonic territory – not because he couldn't respond to its moods but because his natural melodic phrasing didn't fit there. The bathetic and stilted tune of THAT MEANS A LOT contains more than a trace of his uncharacteristically contrived [54] TELL ME WHAT YOU SEE, taped two days earlier. A mix of TICKET TO RIDE and TELL ME WHAT YOU SEE seems on the face of it unlikely – but this is what we hear in THAT MEANS A LOT.

Take 1 of this ill-fated song is fascinating not only for revealing The Beatles in the unfamiliar role of blunderers in the dark, but for its glimpse into the big sound they had discovered on tour while listening to groups like The Who and The Yardbirds. While Lennon used this sonority in TICKET TO RIDE, it shrank somewhat in the mix. Take 1 of THAT MEANS A LOT preserves the group in untamed 'mega' mode – so loud that Lennon's amp vibrato can be heard motorboating as the track begins. The Beatles clearly enjoyed erecting this wall of sound, their excitement palpable in the powerful coda (based on the climactic 'Can't you see?' phrase from the middle eight). The song nonetheless remains a botch, rightly excluded from the *Help!* album.

[56] HELP! *(Lennon–McCartney)*

Lennon double-tracked vocal, acoustic 12-string rhythm guitar;
  McCartney backing vocal, bass; **Harrison** backing vocal, lead
  guitar; **Starr** drums, tambourine
Recorded: 13th April 1965, Abbey Road 2.
  Producer: George Martin. Engineer: Norman Smith.
UK release: 23rd July 1965 (A single/I'M DOWN)
US release: 19th July 1965 (A single/I'M DOWN)

Seven weeks into shooting, The Beatles' second film was still scheduled as *Eight Arms To Hold You*, yet neither Lennon nor McCartney fancied writing a song to accommodate this octopodous concept, and in the end director Richard Lester, perhaps acknowledging the slapdash and directionless tone of the project, decided on *Help!* Written mainly by

---

[1] Lennon may have helped with the lyric, the middle eight, and the initial arrangement.

Lennon at his new home in Weybridge, the title song began in mid-tempo, but was speeded up slightly during recording to make it more commercial. Lennon later resented this for compromising his conception, yet the group needed another hit and the job they did in sprucing up his first thoughts was comparable to the similarly effective work on [3] PLEASE PLEASE ME and [12] SHE LOVES YOU.[1]

In fact, HELP! retains its authenticity through the emotion in its author's voice. Looking back on this song in 1980, Lennon recalled it as a cry for help from the depths of what he referred to as his 'fat Elvis' period. Mentally exhausted by two years of continuous touring, he was isolated and alienated in his multi-roomed mansion in the stockbroker belt of London's western fringe. His marriage damaged by his orgiastic round of whores and groupies on the road, he felt unsustained by his faithful and attentive wife Cynthia, who, concerned for her husband's health, made no secret of disapproving of his drug intake. All of this amounted to a personal malaise that would expand to overwhelming dimensions during the next two years.

Lyrically, Help! distills Lennon's misery, marking a watershed in his life. Here, the shell he had grown around his feelings since his mother's death finally cracks as he admits a need for others. Musically, the song offers neither artifice nor distance. So characteristically horizontal that its verse consists of one repeated note trailing off into a wail, the song opens on an unhappy B minor, climbing stepwise via a sixth to a pleading scream as A major arrives to stabilise the harmony. (This sequence is a condensation of the chorus.) With no relieving middle eight – its role usurped by a repeat of the first verse – HELP! perpetually slides back to the anxiety and tension of B minor. Only in the song's moaning final sixth is this tension wearily resolved.

Despite a recording gap of nearly two months, The Beatles picked up where they'd left off with [55] YOU'RE GOING TO LOSE THAT GIRL, developing a similarly complex backing-vocal pattern, this time anticipating rather than responding to the melody.[2] This arrangement, plus a duplicate of Lennon's lead vocal, were added on takes 9 and 10.[3] To finish, Starr overdubbed tambourine and Harrison taped his guitar part, descending at the end of each chorus on a cross-rhythm

---

[1] McCartney recalls the song as 70-30 to Lennon (Miles, op. cit., p. 199).

[2] This descant to Lennon's 'one-note' melody was written by McCartney (ibid, p. 199).

[3] As with [45] I FEEL FINE, the backing track was taped first (without a guide vocal). This practice from now on became the group's standard method until the 'Get Back' sessions of 1969.

arpeggio run in the style of Nashville guitarist Chet Atkins. (This, and Starr's straight-quaver fills against the song's fast shuffle beat, are good examples of the group's care in painting characterful touches into every corner of their best work.)

Taken into The Beatles' act during 1965, HELP! rose to No. 1 on both sides of the Atlantic. In America it displaced Sonny and Cher's 'I Got You Babe' and was succeeded by Barry McGuire's nuclear protest-song 'Eve of Destruction', representatives of a new style pioneered by Dylan and his acolytes The Byrds: folk-rock. Sold as America's answer to the 'British Invasion' of groups from Liverpool and London in 1964 (see [21], note), the folk-rock phenomenon coincided with the US Labor Department's panicky protectionist move to ban British acts from America. Beatles-business, though, was too lucrative to exclude and they accordingly returned to the States in August 1965 to promote HELP! and the thinly inconsequential film to which it was formally attached (and which they loathed).

[56b] DIZZY MISS LIZZY *(Williams)*

Lennon vocal, rhythm guitar; **McCartney** bass, electric piano;
    Harrison double-tracked lead guitar; **Starr** drums, cowbell
Recorded: 10th May 1965, Abbey Road 2.
Producer: George Martin. Engineer: Norman Smith.
UK release: 6th August 1965 (LP: *Help!*)
US release: 14th June 1965 (LP: *Beatles VI*)

Dodging into Abbey Road after a day's hasty filming for *Help!*, a tired group submitted to an unwanted Monday evening's work in response to urgent pleas from Capitol for new material. By shuffling The Beatles' UK releases and short-changing the US public with fewer titles per LP, EMI's American outlet had managed to eke out six albums from four British ones. In fact, so cunningly had Capitol's A&R department deployed its Beatles product that it had nine tracks in hand — nearly enough for a seventh album. At under twenty-five minutes, however, this was deemed insufficient even for the insatiable US market; hence this hastily arranged session. Having no new songs, the group dutifully knocked off two Larry Williams numbers, DIZZY MISS LIZZY and [56c] BAD BOY (see [32b]). Williams' original DIZZY MISS LIZZY, issued on Specialty in 1958, is a drab twelve-bar boogie with an overheated rhythm section. The Beatles' version, an unprepossessing shambles of *ersatz* hysteria and jumbled double-tracking, is little better.

[56c] BAD BOY *(Williams)*

Lennon vocal, rhythm guitar; **McCartney** bass, electric piano;
  Harrison double-tracked lead guitar; **Starr** drums, tambourine
Recorded: 10th May 1965, Abbey Road 2.
Producer: George Martin. Engineer: Norman Smith.
UK release: 9th December 1966 (LP: *A Collection Of Beatles Oldies*)
US release: 14th June 1965 (LP: *Beatles VI*)

Issued on Specialty in 1959, Larry Williams' BAD BOY was a vain attempt to get back into the charts by imitating Leiber and Stoller's musical 'playlets' for The Coasters. Churned out at the same session as [56b] DIZZY MISS LIZZY, The Beatles' version is pressured hack-work.

[57] I'VE JUST SEEN A FACE *(Lennon–McCartney)*

McCartney vocal, acoustic guitar; **Lennon** acoustic guitar;
  Harrison acoustic lead guitar; **Starr** brushed snare, maracas
Recorded: 14th June 1965, Abbey Road 2.
Producer: George Martin. Engineer: Norman Smith.
UK release: 6th August 1965 (LP: *Help!*)
US release: 6th December 1965 (LP: *Rubber Soul*)

Absorbed in his life with Jane Asher, with whose family he now lodged in Wimpole Street, McCartney had fallen far behind Lennon in output since his solo fling with [23] CAN'T BUY ME LOVE eighteen months before. His partner had written The Beatles' last four singles and sung lead on and written a third of [43] EIGHT DAYS A WEEK, an extra single issued only in America. Lennon's album material, too, had become deeper, more original, and more varied. While never stuck for production ideas, McCartney had ground to a halt with his songwriting, only [44] SHE's A WOMAN standing out among his contributions since [39] EVERY LITTLE THING. Thus far, the only substantial work on the flimsy *Help!* album had been Lennon's. Unless McCartney woke up, he risked losing his equal status in the partnership.

A month having elapsed since their last hastily convened session, The Beatles broke off from post-production work on the film to finish the album. The first of three new numbers by McCartney recorded on 14th June was I'VE JUST SEEN A FACE, the simplest of descending-sequence guitar songs, made indelible by a melody based on an equally simple game with the first three intervals of its A major scale. Because his Auntie Jin liked it, the tune was shortlisted as 'Auntie Jin's Theme' until McCartney added the love-at-first-sight lyric which, with its tumbling internal rhymes and gasping lack of breathing spaces, complements the music perfectly. Taped in six takes, without frills or second thoughts, the song grabbed Capitol's A&R department so firmly that they pulled it off the American version of *Help!* and turned it into the opening track of the American version of *Rubber Soul*, so conspiring to give the US public the impression that the latter was 'The Beatles' folk-rock album' (see [56]). As with [59] YESTERDAY, there is no doubt that had I'VE JUST SEEN A FACE been ready three months earlier, it would have featured in the film. As it was, it lifted the later stages of the *Help!* album with its quickfire freshness – a pop parallel to the fast-cutting impressionism of contemporary Swinging London movies like Richard Lester's *The Knack*, John Schlesinger's *Darling*, and John Boorman's *Catch Us If You Can*.

[58] I'M DOWN *(Lennon–McCartney)*

McCartney vocal, bass; **Lennon** backing vocal, rhythm guitar,
   organ; **Harrison** backing vocal, lead guitar; **Starr** drums, bongos
Recorded: 14th June 1965, Abbey Road 2.
Producer: George Martin. Engineer: Norman Smith.
UK release: 23rd July 1965 (B single/HELP!)
US release: 19th July 1965 (B single/HELP!)

Made between the light [57] I'VE JUST SEEN A FACE and delicate [59] YESTERDAY, this demented raver illustrates McCartney's vocal and stylistic versatility. I'M DOWN, rated a rock-and-roll classic in the USA, is actually a genre prank pushed home at high energy.[1] A straightforward G major twelve-bar warped into a fourteen-bar layout, it's partly a send-up of the blues and partly a tongue-in-cheek response to Lennon's anguished self-exposure in [56] HELP! (and, as such, a kind of anticipation of [139] YER BLUES). Lennon – who takes a zany Jerry Lee Lewis chorus on a Vox Continental organ – clearly relishes the irony even when it's half directed at himself. Casting about for a new direction after the *Help!* sessions, he and McCartney would briefly toy with the idea of 'comedy numbers' [63] – an impulse perhaps partly suggested by the pseudo-hysterics of I'M DOWN which, while exciting, was conceived mainly as a joke.

---

[1] McCartney saw the song as a vehicle for his Little Richard impersonation (Miles, op. cit., pp. 200-201).

[59] YESTERDAY *(Lennon–McCartney)*

McCartney vocal, acoustic guitar; **Tony Gilbert**, **Sidney Sax**
  violins; **Kenneth Essex** viola; **Francisco Gabarro** cello
Recorded: 14th, 17th June 1965, Abbey Road 2.
Producer: George Martin. Engineer: Norman Smith.
UK release: 6th August 1965 (LP: *Help!*)
US release: 13th September 1966 (A single/ACT NATURALLY)

According to George Martin, McCartney wrote YESTERDAY while staying at the George V hotel, Paris, in January 1964 (i.e., during the writing stage for the *A Hard Day's Night* album).[1] If true, it would mean that this famous piece, which holds the *Guinness Book of Records* title as the most 'covered' song in history, was left off two Beatles albums and withheld until the final stages of a third before being considered good enough to record – on the face of it, not very likely. It is, however, true that McCartney was hesitant about YESTERDAY for several months, playing it to friends and asking them, 'Is this by someone else or did I write it?', unable to believe that it hadn't been around for at least a generation.

His uncertainty stemmed from the circumstances of its composition. Waking one day with the tune running through his head, he stumbled to a piano to work out the chords. In effect, YESTERDAY fell, fully-formed, out of the sky. 'When you're trying to write a song,' he later observed, 'there are certain times when you get the essence, it's all there. It's like an egg being laid – not a crack or flaw in it.'[2] While not the only Beatles song to arrive in this quasi-mediumistic way (see [69], [88], [123]), YESTERDAY remains the uncanniest instance of it in the group's discography. (Not that the legend of its flawlessness is justified, its middle eight being perceptibly less inspired than its verse/chorus.)

McCartney sang YESTERDAY accompanied by his Epiphone Texan guitar on the evening of 14th June, only two hours after he had rounded off the afternoon with the shrieking choruses of [58] I'M DOWN. (Though no modern producer would dream of allowing a singer to risk his larynx on a screamer before taping a delicate ballad, this, insists McCartney, is how he was happy to do it.) A score for string quartet – George Martin's first major arranging contribution to The Beatles' discography – was over-dubbed three days later on the

---

[1] Lewisohn, *Sessions*, p. 59.
[2] Eggs were on McCartney's mind in more ways than one where YESTERDAY was concerned (perhaps because the first thing he did after writing it was have breakfast). In the first few days of its existence, the song was code-named 'Scrambled Eggs' and had a second line to rhyme: 'Oh, my baby, how I love your legs.'

afternoon of 17th June, before the recording of [60b] ACT
NATURALLY.[1] McCartney was sceptical about strings and stipulated
that he didn't want it to end up 'like Mantovani'. Even after Martin had
played him some quartet records, he remained adamant that there
should be no *vibrato*.[2] Aware that modern string-players would find
this unnatural, Martin diverted McCartney by asking him to supervise
the arrangement, as a result of which the latter added the cello phrase in
bar 4 of the middle eight (1:25–1:27) and the violin's held high A in the
final verse.[3] The result has an austere clarity which, despite minor
imperfections,[4] deserves the praise showered on it. Issued as a single in
the USA, it defied American popular distaste for the 'highbrow' by
staying at No. 1 for a month.

With its yearning suspended ninths, rapid harmonic movement, and
irregular phrase-lengths, YESTERDAY has been analysed more closely
than any other Beatles composition.[5] Its significance, so far as the
group was concerned, lay less in the song's musical attributes than in
George Martin's disclosure to them of an hitherto unsuspected world of
classical instrumental colour. Restrained by the demands of touring,
they paused a year before putting this discovery to full use.

---

[1] YESTERDAY sounds in F but was probably played in E with a capo on the first
fret.
[2] McCartney may have feared something similar to the ostentatious strings on
Marianne Faithfull's 1964 UK hit 'As Tears Go By'. He offered YESTERDAY to her –
she was married to his friend John Dunbar – but her company was slow on the
uptake and it became a UK hit for the 'singing bus-conductor' Matt Munro.
[3] McCartney may also have asked for the violin harmony to his voice on the
second middle eight. Yet another (this time inadvertent) contribution was the
descending viola line at the end of the first middle eight, which Martin took from the
singer's embellishment to the repeat.
[4] The cello tends to hurry in the verse/choruses; there is, too, residual voice
leakage on the last two bars of the first middle eight (0:54–0:58).
[5] Eg., Wilfrid Mellers (in *Twilight of the Gods*) and Deryck Cooke in his essay 'The
Lennon–McCartney Songs' (reprinted in *Vindications*, 1980). YESTERDAY is composer
Peter Maxwell Davies's favourite Beatles song 'because it demonstrates the generosity
of spirit in Paul McCartney's melodies and their exemplary, instinctive technical
know-how' (*Independent on Sunday*, 7th June 1992).

[60] IT'S ONLY LOVE *(Lennon–McCartney)*

Lennon double-tracked vocal, acoustic rhythm guitar; **Harrison**
    lead guitar; **McCartney** bass; **Starr** drums, tambourine
Recorded: 15th June 1965, Abbey Road 2.
Producer: George Martin. Engineer: Norman Smith.
UK release: 6th August 1965 (LP: *Help!*)
US release: 6th December 1965 (LP: *Rubber Soul*)

A twee make-weight based on a characteristic descending chromatic
sequence, IT'S ONLY LOVE mildly embarrassed Lennon from the
moment that he wrote it.[1] Probably made with another artist in mind
– perhaps Billy J. Kramer, who'd just had a hit with Bacharach and
David's 'Trains and Boats and Planes'[2] – the song is only slightly
redeemed by its vigorous chorus, while the lyric is the hollowest
Lennon ever perpetrated. His own estimate of it can be heard in his
laughing delivery of the lines 'Just the sight of you makes night-time
bright . . . Very bright'. (The song's working title, which gives an idea
of how seriously its author took it, was 'That's A Nice Hat'.)

The production, with different sounds for each of Lennon's vocal
tracks, displays the group's new drive to experiment in the studio.
Significantly, the same layering of tones applies to Harrison's guitar
tracks, the more distant of which involved feeding its signal through a
Leslie 145 cabinet (presumably the one belonging to the Hammond
organ used on [58] I'M DOWN and on one speculative take of [59]
YESTERDAY). This famous item of pop soundware contained a high-
frequency rotary horn balanced by an up-turned bass speaker pointed
into a revolving drum, the two waveforms producing a swimming
'chorus' effect. The Beach Boys often put their guitars through a Leslie
(e.g., the title track of *Pet Sounds*), while The Beatles at one time or
another used it on almost every sound they recorded, including vocals
[77].

---

[1] McCartney helped him with it, estimating the song as 60–40 to Lennon (Miles,
op. cit., p. 200).
[2] Kramer was certainly looking for a Lennon–McCartney song at the time. When
he and McCartney met after The Beatles' TV appearances at the ABC Theatre,
Blackpool, on 1st August 1965, the latter offered him [59] YESTERDAY. Sick of
recording 'nicey nicey' material, Kramer turned it down. 'Six months later,' he
recalled, glumly, 'everyone was having hits with it.' (Leigh, p. 39.)

[60b] ACT NATURALLY *(Morrison-Russell)*

Starr vocal, drums, sticks; **McCartney** harmony vocal, bass;
  Lennon acoustic rhythm guitar; **Harrison** lead guitar
Recorded: 17th June 1965, Abbey Road 2.
Producer: George Martin. Engineer: Norman Smith.
UK release: 6th August 1965 (LP: *Help!*)
US release: 13th September 1966 (B single/YESTERDAY)

Except for their version of the Liverpool folk-ballad [161b] MAGGIE
MAE made during the 'Get Back' sessions in 1969, this was the last of
The Beatles' twenty-four 'main sequence' non-originals (i.e., omitting
those issued in 1994 on *Live at the BBC*). ACT NATURALLY, a country-
and-western hit for Buck Owens in 1963, is the only song by another
artist in the group's recorded output never to have previously featured
in their act. A late replacement for the awful [U54] IF YOU'VE GOT
TROUBLE, this exceedingly simple number needed a dozen takes to get
right with the band effectively reduced to rehearsing it in the studio. In
the end, it proved a shrewd choice. Recorded a month after the end of
filming for *Help!*, the song sat neatly at the top of Side 2 of the album,
lightening the mood after Lennon's intense [47] TICKET TO RIDE and
complimenting Starr's cinematic persona as the deadpan Joe Ordinary
of the group.

The Beatles' version is spritelier than Owens' and contains a
humorous touch in the naively assertive bass-drum pushed up in the
mix at the end of each middle sixteen. Harrison characteristically sorts
out the guitar part into something neater, but McCartney, providing
the Nashville harmony to Starr's lead, oddly neglects the chuckling
double-time bass-runs which accompany it on the original.

[61] WAIT *(Lennon–McCartney)*

Lennon double-tracked vocal, rhythm guitar; **McCartney** double-
  tracked vocal, bass; **Harrison** guitars; **Starr** drums, maracas,
  tambourine
Recorded: 17th June, 11th November 1965, Abbey Road 2.
Producer: George Martin. Engineer: Norman Smith.
UK release: 30th November 1965 (LP: *Rubber Soul*)
US release: 6th December 1965 (LP: *Rubber Soul*)

The Beatles concluded their recording for *Help!* in an evening session
with this, the first full fifty-fifty Lennon–McCartney collaboration since
[37] BABY'S IN BLACK.[1] In the end WAIT was left off the LP – oddly

---

[1] McCartney recalls the song as entirely his (Miles, op. cit., p. 278).

since, while no masterpiece, it was a stronger track than several that were included. Disinterred five months later during the final session for *Rubber Soul*, it was pepped up with some additional percussion and added to that album's second side.

WAIT shows Lennon and McCartney in transition, consciously casting about for the new direction they knew they'd need in the second half of 1965. Part filler, part experiment, it has a hypothetical quality that renders it difficult to feel strongly about. While more considered than usual, the lyric remains contrived − a sequence of heroic-romantic clichés neither of its writers seem to have believed in. The mordant tone of Lennon's verse, dictated by its descending minor sequence,[1] is interestingly, if unconvincingly, dispelled by the chorus's optimistic shift to the relative major. If the key change here was Lennon's, the harmony's ostentatious rise over an octave is more like McCartney, who probably also contributed the rather insipid middle eight.

As a performance, WAIT goes some way to recouping its losses as a composition. The production may be sparse (Harrison and Lennon alike using the volume-pedal introduced on [49] I NEED YOU and [50] YES IT IS), but the track has undeniable drive and character. Much of this comes from Starr, who clearly enjoys the change of rhythm and mood from verse to chorus, and offers one of those unique 'Ringo fills' which pop drummers recall with such fondness: a curt smack at the closed hi-hat followed by a bubbling triplet roll on a slack-tuned high tom-tom.

[62] RUN FOR YOUR LIFE *(Lennon–McCartney)*

Lennon vocal, acoustic rhythm guitar, lead guitar (?); **McCartney**
   harmony vocal, bass; **Harrison** harmony vocal, lead guitar (?);
   Starr drums, tambourine
Recorded: 12th October 1965, Abbey Road 2.
Producer: George Martin. Engineer: Norman Smith.
UK release: 3rd December 1965 (LP: *Rubber Soul*)
US release: 6th December 1965 (LP: *Rubber Soul*)

Immediately after finishing *Help!*, The Beatles left Britain for a fortnight of concerts in France, Italy, and Spain. They then had a month off before their summer tour of America, notable for a famously inaudible

---

[1] Created by holding the two lower notes in the F sharp minor triad whilst moving the top finger down in Lennon's favourite chromatic steps.

appearance at New York's Shea Stadium as well as meetings with celebrities like Dylan and Presley. During a week off in August at a house in Bel Air, Los Angeles, Lennon and Harrison had their second, and Starr his first, encounter with LSD. (McCartney postponed his initiation for another year.) It was on this occasion that Lennon had the experience recorded in [92] SHE SAID SHE SAID. Back in London the group unwound for a month, writing material for their sixth LP, which they began at Abbey Road on 12th October.

The first song for what was to become *Rubber Soul*, RUN FOR YOUR LIFE constituted an inauspicious start. Stealing his opening lines from an old Presley number ('Baby, Let's Play House'), Lennon produced a lazily sexist lyric unmitigated by any saving irony. (Under the influence of Yoko Ono's feminism, he would later renounce such nastiness, with implicit reference to this song.) Recorded, overdubs and all, during one long afternoon, RUN FOR YOUR LIFE leaves its country-and-western idiom only for the chorus's ii chord[1] ('catch you with another *man*'), grimly threatening the song's addressee with the relative minor before swinging back to the home key via a standard C&W turnaround. The performance is slapdash, Lennon muffing his words and 'popping' the microphone several times by getting too near it. The guitar-work, some of which is badly out of tune, is similarly rough, the piercingly simplistic blues solo suggesting that the player was not Harrison but Lennon himself.

[63] NORWEGIAN WOOD (THIS BIRD HAS FLOWN)
(Lennon–McCartney)

Lennon double-tracked vocal, acoustic rhythm guitar; **McCartney**
   harmony vocal, bass; **Harrison** double-tracked sitar; **Starr**
   tambourine, maracas, finger cymbal
Recorded: 12th, 21st October 1965, Abbey Road 2.
Producer: George Martin. Engineer: Norman Smith.
UK release: 3rd December 1965 (LP: *Rubber Soul*)
US release: 6th December 1965 (LP: *Rubber Soul*)

The day after the second session for NORWEGIAN WOOD, McCartney informed *New Musical Express* that he and Lennon had found a new direction: 'We've written some funny songs – songs with jokes in. We think that comedy numbers are the next thing after protest songs.'[2]

---

[1] E minor in first inversion.
[2] *New Musical Express*, 22nd October 1965. Protest songs – then all the rage – were a particular bugbear with the apolitical Beatles, their pet hate at the time being Barry McGuire's 'Eve Of Destruction'.

Whether this was itself a joke or a genuine reflection of their uncertainty at this transitional point in their development is hard to say. Probably it was both. What is beyond doubt is that *Rubber Soul* – the hinge on which the two phases of The Beatles' stylistic development swing – includes several songs written in the form of comic short stories. One, [64] DRIVE MY CAR, even has a punchline.

Clearly Lennon and McCartney were running out of variations on simple romance and knew they had to branch out or dry up. Probably they privately agreed with their publisher Dick James that most of their lyrics didn't 'go anywhere' or 'tell a story'. Certainly they were aware that Bob Dylan, with his tumultuously original singles 'Subterranean Homesick Blues' and 'Like A Rolling Stone', had rolled back the horizons of the pop lyric in a way they must acknowledge and somehow outdo. Indeed several of their English rivals had stolen a march on them by following Dylan's lead. The Rolling Stones with 'Satisfaction', The Kinks' 'See My Friend', The Animals' 'We Gotta Get Out Of This Place', The Who's imminent 'My Generation' – all cut deeper than the standard pop song, offering social and sexual observations that made The Beatles' lyrics seem tame. On the purely technical front, the UK chart during summer 1965 had been unusually rich in mould-breaking singles like The Who's 'Anyway Anyhow Anywhere', The Yardbirds' 'For Your Love', and Unit 4 Plus 2's 'Concrete and Clay'. Even the ostensibly conservative Beach Boys had abandoned surf pop for the subtler sound-world of their dreamy idyll 'California Girls' and the commercially unsuccessful 'The Little Girl I Once Knew' with its novel sonorities and bold 'radio silence' tacets. If The Beatles didn't find a new road soon, they risked appearing *passé* (apart from being boring, pop's only recognised deadly sin).

Begun by Lennon while on a skiing holiday in St Moritz, Switzerland, during January–February 1965, NORWEGIAN WOOD is the first Beatle song in which the lyric is more important than the music. In the spirit of the teasing narratives in Dylan's recent albums, with their enigmatic women and hints of menace, it was hailed as a breakthrough – and, despite the fact that its admired elusiveness was mostly a product of bluff and evasion, found its way into a book of modern verse. For his part, Lennon was uneasy about trespassing on Dylan's territory[1] and when the latter, on his next album *Blonde On Blonde*, produced an

---

[1] According to the ex-Animals' organist Alan Price, Lennon told him before the song was recorded that the other Beatles were 'taking the mickey out of him' for copying Dylan in it. Lennon had at least given up wearing a peaked 'Dylan cap' by then, this job having been assumed by Donovan.

inscrutable parody of NORWEGIAN WOOD called '4th Time Around', the head Beatle was, as he later admitted, 'paranoid': what did that title mean? NORWEGIAN WOOD, I'M A LOSER, YOU'VE GOT TO HIDE YOUR LOVE AWAY, and . . . BABY'S IN BLACK? Or was it the cap?[1] And what was Dylan driving at in those closing lines: 'I never asked for your crutch/Now don't ask for mine' . . .? In the end, the matter was settled amicably when the two met – for the fifth time[2] – in London in April 1966. In truth, Dylan got on reasonably well with Lennon, with whom he had a fair amount in common.[3] Towards McCartney, on the other hand, he was cooler, despising songs like [59] YESTERDAY and [71] MICHELLE as sell-outs to soft pop, unaware that Lennon co-wrote the latter and that McCartney added more than a little to NORWEGIAN WOOD.

Precisely how much McCartney wrote of NORWEGIAN WOOD remains in dispute. Talking to *Playboy* in 1980, Lennon claimed it as 'my song completely'. Some years later, McCartney stated that Lennon at first had only the melody and lyric of the opening line and that he had helped with extending the lyric, contributing the idea that the house should burn down, a dramatic insight into the lyric's casually obscure last three lines.[4] If so, he may also have supplied the title Lennon settled on (having begun with 'This Bird Has Flown').[5] Debatable in terms of its lyric, the musical authorship of NORWEGIAN WOOD is equally vexed. There's no doubt that Lennon wrote the modally-inflected E major tune of the verse/chorus. The lighter E minor middle eight, however, sounds more like McCartney (whose vocal line here is the melody to Lennon's harmony); in fact, when interviewed by *Rolling Stone* in 1970, Lennon attested that this section *was* McCartney's, which makes NORWEGIAN WOOD close to a fifty-fifty collaboration.[6]

Supposedly about an affair Lennon was having with a journalist, the song holds the attention partly through its lyric obliqueness and partly

[1] See previous note.

[2] The previous occasions were: 28th August 1964 at the Hotel Delmonico, New York [38]; after one of Dylan's London gigs in May 1965; 13th and 16th August 1965 at the Warwick Hotel, New York.

[3] Up to a point. See their edgy conversation taped in London in May 1966 (*Mojo*, November 1993).

[4] *Musician* (February 1985); Miles, op. cit., p. 270. For a different explanation, see Shotton, p. 122.

[5] Aside from a reference to the Sixties fashion for Scandinavian pine interiors, Lennon admitted to having no idea why NORWEGIAN WOOD was so-called.

[6] McCartney claims this section in Miles, op. cit., p. 270.

through its unusual instrumental colour, provided by Harrison's doubling of the main descending line on sitar. The Beatles had rented a house on Mulholland Drive in Los Angeles during their 1965 American tour, and it was there, on 24th August, that they met two of The Byrds, Roger McGuinn and David Crosby. During a day spent tripping on LSD, an experience which later found its way into [92] SHE SAID SHE SAID, Lennon and Harrison sat with McGuinn and Crosby playing 12-strings and discussing the music of the Indian sitar-player Ravi Shankar. Harrison had been interested in this instrument since he'd heard it used to spice up the soundtrack of *Help!*,[1] but it was new to Lennon who, sensitised by the 'acid', became fascinated by the exotic *raga* phrases Crosby played to him. Conceivably the sustained E major of his part of NORWEGIAN WOOD represents his version of the drone common to all Indian classical music, while his descending melody may have been a gesture at reproducing the Oriental intervals to which he had been introduced seven weeks earlier by The Byrds.[2]

The sitar posed limiting problems, its sharp waveforms making the VU meter needles leap into the red without leaving much sonority behind. Nor were The Beatles sure of the arrangement, going through four versions in two sessions, including a complete remake.[3] The

---

[1] Giorgio Gomelsky, then manager of The Yardbirds, claims Jimmy Page introduced Harrison to the sitar, having bought one from an Indian musician hired to play on The Yardbirds' 'Heart Full Of Soul' around mid-March/mid-April 1965. (The riff in question ended up performed on guitar by Jeff Beck.)

[2] According to artist Barry Fantoni, The Beatles got their immediate idea for using pseudo-Indian drones from The Kinks' 'See My Friend', released two months before they began work on *Rubber Soul*. Instead of a tambura, Ray Davies plucked the drone chord (E flat major) on his Framus 12-string before standing it near the amp so that feedback sustained it. This sound was then heavily compressed to create a pulsing effect. Pete Townshend identifies this as 'the first reasonable use of the drone' in pop, preferring it to anything comparable by The Beatles and admitting to adapting it – on The Who's *My Generation* album – in his similarly melancholy 'The Good's Gone' (and perhaps also in 'Out In The Street'). The Beatles would certainly have heard 'See My Friend' before they left for their August 1965 American tour and no doubt stole from it, but it would be wrong to conclude that it was the sole cause of their subsequent interest in pseudo-Indian drones. In the first place, a drone is implicit in [47] TICKET TO RIDE, which may well have influenced 'See My Friend'. In the second place, Harrison had started to listen to the music of Ravi Shankar some time before 'See My Friend' was released.

[3] The first version, issued on *Anthology 2*, is badly out of tune, a problem created by the sympathetic strings of the sitar. It includes extra sitar phrases on the middle eight, wisely omitted for the remake, and is (approximately) in D major, a whole tone lower than the version issued on *Rubber Soul*. Since the NORWEGIAN WOOD melody derives from the guitar D chord, the official 1965 release must have been either transposed (unlikely), played with capoed guitars and bass, or (likeliest) varispeeded.

result, from their point of view, was worth the effort. NORWEGIAN WOOD became one of the most popular tracks on *Rubber Soul* and a favourite among folk musicians in Britain and America.

[64] DRIVE MY CAR *(Lennon–McCartney)*

McCartney vocal, piano, lead guitar; **Lennon** vocal; **Harrison** harmony vocal, bass; **Starr** drums, cowbell, tambourine
Recorded: 13th October 1965, Abbey Road 2.
Producer: George Martin. Engineer: Norman Smith.
UK release: 3rd December 1965 (LP: *Rubber Soul*)
US release: 20th June 1966 (LP: *'Yesterday'* . . . *and Today*)

The second of *Rubber Soul*'s 'comedy songs' [63], DRIVE MY CAR started life as a McCartney song about 'a bitch' with a chorus that began 'You can buy me diamond rings'. Since The Beatles had used this cliché twice before ([23], [45]), he and Lennon thought again and, following a pause in which they found themselves uncertain as to how to continue (the nearest they came, recalls McCartney, to a 'dry' writing session),[1] they recast the lyric as a facetious vignette about a 'wannabe' star complete with a jokey pay-off line and an erotic *double-entendre* in the title.

DRIVE MY CAR was taped in an unusually long evening session, The Beatles' first to extend past midnight. McCartney came in with an arrangement in his mind but Harrison had been listening to Otis Redding's 'Respect' (then a minor American hit on the Volt label) and, perceiving the family resemblance between the two numbers, suggested a similar riffing line doubled on bass and low guitar.[2] Having taken much of the session to work it out, he and McCartney, together with Starr on drums, laid it down as the rhythm track,[3] the rest, including the vocals, being overdubbed later. With its resonantly humming foundation, bolstered by piano on the choruses, DRIVE MY CAR has more 'bottom' than any previous Beatles recording, an effect presumably inspired by the bass-heavy sound generated in Redding's Memphis studio. 'Black', too, is its hollered two-part refrain and raunchy tug-of-war between D major and B minor, snapping to the rhythm more tightly than anything The Beatles had done since [44] SHE'S A WOMAN.

---

[1] Miles, op. cit., p. 269.
[2] Harrison's knowledge of soul music was comprehensive. Then a long way ahead of hip taste in Britain in being a fan of Curtis Mayfield and the Impressions, he was effectively The Beatles' scout on new records from America, much as Dave Davies was for The Kinks.
[3] Harrison took over on bass for this (*The Beatles Anthology*, p. 194).

With its parallel-movement three-part chorus, interlocking drum part, and fiercely angular slide guitar solo[1] (very difficult and possibly varispeeded), DRIVE MY CAR is among the group's most closely arranged records and remains one of the most effective starting tracks to any of their albums.[2]

[65] DAY TRIPPER *(Lennon–McCartney)*

> **Lennon** double-tracked vocal, rhythm/lead guitar; **McCartney** double-tracked vocal, bass; **Harrison** lead guitar; **Starr** drums, tambourine
> Recorded: 16th October 1965, Abbey Road 2.
> Producer: George Martin. Engineer: Norman Smith.
> UK release: 3rd December 1965 (A single/WE CAN WORK IT OUT)
> US release: 6th December 1965 (A single/WE CAN WORK IT OUT)

Returning to the studio on Saturday after a day off, The Beatles maintained the bluesy style of [64] DRIVE MY CAR with a song Lennon and McCartney later admitted had been 'forced' by the need for a new single. Conceivably they wrote DAY TRIPPER on Friday after consulting a rough mix of DRIVE MY CAR, which would explain why Thursday's session overran.[3] Entirely dependent on its riff – catchier if far less subtle than the line used on DRIVE MY CAR – DAY TRIPPER repaid what its companion track had stolen from Otis Redding. (Tickled by what he heard, Redding cut his own, madly up-tempo, version of DAY TRIPPER for Stax in 1967.)[4]

Though Lennon had yet to launch himself into his fullscale LSD period, he evidently felt sufficiently versed in the 'counterculture' associated with the drug to poke fun at those who took it without changing their outlook. The lyric of DAY TRIPPER, he later explained, was an attack on 'weekend hippies' – those who donned floral shirts and headbands to listen to 'acid rock' between 9-to-5 office-jobs.

---

[1] Played by McCartney on the Epiphone Casino he first used on the coda of [47] TICKET TO RIDE.

[2] The American version of *Rubber Soul* omitted DRIVE MY CAR and three other tracks, thereby giving a misleading impression that The Beatles had gone for a 'soft' sound in order to differentiate themselves from the harshness of Dylan and those imitating him (see [63]).

[3] They were still sorting the song out during the Saturday session. Lennon's half-sister Julia Baird told Spencer Leigh: 'It seemed like lots of bits and pieces were being put together and I can't understand how they got the final version out of what I heard.' (*Speaking Words of Wisdom*, p. 43.)

[4] Lennon may have arrived at the DAY TRIPPER riff in an attempt to better The Rolling Stones' 'Satisfaction', which Otis Redding also covered in 1966.

While something of the sort may have been in Lennon's mind in October 1965, it must be said that few outside a select circle in America had taken LSD by then, that the word 'hippie' was not coined until 1966, and that 'acid rock' arrived a full year later.[1] (The line recorded as 'she's a big teaser' was originally written as 'she's a prick teaser'.) Either way it isn't very interesting, despite sustaining the strain of ironic narrative introduced in the group's previous two recordings.

Recorded with peculiarly wide stereo separation, DAY TRIPPER starts as a twelve-bar in E which makes a feint at turning into a twelve-bar in the relative minor (i.e., the chorus) before doubling back to the expected B – another joke from a group which had clearly decided that wit was to be their new gimmick. Reaching B by this erratic route the second time round, the song hangs onto it in a twelve-bar pedal-point crescendo over which Lennon solos while Harrison climbs a lengthy scale ending triumphantly in the home key. (Another in-joke occurs in the chorus bars of Starr's drum-part, played with fours on the bass-drum in the style of Al Jackson of The MGs, the Stax house-band.) Musically uninspired by The Beatles' standards and marred by a bad punch-in edit on the vocal track (1:50), DAY TRIPPER was nevertheless scheduled as their new single until the recording of [68] WE CAN WORK IT OUT a few days later. Arguments over which was to be given preference (Lennon wanted DAY TRIPPER) led to the single being marketed as the first 'double A-side'. Airplay and point-of-sale requests soon proved WE CAN WORK IT OUT to be more popular.

[66] IF I NEEDED SOMEONE (Harrison)

Harrison double-tracked vocal, lead guitar; **Lennon** harmony
vocal, rhythm guitar; **McCartney** harmony vocal, bass; **Starr**
drums, tambourine; **George Martin** harmonium
Recorded: 16th, 18th October 1965, Abbey Road 2.
Producer: George Martin. Engineer: Norman Smith.
UK release: 3rd December 1965 (LP: *Rubber Soul*)
US release: 20th June 1966 (LP: *'Yesterday'* . . . *and Today*)

More insider references are concealed in this, Harrison's most successful song to date, the guitar figure being derived from The Byrds' 'The Bells of Rhymney' (a fact conveyed by Beatles publicist Derek Taylor to Roger McGuinn, who had already guessed it). In fact, IF I NEEDED

---

[1] McCartney recalls the song as being about 'a girl who thought she was it', mere egoism being unenlightened compared to the Universal Love ideal of the acid-inspired counterculture – 'whereas we saw ourselves as full-time trippers, fully committed drivers' (Miles, op. cit., p. 209).

SOMEONE was influenced far more by its author's new interest in Indian classical music, being, like Lennon's [63] NORWEGIAN WOOD, founded on a drone – a tonic A which persists beneath the change to G major on the chorus line. In this context, the guitar figure acts as a kind of high-register tambura, which may have been how The Byrds conceived it. Set against this pedal-point, Harrison's syncopated Mixolydian tune gives the verse/chorus a sense of perpetual ascent which, together with the bell-like pealing of his capoed Rickenbacker 12-string and an angelic choir in three-part block harmony, creates a striking, if rather solemn, effect, aptly reinforced by an icy lyric. Sadly, the syncopation's persistence into the middle eight frustrates any intended contrast and the song quickly gets monotonous (an effect made worse by a superfluous verse/chorus between the solo and second middle eight). Like so many Harrison songs, IF I NEEDED SOMEONE has an obstinate quality which, combined with his preference for aloof sentiments and dour progressions, renders it gauche beside McCartney's urbanity and anaemic next to the boldness of Lennon.

[67] IN MY LIFE *(Lennon–McCartney)*

> **Lennon** double-tracked vocal, rhythm guitar; **McCartney** harmony vocal, bass, electric piano (?); **Harrison** harmony vocal, lead guitar; **Starr** drums, tambourine, bells (?); **George Martin** electric piano
> Recorded: 18th, 22nd October 1965, Abbey Road 2.
> Producer: George Martin. Engineer: Norman Smith.
> UK release: 3rd December 1965 (LP: *Rubber Soul*)
> US release: 6th December 1965 (LP: *Rubber Soul*)

During the planning stage of *Rubber Soul*, Lennon and McCartney had broached the idea of writing something about Liverpool. Around the same time, the eminent journalist Kenneth Allsop, whom Lennon admired, challenged him as to why his songs didn't employ the acerbic word-play of his books *In His Own Write* and *A Spaniard In The Works*. Pursuing both leads, Lennon began a haphazard lyric about a bus-ride from his childhood home in Menlove Avenue into Liverpool's town centre, listing every landmark and neighbourhood *en route* (including Penny Lane).[1] When this became unwieldy, he struggled vainly to

---

[1] In The Beatles' pre-Dylan period, their songs usually started from a lyric phrase which would in turn suggest the main musical idea. The remaining words would be ad-libbed along with the developing melody, and the full lyric filled in last. (An exception to this in McCartney's case was [15], where the lyric came first, followed by the tune, and finally the harmony.) According to Pete Shotton (p. 121), the lyrics of Lennon's post-Dylan songs almost always preceded the music. He would put the

condense the material.[1] Finally giving up the effort to be all-inclusive, he sat back from what he'd been doing – and the lyric of IN MY LIFE took shape. A meditation on his past and the mixed pleasures of recollecting it, IN MY LIFE strikes a deeper note than previous Beatles lyrics, embracing thoughts of death without stylising them (as, for example, in [50] YES IT IS). Its calm fatalism gives *Rubber Soul* a weight it might otherwise have lacked, notwithstanding the aura of drug-induced mellowness that makes the album seem more penetrating than its predecessors.

Lennon was proud of this lyric, regarding it as his first serious piece and claiming credit also for the music, except for the verse harmony and the middle eight, which he conceded to McCartney. His partner, on the other hand, recalled taking the words to a keyboard (the latter's Mellotron) and setting them to music from start to finish. While it's hard to agree with McCartney's notion that the tune is 'Miracles inspired', its angular verticality, spanning an octave in typically wide – and difficult – leaps, certainly shows more of his touch than Lennon's, despite fitting the latter's voice snugly.[2] (As for a middle eight, there isn't one, the song alternating between its verse and an extended chorus.)

Recorded – with a verse in the middle left open for an unspecified fill – in the same afternoon as [66] IF I NEEDED SOMEONE, IN MY LIFE was finished four days later when George Martin came in early to dub on a keyboard solo. (He presumably did this so that the group would hear the finished effect, rather than reject it before seeing what he had in mind.) Trying it on organ first, he switched to electric piano, recording his part at half-speed to give it a wiry harpsichord-like tone on playback. A clever baroque pastiche, complete with authentic shakes, it was, after [59] YESTERDAY, his second direct contribution to a Beatles track, becoming one of the most admired instrumental passages on *Rubber Soul*. Whether its dancing lightness and concluding disappearance through the trapdoor of a witty *glissando* really suit the song's mood of sighing introspection is another question.

---

words up on a piano and start poking about on it for a sequence or melody.
[1] Interviewed by *New Musical Express* on 12th November, McCartney spoke of this lyric as a joint effort. It was, he said, 'a number about the places in Liverpool where we were born . . . Places like Penny Lane and the Dockers' Umbrella [the Liverpool Overhead Railway, now demolished] have a nice sound, but when we strung them together in a composition they sounded contrived, so we gave up.'
[2] On the other hand, the chromatic descent, via the minor subdominant, in the second half of the verse suggests Lennon. Perhaps McCartney did the first half of the verse, Lennon the second?

[68] WE CAN WORK IT OUT *(Lennon–McCartney)*

McCartney double-tracked vocal, bass; **Lennon** harmony vocal,
  acoustic rhythm guitar, harmonium; **Harrison** harmony vocal (?);
  Starr drums, tambourine[1]
Recorded: 20th, 29th October 1965, Abbey Road 2.
Producer: George Martin. Engineer: Norman Smith.
UK release: 3rd December 1965 (A single/DAY TRIPPER)
US release: 6th December 1965 (A single/DAY TRIPPER)

The result of by far the largest amount of studio-time devoted to a
Beatles track thus far (eleven hours), WE CAN WORK IT OUT is a classic
instance of Lennon and McCartney collaborating as equals. McCartney
wrote the words and music to the eight-bar verse/chorus, Lennon the
words and music to the sixteen-bar middle. Based on McCartney's
often fractious relationship with Jane Asher,[2] the song unburdens itself
with vivid urgency. The usual critical line, derived from Lennon's
remark to this effect to *Playboy* in 1980, is that his section is impatiently
realistic beside the cajoling optimism of McCartney's part. This,
though, misreads the song, which is not only tersely forthright
throughout, but tough in passages which Lennon had no hand in.
Something of a breakthrough for McCartney, his part of the lyric for
WE CAN WORK IT OUT displays a dramatic instinct which would soon
begin to dominate his work.

  Melodically, McCartney's D major verse is unusually full of
repetitions, implying that (as in the case of [137] and [164]), it was
written under the pressure of emotional necessity rather than out of
purely formal inspiration. With its tense suspensions and irregular
phrase-lengths, it shows him at his most Lennonish, directly expressing
the forcefulness of his lyric. Lennon's middle eight – one of his
cleverest – shifts focus from McCartney's concrete reality to a
philosophical perspective in B minor, illustrating this with a churchy
suspension and a burlesque waltz that prefigures the solemn dance of
Henry the Horse in [101] BEING FOR THE BENEFIT OF MR KITE. This

---

[1] The tambourine on WE CAN WORK IT OUT was the most effective and
influential use The Beatles ever made of the instrument (which, as a result, turned up
on every other 'folk-rock' record made around this time). While some sources say
Harrison played it, it is here credited to Starr on the grounds of probability.
[2] Then still an unreconstructed Northern male chauvinist, McCartney expected
Asher to remain at his domestic beck and call. She, an educated middle-class
southern girl, wished instead to pursue her acting career and refused to be dissuaded
from going on tour with the Old Vic. Other social and cultural differences emerged
as their relationship developed, chiefly revolving around Asher's need for privacy as
against McCartney's frank enjoyment of public recognition (and female adulation).

was probably meant to suggest tiresome struggle, but doubles as an ironic image of the *karmic* roundabout of heedless egoism, a concept with which Lennon would have been familiar from exchanges with Harrison.[1] These passages are so suited to his Salvation Army harmonium that it's hard to imagine them not being composed on it.[2] The swell-pedal crescendos he adds to the verses are, on the other hand, textural washes added in the studio – the first of their kind on a Beatles record and signposts to the enriched sound-palette of *Revolver*.

Produced with restraint despite the twelve hours spent on it, WE CAN WORK IT OUT was an understandable favourite of its authors, who met more closely in a single song only in their masterpiece [96] A DAY IN THE LIFE. It was an inevitable No. 1 on both sides of the Atlantic, becoming The Beatles' fastest-selling single since [23] CAN'T BUY ME LOVE, their previous McCartney-led A-side in Britain. Despite his last-ditch attempt at promoting [65] DAY TRIPPER to the A-side, Lennon must have sensed that his era of dominance over the band's output, begun with [24] YOU CAN'T DO THAT, was over. From now on, his partner would be in the ascendant not only as a songwriter, but also as instrumentalist, arranger, producer, and *de facto* musical director of The Beatles.

[69] NOWHERE MAN *(Lennon–McCartney)*

Lennon double-tracked vocal, acoustic rhythm guitar; **McCartney** harmony vocal, bass; **Harrison** harmony vocal, lead guitar; **Starr** drums
Recorded: 21st–22nd October 1965, Abbey Road 2.
Producer: George Martin. Engineer: Norman Smith.
UK release: 3rd December 1965 (LP: *Rubber Soul*)
US release: 21st February 1966 (A single/WHAT GOES ON)

The third of Lennon's creative confessions of personal inadequacy (see [38], [56]), NOWHERE MAN is both an observation about a very different type of person and a reflection of himself in his 'fat Elvis'

---

[1] Harrison suggested this passage (Miles, op. cit., p. 210). *Karma* is the law of cause and effect held by Hindu religious philosophers to govern the processes of reincarnation. (Sin leads to bad *karma* and rebirth, virtue to good *karma* and spiritual release.) Local dignitaries in the Bahamas presented The Beatles with various Indian scriptures while the group were filming *Help!* there in February 1965. Harrison became interested and was already studying them when he and Lennon were introduced to Hindustani classical music by The Byrds in Los Angeles in August (see [63]).

[2] During the early run-throughs, either Lennon or McCartney fingerpicked in double-time through this section.

period – cut off from reality by the need to play to a public image determined by Brian Epstein, lost in the many-roomed seclusion of his Weybridge mansion, out of love with his wife, and steadily dissolving the boundaries of his identity with a sapping tide of drugs. The weary weight of this dirge-like song all too effectively transfers itself to the listener. Unusually regular for Lennon, its harmony-laden melody sags so graphically that it's a relief to reach the glistening, treble-bright solo so early (after the first middle eight). Played in unison by Lennon and Harrison on their Sonic Blue Fender Stratocasters (see [55], note), this passage, with its peak on a luminous pendant harmonic, is the high point of the record. The song thereafter diminishes in interest, dying of a superfluous third dose of its pleading middle eight.

Like [59] YESTERDAY, NOWHERE MAN was mediumistically 'received' at dawn after a night spent trying to write something for the forthcoming album.[1] As with the lyric of [67] IN MY LIFE, Lennon found that giving up the struggle produced the goods: as soon as his conscious mind let go, the song 'came through' *(sic)*. But where from? If YESTERDAY had seemed sufficiently ready-formed to McCartney for him to wonder whether he hadn't subconsciously pilfered it, NOWHERE MAN, with its sequential repetitions and sleepy predictability of harmonic movement, is equally untypical of Lennon. (The only characteristic touch occurs in the last three bars of the middle eight, where he seems to have got bored and reversed the phrasing against the beat.) Decorated with deep-pile harmonies during the two days of its recording, the track is memorable mostly for the luxury of its production, its massed vocals glowing against a tapestry of saturated guitar-tone while McCartney's new Rickenbacker 4001S bass[2]

---

[1] Lennon described his favourite experiences in songwriting in terms of being passively 'in tune' with 'the music of the spheres': 'My joy is when you're like possessed, like a medium, you know.' (Interview with Andy Peebles for the BBC, 6th December 1980.)

[2] This guitar, the first left-hand model, was offered to McCartney in New York by Rickenbacker's boss F. C. Hall in February 1964. Used to his lightweight Hofner, he declined it – but, after a year of experimenting with new sounds in the studio, was glad to accept it in Los Angeles in August 1965. He used the Rickenbacker only sparingly during the November sessions for *Rubber Soul* – e.g., the tracked 'fuzz bass' on [73] THINK FOR YOURSELF – but, from [80] PAPERBACK WRITER, he favoured it over the Hofner, which he reserved for live work. With its heavier sound, fuller treble tone, and more reliable upper-neck tuning, the Rickenbacker was ideally suited to the high counter-melody bass lines he developed for *Revolver* and *Sgt. Pepper*, and remained his studio bass for the rest of The Beatles' career. In 1967, McCartney painted the guitar psychedelic for the *Magical Mystery Tour* film, stripping

weaves an ornate foundation. (Held back from *Rubber Soul* in America
and released on '*Yesterday*' . . . *and Today*, NOWHERE MAN was issued as
a single in the USA — coupled with [72] WHAT GOES ON — where it
struggled to No. 3.)

[70] I'M LOOKING THROUGH YOU (*Lennon–McCartney*)

McCartney double-tracked vocal, acoustic rhythm guitar, bass, lead
  guitar; **Lennon** harmony vocal, acoustic rhythm guitar; **Harrison**
  guitar (?); **Starr** drums, tambourine, Hammond organ
Recorded: 24th October, 6th, 10th–11th November 1965, Abbey
  Road 2.
Producer: George Martin. Engineer: Norman Smith.
UK release: 3rd December 1965 (LP: *Rubber Soul*)
US release: 6th December 1965 (LP: *Rubber Soul*)

Like [68] WE CAN WORK IT OUT, I'M LOOKING THROUGH YOU
records a hiatus in McCartney's affair with Jane Asher — this time
serious enough to have made him insist on three separate attempts at
getting the recording right.[1] A neat construction in the rare key of A
flat major,[2] the song, which shows signs of having started as an
exercise in the manner of Dylan, uses its changes to underline
ambiguities and questions in the lyric. Even the introductory acoustic
guitar, probably played by McCartney, enters in waltz-time before
slipping, deceptively, into 4/4. To judge by the style of the lead guitar,
McCartney may also have played this, making it possible that Harrison
doesn't appear on the track at all (as may also be the case on WE CAN
WORK IT OUT).[3] With Starr stabbing at a Vox Continental organ,

---

it back to its original maplewood in 1969. (See [125], note.)
[1] The first version in G major (nine hours on 24th October) was slower and
tougher, using a rhythm track of claves, maracas, and drums. Instead of the middle
eight, which did not then exist, the group used two instrumental passages in blues
form, with lead guitar in blues style (*Anthology 2*). The second version (six hours on
the evening of 6th November) adopted an up-tempo country-and-western approach.
The third attempt (eight hours on 11th November) was the version selected for the
album.
[2] Since the song was originally in G major, the final key must have come about
either by the use of a capo or (more probably in this instance) by varispeeding.
[3] According to engineer Norman Smith, the perfectionist McCartney had begun
to insist on Harrison playing predetermined solos. If the latter failed to get them
precisely right, he would play them himself, a luxury afforded by four-track
recording procedures in which solos and other overdubs could be added on spare
tracks. Though infuriated by this, Harrison kept quiet about it during these sessions
(which were also, observes Smith, characterised by tension between Lennon and

McCartney yells the choruses indignantly at the top of his chest register, imparting a recurring kick to a thoughtful minor recording.[1]

[71] MICHELLE *(Lennon–McCartney)*

> **McCartney** vocal, acoustic guitars, lead guitar, bass, drums (?);
> **Lennon** backing vocal (?); **Harrison** backing vocal (?); **Starr** drums (?)
> Recorded: 3rd November 1965, Abbey Road 2.
> Producer: George Martin. Engineer: Norman Smith.
> UK release: 3rd December 1965 (LP: *Rubber Soul*)
> US release: 6th December 1965 (LP: *Rubber Soul*)

In line with the 'comedy song' strategy mooted around this time (see [63]), McCartney dug up a wordless six-bar fragment of a Gallic-tinged tune which he had occasionally busked in fake French to attract women while hanging out with Lennon at the Liverpool Institute during 1959.[2] Short of new songs for *Rubber Soul*, he played it on request to Lennon, who, by stealing a line from Nina Simone's 'I Put A Spell On You' (a minor UK hit in August 1965) took it into its F minor middle section with a passionate outburst of triplets ('I love you, I love you, I love you'). They then collaborated on the rest, calming the melody over a suspension, and returning it to F major via a chromatic descent.[3] Recruiting the teacher wife of Lennon's school friend Ivan Vaughan to provide a line of authentic French[4], they finished the lyric and took the song into the studio.

MICHELLE was made in nine hours and seems to have been played mostly, if not entirely, by McCartney using overdubs. Featuring a

McCartney).
[1] McCartney recalls the song as being sparked by his disillusionment over Jane Asher's single-minded focus on her theatre career at the Bristol Old Vic—a feeling of irritation with her discharged by writing about it (Miles, op. cit., p. 276).
[2] He recalled it as finger-picked progression based on Chet Atkins' 'Hambone' (Miles, op. cit., p. 273).
[3] With its one-note melody, this passage suggests Lennon's hand, and McCartney appears to have had trouble deciding on a bass part to accompany it. Speaking to Mark Lewisohn in 1987 about the bass line to MICHELLE (which he dubbed on last), McCartney described it as 'a kind of Bizet thing'. He must have meant the final four bars of this middle section (extracted for the intro), in which the guitars' chromatic descent from F to C recalls 'L'amour est un oiseau rebelle' from *Carmen*. (The reference is to his see-sawing tonic-dominant-octave figure as a version of Bizet's *habañera* bass line.)
[4] McCartney later 'sent a cheque' round to Jan Vaughan as 'virtually a co-writer' (Miles, op. cit., p. 274).

subtle ritard through the final chorus and fade-out, the recording would constitute the first McCartney solo track if it weren't for Lennon and Harrison's tricky two-part backing vocals (if they are, indeed, Lennon and Harrison, and not McCartney again). Harmonically one of the Beatles' richest songs, MICHELLE was a favourite among folk guitarists. Yet, despite its refinement, it fails to escape its ironic quotation-marks, remaining a tongue-in-cheek genre exercise. (A trace of the original joke survives in the lines 'I want you, I want you, I want you/I think you know by now'.) Though never as popular as [59] YESTERDAY, MICHELLE was mooted as a Beatles single until a jealous Lennon quashed the idea (see [68]). It was left to The Overlanders to take the song to the UK No. 1 spot for three weeks in February 1966.

[72] WHAT GOES ON *(Lennon–McCartney–Starkey)*

Starr vocal, drums; **Lennon** harmony vocal, rhythm guitar;
  McCartney harmony vocal, bass; **Harrison** lead guitar
Recorded: 4th November 1965, Abbey Road 2.
Producer: George Martin. Engineer: Norman Smith.
UK release: 3rd December 1965 (LP: *Rubber Soul*)
US release: 21st February 1966 (B single/NOWHERE MAN)

Starr's feature on *Rubber Soul*, WHAT GOES ON has the same sloppy country-and-western ambience as [60b] ACT NATURALLY. A primitive early number by Lennon – of which an earlier version was nearly recorded at the [10] FROM ME TO YOU session on 5th March 1963 – it was resurrected in late 1965 with the addition of what Lennon later described as a middle eight by McCartney. There is, though, no middle eight in WHAT GOES ON; only a protracted twenty-bar chorus and a somewhat snappier fourteen-bar verse. If McCartney wrote the latter, as it seems he did, the song amounts to a fifty-fifty collaboration. Starr, though, seems to have contributed to the lyric (notable for its pseudò-Dylanesque 'tides of time').

Falling behind schedule, The Beatles were now forced to record into the early hours. WHAT GOES ON was accordingly knocked off in a session scheduled between 11pm and 2.30am (most of which was devoted to an unreleased instrumental track logged as [U73] 12-BAR ORIGINAL). Starr sings dolefully, Harrison trots out his Chet Atkins clichés, and another two minutes and forty-five seconds are filled.

[U73] **12-BAR ORIGINAL** *(Lennon–McCartney–Harrison–Starkey)*

Harrison lead guitar; **Lennon** lead guitar; **McCartney** bass; **Starr**
drums; **George Martin** harmonium
Recorded: 4th November 1965, Abbey Road 2.
Producer: George Martin. Engineer: Norman Smith.
UK release: 18th March 1996 (CD: *Anthology 2*)
US release: 18th March 1996 (CD: *Anthology 2*)

Recorded in the early hours immediately after [72] WHAT GOES ON,
this unreleased instrumental, while musically a mess, is conceptually
significant in that it appears to have been intended – at least at the time
it was recorded – for inclusion on *Rubber Soul* (presumably as a fade-out
final track).[1] This confirms how far The Beatles saw the album in
terms of its influences from soul music (see [74]), for this track is a loose
but unmistakable copy of Booker T and The MGs' 1962 cult hit
'Green Onions'.

In the version of 12-BAR INSTRUMENTAL presented on *Anthology 2*,
Harrison (on the right channel) leads off, George Martin joining with
Hammond-style trills played on Lennon's harmonium.[2] Starr switches
to ride cymbal on the third chorus while Harrison plays a mutation of
the 'Green Onions' riff, after which he and Lennon exchange very
provisional solos, Harrison toying uncertainly with his volume-pedal.
On the sixth chorus (2:09–2:16), Harrison – presumably playing either
his Stratocaster or McCartney's Fender Esquire – busks a few bars in
straight Steve Cropper style.

The sketchy nature of the surviving tape suggests that, unsure of
being able to fill fourteen tracks for *Rubber Soul* by the following
Thursday, The Beatles were here trying out a filler in case they should
find themselves one track short at the last minute.

---

[1] The last week of recording for *Rubber Soul* was unusually rushed even for The
Beatles, with five tracks – [73] THINK FOR YOURSELF, [74] THE WORD, the re-
remake of [70] I'M LOOKING THROUGH YOU, [75] YOU WON'T SEE ME, and [76]
GIRL – being done in four days amid a hectic schedule of mono and stereo mixing,
and the taping of 'The Beatles' Third Christmas Record'.
[2] The Beatles had used a Hammond on several previous tracks (e.g., [38b] MR
MOONLIGHT and [58] I'M DOWN), and there was one in the studio a week later for
[75] YOU WON'T SEE ME, so why Martin chose to play a Booker T part on the
harmonium is puzzling – unless take 2 of 12-BAR ORIGINAL was merely a try-out for
a full version to be done, if needed, the following week.

[73] THINK FOR YOURSELF *(Harrison)*

Harrison vocal, lead guitar; **Lennon** harmony vocal, electric piano
(?); **McCartney** harmony vocal, bass; **Starr** drums, maracas,
tambourine
Recorded: 8th November 1965, Abbey Road 2.
Producer: George Martin. Engineer: Norman Smith.
UK release: 3rd December 1965 (LP: *Rubber Soul*)
US release: 6th December 1965 (LP: *Rubber Soul*)

Another early-hours session produced Harrison's second contribution
to *Rubber Soul*: a typically sour jibe, allegedly 'political' in inspiration.
Oddly mixed (as if to disguise leakage missed during a bounce-down),
the track features two basses – one recorded conventionally from a Vox
amp in the studio, the other played through a distortion unit[1] and
recorded by direct injection. The second bass line seems to have been
added to help the listener through Harrison's violent chord-changes (an
angry circular progression from A minor, via D minor, to a remote B
flat and back through C and G). Underrated beside the pious [66] IF I
NEEDED SOMEONE, THINK FOR YOURSELF is less ingratiating but more
incisive. While the performance might have been better, it serves its
purpose and McCartney's harmony at the chorus's descent to E flat
major has real fervour.

[74] THE WORD *(Lennon–McCartney)*

Lennon vocal, rhythm guitar; **McCartney** vocal, bass, piano;
 Harrison vocal, lead guitars; **Starr** drums, maracas; **George
 Martin** harmonium
Recorded: 10th November 1965, Abbey Road 2.
Producer: George Martin. Engineer: Norman Smith.
UK release: 3rd December 1965 (LP: *Rubber Soul*)
US release: 6th December 1965 (LP: *Rubber Soul*)

Taped at the end of the evening before going on to record the final
version of [70] I'M LOOKING THROUGH YOU in the early hours, THE
WORD was a late lucky strike in the *Rubber Soul* sessions. A D blues[2]

---

[1] Often referred to as a fuzz-box (or 'fuzz bass'), this overload gadget was custom-
built by Abbey Road engineers. The first fuzz-box, the Gibson Maestro Fuzztone
marketed in 1962, was experimented with by The Beatles as early as 1963 (Babiuk,
Beatles Gear, p. 96) and had been used by The Rolling Stones' Keith Richards on
their October 1965 UK hit 'Satisfaction', though the effect itself had been known for
years, usually through accidental damage to output valves or speakers. For a while,
guitarists took to slashing their speaker cones to obtain the sound (e.g., Dave Davies
on The Kinks' 1964 hit 'You Really Got Me').
[2] While the chords are major, the tune's clashing F natural (flat third) is minor, a

with a four-bar bridge, its rhythm shows the distant influence of contemporary soul singles like Wilson Pickett's 'In The Midnight Hour' and James Brown's 'Papa's Got A Brand New Bag', then prominent in the UK charts. (Though The Beatles' absorption of elements from black American music was so idiosyncratic as to be undetectable, they always assumed that these influences were blatantly obvious – hence the feeble pun of the album's title.[1] Courtesy of Capitol's resequencing policy, *Rubber Soul* was misleadingly marketed in America as 'folk-rock'.)

Described by McCartney as an attempt to write a song on one note, THE WORD was a collaboration by Lennon (verse/chorus, lyric) and McCartney (bridge?). In effect, it marks the climax of the group's marijuana period: a song predicting Love Militant as a social panacea and the accompanying rise of the 'counterculture'. In this, The Beatles were ahead of the game. In November 1965, the countercultural lifestyle was still the preserve of an LSD-using élite in California and London's Notting Hill. Even the word 'hippie' had yet to be coined, while the 'Summer of Love' was still eighteen months away. To celebrate the birth of this song, Lennon and McCartney smoked a joint and wrote out the lyric in coloured crayons as 'a psychedelic illuminated manuscript'.[2]

McCartney's zany piano introduction forecasts the group's impending experimental period. Derived from the comic piano passages in The Goon Show – much loved by The Beatles and the model for [112] YOU KNOW MY NAME (LOOK UP THE NUMBER) – the same sort of playing would soon appear at the end of their first 'psychedelic' record: [77] TOMORROW NEVER KNOWS. Sharing the latter's incantatory monotony, THE WORD is a syncopated rocker which builds to a mini-revelation of falsetto harmonies against a halo of suspended chords on harmonium (see [68]). Starr provides a feast of eccentric 'backwards fills' (see [10], note), while McCartney, liberated by his high-register

---

melodic/harmonic ambiguity which carries on through the bridge.

[1] At the end of take 1 of [58] I'M DOWN *(Anthology 2)*, McCartney comments 'Plastic soul, man, plastic soul'. See also the Otis Redding connection in [64] DRIVE MY CAR and [65] DAY TRIPPER, the alleged Miracles' influence on [67] IN MY LIFE, the blues-tinged first version of [70] I'M LOOKING THROUGH YOU *(Anthology 2)*, the Booker T-style instrumental [U73] 12-BAR ORIGINAL *(Anthology 2)*, and the part played by The Four Tops in [75] YOU WON'T SEE ME.

[2] Miles, op. cit., p. 272. The manuscript later became a present to John Cage for his fiftieth birthday. McCartney observes that they usually stayed sober during writing sessions to avoid getting 'clouded up'.

line in [71] MICHELLE, delivers his most spontaneous bass-part to date, including a flourish (1:15) later developed at length on [81] RAIN.

[75] YOU WON'T SEE ME *(Lennon–McCartney)*

McCartney vocal, bass, piano; Harrison backing vocal, lead guitar;
   Lennon backing vocal; Starr drums, tambourine, hi-hat;[1] Mal
   Evans Hammond organ[2]
Recorded: 11th November 1965, Abbey Road 2.
Producer: George Martin. Engineer: Norman Smith.
UK release: 3rd December 1965 (LP: *Rubber Soul*)
US release: 6th December 1965 (LP: *Rubber Soul*)

Another number marking McCartney's disenchantment with Jane Asher (who had temporarily left him to work in rep in Bristol), YOU WON'T SEE ME is a three-chord trick based on The Four Tops' then-current hit, 'It's The Same Old Song'.[3] Pitched a minor third below its model, McCartney's tune opens the intervals out (B, D, A instead of E, F, D), but the debt is still clear.[4] (Ironically, Holland–Dozier–Holland had chosen the title because their song was a shameless rewrite – shuffling a C–Dm–F–G progression – of their previous number for The Four Tops, 'I Can't Help Myself'.)

YOU WON'T SEE ME shared the weariness of [69] NOWHERE MAN and needed something to lift it. Unfortunately, the group were too tired by late nights to come up with anything, and simply repeated NOWHERE MAN's irritating 'oo-la-la-la' backing-vocal formula. This would have mattered less if they hadn't decided to programme the two tracks next to each other: the most inept piece of sequencing on any Beatles LP. Redeemed by the interest of its bass line – very free in McCartney's liberated new style – YOU WON'T SEE ME soon founders under the weight of its own self-pity and expires long before straggling to the end of an unusually protracted fade.

---

[1] A separate part (in triplets) overdubbed in addition to the 'kit' hi-hat.
[2] A single note (A) held throughout the final verse/chorus.
[3] These are also the chords of [43] EIGHT DAYS A WEEK. Talking to *Playboy* in December 1984, McCartney grinningly admitted: 'We were the biggest nickers in town. Plagiarists extraordinaires.'
[4] Recalling the inspiration as a descending semitonal stepwise movement, McCartney describes the song as 'very Motown-flavoured' with 'a James Jamerson feel' (Miles, op. cit., p. 271).

[76] **GIRL** *(Lennon–McCartney)*

> **Lennon** vocal, acoustic guitars; **McCartney** backing vocal, bass;
>   **Harrison** lead acoustic guitar; **Starr** drums
> Recorded: 11th November 1965, Abbey Road 2.
> Producer: George Martin. Engineer: Norman Smith.
> UK release: 3rd December 1965 (LP: *Rubber Soul*)
> US release: 6th December 1965 (LP: *Rubber Soul*)

The last number to be recorded for *Rubber Soul*, GIRL is Lennon's answer to McCartney's [71] MICHELLE: another Euro-song, replacing his partner's suave mock-French with a decadent German two-step crossed with Mikis Theodorakis's music for *Zorba the Greek*.[1] Moving languidly from C minor verse to E flat major chorus, GIRL's capoed guitars suggest both bazoukis and the Viennese mandolins and accordions the group must have heard on the radio during their Hamburg seasons in 1960–2. The frustrated pacing to-and-fro of the middle eight is sardonically framed by chanted backing vocals ('tit, tit, tit, tit'), while the hiss of indrawn breath on the chorus is so grossly lascivious that it's impossible not to picture Lennon laughing off-mike. Faithful to its idiom, the world-weary lyric is one of his most polished.[2] Reminiscing in 1980, he observed that the song's 'dream girl' had been a recurring fantasy, and that he had finally found her in Yoko Ono.[3] His ideal – an enigmatic bohemian artist la Juliette Greco – may have been partly fulfilled by his friend Stuart Sutcliffe's German girlfriend Astrid Kirchherr and her image may lurk in these verses, too.[4]

With *Rubber Soul*, The Beatles recovered the sense of direction that had

---

[1] A summer 1965 hit for Marcello Minerebi. Cf. [U13o] THE HONEYMOON SONG *(Live At The BBC).*

[2] McCartney claims to have written some of the lyric of the third verse (Miles, op. cit., p. 275).

[3] Talking to *Rolling Stone* in 1970, Lennon revealed that the third verse veers into a discussion he was then having with himself about Catholicism's guilt-ridden association of sexual pleasure with punishment. Coincidentally (?), his name for Ono was Mother Superior (see [148], [156]).

[4] Along with Klaus Voormann (who designed the front cover of *Revolver* and played bass on *John Lennon/Plastic Ono Band*), Astrid Kirchherr became a friend of The Beatles during their Hamburg period 1960–62. An 'Exi' – Lennon and McCartney's word for the German versions of the Parisian 'Left Bank' Existentialists – she is, among other things, credited with creating the group's early 'mop top' haircuts (although contemporary Liverpudlians recall this – local – hairstyle as the 'Julius Caesar').

begun to elude them during the later stages of work on *Beatles For Sale* and which, due to their indulgence in cannabis, almost completely evaporated during *Help!* Gradually realising, from Dylan's example, that they didn't have to segregate their professional work from their inner lives, they consciously experimented in much of the *Rubber Soul* material, feeling their way towards a new style – one which, defining the second half of their career together, would be inspired by their encounter with one of the biggest influences on life and culture in the late Sixties: LSD.

Part 2
The Top

With our love we could save the world.

[77] TOMORROW NEVER KNOWS (Lennon–McCartney)

Lennon vocal, organ, tape-loops; **McCartney** bass, tape-loops;
  Harrison guitars, sitars, tambura, tape-loops; **Starr** drums,
  tambourine, tape-loops; **George Martin** piano
Recorded: 6th–7th April 1966, Abbey Road 3; 22nd April 1966,
  Abbey Road 2.
Producer: George Martin. Engineer: Geoff Emerick.
UK release: 5th August 1966 (LP: *Revolver*)
US release: 8th August 1966 (LP: *Revolver*)

Straight after finishing *Rubber Soul*, The Beatles wearily embarked on
their final tour of Britain – thankfully brief compared with earlier ones
and followed by three idle months, the longest period of free time
they'd had since 1962. During this lay-off, they went on holiday, hung
out in the latest clubs in London, decorated their houses, bought
themselves new cars, and absorbed ideas and influences useful for their
next album.

While Harrison devoted himself to Indian music and McCartney to
classical, Lennon had become interested in exploring his mental 'inner
space' with LSD. Since there was no 'acid' subculture in Britain in
1966, he lacked any guidance to this dangerous drug and so turned to a
product of the American scene: *The Psychedelic Experience*, a manual to
mind expansion by renegade Harvard psychologists Timothy Leary and
Richard Alpert.

Wishing to give the unpredictable acid 'trip' a frame of reference
comparable with the mystical systems of Catholicism and Islam, Leary
and Alpert had selected *The Tibetan Book of the Dead*, an ancient tome
designed to be whispered to the dying so as to steer them through the
delusory states which, according to Tibetan Buddhism, hold sway
between incarnations. Leary and Alpert chose this holy book because
they believed LSD to be a 'sacramental chemical' capable of inducing
spiritual revelations. Leary had met Aldous Huxley, another Lennon
fancy, in 1960 and been struck by his prediction that the drug would
make mystical experience available to the masses and produce a 'revival
of religion which will be at the same time a revolution'. Huxley,

though, had been talking, in characteristically patrician terms, of 'self-transcendence', a state in which both individual consciousness and the material universe around it cease to seem real – a wildly impractical basis for anything structured enough to be called a religion. Leary, moreover, tended to vulgarise Huxley by speaking of self-transcendence and LSD as if they were the same thing, thereby turning a chemical process into an end in itself.[1] The indulgent self-gratification this implied had no religious connotations at all. In fact, the religious camouflage disguising Leary's psychedelic[2] ideology concealed a hidden agenda which would have been sinister if it hadn't been motivated chiefly by arrogant naivety.

Among the commonest of the 'altered states' induced by LSD is depersonalisation or 'ego-loss'. In this condition, awareness of self as a separate entity dissolves in what Jung termed 'oceanic consciousness': the sense that all things are one and individual awareness an illusion. It was the resemblance between depersonalisation and the self-transcendence of mysticism that impressed Huxley when he took mescalin and LSD in the mid-Fifties. Mystics, though, usually work within systems of controlled development through meditation. Depersonalisation – if that is what they experience, and not something quite different – could never take them by surprise. By contrast, the LSD trip, while steerable to a limited extent, is produced by an invasive force interacting at unpredictable strengths with the body's own fluctuating chemistry. The drug, not the subject, is in control.

That LSD was Russian roulette played with one's mind must have been clear to Leary, yet so excited was he by its 'revolutionary' potential that he threw caution to the wind by advocating it as a social cure-all. The revolution he envisaged had nothing in common with Lenin's, being based on a blend of post-Freudian psychology, Zen, and New Left utopianism. The enemy was The System: the materialistic machine which processed crew-cutted US youths through high school

---

[1] Eg., 'Drugs are the religion of the twenty-first century.' (*The Politics of Ecstasy*, p. 38.)

[2] Usually paraphrased as 'mind-expanding', this word was coined by Dr Humphrey Osmond in a letter to Huxley written in 1956 (from the Greek *psyche*, mind or soul, and *delos*, to reveal or manifest): 'To fathom Hell or soar angelic/Just take a pinch of psychedelic.' Ten years after he invented it, Osmond's hermetic word, intended for technical use among academics and intellectuals, was universally adopted. 1966 saw the appearance of psychedelicatessens: West Coast shops selling hippie paraphernalia including magic mushrooms, hookahs, and badges bearing the slogan 'Psychedelicize suburbia'.

into faceless corporations or the army – an 'uptight' society of 'straights' so estranged from their bodies and feelings that sex had become a source of guilt for them assuageable only by setting fire to the living flesh of Vietnamese peasants. The core of this System, according to the acid analysis, was the unfeeling rational intellect, the mind divorced from its body, the ego separated from the rest of creation. In some brands of humanist psychology, this disembodied ego was seen as a censorious inner parent whose role was to thwart the natural (and thus, to new wave theorists, unquestionably healthy) desires of the childlike Id. Soon the ego would become identified by the peace movement with the military-industrial complex (manifested in the form of the Pentagon), by feminists with 'patriarchy', and by Left radicals with the bourgeois 'privilege' of privacy. During 1965-8 – the height of Leary's influence – the ego was colloquially referred to as 'the head': a citadel of fearful mirrors to be 'liberated' by acid invasion.[1] In short, during the late Sixties the ego was thought of as something nasty to get rid of, which is why depersonalisation under LSD so interested Leary.

Unfortunately, playing with concepts like *satori*[2] and 'ego-death' is exceedingly dangerous. So real, for example, is the individual soul to Tibetan Buddhism that *The Tibetan Book of the Dead* assumes there to be little chance of stopping it reincarnating. Leary and Alpert's *The Psychedelic Experience*, on the other hand, amounts to a humanist soft-sell for the vague proposition that, through losing self-importance and seeing life as a game, we cease struggling and become reconciled to a meaningless – and hence goalless, and hence peaceful – existence. Leaving aside the desirability of a world peopled by passive adherents of 'the cosmic giggle' (and passing over the tenuous link between meaninglessness and peacefulness), there is, contrary to Leary's assurances, no guarantee of predictable results from LSD, which is capable of inducing anything from suicidal self-negation to paranoid megalomania. All that is certain is that if you exhort people to sacrifice their sense of self to a drug, the chances of disaster are high. Accordingly, as the use of LSD spread under Leary's influence, a trail of 'acid casualties' followed in its wake – individuals who had left their identity in some uncharted

---

[1] Confusingly, hippies sometimes called themselves 'heads' (short for 'pot-heads' or 'acid-heads').

[2] *Satori*. Zen Buddhist word for 'enlightenment', implying release from the bondage of reincarnation. Hippies drew a parallel between LSD and the clarity supposedly experienced during *satori*.

zone of inner space and were now incapable of functioning in the supposedly illusory real world. Among those thus permanently disabled over the next few years were some of the most sensitive and talented people in pop. John Lennon nearly became one of them.

According to Albert Goldman, Lennon took LSD for the third time in January 1966.[1] Apparently intending a serious voyage of self-discovery, he used the instructions given in *The Psychedelic Experience*, reading its paraphrase of *The Tibetan Book of the Dead* onto a tape-recorder and playing it back as the drug took effect. The result was spectacular and he hastened to capture it in song, taking many of his lines directly from Leary and Alpert's text – above all its rapturous invocation of the supposed reality behind appearances: The Void. As 'The Void', the song was the first to be recorded for *Revolver*.[2] Under its eventual title, TOMORROW NEVER KNOWS, it introduced LSD and Leary's psychedelic revolution to the young of the Western world, becoming one of the most socially influential records The Beatles ever made.

While later thankful to have escaped its clutches, Lennon always acknowledged that LSD changed him in some ways for the better. Those who knew him in 1966 say his personality suddenly softened, his aggression giving way to a noticeably mellower mood.[3] The drug had a similar impact on his music, playing a role in his most imaginative creations: [93] STRAWBERRY FIELDS FOREVER, [96] A DAY IN THE LIFE, and [116] I AM THE WALRUS. Yet of all Lennon's LSD-driven songs, TOMORROW NEVER KNOWS is most directly about the drug. Commencing with a line from *The Psychedelic Experience*, the song takes its title from a saying of Starr's, analogous to the hippie maxim 'Be here now'.[4] Typically horizontal, Lennon's lazy Mixolydian melody rises

---

[1] *The Lives of John Lennon*, pp. 197–8. (See [47], [63].)

[2] The recording sheet for 6th April lists the song as 'Mark I'. According to Lennon, who would have preferred 'The Void', he changed the title in order to avoid being charged with writing a drug song.

[3] This was the outward effect of his LSD 'addiction'. In effect, his gentler side was sufficiently intensified by the drug to quieten his aggression. Later, his toughness revived, firstly in his music during 1968–70, and later in his personal life between 1973 and 1975.

[4] *Be Here Now* was later the title of a book by Leary's partner Richard Alpert (Baba Ram Dass). The slogan paraphrases the Vedic teaching that to dwell on past or future is to be dead to the present. Enlightenment consists of living continuously in the present – a philosophical paradox in that to do so requires will, yet will is time-bound, depending on memory and anticipation (consciousness of the past and the

and falls over a C drone on bass, tambura, and sitar, producing a mild polychord when it drifts to B flat (as in Harrison's [66] IF I NEEDED SOMEONE). The influence of Indian music is obvious, but there is a precedent for both the high-lying one-note bass and the track's broken drum-pattern: [47] TICKET TO RIDE. (Both drum-patterns were suggested by McCartney.)[1]

In his account of the *Sgt. Pepper* sessions, Goldman remarks that, compared with contemporary American studios, Abbey Road was primitive and The Beatles were fools to put up with its limitations when they could have followed The Rolling Stones to Los Angeles and obtained the same effects with half the trouble. Indeed, The Beatles were often frustrated by EMI's rigid studio regime and obtuse slowness in upgrading to eight-track. (McCartney has recently revealed that the group briefly considered recording in America in 1966 but found that EMI's contractual clauses made this option prohibitively expensive.) Yet Goldman misses the point. Apart from familiarity and convenience of access, Abbey Road offered a very particular sound, not to mention an aura of homely English eccentricity which colours and arguably fostered the character of The Beatles' best work.[2] More than this, its shoestring ethos mothered the most dazzling aural invention to emerge

---

future).

[1] In the primitive 'Mark 1'/Take 1 *(Anthology 2)*, there is no harmonic movement at all – only a muddy wash made from a pair of simple loops. If this was Lennon's first attempt at realising what was in his mind, it suggests that McCartney's role in clarifying harmony and texture was crucial.

[2] Despite its former limitations, the studio is fondly remembered by McCartney: 'Abbey Road was somewhere we *loved* to go.' (Q, June 1997.) However irksome a restriction, the fact that the group had to work in EMI's London studio almost certainly forced more creativity than would have an easy abundance of means in a foreign climate. Had The Beatles recorded in California during 1966–9, with or without George Martin and Geoff Emerick, the nature and evolution of their lives and music would, beyond any doubt, have been fundamentally different. Speculation on this 'parallel universe' idea is potentially boundless – yet something comparable happened, in reverse, to The Kinks. Blacklisted by the American Federation of Musicians for their wild behaviour on tour in the USA in summer 1965, they were unable to play there again until 1969. Their consequent isolation from American influence steered them away from the blues-based riffing of their early material, producing the determined Englishness of what became their most creative period. Once their exile was over, The Kinks' music almost immediately began to revert to its original transatlantic idiom, e.g., 'Victoria' (from the album *Arthur, Or The Decline And Fall Of The British Empire*), a song retaining an incongruously 'English' lyric while musically styled after the American blues band Canned Heat (see [160]). At this point, the group's era of classic songwriting ceased nearly overnight.

from any studio in Britain or America during the late Sixties (or since). With his engineers Geoff Emerick[1] and Ken Scott, George Martin created a sound-world for The Beatles which astonished their better-equipped counterparts in the USA. American singer/producer Tommy James recalls whole studios being torn apart and put back together again in search of a drum sound The Beatles could get that American technicians couldn't: 'What they did, everything they did, became state of the art.'[2]

The first of these unique drum sounds was created for Starr's mesmeric part for TOMORROW NEVER KNOWS. Performed mainly on a pair of slack-tuned tom-toms – damped, compressed, and recorded with massive echo – it created the image of a cosmic tabla played by a Vedic deity riding in a storm-cloud. This, though, was only the start of a production which, in terms of textural innovation, is to pop what Berlioz's *Symphonie fantastique* was to 19th-century orchestral music. Beginning on 6th April with the basic rhythm track (tambura drone, guitars, bass, drums, organ, piano, tambourine), the group continued the following day by overdubbing tape-loops made by McCartney at home on his Brennell recorders.[3] The tape-loop – a length of taped sound edited to itself to create a perpetually cycling signal – is a staple of sound-effect studios and the noise-art idiom known as *musique concrète* (see [U96], note). Pop music, though, had heard nothing like this before, and the loops created for TOMORROW NEVER KNOWS were especially extraordinary.

There were five in all, each running on an auxiliary deck fed onto the multitrack through the Studio 2 desk and mixed live: (1) a 'seagull'/ 'Red Indian' effect (actually McCartney laughing) made, like most of the other loops, by superimposition and acceleration (0:07); (2) an orchestral chord of B flat major (0:19); (3) a Mellotron played on its flute setting (0:22); (4) another Mellotron oscillating in 6/8 from B flat

[1] Though TOMORROW NEVER KNOWS was a group effort, a major contribution was made by Emerick, a technician in the tradition of English audio experimentalists (of whom Joe Meek is pop's UK pioneer). In 1962, aged 16, he engineered Rolf Harris's highly original 'Sun Arise'. This brought him to Martin's attention and Emerick served as tape-op to Norman Smith on a number of Beatles tracks during 1963–5: [8], [11], [12], [13], [13b], [21], [22], [31], [38b], [43], [44b], [45], [46], [46b], [46c], [46d].

[2] Somach and Somach, p. 93.

[3] Miles, op. cit., p. 291. Harrison and Starr also claim to have brought in loops, although these do not appear to have been used (*The Beatles Anthology*, p. 210).

to C on its string setting (0:38); and (5) a rising scalar phrase on a sitar, recorded with heavy saturation and acceleration (0:56). The most salient of these are (5), which forms the first four bars of the central instrumental break and subsequently dominates the rest of the track, and (4) which, working in cross-rhythm, invites the audience to lose its time-sense in a brilliantly authentic evocation of the LSD experience. (The second half of the instrumental break consists of parts of McCartney's guitar solo for [84] TAXMAN slowed down a tone, cut up, and run backwards [81].)[1]

With its fade-out Goons-style piano [74], the soundscape of TOMORROW NEVER KNOWS is a riveting blend of anarchy and awe, its loops crisscrossing in a random pattern of colliding circles. Even Lennon's voice track is unprecedented. During the first half of the song, it was put through a new Abbey Road invention: artificial double-tracking (ADT). For the second half, Lennon wanted to sound like the Dalai Lama and thousands of Tibetan monks chanting on a mountain top. George Martin solved this by sending the voice track through the revolving speaker in a Leslie cabinet, a process which required physically breaking into the circuitry. (Though the effect was startling – the last aural coup in an album of stunning effects – Lennon remained unsatisfied, wishing the monks had been hired instead.)

As a pure sound-event, TOMORROW NEVER KNOWS remains exhilarating – yet it is easy, thirty years later, to underestimate its original cultural impact. Part of this is due to an intervening change in Western musical habits. Wheeling in on a fade-up, the whirring drone of darkly glittering sitar-tambura harmonics, seemed, in 1966, like an unknown spiritual frequency tuning in – an impact lessened for subsequent generations conditioned to pedal-point harmony by 'ambient' synthesiser pieces and monochordal 'rave' music. WHEN TOMORROW NEVER KNOWS appeared, drones had been absent from Western music since the passing of the religious 'organum' style in the 12th century.[2] Only the fringe experimentalist La Monte Young was ahead of The Beatles in embracing the Indian drone with reference to its original context: a cosmic keynote resounding through space – the

---

[1] This must have been done on 22nd April when both TAXMAN and TOMORROW NEVER KNOWS were receiving their final overdubs. The tell-tale octave leap on D of the Taxman solo can be heard on TOMORROW NEVER KNOWS (reversed and transposed down to C) at 1:15.

[2] This, of course, excludes folk music, where the drone is intrinsic to bagpipes and hurdygurdy.

reverberation of the universe-engendering voice of Brahma the creator.[1] Serving notice that the ensuing music will contain no tonal 'progress' – no change of key or chord (not quite true in the case of TOMORROW NEVER KNOWS) – the Indian drone, as brought into First World culture by this track, challenges not only seven centuries of Western music, but the operating premise of Western civilization itself. When Lennon's voice rises out of the seething dazzle of churning loops, the first words it utters, 'Turn off your mind', are a mystic negation of all progressive intellectual enterprise. The message: it is not the contents of one's mind which matter; rather, what counts is the quality of the containing mind itself – and the emptier, the better. This proposition, now a truism in Western fringe thinking, and happily travestied in the Ecstasy subculture of 'psychedelic' dance music, was radically subversive in 1966. TOMORROW NEVER KNOWS launched the till-then élite-preserved concept of mind-expansion into pop, simultaneously drawing attention to consciousness-enhancing drugs and the ancient religious philosophies of the Orient, utterly alien to Western thought in their anti-materialism, rapt passivity, and world-sceptical focus on visionary consciousness.

In Britain, the fourteen tracks from *Revolver* were released to radio stations in twos and threes throughout July 1966, building anticipation for what would clearly be a radical new phase in the group's recording career. The most extreme departure on the album, TOMORROW NEVER KNOWS was held back till last, resounding over the airwaves only days before *Revolver*, with its groundbreaking black-and-white psychedelic cover, finally appeared in the shops. The strategy served to establish that The Beatles had initiated a second pop revolution – one which, while galvanising their existing rivals and inspiring many new ones, left all of them far behind.

Lennon, meanwhile, became psychologically addicted to LSD, taking it daily and living in one long, listless chemically altered state. Gradually fatigue and sensory overload conspired with Leary's prescription for voluntary ego-death to dissolve his sense of self. For the next two years, by his own account, he had little grasp of his own identity. Living in a passive, impressionable condition dominated by LSD, he clung to the ideology of the psychedelic revolution despite an increasing incidence of the 'bad trips' which Leary had claimed were impossible after ego-death. By 1968 – at which point Leary was merrily

---

[1] Young: 'Get into the Sound: the Sound is God; I am the Sound that is God.'

hailing The Beatles as 'Divine Messiahs, the wisest, holiest, most effective avatars the human race has yet produced, prototypes of a new race of laughing freemen' – Lennon was a mental wreck struggling to stitch himself back together. Luckily, his constitution was robust enough to avert physical collapse, while the scepticism that balanced his questing gullibility warded off a permanent eclipse of his reason. Many others like him never came back.

[78] GOT TO GET YOU INTO MY LIFE *(Lennon–McCartney)*

McCartney double-tracked vocal, bass; **Lennon** rhythm guitar (?); **Harrison** lead guitar; **Starr** drums, tambourine; **George Martin** organ; **Eddie Thornton, Ian Hamer, Les Condon** trumpets; **Alan Branscombe, Peter Coe** tenor saxes
Recorded: 7th May 1966, Abbey Road 3; 8th, 11th April, 18th May, 17th June 1966, Abbey Road 2.
Producer: George Martin. Engineer: Geoff Emerick.
UK release: 5th August 1966 (LP: *Revolver*)
US release: 8th August 1966 (LP: *Revolver*)

Next to its futuristic predecessor, McCartney's first contribution to *Revolver* was distinctly conservative, being a pastiche of Holland–Dozier–Holland's recent hits for The Supremes.[1] During The Beatles' lay-off at the beginning of the year [77], he and Jane Asher were often seen in such London nightclubs as the Bag O'Nails in Kingly Street, Soho, where they heard the leading English soul-jazz stylist Georgie Fame. When it came to adding brass to GOT TO GET YOU INTO MY LIFE, McCartney hired two of Fame's group The Blue Flames, Eddie Thornton and Peter Coe. The others on the session were freelance jazzmen.

Slightly out of his neighbourhood in this idiom, McCartney seems to have had no firm idea of how he wanted the song done, and it took two days of trial and error to record the basic track, using a harmonium 'pad'.[2] He wisely chose to leave the result for a month before hiring

[1] Though the even crotchet beat recalls the early Supremes hits 'Where Did Our Love Go' and 'Baby Love', the model for GOT TO GET YOU INTO MY LIFE was probably Motown's bid to revive the formula in January 1966 with 'I Hear A Symphony', whose descending chromatic sequence is echoed in its bridge.
[2] Take 5 *(Anthology 2)*. The pad gives a drone effect common to many other Beatles songs of this period – notably [77] TOMORROW NEVER KNOWS and [80] PAPERBACK WRITER – which suggests that the song might have started from a pseudo-Indian ('one chord') idea before acquiring its Motown characteristics. Take 5 of GOT TO GET YOU INTO MY LIFE is a sketch of the general lay-out, plus some rather wayward vocal harmony ideas. A central climactic passage ('I need your love'), omitted in the final version, recalls Sandie Shaw's 1964 No. 1 'Always Something

the brass and working up a 'chart' with George Martin while Lennon co-ordinated affairs from the control-room. Following a month's further cogitation, more guitar, a new vocal, and a desynchronised copy of the brass track were overdubbed. By this time, the production had become messy, with raggedly matched lead vocals and leakage from the brass onto one of the guitar tracks.

Holding a one-note bass line for its first eight bars, GOT TO GET YOU INTO MY LIFE is a taut design that relieves its tension only in the climactic shout of its chorus. Closely miked and limited for a punchy sound, the brass maintains the mood, driving the track to the release of a screaming fade. Starr's drum fills are slightly stiff, as if inhibited by the metronomic beat, but Harrison's guitar crescendo precisely captures the wound-up urgency of the music.[1]

[79] LOVE YOU TO (Harrison)

Harrison multitracked vocal, acoustic guitar, electric guitar, sitar (?);
   McCartney harmony vocal (?); **Starr** tambourine; **Anil
   Bhagwat** tabla; **Other unnamed Indian musicians** sitar,
   tambura
Recorded: 11th April 1966, Abbey Road 2; 13th April 1966,
   Abbey Road 3.
Producer: George Martin. Engineer: Geoff Emerick.
UK release: 5th August 1966 (LP: *Revolver*)
US release: 8th August 1966 (LP: *Revolver*)

The first product of Harrison's interest in Indian music [63], LOVE YOU TO[2] is distinguished by the authenticity of its Hindustani classical instrumentation and techniques. Based on the upper five notes of the C minor Dorian mode, the melody is sourly repetitious in its author's usual saturnine vein, but the design – free-tempo improvisatory prelude *(alap)* followed by slow and fast *gat* – is well-managed considering that he'd had no tuition in the genre. The lyric (part philosophical, part love-song to his wife Patti) develops the scepticism of [73] THINK FOR YOURSELF. For the recording, players from the North London Asian Music Circle were hired, including an uncredited sitarist who played most of what was once attributed to Harrison.

There To Remind Me'.
[1] In 1980, Lennon observed that he thought the lyric, which he particularly liked, referred to McCartney's belated experience of LSD. According to McCartney, the song is 'an ode to pot, like someone else might write an ode to chocolate or a good claret' (Miles, op. cit. p. 290). (See [95], note.)
[2] The meaning of the title, added at the last minute, is obscure. During recording, the song was codenamed 'Granny Smith' (after the apple).

[80] PAPERBACK WRITER *(Lennon–McCartney)*

McCartney vocal, bass; **Lennon** backing vocal, rhythm guitar;
  Harrison backing vocal, lead guitar; **Starr** drums, tambourine
Recorded: 13th–14th April 1966, Abbey Road 3.
Producer: George Martin. Engineer: Geoff Emerick.
UK release: 10th June 1966 (A single/RAIN)
US release: 30th May 1966 (A single/RAIN)

The Beatles' twelfth British single was their first since [12] SHE LOVES
YOU not to go straight to No. 1 in the UK. Written mainly by
McCartney[1] – the second of a run of three consecutive A-sides by him
– it strained too hard to define a new style for the group, its air of
contrivance sounding flashy after the ideal balance of form and feeling
in [68] WE CAN WORK IT OUT. Displaying The Beatles' cannabis-
induced fascination with getting the maximum out of one chord (see
[66], [74], [77]), PAPERBACK WRITER offers a jokey lyric reflecting its era
of classless ambition: the generation of 'young meteors' who in the
mid-Sixties rose from provincial and working-class backgrounds to
dazzle the heights of British fashion, film, and print.[2] Beyond this
social observation any potential poignancy is sacrificed to excitement,
word-games, and studio-effects. In the end, this is a record less about its
time and place than about pop records in early 1966. Intermittently
glimpsed in The Beatles' music, 'Swinging London' was less interesting
to them as visiting northerners than it was to cynical locals like The
Kinks and The Rolling Stones.[3]

Now living within walking distance of Abbey Road (in Cavendish
Avenue, St John's Wood), McCartney was often at the studio before
the others, trying out musical ideas and production effects which he
then presented to them as *faits accomplis*. While the group benefited
immensely from his energetic attention to detail, it didn't make him
popular and his pedantic insistence on Harrison playing every guitar

---

[1] With possibly fifty-fifty assistance from Lennon on the music (Miles, op. cit., p.
279).
[2] Salewicz (p. 179) suggests that the subject occurred to McCartney while helping
The Beatles' friend John Dunbar catalogue the stock of his Indica book shop and
gallery in Mason's Yard. English culture of this period benefited immensely from the
patronage of Jenny Lee, Harold Wilson's Minister for the Arts. Under her direction,
theatres, concert halls, galleries, and libraries received vital funding while the Arts
Council, chaired by Lord Goodman, gained new grant-giving powers and expanded
financial resources. In this atmosphere, creativity flourished in every walk of cultural
life.
[3] Eg., The Kinks: *Face To Face* (October 1966); *Something Else* (September 1967);
The Rolling Stones: *Aftermath* (April 1966); *Between The Buttons* (January 1967).

line *just so* often caused tension. (Whether he or Harrison recorded the guitar riff on PAPERBACK WRITER is unknown, though it's clearly McCartney's idea – based, as Lennon later remarked, on the similar figure in [65] DAY TRIPPER.)[1]

Made in eleven hours, the track has a widely divided stereo image using, among other novelties, a drum part channelled separately across the spectrum (snare and cymbals left, tom-toms centre, bass-drum right). For his prominent high-register bass part, McCartney swapped his Hofner for the long-scale Rickenbacker (see [69], note), a guitar with a solid, cutting treble tone which he modified by miking his amp through a second speaker and rolling off the top with compression to get a smoother sound.[2] With a tape-echoed chorus, the vocal arrangement includes passages of four-part polyphony modelled on The Beach Boys, whose 'Sloop John B' had just entered the UK charts. That Lennon and Harrison were not entirely serious in performing their falsetto parts can be heard in the gasps of laughter audible on a very 'dirty' vocal track (and the fact that, during the second verse/chorus, they are chanting 'Frère Jacques').

[81] RAIN *(Lennon–McCartney)*

Lennon vocal, rhythm guitar; **McCartney** backing vocal, bass;
    Harrison backing vocal, lead guitar; **Starr** drums, tambourine
Recorded: 14th April 1966, Abbey Road 3; 16th April 1966,
    Abbey Road 2.
Producer: George Martin. Engineer: Geoff Emerick.
UK release: 10th June 1966 (B single/PAPERBACK WRITER)
US release: 30th May 1966 (B single/PAPERBACK WRITER)

Generally agreed to be The Beatles' finest B-side, RAIN – which McCartney assigns '70-30' to Lennon[3] – expresses the vibrant lucidity of a benign LSD experience. However, the weather imagery would be banal were it solely metaphorical. What alters this is the track's sheer sonic presence – an attempt to convey the lustrous *weight* of the world

---

[1] During one take, McCartney moved to lead guitar, playing the riff with his Epiphone Casino [47] while Harrison took up a short-scale Burns Nu-Sonic bass. Otherwise, Harrison played a Gibson SG Standard and Lennon a hollow-bodied Gretsch Nashville (their respective guitars for [81] RAIN, too, and most of *Revolver*).
[2] Microphones and speakers work by opposite principles: air-movement to electrical impulse (or vice versa). McCartney's bass amp made the sound-wave which, vibrating the cone of the second speaker, transduced voltage in its moving coil, creating a second signal. This was presumably done for colouration rather than signal boosting. (The larger the second speaker, the lower the available frequencies.)
[3] Miles, op. cit., p. 280.

as it can appear to those under the drug's influence. The song's 'rain' and 'sun' are physical phenomena experienced in a condition of heightened consciousness, the record portraying a state of mind in which one is peacefully at home in an integrated universe (as distinct from those who see only disparate elements to be manipulated or feared). As such, RAIN is the first pop song to draw an 'us and them' line between the children of Leary's psychedelic revolution and the supposedly unknowing materialism of the parental culture. Here, the post-war 'generation gap' acquires a philosophical significance which would soon seize the imagination of Western youth.

A spiritual revolt against the constraints of cultural form and social formality, the hippie movement had been proclaimed at the Trips Festival in San Francisco three months before The Beatles went into Abbey Road to begin *Revolver*. The hippies, as psychedelic descendants of the free-speech/anti-racist/anti-nuclear movements of the early Sixties, rejected straight society in favour of a communal utopia in which sex was free, the intellect ('the head') distrusted, and peaceful self-determination valued above all. LSD-inspired, the movement's underlying ideal was a return to Eden: a regaining of the unprejudiced vision of the child. While a similar vision is displayed in RAIN, what redeems it (and Lennon's later child's-eye-view songs) is its acerbic quality. There is nothing innocent here, the observing eye is critical, and the song's chanting phrases verge on a sneer ('Can you *hear* me?').

The Beatles created the sense of weight and depth they achieved in RAIN by recording the basic track at a faster tempo and then slowing it down (probably by a tone) so as to alter the frequencies of their instruments. The result of sixteen hours of careful bouncing down and overdubbing, this clangorously saturated texture resonates around McCartney's bass, mixed large and played high in the style he had begun to explore in the final tracks for *Rubber Soul*.[1] Above this, varispeeded and multitracked vocals clash symbolically as the guitars ring out C major against an unyielding G, a variation of the similar effect in [66] IF I NEEDED SOMEONE. (The drone-like pull of G

---

[1] Compare [80] PAPERBACK WRITER. While difficult to do, some of these high bass lines (*not* the one for Rain) may have been played with a capo. Photos of McCartney during the *Rubber Soul* sessions show him with his Rickenbacker capoed at the third fret. Asked about this (*Bass Player*, July/August 1995), he replied that, in that period, he was continually experimenting: 'I'd try anything!' One possibility is that, having written a song using a capo, he only knew it in that key and, rather than adapt, chose to capo his bass. Alternatively, he might have done this to obtain a higher pitch or a different sound. (He would occasionally tune the Rickenbacker down a whole tone for similar reasons.)

throughout the track shows the growing influence of the Indian classical style in The Beatles' music of 1966, confirmed by exotic melismas in the bass part and chorus vocals.)[1]

Instrumentally, the twin focuses of RAIN are Starr's superb soloistic drumming (which he reckons his best recorded performance), and McCartney's high-register bass, sometimes so inventive that it threatens to overwhelm the track. With its density of sound and intuitive playing, RAIN is a cross between the clipped discipline of pop and the heavily-amplified, improvisatory sound of 'rock' – a genre which, in step with the acid counterculture, emerged in 1967–8. More significant for The Beatles' own style was an effect used in the fade-out, where the opening lines of the song are spooled backwards, a device discovered while playing with the loops made for [77] TOMORROW NEVER KNOWS.[2] Suiting the sense of RAIN by echoing the lyric's mystic indifference to the phenomenal world, this backwards effect was for a while, like the Leslie rotary speaker, applied to almost everything the group recorded.

[82] DOCTOR ROBERT *(Lennon–McCartney)*

Lennon vocal, rhythm guitar, harmonium; **McCartney** harmony
  vocal, bass; **Harrison** lead guitar, maracas; **Starr** drums
Recorded: 17th, 19th April 1966, Abbey Road 2.
Producer: George Martin. Engineer: Geoff Emerick.
UK release: 5th August 1966 (LP: *Revolver*)
US release: 20th June 1966 (LP: *'Yesterday' . . . and Today*)

DOCTOR ROBERT, though minor, is one of The Beatles' most incisive pieces. Concerning a New York doctor who habituated his socialite

---

[1] Bootlegs of RAIN without the vocal track reveal a resemblance between its opening chords (I–IV–V) and those of Dylan's 'Visions of Johanna'. (The way Lennon – or perhaps Harrison? – picks this sequence mirrors the second phrase of Dylan's melody, e.g., '. . . to play tricks when you're trying to be so quiet'. Thereafter the sequences diverge and the melodic echoes cease.) While songwriters often 'borrow' in this way to get started, it would seem that this particular case is coincidental. Written by mid-December 1965 when Dylan is thought to have played an electric version at a gig in California, 'Visions Of Johanna' was taped in Nashville on 14th February 1966, two months before RAIN was recorded in London. Yet, unless someone sent Lennon a tape of the track, he couldn't have heard it before Dylan's tour arrived in Europe in late April. (It's conceivable that Dylan himself sent Lennon a tape – he played McCartney acetates of *Blonde On Blonde* in London on 2nd May – but the possibility seems remote.)

[2] Lennon claimed to have chanced on this effect at home by threading the tape of a rough mix back-to-front. George Martin insists that he created the effect in the studio, playing it to Lennon when he arrived. (The latter was apparently so excited by this that he wanted the whole track to be released in reverse.)

clients to narcotics by mixing methedrine with vitamin shots, the song shifts key evasively, stabilising only in its middle eight – an evangelical sales-pitch backed by pious harmonium and warbling choirboys. Lennon's caustic vocal, recorded with ADT and split across the stereo spectrum, is matched by McCartney's huckstering harmony in fourths ('he's a man you must believe') and by Harrison's double-tracked guitar, with its unique blend of sitar and country-and-western. Tonally inconclusive, the song can be heard as a rebellious message from Lennon's subconscious concerning the trustworthiness of 'Doctor' Timothy Leary [77].

[83] AND YOUR BIRD CAN SING *(Lennon–McCartney)*

Lennon vocal, rhythm guitar, handclaps; **McCartney** harmony vocal, bass, handclaps; **Harrison** harmony vocal, lead guitar, handclaps; **Starr** drums, tambourine, handclaps
Recorded: 20th, 26th April 1966, Abbey Road 2.
Producer: George Martin. Engineer: Geoff Emerick.
UK release: 5th August 1966 (LP: *Revolver*)
US release: 20th June 1966 (LP: *'Yesterday'* . . . *and Today*)

During the high-pressure final dates for *Rubber Soul*, The Beatles had been allowed to arrange their sessions more or less as they pleased and had grown accustomed to camping out in Abbey Road for days at a time, evolving songs in the studio and recording them as they went along. AND YOUR BIRD CAN SING took most of two twelve-hour sessions (including a complete remake) and went through many variations before arriving at its finished form in the early hours of 27th April. In what he later dismissed as a throwaway, Lennon[1] elaborates the hipper-than-thou psychedelic omniscience of [81] RAIN, taunting the limitations of the analytical mind which, no matter how educated, can never comprehend creativity.[2] Ending on the raised eyebrow of an unresolved subdominant, the track is memorable mainly for its rolling swing (probably based on The Merseys' contemporary UK hit 'Sorrow') and the intricacy of its guitar parts, including an arpeggiated chromatic passage and a recurring arabesque in parallel thirds played by Harrison and McCartney (or possibly Lennon).[3]

---

[1] McCartney claims to have helped on the lyric, estimating the song as '80-20 to John' (Miles, op. cit., p. 288).
[2] The song's working title was 'You Don't Get Me'. Counting the song in at the start of the second day, Lennon mocked the pedantry of popular sheet music: 'Okay, boys – quite brisk, moderato, foxtrot.'
[3] One of the early versions of this track *(Anthology 2)* shows the group using a stop chord on the final 'me' of the last chorus. This allows a break from the track's dense

[84] TAXMAN *(Harrison)*

Harrison vocal, lead guitar; **Lennon** backing vocal; **McCartney**
  backing vocal, bass, lead guitar; **Starr** drums, tambourine,
  cowbell
Recorded: 20th–22nd April, 16th May 1966, Abbey Road 2; 21st
  June 1966, Abbey Road 3.
Producer: George Martin. Engineer: Geoff Emerick.
UK release: 5th August 1966 (LP: *Revolver*)
US release: 8th August 1966 (LP: *Revolver*)

Capitalising on the disillusioned impatience of his recent songs ([73],
[79]), Harrison stops beating about the bush and attacks the nineteen-
shillings-and-sixpence-in-the-pound top rate of income tax under
Harold Wilson's Labour government. At this stage Harrison was more
business-minded than his colleagues and had just realised how much of
the group's income was being siphoned off by the Treasury (in effect,
the price of their MBEs, nominated, in recognition of their foreign
earnings, by Wilson a year earlier). Greeted charily by those in the
high-earning pop business, the landslide re-election of the Labour
government at the end of March 1966 worried even stars with social
scruples, anxious not to lose out financially while they were at their
peak. This, though, was difficult to voice if one also happened to
sympathise with the underdog. Hence, the dig at Wilson in this Beatle
'protest' lyric, part-written by Lennon, is balanced by a conscience-
saving (and controversy-evading) snipe at Conservative opposition
leader Edward Heath.[1]

TAXMAN, a tight twelve-bar design in bluesy sevenths, shows signs
of rhythmic influence from several black or black-influenced British
hits of March 1966: James Brown's 'I Got You', Lee Dorsey's 'Get Out
Of My Life Woman', and The Spencer Davis Group's 'Somebody
Help Me'. Considering that it evolved over about twenty hours, the
track is surprisingly stark, consisting mainly of a bass riff against fuzz-
toned off-beat guitar chords. The mix accentuates this by keeping the
right channel open for tambourine and the falling 'coins' of an echoed
cowbell until the entry of McCartney's startling guitar solo: a savage

---

texture, momentarily revealing the vocal harmony by itself – an effective device for
some reason later dropped.
  [1] A similar dilemma was likewise skirted around by Ray Davies of The Kinks,
who, in 'Sunny Afternoon', used a millionaire persona to complain about Harold
Wilson's deflationary clamp on credit ('Save me, save me, save me from this
Squeeze') before offsetting this with a Dickensian portrayal of urban poverty in the
group's follow-up single 'Dead End Street'.

seven-bar affair that picks up the octave jump in the riff, adding a scintillating pseudo-Indian descending passage *en route*.[1]

With its studio-*verité* introduction, TAXMAN was a natural choice for the opening track of *Revolver*, where its shouted count-in recalled the beginning of *Please Please Me* and was inevitably interpreted as symbolising a new start in the group's recording career. While Harrison was rightly praised for this track, it should be heard as an ensemble effort, with McCartney's contribution bulking largest. Apart from his outstanding guitar solo, he plays some remarkable bass, taking advantage of the hard-hitting treble range of his Rickenbacker 4001S, particularly in his agitated secondary riff during the song's third verse.[2]

[85] I'M ONLY SLEEPING (Lennon–McCartney)

Lennon double-tracked vocal, acoustic rhythm guitar; **McCartney**
  harmony vocal, bass; **Harrison** harmony vocal, lead guitar; **Starr**
  drums
Recorded: 27th, 29th April, 5th May 1966, Abbey Road 3; 6th
  May 1966, Abbey Road 2.
Producer: George Martin. Engineer: Geoff Emerick.
UK release: 5th August 1966 (LP: *Revolver*)
US release: 20th June 1966 (LP: 'Yesterday' . . . *and Today*)

Obliquely influenced by The Kinks' change of direction into down-at-heel English musical-hall with 'Well-Respected Man' and 'Dedicated Follower Of Fashion', this evocative number, co-written according to McCartney,[3] represents Lennon's first use of an idiom outside his usual range since the German ballad style of [76] GIRL (accounting for the paradox that a song about lethargy was harmonically more active than anything he had written since GIRL itself). Lyrically, the subject was close to home, living as he was in a permanent psychedelic reverie

---

[1] Performed on McCartney's Epiphone Casino, this goes far beyond anything in the Indian style Harrison had done on guitar, the probable inspiration being Jeff Beck's ground-breaking solo on The Yardbirds' astonishing 'Shapes Of Things' (a UK hit in March 1966).
[2] Take 11 *(Anthology 2)* shows that the track originally came to a sudden close before the final guitar solo (which was copied from the middle of the recording and spliced to the end with an added fade-out during a mixing session on 21st June – a fundamental change effected at the very last minute!). In place of their 'Ah ah, Mr Wilson/Mr Heath' backing vocals, Lennon and McCartney can be heard gabbling 'Anybody got a bit of money?' Fortunately this was rectified the following day (22nd April).
[3] Miles, op. cit., p. 285.

(see [77]). A personal confession disguised as the murmurings of a modern Oblomov,[1] I'M ONLY SLEEPING dismisses the empty business of the mundane world with an indolence that holds the seeds of Lennon's later heroin addiction.[2]

Recording was begun after a break for mixing the tracks already taped for *Revolver*. This was the first such session The Beatles had ever attended, an indication of how concerned they were with the integrity of the new sound-world they were creating. In about twenty-four hours of recording spread over four days, they worked hard to obtain the timbres they wanted, using varispeed to alter frequencies. (The thin, papery old man's voice Lennon wanted was obtained by a circuitous process of speeding up and down which ended with the track a semitone below its original key of E minor.) Most striking of the effects used was the backwards guitar part, constructed by Harrison during a painstaking six-hour session. Having worked out his Indian-style line in normal sequence, he had Martin transcribe it in reverse and then recorded it thus, subsequently dubbing the result on backwards to obtain the characteristic smeared crescendi and womblike sucking noises. Only the radiant free-tempo fade-out uses serendipity, combining a cyclic arpeggio with part of the 'fast *gat*' from [79] LOVE YOU TO (played on guitar instead of sitar).

While not as showy as that of TOMORROW NEVER KNOWS, the texture of I'M ONLY SLEEPING, with its dreamy multitracking, dim halo of slowed cymbal sound, and softly tiptoeing bass, is equally deep in artifice. The Beatles were no longer interested in simulating their live sound under studio conditions, instead creating a new sonic environment in each successive track.[3]

---

[1] Lennon would certainly have seen Spike Milligan's legendary performances in *Oblomov* (New Lyric Theatre, Hammersmith, October–November 1964) and *Son Of Oblomov* (Comedy Theatre, 2nd December 1964–30th April 1966), but we can only conjecture as to whether he had these in mind while writing I'M ONLY SLEEPING. A lifelong fan of the Goons, he also knew Milligan through Dick Lester, who directed *The Running, Jumping, and Standing Still Film* (1959) and *The Bed Sitting Room* (1969).

[2] According to McCartney, the lyric related to the differences between the hours of his day and the hours Lennon kept. The former would arrive at Lennon's Weybridge home for writing sessions for which he'd have to wake Lennon up. (Miles, op. cit., pp. 284–5.)

[3] In terms of the way groups used recording studios, 1965–6 was a pivotal period. Until then, recorded songs differed little from their live versions. By mid-1966, cutting-edge pop records were harder, if not impossible, to perform onstage. For example, The Lovin' Spoonful could only roughly attempt a live version of 'Summer in the City'. (John Sebastian couldn't sing and play the piano part at the same time, so drummer Joe Butler had to take lead vocal.) The Yardbirds struggled to reproduce 'Shapes of Things' live, while The Beach Boys had slim hopes of performing

[86] ELEANOR RIGBY *(Lennon–McCartney)*

McCartney vocal; Lennon harmony vocal; Harrison harmony
vocal; Tony Gilbert, Sidney Sax, John Sharpe, Jurgen Hess
violins; Stephen Shingles, John Underwood violas; Derek
Simpson, Norman Jones cellos
Recorded: 28th April 1966, Abbey Road 2; 29th April, 6th June
1966, Abbey Road 3.
Producer: George Martin. Engineer: Geoff Emerick.
UK release: 5th August 1966 (LP: *Revolver*)
US release: 8th August 1966 (LP: *Revolver*)

Death is a subject normally avoided in pop music. Where acknowledged, it is either sanitised with heavenly choirs or treated as a black
joke (e.g., The Shangri-Las' camp 1965 classic 'Leader of the Pack').
Consequently the downbeat demise of a lonely spinster in ELEANOR
RIGBY – not to mention the brutal image of the priest 'wiping the dirt
from his hands as he walks from the grave' – came as quite a shock to
pop listeners in 1966. Taken together with George Martin's wintry
string octet arrangement, the impact was transfixing.

In fact, the song's grim final verse was settled on only after much
head-scratching and at the last minute. According to McCartney,
ELEANOR RIGBY began as a plain tune with a melancholy descending
phrase and the image of a spinster, Miss Daisy Hawkins, sweeping up
the rice in a church after a marriage.[1] Meeting Jane Asher in Bristol,
where she was working in rep, McCartney allegedly got the name
Rigby from a clothes shop, adding 'Eleanor' from Eleanor Bron, the
actress who had played the female lead in *Help!* Against this is the fact
that the Rigbys were a well-known local family in Liverpool, of whom
one, Eleanor (1895–1939), lies buried in the churchyard of St Peter's in
Woolton, close to McCartney's home suburb of Allerton.[2]

Armed with only the first verse, McCartney headed for Lennon's
house at Weybridge where, during an informal evening with friends,
he and the other Beatles pieced the rest of the song together. Starting as
Father McCartney, the priest in the second verse soon became the
more neutral Father McKenzie, a name found by consulting a

---

anything from *Pet Sounds* in concert.
[1] According to Donovan, the first version of the lyric consisted of an almost
random array of words thrown in to give a provisional form to the melody line, a
sketch method McCartney often used when working fast. (See Miles, op. cit., pp.
281-2.)
[2] Lionel Bart has a third version, claiming the character started out as Eleanor
Bygraves – 'and I asked them to change it'. (Leigh, p. 45.)

telephone directory. Starr suggested the idea of him 'darning his socks in the night'. The refrain 'Ah look at all the lonely people' seems to have been designed by committee, possibly later in the studio (where some say the last verse was decided); others maintain that the song was completed during the same evening. (Lennon, who subsequently claimed 'about 70 per cent' of the lyric, apparently tried to quash the idea of its two characters 'meeting' at the end.)[1]

Given its chaotic genesis, ELEANOR RIGBY is extraordinarily cogent and concentrated. The face that the heroine 'keeps in a jar by the door' (to mask the despair inadmissible by English middle-class etiquette) remains the single most memorable image in The Beatles' output.[2] Yet the lyric's televisual vividness ('Look at him working') is never gratuitous, being consistently at the service of the song's relentless despondency. Eleanor Rigby dies alone because unable to tell anyone how she felt. McKenzie's sermon won't be heard – not that he cares very much about his parishioners – because religious faith has perished along with communal spirit ('No one was saved'). Often represented as purveyors of escapist fantasy, The Beatles were, at their best, more poignantly realistic about their society than any other popular artists of their time.[3]

The monochrome pessimism of the lyric is paralleled in the naked simplicity of the music: a plain E Dorian melody over what amounts to two chords.[4] Arranged by Martin from a rough idea by McCartney,[5]

---

[1] According to McCartney – and Pete Shotton (pp. 122–3) – he contributed almost nothing.

[2] The novelist A. S. Byatt, for whom this lyric displays 'the minimalist perfection of a Beckett story', points out that, had Eleanor's 'face' been kept in a jar by a mirror, it would suggest the less disturbing idea of makeup. Instead, the image implies that behind her door, inside her house, Miss Rigby 'is faceless, is nothing'. (Talk on BBC Radio 3, 11th May 1993.)

[3] Explaining why The Beatles took up meditation in 1967, McCartney (Green, *Days in the Life*, p. 160) refers to the Church's failure to account for the suffering in the world. Where Christianity prescribes faith and prayer, Hindu philosophy answers the question directly (see [68], note), while meditation supposedly alters the individual's entire experience of reality. A key figure in conveying Oriental religious concepts to the West was the German writer Hermann Hesse, whose novels *Demian* (1919), *Siddhartha* (1922), *Steppenwolf* (1927), and *The Glass Bead Game* (1943) became cult reading during the late Sixties.

[4] McCartney describes it as a tune 'danced over the top of' an E minor vamp – a tune, moreover, 'with almost Asian Indian rhythms' (Miles, op. cit., p. 281).

[5] McCartney suggested something in the style of Vivaldi, to whose music he had recently been introduced by Jane Asher. Martin, though, based his arrangement on Bernard Herrmann's score for Francois Truffaut's *Fahrenheit 451*, then being screened in London.

the string accompaniment was recorded along with a guide vocal in a standard three-hour session, the final vocals being added later. Issued as a single (coupled with [88] YELLOW SUBMARINE), ELEANOR RIGBY held the UK No. 1 spot for four weeks during August and September. (The comparatively hollow [80] PAPERBACK WRITER lasted only two weeks at the top.) In militantly optimistic America, however, the combination fared less well, YELLOW SUBMARINE's light relief proving more popular. Neither reached the top of the chart.

[87] FOR NO ONE (Lennon–McCartney)

McCartney vocal, bass, piano, clavichord; **Starr** drums, tambourine; **Alan Civil** horn
Recorded: 9th, 16th May 1966, Abbey Road 2; 19th May 1966, Abbey Road 3.
Producer: George Martin. Engineer: Geoff Emerick.
UK release: 5th August 1966 (LP: *Revolver*)
US release: 8th August 1966 (LP: *Revolver*)

Written in March 1966 on holiday with Jane Asher in Switzerland, FOR NO ONE is a curiously phlegmatic account of the end of an affair, as matter-of-fact in its recognition of deceased love as [86] ELEANOR RIGBY in its tale of lonely death. (The song's original title was 'Why Did It Die?') The only emotion shown in this elegant '4/4 waltz' comes in a puzzled actuarial reckoning: 'a love that should have lasted years'. Neither partner in McCartney's cool scenario commands much sympathy, his detachment precluding the compassion of ELEANOR RIGBY. An enthusiastic film-goer, he may have been aiming at something with the dry cinematic eye of John Schlesinger's *Darling*.

FOR NO ONE is formally one of McCartney's most perfect pieces, constructed with its author's customary logic and moving methodically through its classical steps like a chess player. Whether by accident or design, this progress precisely reproduces his hero's obsessive examination of his predicament: exhausting every possibility, yet hesitating (over a suspension at the end of each chorus) before going round again to make sure all the options have been covered. (At the end, as though unable to face an unwelcome conclusion, the song ceases on the unresolved dominant.)

The classicism of FOR NO ONE suggested a French horn to Martin, who hired one of Britain's most distinguished players, Alan Civil. The track having been varispeeded for McCartney's vocal, Civil was disconcerted to find it presented to him in the quarter-tone gap between B and B flat. Once the capstan speed had been lowered, probably by several keys, he recorded his self-composed solo, took the standard session fee, and left.[1] Universally admired down the years, this passage, while memorable and accomplished, has little to do with the mood or sense of the song, adding only another kind of immaculate indifference.

[88] YELLOW SUBMARINE (Lennon–McCartney)

> **Starr** vocal, drums; **McCartney** backing vocal, shouting, bass;
> **Lennon** backing vocal, shouting, acoustic guitar; **Harrison**
> backing vocal, tambourine; **Mal Evans** bass drum; **Mal Evans,**
> **Neil Aspinall, George Martin, Geoff Emerick, Patti**
> **Harrison, Brian Jones, Marianne Faithfull, Alf Bicknell**
> backing vocals
> Recorded: 26th May 1966, Abbey Road 3; 1st June 1966, Abbey
> Road 2.
> Producer: George Martin. Engineer: Geoff Emerick.
> UK release: 5th August 1966 (LP: *Revolver*)
> US release: 8th August 1966 (LP: *Revolver*)

Written in bed one night as a children's song,[2] McCartney's YELLOW SUBMARINE may have been a musical spin-off from Bob Dylan's march-tempo 'Rainy Day Women Nos. 12 and 35', which entered the UK chart a fortnight before. The Beatles met Dylan[3] at the Savoy Hotel the evening before they began the track, where they also ran into Donovan,[4] with whom they got on well. The following day McCartney stopped off at Donovan's apartment and played him YELLOW SUBMARINE, asking for a suggestion for the closing lines. The latter obliged with 'Sky of blue, sea of green'. That evening, after much rehearsal, the group taped a rhythm track with vocals, returning a week

---

[1] McCartney recalls that the arrangement involved a high D normally considered above the range of Civil's instrument, but which he nevertheless managed. (Miles, op. cit., p. 289.) However, since the track was varispeeded, it may be that the solo was recorded in a lower key at a slower speed.

[2] In Part 6 of the *Anthology* video, McCartney recalls this as a hypnagogic inspiration (i.e., similar to those of [59] YESTERDAY, [69] NOWHERE MAN, and [123] ACROSS THE UNIVERSE).

[3] He was in London for his Albert Hall concerts with The Band (26th and 27th May). On 27th May, D. A. Pennebaker filmed Lennon and Dylan riding in a limousine from Weybridge to Mayfair, footage intended for the abandoned movie *Eat The Document*. A transcript of their conversation, with Dylan on menacing form and Lennon justifiably uneasy, appeared in the first issue of *Mojo* (November 1993).

[4] Donovan accompanied them to Rishikesh in 1968. A duet with McCartney on the latter's 'Heather' (dedicated to his stepdaughter and recorded in 1969) can be found on some Beatles bootlegs.

later to throw a party in Studio 2 and dub on sound-effects. Directed by George Martin, whose experience as a producer of comedy records now came into its own, they raided Abbey Road's 'trap room' for its trove of noise-making implements, including chains, whistles, hooters, hoses, handbells, and an old tin bath. In his element, Lennon filled a bucket with water and blew bubbles in it while the group's chauffeur Alf Bicknell rattled chains in the bath and Brian Jones of The Rolling Stones clinked glasses. Other effects were obtained from records, including an uncredited 78rpm snippet of a brass band march cut up by Martin and cleverly pasted into the last two bars of the second verse.[1] For the central section, Lennon and McCartney went into the studio's echo chamber to yell meaningless nauticalisms, Lennon remaining there to repeat Starr's lines, Goon-style, throughout the final verse. All told, this process took nearly twelve hours[2] – time well-spent in producing a sparkling novelty song impossible to dislike.

[89] I WANT TO TELL YOU *(Harrison)*

Harrison double-tracked vocal, lead guitar, handclaps; **McCartney**
  harmony vocal, bass, piano, handclaps; **Lennon** harmony vocal,
  tambourine, handclaps; **Starr** drums, maracas, handclaps
Recorded: 2nd–3rd June 1966, Abbey Road 2.
Producer: George Martin. Engineer: Geoff Emerick.
UK release: 5th August 1966 (LP: *Revolver*)
US release: 8th August 1966 (LP: *Revolver*)

An unprecedented third Harrison contribution to a Beatles album, I WANT TO TELL YOU resembles [73] THINK FOR YOURSELF in using chord changes as expressive, rather than functional, devices.[3] A song,

---

[1] George Martin (personal communication). The march is probably 'Le Rêve passe' (Krier–Helmer, 1906).
[2] This included a fifteen-second spoken introduction (supposedly a 'tribute' to Dr Barbara Moore and her 1960 charity walk from Land's End to John O'Groats) made available on the *Real Love* single.
[3] The only Beatle to mention chords in his lyrics [100], Harrison – like most lead guitarists – came to songwriting uncertainly, fumbling over words and melody and with ears tuned more to the emotional resonances of harmonic progressions. With a narrow vocal range, he began closer to Lennon as a songwriter, his melodies rising and falling only minimally over minor sequences. This led to his use of diminished chords – e.g., I WANT TO TELL YOU (2nd and 6th bars of the middle eight), [117] BLUE JAY WAY ('We'll be over soon they said'), [147] PIGGIES ('to play around in') – though it is easy to exaggerate this trait in his writing. (Diminished chords are proportionally almost as common in Lennon and McCartney's work). In his later Beatles songs, liberated by Indian music's focus on scales rather than harmony, he found his melodic voice and gravitated more in McCartney's direction.

in its author's words, about 'the avalanche of thoughts that are so hard to write down or say', it couches communication problems in Oriental terms, seeing them as contradictions between different levels of being ('it's only me, it's not my mind/That is confusing things'). Thus his eleven-bar sequence aspires upwards from A major to B major only to proceed from there in two directions at once, creating a frustrated bitonal dissonance (G sharp 7 diminished against E7, or E7 flat 9) before falling back on the home triad.[1] Similarly, the restlessly irregular phrases of the middle eight (doggedly pressing on with the syncopated crotchets of [66] IF I NEEDED SOMEONE) revolve dejectedly around B minor until inner light dawns and resolve returns with an ascent to a suspended fourth on A major, fiercely reinforced by Starr's battering drums. The underlying Hindu outlook in the lyric – a *karmic* reference to time in the final lines – is confirmed by a descending melisma in the fade-out (sung by McCartney?).

If not the most talented then certainly the most thoughtful of the songwriting Beatles, Harrison was regarded by Lennon and McCartney as a junior partner, and I WANT TO TELL YOU was despatched swiftly compared with the time lavished on their material. He, meanwhile, patiently pursued his own course, developing his interest in all things Indian. During June 1966 Ravi Shankar visited his Esher home with his colleague the tabla-player Alla Rakha and played for the assembled Beatles. The guitarist quickly became one of Shankar's Western protégés and, within a year, his fascination with Eastern philosophy was dominating the social life of the group.

---

[1] Implying an Oriental variant of the A major scale wherein the sixth is flat: more Arabic than Indian. A precedent was set by recording the rhythm track without bass, taping it later on a separate track, a decision which may have originated in uncertainty over whether to play E or F in the sixth bar. Then influenced by Brian Wilson's chord-defining bass-parts for The Beach Boys, McCartney realised that recording like this allowed him to control the harmonic structure of the music. Hence most Beatles tracks made from late 1966 to 1968 were initially recorded without bass – McCartney playing keyboard or guitar – or by using only a 'guide' bass track, replaced at a later stage. McCartney's other big influence on bass around this time was Motown sessionman James Jamerson, whose lines suddenly took on a guitar-like freedom and busy triplet complexity from the second half of 1965. (Some of these famous bass-parts – e.g., 'Reach Out I'll Be There' and 'Bernadette' by The Four Tops – are said by several witnesses to have been created not by Jamerson in Detroit but in Los Angeles by Carol Kaye, a session guitarist before she switched to bass in 1964.)

[90] GOOD DAY SUNSHINE *(Lennon–McCartney)*

McCartney vocal, bass, piano, handclaps; **Lennon** harmony vocal,
guitar (?), handclaps; **Harrison** harmony vocal, handclaps; **Starr**
drums, handclaps; **George Martin** piano
Recorded: 8th–9th June 1966, Abbey Road 2.
Producer: George Martin. Engineer: Geoff Emerick.
UK release: 5th August 1966 (LP: *Revolver*)
US release: 8th August 1966 (LP: *Revolver*)

The summer of 1966 was particularly glorious and McCartney's GOOD
DAY SUNSHINE, written one hot afternoon at Lennon's mansion, was
one of several records to capture the atmosphere.[1] Made quickly and
easily in two sessions, the song is both blissfully simple and full of the
free-spirited musical jesting with which The Beatles amazed classical
critics. (It was a particular favourite of Leonard Bernstein.) Stealing up
through the deceptive shade of E major, it leaps joyously into the light
of the dominant – dropping beats left, right, and centre – before
landing, in barrelhouse 4/4, on A major. Lest this become too familiar,
the second verse cuts itself short for a rolling piano excursion to D,
played with aplomb (and varispeed) by George Martin, before
modulating in a telescoping coda of canonic entries from all parts of the
stereo spectrum.[2] Superbly sung by McCartney and exquisitely
produced by Martin and his team, GOOD DAY SUNSHINE displays The
Beatles at their effortless best.

---

[1] Based on The Lovin' Spoonful's similarly summery 'Daydream' (a UK hit from
April to July), GOOD DAY SUNSHINE was recorded in the same week that The Kinks'
'Sunny Afternoon' entered the British charts. In New York, where the heat was
intense, The Lovin' Spoonful followed up their hit with the powerful anti-idyll
'Summer in the City'. The Rolling Stones likewise opted for a darker view with
their sitar-driven summer hit 'Paint It Black'. Donovan, meanwhile, had an
American hit with the jazzy 'Sunshine Superman'.

[2] Beginning the second side of *Revolver*, GOOD DAY SUNSHINE is the first of a
sequence of four songs to finish in a key other than the one they start in.

[91] HERE, THERE AND EVERYWHERE *(Lennon–McCartney)*

McCartney double-tracked vocal, acoustic guitar, bass, finger-snaps;
   Lennon backing vocal, finger-snaps; **Harrison** backing vocal,
   lead guitar, finger-snaps; **Starr** drums, finger-snaps
Recorded: 14th, 16th–17th June 1966, Abbey Road 2.
Producer: George Martin. Engineer: Geoff Emerick.
UK release: 5th August 1966 (LP: *Revolver*)
US release: 8th August 1966 (LP: *Revolver*)

Written by Lennon's pool at Weybridge, McCartney's lullaby love-song[1] is often spoken of as influenced by Brian Wilson's lushly romantic 1966 compositions for The Beach Boys (in particular the sublime 'God Only Knows', perhaps the most perfect pop record ever made). However, while *Pet Sounds*, conceived as a 'reply' to *Rubber Soul* (see [93], note), deeply impressed McCartney and spurred him to better it in The Beatles' next album *Sgt. Pepper*, Wilson's masterpiece wasn't issued in Britain until July. Even supposing McCartney to have had an advanced copy, no musical link exists between HERE, THERE AND EVERYWHERE and anything on *Pet Sounds*, although the mood of 'Don't Talk (Put Your Head On My Shoulder)' is similar.

The track took three days to record, care being taken over the texture of its three-part backing vocals (which, as arranged by Martin, follow the sequence in block harmony, while sounding richer and more complex). Mandolin-toned guitar was obtained through the Leslie cabinet and, in the final bars, given a horn-like timbre by the use of the volume-pedal [61]. McCartney's favourite among his songs ('with "Yesterday": a close second'), HERE, THERE AND EVERYWHERE is a pretty melody, cunningly worked out and prefaced by a three-bar intro which subtly and skilfully introduces its G/B flat major tonality. While the lyrics seek to match the ingenuity of the music, they fail to avoid sentimentality, and for all its soft-focus charm the song's overall effect is chintzy and rather cloying.

---

[1] He wrote most of it whilst waiting for Lennon to get up. Lennon helped him finish it. McCartney estimates authorship at '80-20' to him. (Miles, op. cit., p. 286.)

[92] SHE SAID SHE SAID *(Lennon–McCartney)*

Lennon vocal, rhythm guitar, Hammond organ; **Harrison** backing
vocal, bass, lead guitar; **Starr** drums, shaker
Recorded: 21st June 1966, Abbey Road 2.
Producer: George Martin. Engineer: Geoff Emerick.
UK release: 5th August 1966 (LP: *Revolver*)
US release: 8th August 1966 (LP: *Revolver*)

The antithesis of McCartney's impeccable neatness, Lennon's
anguished SHE SAID SHE SAID is a song of tormented self-doubt
struggling in a lopsided web of harmony and metre. Resembling the
jangling mid-tempo style of The Byrds, it draws its inspiration from the
day in August 1965 when Lennon took LSD with Roger McGuinn
and David Crosby in Los Angeles (see [63]). He had just watched and
been severely bored by Jane Fonda's new film *Cat Ballou* when her
actor brother Peter turned up and insisted on telling him about a
hospital operation during which he'd had a near-death experience.
Already annoyed by Fonda's sister, Lennon was exasperated by his
disturbing claim that he knew what it was like to be dead and, fearing a
bad trip, had him thrown out. The unease of the encounter stayed with
him and seems to have blended with his experience of 'ego-death'
during early 1966 (see [77]) to become the lyric of SHE SAID SHE SAID,
yet another of his creative admissions of spiritual disorientation. (Cf.
[38], [40], [50], [53], [56], and [69].)

The last track recorded for *Revolver*, SHE SAID SHE SAID strings an
endlessly uncoiling B flat Mixolydian melody around a standard three-
chord progression from which it struggles to break free, managing to
escape only twice, and very briefly, to the 3/4 childhood haven of F
('When I was a boy').[1] Rhythmically one of the most irregular things
Lennon ever wrote, it required the lion's share of its nine-hour session
to rehearse, and the result justifies every minute. As a performance, SHE
SAID SHE SAID is the outstanding track on *Revolver*, emotionally tense
and as moving in its unhappy way as [86] ELEANOR RIGBY. Whenever
the feeling is real, Starr rises to the occasion, and here he holds the track
together with drumming technically finer than that of his other *tour-de-
force* [81] RAIN.

With help from Harrison on vocal harmonies and lead guitar,
Lennon (as with [76] GIRL on *Rubber Soul*) pulls off a last-minute coup
with this track, going some way towards evening up the score in his

---

[1] Harrison recalls helping Lennon piece the song together from two separate
sections he had written (*The Beatles Anthology*, p. 97).

ongoing competition with McCartney (who, following an argument in the studio, does not appear on this track). In truth, however, *Revolver* – regarded by many as The Beatles' finest album – has far more of McCartney's fingerprints on it than Lennon's. While the group's former leader mused in his psychedelic daydream, his versatile partner was taking over – and, luckily for the group, doing so as he approached the summit of his creativity.

[93] STRAWBERRY FIELDS FOREVER *(Lennon–McCartney)*

1st version: **Lennon** vocal, acoustic guitar; **McCartney** Mellotron, bass; **Harrison** electric slide guitar; **Starr** drums

2nd version: **Lennon** vocal, acoustic guitar, bongos, Mellotron; **McCartney** Mellotron, bass, electric guitar, timpani, bongos; **Harrison** electric slide guitar, svarmandal, timpani, maracas; **Starr** drums, percussion; **Mal Evans** tambourine; **Neil Aspinall** guiro; **Terry Doran** maracas; **Tony Fisher**, **Greg Bowen**, **Derek Watkins**, **Stanley Roderick** trumpets; **John Hall**, **Derek Simpson**, **Norman Jones** cellos

Recorded: 24th, 28th–29th November, 8th–9th, 15th, 21st–22nd December 1966, Abbey Road 2.

Producer: George Martin. Engineer: Geoff Emerick.

UK release: 17th February 1967 (A single/PENNY LANE)

US release: 13th February 1967 (A single/PENNY LANE)

In summer 1966, The Beatles' career was in a state of acute self-contradiction. Having evolved a new musical identity in the studio, they were obliged by touring commitments to step back into their earlier pop style and trudge around the world churning out under-rehearsed sets to audiences screaming too loudly to notice how bad they were. A mere two days after finishing *Revolver* (barely a note of which could be reproduced live), the reluctant group was toiling grimly through Germany[1] and Japan.[2] Arriving in the Philippines, they

---

[1] This trip involved a gig in Hamburg on 26th June which returned The Beatles to the beginning of their career. Lennon took the opportunity to drop in on Astrid Kirchherr and reminisce about Stuart Sutcliffe, while McCartney visited the Indra and the Star-Club.

[2] Hitherto *personae non grata* in conservative Japan, The Beatles became acceptable once the British establishment had officially acknowledged the group by awarding them MBEs. Their first concert at the Nippon Budokan Hall in Tokyo (30th June 1966) was greeted with a respectful restraint which took them by surprise, not least because it exposed how far they'd declined as live performers under the barrage of screams which greeted them in less inhibited societies.

enraged the egregious Imelda Marcos by not paying court to her as expected and consequently found themselves manhandled by her husband's thugs at Manila airport. They were already fed up with Brian Epstein for making them tour and rounded on him furiously for exposing them not only to an unrealistically demanding schedule but also to police brutality. Asked what next for The Beatles on returning to London, a glum Harrison replied: 'We'll take a couple of weeks to recuperate before we go and get beaten up by the Americans.'

Thanks to an unwise remark by Lennon to a journalist about the relative popularity of Jesus and The Beatles,[1] Harrison's prediction turned out all too true: by the time they arrived in America for their third and final tour, the group had become hate-figures in the Bible Belt, where all merchandise linked with them was being cast triumphantly onto sacrificial pyres. A public apology by Lennon in Chicago quelled the uproar but the tour itself was a misery of half-empty stadia and half-baked logistics with The Beatles playing, on their own admission, appallingly badly and a demented Lennon screaming inaudible obscenities into the incessant aviary din of female shrieking. After their last concert at San Francisco's Candlestick Park, Harrison flatly informed Epstein that he was leaving the group and, for a while, it was touch and go whether The Beatles would carry on. Epstein's chastened promise that there would be no more touring took the sting out of the situation, while a four-month cooling-off period and the generally ecstatic reaction to *Revolver* gradually restored morale.

Lennon's ironic estimate of The Beatles' god-like status, debatable before *Revolver*, appeared fairly realistic after it. The album's aural invention was so masterful that it seemed to Western youth that The Beatles *knew* – that they had the key to current events and were somehow orchestrating them through their records. Expectations aroused by the sequel to *Revolver* were intense, and not only among the group's fans. Since 1965, the major British and American pop acts had been waging a friendly competition to come up with the most extraordinary music, and in 1966–7 this produced a major structural change in the music business. The hit-and-miss turnover of mass-produced 'artistes' suddenly gave way to a more stable scene based on self-determining 'artists' no longer manipulated by record companies. This difference was measurable in hard market terms, the turnover of

---

[1] 'Christianity will go. It will vanish and shrink. We're more popular than Jesus now.' (*London Evening Standard*, 4th March 1966.)

disposable pop acts plummeting in inverse proportion to the rising sales and prestige of the new pop/rock aristocracy. Moreover, rather than peddle pap for profit, the latter were keen to express their times – which, already exciting, consequently became thrilling.

While 1966 produced many futuristic singles,[1] the new focus of competition was the LP, seen as the natural format for an idiom bursting its commercial and creative limits. In the months before The Beatles began *Sgt. Pepper's Lonely Hearts Club Band*, a queue of artists stepped up to roll back the perceived limits of the pop album. The Rolling Stones' *Aftermath,* The Who's *A Quick One,* Bob Dylan's epic *Blonde On Blonde,* The Byrds' *Fifth Dimension,* and The Mothers of Invention's *Freak Out*[2] all opened new vistas, setting fresh standards of achievement. Yet the key release of 1966 so far as The Beatles were concerned was The Beach Boys' *Pet Sounds.* Consciously created by leader Brian Wilson as a riposte to *Rubber Soul,* this lush homage to Californian adolescence was launched onto the market a few weeks after The Beatles finished *Revolver.*[3] Though Lennon was cool about it – or wished to appear so in hindsight (press interviews of the period

---

[1] The Beach Boys' 'Good Vibrations', The Byrds' 'Eight Miles High', The Yardbirds' 'Shapes Of Things', The Lovin' Spoonful's 'Summer In The City', The Who's 'I'm A Boy', The Four Tops' 'Reach Out I'll Be There', The Supremes' 'Love Is Here And Now You're Gone', The Rolling Stones' 'Have You Seen Your Mother Baby Standing In The Shadow', The Easybeats' 'Friday On My Mind', Cream's 'I Feel Free', etc.

[2] McCartney, who assiduously vetted the competition, regarded *Sgt. Pepper* as 'our *Freak Out!*'

[3] British and European readers should bear in mind that the *Rubber Soul* which so impressed Wilson and the US folk-rockers was a composite, missing four tracks: Side A/[57] I'VE JUST SEEN A FACE; [63] NORWEGIAN WOOD; [75] YOU WON'T SEE ME; [73] THINK FOR YOURSELF; [74] THE WORD; [71] MICHELLE; Side B/[60] IT'S ONLY LOVE; [76] GIRL; [70] I'M LOOKING THROUGH YOU; [67] IN MY LIFE; [61] WAIT; [62] RUN FOR YOUR LIFE. By short-changing American fans, Capitol managed to squeeze out an extra Beatles LP for the US market less than two months before *Revolver* was released. This was *'Yesterday' . . . (and Today* (notorious for its banned 'butcher' cover and resented by British fans at the time for featuring three tracks, subsequently to be issued on *Revolver,* which America heard first and which were meanwhile placed under radio-embargo in the UK): Side A/[64] DRIVE MY CAR; [85] I'M ONLY SLEEPING; [69] NOWHERE MAN; [82] DOCTOR ROBERT; [59] YESTERDAY; [60b] ACT NATURALLY; Side B/[83] AND YOUR BIRD CAN SING; [66] IF I NEEDED SOMEONE; [68] WE CAN WORK IT OUT; [72] WHAT GOES ON; [65] DAY TRIPPER. As a result of this, *Revolver* was released in America with only eleven tracks, a mutilation which infuriated The Beatles for whom this album, more than anything they'd recorded before, was an integral set. (Only with *Sgt. Pepper* did US Beatles albums begin to synchronise with British ones.)

show him enthusing about Wilson's talent as a writer-arranger) – his colleagues were deeply impressed. Declaring *Pet Sounds* to be 'the album of all time', McCartney conceded that The Beatles would need to surpass anything they had done to equal it. As it happened, Wilson was already struggling to match *Revolver* and, by the time *Sgt. Pepper* appeared, had pushed himself into a creative breakdown from which he never recovered. (Others were feeling the heat, too. In mid-1966, Wilson's hero Phil Spector, maddened by what he saw as an industry conspiracy to suppress his self-proclaimed masterpiece 'River Deep, Mountain High', downed tools and did not work again for nearly four years. An exhausted Dylan meanwhile crashed out of his touring schedule and went into retreat,[1] while The Rolling Stones, bingeing on LSD, were on the verge of losing the plot completely.)

Gathering, refreshed, at Abbey Road on Thursday 24th November 1966, The Beatles got down to their new album with a blend of confidence and competitive resolve. With open-ended evening sessions and no budget limit,[2] they could at last work without pressure. Better still, they had a fair idea of what they were aiming at: an autobiographical album developing the Liverpudlian resonances of records like [67] IN MY LIFE and [86] ELEANOR RIGBY.[3]

---

[1] Touring continuously from September 1965 to June 1966, he had burned himself out with drugs and was in a suicidal state, unable to face more commitments. On 29th July, he had a motorcycle accident which became an excuse for breaking his existing contracts. Between then and autumn 1967, he lived quietly at Woodstock, N. Y., recording informally with The Band. His career never recovered its impetus and the quality of his work went into permanent decline.

[2] Since EMI owned both Abbey Road and The Beatles' recordings, studio time wasn't deducted from the group's royalties.

[3] McCartney has since denied this (*Mojo*, November 1995): 'There wasn't any conscious we'll-sit-down-and-remember-our childhood'. This, though, is clearly untrue of songs like [67] IN MY LIFE, [93] STRAWBERRY FIELDS FOREVER, and [95] PENNY LANE. Moreover, McCartney effectively admits that the 'Northern childhood' concept continued to act as a 'device' (*sic*) during *Sgt. Pepper* itself. He describes the cover, for example, as 'an idea which is a bit Northern and a bit to do with our childhood, which was to be a floral clock. I'd seen them up North, a clock all made out of flowers in the park. I wanted us to be above a floral clock being given a mayorial presentation, meeting the Lord Mayor of Halifax or something.' Compare these motifs with the Northern brass band and Northern 'palace of varieties' style of music-hall in the title track (e.g., 'You're such a lovely audience/We'd like to take you home with us'); the evocation of childhood and of Lennon's childhood reading

The inaugural song was to be another of Lennon's hallucinogenic ventures into the mental interior: STRAWBERRY FIELDS FOREVER. Taking up where [92] SHE SAID SHE SAID had left off, STRAWBERRY FIELDS further pursued the theme of sensations too confusing, intense, or personal to articulate (an effect, reproduced in his deliberately stumbling lyric, which Lennon may have borrowed from The Who's 'My Generation'). This time, the character finding it hard to express herself was an orphan at Strawberry Field, a girls' reform school in Beaconsfield Road near Lennon's childhood home in Woolton. Never one to repeat himself, he turned the anxious disorientation of SHE SAID SHE SAID into something more ambiguous: on the one hand, a study in uncertain identity, tinged with the loneliness of the solitary rebel against all things institutional; on the other, an eerie longing for a wild childhood of hide-and-seek and tree-climbing: the visionary strawberry fields of his imagination.[1] This second aspect of the song effectively inaugurated the English pop-pastoral mood explored in the late Sixties by groups like The Pink Floyd, Traffic, Family, and Fairport Convention. More significant, though, was the song's child's-eye-view – for the true subject of English psychedelia was neither love nor drugs, but nostalgia for the innocent vision of the child. Initiated by Lennon and McCartney with the single STRAWBERRY FIELDS FOREVER/[95] PENNY LANE, pop's late-Sixties preoccupation with the lost domain of childhood drew predictably facile responses from songwriters who, in taking up the idea, were merely following fashion (e.g., Keith West in 'Excerpt from A Teenage Opera'). For Lennon, though, childhood had

habits in [103] LUCY IN THE SKY WITH DIAMONDS; the rueful reference to school days in [104] GETTING BETTER; the Northern (Rochdale) inspiration for [101] BEING FOR THE BENEFIT OF MR KITE; McCartney's self-avowed 'parody on Northern life' in [94] WHEN I'M SIXTY-FOUR; the strong Northern tint to the images of the town in [98] GOOD MORNING GOOD MORNING; and the recollection of McCartney's Liverpudlian youth in his section of [96] A DAY IN THE LIFE. Even the LP's closing reference to Blackburn, Lancashire, can be said to be part of this pattern since The Beatles only began to be specific with place names on the single [93] STRAWBERRY FIELDS FOREVER/[95] PENNY LANE, after which Northern/Liverpudlian allusions crop up throughout the rest of their work (although nowhere more intensively than on *Sgt. Pepper*). The 'Northern childhood' motifs in *Sgt. Pepper* are too pervasive to ignore, whether or not actively co-ordinated; indeed the title of Harrison's rejected [100] ONLY A NORTHERN SONG suggests the theme *was* informally voiced by the group during the album's early stages.

[1] As a boy he had roamed in the grounds of Strawberry Field with his friends Pete Shotton and Ivan Vaughan. His Aunt Mimi also took him to the annual open-air party where a Salvation Army band played.

been a very mixed experience, and only The Incredible String Band, in whom he and the other Beatles took a close interest during 1967–8, were able to evoke the same ambiguous landscape at comparable emotional intensity.

Like SHE SAID SHE SAID, STRAWBERRY FIELDS FOREVER was the product of a period of intense self-doubt for its author. Having shifted his outlook, LSD was undermining his confidence (so much so that, in private, after apologising for his 'anti-Jesus' comments at an American press-conference in August, he broke down and wept). All this put pressure on his beleaguered marriage, itself further weakened when he met Yoko Ono at the Indica gallery shortly before recording STRAWBERRY FIELDS – a moment which, in his precarious state, he recalled as equivalent to encountering Castaneda's Don Juan.[1] Piecing the song together on acoustic guitar during breaks from filming *How I Won The War* in Spain in September, he seems to have lost and rediscovered his artistic voice, passing through an interim phase of creative inarticulacy reflected in the halting, childlike quality of his lyric.[2] The music, too, shows Lennon at his most somnambulistic, moving uncertainly through thoughts and tones like a momentarily blinded man feeling for something familiar.

In fact, so unusual was the direction Lennon took with STRAW-BERRY FIELDS that he had no clear idea of what he wanted[3] and the first three days of recording amounted to a sustained false start. This began (24th November) with a studio demo (take 1) now available on *Anthology 2* – a thin sketch in which the chorus is held back for two verses. (This marks the first appearance of Harrison's distinctive slide

---

[1] The reference is to Carlos Castaneda's influential sequence of books purporting to be about a Mexican Indian shaman, of which the first volume appeared in 1968. Lennon attended a preview of Ono's show *Unfinished Paintings and Objects* on 9th November. At this stage Conceptual Art was still new and thus potent, particularly when mixed with Zen-like Oriental dislocations – and by a woman.

[2] The first verse ('Living is easy with eyes closed') seems less like a prelude to what follows than a postscript to the experience dealt with in SHE SAID SHE SAID (although Lennon later spoke of it as if it referred not to him but to the world at large). Recalling the song in 1980, he declared that even when very young he had felt unique, as if seeing things in a way unlike others ('No one I think is in my tree'). He was never sure whether this was a sign of genius or madness ('it must be high or low').

[3] In the home demo of November 1966 (*Anthology 2*), he begins by trying to fingerpick the chords but breaks off muttering 'I cannae do it' and continues with simple strumming. (For the 'first version', Harrison fingerpicked the chords on electric guitar.)

guitar style, later to dominate his first solo album *All Things Must Pass*.) With the chorus brought to the front, the slower 'first version' of STRAWBERRY FIELDS was commenced on 28th November, five takes of this being accumulated by the end of the next day and the last mixed down ('take 7'/reduction mix 1)[1] on the assumption that it would be the basic track. Lennon, though, was uneasy and, after a week's break, he and George Martin agreed to start from scratch using different instrumentation: trumpets and cellos. A faster, denser rhythm track was created on 8th–9th December in Studio 1 ('take 25'/reduction mix 2) and a week later the session players, scored by Martin, performed their overdubs ('take 26'/reduction mix 3).

Lennon remained unsatisfied. Finally, after a further week of pondering, he announced that he wanted the first part of the original version to be spliced to the second part of the new one, a task which would involve matching two takes recorded at different speeds and a semitone apart in pitch. Martin ventured mildly that this would be impossible; Lennon was adamant – and turned out to be right. By sheer fluke, it happened that the difference in tempi between the two tracks was in nearly exact ratio to the difference in their keys. By varispeeding the two takes to approximately the same tempo, Martin and his engineer Geoff Emerick pulled off one of the most effective edits in pop, detectable only in a change in ambience (at 1:00).[2] This swoop from the airiness of the first chorus/verse into something more shadowy, serious, and urgent was what Lennon had been groping for all along, yet ultimately it had to be achieved through controlled accident. (Lennon later confessed himself unsatisfied by the result, claiming it didn't represent what was in his mind and threatening to record the song yet again.)

More controlled accident lies behind the track's peculiar 'swimming' sound, derived from the varispeeding techniques developed

---

[1] Here the distinction between a live take and a mix-down was blurred for convenience's sake.

[2] This was done using a 'lash-up' created by EMI's Chief Engineer Ken Townsend: a valve-powered 'washing-machine lookalike' known as the frequency-changer (Martin, *Summer Of Love*, p. 22). The final version of STRAWBERRY FIELDS spliced 'take 7' to 'take 26'. Take 7, though, had a different structure to take 26: instead of the second chorus (after 'It doesn't matter much to me'), it went straight to the next verse. In other words, as well as joining two takes at different speeds and in different keys, Martin and Emerick also added an extra chorus – a significant improvement to the song's lay-out.

during the *Revolver* sessions. In fact, so much varying of the capstan speed went on during the making of STRAWBERRY FIELDS that the final mix wanders in a microtonal borderland between keys. (The track begins in an untempered A sharp before sliding imperceptibly into orthodox B flat.) An idea of how much acceleration needed to be applied to the first version to match it to the second can be had by comparing Starr's high-frequency snare sound in the opening minute with its more natural pitch thereafter. Not that this should be exaggerated; the percussion tracks for STRAWBERRY FIELDS – tape-reversed hi-hat on the verses, ringing tom-toms, double-time timpani and bongos on the later choruses – were carefully put together.

Though *par excellence* a Lennon song, STRAWBERRY FIELDS drew sharp contributions from all involved. Apart from Starr's indispensable foundation work, the main features of the texture were supplied by a Mellotron played by McCartney[1] and a sort of Indian zither called a *svarmandal* used by Harrison for the descending *raga* scale which pans across the stereo spectrum at the ends of the central choruses. Picking up on this Indian inflection, George Martin wove his cellos exotically around McCartney's sitar-like guitar-fills in the fade, his one-note brass fanfare (probably based on scatting by Lennon, McCartney, and Harrison in the original version)[2] emerging as the most exciting feature of a superbly climactic arrangement. (Famous in the studio world for its resonant drum sounds, STRAWBERRY FIELDS – along with [116] I AM THE WALRUS – is also especially esteemed for its cello parts, on which groups like The Electric Light Orchestra and Wizzard based entire careers.)

Devouring an unprecedented fifty-five hours of studio-time, STRAWBERRY FIELDS FOREVER extended the range of studio techniques developed on *Revolver*, opening up possibilities for pop which, given sufficient invention, could result in unprecedented sound-images. Such moods and textures had formerly been the province of classical music, and when George Martin described the recording as 'a complete tone

---

[1] He wrote the four-bar introduction on this instrument. Lennon used its master-speed control knob (forerunner of the modern synthesiser's pitch-wheel) for the downward glissando from verse to chorus. He also found a way of making it generate random notes in the 'fade-back' section at the end.

[2] The Beatles often 'wrote' instrumental lines in this way. Most of Martin's brass and wind arrangement on [95] PENNY LANE was derived from such vocal ad-libbing. However he also recalls 'lifting' some 'very groovy' brass ideas from American records of the time (*Summer Of Love*, p. 21).

poem – like a modern Debussy', he did so with a certain justification. Genres apart, the main difference between a Debussy piece and a song like STRAWBERRY FIELDS lies less in expressive aspiration than in range of colour and fluency of articulation. Here, The Beatles show that technical shortcomings, far from constraining the imagination, can let it expand into areas inaccessible to the trained mind. Heard for what it is – a sort of technologically-evolved folk music – STRAWBERRY FIELDS FOREVER shows expression of a high order. While there are countless contemporary composers qualified to write music hugely more sophisticated in form and technique, few if any are capable of displaying feeling and fantasy so direct, spontaneous, and original.

[94] WHEN I'M SIXTY-FOUR *(Lennon–McCartney)*

McCartney vocal, backing vocal, piano, bass; Lennon backing
vocal, guitar; Harrison backing vocal; Starr drums, chimes;
Robert Burns, Henry MacKenzie, Frank Reidy clarinets
Recorded: 6th December 1966, Abbey Road 2; 8th December,
Abbey Road 1; 20th–21st December 1966, Abbey Road 2.
Producer: George Martin. Engineer: Geoff Emerick.
UK release: 1st June 1967 (LP: *Sgt. Pepper's Lonely Hearts Club
Band*)
US release: 2nd June 1967 (LP: *Sgt. Pepper's Lonely Hearts Club
Band*)

The Beatles' versatility was a facet their rivals could only envy. Taped between sessions for [93] STRAWBERRY FIELDS FOREVER, this McCartney song could hardly have stood in greater contrast: light in tone and texture, musically backward-looking, and delivered with cute insouciance. Casting back to the music-hall of George Formby and the seaside postcards of Donald McGill, WHEN I'M SIXTY-FOUR seems, on the face of it, typical of the mid-Sixties taste for pastiches of pre-war English pop dealt in by groups like The Temperance Seven, The New Vaudeville Band, and The Bonzo Dog Doo-Dah Band. In fact, it was one of McCartney's earliest instrumental pieces and had been used by the group in their club days as a filler when the PA system broke down. Brought to its writer's mind when his father Jim turned sixty-four on 2nd July 1966, it was equipped with a lyric (described by McCartney as 'a parody on Northern life') and placed, like a comic brass fob-watch suspended from a floral waistcoat, amid the multi-layered psychedelic textures of *Sgt. Pepper*, providing a down-to-earth interlude after Harrison's complex and serious [106] WITHIN YOU WITHOUT YOU.

Few Beatles arrangements are as sparse, its main features being McCartney's sedately plodding bass, George Martin's cheeky clarinet lines, and some unusually florid backing voices.[1] Capped with one of McCartney's most winsome vocals – made more larkish by speeding the track up a key – WHEN I'M SIXTY-FOUR was aimed chiefly at parents, and as a result got a cool reception from the group's own generation.

[95] PENNY LANE *(Lennon–McCartney)*

> **McCartney** vocal, pianos, bass, harmonium, tambourine, effects; **Lennon** backing vocal, pianos, guitar, congas, handclaps; **Harrison** backing vocal, guitar; **Starr** drums, handbell; **George Martin** piano; **Ray Swinfield, P. Goody, Manny Winters, Dennis Walton** flutes, piccolos; **David Mason, Leon Calvert, Freddy Clayton, Bert Courtley, Duncan Campbell** trumpets, flugelhorn; **Dick Morgan, Mike Winfield** oboes, cor anglais; **Frank Clarke** doublebass
>
> Recorded: 29th–30th December 1966; 4th–6th, 9th January 1967, Abbey Road 2; 10th, 12th January 1967, Abbey Road 3; 17th January 1967, Abbey Road 2.
>
> Producer: George Martin. Engineer: Geoff Emerick.
>
> UK release: 17th February 1967 (A single/STRAWBERRY FIELDS FOREVER)
>
> US release: 13th February 1967 (A single/STRAWBERRY FIELDS FOREVER)

Anyone unlucky enough not to have been aged between 14 and 30 during 1966–7 will never know the excitement of those years in popular culture. A sunny optimism permeated everything and possibilities seemed limitless. Bestriding a British scene that embraced music, poetry, fashion, and film, and in which English football had recently beaten the world, The Beatles were at their peak and looked up to in awe as arbiters of a positive new age in which the dead customs of the older generation would be refreshed and remade through the creative energy of the classless young. With its vision of 'blue suburban skies' and boundlessly confident vigour, PENNY LANE distills the spirit of that time more perfectly than any other creative product of the mid-Sixties. Couched in the primary colours of a picture-book, yet observed with

---

[1] Apart from backing vocals, Lennon contributes some anomalous folk-blues guitar picking to the final verse/chorus (2:17–2:29) – a style joke that provokes an audible grin from McCartney (2:23).

the slyness of a gang of kids straggling home from school, PENNY LANE is both naive and knowing – but above all thrilled to be alive.

Lennon and McCartney had toyed with this title for eighteen months, having made a list of Liverpool place-names during a writing session for *Rubber Soul* (see [67]). While it was Lennon who picked the neighbourhood in question,[1] it was McCartney who went on to set it to music. Both, though, contributed to the pictorial lyric which was very specific to the actual place. As Lennon later told *Rolling Stone*: 'The bank was *there*, and *that* was where the tram sheds were and people waiting and the inspector stood *there*, the fire engines were down *there*. It was just reliving childhood.'[2]

The track's distinctive staccato piano chords (to become a cliché in the hands of imitators) recycle the style first tried in [78] GOT TO GET YOU INTO MY LIFE. So successful was the effect in PENNY LANE that McCartney quickly repeated it in different tempi in four more songs: [99] FIXING A HOLE, [104] GETTING BETTER, [107] WITH A LITTLE HELP FROM MY FRIENDS, and [115] YOUR MOTHER SHOULD KNOW. If, in PENNY LANE, this device seems simple, the actual sound of it was the product of hard work, guided by its author's interest in production effects. Presumably playing to a click-track, he began with a basic take of piano chords. Having added a second piano (sent, with reverb, through a Vox amp), he recorded a third at half-speed, thereby altering the instrument's overtones. On top of this three-decked super-piano were layered various 'treated' percussion effects and some high-frequency tones from a harmonium. Bounced down to accommodate a guide-vocal (taped, for some reason, at reduced speed), the track was left to mature over Christmas. Work on it resumed early in January 1967 with a fourth piano layer overdubbed by Lennon and, two days later, yet more piano from Lennon and Martin. At this point McCartney finally approved the sound.[3] Further slowed recording was

---

[1] Penny Lane, though also a street, is usually thought of in Liverpool as an area. Thus, Lennon lived 'in' Penny Lane as a small boy, though his actual address was Newcastle Road.

[2] The barber in Penny Lane was where McCartney and his brother Mike were taken by their father for their 'short-back-and-sides' during the late Forties and early Fifties. The Liverpool sexual slang phrase 'finger pie' was probably contributed by Lennon.

[3] The finished 'piano' part is subtly varied throughout the track with the maximum weight and range of the keyboards involved in it used only at key points. Other emphases are applied with spot reverb on the percussion and moments of double-tracked bass. (A stereo remix for *Anthology 2* reveals other aspects of Martin's elaborate arrangement.)

applied to his bass guitar and most of the rest of the group's other overdubs; however, the famous B-flat piccolo trumpet solo added on the final day of recording was, contrary to legend, taped in real time and not speeded up. (Or so says David Mason, the Philharmonia trumpeter who performed the part. Few would doubt his claim that he can, to this day, play the line along with the record, but this is no proof that the track wasn't varispeeded – without his knowledge – during the recording.)[1]

Following the style created in *Revolver*, PENNY LANE is packed with illustrative sound-effects and arrangement touches, ranging from the obvious (the fireman's handbell) to the virtually inaudible (an arthritic doublebass depicting the Banker lowering himself into the Barber's chair for a trim). While a team-effort in terms of performance, the track is as essentially McCartneyesque as [93] STRAWBERRY FIELDS FOREVER is Lennonian. Breezily vertical in tune and harmony where STRAWBERRY FIELDS is lazily horizontal, PENNY LANE's jaunty triplet melody, counterpointed by a high-lying bass, could have come from no other songwriter. Credit must also be given to him for David Mason's quasi-baroque trumpet solo. Though Martin wrote it out, the line, like other details of the arrangement, was sung to him by McCartney in imitation of Bach's Second Brandenburg Concerto, which he had heard on television, played by Mason, a week earlier. (Note, too, the subtle motivic quotation from the song's melody in the solo's seventh bar.)

As much a triumph for McCartney as STRAWBERRY FIELDS was for Lennon, PENNY LANE fathered a rather smug English pop vogue for brass bands and gruff Northern imagery. However, as the film of *Yellow Submarine* later showed by using similar images in a psychedelic context, the song is every bit as subversively hallucinatory as STRAWBERRY FIELDS. Despite its seeming innocence, there are few more LSD-redolent phrases in The Beatles' output than the line (sung with an ecstatic shiver of grace-notes) in which the Nurse 'feels as if she's in a play' . . . and 'is, anyway'.[2]

---

[1] The initial pressings of PENNY LANE, sent out to DJs and played on the radio during the first weeks of February, included an extra two-bar phrase by Mason in the final bars, bringing the song to a full close in B major *(Anthology 2)*. This vanished from all subsequent copies of the track.

[2] Seemingly naturalistic, the lyric scene is actually kaleidoscopic. As well as raining and shining at the same time, it is simultaneously summer and winter (the Nurse is selling poppies for Remembrance Day: 11th November). The last Beatle to try LSD, McCartney was the first to admit to it (to a *Life* reporter in May 1967); consequently the usual guess is that he took the drug in early 1967. PENNY LANE suggests it may have been towards the end of 1966. This guess is confirmed by Miles (op. cit., p. 380), who dates McCartney's first 'trip', in company with Tara Browne, to around

[U96] CARNIVAL OF LIGHT *(McCartney–Lennon–Harrison–Starr)*

McCartney, Lennon, Harrison, Starr voices, organ, guitar,
  tambourine, effects, loops[1]
Recorded: 5th January 1967, Abbey Road 2.
Producer: George Martin. Engineer: Geoff Emerick.
Never officially released.[2]

Rejected for *Anthology 2* – supposedly by Harrison but probably also by
others involved – this 13:48 'freak-out' was taped by The Beatles
during an evening session following a vocal overdub on [95] PENNY
LANE. For various reasons, it will never be released, although it may, of
course, eventually find its way onto a bootleg. Almost no one outside
the Apple circle has heard it and interest in it among 'Beatleologists' is
consequently high. In fact, an enterprising fraudster could easily
counterfeit a black-market version, since the real thing sounds nothing
like The Beatles.

A free-form piece without beat or key, CARNIVAL OF LIGHT was
instigated and directed by McCartney eighteen months before Lennon's [127] REVOLUTION 9. For this reason, if nothing else, McCartney
is proud of it and apparently still hankers for it to be in the public
domain.[3] Yet while it establishes his 'underground' credentials ahead
of Lennon's, CARNIVAL OF LIGHT cannot be compared with REVOLU-
TION 9.

For more than a year before The Beatles recorded this track,
McCartney had been playing at his home in Cavendish Avenue with
tape loops (see [77]) and *musique concrète*,[4] as well as experimenting

---

November 1966 (information confided in conversation).

[1] No record was kept of who played which instruments.

[2] I am grateful to Dave Vaughan, the organiser of the Carnival of Light, and to
Miles for information contained in this entry. (See also 'The Beatles & Psychedelia',
Record Collector No. 166, June 1993.)

[3] McCartney was at this stage far more involved with the London countercultural
avant-garde than Lennon who, leading the life of a married man in Weybridge, had
to commute in order to record at Abbey Road. Nor, until he encountered LSD, had
Lennon been much interested in expanding his horizons. ('Avant-garde,' he was
fond of remarking, 'is French for bullshit'.) It was not until he met Yoko Ono that
he began to catch up with McCartney in this respect.

[4] A form of tape music in which natural sounds are composed by being cut,
spliced, and altered by signal-processing, *musique concrète* was invented by Pierre
Schaeffer, a Radio France audio technician, who in 1948 broadcast his first essay in
the genre: a four-minute collage of the sounds of trains. During the early Fifties,
Stockhausen used a pulse-generator at WDR Cologne to blend pure electronics with
altered natural sounds (the voice of a boy chorister in Cologne Cathedral), thereby
creating *Gesang der Jünglinge*, generally reckoned the masterpiece of this idiom (and,
as such, an influence on Frank Zappa, The Grateful Dead, Pink Floyd, and Faust). In

with *montage* home movies. Through Miles, he knew the music of AMM, a free-jazz trio founded in 1965[1] who often performed in darkness, incorporating randomly scanned broadcasts by 'playing' transistor radios (cf. [116]). McCartney clearly had this sort of music in mind during the recording of CARNIVAL OF LIGHT and [96] A DAY IN THE LIFE.[2] The major discovery of his interaction with the mid-Sixties classical and jazz avant-garde was 'random' – the realisation that chance elements, with which The Beatles had already casually toyed, could produce striking results when actively sought after.[3] The difference was that AMM – following the contemporary ideal of transcending the ego (see [77]) – specialised in a sensitive form of collective improvisation in which players not only listened intently to each other but interacted spontaneously with everything around them, including their audiences. In CARNIVAL OF LIGHT, The Beatles merely bashed about at the same time, overdubbing without much thought, and relying on the Instant Art effects of tape-echo to produce something suitably 'far out'. That said, it would be unfair to expect anything much more considered, given that, unlike REVOLUTION 9 which was recorded for *The Beatles* and took five days, CARNIVAL OF LIGHT was knocked off quickly as an informal commission for a 'mixed media' event held on 28th January and 4th February 1967 at The Roundhouse Theatre in Camden Town, North London.[4]

1960, Schaeffer gave up *musique concrète* and turned to writing science fiction novels. His role was filled by his colleague Pierre Henry whose collaborations with choreographer Maurice Béjart puzzled ballet audiences during the Sixties. McCartney admired *Gesang der Jünglinge* and may also have known Henry's *Mass for the present time* (1967).

[1] Eddie Prévost (drums, percussion), Keith Rowe (guitar, electronics), and Lou Gare (tenor sax).

[2] AMM was joined in 1966 by left-wing composer Cornelius Cardew, whose *Treatise*, premiered in 1967, was an 'indeterminate' graphical score in which players interpreted their parts subjectively as they went along. This produced random sounds similar to the orchestral crescendos in [96] A DAY IN THE LIFE. In 1969 Cardew founded the Scratch Orchestra in which anyone, regardless of ability, could 'play' the classics on the basis that everyone was an artist. (He later became a Maoist, denouncing his former hero Stockhausen as an imperialist, and was killed in London by a hit-and-run driver in 1981.)

[3] See [127], [144], and Index references.

[4] The Roundhouse, a circular structure resembling a miniature Albert Hall, began as a 19th-century turntable shed built by the London and Birmingham Railway. Semi-derelict, it was bought by Arnold Wesker's Centre 42 in 1964 and taken over by the launch party for *International Times* in October 1966, after which it became the main arts venue of the London underground, hosting the Uncommon Market (a sort of hippie bazaar) as well as many rock events, the most famous of which, in 1968, featured The Doors and The Jefferson Airplane.

Organised by a trio of then-vogueish underground artists, (Douglas) Binder, (Dudley) Edwards, and (Dave) Vaughan, the Carnival Of Light Rave was a genuine countercultural 'happening' – a gathering of the English 'heads' three months before the larger and better-remembered 14-Hour Technicolor Dream held at Alexandra Palace on Muswell Hill. For the Carnival, the inside of The Roundhouse was turned into an 'environment' by being draped in sheets for light-shows. As at the Technicolor Dream and similar hippie events, the audience wandered amid art-objects and installations as films were projected and music was performed.[1] Personally delivered to Binder, Edwards, and Vaughan on quarter-inch tape by McCartney, The Beatles' soundtrack to these proceedings was played several times during both evenings.

The unstable mixture of naive 'flower power' idealism, confrontational street politics, and commercial opportunism which comprised, and finally compromised, the counterculture was epitomised by the Carnival Of Light. Faced with the evils of prejudice, war, poverty, and starvation, the underground was uncertain whether to attack these head-on with disruptions of the sort favoured by the Situationists (see [127]) or by-pass them by invoking love and peace. Was it better to argue the toss with people supposedly too brainwashed to understand one's language or simply 'love-bomb' them with flowers and smiles? In truth, a movement ranging, at its extremes, from dogmatic Left-wingers to LSD-in-the-reservoirs anarchists had as many 'communication hang-ups' within its own ranks as with the 'straight' world outside.

Binder, Edwards, and Vaughan, for example, were split between wanting success in a commercial sense and (almost certainly mutually contradictory) success in the idealistic sense of changing the world. Since they had to live and lived to paint, they decorated boutiques, provided murals for clubs, and let groups like The Kinks pose with their trademark, a psychedelically embellished Buick convertible in which they cruised their territory in Gloucester Road and Ladbroke Grove. McCartney met them through Tara Browne (see [96]), who recommended them as artists competent to paint his upright piano for him. Partly in return for this, but mainly because he was genuinely sympathetic to some of the counterculture's ideals, McCartney agreed to Vaughan's request to provide a soundtrack for the Carnival Of Light. Apart from this, the aims of the event were as discordant as the

---

[1] One of the acts at the Carnival was the newly-formed Jimi Hendrix Experience. Afterwards, Hendrix's Stratocaster was stolen, the thief being unsuccessfully pursued up Haverstock Hill. Hendrix's manager, ex-Animal Chas Chandler, had to sell his own bass guitar in order to buy a replacement.

'alternative society' itself: an avowed attempt to replace the mono-chrome seriousness of CND with something in the same anti-war spirit but 'lighter', while at the same time protesting against Vietnam and celebrating dope. Whether the nightmareish nature of CARNIVAL OF LIGHT came about as a response to this war/peace ambiguity, let alone to the specific reference to Vietnam, remains unclear even to the participants.[1] Within a year, such confusing confluences of light, dark, and drugs would begin to destroy the counterculture. Already, in January 1967, gangsters were at the doors of The Roundhouse demanding protection money. By January 1968, the sense of commu-nion which had inspired the English underground in the summer of 1965, carrying it through 1966 to the brief zenith of 1967, was gone.

[96] A DAY IN THE LIFE *(Lennon–McCartney)*

Lennon double-tracked vocal, acoustic guitar, piano; **McCartney** vocal, piano, bass; **Harrison** maracas; **Starr** drums, bongos; **Erich Gruenberg, Granville Jones, Bill Monro, Jurgen Hess, Hans Geiger, D. Bradley, Lionel Bentley, David McCallum, Donald Weekes, Henry Datyner, Sidney Sax, Ernest Scott** violins; **John Underwood, Gwynne Edwards, Bernard Davis, John Meek** violas; **Francisco Gabarro, Dennis Vigay, Alan Dalziel, Alex Nifosi** cellos; **Cyril MacArthur, Gordon Pearce** doublebasses; **John Marston** harp; **Basil Tschaikov, Jack Brymer** clarinets; **Roger Lord** oboe; **N. Fawcett, Alfred Waters** bassoons; **Clifford Seville, David Sandeman** flutes; **Alan Civil, Neil Sanders** French horns; **David Mason, Monty Montgomery, Harold Jackson** trumpets; **Raymond Brown, Raymond Premru, T. Moore** trombones; **Michael Barnes** tuba; **Tristan Fry** timpani, percussion
Recorded: 19th–20th January, 3rd February 1967, Abbey Road 2; 10th February 1967, Abbey Road 1; 22nd February 1967, Abbey Road 2.
Producer: George Martin. Engineer: Geoff Emerick.
UK release: 1st June 1967 (LP: *Sgt. Pepper's Lonely Hearts Club Band*)
US release: 2nd June 1967 (LP: *Sgt. Pepper's Lonely Hearts Club Band*)

With [93] STRAWBERRY FIELDS FOREVER and [95] PENNY LANE in the can, The Beatles were confident that their reply to The Beach Boys' *Pet*

[1] It certainly doesn't seem to have been explained to Lennon, the Beatle most overtly 'against Vietnam'; nor do his bellows of 'Barcelona!' suggest parallelistic allusions to the Spanish Civil War.

Sounds was well under way. Capitol, though, needed a new single and the tracks were accordingly requisitioned for a double A-side in February 1967. Since UK chart protocol in the Sixties was that anything issued as a single could not be included on an LP released in the same year, the group submitted to this with ill grace.[1] Apart from putting them back to square one with the new album, the decision killed the informal concept of an LP drawing inspiration from their Liverpool childhoods.[2] Fortunately, they were at the peak of their powers and, only two days after finishing PENNY LANE, they were back in Abbey Road working on their finest single achievement: A DAY IN THE LIFE.

More nonsense has been written about this recording than anything else The Beatles produced. It has been described as a sober return to the real world after the drunken fantasy of 'Pepperland'; as a conceptual statement about the structure of the pop album (or the artifice of the studio, or the falsity of recorded performance); as an evocation of a bad trip; as a 'pop *Waste Land*'; even as a morbid celebration of death. Most of this misinterpretation stems from ignorance of the fact that – apart from the relatively trivial [94] WHEN I'M SIXTY-FOUR – A DAY IN THE LIFE was the first track begun for *Sgt. Pepper*. At this stage, The Beatles had little idea what the new LP was going to be about (if anything). Conceived on its own terms, A DAY IN THE LIFE fell into place at the end of the finished work four months later with a naturalness that could hardly have been apparent at the time it was recorded. Still less likely is that The Beatles would have set about constructing an album to be 'subverted' or 'commented upon' by a piece of music unlike anything they'd ever done before (not least in being two minutes longer than the longest track in their discography to date: 5:03). Far from a purpose-built grand finale to a masterplan, it was merely a further speculative episode in the parallel developments of its authors.

If anything predetermined A DAY IN THE LIFE, it was LSD. A song about perception – a subject central both to late-period Beatles and the counterculture at large – A DAY IN THE LIFE concerned 'reality' only to the extent that this had been revealed by LSD to be largely in the eye of the beholder. A scepticism about appearances had figured in some of the songs for *Rubber Soul*, later coming to the fore in [81] RAIN, [83] AND YOUR BIRD CAN SING, and [77] TOMORROW NEVER KNOWS.

---

[1] In retrospect, George Martin describes his decision to pull STRAWBERRY FIELDS and PENNY LANE off the album as 'the biggest mistake of my professional life' (*Summer Of Love*, p. 26).

[2] See [93] STRAWBERRY FIELDS FOREVER, note, p. 191.

STRAWBERRY FIELDS FOREVER and PENNY LANE are further links in a chain of songs about perception and reality of which A DAY IN THE LIFE is an explicit culmination.

A song not of disillusionment with life itself but of disenchantment with the limits of mundane perception, A DAY IN THE LIFE depicts the 'real' world as an unenlightened construct that reduces, depresses, and ultimately destroys. In the first verse – based, like the last, on a report in the *Daily Mail* for 17th January 1967 – Lennon refers to the death of Tara Browne, a young millionaire friend of The Beatles and other leading English groups. On 18th December 1966, Browne, an enthusiast of the London counterculture and, like all its members, a user of mind-expanding drugs, drove his light blue Lotus Elan at high speed through red lights in South Kensington, smashing into a parked mini-van and killing himself. Whether or not he was tripping at the time is unknown, though Lennon clearly thought so. Reading the report of the coroner's verdict, he recorded it in the opening verses of A DAY IN THE LIFE, taking the detached view of the onlookers whose only interest was in the dead man's celebrity. Thus travestied as a spectacle, Browne's tragedy became meaningless – and the weary sadness of the music which Lennon found for his lyric displays a distance that veers from the dispassionate to the unfeeling.[1]

On the next page in the same newspaper, he found an item whose absurdity perfectly complemented the Tara Browne story: 'There are 4,000 holes in the road in Blackburn, Lancashire, or one twenty-sixth of a hole per person, according to a council survey.' This – intensified by a surreal reference to the circular Victorian concert venue the Albert Hall (also in South Kensington)[2] – became the last verse. In between, Lennon inserted a verse in which his jaded spectator looks on as the English army wins the war. Prompted by his part in the film *How I Won The War* three months earlier, this may have been a veiled allusion to

---

[1] This may not have been entirely simulated. According to Goldman, during the *Sgt. Pepper* period, The Beatles used not only cannabis and LSD but also 'speed-balls' – cocktails of heroin and cocaine. McCartney admits to using cocaine in this period (*Rolling Stone*, 11th September 1968). Miles confirms that speed-balls were 'around' during the sessions, but is unable to remember whether The Beatles themselves participated. (While recording, the group usually aimed to maintain sobriety.)

[2] Constructed during 1868–70 – partly on the profits from the Great Exhibition of 1851 which took place in the original Crystal Palace in Hyde Park, opposite the present site – the Albert Hall, along with the Albert Memorial which faces it, is the grandest architectural symbol of Victoria's reign. As such, it is held in obstinate affection by the English, despite its notorious echo which, say wags, makes it the only concert hall in the country in which a British composer can be sure of hearing his work twice.

Vietnam which, though a real issue to Lennon, would have overheated the song if stated directly.

At one level, A DAY IN THE LIFE concerns the alienating effect of 'the media'. On another, it looks beyond what the Situationists called 'the society of the Spectacle' to the poetic consciousness invoked by the anarchic wall-slogans of May 1968 in Paris (e.g., 'Beneath the pavement, the beach'). Hence the sighing tragedy of the verses is redeemed by the line 'I'd love to turn you on', which becomes the focus of the song. The message is that life is a dream and we have the power, as dreamers, to make it beautiful. In this perspective, the two rising orchestral glissandi may be seen as symbolising simultaneously the moment of awakening from sleep and a spiritual ascent from fragmentation to wholeness, achieved in the resolving E major chord. How the group themselves pictured these passages is unclear, though Lennon seems to have had something cosmic in mind, requesting from Martin 'a sound like the end of the world' and later describing it as 'a bit of a *2001*'. All that is certain is that the final chord was not, as many have since claimed, meant as an ironic gesture of banality or defeat. (It was originally conceived and recorded – Beach Boys style – as a hummed vocal chord.) In early 1967, deflation was the last thing on The Beatles' minds – or anyone else's, with the exception of Frank Zappa and Lou Reed.[1] Though clouded with sorrow and sarcasm, A DAY IN THE LIFE is as much an expression of mystic-psychedelic optimism as the rest of *Sgt. Pepper's Lonely Hearts Club Band*. The fact that it achieves its transcendent goal via a potentially disillusioning confrontation with the 'real' world is precisely what makes it so moving.

The Beatles began recording A DAY IN THE LIFE two days after Lennon was inspired to write its verses. In the intervening period, McCartney added the double-time middle section, a fragment of a number about his schooldays which, in its new context, became a vignette of a vacantly busy life of routine. (The 'smoke' was originally a Woodbine but, as McCartney and Lennon agreed, 'Bugger this, we're going to write a real turn-on song!') At this stage, the composition was so new that they hadn't had time to work out how to join Lennon's section to McCartney's and so had to record the basic track leaving two

---

[1] Derek Taylor describes The Beatles as being very happy and relaxed during the *Sgt. Pepper* sessions. (In the country as a whole, economic strictures imposed in the second half of 1966 were beginning to undermine confidence in the Labour government, yet such was the festive atmosphere in English pop culture that disturbances in the political sphere did not intrude significantly until 1968.)

arbitrary gaps of twenty-four bars (counted by road manager Mal Evans, whose reverbed voice remains on the finished recording).[1] The recording was subsequently built up over the next three weeks – Lennon and McCartney redoing their vocals, McCartney and Starr replacing their bass and drum parts – until the desired effect was obtained.

For the final overdubs, a party was thrown in Studio 1 on Friday 10th February, much as had been done on 1st June 1966 for [88] YELLOW SUBMARINE, except that this time an orchestra was involved. McCartney – who had listened to music by John Cage and Luciano Berio and heard performances by AMM (see [U96]) at the Royal College of Art – decided that the twenty-four bar bridges would be filled by a symphony orchestra going from its lowest to its highest note in an unsynchronised slide: a 'freak- out' or aural 'happening'. Charged with realising this, George Martin halved the number of players and scored the *glissando* individually to ensure the right 'random' effect. Rather than a chaotic tone-cluster, each player was asked to finish on whichever note in the E major triad was nearest the highest on his instrument. A second four-track tape machine was slaved to the one running The Beatles' own stereo track (the first time this had ever been tried in a British studio) and each orchestral *glissando* was recorded in mono four times before being mixed back to the master as a single monstrous noise (presumably remixed with ADT to take up the spare track). At the end of a festive evening, those in the studio spontaneously applauded the result.[2] The final chord, played by Lennon, McCartney, Starr, Evans, and Martin on three pianos (and 'tracked' four times), was recorded separately twelve days later.

Made in a total of around thirty-four hours, A DAY IN THE LIFE represents the peak of The Beatles' achievement. With one of their most controlled and convincing lyrics, its musical expression is breathtaking, its structure at once utterly original and completely natural. The performance is likewise outstanding. Lennon's floating, tape-echoed vocal contrasts ideally with McCartney's 'dry' briskness;[3]

---

[1] These counts, starting at 1:41 and 3:46, suggest that the final line of Lennon's section ('I'd love to turn you on') was added later. He later credited this line to McCartney. The end of the first of these bridges was marked by an alarm clock, fortuitously anticipating McCartney's middle section.

[2] The orchestral session for A DAY IN THE LIFE was filmed on 16mm hand-held cameras. Some of this footage appears in Part 6 of the *Anthology* video.

[3] Lennon asked for a sound similar to the echo used on Presley's voice in 'Heartbreak Hotel'. Geoff Emerick came up with a unique twittering effect by feeding Lennon's voice to a mono deck whose record and replay heads rapidly fed

Starr's drums hold the track together, beginning in idiosyncratic dialogue with Lennon on slack-tuned tom-toms;[1] McCartney's contributions on piano and (particularly) bass brim with invention, colouring the music and occasionally providing the main focus. A brilliant production by Martin's team, working under restrictions which would floor most of today's studios, completes a piece which remains among the most penetrating and innovative artistic reflections of its era.

[97] SGT. PEPPER'S LONELY HEARTS CLUB BAND
(Lennon–McCartney)

McCartney vocal, bass, lead guitar; **Lennon** harmony vocal;
Harrison harmony vocal, guitar; **Starr** drums; **James W. Buck,
Neil Sanders, Tony Randall, John Burden** French horns
Recorded: 1st–2nd February, 3rd, 6th March 1967, Abbey Road 2.
Producer: George Martin. Engineer: Geoff Emerick.
UK release: 1st June 1967 (LP: *Sgt. Pepper's Lonely Hearts Club Band*)
US release: 2nd June 1967 (LP: *Sgt. Pepper's Lonely Hearts Club Band*)

During The Beatles' final US tour, McCartney had been struck by the fanciful names adopted by the new American groups and the graphical blend of psychedelia and vaudeville used in West Coast pop posters. Such anarchic free-association made 'The Beatles' seem as *passé* as the performing career the group were about to abandon. Musing on this, he conceived the idea of a reborn Beatles in the form of a corporate *alter ego*: Sgt. Pepper's Lonely Hearts Club Band: 'I thought it would be nice to lose our identities, to submerge ourselves in the persona of a fake group. We could make up all the culture around it and collect all our heroes in one place.'[2] An idea later revived by the theatrical 'glam rock' artists of the Seventies, McCartney's brainwave didn't immediately appeal to Lennon, but he came round to it as the album progressed. Made passively tolerant by LSD, he was happy to sit back

---

back on themselves before the final signal was taken as output to the multitrack. McCartney was initially recorded with the same tape-echo, but this was dropped because the shorter note-values of his section conflicted with the repeat-interval (see *Anthology 2*).
[1] The deep drum-sounds suggest that this section was recorded at higher speed and slowed down. Starr recalls that he played his fills illustratively, tracing the feeling of the song. For example, at the line 'four thousand holes in Blackburn, Lancashire', he 'played the disenchanting mood' (*The Beatles Anthology*, p. 80).
[2] Some claim the name was invented by the group's road manager Mal Evans.

and let McCartney (who, with Jane Asher on drama tour in America, had energy to spare) run the show.

Not so much a song as a purpose-designed overture, SGT. PEPPER'S LONELY HEARTS CLUB BAND is a shrewd fusion of Edwardian variety orchestra and contemporary 'heavy rock'.[1] On the one hand, McCartney was thinking of the period fashion then on sale in London shops like I Was Lord Kitchener's Valet and Granny Takes A Trip; on the other, he was influenced by The Jimi Hendrix Experience, which he and Lennon heard at Brian Epstein's Saville Theatre two nights before recording this track.[2] Thus, SGT. PEPPER'S LONELY HEARTS CLUB BAND adopts a symmetrical form embracing both idioms: a three-chord verse with screaming heavy rock vocal and guitar; a gently anachronistic five-bar bridge played by a quartet of horns (arranged by George Martin from lines sung to him by McCartney); a central chorus mingling the two; a vocal rerun of the bridge; and a final return to the verse.[3] Like The Beatles' later studio-bound attempts at the heavy style (see [134]), the track evokes the image of a mild middle-weight puffing himself up to resemble a bullish heavy with McCartney's shrieking guitar sounding more petulant than powerful.[4] On the other hand, Starr's kit sound, achieved by new techniques of damping and

---

[1] The prototype for what later became known as 'heavy metal', this genre was founded on LSD, high amplification, and a more prominent rhythm section. The typical quartet instrumental line-up of earlier Sixties pop gave way to a trio format (The Who, The Jimi Hendrix Experience, Cream, etc.) in which the absence of a rhythm guitarist demanded more active – and louder – bass and drums.

[2] See [U96], note. Lennon and McCartney were early fans of Hendrix, McCartney ensuring his invitation to play at the Monterey Festival in June 1967. By way of acknowledgment, Hendrix began playing a concert version of SGT. PEPPER'S LONELY HEARTS CLUB BAND only two days after the album hit the shops. This cameraderie was typical of the Sixties pop/rock scene on both sides of the Atlantic, a mood reflecting the prevailing atmosphere of 'stateless' communal idealism (the 'international feel' later anthemised by Todd Rundgren). However, it was also based on the common interests of musicians in what was then still a new idiom, developing at dizzying speed. Not only did artists hang out with each other at London nightclubs like Blaises, the Bag O'Nails, the Cromwellian, and the Scotch of St James; they also frequently dropped in on each other's recording sessions and routinely jammed together at sound-checks before gigs. Such gregariousness did not exclude intense and even jealous competition, but this was expressed in creative ways, while the mutual fascination and respect between those presented in the press as rivals was real.

[3] The scene-setting sound-effects of audience murmur and orchestral tuning were combined from Martin's record of the comedy show *Beyond the Fringe* (Fortune Theatre, London, 1961) and between-takes noises from the 10th February orchestral session for [96] A DAY IN THE LIFE.

[4] McCartney replaced a Harrison solo that had taken seven hours to record (Martin, *Summer of Love*, pp. 66–7). This may have contributed to Harrison's somewhat distant role throughout *Sgt. Pepper*.

close-miking, is remarkably three-dimensional for its time, its gated snare crashing ferociously as bass-drum and tom-toms punch through the texture around it. (American engineers hastened to copy these sound-techniques and, like many other Beatle recording experiments, they became standard studio procedures.)

As a song, like many of the *Sgt. Pepper* tracks, this is clearly inferior to the average number on *Revolver*, yet the comparison is unfair. Different in scope, the later album demands to be taken as a whole, and in that perspective SGT. PEPPER'S LONELY HEARTS CLUB BAND serves its purpose well. Moreover, for the group, content was becoming more important than form. Allen Ginsberg has pointed out that, with *Sgt. Pepper*, The Beatles offered an inclusive vision which, among other things, worked to defuse the tensions of the generation gap. Had they been created in America, where the clash between establishment and counterculture was already violent, Sgt. Pepper would have been a reactionary pig, Lovely Rita an uptight bureaucrat. The Beatles, their age-prejudice dissolved by LSD, were having none of this. Theirs was an optimistic, *holistic* view. *Sgt. Pepper* surpasses *Revolver* not in form but in spirit.

[98] GOOD MORNING GOOD MORNING
(Lennon–McCartney)

Lennon double-tracked vocal, rhythm guitar; **McCartney** backing
  vocal, lead guitar, bass; **Harrison** backing vocal, lead guitar;
  Starr drums, tambourine; **Barrie Cameron, David Glyde,**
  Alan Holmes saxes; **John Lee, Unknown** trombones;
  Unknown French horn
Recorded: 8th February 1967, Abbey Road 2; 16th February 1967,
  Abbey Road 3; 13th March, 28th–29th March 1967, Abbey
  Road 2.
Producer: George Martin. Engineer: Geoff Emerick.
UK release: 1st June 1967 (LP: *Sgt. Pepper's Lonely Hearts Club*
  Band)
US release: 2nd June 1967 (LP: *Sgt. Pepper's Lonely Hearts Club*
  Band)

Later dismissed by Lennon as 'a throwaway, a piece of garbage', GOOD MORNING GOOD MORNING is, in effect, a bilious riposte to McCartney's blithe [90] GOOD DAY SUNSHINE.[1] Born from its author's habit of

---

[1] McCartney sees the song as Lennon kicking against his confinement as a husband in Weybridge (Miles, op. cit., p. 321).

working with the television on in the background, it was inspired by an irritating Kellogg's cornflakes commercial and contains a sneering reference to a middlebrow British sitcom of the period, *Meet the Wife*. No one in pop cursed more entertainingly than Lennon, and only a corpse would fail to chuckle at the splenetic gusto with which he lays about him here. A disgusted canter through the muck, mayhem, and mundanity of the human farmyard, GOOD MORNING GOOD MORNING belies the airy-fairy reputation *Sgt. Pepper* has acquired in hindsight, being one of the earthiest things The Beatles ever made.[1]

Rhythmically unruly, the track proceeds in a clumsy sideways gallop lashed on by mighty pugilistic smashes on the crash cymbal.[2] Martin's production maximises the aggression by viciously compressing everything, picking up the 'a-hunting we will go' mood in a rollicking brass score played by a line-up including members of Britain's top Sixties session backing group, Sounds Incorporated. Starr contributes a fine performance, superbly recorded, and the track is whipped to a climax by a coruscating pseudo-Indian guitar solo from McCartney (see [84]).[3]

[99] FIXING A HOLE (*Lennon–McCartney*)

McCartney double-tracked vocal, lead guitar, bass; **Harrison** backing vocal, double-tracked lead guitar; **Lennon** backing vocal; **Starr** drums, maracas; **George Martin** harpsichord

Recorded: 9th February 1967, Regent Sound Studio; 21st February 1967, Abbey Road 2.

Producer: George Martin; Engineers: Adrian Ibbetson/Geoff Emerick

UK release: 1st June 1967 (LP: *Sgt. Pepper's Lonely Hearts Club Band*)

US release: 2nd June 1967 (LP: *Sgt. Pepper's Lonely Hearts Club Band*)

Deriving its images from McCartney's mood of casual, marijuana-inspired artistic improvisation, this song was for a while rumoured to

---

[1] The apparently random farmyard noises during the fade are actually designed, on Lennon's insistence, as a sequence in which each successive animal is capable of eating its predecessor.

[2] Take 8, issued on *Anthology 2*, illustrates the extraordinary rhythm-tracks the post-STRAWBERRY FIELDS Beatles were now using – a mixture of live drums, percussion, and backwards tapes. Especially anarchic, the introduction offers pointers for [110] BABY, YOU'RE A RICH MAN.

[3] This was played on a Fender Esquire, a single-pickup Telecaster which McCartney used throughout the *Sgt. Pepper* sessions (e.g., [97] SGT. PEPPER'S LONELY HEARTS CLUB BAND).

refer to heroin.[1] Like [91] HERE, THERE AND EVERYWHERE, it sets out its harmonic wares in a brief prelude, after which a wistfully introspective minor verse/chorus alternates with a more confident major middle eight, the chords placed on the beat as in [78], [95], [104], [107], and [115].

FIXING A HOLE was the only track on *Sgt. Pepper* not to have had its bass part dubbed on later. (Because of this, a minor mistake had to be let through at 1:09.) Recorded with ADT to get a fretless tone, McCartney's rather uncertain line, where not restricted to a root-fifth seesaw, uses a rising figure with airy octave shifts, suggesting Brian Wilson's lines for The Beach Boys (e.g., 'Good Vibrations').[2] A distracted and introverted track, FIXING A HOLE trades its author's usual smooth design for something more preoccupied, a mood captured in the guitar solo (played by Harrison on his Stratocaster with treble-heavy settings similar to the solo on [69] NOWHERE MAN).

[100] ONLY A NORTHERN SONG (Harrison)

Harrison vocal, organ, tape-effects, noises; **McCartney** bass, trumpet (?), tape-effects, noises; **Lennon** piano, glockenspiel (?), tape-effects, noises; **Starr** drums
Recorded 13th–14th February, 20th April 1967, Abbey Road 2.
Producer: George Martin. Engineer: Geoff Emerick.
UK release: 17th January 1969 (LP: *Yellow Submarine*)
US release: 13th January 1969 (LP: *Yellow Submarine*)

In the context of Harrison's minimal role in the *Sgt. Pepper* project thus far, this self-indulgent dirge suggests that, six months after threatening to leave the group, he had yet to recover his enthusiasm for being a Beatle. A slapdash rerun of the verse/chorus of [66] IF I NEEDED SOMEONE, it was recorded, according to its author, as a 'joke' to fulfil a contractual obligation to Northern Songs, the publishing company set up for The Beatles by Dick James (and part-owned by Lennon and McCartney) to which Harrison was resentfully signed as a songwriter.[3]

---

[1] See Miles, op. cit., pp. 314-15.
[2] Engineer Richard Lush recalls this line as played by Lennon on a Fender bass (Babiuk, *Beatles Gear*, p. 200).
[3] It seems probable that the title came to him as result of discussions, during the early stages of *Sgt. Pepper*, of the 'Northern childhood' device (see [93] note). Like most Harrison tracks in their early stages, it was untitled during recording and thus referred to as 'Not Known'. Similarly, an unused 22-minute drums-and-percussion track recorded on 22nd February was logged as 'Anything', while Harrison's [105]

His suppressed bitterness is coded in a mild dissonance ('you may think the chords are going *wrong*')[1] prior to shifting key from obstinate A major to nasally sarcastic B minor. Quickly set aside and forgotten, ONLY A NORTHERN SONG was later issued, along with some similarly dismal rejects, on the soundtrack of the cartoon feature *Yellow Submarine*.

[101] BEING FOR THE BENEFIT OF MR KITE!
(Lennon–McCartney)

> **Lennon** double-tracked vocal, Hammond organ; **McCartney** bass, guitar; **Harrison** harmonica; **Starr** drums, tambourine, harmonica; **George Martin** harmonium, Lowery organ, glockenspiel (?), tape-effects; **Mal Evans, Neil Aspinall** harmonicas
>
> Recorded: 17th February 1967, Abbey Road 2; 20th February 1967, Abbey Road 3; 28th–29th, 31st March 1967, Abbey Road 2.
>
> Producer: George Martin. Engineer: Geoff Emerick.
>
> UK release: 1st June 1967 (LP: *Sgt. Pepper's Lonely Hearts Club Band*)
>
> US release: 2nd June 1967 (LP: *Sgt. Pepper's Lonely Hearts Club Band*)

While The Beatles were filming a promo for [93] STRAWBERRY FIELDS FOREVER in Sevenoaks, Kent, on 31st January, Lennon wandered into an antiques shop and picked up a Victorian circus poster advertising 'the last night but three' of a show put on by some travelling tumblers in Rochdale in 1843.[2] This appealed to his sense of the ridiculous and,

---

WITHIN YOU WITHOUT YOU was short-listed as 'India'.

[1] Bm7 over A with the bass holding E (Bm7/11).

[2] The text of the poster is as follows: 'Pablo Fanque's Circus Royal, Town-Meadows, Rochdale. Grandest Night of the Season! And positively the LAST NIGHT BUT THREE! Being for the BENEFIT OF MR KITE (late of Wells's Circus) and MR J. HENDERSON, the celebrated somerset thrower! Wire dancer, vaulter, rider, etc. On Tuesday Evening, February 14th, 1843. Messrs. Kite & Henderson, in announcing the following Entertainment, assure the Public that this Night's Production will be one of the most Splendid ever produced in this Town, having been some days in preparation. Mr Kite will, for this Night only, introduce the celebrated HORSE, ZANTHUS! Well known to be one of the best Broke Horses IN THE WORLD!!! Mr Henderson will undertake the arduous Task of THROWING TWENTY ONE SOMERSETS on the solid ground. Mr Kite will appear, for the first time this season, On the Tight Rope, When Two Gentleman Amateurs of this Town will perform with him. Mr Henderson will, for the first time in Rochdale, introduce his extraordinary TRAMPOLINE LEAPS and SOMER-SETS! Over Men & Horses, through Hoops, over Garters, and lastly, through a Hogshead of REAL FIRE! In this branch of the profession, Mr H. challenges THE

when the new album called for another composition from him, he hung the poster on the wall of his home studio and, playing his piano, sang phrases from it until he had a song.[1] Taking it to Abbey Road, he asked George Martin for a 'fairground' production wherein one could smell the sawdust – which, while not in the narrowest sense a musical specification, was, by Lennon's standards, a clear and reasonable request. (He once asked Martin to make one of his songs sound like an orange.) While The Beatles' producer worked more naturally with the conventionally articulate McCartney, the challenge of catering to Lennon's intuitive approach generally spurred him to his more original arrangements, of which BEING FOR THE BENEFIT OF MR KITE! is an outstanding example. Using harmonium, harmonicas, and a tape of Victorian steam organs and calliopes cut up and edited into a kaleidoscopic wash, he created a brilliantly whimsical impression of period burlesque, ideally complementing Lennon's dry nasal delivery. Few producers have displayed a tenth of the invention shown here.

Lennon was happy with the effect but not with the song, which he considered facile. Most would beg to differ. Ingeniously matching its serpentine melody, the lyric elaborates on its poster text with real wit, while, with its irresistible image of a solemnly waltzing horse, the track as a whole offers a grotesque sequel to McCartney's wholesome [88] YELLOW SUBMARINE which only a professional misanthrope could fail to enjoy. Yet Lennon was by nature – and later on principle – distrustful of objective art (i.e., anything that didn't directly concern himself). Unable to appreciate the pleasure his imagination brought to others, he fashioned things like this with fluent ease only to reject them for having entailed none of the pain by which he measured creative authenticity. A spontaneous expression of its author's playful hedonism, BEING FOR THE BENEFIT OF MR KITE! was repudiated by the puritan in him.

WORLD!'

[1] McCartney, however, recalls the song as 'quite co-written' (Miles, op. cit., p. 318).

[102] LOVELY RITA *(Lennon–McCartney)*

McCartney vocal, piano, bass, comb and paper; **Lennon** backing vocal, 'vocal percussion', acoustic rhythm guitar, comb and paper; **Harrison** backing vocal, electric slide guitar, acoustic rhythm guitar, comb and paper; **Starr** drums, comb and paper; **George Martin** piano
Recorded: 23rd–24th February, 7th March, 21st March 1967, Abbey Road 2.
Producer: George Martin. Engineer: Geoff Emerick.
UK release: 1st June 1967 (LP: *Sgt. Pepper's Lonely Hearts Club Band*)
US release: 2nd June 1967 (LP: *Sgt. Pepper's Lonely Hearts Club Band*)

What Lennon distrusted in songs like [101] BEING FOR THE BENEFIT OF MR KITE! came naturally to the extrovert McCartney. Referring to LOVELY RITA, Lennon later poured scorn on his partner's 'novelist' songs: 'These stories about boring people doing boring things – being postmen and secretaries and writing home. I'm not interested in third-party songs. I like to write about me, cos I *know* me.' Rooted in egoism, Lennon's prejudice was hardened into dogma by Yoko Ono, who cleaved to the postmodern theory that objectivity is illusory and all creativity inescapably self-referential. Too practical to fall for such anti-social solipsism, McCartney was healthier in his outlook, if often shallower. LOVELY RITA is a good example – a silly song in many ways, but imbued with an exuberant interest in life that lifts the spirits, dispersing self-absorption. (Allegedly based on a friendly encounter with a traffic warden called Meta Davis in Garden Road, St John's Wood,[1] the lyric began as a satire on authority with its heroine a hate-figure – until, in keeping with the warm mood of the time, McCartney decided 'it'd be better to love her'.)

Plastered with the ubiquitous *Sgt. Pepper* tape-echo, the track was subjected to much varispeeding, ending up in E flat major, a brass band key not much used in pop. George Martin played the piano solo (speeded up and wobbled to simulate a honkytonk sound)[2] while Lennon contributed percussive mouth noises of the sort later used on [116] I AM THE WALRUS. An eccentric mix confines the drums to the left channel, rendering McCartney's walking bass line, dubbed on later in the group's now standard manner, unnaturally prominent.

---

[1] According to McCartney, this was merely a coincidence (Miles, op. cit., p. 320).
[2] This involved weighting the capstan with sticky tape during the tape-echo process.

[103] LUCY IN THE SKY WITH DIAMONDS
(Lennon–McCartney)

Lennon double-tracked vocal, lead guitar; **McCartney** harmony
  vocal, Lowery organ, bass; **Harrison** harmony vocal, lead guitar,
  acoustic guitar, tambura; **Starr** drums, maracas
Recorded: 28th February, 1st–2nd March 1967, Abbey Road 2.
Producer: George Martin. Engineer: Geoff Emerick.
UK release: 1st June 1967 (LP: *Sgt. Pepper's Lonely Hearts Club
  Band*)
US release: 2nd June 1967 (LP: *Sgt. Pepper's Lonely Hearts Club
  Band*

One of Lennon's dreamier songs, LUCY IN THE SKY WITH DIAMONDS
circles lazily on melodic eddies in an iridescent stream of sound. Taking
its title from a pastel drawing by his four-year-old son Julian and its
atmosphere from a hallucinatory chapter in Lewis Carroll's *Through the
Looking-Glass*,[1] it was naturally assumed to be a coded reference to
LSD. In fact, no such code was intended and, though the lyric
explicitly recreates the psychedelic experience, The Beatles were
genuinely surprised when it was pointed out to them. Lennon, who
wrote most of the words (with help from McCartney on a few images),
later thought them contrived. With hindsight, he also hated the
production – made unusually rapidly for *Sgt. Pepper*[2] – and expressed a
wish to re-record it.

What he had in mind is unknown, but the probability is that, as
with [93] STRAWBERRY FIELDS FOREVER, his original impulse got lost in
the studio, shedding a sentimental gentleness akin to that of [130]
GOOD NIGHT and [156] JULIA.[3] The first day of recording consisted of
an eight-hour session in which Lennon composed much of the song

[1] 'Wool and Water'. Carroll was Lennon's favourite writer; indeed, he harboured
an ambition to 'write an *Alice*' (Shotton, p. 33). The *Alice* books were canonised by
the counterculture for their surreal wit and drug-dream undertones, the outstanding
example of this being The Jefferson Airplane's 'White Rabbit', recorded in a
tremendous performance for their album *Surrealistic Pillow* (1967).
[2] It contains one of the few instances of bad editing on the album: an uncleaned
lead vocal track at 1:32.
[3] The scene where Alice gathers scented rushes is the most overtly sentimental
and nostalgic passage in Carroll's book. The 'girl with kaleidoscope eyes'
(McCartney: 'God, the big figure, the white rabbit') was, for Lennon, the lover/
mother of his most helpless fantasies: 'the image of the female who would someday
come save me.' This mysterious, oracular woman – mourned for in [50] YES IT IS,
bewildered by in [92] SHE SAID SHE SAID – was originally his mother Julia, a role
subsequently assumed by Yoko Ono [156].

'on the hoof'.[1] A single part can fundamentally alter a piece of music and, in view of Lennon's passive and pliant frame of mind (see [77]), it could be that he accepted McCartney's glittering countermelody[2] when all he really wanted was the cyclic cloud-drift of his verse sequence with its descending chromatic bass line (later reused in [143] DEAR PRUDENCE).[3] Certainly the most effective section of the recording is the lightest: the bridge, with its subtly harmonised D drone and featherweight bass.[4] Unfortunately a clodhopping shift to three-chord 4/4 rock for the chorus shatters the lulling spell the track has taken such pains to cast. The truth is that LUCY IN THE SKY WITH DIAMONDS is poorly thought out, succeeding more as a glamorous production (voice and guitar through the Leslie cabinet; echo and varispeed on everything) than as an integrated song.

[104] GETTING BETTER *(Lennon–McCartney)*

McCartney double-tracked vocal, bass; **Lennon** backing vocal, lead guitar; **Harrison** backing vocal, lead guitar, tambura; **Starr** drums, congas; **George Martin** piano, pianette
Recorded: 9th–10th March, 21st, 23rd March 1967, Abbey Road 2.
Producer: George Martin; Engineers: Malcolm Addey/Geoff Emerick
UK release: 1st June 1967 (LP: *Sgt. Pepper's Lonely Hearts Club Band*)
US release: 2nd June 1967 (LP: *Sgt. Pepper's Lonely Hearts Club Band*)

In terms of sound and feeling, GETTING BETTER plays a role on *Sgt. Pepper* similar to that of [90] GOOD DAY SUNSHINE on *Revolver*. With its clipped, metronomic guitars, the track threatens to be little more than a pale revamp of [95] PENNY LANE, yet thanks to the kick of its production and the most ebullient performance on *Sgt. Pepper*, it comes off with flying colours.

---

[1] Martin, *Summer of Love*, p. 103.
[2] This sound, often said to resemble a celesta but more like a cross between a harpsichord and a glockenspiel, was produced on a Lowrey organ (Martin, *Summer of Love*, p. 101).
[3] The remix of early takes issued on *Anthology 2* also shows how fundamental McCartney's late-added bass lines could be (e.g., the counter-melody through the chorus, absent until the final stages).
[4] As well as contributing tambura, Harrison plays on guitar what he thought of as a sarangi-style doubling of Lennon's vocal line through this section (*The Beatles Anthology*, p. 243).

The title occurred to McCartney a few days before the recording when the sun had come out while he was walking his dog Martha in Hampstead. (Originally the wan refrain of Jimmy Nicol, Starr's replacement in Australia during 1964, the phrase had for a while been a running joke among The Beatles, Lennon finding it particularly hilarious.) Having prepared the music, McCartney invited his partner to his house in St John's Wood to write the lyric with him – hence the allusions to angry youth, problems at school, and woman-beating (not to mention the typically sarcastic rejoinder to the title phrase: 'It can't get much worse').[1]

Musically, GETTING BETTER is blithely unorthodox. Perhaps harmonically influenced by the verse of [103] LUCY IN THE SKY WITH DIAMONDS, the track begins with the simultaneous sounding on two guitars of the subdominant (left) against the dominant (right): an F major ninth from which the tonic C emerges as the verse begins. Built from scalar chords, the song never relinquishes this staccato dominant, which, reinforced in octaves by the bass and later by plucked piano strings, acts as a drone (and yet another 'Indian' ingredient, jokingly underlined in the use of tambura during the third verse). The production, masterminded by McCartney, hangs on his airy bass line, dubbed over the basic track by direct injection with ADT.[2]

---

[1] The pre-LSD Lennon had been cruel to women: 'I couldn't express myself, and I hit.' During the session on 21st March, he got his supply of pills confused and found himself tripping while trying to sing backing vocals. Considering the subject-matter of the song and the fact that the drug tends to confront its users with their personal contradictions, this must have been a disturbing experience. (McCartney is said to have taken his shaken friend back to his house in St John's Wood and 'turned on' to keep him company.)

[2] During the second session for this track, The Beatles' former engineer Norman Smith introduced them to his psychedelic protégés The Pink Floyd, then recording their remarkable debut album *Piper At The Gates of Dawn* in Abbey Road's Studio 2. The encounter was cautious – a shame in that, at this stage, the Floyd's music more closely resembled The Beatles' than any other group in the country. Lennon and Syd Barrett had much in common as songwriters, but it was McCartney who had heard the Floyd at UFO, London's first underground club, and complimented them on the musical direction they were taking. (Pink Floyd dropped the 'The' after Barrett, the first major casualty of LSD and probably the greatest of such losses to English pop/rock, was eased out of the group at the end of 1967.)

[105] WITHIN YOU WITHOUT YOU *(Harrison)*

Harrison vocal, sitar, acoustic guitar, tambura; **Uncredited Indian musicians** dilrubas, svarmandal, tabla, tambura; **Erich Gruenberg, Alan Loveday, Julien Gaillard, Paul Scherman, Ralph Elman, David Wolfsthal, Jack Rothstein, Jack Greene** violins; **Reginald Kilbey, Allen Ford, Peter Beavan** cellos; **Neil Aspinall** tambura

Recorded: 15th, 22nd March, Abbey Road 2; 3rd April 1967, Abbey Road 1; 4th April 1967, Abbey Road 2.

Producer: George Martin. Engineer: Geoff Emerick.

UK release: 1st June 1967 (LP: *Sgt. Pepper's Lonely Hearts Club Band*)

US release: 2nd June 1967 (LP: *Sgt. Pepper's Lonely Hearts Club Band*)

Harrison's WITHIN YOU WITHOUT YOU finishes with a spasm of embarrassed laughter added by its composer during the final day of work on it (the last day of recording for *Sgt. Pepper* as a whole).[1] His wryness was prescient: this ambitious essay in cross-cultural fusion and meditative philosophy has been dismissed with a yawn by almost every commentator since it first appeared. Bored by the track's lack of harmonic interest, critics have focused on the lyric, attacking it as didactic and dated.

Apart from its offence to the Me Generation in pointing out how small we are, the trouble with WITHIN YOU WITHOUT YOU for most of its detractors lies in the song's air of superiority and sanctimonious finger-wagging at those 'who gain the world and lose their soul' ('Are you one of them?'). Yet, seeing the world from the metaphysical perspective of Indian philosophy, it was only natural that Harrison should find himself wailing that people could save the world 'if they only knew'. As for the accusatory finger – bad manners in times of relativism and making-do – this is a token of what was then felt to be a revolution in progress: an inner revolution against materialism. For better or worse, it is impossible to conduct a revolution without picking a side and pointing out the drawbacks of its rivals.

Harrison wrote the song on a harmonium at the home of his friend Klaus Voormann after a dinner in which the conversation had dwelt on the spiritual aridity of modern life ('the space between us all ... the love that's gone so cold'). As such, WITHIN YOU WITHOUT YOU is the conscience of *Sgt. Pepper's Lonely Hearts Club Band*: the necessary

---

[1] This is a snippet of The Beatles laughing after an unknown take during the *Sgt. Pepper* sessions (Martin, *Summer of Love*, p. 129).

sermon that comes with the community singing. Described by those with no grasp of the ethos of 1967 as a blot on a classic LP, WITHIN YOU WITHOUT YOU is central to the outlook that shaped *Sgt. Pepper* – a view justifiable then, as it is justifiable now (see [114]).

Once it was clear that [100] ONLY A NORTHERN SONG wouldn't be included on the album, Harrison seems to have shaken himself out of his disenchantment and concentrated on making this track count. Doubling his slow-moving melody with a multitracked bowed lute called a dilruba (varispeeded to produce deeper tones), he decided the track needed more and asked Martin for a string arrangement.[1] In the central *gat* in 5/8, his sitar dialogues first with the dilruba and then with the string ensemble, after which a harp-like scale on svarmandal (see [93]) prefaces a free-tempo exchange between sitar and solo cello. (At this point – 3:46 – Harrison can be heard softly counting in the tabla player.) Recorded with uncredited musicians from the Asian Music Centre sitting on a carpet in Studio 2, lights low and incense burning, WITHIN YOU WITHOUT YOU was mixed with global ADT and heavy compression on closed-miked tabla. Stylistically, it is the most distant departure from the staple Beatles sound in their discography – and an altogether remarkable achievement for someone who had been acquainted with Hindustani classical music for barely eighteen months.[2]

---

[1] A less than enthusiastic Martin did his best to catch the idiom, carefully marking in the microtonal slides his London Symphony Orchestra players were required to imitate. Unimpressed by WITHIN YOU WITHOUT YOU at the time, he revised his opinion in retrospect: 'A very good track indeed.' (His orchestral score for *Yellow Submarine* contains an affectionate quotation from this song: 'Sea of Time'.)

[2] Harrison based WITHIN YOU WITHOUT YOU on a suite-like composition by Ravi Shankar for All-India Radio, making it in three edit-sections which he then pieced together. The work-in-process backing track on *Anthology 2* shows that the song was varispeeded up a semitone from its original 'key' of C for release on *Sgt. Pepper.*

[106] SHE'S LEAVING HOME *(Lennon–McCartney)*

McCartney double-tracked vocal, backing vocal; **Lennon** double-tracked vocal, backing vocal; **Erich Gruenberg, Derek Jacobs, Trevor Williams, José Luis Garcia** violins; **John Underwood, Stephen Shingles** violas; **Dennis Vigay, Alan Dalziel** cellos; **Gordon Pearce** double-bass; **Sheila Bromberg** harp
Recorded: 17th, 20th March 1967, Abbey Road 2.
Producer: George Martin. Engineer: Geoff Emerick.
UK release: 1st June 1967 (LP: *Sgt. Pepper's Lonely Hearts Club Band*)
US release: 2nd June 1967 (LP: *Sgt. Pepper's Lonely Hearts Club Band*)

SHE'S LEAVING HOME was inspired by a story in the *Daily Mirror*[1] and pursues the cinematic style of [86] ELEANOR RIGBY and [87] FOR NO ONE, this time focusing on the post-war 'generation gap' (see Introduction). The pictorial poignancy of Mike Leander's arrangement, making the most of McCartney's rich ninths and elevenths, has been criticised for lack of restraint compared with Martin's similar instrumentation on ELEANOR RIGBY.[2] Yet, where Eleanor's tragedy is stark and final, the failure of the heroine's parents to understand their child in SHE'S LEAVING HOME is at least recoverable, rendering the track's heart-tugging sentiment entirely apt. Indeed, for some, this is the single most moving song in The Beatles' catalogue. Its succinct and compassionately observed lyric[3] is McCartney's except for Lennon's lines in the chorus, based on typical sayings of his Aunt Mimi. With its hopeful upward movement, the music of the verse is by McCartney; the chorus, in which the mother and father grieve in huddled descending phrases, was effectively co-written.[4] Made in two days, SHE'S LEAVING HOME represents, with [96] A DAY IN THE LIFE, the finest work on *Sgt. Pepper* – imperishable popular art of its time.[5]

---

[1] 27th February 1967. The 'she' of the title was 17-year-old runaway Melanie Coe. By chance, the lyric accurately guessed much of the detail of her life. (See Turner, *A Hard Day's Write*, pp. 125–6.)
[2] As a freelance, Martin had other acts to look after and was busy when an excited McCartney phoned demanding an instant arrangement. Unable to comply, he was upset next day to discover that McCartney had commissioned Leander in his place. He conducted Leander's score with only minor modifications.
[3] Songwriter Nick Heyward: 'You don't get words like "clutching" in songs any more.' (*Independent*, 16th December 1993.)
[4] George Martin *(Summer of Love*, p. 133) describes SHE'S LEAVING HOME as 'not, strictly speaking, a Beatles song at all . . . pure McCartney, from start to finish'. Yet, unless McCartney wrote the music for the chorus phrases Lennon sings and wrote words for – which seems unlikely – this isn't quite true.
[5] On holiday in America with Jane Asher after *Sgt. Pepper*, McCartney visited The

[107] WITH A LITTLE HELP FROM MY FRIENDS
(Lennon–McCartney)

Starr vocal, drums, tambourine; **McCartney** backing vocal, piano,
  bass; **Lennon** backing vocal, cowbell; **Harrison** lead guitar;
  George Martin Hammond organ
Recorded: 29th–30th March 1967, Abbey Road 2.
Producer: George Martin. Engineer: Geoff Emerick.
UK release: 1st June 1967 (LP: *Sgt. Pepper's Lonely Hearts Club
  Band*)
US release: 2nd June 1967 (LP: *Sgt. Pepper's Lonely Hearts Club
  Band*)

With pressure from EMI to finish the album, The Beatles upped their
work-rate around the end of March 1967 – though, if Hunter Davies'
account in his contemporary biography of the group is anything to go
by, this relative urgency was undetectable to observers of their
composing methods. Bringing the chords of WITH A LITTLE HELP
FROM MY FRIENDS (then called 'Bad Finger Boogie') to Lennon's
house, McCartney and his partner banged away abstractedly at a piano,
singing phrases that popped into their heads or occurred in the
conversation of their friends in the same room. This process went on
for hours, broken by outbursts of laughter, long intervals spent in
flipping casually through magazines, and random diversions into other
songs and styles (including, without announcement or comment, a new
number by McCartney: [117] THE FOOL ON THE HILL). Davies'
description is of creativity as a dreamlike process, The Beatles groping
along in a sort of light trance. While drugs must have played a part in
this, there was probably a fair degree of method to it too. Both
McCartney ([59], [88]) and Lennon ([67], [69]) had found inspiration in
moments in which their conscious minds had fallen into abeyance.
Much of what Davies witnessed was probably a strategy to keep the
imaginative current flowing. After ten years of songwriting on guitars
and pianos, Lennon and McCartney were aware of deadening habit and
careful to vary their methods so as to retain an element of self-surprise.

Quite apart from their intuitive and lateral methods, The Beatles
were singularly in touch with their unconscious minds and childhood
memories. Punctuated by sharp *aperçus*, Lennon's mentality was

---

Beach Boys' Los Angeles studio, where they were slowly recording *Smile*, their
follow-up to *Pet Sounds* and reply to *Revolver*. Before leaving, McCartney sat at a
piano and sang SHE'S LEAVING HOME, cheerfully warning Brian Wilson as he left:
'You'd better hurry up!' In fact, Wilson had lost his way and *Smile* was not released
until 2004.

otherwise so dreamy that, during his LSD period, he depended on the others to stop him drifting away for good: 'If I'm on my own for three days, doing nothing, I almost leave myself completely. I'm up there watching myself, or I'm at the back of my head. I can see my hands and realise they're moving, but it's a robot who's doing it.'[1] With the same Celtic blood in his veins, McCartney admitted similar tendencies. Because of these shared traits, The Beatles were unusually close, particularly in 1967 – a quartet of seemingly telepathic minds recalled by many who met them as a sort of *Gestalt*. While they tried not to depend on each other too much – efforts at which Harrison was the most successful – other people rather bored them, and they found themselves endlessly recombining like some insoluble chemical compound.[2]

At the same time, the countercultural spirit of 1966–9 was essentially communal, and The Beatles were, for a while, convinced that the coming Arcadia would be tranquilly collective. This assumption (thematic in *Magical Mystery Tour* and implied in their TV versions of [114] ALL YOU NEED IS LOVE and [137] HEY JUDE) first entered their music in a song absent-mindedly evolved in a roomful of chattering acquaintances: WITH A LITTLE HELP FROM MY FRIENDS. At once communal and personal, it's a song of comfort – an acid lullaby. Touchingly rendered by Starr, it was meant as a gesture of inclusivity: everyone could join in. Anthemised by Joe Cocker, it became a countercultural totem, a symbol of 'Woodstock Nation'. Yet the lines that resonated most for its late Sixties audience seemed mysterious beyond paraphrase: 'What do you see when you turn out the light?/I can't tell you but I know it's mine.' These words had the appearance of emerging from beyond the rational mind, and, in 1967, seemed convincing precisely because of that.[3] No accident, then, that chance-determination was becoming central to The Beatles; and no mystery that they would soon begin to lose their ability to discriminate between creativity and self-indulgence.

---

[1] Davies, p. 380. Lennon's description conforms to a standard type of out-of-body experience.

[2] When, in 1965, The Byrds' Roger McGuinn asked Harrison whether he believed in God, he was fascinated by the reply: 'Well, we don't know about that yet.' Self-educated, The Beatles advanced through their twenties as a sort of sensory phalanx, picking up facts and impressions and pooling them between each other. 'It was,' recalls McGuinn, 'like they had combined minds. It was really a tight unit.' (Somach and Somach, p. 167.)

[3] McCartney has an earthier explanation for these lines (see Miles, op. cit., p. 310). His version, though, doesn't square with Hunter Davies' account.

[108] SGT. PEPPER'S LONELY HEARTS CLUB BAND (Reprise) *(Lennon–McCartney)*

McCartney vocal, organ, bass; **Lennon** vocal, rhythm guitar;
  Harrison vocal, lead guitar; **Starr** vocal, drums, tambourine,
  maracas
Recorded: 1st April 1967, Abbey Road 1.
Producer: George Martin. Engineer: Geoff Emerick.
UK release: 1st June 1967 (LP: *Sgt. Pepper's Lonely Hearts Club
  Band*)
US release: 2nd June 1967 (LP: *Sgt. Pepper's Lonely Hearts Club
  Band*)

Apart from the string overdubs on [105] WITHIN YOU WITHOUT YOU (and the snippet of gibberish taped for the run-out groove on 21st April), this was the last thing to be recorded for *Sgt. Pepper*, and something of an afterthought. The Beatles had been playing with running-orders for the album and had come up with a provisional solution for Side 1.[1] The second side, though, needed something else. Neil Aspinall, The Beatles' factotum, suggested to McCartney that, since the album opened with 'Sgt Pepper' introducing the show, the character should also make a few closing remarks. Translated into formal terms, this meant that [97] SGT. PEPPER'S LONELY HEARTS CLUB BAND should be reprised in abbreviated form to book-end the album and *segue* into [96] A DAY IN THE LIFE. Shortly afterwards, Lennon grinned sardonically as he walked past Aspinall, saying 'Nobody likes a smart-ass'. ('That,' recalls Aspinall, 'was when I knew that John liked it and that it would happen.'[2])

The recording took less than a day and the excitement in the studio is tangible in the result. When the LP was sequenced and cross-faded a few days later, the reprise made an eruptive transition between [98] GOOD MORNING GOOD MORNING and the finale, McCartney's whooping master of ceremonies nicely balanced by Lennon's slyly ambiguous 'Bye!'

With *Sgt. Pepper's Lonely Hearts Club Band* finished, the group left

---

[1] [97] SGT. PEPPER'S LONELY HEARTS CLUB BAND, [107] WITH A LITTLE HELP FROM MY FRIENDS, [101] BEING FOR THE BENEFIT OF MR KITE!, [99] FIXING A HOLE, [103] LUCY IN THE SKY WITH DIAMONDS, [104] GETTING BETTER, [106] SHE'S LEAVING HOME.
[2] Derek Taylor, p. 26.

Abbey Road at dawn bearing an acetate and drove to 'Mama' Cass Elliott's flat off the King's Road where, at six in the morning, they threw open the windows, put speakers on the ledge, and played the album full blast over the rooftops of Chelsea. According to Derek Taylor, 'all the windows around us opened and people leaned out, wondering. It was obvious who it was on the record. Nobody complained. A lovely spring morning. People were smiling and giving us the thumbs up.'[1]

When *Sgt. Pepper* was released in June, it was a major cultural event. Young and old alike were entranced. Attending a party with a group of rich older women, EMI boss Sir Joseph Lockwood found them so 'thrilled' by the album that they sat on the floor after dinner singing extracts from it. In America normal radio-play was virtually suspended for several days, only tracks from *Sgt. Pepper* being played. An almost religious awe surrounded the LP. Paul Kantner of the San Francisco acid rock band Jefferson Airplane remembers how The Byrds' David Crosby brought a tape of *Sgt. Pepper* to their Seattle hotel and played it all night in the lobby with a hundred young fans listening quietly on the stairs, as if rapt by a spiritual experience. 'Something,' says Kantner, 'enveloped the whole world at that time and it just exploded into a renaissance.'[2]

The psychic shiver which *Sgt. Pepper* sent through the world was nothing less than a cinematic dissolve from one *Zeitgeist* to another. In *The Times*, Kenneth Tynan called it 'a decisive moment in the history of Western civilisation', a remark now laughed at but nonetheless true, if perhaps not quite in the way that it was intended. As the shock wore off, voices from an earlier age began to complain that this music was absolutely saturated in drugs. Not wishing to promote LSD, the BBC banned [96] A DAY IN THE LIFE and [103] LUCY IN THE SKY WITH DIAMONDS, while others found drug references in [99] FIXING A HOLE and [107] WITH A LITTLE HELP FROM MY FRIENDS. More bizarrely, [106] SHE'S LEAVING HOME was attacked by religious groups in America as a cryptic advertisement for abortion.

While half these claims were spurious, it would be silly to pretend that *Sgt. Pepper* wasn't fundamentally shaped by LSD. The album's sound – in particular its use of various forms of echo and reverb – remains the most authentic aural simulation of the psychedelic experience ever created. At the same time, something else dwells in it: a

[1] Ibid., p. 41.
[2] Ibid., p. 5.

distillation of the spirit of 1967 as it was felt by vast numbers across the Western world who had never taken drugs in their lives. If such a thing as a cultural 'contact high' is possible, it happened here. *Sgt. Pepper's Lonely Hearts Club Band* may not have created the psychic atmosphere of the time but, as a near-perfect reflection of it, this famous record magnified and radiated it around the world.

Part 3
Coming Down

When you get to the top, there is nowhere to go but down.
But the Beatles could not get down.

(Philip Larkin)

[109] MAGICAL MYSTERY TOUR *(Lennon–McCartney)*

McCartney vocal, piano, bass; **Lennon** harmony vocal, acoustic
   rhythm guitar; **Harrison** harmony vocal, lead guitar; **Starr**
   drums, tambourine; **Mal Evans, Neil Aspinall** cowbell, maracas,
   tambourine; **David Mason, Elgar Howarth, Roy Copestake,
   John Wilbraham** trumpets
Recorded: 25th–27th April, 3rd May 1967, Abbey Road 3.
Producer: George Martin. Engineer: Geoff Emerick.
UK release: 8th December 1967 (2-EP: *Magical Mystery Tour*)
US release: 27th November 1967 (LP: *Magical Mystery Tour*)

Rather than rush to fill a three-month album schedule as had been
necessary while touring, The Beatles now settled into a regime of
continuous low-intensity recording. This suited their more relaxed life-
style, but it had a workaday quality about it – an intrinsic lack of tension
which was bound to colour the resulting material. Since they paid no
studio-fees, they needed only to find free time in the Abbey Road
schedules and turn up, whether or not they had anything ready to
record. Consequently many of the hours they now spent in Studio 2
were occupied not with recording or even rehearsing, but with writing
songs. In practice, this meant that the Beatle with the main idea had to
worry it into shape with the half-attentive help of the others, a tedious
procedure for anyone not immediately involved (such as Starr and the
studio staff).[1] At the same time, the group's drug-intake had begun to
loosen their judgement, lowering their standards of self-criticism.

   These effects colluded with The Beatles' ambivalent attitude to
their own talent to induce an uncharacteristic carelessness in their work.
Press statements of this period show them casually acknowledging the
fact that they were the world's best pop group while maintaining that
all they did was put in the hours and that anyone could achieve the
same if they tried hard enough. This reflexive self-deprecation was

---

[1] During this period, Starr and Neil Aspinall taught themselves chess to while
away the time.

partly a stock-in-trade of Northern English culture, with its bias to the ordinary and instinctive dislike of anything 'fancy' or 'affected'. McCartney's family background made him a sucker for such populist anti-élitism and his various attempts to find projects to keep The Beatles going during their last three years were invariably marked by it. By contrast, Lennon and Harrison had fled Liverpool precisely to escape the stultifying effects of this inverted snobbery; yet such was its hold on them that both quickly found substitutes for it – Harrison in Indian religion with its distrust of worldliness and stress on the simple things in life, Lennon with his compulsion to debunk 'culture' and his sardonic delight in the ridiculous and grotesque.

Harrison, who had been comparatively inactive during the *Sgt. Pepper* sessions, was the earliest of the group to become disenchanted with The Beatles and the first to sanction a consciously slovenly piece of work [100]. Despite this, he kept his reservations quiet. The less guarded Lennon, on the other hand, was capable of outspoken dismissals of the group's work and worth, veering easily from boastful claims that they were as good as Beethoven to cynical rejections of The Beatles as talentless con artists.

With his careerist commitment to the group, the extrovert McCartney sensed this malaise setting in soon after they had given up touring, and it was his pestering that initiated and maintained the impetus behind *Sgt. Pepper*, without which they might well have broken up around the end of 1966. The same danger, in his anxious judgement, reasserted itself towards the end of the *Pepper* sessions, and he began looking for a new project ('To keep us together, keep us going, give us something new to do'). Joining Jane Asher on her theatre tour of America in April 1967, he was impressed by the dedication of the West Coast hippies compared with their more flippant British cousins, and was particularly struck by Ken Kesey's LSD-apostles the Merry Pranksters and their dayglo-painted touring coach. A cinema-fan and a maker of 'underground' home-movies, McCartney saw the motif of a psychedelic roadshow as the basis for a film, which he accordingly roughed out on a sheet of paper while flying back to Britain. Mixing for *Sgt. Pepper* was still going on when he arrived, and it might have been wiser to let everyone have a couple of months' rest before pushing on with a new project, but Brian Epstein liked the idea and McCartney, as ever, was impatient to start. Thus, a mere four days after *Pepper* was put to bed, the jaded Beatles were back in Abbey Road, taping the title track for *Magical Mystery Tour*.

In an apparent attempt to keep things spontaneous, McCartney arrived at the studio with only three chords and the opening line of the lyric. Evolving the music and rehearsing it as the session progressed, he kept the others' attention by getting them to shout out phrases and bash any percussion instruments to hand. Despite this, they soon lost interest and he had to assume the role of bandmaster, drilling them through a backing track and asking George Martin for traffic sound-effects and a trumpet section. Two further days of erratically inspired labour on the track was followed by a chaotic session for trumpet overdubs in which McCartney again turned up with only vague ideas, leaving Elgar Howarth to dash off a score. While energetic, the result is manufactured, its thin invention undisguised by a distorted production tricked out with unconvincing time and tempo changes. (The main idea – 'Roll up', etc. – is shop-worn, while the contrasting section – 'The Magical Mystery Tour is coming', etc. – does little more than transpose the verse sequence of [103] LUCY IN THE SKY WITH DIAMONDS.)

The extent of the others' enthusiasm for *Magical Mystery Tour* is clear from the fact that no further work was done on the soundtrack for another four months. Yet, while Lennon and Harrison postponed thinking about the project for as long as they could, they enjoyed the actual filming and were as unprepared as McCartney for the critical roasting the programme suffered when it was transmitted by the BBC on 26th December.[1] The general view was that The Beatles had finally overreached themselves and perpetrated their first career howler. Only the *Guardian*'s Keith Dewhurst took a deeper look: 'An inspired freewheeling achievement . . . a deliberate parody of mass communication . . . a fantasy morality play about the grossness and warmth and stupidity of The Beatles' audience . . .'

Paradoxically, far from a case of self-indulgent hubris, such as has become a standard ingredient in pop/rock conceptual disasters since 1968, the failure of *Magical Mystery Tour* was a product of the group's false modesty. Regarding themselves both as the best in their field and (so as not to get big-headed about it) as nothing special, they wandered, drug-dozy, into the medium of film, assuming that anyone with a few

---

[1] Assuming the role of impresario after Brian Epstein's death, McCartney pulled *Magical Mystery Tour* out of mothballs in September 1967, intending to finish it by November and sell it to the BBC. The Beatles, though, were still sloppy from LSD and in any case lacked Epstein's gift for organisation. Ransacking *Spotlight* for a cast, they hired a crew and a coach, setting off for Cornwall with neither shooting script nor production board. Ten hours of spontaneous filming in Newquay, RAF West Malling, and Raymond's Revue Bar had to be edited to 52 minutes, for which they budgeted a hopeful week in Old Compton Street. In the event, licking *Magical Mystery Tour* into shape took three months slowed by further continuity filming and a cut-and-recut struggle between McCartney and Lennon.

ideas could turn out something watchable. (With his usual sublime confidence, McCartney had the cheek to show some of his home movies to Michelangelo Antonioni while he was shooting *Blow Up* in London in 1966.) As it happens, the group's fans enjoyed *Magical Mystery Tour* and the film-and-record package did healthy business in America, recouping its £40,000 outlay from the advance orders for the soundtrack weeks before it was screened. Nor was the programme quite as ineptly haphazard as is often claimed. As a prototype of both the 'road movie' genre inaugurated two years later by *Easy Rider* and of the brief Eighties' vogue for 'long-form' videos, it even has a modest place in film history.

In terms of The Beatles' career, *Magical Mystery Tour* marks the breakdown of the cross-generational consensus on them, established in 1964 by *A Hard Day's Night*. Notwithstanding McCartney's eagerness to please ([115], [119]), this is where parents began to part company with their sons and daughters over the group, rightly suspecting a drug-induced pretension setting in. At the same time, The Beatles remained their debunking selves and the subversive agenda of *Magical Mystery Tour* – sending up consumerism, showbiz, and the clichés of the media – was very much their version of the counterculture's view of mainstream society. While in America the hippies openly jeered the 'middle-aged, middle-class, middle-brow'[1] customs of the parental generation, *Magical Mystery Tour* did the same for Britain in a slyer, less confrontational way. The Beatles' much-criticised 'aimlessness' in this project was partly satirical, gently embarrassing the 'great British public' on its most bloated day of the year. At the very least the film marked an advance in content over the disarmingly boyish *A Hard Day's Night* and genuinely directionless *Help!*

---

[1] Part of a chant by The Fugs, a group of second generation Beats formed in Greenwich Village in 1964 by poets Ed Sanders and Tuli Kupferberg. Dylan, The Beatles, Jimi Hendrix, and Donovan were all Fugs fans.

[110] BABY, YOU'RE A RICH MAN *(Lennon–McCartney)*

Lennon double-tracked vocal, harmony vocal, clavioline, piano;
   McCartney harmony vocal, piano, bass; **Harrison** harmony
   vocal, guitar, handclaps; **Starr** drums, tambourine, maracas,
   handclaps; **Eddie Kramer** vibraphone; **Mick Jagger (?)** harmony
   vocal
Recorded: 11th May 1967, Olympic Sound Studios.
Producer: George Martin. Engineer: Keith Grant.
UK release: 7th July 1967 (B single: ALL YOU NEED IS LOVE)
US release: 17th July 1967 (B single: ALL YOU NEED IS LOVE)

That The Beatles in mid-1967 were easing their standards and relaxing their creative focus is confirmed by the fact that, two days before recording this song, they spent seven hours in Abbey Road's Studio 2 vaguely doodling a sixteen-minute instrumental track to which they never afterwards returned.[1] Without doubt, drugs were now leading their decisions.

If amphetamines ('speed') were the characteristic pharmaceuticals of the high-energy early Sixties, the late Sixties were dominated by cannabis and LSD, drugs which slow thought and amplify sensation, rendering the commonplace fascinating and making it hard to judge the worth of one's impressions. As a result, pop's sense of time expanded and the discipline of the two-and-a-half minute single gave way to open-ended album-length forms governed by slower rates of harmonic change and louder and less precisely defined sounds: the large-hall idiom later christened 'rock'. (An example of this transition can be heard in the contrast between the aggressive sharpness of The Who's early 'speed'-influenced style and the humourless grandiloquence of their first acid-inspired record 'I Can See For Miles'.)

Given that all beat-driven music is primarily physical in impact, the main difference between pop and rock (besides signal-volume) is that classic pop captures a mood or style in a condensed instant that speaks mainly to the mind and emotions, whereas rock broadcasts across a wide waveband to the senses in general. Moreover, in rock's more relaxed or 'laid-back' forms, the sensuality of the rhythm can easily become the sole *raison d'être* of the song. Influenced by black dance idioms, such 'feel' music ideally suited the sense-enhancing drugs of the

---

[1] A possible influence may have been the improvisations of The Pink Floyd whose debut LP was being made at Abbey Road. The Floyd's then-manager Peter Jenner suggests (*Mojo* 34, p. 54) that, during the *Sgt. Pepper* sessions, The Beatles were 'copying' what they could hear coming from The Floyd's studio, and vice-versa (e.g., the Farfisa organ in 'Scarecrow' on *Piper At The Gates Of Dawn*).

late Sixties and early Seventies and accordingly became a staple of that era's vast open-air summer festivals.

With its lazily swinging off-beat and chugging pseudo-march rhythm (probably stolen from The Four Tops' contemporary single 'Reach Out I'll Be There'), BABY YOU'RE A RICH MAN is The Beatles' first full-blown 'feel' record.[1] With heavy compression on almost everything in the track, the mix reinforces the sensual impact of the sound. The result – taped in a mere six hours at Olympic Sound Studio[2] – is, in its ruthless concentration on 'the groove', a canny anticipation of musical things to come. Even while The Rolling Stones were still stumbling, acid-fuddled, through a doomed imitation of *Sgt. Pepper*, The Beatles had grasped the principle of the black-white, acid-dance fusion their rivals would begin to arrive at a year later.

The one thing missing from BABY YOU'RE A RICH MAN – as is generally the difference between pop (at its best) and rock – is well-crafted music. Created separately, Lennon's falsetto verse and McCartney's monotone chorus dovetail lyrically but are harmonically too alike to provide a sense of development or release. The song arrives, dwells unchanged for a while before our ears, and departs – much like a modern dance record.

While the group were obviously excited about the track as a sound-event, there is a stoned sloppiness about the writing (particularly in the chorus) which spoils the effect. Drugs and overconfidence here fool The Beatles into accepting their initial inspiration as a creative 'found' object. Gone are the days when, as McCartney recalls, they sweated over every bar of a song. Even the didactic lyric, which Harrison insists was intended to show people that they were rich in themselves, mixes clarity with cloudiness. (Its high-flown sentiment is undermined by Lennon's inability to resist singing, on some of the later choruses, 'Baby you're a rich fag Jew' – a supposed reference to Brian Epstein.)[3]

---

[1] [81] RAIN has some prior claim to this title, Starr's work on both tracks being much admired by American drummers, the masters of 'feel' playing – e.g., the characteristic fill at 0:49–0:53: a 'backwards' snare roll into a rim-shot followed by two 'backwards' triplets from (low-tuned) high tom-tom to (high-tuned) snare.

[2] This was The Beatles' second British EMI session outside Abbey Road (after the 9th February 1967 date for [99] FIXING A HOLE at Regent Sound Studio).

[3] The 'beautiful people' was what the West Coast hippies called themselves. The 14-Hour Technicolor Dream, an all-night festival at Alexandra Palace on 29th April 1967 which Lennon attended, was the first tribal gathering of the British 'beautiful people'. This, and the fact that the session for BABY YOU'RE A RICH MAN was

Musically, the most cogent and original element is purely instrumental: a speeded-up imitation of the harsh Oriental oboe known in India as a shehnai and in the Arab world as a nay. Played by Lennon on a now-forgotten monophonic keyboard called a clavioline,[1] this ornamental line wends in and out of the vocals, lending the track a beguiling joss-stick exoticism.

[111] ALL TOGETHER NOW *(Lennon–McCartney)*

McCartney vocal, acoustic guitar, bass, handclaps; **Lennon** backing
  vocal, acoustic guitar, ukelele, harmonica, handclaps; **Harrison**
  backing vocal, handclaps; **Starr** drums, finger cymbals, handclaps
Recorded: 12th May 1967, Abbey Road 2.
Producer: Paul McCartney. Engineer: Geoff Emerick.
UK release: 17th January 1969 (LP: *Yellow Submarine*)
US release: 13th January 1969 (LP: *Yellow Submarine*)

Self-produced (for the planned *Yellow Submarine* cartoon feature) in one six-hour session, this repetitive McCartney singalong displays the group's misplaced faith in the childlike, being trite enough to have been chanted for several seasons on English football terraces.

[112] YOU KNOW MY NAME (LOOK UP THE NUMBER)
  (Lennon–McCartney)

Lennon vocal, guitar, maracas; **McCartney** vocal, piano, bass;
  Harrison backing vocal, guitar, vibes; **Starr** vocal, drums,
  bongos; **Mal Evans** spade in gravel; **Brian Jones** alto saxophone
Recorded: 17th May, 7th–8th June 1967, Abbey Road 2; 30th
  April 1969, Abbey Road 3.
Producer: George Martin. Engineer: Geoff Emerick.
UK release: 6th March 1970 (B single/LET IT BE)
Us release: 11th March 1970 (B single/LET IT BE)

During much of the summer of 1967, The Beatles were, in effect, just messing about at random in the echo of *Sgt. Pepper*. Whether, stoned as they were, they *knew* they were messing about is beside the point; all that matters is that most of what they recorded then was a transparent

---

arranged at short notice, suggest that the song was inspired by the event.
[1] A small three-octave organ designed to be attached to and played from a piano. It appears prominently on Del Shannon's 'Runaway' (1961) and The Tornados' 'Telstar' (1962).

waste of studio time. Unfortunately, since EMI was paying for it, there was no pressure for self-discipline.

You Know My Name (Look Up The Number) is a fair indication of the state they were in. Lennon conceived its opening section as the beginning of a long, chant-like freakout consisting solely of the title-phrase ('like a mantra'). This didn't work and the concept altered many times, expanding at one point to a twenty-minute design in multiple parts before being left for nearly two years and edited down into a Goon-like novelty song issued on the B-side of The Beatles' final single. The result of all this blind-flying is, thanks to the band's natural humour, quite funny, while the track remains interesting as a glimpse of their creative process preserved in its inchoate initial stages. (The stereo version issued on *Anthology 2* has an extra section: a ska parody later cut by Lennon.)[1]

[113] It's All Too Much *(Harrison)*

Harrison double-tracked vocal, lead guitar, Hammond organ;
   McCartney harmony vocal, bass; **Lennon** harmony vocal, lead
   guitar; **Starr** drums, tambourine; **David Mason (and 3 others)**
   trumpets; **Paul Harvey** bass clarinet
Recorded: 25th–26th May/2nd June 1967, De Lane Lea Studios,
   Kingsway.
Producer: None/George Martin.[2] Engineer: Dave Siddle.
UK release: 17th January 1969 (LP: *Yellow Submarine*)
US release: 13th January 1969 (LP: *Yellow Submarine*)

Composed in 'a childlike manner' by Harrison under the influence of LSD, this protracted exercise in drug-mesmerised G-pedal monotony amounts to automatic writing. The result – pieced together during three lackadaisical days in De Lane Lea Studios – is marked by hamfisted feedback guitar, a trumpet quotation from Jeremiah Clarke's *Prince of Denmark's March* (anticipating [114]), and a meaningless snatch of The Merseys' 1966 hit 'Sorrow' (see [83]). Lyrically, It's All Too

---

[1] The smarmy nightclub crooner Dennis O'Bell – Dennis O'Dell was head of Apple's film division – is supposedly sung by Starr, though it sounds more like Harrison imitating his friend Neil Innes of The Bonzo Dog Doo-Dah Band, whose style the track most resembles. (The Bonzos appeared in *Magical Mystery Tour*. Lennon wanted a 'period' group and proposed The New Vaudeville Band, but McCartney's brother Mike McGear, then a member of Scaffold, suggested the Bonzos instead.)
[2] Martin was absent during the first two days of recording, which seem to have been produced by the group.

MUCH is the *locus classicus* of English psychedelia: a cozy nursery rhyme in which the world is a birthday cake and the limits on personal transformation are settled in the line 'Show me that I'm everywhere and get me home for tea'. The revolutionary spirit then abroad in America and Europe was never reciprocated in comfortable (and sceptical) Albion, where tradition, nature, and the child's-eye-view were the things which sprang most readily to the LSD-heightened Anglo-Saxon mind (see [93], [95], [120]).

[114] ALL YOU NEED IS LOVE *(Lennon–McCartney)*

> **Lennon** vocal, harpsichord, banjo; **McCartney** harmony vocal,
> string bass, bass guitar; **Harrison** harmony vocal, violin, guitar;
> **Starr** drums; **George Martin** piano; **Sidney Sax, Patrick**
> **Halling, Eric Bowie, Jack Holmes** violins; **Rex Morris, Don**
> **Honeywill** tenor saxes; **Stanley Woods, David Mason**
> trumpets; **Evan Watkins, Harry Spain** trombones; **Jack**
> **Emblow** accordion; **Mick Jagger, Keith Richards, Marianne**
> **Faithfull, Jane Asher, Mike McCartney, Patti Harrison,**
> **Eric Clapton, Graham Nash, Keith Moon, Hunter Davies,**
> **Gary Leeds (and others)** chorus; **Mike Vickers** conductor
> Recorded: 14th June 1967, Olympic Sound Studios; 19th June
> 1967, Abbey Road 3; 23rd–25th June 1967, Abbey Road 1.
> Producer: George Martin. Engineers: Eddie Kramer/Geoff Emerick.
> UK release: 7th July 1967 (A single/BABY YOU'RE A RICH MAN)
> US release: 17th July 1967 (A single/Baby YOU'RE A RICH MAN)

One of The Beatles' less deserving hits, Lennon's ALL YOU NEED IS LOVE owes more of its standing to its local historical associations than to its inspiration which, as with their other immediate post-*Pepper* recordings – [109] to [113] – is desultory. Thrown together for *Our World*, a live TV broadcast linking twenty-four countries by global satellite on 25th June 1967, the song is an inelegant structure in alternating bars of 4/4 and 3/4, capped by a chorus which, like its B-side, [109] BABY YOU'RE A RICH MAN, consists largely of a single note. The order in which the group's recordings of this period were issued concealed the slapdash atmosphere in which they were made and to some extent disguised the sloppiness on show in ALL YOU NEED IS LOVE (a false impression reinforced by the razzmatazz surrounding it). The fact was, though, that The Beatles were now doing willfully substandard work: paying little attention to musical values and settling for lyric first-thoughts on the principle that everything, however haphazard, meant *something* and if it didn't – so what? Their attention to production, so painstaking during the *Pepper* sessions, had likewise faded. (The engineers at Olympic, where the backing track was prepared for the TV broadcast, were shocked by the carelessness with which the mixdown was made.)[1]

Drug-sodden laziness was half the problem (see [110]). In Lennon's case, this was complicated by his oscillating confidence, which had him either wildly overestimating The Beatles ('We're as good as Beethoven') or flatly dismissing them (and art in general) as 'a con' (see [109]). The rest of the trouble sprang from the ethos of 1967 itself – a passive atmosphere in which anything involving struggle, conflict, or difficulty seemed laughably unenlightened. 'It's *easy*' – the half-ingenuous, half-sarcastic refrain of ALL YOU NEED IS LOVE – expressed both this starry-eyed mood and The Beatles' non-evaluative attitude to their music in the dazzling light of LSD. All you had to do was toss a coin, consult the *I Ching*, or read a random paragraph from a newspaper – and then start playing or singing. Anyone could do it, everyone could join in. ('All together now . . .')[2]

The communality of the hippies, like that of the 17th-century nonconformists to whom they looked for precedents, was essentially egalitarian. There was little room in this outlook for 'special' individuals and thus (theoretically, at least) small scope for artistic genius. Creativity was merely the childlike play of the imagination; we were *all* artists. When The Pink Floyd made a TV appearance to promote their extraordinary second single 'See Emily Play', they were surrounded by a kaftan-clad crowd of beatific followers resembling fey emissaries from some future Eden. Shortly afterwards, The Beatles repeated the trick by performing ALL YOU NEED IS LOVE knee-deep in garlanded hangers-on, going one better by having them all sing along.

If the lotus-eating delusion of an egalitarian life of ease was seductive, its concomitant worship of benign chance was positively enervating. During the chaotic sessions for [113] IT'S ALL TOO MUCH, the group filled several tapes with instrumental ramblings to which they never later returned, although they were presumably under the impression that they were doing something worthwhile at the time. By mid-1967, their enthusiasm for 'random', which had begun as a sensible instinct for capitalising on fortuitous mistakes, was starting to degenerate into a readiness to accept more or less anything, however daft or irrelevant, as divinely dispensed. Lennon's lyric for ALL YOU NEED IS

---

[1] Lewisohn, *Sessions*, p. 116.
[2] During the sessions for ALL YOU NEED IS LOVE, Harrison insisted on playing violin, an instrument he'd never previously touched.

LOVE shows the rot setting in: a shadow of sense discernible behind a cloud of casual incoherence through which the author's train of thought glides sleepily backwards. The various musical quotations[1] – collaged onto the backing track by George Martin, working to The Beatles' offhand instructions – are in the same vein, if more to the point, underlining an ambiguity implicit in the orchestra's blowsily derisive rejoinders to the chorus. The presiding spirit of ALL YOU NEED IS LOVE nonetheless has more to do with comfortable self-indulgence than redeeming self-parody.

During the materialistic Eighties, this song's title was the butt of cynics, there being, obviously, any number of additional things needed to sustain life on earth. It should, perhaps, be pointed out that this record was not conceived as a blueprint for a successful career. 'All you need is love' is a transcendental statement, as true on its level as the principle of investment on the level of the stock exchange. In the idealistic perspective of 1967 – the polar opposite of 1987 – its title makes perfect sense.

[115] YOUR MOTHER SHOULD KNOW *(Lennon–McCartney)*

McCartney vocal, backing vocal, piano, bass; **Lennon** backing vocal, organ; **Harrison** backing vocal, guitar; **Starr** drums, tambourine

Recorded: 22nd–23rd August, Chappell Studios; 16th September 1967, Abbey Road 3; 29th September 1967, Abbey Road 2.

Producer: George Martin. Engineers: John Timperley; Geoff Emerick; Ken Scott.

UK release: 8th December 1967 (2-EP: *Magical Mystery Tour*)

US release: 27th November 1967 (LP: *Magical Mystery Tour*)

After [114] ALL YOU NEED IS LOVE, The Beatles took a two-month break, their first substantial time away from recording since beginning [93] STRAWBERRY FIELDS FOREVER in late November 1966. Despite the sedentary atmosphere of the high summer of 1967, their native sharpness began to recover its edge. Intuitive as Lennon and McCartney were, their creative drive had always been governed by practicality and hard graft. (When preparing a new album, they would scrupulously check their previous work to see where they'd got to and how it compared with that of their competitors.) While it never fully returned

---

[1] The 'Marseillaise', a Bach two-part invention, *Greensleeves*, and Glenn Miller's 'In The Mood'. (The last was still in copyright and The Beatles later made an out-of-court settlement with its publisher.)

after *Sgt. Pepper*, this sense of perspective had reasserted itself enough by August for them to see that they needed to raise their game if the slackness of their recent efforts was to be overcome.

Its title taken from a line from the screenplay of *A Taste of Honey*, McCartney's YOUR MOTHER SHOULD KNOW shows him finding his way back to discipline and, in so doing, paying respects to the old-fashioned values of his father Jim's musical era. The song's regular crotchet piano chords suggest that he'd been reviewing his clutch of recent numbers featuring this trait – [78], [95], [99], [104] – though without quite regaining their creative energy. That he was trying to is clear from the ascending phrase that begins the song's long-breathed, winding melody. 'Let's all get up,' urges McCartney, addressing his fellow Beatles as much as the world at large. Yet, aware as he was of the group's need to recover its dynamism, his own indulgence in psychedelic drugs had left him only half in charge of his ambitions. While innovative, the stereo panning in each verse of the song is really a trick to conceal the fact that its author hadn't managed to think up a middle eight for it. Those sensitive to tempo will likewise note that the second verse gradually slows down – a reliable sign of jadedness, and very unusual for Starr (who, to do him justice, may have had to dub his drums on against McCartney's pre-recorded piano track).

[116] I AM THE WALRUS *(Lennon–McCartney)*

> **Lennon** double-tracked vocal, electric piano; **McCartney** backing
> vocal, bass; **Harrison** backing vocal, lead guitar; **Starr** drums;
> **Sidney Sax, Jack Rothstein, Ralph Elman, Andrew McGee,
> Jack Greene, Louis Stevens, John Jezzard, Jack Richards**
> violins; **Lionel Ross, Eldon Fox, Bram Martin, Terry Weil**
> cellos; **Gordon Lewin** clarinet; **Neil Sanders, Tony Tunstall,
> Morris Miller** horns; **The Mike Sammes Singers** backing
> vocals
> Recorded: 5th September 1967, Abbey Road 1; 6th September
> 1967, Abbey Road 2; 27th September 1967, Abbey Road 1;
> 28th–29th September 1967, Abbey Road 2.
> Producer: George Martin. Engineer: Geoff Emerick.
> UK release: 24th November 1967 (B single/HELLO, GOODBYE)
> US release: 27th November 1967 (B single/HELLO, GOODBYE)

When The Beatles ceased touring in August 1966, Brian Epstein lost what he saw as his main function in life. While holding him in real affection and respectful of his business sense, the group had never taken his musical judgement seriously. Feeling superfluous to their new studio-bound career, he fell into a cycle of binge and depression, quickly becoming addicted to the prescription drugs with which he maintained a semblance of normality. A lonely and hypersensitive homosexual, he was easily hurt by his protégés' flippant jibes. No harm was meant by any of this banter, however, and the sad truth is that Epstein's private life was by then a tormented mess beyond outside influence, helpful or otherwise. While witnesses differ over his mood in August 1967, he was long on the road to ruin, and his death from an apparently accidental overdose on the 27th had been imminent for at least a year.

The Beatles were nonetheless shattered by the news. Only four days earlier, Epstein had paid his final visit to one of their recording sessions (at Chappell, the second of two for [115] YOUR MOTHER SHOULD KNOW). The following evening, the group had attended a lecture by the Maharishi Mahesh Yogi at the London Hilton, and had been excited enough to cancel a further studio date on the 25th to pursue the guru to a weekend retreat in Wales. Learning of Epstein's death, they cut their stay short and reconvened at McCartney's house in St John's Wood on 1st September to decide what to do. McCartney knew that the psychological force holding them together would soon dissipate without some new creative focus, and argued that they must now get on with the *Magical Mystery Tour* project. The others glumly agreed, Lennon acquiescing despite seeing with his usual withering clarity that, without Epstein, The Beatles would soon fall apart. (Why they chose one of his songs to continue with is unknown. Possibly it was a smart move on McCartney's part, based on the calculation that his partner, if allowed to brood, might become intractable.)

Lennon's mood in August 1967, when he wrote I AM THE WALRUS, was, as usual, paradoxical. Passively introspective, he was interested mostly in his own LSD-enhanced impressions, though also fascinated by the spiritual issues these raised [77]. In this respect, he was closest to Harrison, whose regard for Hindu religion he shared [121] and who, by way of returning the compliment, admired Lennon's recent 'message' songs of peace and tolerance ([110], [114]). (During a visit to San Francisco on 8th August, Harrison strolled, minstrel-style, through the city's hippie enclave Haight-Ashbury, playing guitar and singing BABY, YOU'RE A RICH MAN.) At the same time, Lennon's astringent cynicism remained as a balancing factor and, during 1967's 'Summer of Love', this found much to feed on. It was then that the British establishment, disconcerted by the explosion of the counterculture in the UK and aware of the unrest and civil disobedience associated with its parent movement in America, moved to stifle it at home by making examples of its leading representatives (notably the underground paper *International Times*, raided for 'subversive material' by the police in March). Though the MBE-inoculated Beatles were immune, their outrageous colleagues The Rolling Stones were fair game and within months Mick Jagger, Keith Richards, and Brian Jones had all been arrested on drugs charges.[1] With the trial of Jagger and Richards impending, Lennon and McCartney (who had recently publicly admitted to taking LSD) made a gesture of solidarity by singing backing vocals on the Stones' opportunistic protest single 'We Love You'.[2] Jailed, respectively, for three months and one year, Jagger and Richards were freed only after the editor of *The Times* took up their case, famously demanding to know, in the words of Alexander Pope, 'Who Breaks A Butterfly Upon A Wheel?' Soon after this, despite an outcry from the country's younger generation, Britain's hugely popular and perfectly harmless 'pirate' radio stations were officiously banned. The times they were a-changing.

At home in Weybridge around this time, Lennon was prodding about on his piano when he heard the droning two-note siren of a police-car in the distance. Whether or not as a symbol of mean-spirited authority, he instantly absorbed this semitonal seesaw into an obsessive musical structure built round a perpetually ascending/descending M. C. Escher staircase of all the natural major chords – the most unorthodox and tonally ambiguous sequence he ever devised.[3] The words took longer to come, arriving over several acid-heightened weekends and passing through a number of phases. According to Lennon's friend Pete Shotton, the original inspiration was a letter from a boy at their old school Quarry Bank, describing how his English class was analysing the Beatles' lyrics, a fact which Lennon found hilarious. (His teachers at Quarry Bank, particularly his English teachers, had always dismissed

---

[1] Further drug 'busts' among London's hippie community soon afterwards led to a pro-cannabis rally in Hyde Park and the founding of Release. Lennon remained inviolable only so long as he 'played the game' (i.e., remained a sort of eccentric national jester). As soon as he broke the compact by appearing nude with a Japanese woman on the sleeve of *Two Virgins* (publicised before its release), he was immediately busted – and 'planted', if Pete Shotton, who witnessed the raid, is to be believed (*John Lennon in My Life*, p. 185).

[2] This was accompanied by a promotional film featuring Jagger as Oscar Wilde, Marianne Faithfull as Lord Alfred Douglas, and Richards as the Marquess of Queensberry. The Who joined the protest by issuing a cover of an appropriate Jagger–Richards song, 'Under My Thumb'.

[3] It is odd that classical critics, in their rush to lionise [59] YESTERDAY, have overlooked this extraordinary song with its mind-bending *Through the Looking-Glass* harmonic structure.

him as a talentless disrupter – a rejection which left deep scars.)[1] Reminiscing, he and Shotton recalled a typical playground nonsense chant: 'Yellow matter custard, green slop pie/All mixed together with a dead dog's eye.' Returning to the song, Lennon wrote 'Yellow matter custard dripping from a dead dog's eye', adding a string of the most meaningless images he could think of.[2] Yet as the lyric progressed, it grew more pointed, rising above the level of a schoolboy nose-thumb to embrace his festering resentment of the British establishment as a whole. Gradually turning into an angry sequel to the darkly melancholic [93] STRAWBERRY FIELDS FOREVER, I AM THE WALRUS became its author's ultimate anti-institutional rant – a damn-you-England tirade that blasts education, art, culture, law, order, class, religion, and even sense itself. The hurt teenager's revenge on his 'expert textpert' schoolmasters ('I'm *crying*') broadens into a surreal onslaught on straight society in general – an anti-litany of smiling pigs in a sty, city policemen in a row, corporation vans, and the guardians of conventional morality beating up a fellow psychedelic rebel (the opium-addicted surrealist Edgar Allan Poe). A trace of the more peaceably philosophical Lennon remains in the song's opening line, but the rest is pure invective.[3]

Usually regarded as a cheerful exercise in anarchic nonsense, I AM THE WALRUS takes on a different cast when seen in context. This is not, however, to underestimate its element of pure linguistic mischief. Apart from attacking his old teachers and the establishment, Lennon was satirising the fashion for fanciful psychedelic lyrics cultivated by Dylan's then much-discussed output of 1965–66.[4] Yet here, too, he was

---

[1] Trying to judge Lennon's outlook from his own words is an exercise complicated by the emotional instability which could tip him into wild exaggerations. In the *Rolling Stone* interview (1970), this happens when Jann Wenner probes his childhood memories of being 'difficult' and misunderstood. Cursing uncontrollably, Lennon careers into a violent diatribe about the pain and resentment of being 'looked down on'. (Wenner, pp. 163–4.)

[2] One of these – policemen flying 'like Lucy in the sky' – alludes to the misinterpretation of [103] LUCY IN THE SKY WITH DIAMONDS as a code for LSD (Shotton, p. 124).

[3] This includes a snipe at the mechanical mantra-chanting of the *Hare Krishna* movement, to which Harrison was amiably disposed. Lennon later claimed that this was a dig at Beat poet Allen Ginsberg, whose recitals around this time chiefly consisted of him playing a harmonium and chanting mantras.

[4] Recalling his mood at the time of writing I AM THE WALRUS, Lennon remarked: 'Dylan got away with murder. I thought, I can write this crap, too.' (He later wrote a Dylan parody entitled 'Stuck Inside Of Lexicon With The Roget's Thesaurus Blues Again'.)

ambivalent. If there was a model for I AM THE WALRUS it was Procol Harum's 'A Whiter Shade of Pale', his favourite record of summer 1967 and famous in the pop world for taking portentous meaninglessness to rococo lengths (a fact which did not prevent it justly delighting the British public enough to keep it at No. 1 for six weeks). While 'A Whiter Shade of Pale' and I AM THE WALRUS are related mainly by mood and tempo, it is no secret that Lennon loved such nonsense for the sake of it – indeed, his favourite author, Lewis Carroll, provided the title of the song (a garbled reference to his poem *The Walrus and the Carpenter*)[1]. The nonsense of I AM THE WALRUS is, though, anything but whimsical. A song of self-definition amounting to a manifesto, it is defensive to the point of desperation. Confronting his boyhood dilemma over whether he was mad or a genius [93], Lennon here concludes (after the style of contemporary radical psychologist R. D. Laing) that his madness is at least more real to him than the repressive *mores* of an insane world.[2] In short I AM THE WALRUS marks the start of a period in which its author allowed expressive integrity to override ordinary sense completely. (With an irony Lennon must have relished, his satire on repressive inflexibility was banned by the BBC for its use of the revolutionary codeword 'knickers'.[3])

---

[1] Lennon later regretted picking the Walrus after re-reading Carroll's poem and realising that he was 'the bad guy' [103].

[2] In the film of *Magical Mystery Tour*, Lennon mimed I AM THE WALRUS wearing an 18th-century madman's cap. The line that inspired this, 'I am the Eggman', may also refer to another *Through the Looking-Glass* character, Humpty Dumpty.

[3] Despite a long-standing campaign of subversive provocation in Britain's radical theatres, official censorship was then still in force in Britain. During 1967, *Last Exit To Brooklyn* was on trial in the High Court for obscenity and the Royal Court's production of Edward Bond's *Early Morning* was bowdlerised by the Lord Chamberlain. Inevitably, the paternalistic attitude that accompanied this shaped the BBC's decisions on what, and what not, to broadcast. Yet this situation was on the point of changing. Towards the end of 1967, abortion and homosexuality were legalised, and contraception was regulated in the Family Planning Act. In September 1968, the role of Lord Chamberlain was abolished, ending theatre censorship, an event celebrated at the premiere of the London production of the 'hippie musical' *Hair*, at which the cast appeared in 'full frontal nudity' onstage (the thespian equivalent of the fade-out chant of 'Everybody's got one' in I AM THE WALRUS). Within two years, Kenneth Tynan's explicit erotic revue *Oh! Calcutta* opened in London to blasé reviews. In the cinema, sexual censorship began to soften around 1966, while the rules on screen violence in Britain were significantly loosened by the X-certification of William Penn's *Bonnie and Clyde* in 1968. Later stages in the relaxation of control on violence in the cinema were marked by Sam Peckinpah's *The Wild Bunch* (1969) and *Straw Dogs* (1971) and by Stanley Kubrick's *A Clockwork*

Lennon enjoyed himself recording it, but this song was close to home and the fact that work on it began only nine days after Epstein's death must have exacerbated its bitterness. (His vocal was snarled so harshly into the microphone that the mix barely masks the resulting peak-distortions.) Fired by Lennon's imagination, George Martin created his finest arrangement for any Beatles song, developing aspects of the lyric and backing-track just as he had with [93] STRAWBERRY FIELDS FOREVER.[1] Only the final mix – complete with a random radio scan (by Lennon) which broke into a Third Programme broadcast of *King Lear* – leaves anything to be desired, its alterations of timbre and balance achieved at the cost of bass-response.[2]

Representing Lennon's final high-tide of inspiration for The Beatles, I AM THE WALRUS is (with the possible exception of Dylan's surrealistic anti-nuclear nightmare 'A Hard Rain's A-Gonna Fall') the most idiosyncratic protest-song ever written. Though its author continued to write exceptional songs for the group, he never rose to this stunning level again.

[117] BLUE JAY WAY *(Harrison)*

Harrison double-tracked vocal, backing vocal, Hammond organ;
  McCartney backing vocal, bass; **Lennon** backing vocal; **Starr**
  drums, tambourine; **Uncredited** cello
Recorded: 6th–7th September, 6th October 1967, Abbey Road 2.
Producer: George Martin. Engineer: Geoff Emerick.
UK release: 8th December 1967 (2-EP: *Magical Mystery Tour*)
US release: 27th November 1967 (LP: *Magical Mystery Tour*)

Unlike Lennon, Harrison had yet to escape The Beatles' summer doldrums, and his contribution to *Magical Mystery Tour* was as unfocused and monotonous as most of the group's other music of this

---

Orange (1971), a film subsequently withdrawn from British circulation by its director following 'copycat' incidents. The last watershed for UK cinema censorship (sex *and* violence) was William Friedkin's *The Exorcist* (1973). The – to date – final showdown on the grounds of literary obscenity in Britain took place at the OZ trial in June–July 1971.
[1] The pre-bass, pre-orchestration version of I AM THE WALRUS on *Anthology 2* gives a good idea of how crucial Martin's contribution was to the final effect.
[2] The final version joins two reduction mixes at the middle section: 'Sitting in an English garden . . .'

period. Written in the fog-bound Hollywood Hills of Los Angeles on 1st August 1967, the blurred harmonic oscillation between C major and C diminished which is almost the entire musical matter of BLUE JAY WAY all too successfully conveys its author's jet-lagged dislocation while waiting for publicist Derek Taylor to arrive. A four-minute pedal-drone laden with ADT, phasing, and backwards tapes, it numbingly fails to transcend the weary boredom that inspired it.

[118] **FLYING** *(Harrison–Lennon–McCartney–Starkey)*

> **Lennon** vocal, organ, Mellotron; **Harrison** vocal, guitar;
>   **McCartney** vocal, guitar, bass; **Starr** vocal, drums, maracas
> Recorded: 8th September 1967, Abbey Road 3; 28th September
>   1967, Abbey Road 2.
> Producer: George Martin. Engineers: Geoff Emerick/Ken Scott.
> UK release: 8th December 1967 (2-EP: *Magical Mystery Tour*)
> US release: 27th November 1967 (LP: *Magical Mystery Tour*)

In their club days, The Beatles paced their sets with many instrumentals, some original, others covers.[1] Initially entitled 'Aerial Tour Instrumental' and vaguely intended for a segment of the *Magical Mystery Tour* soundtrack, FLYING, a sleepy C blues decorated with pseudo-Indian melismas and some beautiful varispeeded Mellotron by Lennon, was gently doodled in two casual sessions at either end of a chaotic fortnight's filming for the programme.

---

[1] Eg., [E4] CRY FOR A SHADOW. Featured in the group's set from 1958 to 1962, McCartney's 'Catswalk' was later recorded by Chris Barber as 'Catcall'. Another McCartney instrumental from 1957–9, 'Hot As Sun', was recorded on his first solo album in 1970. Two more originals, 'Winston's Walk' and 'Looking Glass', date from the same period. During 1960, The Beatles occasionally played The Shadows' 'Apache' and a version of 'Harry Lime (Theme from The Third Man)'. Other such covers included Duane Eddy's 'Three Thirty Blues', and Jet Harris and Tony Meehan's 1963 UK No. 1 'Diamonds'.

[119] THE FOOL ON THE HILL *(Lennon–McCartney)*

McCartney vocal, piano, acoustic guitar, recorder, bass; **Lennon**
harmonica, jaw's harp (?); **Harrison** acoustic guitar, harmonica;
Starr drums, maracas, finger cymbals; **Christopher Taylor,**
Richard Taylor, Jack Ellory flutes
Recorded: 25th–27th September, Abbey Road 2; 20th October
  1967, Abbey Road 3.
Producer: George Martin. Engineer: Ken Scott.
UK release: 8th December 1967 (2-EP: *Magical Mystery Tour*)
US release: 27th November 1967 (LP: *Magical Mystery Tour*)

McCartney wrote this poignantly expressive D major-minor melody[1]
during the *Sgt. Pepper* sessions in March 1967 and showed it to Lennon
while they were working on [107] WITH A LITTLE HELP FROM MY
FRIENDS. Like many other Beatles songs of the period, its origin on the
(to them) foreign medium of the piano is clear in its regular crotchet
beat; indeed Lennon may have had it in the back of his mind during the
early stages of [116] I AM THE WALRUS, written in a similar way.

With its high *tessitura* and perpetually ascending chorus, THE FOOL
ON THE HILL is an airy creation, poised peacefully above the world in a
place where time and haste are suspended. Part intuited from the key-
scheme and part rationalised, McCartney's lyric skirts sentiment by
never committing itself, remaining open to several interpretations.[2]
The timeless appeal of THE FOOL ON THE HILL lies in its paradoxical air
of childlike wisdom and unworldliness, an effect created by a
melancholy revolving harmony in which the world turns in cycles of
struggle and rest, shadowed by clouds drifting indifferently across the
sky.

---

[1] In his studio demo *(Anthology 2)*, the musicianly McCartney characteristically
follows classical practice by 'stating' this tonal ambiguity in a four-bar piano
introduction (cf. [91]). Shorn of its repeat, this survived into the first group–recorded
version *(Anthology 2)*, but was dropped for the remake begun on 26th September
1967.
[2] He was partly thinking of the Maharishi and partly of The Fool in the Tarot
pack, a paradoxical symbol, numbered 0 or 22, which stands for 'redeeming
ignorance'. Along with interest in Hindu and Tibetan religion, LSD created a revival
of Western occultism and a fascination with figures like the French mage Eliphas
Lévi and the magicians of The Golden Dawn. As a result, Pamela Coleman Smith's
art nouveau illustrations for A. E Waite's Golden Dawn Tarot became, with the *I*
Ching, a standard item of hippie furniture. (The Dutch artists Simon Posthuma and
Marijke Koger, who later painted a short-lived psychedelic design on the exterior of
the Apple shop, took their trade-name, The Fool, from the same Tarot card.)

[120] HELLO, GOODBYE *(Lennon–McCartney)*

McCartney double-tracked vocal, backing vocal, piano, bass,
   bongos, conga; **Lennon** backing vocal, lead guitar, organ;
   Harrison backing vocal, lead guitar; **Starr** drums, maracas,
   tambourine; **Kenneth Essex, Leo Birnbaum** violas
Recorded: 2nd October 1967, Abbey Road 2; 19th October 1967,
   Abbey Road 1; 25th October 1967, Abbey Road 2; 2nd
   November 1967, Abbey Road 2.
Producer: George Martin. Engineer: Ken Scott/Geoff Emerick.
UK release: 24th November 1967 (A single/I AM THE WALRUS)
US release: 27th November 1967 (A single/I AM THE WALRUS)

Recorded after most of the filming for *Magical Mystery Tour* was
finished, this blandly catchy McCartney song became The Beatles' first
post-Epstein single (much to Lennon's disgust, his [116] I AM THE
WALRUS being harmlessly diverted to the B-side). According to group
assistant Alistair Taylor, HELLO, GOODBYE began as an exercise in
'random' in which he and McCartney struck alternate notes on a
harmonium while playing a word-association game. Childlike lyrics,
another by-product of LSD, were then fashionable, McCartney
catching a mood set in such 1967 hits as The Pink Floyd's 'See Emily
Play' and Traffic's 'Hole In My Shoe'.[1] Built on a descending
sequence in C, the song's characteristic scalar structure offers a brief
touchdown on A flat as its only surprise, yet this, plus its plaintively
simple melody and heavily echoed 'Maori finale' – a mistake for
'Hawaiian' *(aloha)* – proved sufficient to secure a big hit. (McCartney
took particular care over the bass line which, like most of those after
[89] I WANT TO TELL YOU, was recorded at a late stage on its own
track.)[2]

That HELLO, GOODBYE spent seven weeks at No. 1 in the UK, The
Beatles' longest stay at the top since [12] SHE LOVES YOU, says more
about the sudden decline of the singles chart than the quality of the
song itself. Following a period in which Tin Pan Alley and the major
labels had lost control to self-reliant groups, a new generation of young
female listeners – a segment of the market soon formally categorised as

---

[1] Around the time HELLO, GOODBYE was written (late September), Traffic's pop
nursery-rhyme 'Here We Go Round The Mulberry Bush' had been scheduled for
inclusion in *Magical Mystery Tour*.
[2] The almost-finished but still bass-less multitrack was remixed for *Anthology 2*,
revealing some superfluous (and subsequently erased) Harrison guitar interjections on
the opening lines.

teenyboppers – was being targeted by old-style manufactured acts masterminded by traditional writer/producer studio teams.[1] These along with pseudo-Beatles like The Monkees and The Bee Gees, lightweight exploitations of San Franciscan 'flower-power', and the histrionic bellowing of proto-'heavy metal' quartet Vanilla Fudge, represented a significant decline in pop's inspiration from its peak of 1965 to mid-1967. As the divide between pop and rock widened during the next few years, the brighter writer-performers would move *en masse* into the album market, leaving the singles charts to the sort of shallow 'bubblegum' last dominant in the 1959–62 interregnum between Presley and The Beatles.

[U121] CHRISTMAS TIME (IS HERE AGAIN)
(Lennon–McCartney–Harrison–Starkey)

> **McCartney** double-tracked vocal, piano; **Lennon** double-tracked
>   vocal, bass-drum; **Harrison** double-tracked vocal, acoustic guitar;
>   **Starr** double-tracked vocal, drums; **George Martin, Victor**
>   **Spinetti** double-tracked vocals
> Recorded: 28th November, 6th December 1967, Abbey Road 3.
> Producer: George Martin. Engineer: Geoff Emerick.
> UK release: 4th December 1995 (CD single: *Free As A Bird*)
> US release: 4th December 1995 (CD single: *Free As A Bird*)

Made for The Beatles' fifth fan club Christmas EP, this brief blues-structured chorus was edited down and interspersed with the usual clowning around on the rest of the disc, which, on this occasion, included some parody advertisements and a tantalising excerpt from The Ravellers' legendary 'Plenty Of Jam Jars'. Sadly, the version issued on the [187] FREE AS A BIRD single omits most of this. The original six-minute take is still in the Abbey Road archive.

---

[1] Aka pretty boys singing fluff, a perennial genre. In Britain: The Tremeloes, Dave Dee, Dozy, Beaky, Mick, and Tich, The Herd, Love Affair, Marmalade, *et al*; in the USA: Tommy James and the Shondells, The 1910 Fruitgum Co., Ohio Express, Union Gap, etc.

[121] THE INNER LIGHT *(Harrison)*

> Harrison vocal; Lennon backing vocal; McCartney backing vocal;
> Sharad Ghosh or Hanuman Jadev shehnai; Hariprasad
> Chaurasia or S. R. Kenkare flute; Ashish Khan sarod;
> Mahapurush Misra tabla, pakavaj; Rij Ram Desad harmonium
> Recorded: 12th January 1968, EMI Bombay; 6th February 1968,
>   Abbey Road 1; 8th February 1968, Abbey Road 2.
> Producer: George Martin. Engineers: J. P. Sen, S. N. Gupta/Geoff
>   Emerick.
> UK release: 15th March 1968 (B single/LADY MADONNA)
> US release: 18th March 1968 (B single/LADY MADONNA)

Harrison's post-touring mood of introspection finally came to an end
when he was invited by director Joe Massot to write a score for a now-
forgotten Swinging London film called *Wonderwall*, starring Jane Birkin
and Jack MacGowran. During the three months it took to record his
Indian-influenced soundtrack, he flew to Bombay and taped a number
of instrumentals at the EMI India studio using, among others, the
celebrated flute/santoor duo Hariprasad Chaurasia and Shivkumar
Sharma. Among the results was the basic track for what, back in Abbey
Road, became THE INNER LIGHT, a song based on a section from Lao-
Tse's Taoist holy book, the *Tao Te Ching*.

On 29th September 1967, Harrison and Lennon had appeared on
an edition of David Frost's *The Frost Programme* devoted to the subject
of Transcendental Meditation.[1] So much interest was created by this
that they were invited back on 4th October to take part in a discussion
with members of the audience and some specialist intellectuals. Among
the latter was Juan Mascaro, a Cambridge Sanskrit scholar, who shortly
afterwards sent Harrison a copy of his anthology *Lamps of Fire*, pointing
out the musical potential of a passage from the *Tao Te Ching* – the text
of which became THE INNER LIGHT. (Harrison's decision to take up
Mascaro's suggestion may have been inspired by the example of The
Pink Floyd's Syd Barrett in his 1967 song 'Chapter 24' which similarly
sets an excerpt from the Chinese *I Ching* or Book of Changes.)

Embarrassed by the high singing key he had left himself, Harrison
had to be cajoled by McCartney and Lennon before he would abandon
his native caution and commit himself. In the event, the others liked

---

[1] Immediately after the programme was taped for transmission later that evening,
they drove from Rediffusion's Wembley studio to Abbey Road, where they worked
on the final mix of [116] I AM THE WALRUS (including Lennon's radio scan of Act
IV Scene 6 of a BBC production of *King Lear*).

the song so much that they put it on the B-side of their final Parlophone single. With the studied innocence and exotic sweetness of The Incredible String Band, THE INNER LIGHT is both spirited and charming – one of its author's most attractive pieces.

[122] LADY MADONNA *(Lennon–McCartney)*

> **McCartney** double-tracked vocal, piano, bass, handclaps; **Lennon** backing vocal, lead guitar, handclaps; **Harrison** backing vocal, lead guitar, handclaps; **Starr** drums, handclaps; **Ronnie Scott, Bill Povey** tenor saxes; **Harry Klein, Bill Jackman** baritone saxes
>
> Recorded: 3rd February 1968, Abbey Road 3; 6th February 1968, Abbey Road 1.
> Producer: George Martin. Engineers: Ken Scott/Geoff Emerick.
> UK release: 15th March 1968 (A single/THE INNER LIGHT)
> US release: 18th March 1968 (A single/THE INNER LIGHT)

As if to prove himself unaffected by the critical savaging inflicted on *Magical Mystery Tour* [109], McCartney bounced back with another A-side, the second in a row to oust a rival offering from Lennon ([120], [123]). LADY MADONNA, a song uncontroversially in praise of motherhood, was inspired by a magazine picture of an African woman suckling her baby over the caption 'Mountain Madonna'.[1] Styled after Fats Domino, the music's immediate source was Johnny Parker's boogiewoogie piano line on Humphrey Lyttleton's 'Bad Penny Blues', produced by George Martin in 1956. As such, LADY MADONNA was the first Beatles song (not counting the instrumental [118] FLYING) to use a blues scale since [90] GOOD DAY SUNSHINE – which suggests that McCartney may have been trying to guide the group back to earth after its disembodied LSD phase. If so, the attempt was superficial, for the lyric is tinged with the acid-fuelled unreality that had hung over The Beatles since *Sgt. Pepper* (and which was about to shape the ill-fated Apple project). While the words of the verse/chorus hang together, the middle eight wanders off into a string of vaguely associated images, climaxing, on a hymnic suspension, with a pointless allusion to [116] I AM THE WALRUS. Whether this was done to please Lennon or, in a spirit of playfulness, to add another link to an ongoing chain of

---

[1] Interviewed by Barry Miles (op. cit., p. 449), McCartney makes no mention of this explanation, instead relating the song directly to the Virgin Mary.

references ([103], [116]), it amounted to wanton – and perilous – self-mythologisation (see [144]).

Most of the work on LADY MADONNA took place on one day in Studio 3, with a separate late-night session for overdubs. Following his usual practice, McCartney began by taping the piano track plus a guide vocal, accompanied by Starr on brushed snare. (An old microphone was used to obtain the right period piano sound.) After Lennon and Harrison had doubled the riff on fuzz-toned guitars played together through the same amp, McCartney and Starr added their rhythm-section, the rolling bass line matched by a syncopated bass–drum pattern akin to the swing-beat of the late Eighties. Achieved by limiting, the thunderous low-frequencies of bass and piano were also applied to Starr's kit, in particular the snare sound in the coda. After redoing his Presleyesque vocal, McCartney hired four jazz saxophonists without preparing parts for them, an 'unprofessional' lapse which provoked an audibly exasperated tenor solo from Ronnie Scott. The result was a moderately entertaining let-down after the psychedelic heights of early 1967. Significantly, LADY MADONNA became the first purpose-built Beatles single not to reach No. 1 in America since ELEANOR RIGBY.

[123] ACROSS THE UNIVERSE *(Lennon–McCartney)*

> Lennon vocal, backing vocal, acoustic rhythm guitar, lead guitar;
>   McCartney backing vocal, piano; Harrison backing vocal, sitar,
>   tambura; Starr maracas; George Martin Hammond organ;
>   Lizzie Bravo, Gayleen Pease backing vocals; Uncredited
>   strings and choir
> Recorded: 4th February 1968, Abbey Road 3; 8th February 1968,
>   Abbey Road 2.
> Producer: George Martin. Engineer: Ken Scott.
> UK release: 12th December 1969 (LP: *No One's Gonna Change Our
>   World*)
> US release: 12th December 1969 (LP: *No One's Gonna Change Our
>   World*)

After the aggressive sarcasm of [116] I AM THE WALRUS, it is sad to find Lennon, some months and several hundred acid trips later, chanting this plaintively babyish incantation.[1] His most shapeless song, ACROSS THE

---

[1] According to those who knew him around this time, his LSD intake was so enormous that he was almost permanently tripping.

UNIVERSE, like [67] IN MY LIFE and [69] NOWHERE MAN, came out of a mentally drained state in the early hours of the morning: a trancelike succession of trochees which presently extended to three verses. Lennon was impressed with this lyric, trying on several later occasions to write in the same metre. Sadly, its vague pretensions and listless melody are rather too obviously the products of acid grandiosity rendered gentle by sheer exhaustion.

Lennon always spoke highly of ACROSS THE UNIVERSE, claiming that McCartney had sabotaged it by not taking it seriously. Yet the fact that he failed to provide a contrasting middle eight suggests that he was too close to the song to judge it properly, an impression confirmed by his directionless attempts to record it. Planned as a Beatles A-side, it gradually dissolved into a morass of out-of-tune wahwah guitar and squeaky backing vocals by two of the band's teenage girl fans who stood sentinel all day outside Abbey Road and who were asked in on the spur of the moment. In the end Lennon withdrew the song as a candidate for The Beatles' next single, agreeing to the substitution of McCartney's [122] LADY MADONNA. Uncertain what to do with it, he let ex-Goon Spike Milligan use it on a World Wildlife Fund charity LP, for which it was speeded up a semitone from its original D major and spattered with bird noises. Finally Phil Spector was given the tape and asked to make something of it for *Let It Be*. Sadly his solution – slowing it to D flat and plastering it with Disney strings and lullaby voices – merely emphasised the song's insipid lethargy. While a Beatle, Lennon was rarely boring. He made an unwanted exception with this track.

[124] HEY BULLDOG *(Lennon–McCartney)*

Lennon double-tracked vocal, piano, lead guitar; **McCartney**
  harmony vocal, bass; **Harrison** guitar; **Starr** drums, tambourine
Recorded: 11th February 1968, Abbey Road 3.
Producer: George Martin. Engineer: Geoff Emerick.
UK release: 17th January 1969 (LP: *Yellow Submarine*)
US release: 13th January 1969 (LP: *Yellow Submarine*)

Convened for the purpose of filming a promo for [122] LADY MADONNA, this session evolved into another new track. Lennon had a half-sketched idea entitled 'Hey Bullfrog' which he showed to McCartney – upon which they finished it and spent the day recording it for the *Yellow Submarine* soundtrack. Based on a variation of [13c] MONEY, the song is bluesy after the fashion of LADY MADONNA, and follows [119] THE FOOL ON THE HILL in moving to the minor for its chorus. The lyric, which Lennon claimed to be meaningless and which was to some extent rationalised during the session,[1] is actually, like that of [116] I AM THE WALRUS, rather menacingly pointed (possibly at McCartney). The unbalanced mix emphasises an over-spontaneous bass line, but the rest, particularly Lennon's scathing delivery of the rising augmented chorus, is rawly exciting. Showing how fast he could snap out of introversion [123], HEY BULLDOG signals the end of his dissociated acid phase. It also opens the final phase in The Beatles' career in that present throughout the day's recording was his future muse Yoko Ono.

[U125] JUNK *(McCartney)*

McCartney vocal, acoustic guitar
Recorded: Last week of May 1968, Esher.
Producer: None. Engineer: None.
UK release: 28th October 1996 (2-CD: *Anthology 3*)
US release: 28th October 1996 (2-CD: *Anthology 3*)

In February 1968 The Beatles and their wives flew to India to stay at the Maharishi Mahesh Yogi's Himalayan meditation centre at Rishikesh. Unable to stomach the vegetarian food, Starr returned to Britain at the end of the month; a noncommittal McCartney stuck it out till mid-March. More interested in Hindu religion, Lennon and Harrison remained until April, whereupon they allegedly discovered something rotten in the state of higher awareness (see [135]) and decamped in disillusionment.

Apart from mountain air and Transcendental Meditation, the most significant thing about The Beatles' stay in Rishikesh was that they were almost entirely drug-free. (Though they smuggled in enough marijuana for a regular evening joint, they foreswore LSD.) This undoubtedly cleared their minds and helped them recharge their batteries; indeed their creativity revived so sharply that they wrote more than thirty new songs between them.

Before going into Abbey Road on 30th May 1968 to begin the sessions for *The Beatles*, the group gathered amid the Indian decor of Harrison's Esher bungalow to tape twenty-six very rough demos: seven

---

[1] The line 'measured out in you' began as 'measured out in news'. (McCartney made this improvement by affecting to have misread Lennon's handwriting.)

by McCartney,[1] five by Harrison,[2] and no fewer than fourteen by Lennon[3] (a measure of the extent to which the mesmeric influence of LSD had been depressing his energy).

Typical of McCartney's demos, JUNK is virtually finished in the sketch now available on *Anthology 3*. All that needed to be done was to take the arrangement into the studio and tape it. In the event, its author's contribution to the 'White Album' was so prolific that this gentle exercise in sentimental nostalgia had to wait a further eighteen months before finding a place on his eponymous debut solo album.

[U126] CHILD OF NATURE (Lennon)

Lennon double-tracked vocal, double-tracked acoustic guitar; **Starr** shaker (?)
Recorded: Last week of May 1968, Esher.
Producer: None. Engineer: None.
Never officially released.

Unreleased on *Anthology 3*, and hence not part of The Beatles' official EMI discography, this Esher demo is nevertheless included here for the sake of the light it throws on Lennon's state of mind at the time it was recorded. Long circulated on bootlegs, this track fascinatingly reveals that what later became the painfully self-analytical 'Jealous Guy' (*Imagine*, 1971) started life as an unguarded confession of religious faith apparently provoked by a few heady weeks of fresh air and meditation in Rishikesh. (A few days before demoing CHILD OF NATURE, its still spaced-out author convened an official group meeting at Apple to inform the others that he was Jesus.)

---

[1] [U125] JUNK (*Anthology 3*), [128] BLACKBIRD, [131] OB-LA-DI, OB-LA-DA, [138] MOTHER NATURE'S SON, [140] ROCKY RACCOON, [142] BACK IN THE USSR, and [149] HONEY PIE (*Anthology 3*).
[2] [136] WHILE MY GUITAR GENTLY WEEPS, [147] PIGGIES (*Anthology 3*), 'Circles', 'Sour Milk Sea' (given to Apple artist Jackie Lomax in June 1968), and [U138] NOT GUILTY (*Anthology 3*). Harrison's demo of 'Sour Milk Sea' was little more than a casual indication using double-tracked voice and guitar with McCartney on bass and shaker by Starr. 'Circles', a typically perceptive, if deeply gloomy, song about *karma*, was accompanied by its composer on harmonium and shadowed by a tentative McCartney bass line. Harrison later recorded it for his 1982 album *Gone Troppo*.
[3] [U126] CHILD OF NATURE, [125] REVOLUTION 1, [129] EVERYBODY'S GOT SOMETHING TO HIDE EXCEPT ME AND MY MONKEY, [133] CRY BABY CRY, [135] SEXY SADIE, [139] YER BLUES, [143] DEAR PRUDENCE, [144] GLASS ONION (*Anthology 3*), [153] I'M SO TIRED, [154] THE CONTINUING STORY OF BUNGALOW BILL, [156] JULIA, [U140] WHAT'S THE NEW MARY JANE (*Anthology 3*), [182] MEAN MR MUSTARD (*Anthology 3*), and [183] POLYTHENE PAM (*Anthology 3*).

His double-tracked voice earnest with vibrato, Lennon here revisits the idealistic domain of [123] ACROSS THE UNIVERSE, insisting, contrary to his bitterly revised views of two years later, that 'the dream I had was true'. It is puzzling that, having left Rishikesh only a month earlier because of the disillusioning experience referred to in [135] SEXY SADIE, he should still have sincerely identified with lines like 'Underneath the mountain ranges/Where the wind that never changes/ Touched the windows of my soul'. A lyric in which all his barriers are down, CHILD OF NATURE shows its composer, according to one's bias, either egolessly close to God or foolishly self-surrendered to a delusion. The transformation of the song into a poignant confession of passionate egocentricity in 'Jealous Guy' offers a signal insight into how circuitous the creative process can be. Except for the chorus chords, nothing changes – yet the mood of reconciliation in melody and harmony works at least as effectively (if not far more so) in the service of an almost diametrically different lyrical outlook.

[125] REVOLUTION 1 *(Lennon–McCartney)*

Lennon vocal, acoustic guitar, lead guitar; **McCartney** backing
  vocals, piano, Hammond organ, bass; **Harrison** backing vocals,
  lead guitar; **Starr** drums; **Derek Watkins, Freddy Clayton**
  trumpets; **Don Lang, Rex Morris, J. Power, Bill Povey**
  trombones
Recorded: 30th May 1968, Abbey Road 2; 31st May–4th June
  1968, Abbey Road 3; 21st June 1968, Abbey Road 2.
Producer: George Martin. Engineers: Geoff Emerick/Peter Bown.
UK release: 22nd November 1968 (LP: *The Beatles*)
US release: 25th November 1968 (LP: *The Beatles*)

If nothing else, The Beatles' Rishikesh experience (see [U125]) cleared their heads and regenerated their energies. Unfortunately, once back in the familiar surroundings of London, they soon returned to their old regime of irregular hours and recreational drugs, a lifestyle unconducive to sustained acquaintance with the everyday world. Despite the panning administered to *Magical Mystery Tour* [109], they still seemed to believe that everything they did, however casual, would somehow turn to gold if they persisted along intuitive lines, regardless of time or cost. In business terms, this attitude quickly led to the tax-manoeuvre-cum-investment-disaster of Apple Corps, a semi-philanthropic enterprise which, within a year, had all but emptied The Beatles' coffers in the pursuit of witless follies and gargantuan expense-accounts. At the level of working detail, it led to a creative embrace of coincidence and a willingness to see accidents as meaningful, from which it was a perilously short step to regarding meaning as accidental. Though the last song to be recorded for their next venture *The Beatles*, Lennon's [156] JULIA contains a rationale for the obscure and often random lyrics which adorn most of this rambling double-album: 'Half of what I say is meaningless/But I say it just to reach you.'[1] A *précis* of the counterculture's attitude towards straight society, Lennon's insistence that expression was more important than form was, up to a point, something anyone could accept. Beyond a certain limit, however, such whimsy risked sliding into incoherence, a danger compounded by The Beatles' self-taught wilfulness and herculean drug-intake.

In Lennon's case, drugs were especially hazardous in that they intensified his introspection during a time when his sense of self was shifting under the new pressure of his relationship with Yoko Ono. (They finally consummated their affair at his house in Surrey on 19th May 1968 while his wife Cynthia was on holiday, spending all night recording their *Unfinished Music No. 1: Two Virgins* before making love at dawn.) By late 1967 – the period of [123] ACROSS THE UNIVERSE – Lennon had come so close to erasing his identity with LSD that The Beatles' publicist Derek Taylor had to risk a powerful therapeutic 'trip' with him in which he went through the group's songs pointing out to their dazed author which ones he'd written and how good they were. Yet, while Lennon's love for Ono helped him escape the debilitating clutches of acid, it was a fragile *détente* and, within a year, wounded by hostile media coverage, the couple were experimenting not merely with artistic conventions but with heroin.

These influences played to the interest in threshold consciousness Lennon had been exploring since [77] TOMORROW NEVER KNOWS, a fascination which resurfaced during the initial session for REVOLUTION 1. Begun, with no anticipation of sequels, as an unnumbered REVOLUTION, this song was the first to be taped during the sessions for the thirty-track epic *The Beatles*, the group having earmarked it as a possible next single. As they played and replayed it, however, it began to drift from the necessary immediacy of a 45 into something more subtle. 'Laying back' on its lazy two-chord shuffle-beat at the end of take eighteen, The Beatles played on, Lennon turning his rasped 'Alright' into orgasmic gasps and screams as the song unravelled in a ten-minute 'happening' similar to the free-form ad-libs on The

---

[1] The phrase adapts a line from Kahlil Gibran's *Sand and Foam* [156].

Mothers of Invention's 1966 album *Freak Out!* The excitement must have seemed auspicious: the new album had started with a bang.[1]

Discarding the earlier takes, Lennon took Ono into the studio with him and overlaid the last six minutes of this unplanned long version with further vocalisations and effects.[2] Further overdubs by the group were added during the following week, including a new lead vocal recorded by Lennon lying flat on his back on the studio floor (the only position in which he felt he could get a sufficiently relaxed sound). Second thoughts set in on 6th June, when he decided to lop off the orgiastic end-section and turn it into the basis of an independent entity, [127] REVOLUTION 9. A fortnight later, the shortened version was completed by the addition of an oddly bottom-heavy brass section. From start to final mix, the process had taken around forty hours – ominously long considering the simplicity of the arrangement.

Since Lennon experimented obsessively with vocal sounds throughout his career, guessing why he chose a particular technique in a given song is bound to be speculative. Lying down to get a loose, breathy sound makes sense on its own terms and he may have done it merely because he liked the effect. This, on the other hand, was the first Beatles recording touched by the disturbing influence of Yoko Ono, whose background in the radical arts scene had grounded her in the sex-politics then being sold by the counterculture as an alternative to the Maoism of the revolutionary student left.[3] Based on the writings of Wilhelm Reich, Herbert Marcuse, and Norman O. Brown (and promoted in Britain by *International Times* and *OZ*), this philosophy aimed to relax the Left's tight-minded totalitarian reflex by bringing it to its senses with a Dionysiac diet of 'dope, rock-and-roll, and fucking in the streets'. While Lennon had been interested in the British counterculture for at least a year, it was not until he met Ono that he became personally confronted by this erotic ideology. ('When we weren't in the studio,' Lennon later admitted, 'we were in bed.')

---

[1] The studio tapes for this session show The Beatles loosening up with several chaotic blues jams between takes. Such spontaneous improvisations were frequent during the 1968–9 studio recordings.

[2] In a revealing passage recorded while Lennon and Ono were having their microphone levels set, they sang to each other in mock-recitative. Lennon: 'I 'ave been stabbed in the brass vertebrae.' Ono: 'Who did that?' Lennon: 'I did it myself.' Ono (laughing): 'Don't you ever do that.' Lennon: 'I must do it now and then to keep myself in tune.' Ono (laughing): 'You mustn't do anything without me.' Lennon: 'I wasn't exactly doing it without you. I was just doing it in the corner, oh Mother McCrae . . .'

[3] For Ono's background, see Goldman, pp. 209–47.

REVOLUTION 1, or at least its unissued long version, seems to have been his first expression of this; hence, perhaps, his decision to lie down to sing it.[1]

Another motive for Lennon's desire to be fully relaxed while singing this song was unease about the lyric. The immediate inspiration for the REVOLUTION sequence ([127], [132]) was the May '68 student uprising in Paris, which reached its crescendo with de Gaulle's dissolution of the French National Assembly the very evening that REVOLUTION 1 was being laid down in London. Fanfared by the Tet Offensive,[2] 1968 had burst violently into the floating utopian fantasy of the previous year, thrusting Vietnam to the top of the protest agenda and sparking a pitched battle between police and 100,000 anti-war marchers outside the US embassy in Grosvenor Square. As if to drive the point home, Martin Luther King's assassination a few weeks later confirmed a brutal *Zeitgeist* shift from love and peace to politics and struggle. In Revolution 1, Lennon was consciously addressing such issues; and in refusing to relinquish love and peace for the grim priorities of the new era, he knew he risked alienating The Beatles' world audience of rapidly radicalising youth. Echoing the turmoil in France, British students had begun taking over their own universities the week before the group began the new album; indeed, at the precise moment that The Beatles were freaking out on the extended version of REVOLUTION 1, students at Hornsey College of Art were declaring a 'state of anarchy' and a 'sit-in' in solidarity with their disaffected peers at Nanterre, the Sorbonne, and the London School of Economics.

When [132] REVOLUTION was released ahead of the new album in August (as the B-side of [137]), the more politicised students scorned what they saw as Lennon's bland rich-man's assurances that everything was somehow going to be 'alright', resenting his wish to be counted out of any impending 'destruction'. The New Left press was likewise offended, especially in America, where REVOLUTION was branded 'a betrayal' and 'a lamentable petty bourgeois cry of fear'. (The jazz singer Nina Simone recorded a 'reply' record in which she attacked Lennon for his apoliticism and advised him to 'clean' his brain.) Meanwhile,

---

[1] If this kind of associational thinking strikes today's more matter-of-fact audience as implausibly naive, it was the very stuff of '68, and no grasp of the period is possible without taking it into account.

[2] Tet, the Vietnamese New Year festival and traditionally a truce period, was chosen by the Vietcong in February 1968 for guerrilla attacks all over South Vietnam. As the Tet Offensive escalated, television pictures of the carnage brought the Vietnam war into Western living rooms, provoking angry protest marches against it in America and Europe.

Time magazine devoted an article to the song, approving its 'exhilarating' criticism of radical activists, while American right-wingers argued on the contrary that The Beatles were merely middle-of-the-road subversives warning the Maoists not to 'blow' the revolution by pushing too hard.[1] In fact, Lennon had agonised about these points even when writing the song in India, and while recording it he constantly changed his mind about being counted 'out' and 'in', in the end opting for both.[2] When this equivocal version hit the shops as the opening track of Side 4 of *The Beatles* in November, it looked like a recantation of his earlier position and, as such, went down well on campus. But the truth was that Lennon had actually hardened his apoliticism after REVOLUTION 1 and, by the time he recorded its savage sequel [132] in July, he was no longer unsure of his feelings. By then, he was committed to peace and, in effect, already pledged to the series of Dadaish demonstrations on its behalf which would eventually bring the derision of both Left and Right down on him, driving him into isolation.[3]

The 'out/in' dilemma is the only equivocation in a song which otherwise avoids the obscurity of so many of Lennon's lyrics of this period. His rejection of 'minds that hate' and dry demand to be shown 'the plan' shows an intuitive grasp of the tangled issue of ideology, while the juxtaposition of Maoism with 'making it' in the closing lines confirms his approval of the counterculture's pyschosexual analysis. Formally, like many Lennon songs from The Beatles' later years, REVOLUTION 1 is a metrically dishevelled and sectionally distended blues. Beginning on A, he delays the expected move to D with an interjected bar of 2/4 ('We-e-ell') – a wry musical face-pull with the simultaneous effect of making the song seem to reverse and start again. Similarly, the last note in the bridge is 'pushed' by means of another 2/

---

[1] This was exactly what Lennon had in mind vis-à-vis the Maoists, whom he saw as prejudicing chances of real social change by baiting the establishment with red flags. (For a fuller account of the Western Left intelligentsia's reaction to REVOLUTION, see Wiener, pp. 60–63.)

[2] The phrase 'it's gonna be alright' arose from Lennon's experiences while meditating in Rishikesh, his idea being that God would take care of the human race whatever happened politically. He later confessed that he'd dabbled in politics during the late Sixties out of guilt and against his instincts.

[3] Responding angrily to an attack on REVOLUTION in the Trotskyite organ of the Vietnam Solidarity Committee *Black Dwarf* in January 1969, he declared himself against both establishment and New Left: 'I'll tell you what's wrong with the world: people. So do you want to destroy them? Until you/we change our heads, there's no chance. Tell me of one successful revolution. Who fucked up communism, Christianity, capitalism, Buddhism, etc? Sick heads, and nothing else.'

4 bar so as to stress the final word in the 'Count me/Out' phrase. (Such brusquely direct devices, typical of him, were rarely resorted to by the more musicianly McCartney.)[1]

The blues basis of REVOLUTION 1, together with its rough and ready dislocations, served to identify it with contemporary street culture and, as such, mark the beginnings of an increasingly extreme reaction on Lennon's part against the 'bourgeois' artifice of 1966–7. This *volte-face* took place in the context of a general return to basics during the late Sixties. In Britain, a new emphasis on live music had brought previously marginalised club musicians to centre stage in the so-called 'blues boom' (see [140]), while America was witnessing the first stirrings of a reconciliation between radical middle-class rock and conservative working-class country music. Both trends were conditioned by national characteristics. For young Americans, 'country rock' implied an earnest search for spiritual roots and a traditional foundation for their hippie communality. To the British, unworried about cultural identity, the popularity of blues represented little more than a change of style: a typical pendulum swing from the flowery cavalier vagaries of psychedelia to the gritty roundhead bluffness of twelve-bars about sex and booze. Apart from Lennon, only Mick Jagger and Keith Richards of The Rolling Stones spotted the parallel between this new musical proletarianism and the rise of the revolutionary Left, shrewdly plaiting the two strands in their album *Beggars Banquet* (released soon after *The Beatles* and a big hit with the student constituency).[2] For the intensely

---

[1] The track features Lennon's first recorded use of his Epiphone Casino semi-acoustic. Impressed by McCartney's Casino-playing on [47] TICKET TO RIDE, [64] DRIVE MY CAR, and [84] TAXMAN, Lennon bought his own in 1966. In 1968, he stripped the instrument of its veneer on the then-vogueish assumption that this would improve its resonance; the fact that the unvarnished wood also gave it a look of deglamourised frankness presumably had its appeal. (McCartney and Harrison had painted their Fenders in psychedelic colours for *Magical Mystery Tour*.) The stripped Casino became Lennon's main guitar and a key part of his image during The Beatles' last two years (e.g., the 'rooftop concert').

[2] See Wiener, pp. 65–9. In fact, The Rolling Stones were even less radical than The Beatles. Interviewing Jagger for ITV's *World in Action* on 31st July 1967, the editor of *The Times*, Sir William Rees-Mogg, was astonished to discover 'a right-wing libertarian – straight John Stuart Mill!' During 1968, Jagger flirted briefly with a revolutionary attitude, declaring himself against private property, joining the Trotskyite-organised anti-Vietnam demonstration in Grosvenor Square, and writing 'Street Fighting Man', a song as powerful and ambivalent as Lennon's REVOLUTION. (A subversive variation on Martha and the Vandella's 'Dancing in the Street', it was immediately banned by the BBC.) However, after the fiasco at Altamont Speedway on 9th December 1969, when a gang of Hell's Angels rioted, killing one of his audience (see the film *Gimme Shelter*, 1970), he reverted to his former stance.

individual Lennon, the shift towards simplicity registered in REVOLU-
TION 1 went far deeper, embodying a need for honesty forced on him
by the pressure for personal reassessment created by the break-up of his
marriage. This shedding of pretence became progressively more
obsessive until, two years later, it reached an agonised climax in the
naked 'primal' expiation of his first solo album.

Lennon's urgent ambition to make REVOLUTION 1 The Beatles'
next single alarmed McCartney, who blanched at the prospect of an
overt political statement. Arguing (with Harrison's support) that the
track was too slow, he suggested that they wait a bit before coming to a
decision. If he had assumed Lennon would give up at this point, he was
disappointed. For too long immersed in LSD to be bothered with
fighting his corner, Lennon had 'come awake' *(sic)* when he met Yoko
Ono and now obstinately refused to be manipulated. If the track was
too slow, he replied, they'd simply have to do it again, faster; one way
or another, it was going out as a single.

The first serious crack in The Beatles' corporate façade, REVOLU-
TION 1 is one of the major period-inaugurating songs in Lennon's
development: a successor to key creations like [56] HELP! and [93]
STRAWBERRY FIELDS FOREVER, and the last such turning-point in his
career as a Beatle.

[126] DON'T PASS ME BY *(Starkey)*

Starr vocal, drums, sleigh bell, piano; **McCartney** piano, bass; **Jack
Fallon** violin

Recorded: 5th June 1968, Abbey Road 3; 6th June 1968, 12th July
1968, Abbey Road 2; 22nd July 1968, Abbey Road 1.

Producer: George Martin. Engineers: Geoff Emerick/Ken Scott.

UK release: 22nd November 1968 (LP: *The Beatles*)

US release: 25th November 1968 (LP: *The Beatles*)

Referred to during the early stages of recording as 'This Is Some
Friendly', Starr's first solo composition for The Beatles is a rudimentary
invention in country-and-western style embellished with bluegrass
violin (plus some disorganised busking at the end, retained, in the
prevailing spirit of 'random', despite the player's embarrassed protests).
That his lyric is a personal plea seems confirmed by the fact that Starr
had been toying with a song of this title for five years.[1]

---

[1] *Anthology 3* begins with an orchestral prelude written by George Martin for
DON'T PASS ME BY – a brief piece in the style of Ravel recorded at the 22nd July
Studio 1 session for [130] GOOD NIGHT, but later rejected. The composer explains:

[127] REVOLUTION 9 *(Lennon–McCartney)*

Sound collage

Recorded: 6th June 1968, Abbey Road 2; 10th June 1968, Abbey
Road 3; 11th June 1968, Abbey Road 2; 20th–21st June 1968,
Abbey Road Studios 1-3.

Producer: George Martin. Engineer: Geoff Emerick.

UK release: 22nd November 1968 (LP: *The Beatles*)

US release: 25th November 1968 (LP: *The Beatles*)

q0115

By far The Beatles' most extreme venture into 'random', this eight-minute exercise in aural free association is the world's most widely distributed avant-garde artefact. Around a million households owned copies of it within days of its release and, a quarter of a century later, its hearers number in the hundreds of millions. One of the most striking instances of the communicative power of pop, REVOLUTION 9 achieved a global exposure never imagined by the artists who pioneered its techniques. While the cut-up texts of Burroughs, the collages of Hamilton, and the *musique concrète* experiments of Cage and Stockhausen ([U96], note) have remained the preserve of the modernist intelligentsia, Lennon's sortie into sonic chance was packaged for a mainstream audience which had never heard of its progenitors, let alone been confronted by their work.

The probability that few who bought the album ever bothered to listen to REVOLUTION 9 more than once was, from the perspective of the avant-garde, irrelevant. This type of art was designed to change the way its beholders experienced reality – to disrupt the habit-dictated hierarchy of incoming sense data, rendering its connective and peripheral parts as significant as its central elements. Merely to be exposed to it was (in theory) to disperse the stale, institutionalised consciousness which class-stratified society supposedly exuded like a kind of cognitive smog. Whether such anarchicising effects, hoped for by art groups like Fluxus and the Situationists, really contributed to the changes in custom and morality seen in the West since the Sixties, is hard to say;[1] clearly factors like material and sexual consumerism

---

'It was for John that I did an off-the-wall introduction, because we hadn't a clue what to do with Ringo's song. In the event, the intro was too bizarre for us to use, and the score was scrapped.' (Personal communication.) Other classical allusions – Mozart, Bach, Webern – occur in Martin's *Yellow Submarine* score.

[1] Fluxus (meaning 'flow' or 'change') was an international Sixties movement dedicated to disrupting the routines of bourgeois life with live events ('actions' or 'happenings') often held in the streets. As such Fluxus was less an aesthetic style than a culturally revolutionary state of mind. Fluxus artists included George Maciunas,

played greater roles in this than anything the most ingenious Deconstructionist ever dreamt up. Yet many consider the violent discontinuity of modern life to be rooted in the revolutionary disruptions of the Sixties, and as such REVOLUTION 9 (the best-known evocation of these events) must be counted, if only socio-culturally, as one of the most significant acts The Beatles ever perpetrated.

Reflecting on REVOLUTION 9 in an interview with Robin Blackburn and Tariq Ali in 1971, Lennon observed: 'I thought I was painting in sound a picture of revolution – but I made a mistake. The mistake was that it was anti-revolution.'[1] Never stable, Lennon's politics in 1971 were passing through a Maoist phase which he later repudiated. His claim that REVOLUTION 9 was conceived as a picture of revolution should be judged against the probability that what he'd actually been doing in 1968 (as distinct from what he thought left-wing ideologues wanted him to say three years later) was far closer to Yoko Ono's conceptual work of the mid-Sixties than to any supposed attempt to create an impression of contemporary unrest in France and Germany.[2] In fact his 1971 rationale of his original motives – that he'd wanted to wake the workers from their dream of material contentment – has more in common with the ideas of Maciunas and Debord than with those of Mao or Lenin. Made only three weeks after Lennon and Ono became lovers and recorded the similarly experimental *Two Virgins* in celebration, REVOLUTION 9 is unlikely to have embodied much, if anything at all, in the way of 'theory'. To the extent that Lennon conceptualised the piece at all, it is likely to have been as a sensory attack on the citadel of the intellect (see [77]): a revolution in the head aimed, as he stressed at the time, at each individual listener – and not a

---

Joseph Beuys, George Brecht, La Monte Young, Nam June Paik, and Yoko Ono. A socially-engaged offspring of the Surrealist movement, the Situationist International (1957–72) dealt in conceptual art designed to break the hypnosis of the mass-media 'spectacle' which it saw as a capitalist conspiracy to lull the workers into apathy. Situationist slogans appeared on the walls of Paris during the May '68 uprising and later inspired the punk 'anarchy' movement in the UK (1976–7). Leading Situationists included Guy Debord, André Bertrand, Asger Jorn, Giuseppe Pinot Gallizio, and the Spur Group.

[1] *Red Mole*, 8th–22nd March 1971.

[2] Like Communist statesmen, Lennon was given to regularly revising his past. By 1970, he had allowed himself to be persuaded that the megalomaniac mass-murderer Mao Tse-tung was 'doing a good job' (*sic*). Interviewed in April 1972, he accordingly expressed regret about the slighting reference to Mao in [125/132] REVOLUTION, claiming that he had added it at the last minute in the studio – whereas, in fact, he had written the song in tranquillity in India and considered its lyric with unusual care.

Maoist incitement to social confrontation, still less a call for general anarchy. (Lennon and Ono disliked the negativity of late Sixties radicalism, taking a particularly dim view of the Chicago riots of August 1968. Instead of asking what we are against, they reasoned, we should be working out what we are *for*.)

Working as ever intuitively, Lennon was, in effect, externalising the unconscious elements of his creativity in their raw state. Here, in the random interaction of scores of tape fragments – some looped, others spun backwards – is a representation of the half-sceptical, half-awake, channel-hopping state of mind he liked to relax in (and which, twenty-five years on, has become characteristic of a generation). On one level, REVOLUTION 9 is another Lennonian evocation of the domain between sleeping and waking, its wavelength-wandering radio-babble resembling the sound an infant might have apprehended in a suburban garden during a typical post-war summer.[1] On another, it is a sarcastic homage to cliché so impartially targeted that even its fade – on the sound of chanting crowds – becomes ambiguous, if not actively ironic. The common factor is consciousness itself; indeed, if REVOLUTION 9 can be said to be about any one thing it would be the abiding concern of the Sixties counterculture: quality of awareness. 'Do not adjust your brain, there is a fault in reality', ran a hippie slogan of the time. REVOLUTION 9 restates that slogan in sound.

Intentions apart, the actual experience of listening to this track, where not merely boring or baffling, often inclines to the sinister, an effect ascribable to the twin driving forces behind it: chance determination and drugs. Sold as everything from a creative aid to a psychotherapeutic panacea, LSD was the dominant influence on late Sixties pop. That it was individually harmful is well-established, particularly among the period's best songwriters, whose minds all too readily ran riot (and in some cases collapsed) under its influence. Artists, though, have always been given to playing games with their imaginations. More remarkable is that taking LSD, an act equivalent to gambling with sanity itself, became for many young people at this time a part of everyday behaviour. Nothing about such a drug (least of all its strength) is predictable: one may experience beatific visions, pleasantly dotty distortions of normal perception, paranoia, hellish hallucinations, even mental annihilation. To surrender to such a range of possibilities is

---

[1] It is in this perspective that McCartney's 'Can you take me back?' introduction is so apt. Rather than anticipating political revolution, the track depicts the *psychologically* revolutionary forces lurking in the depths of memory, waiting to be found, activated, and (with luck) integrated.

to cast one's identity to the wind, an astonishing measure of the counterculture's revolt against what it saw as the obsolete certainties of previous generations. There is, furthermore, an analogy between the generational surrender to chance implicit in the mass use of LSD and the creative randomness embraced by The Beatles in their music of the period. To place a priority on one or the other would be invidious, since to some extent they merely coincided. This would not, however, overestimate The Beatles' influence on young people at the time. More seriously, it would place some responsibility upon the group for the harmful consequences of fostering such a randomised sensibility. They had, after all, for several years been playing with exactly the sort of half-intended hidden messages which Charles Manson later read into songs like [134] HELTER SKELTER and [147] PIGGIES. Indeed, REVOLUTION 9 itself became for the Manson family a prophesy of the impending apocalypse and an artistic justification for their murders. (Careless of the consequences of what he and the group were doing, Lennon went on to acknowledge this penchant for mischief – and express his disdain for those who fell for it – in the complacently sarcastic [144] GLASS ONION, recorded two months later.)

On *The Beatles*, REVOLUTION 9 segues from Lennon's eerie [133] CRY BABY CRY via an apposite, if fortuitous, fragment of between-takes ad-libbing by McCartney [145]. Following a whimsical control-room exchange between Apple office manager Alistair Taylor and George Martin, the track proper starts with the looped announcement 'number nine', taken from examination tapes for the Royal Academy of Music once stored at Abbey Road. As analysed by Mark Lewisohn from the original four-track tape, the main elements of what ensues include a backwards Mellotron, part of the orchestral overdub for [96] A DAY IN THE LIFE, and 'miscellaneous symphonies and operas'. (One of the latter is a loop of the final chord of Sibelius's Seventh Symphony which recurs several times between 2:13 and 5:53.) Lennon took two days to prepare REVOLUTION 9, working with Ono to assemble effects and loops before taking over Abbey Road on 20th June for the final session. As with [77] TOMORROW NEVER KNOWS, this consisted of spinning in sounds from numerous auxiliary recorders onto the main deck in Studio 1. The basic element was the amputated final six minutes of the original [125] REVOLUTION 1, from which are discernible various cries of 'Alright!' and some talking by Ono (including the famous closing statement 'You become naked'). Since each pass took eight minutes, the Abbey Road echo tape-delay ran out during one take and had to be rewound live (3:25–3:37).

McCartney was in New York during this session, leaving Lennon and Harrison to add a track of random interjections ('the Watusi . . . the Twist . . . Eldorado', etc.) which was subsequently faded in and out with the other sources. Though underwhelmed by the results when he returned five days later, he was not, as has usually been supposed, expressing a middlebrow conservatism. On the contrary, he admired Stockhausen's early electronic composition *Gesang der Jünglinge* and had led The Beatles through a similar chance-determined piece eighteen months earlier (see [U96]). Probably what he disliked about the track was not so much its presumption in representing itself as a Lennon–McCartney composition as its cynical darkness of tone. While Lennon needed lessons in cynicism from no one, it is possible that he was influenced in this instance by Stockhausen's huge 1967 collage *Hymnen*, a mordant satire on nationalism which inhabits a similar sound-world. Yet his main artistic guide in 1968, apart from Yoko Ono, was his own imagination – and it is this reliance on creative instinct which makes REVOLUTION 9 in retrospect superior to its more organised and articulate 'serious' equivalents. One need only compare Lennon's work with Luigi Nono's similar *Non consumiamo Marx* (1969)[1] to see how much more aesthetically and politically acute Lennon was than most of the vaunted avant-garde composers of the time. Invoking the word *'l'imagination'* without actually showing any (as if merely referring to it sufficed), Nono's piece entirely lacks the pop-bred sense of texture and proportion manifested in REVOLUTION 9. Like that of his colleagues in late Sixties 'revolutionary' music, Nono's art is an expression of the detached analytic mind – of 'the head'. As such, it is itself as much a target of Revolution 9 as the media and vernacular clichés Lennon's track sarcastically subverts.

[128] BLACKBIRD *(Lennon–McCartney)*

McCartney vocal, acoustic guitar
Recorded: 11th June 1968, Abbey Road 2.
Producer: George Martin. Engineer: Geoff Emerick.
UK release: 22nd November 1968 (LP: *The Beatles*)
US release: 25th November 1968 (LP: *The Beatles*)

In stressing the blues and country roots of modern pop, rock-based critics tend to underestimate the heritage of Tin Pan Alley and, in the UK, of folk music. Important to the technique of much British pop in

---

[1] A collage made up of slogans recorded on the streets of Paris during the May '68 uprising. The title ('We don't consume Marx') reflects ideas then current in Situationism.

the Sixties and early Seventies were the finger-picking styles defined by folk-club guitarists like Davey Graham, Archie Fisher, John Renbourn, and – in particular – Bert Jansch. (This tradition was effectively erased in the UK by the New Wave 'thrash' style of 1976–8 and consequently of almost no influence on the wall-of-sound Indie bands of the Eighties.) Beyond the reach of electricity in the Maharishi's retreat at Rishikesh during the spring of 1968, The Beatles could use only their Martin D-28 acoustic guitars, which meant either strumming or brushing up on the arpeggio patterns used by folk guitarists to sustain their chords. The results of this forced technical restriction can be heard in [138] MOTHER NATURE'S SON, [143] DEAR PRUDENCE, [148] HAPPINESS IS A WARM GUN, and [156] JULIA.

From the songwriter's point of view, one of the secrets of the arpeggiated guitar style is that it exploits the instrument's scope for retuning, creating unexpected chords and scales, and even generating melodies. The best example of this on *The Beatles* is provided by the present song which, as folk guitarist Richard Digance has pointed out,[1] owes its distinctiveness (and probably its existence) to a tuning in which the E-strings are dropped to D and the chords carried mostly on the second and fourth strings.[2] Recorded by its composer McCartney in Studio 2 (with Lennon next door in Studio 3 working on [127] REVOLUTION 9), this haunting thing was taped and mixed, including a warbling blackbird from the Abbey Road effects library, in six hours.[3]

---

[1] Leigh, p. 67.

[2] McCartney recalls the inspiration for the song as 'a well-known piece by Bach' (Miles, op. cit., p. 485).

[3] For McCartney, BLACKBIRD was a metaphor for the civil rights struggle in America, the subject being a black woman (Miles, op. cit., pp. 485-6); Charles Manson made precisely this interpretation (Bugliosi and Gentry, pp. 241–2). McCartney sat on a windowsill and played BLACKBIRD to the girl fans camped outside his house the first night his future wife Linda Eastman came over and stayed. (An early, casual take on *Anthology 3* shows McCartney loosening up on the song.)

[129] EVERYBODY'S GOT SOMETHING TO HIDE EXCEPT ME AND MY MONKEY *(Lennon–McCartney)*

Lennon vocal, guitar, percussion, handclaps; **Harrison** backing
vocal, lead guitar, percussion, handclaps; **McCartney** backing
vocal, bass, percussion, handclaps; **Starr** drums, percussion,
handclaps

Recorded: 26th–27th June; 1st, 23rd July 1968, Abbey Road 2.
Producer: George Martin. Engineer: Geoff Emerick/Ken Scott.
UK release: 22nd November 1968 (LP: *The Beatles*)
US release: 25th November 1968 (LP: *The Beatles*)

After a week of mixing, The Beatles returned to recording with this
simple rocker – another number built, if circuitously, from blues
changes. (Musically, it marks a further stage in the post-psychedelic re-
emergence of Lennon the rock-and-roller, signaled in [124] HEY
BULLDOG.)

As with [125] REVOLUTION 1, the group rehearsed the song
through multiple takes until, after two days, they arrived at what they
wanted. Much of the excitement derives from the frantic rattling of a
handbell in the left channel against two guitars in the right, one
generating a continuous *obbligato*, the other (mixed brightly to make it
cut through) playing the Spanish-tinged basic riff. An extra kick was
added later by slightly speeding up the tape. Having left the result to
stand for three weeks, Lennon redid his tracked vocals during a final
session in which the others joined him to gabble the 'C'mon's at the
top of the fade-out. From start to final mix, the record took thirty-two
hours.

EVERYBODY'S GOT SOMETHING TO HIDE is an exuberant 'tails' to
the ruminative 'heads' of REVOLUTION 1, taking the latter's subversion
and giving it an upbeat twist. Though nothing is explicit and the words
are genially close to gibberish, the seditious intent is clear and a *double-
entendre* on 'come' more than likely.[1]

---

[1] According to Harrison, the song's title was adapted from a saying of the
Maharishi ('apart from that bit about the monkey'). McCartney believes 'monkey'
was a reference to Lennon's heroin habit (Miles, op. cit., pp. 486-7.)

[130] GOOD NIGHT *(Lennon–McCartney)*

Starr vocal; **George Martin** celesta; **The Mike Sammes Singers**
backing vocals; **Uncredited** 12 violins, 3 violas, 3 cellos, double-
bass, 3 flutes, clarinet, horn, vibraphone, harp
Recorded: 28th June/2nd July 1968, Abbey Road 2; 22nd July
1968, Abbey Road 1.
Producer: George Martin. Engineers: Geoff Emerick/Peter Bown/
Ken Scott.
UK release: 22nd November 1968 (LP: *The Beatles*)
US release: 25th November 1968 (LP: *The Beatles*)

Placed at the end of *The Beatles* after REVOLUTION 9, this 'very slow and
dreamy' Lennon ballad – an inadvertent variation on Cole Porter's
'True Love', one of the group's old Hamburg standards – could hardly
help seeming almost nastily ironic. In fact, it was conceived as a lullaby
for Lennon's five-year-old son Julian and, though partly tongue in
cheek, its sentimentality was genuine. George Martin's adroitly treacly
arrangement (Lennon: 'possibly over lush') makes the most of this,
complete with knowing winks at Hollywood. So uncharacteristic of
Lennon is this track that many initially assumed both song and vocal to
be by McCartney.

[131] OB-LA-DI, OB-LA-DA *(Lennon–McCartney)*

McCartney vocal, bass, drums (?), handclaps, 'vocal percussion';
  Lennon backing vocals, piano, handclaps, 'vocal percussion';
  Harrison backing vocals, acoustic guitar, handclaps, 'vocal
  percussion'; **Starr** drums (?), bongos, percussion, handclaps, 'vocal
  percussion'; **Uncredited** 3 saxes
Recorded: 3rd–5th, 8th July 1968, Abbey Road 2; 9th, 11th July
1968, Abbey Road 3; 15th July 1968, Abbey Road 2.
Producer: George Martin. Engineer: Geoff Emerick.
UK release: 22nd November 1968 (LP: *The Beatles*)
US release: 25th November 1968 (LP: *The Beatles*)

One of the most spontaneous-sounding tracks on *The Beatles*, McCartney's rather approximate tribute to the Jamaican ska idiom took a
laborious forty-two hours to complete, its composer's perfectionism
provoking some ominously fraught scenes *en route*. An initial version
(with heavy acoustic guitars and including some session overdubs) had
been in progress for three days when McCartney decided it wasn't
happening and scrapped it. On the fourth day, a stoned and frustrated

Lennon injected some energy by pounding out a mock music-hall piano introduction at faster tempo. Despite an attempt by McCartney to begin yet another remake, this take became the final version.[1]

With its desperate levity, cheerfully silly lyric,[2] and punchy sound (created by liberal use of compression and a heavily overloaded acoustic guitar doubling the bass line), OB-LA-DI, OB-LA-DA was the most commercial track on the album, if trite by McCartney's standards. Fed up with it, the others vetoed it as a single and Marmalade cashed in, taking it to No. 1.

[132] REVOLUTION *(Lennon–McCartney)*

Lennon double-tracked vocal, lead guitar, handclaps; **McCartney** bass, Hammond organ, handclaps; **Harrison** lead guitar, handclaps; **Starr** drums, handclaps; **Nicky Hopkins** electric piano

Recorded: 9th–11th July 1968, Abbey Road 3; 12th July 1968, Abbey Road 2.

Producer: George Martin. Engineer: Geoff Emerick.

UK release: 30th August 1968 (B single/HEY JUDE)

US release: 26th August 1968 (B single/HEY JUDE)

Lennon's dry response to the growing calls for revolution among the once-pacifist counterculture hit the shops in America days before Mayor Richard Daley's Chicago police rioted at the city's Democratic Convention, attacking Vietnam protesters and beating delegates on the sidewalk in full view of TV cameras. Lennon's unambiguous revision of his first thoughts ('Count me out') could not have arrived at a more polarised moment and the reaction, from New Left radicals to the least political of rock critics, was vengeful [125]. REVOLUTION became a subject of heated media debate and McCartney's worst fears of political

---

[1] McCartney recalls the session which Lennon kickstarted as accomplished 'in a very good mood' and the two of them having 'a whale of a time' over recording the track (Miles, op. cit., p. 492). In *The Beatles in Rishikesh* (pp. 78-87), Paul Saltzman records McCartney and Lennon playing the chorus over and over again at the Maharishi's ashram, the song at that stage lacking a verse.

[2] Desmond doing 'his pretty face' was a singing mistake (it should have been Molly again) which McCartney left in 'to create a bit of confusion'. The title was borrowed from Jimmy Scott, a Nigerian friend in London, who, not unreasonably, demanded a cut when he heard the song. Scott played bongos on the rejected first version of OB-LA-DI, OB-LA-DA *(Anthology 3)*, which shows that the song, written in A major, was varispeeded up a tone during the master-mix.

controversy were fulfilled. Up against a hip consensus, Lennon stuck to his guns for a year and a half ('Don't expect me to be on the barricades unless it's with flowers') before finally capitulating in New York by donning a Mao badge and regulation black beret and leather gloves. Tiananmen Square, the ignominious collapse of Soviet communism, and the fact that most of his radical persecutors of 1968–70 now work in advertising have belatedly served to confirm his original instincts.

The most distorted production ever applied to a Beatles song sees Starr's drums scrunched into a thunderously compressed ball on one channel with a pair of fuzz-toned guitars, overloaded by direct injection, wrangling on the other. Between them, McCartney's limiter-muffled bass shambles behind Lennon's jeering vocal, the latter tracking himself with a rough and careless spontaneity that becomes a point in itself.[1] Raw directness, forecasting the minimalism of his first solo album, here displaces the elaborate artifice of [116] I Am The Walrus. While the substance of the two tracks – only ten months apart – is closer than superficially appears, the distance between them in terms of style and sound remains the broadest encompassed by any pop artist.[2]

Originally a troubled message about something vital, by 1987, as the soundtrack to a Nike ad, Revolution had turned into a song about training shoes. Enough said.

[133] CRY BABY CRY (Lennon–McCartney)

Lennon vocal, acoustic guitar, piano, organ; **McCartney** bass;
  Harrison lead guitar; **Starr** drums, tambourine; **George Martin**
  harmonium
Recorded: 15th, 16th, 18th July 1968, Abbey Road 2.
Producer: George Martin. Engineers: Geoff Emerick/Ken Scott.
UK release: 22nd November 1968 (LP: *The Beatles*)
US release: 25th November 1968 (LP: *The Beatles*)

Written in India, Lennon's CRY BABY CRY revolves around a verse which, like [143] DEAR PRUDENCE, makes a descending sequence out of one chord (E minor). Lennon later dismissed it as 'a piece of rubbish',

---

[1] Pitched a semitone higher than [125], the track was presumably varispeeded rather than actually played in B flat major.
[2] Dylan's journey from the folk-blues idiom of his first album to the sophistication of 'Like A Rolling Stone' represents a larger stride than Lennon's in terms of complexity of thought. Musically, however, his range is markedly narrower, while the possibilities of production and arrangement interest him hardly at all.

but his retrospective views were often coloured by the puritanism of the reformed sinner and CRY BABY CRY remains a haunting and haunted creation.[1] Supposedly based on a TV commercial, the lyric began as 'Cry baby cry, make your mother buy' before developing into something resembling the nursery rhyme 'Sing a song of sixpence'. The rhyme's reference to blackbirds suggest that Lennon heard McCartney singing [128] BLACKBIRD in Rishikesh and free-associated his own ironic and sinister train of thought. Whatever the truth, CRY BABY CRY exudes a memorably creepy atmosphere created partly by verbal ambiguity and partly by an ominously recurring blues B flat which belongs in neither the chorus's G major nor its related minor. Of all The Beatles, Lennon had the most direct access to childhood, and this song, with its deceptive sunshine and mysterious laughter behind half-open doors, is one of the most evocative products of that creative channel.

[134] HELTER SKELTER *(Lennon–McCartney)*

McCartney vocal, lead guitar, bass; Lennon backing vocals, lead guitar, bass, tenor sax; Harrison backing vocals, rhythm guitar; Starr drums; Mal Evans trumpet
Recorded: 18th July, 9th–10th September 1968, Abbey Road 2.
Producer: George Martin. Engineer: Ken Scott.
UK release: 22nd November 1968 (LP: *The Beatles*)
US release: 25th November 1968 (LP: *The Beatles*)

The 'heavy metal' idiom of the Seventies originated in the mid-Sixties switch from the low-volume standard pop four-piece to the vastly amplified rock 'power trio', a format change in which the redundant rhythm guitarist was replaced by turning up the bass, close-miking the drums, and adding a range of signal-distortion effects to the lead guitar. Led by groups like The Who, Cream, and The Jimi Hendrix Experience, this move was, to some extent, an inevitable consequence of bigger and better amps and speakers designed for larger and more remunerative venues.[2] Yet the loss of the craft of the rhythm guitarist

---

[1] The atmosphere in the studio during the recording (immediately after the tense sessions for [131] OB-LA-DI, OB-LA-DA), was so stormy that engineer Geoff Emerick, George Martin's right-hand man since [77] TOMORROW NEVER KNOWS, couldn't stand it and left.

[2] To wit, the Marshall 100-watt stack. Amplification is a science in itself. In order to make themselves heard through the barrage of screaming girls during Beatlemania, The Beatles had to double the power of their Vox amps every year after 1962. By 1966, each was using 150-watt amps through 4x12" horn cabinets. After Fender

was soon felt in a degradation of texture and a decline in overall musical subtlety. Rhythm guitarists were usually songwriters, and the variety of articulation and accenting techniques they used also shaped their compositions. The average power trio, lacking such a musical brain, was in effect an excuse to replace songs with riffs and discard nuance for noise. When a second guitarist appeared, it was solely to bolster the riff while the lead guitarist was taking his protracted and invariably garish solos. More a sonic contact sport than a musical experience, heavy metal naturally became hugely popular and, in various guises, has ruled mainstream rock since the mid-Seventies.

The Beatles' interest in musical developments around them was keen and usually productive, but their attempts at emulating the heavy style were without exception embarrassing. The quintessential Sixties four-piece, their natural inclinations were for balance, form, and attention to detail, and in straining to transcend these obsolete values in HELTER SKELTER they comically overreached themselves, reproducing the requisite bulldozer design but on a Dinky Toy scale. Provoked by hearing that The Who had gone all out on their latest track to achieve the most overwhelming racket imaginable – it being about this time that an acid-inflated Pete Townshend all but ceased to write songs focused enough to produce hits – McCartney came up with this clumsy attempt to outdo them. In one early version, HELTER SKELTER persisted for a grandiose twenty-seven minutes.[1] Condensed for release on 9th September, the result was nonetheless ridiculous, McCartney shrieking weedily against a massively tape-echoed backdrop of out-of-tune thrashing. Critics differ over whether it is Starr or Lennon who at the end complains of having incurred superficial damage to his digits. Few have seen fit to describe this track as anything other than a literally drunken mess.[2]

---

wooed them with two Stratocasters in 1965 (see [55]), they added Showman amps and cabinets to their backline for the *Revolver* sessions. For the 1967 recordings, Lennon and Harrison used Selmer amps, while McCartney put his Rickenbacker through the 100-watt Fender Bassman he subsequently stuck with. The others finally abandoned Vox in 1968, changing to Fender Twin Reverbs.

[1] An edit of the 12-minute take 2 from 18th July on *Anthology 3* shows that the song was then being treated as a brutal monochordal blues vamp – surprisingly close to the raw minimalism Lennon began to move towards in [139] YER BLUES and later used as the basis for *John Lennon/Plastic Ono Band*.

[2] Apparently unaware that a helter skelter is a spiral slide in English funfairs, Charles Manson assumed the track had something to do with hell, taking it as a code for the apocalyptic race-war which his 'family' attempted to inaugurate with the grisly Tate–La Bianca murders in August 1969. (Bugliosi and Gentry, pp. 239–48.)

[135] SEXY SADIE *(Lennon–McCartney)*

Lennon double-tracked vocal, backing vocal, acoustic guitar,
electric rhythm guitar, Hammond organ; **McCartney** backing
vocal, bass, piano; **Harrison** backing vocal, lead guitar; **Starr**
drums, tambourine
Recorded: 19th, 24th July; 13th, 21st August 1968, Abbey Road 2.
Producer: George Martin. Engineer: Ken Scott.
UK release: 22nd November 1968 (LP: *The Beatles*)
US release: 25th November 1968 (LP: *The Beatles*)

Written in an acidulous mood during the final hours of his stay in
Rishikesh, Lennon's SEXY SADIE was originally titled 'Maharishi' and
referred, in explicitly insulting terms, to the altercation which
concluded The Beatles' stay there.[1] Rewritten to avoid a court case, it
was recorded in a haphazard manner involving fifty-two takes, two re-
makes,[2] around thirty-five hours of studio time, and a great deal of
clowning about. As usual with Lennon, meaning and musical expression are integrally linked, from the dry chiding of the song's opening
phrase to its endlessly manoeuvring chord sequence, shifting as
evasively as its heroine slips between compromising situations. (The
five-bar middle section uses the same chords as McCartney's [91] HERE
THERE AND EVERYWHERE.) With a duplicitous echo on the piano,
hypnotic phasing on the backing vocals, and an insidious guitar *obbligato*
from Harrison, Sexy Sadie is all of an unprepossessing piece.

---

[1] See Lewisohn, *Sessions*, p. 144. The scandal allegedly involved special tuition
given by the guru to a female member of The Beatles' entourage. Harrison suggested
the title SEXY SADIE (*The Beatles Anthology*, p. 286).
[2] One of these early versions, considerably more relaxed and consequently far less
caustically menacing (not to say boring), is available on *Anthology 3*.

[136] WHILE MY GUITAR GENTLY WEEPS *(Harrison)*

Harrison double-tracked vocal, backing vocal, acoustic guitar,
  Hammond organ; **McCartney** backing vocal, piano, organ, 6-
  string bass; **Lennon** lead guitar; **Starr** drums, tambourine; **Eric
  Clapton** lead guitar
Recorded: 25th July; 16th August; 3rd, 5th–6th September 1968,
  Abbey Road 2.
Producer: George Martin. Engineer: Ken Scott.
UK release: 22nd November 1968 (LP: *The Beatles*)
US release: 25th November 1968 (LP: *The Beatles*)

In its final version, WHILE MY GUITAR GENTLY WEEPS is another
venture in the heavy idiom (see [134]); yet, like the majority of the
songs on *The Beatles*, it was largely written in India on acoustic guitar
and, when first recorded at Abbey Road on 25th July, was played this
way with no other accompaniment.[1] Speaking of the Rishikesh
interlude, Donovan has recalled how he taught Lennon a finger-
picking style which the latter used in [143] DEAR PRUDENCE and [156]
JULIA – a technique borrowed from the Edinburgh folk guitarists with
whom Donovan learned his craft (see [128]). While there is no trace of
a finger-picking style in the recorded versions of WHILE MY GUITAR
GENTLY WEEPS, there may well have been to begin with, since
Harrison is bound to have noticed Lennon learning a new style. (If
Donovan showed him the technique used in his friend Davey Graham's
famous folk instrumental 'Anji', Harrison may have evolved WHILE MY
GUITAR GENTLY WEEPS from it. Both are in A minor and both feature
stepped descending bass lines – though Harrison's is chromatic,
changing the sequence, and the 'Anji' picking technique is not
reproduced.[2])

Unhappy with his first attempt at recording the song – because, he
felt, the other Beatles weren't taking the song seriously enough[3] –
Harrison took about thirty-seven hours, including two re-makes, to get
what he wanted. During this, The Beatles obtained one of the first
eight-track machines used in Britain and devoted two sessions to a

---

[1] Issued on *Anthology 3*, this version includes an extra verse.
[2] The out-take version is in G minor. Whether it was written as such or lowered
by Harrison to make it easier to sing is unclear. ([73] THINK FOR YOURSELF is in G
minor–major.)
[3] The Beatles Anthology, p. 306.

version they thereupon scrapped.[1] Harrison, who had spent eight hours vainly striving to get a 'weeping' effect from a backwards guitar track, found no solution till the fifth day of work on the song when, driving into London with his old friend Eric Clapton,[2] he invited him to play the guitar solo. Clapton was then with Cream, the heaviest blues-rock group in the UK, yet his style suited the final version of WHILE MY GUITAR GENTLY WEEPS, which by then had become ponderously weighty. Using his cherry red Gibson Les Paul for its plangent sustained tone, Clapton had it 'wobbled' with ADT to make the sound less bluesy.[3]

The characteristically accusatory lyric, written after returning from India, originated in one of the many random impulses The Beatles resorted to around this time, Harrison finding the phrase 'gently weeps' by chance in a book.[4] While meaningful, the quadruple internal rhymes of his middle sixteens are pedantically contrived and, as a whole, the track exudes a browbeating self-importance which quickly becomes tiresome. Later popular at concerts, WHILE MY GUITAR GENTLY WEEPS enshrines, in its plodding sequence, rock's typical rhythmic overstatement and slow rate of harmonic change. The energetic topicality of pop is here supplanted by a dull grandiosity predictive of the simplified stadium music of the Seventies and Eighties.

---

[1] The Beach Boys' *Pet Sounds* was recorded on an eight-track, while Motown had been using eight-track since 1964. The first commercially successful eight-track recordings were made in 1958 by The Coasters ('Charlie Brown', 'Yakety Yak'), engineered by Tom Dowd at Atlantic Studios in New York.

[2] They met in 1964 when Clapton, then with The Yardbirds, shared some bills with The Beatles.

[3] After the session, Clapton gave Harrison this guitar (called Lucy in homage to Albert Collins' Telecaster of the same name). The latter subsequently used it on [135] SEXY SADIE, [133] CRY BABY CRY, [170] SOMETHING, and much of *Abbey Road* (including his Claptonesque breaks on [180] THE END).

[4] He chose the phrase thus in accordance with his understanding of Indian teaching that there is no such thing as coincidence, that meaning inheres in every moment (*The Beatles Anthology*, p. 306).

[137] HEY JUDE *(Lennon–McCartney)*

McCartney vocal, piano, bass; **Lennon** backing vocal, acoustic
guitar; **Harrison** backing vocal, lead guitar; **Starr** backing vocal,
drums, tambourine; **Uncredited** 10 violins, 3 violas, 3 cellos, 2
doublebasses, 2 flutes, 2 clarinets, 1 bass clarinet, 1 bassoon, 1
contrabassoon, 4 trumpets, 2 horns, 4 trombones, 1 percussion;
All backing vocals, handclaps
Recorded: 29th–30th July, 1968, Abbey Road 2; 31st July, 1st
August 1968, Trident Studios.
Producer: George Martin. Engineers: Ken Scott/Barry Sheffield.
UK release: 30th August 1968 (A single/REVOLUTION)
US release: 26th August 1968 (A single/REVOLUTION)

McCartney's HEY JUDE was scheduled as a Beatles single from the
moment it was written. Composed while its author was driving to visit
Cynthia Lennon in June 1968, the song was originally sung as if to
John's five-year-old son Julian ('Hey Jules') before McCartney changed
it to 'something a bit more country and western'. Demoing it on piano,
he took the tape to Lennon, apologising for the lyric as the first words
that had come into his head. His partner would have none of this,
dismissing McCartney's embarrassment over the line 'the movement
you need is on your shoulder' and declaring HEY JUDE all but finished
as it stood. (He later described the song as the best his partner ever
wrote.)

After some more work on it on 26th July (probably the harmony
on the final verse and the coda melody), the group spent two days
trying it out in Abbey Road before deciding they needed an orchestra.
So as not to have to repeat the laborious mix-downs entailed by the
orchestral recording for [96] A DAY IN THE LIFE, they moved to Soho's
Trident Studios, an eight-track which Apple had been using to record
acts like Jackie Lomax, Mary Hopkin, and James Taylor.[1] Here, on
Thursday 1st August, they packed thirty-six highly-trained classical
musicians into a small room to play four chords over and over again,
closing the evening by requesting them to clap and sing along.
Persuaded by a double fee, all but one complied.

The monumentality of the orchestral contribution to HEY JUDE – so

---

[1] Abbey Road had recently acquired its own eight-track which, unknown to The
Beatles, was then being tested and adapted elsewhere in the building. The group
subsequently discovered and hijacked it on the 3rd September session for [136]
WHILE MY GUITAR GENTLY WEEPS.

simple, so surprising – was typical of The Beatles. Their instinct for what worked was rarely sharper, the huge chords suggesting both Jude's personal revelation and, along with the accompanying chorale, a vast communality in which artists and audience joined in swaying to a single rhythm all around the world – an effect which the more casual and ironic [114] ALL YOU NEED IS LOVE had not quite managed to conjure. The first of many such anthem-like singalongs to arise in response to rock's compulsive self-mythologisation, HEY JUDE is a pop/rock hybrid drawing on the best of both idioms. Partly because conceived without an instrument to hand, partly because driven more by feeling than form, its verse/chorus lacks its composer's usual elegant construction, cadencing so often on the tonic that the plain seventh leading to the middle eight seems like the sun coming out. So expressive is the melody, however, that reservations are academic.

The work put in at rehearsal shows in the subtlety of the group's arrangement during the song proper with bass and piano working off drums and tambourine to give the foursquare rhythm a characteristic rolling swing.[1] Faced with a sententious lyric demanding 'interpretation' (and a lot of space in which to do it), McCartney gives a tasteful performance at the bottom of his range, making spare use of gospel-style melismas. His ill-advised pseudo-soul shrieking in the fade-out may be a blemish (as is the curse over a fluffed backing vocal at 2:58), but otherwise HEY JUDE, for all its inordinate length,[2] is a self-evident success. The group's biggest-selling American hit, it held the US No. 1 position for an astonishing nine weeks.

Disputes over who the song was about (the press assumed it was aimed at Dylan) even affected the group. On hearing it, Lennon exclaimed 'It's me!', to which a surprised McCartney countered 'No – it's me!'[3] In fact, HEY JUDE strikes a universal note, touching on an

---

[1] This is absent from the sketch made on 29th July and released on *Anthology 3*, where Starr plays a straight, unsyncopated two-crotchet bass-drum part. (This take is useful for illustrating the damping technique he and Geoff Emerick had by then developed for his drum kit – particularly the tom-toms.)

[2] American composer Jimmy Webb, who visited The Beatles at Abbey Road around this time, thinks HEY JUDE was edited to last one second more than his unprecedentedly long, suite-like song for Richard Harris, 'MacArthur Park', a big hit in Britain a few weeks before HEY JUDE was recorded.

[3] Both were then moving between long-term relationships. Lennon was living with Ono at Starr's flat in Montagu Square, waiting to start divorce proceedings with his wife Cynthia. McCartney, whose engagement to Jane Asher had been broken off by her soon after he returned from India, was living at his house in Cavendish

archetypal moment in male sexual psychology with a gentle wisdom one might properly call inspired.

[U138] NOT GUILTY *(Harrison)*

Harrison vocal, guitars, harpsichord (?); **McCartney** bass, drums (?); **Lennon** harpsichord (?); **Starr** drums
Recorded: 7th–9th, 12th August 1968, Abbey Road 2.
Producer: George Martin. Engineer: Ken Scott.
UK release: 28th October 1996 (2-CD: *Anthology 3*)
US release: 28th October 1996 (2-CD: *Anthology 3*)

A tortuous song about conscience and anger, NOT GUILTY was, metrically and harmonically, sufficiently intricate that the first 18 takes had to be devoted solely to rehearsing its introduction. Of the next 27 takes, only five managed to negotiate Harrison's melancholy maze of half-bars, clashing tonalities, and switched time-signatures. On the second day, the group battled through a further fifty takes, replacing the original electric piano with the rhythmically clearer sound of a harpsichord.[1] By take 99 (!), Harrison was ready to settle for what he'd got – yet in truth it still wasn't there and would never be used.

In terms of the arrangement, the solution was obvious and it is amazing that old hands like The Beatles and their production team failed to spot it. As was the case with several other Harrison numbers (e.g., [73] THINK FOR YOURSELF), NOT GUILTY featured a set of changes too tartly elusive to survive a staccato attack; instead, they needed some sustained support to guide the listener's ears – a 'pad', as it is called in the studio world. In his slower remake for the *George Harrison* album eleven years later, the composer solved his quandary by precisely this method, extravagantly hiring no less a light than Steve Winwood to play a simple pad on harmonium in the bridge-chorus sequence. Yet even the 1979 solution would have been insufficient to rescue the original version of NOT GUILTY, which was additionally hamstrung by the gratuitous entanglement of six bars of 3/8 after the solo and Harrison's generally uncertain lead lines. Very far from a total loss (and certainly preferable to the dreadful [147] PIGGIES), this difficult track would nonetheless have required a basic rethink in order to qualify for a place on *The Beatles*.

Avenue, St John's Wood, with his future wife Linda Eastman.
[1] This was presumably the instrument later used on [147] PIGGIES, which must mean that at least one of these sessions took place in Studio 1.

What chiefly stymied Harrison in 1968 was an awful atmosphere in which The Beatles had temporarily given up helping each other and taken to snapping at the studio staff [138].[1] There again, NOT GUILTY is, in its dejected way, as irritated as PIGGIES, and its composer would probably have resented much interference with it.[2] Whether or not because obliged to do so, he seems to have taken it solely upon himself to fathom the track out. After thickening the texture with additional guitar, bass, and drums (the last sounding more like McCartney's 'floppy' style than Starr's sturdy playing), he spent a day blasting morosely away at his solo lines, having set up his stack at one side of the studio, miked it from the other, and retreated into the control-room on the end of a long lead in order to save his ears. A week later, deeply cheesed off, he bailed out to clear his head with a few days in Greece.

[138] MOTHER NATURE'S SON (Lennon–McCartney)

McCartney double-tracked vocal, acoustic guitars, drums, timpani;
  Uncredited 2 trumpets, 2 trombones
Recorded: 9th, 20th August 1968, Abbey Road 2.
Producer: George Martin. Engineer: Ken Scott.
UK release: 22nd November 1968 (LP: *The Beatles*)
US release: 25th November 1968 (LP: *The Beatles*)

Written in India under the influence of a lecture by the Maharishi (as was Lennon's [U126] CHILD OF NATURE), MOTHER NATURE'S SON is a plain and simple evocation of rural peace.[3] Unlike the metropolitan pop mainstream, the burgeoning rock idiom (then referred to as progressive or underground music) was, owing to its roots in countercultural values, strongly back-to-nature in spirit. Indeed so conscious were contemporary rock musicians of this symbolic divide

---

[1] During the 1st August date for [137] HEY JUDE, there had been a tense moment when McCartney rejected Harrison's idea for a guitar line. Harrison spent the rest of the session in the control room.
[2] The 1979 remake, which drops the 3/8 section and is noticeably blander, offers extra lines in the second verse ('For being on your street/Getting underneath your feet'). It's unlikely that Harrison wrote these for the occasion and it seems reasonable to assume that he was prevailed upon to drop them during the 1968 sessions. (This might explain his audibly gritted teeth at 'No use handing me a writ/While I'm trying to do my bit'. In fact, the whole song can be said to reflect its author's resentment, not only of the general obligations of *karma*, but of the particular annoyances of being a Beatle.)
[3] McCartney draws a parallel with Eden Ahbez's song 'Nature Boy', as recorded by Nat King Cole (Miles, op. cit., p. 490).

between the two genres that their mandatory retreats for the purpose of 'getting our heads together in the country' became a standing joke among the urban cynics of the UK music press. As such, MOTHER NATURE'S SON should be heard in the context of tracks like The Pink Floyd's 'Scarecrow', Traffic's 'Berkshire Poppies', and The Incredible String Band's 1967–8 output in general (as well as the then-nascent folk-rock and country-rock movements in Britain and America respectively).

Founded on familiar guitarists' games with the D chord, McCartney's melody rises over a hint of a rustic drone, suggesting rootedness and rest. Harmonically similar to [119] THE FOOL ON THE HILL, it has the same remote, cyclical quality – a mood piece with murmuring onomatopoeic words to match. Paradoxically, it was recorded at a time when the underlying tensions within The Beatles were surfacing with a vengeance. Running Apple Corps was testing their limited patience and, just before the last session for [137] HEY JUDE, they had been forced to close the loss-making boutique in Baker Street. With a busy George Martin less in evidence at Abbey Road, they had taken to producing themselves, as a result of which sessions were starting to ramble badly with frequent stories of unpleasantness to the studio staff. McCartney seems to have got bored during umpteen run-throughs for Lennon's [139] YER BLUES and took no part at all in the chaotic proceedings for [U141] WHAT'S THE NEW MARY JANE. Meanwhile, having struggled vainly for two days with [U138] NOT GUILTY, Harrison summarily decamped for Greece, leaving the others to cancel a session at short notice. On 20th August, Lennon and Starr, then working in Studio 3 on [139] YER BLUES, visited Studio 2 where McCartney was finishing MOTHER NATURE'S SON. According to those present, the atmosphere instantly froze. Two days later, during the first session for [142] BACK IN THE USSR, Starr walked out, declaring that he was leaving the group.

While it's tempting to hear the flat seventh in the final brass chord of MOTHER NATURE'S SON as an ironic token of this sour background, it's likelier to have been an accident of George Martin's orchestration. McCartney's spirits were high and he spent much of the session playing about with the position of his drums, eventually recording them halfway down the corridor outside the studio. Before packing up, he taped two extra numbers: [141] WILD HONEY PIE and a song called 'Etcetera' which was never heard of again.

[139] YER BLUES *(Lennon–McCartney)*

Lennon vocal, backing vocal, lead guitar; **McCartney** bass;
Harrison lead guitar; **Starr** drums
Recorded: 13th–14th August 1968, Abbey Road 2; 20th August
1968, Abbey Road 3.
Producer: George Martin. Engineer: Ken Scott.
UK release: 22nd November 1968 (LP: *The Beatles*)
US release: 25th November 1968 (LP: *The Beatles*)

Half-satirical, half-earnest, Lennon's YER BLUES was written in India ('up there trying to reach God and feeling suicidal').[1] A gutbucket 6/4 blues shuffle in E with a ragged additional 2/4 bar interjected for verisimilitude, the song mockingly acknowledges the British 'blues boom' of 1968 in which groups like John Mayall's Bluesbreakers, Fleetwood Mac, and Chicken Shack discovered an audience for dirty realism beyond its traditional haunts on the club scene and at the Reading Festival. (In the pop press, the controversy of the day was 'Can white men sing the blues?', a hotly disputed topic which prompted The Bonzo Dog Doo-Dah Band to offer a radical deconstruction of the debate in 'Can Blue Men Sing the Whites?')

Another foray into what, for The Beatles, was the foreign territory of heavy music (see [134]), YER BLUES was taped, live and extremely loud, in a small room next to Studio 2, with ADT and Leslie-tone ladled liberally onto both lead guitars. Featuring a savage edit at 3:17 and a final verse yelled ineffectually into a dead microphone, the track takes *audio verité* authenticity to consciously absurd lengths, Lennon's two-note shuffle-beat solo vying for laconicism with Keith Richards' outburst on The Rolling Stones' 'It's All Over Now'. That the pain expressed here was nonetheless real is confirmed by the fact that this was the only Beatles track Lennon saw fit to record during his appearance at The Rolling Stones' 'Rock and Roll Circus' on 11th December 1968[2] and with The Plastic Ono Band on *Live Peace in Toronto* in 1969. (The Fifties echo on the third verse anticipates the sound later used on his confessional first solo album.)

---

[1] Yoko Ono, who was sending Lennon postcards from England, is presumably the 'girl' of the refrain.
[2] With Eric Clapton (guitar), Keith Richards (bass), and Mitch Mitchell (drums). (CD: Abkco 1268-2.)

[140] ROCKY RACCOON *(Lennon–McCartney)*

McCartney vocal, acoustic guitar; **Lennon** backing vocal,
   harmonica, harmonium, 6-string bass; **Harrison** backing vocal;
   Starr drums; **George Martin** piano
Recorded: 15th August 1968, Abbey Road 2.
Producer: George Martin. Engineer: Ken Scott.
UK release: 22nd November 1968 (LP: *The Beatles*)
US release: 25th November 1968 (LP: *The Beatles*)

Both leading Beatles were adept at jokey ad-libs in various styles. Here
McCartney spins a Tom Mix/Harry Langdon silent-cinema yarn about
comedy cowboys, a song which, in earlier days, would have remained a
private joke but which, in the anything-goes atmosphere prevailing at
Abbey Road, was given a swift polish and accepted for the forthcoming
album. (According to George Martin, who tried to persuade The
Beatles to halve their new material and issue one strong LP instead of
two weak ones, they were recording such fillers in order to fulfil their
EMI contract faster.) Having begun as a jam with Lennon and
Donovan in Rishikesh, ROCKY RACCOON became a shaggy-dog story
sustained by a lyric which seems to be leading somewhere until its glib
closing lines. Taped in one night, it's a faintly amusing squib adorned
with a barrelhouse piano faked with ADT and varispeed.

[U141] WHAT'S THE NEW MARY JANE *(Lennon–McCartney)*

Lennon vocal, double-tracked piano, effects; **Harrison** vocal,
   double-tracked acoustic guitar; **Yoko Ono** vocal, effects; **Mal
   Evans** (?) handbell
Recorded: 14th August 1968, 26th November 1969, Abbey Road
   2.
Producers: George Martin/Geoff Emerick/John Lennon. Engineers:
   Ken Scott/Mike Sheady.
UK release: 28th October 1996 (2-CD: *Anthology 3*)
US release: 28th October 1996 (2-CD: *Anthology 3*)

Probably written in the informal air of Rishikesh, this sardonic nursery-
rhyme appears to be a fairly specific attack on a would-be recruit to the
Apple entourage. The usual explanation – that 'Mary Jane' is slang for
marijuana – fails to account for most of the lyric, which seems to consist
of in-crowd references to a person known to the participants (someone
female, black, possibly American, and perhaps seeking UK residency via
a convenience marriage). Not that the mystery is very tantalising, for

the song, musically trite, is conspicuously unredeemed by a rambling free-form extension seemingly intended to evoke an unpleasant drug experience. (On the longest of its three initial versions, this prolonged the track to 6:31.) Left off *The Beatles* because it simply didn't fit, WHAT'S THE NEW MARY JANE was revived by Lennon fifteen months later as a projected single coupled with [112] YOU KNOW MY NAME (LOOK UP THE NUMBER), to be issued under the auspices of The Plastic Ono Band. This was quashed (by EMI or the other Beatles) and the track stayed in the Abbey Road vaults, gaining an undeserved reputation as a suppressed anarchic masterpiece.

[141] WILD HONEY PIE *(Lennon–McCartney)*

McCartney vocals, acoustic guitars, drums
Recorded: 20th August 1968, Abbey Road 2.
Producer: George Martin. Engineer: Ken Scott.
UK release: 22nd November 1968 (LP: *The Beatles*)
US release: 25th November 1968 (LP: *The Beatles*)

A throwaway based on a Rishikesh singalong, WILD HONEY PIE was taped at the end of the second session for [138] MOTHER NATURE'S SON and uses the same corridor drum set-up.

[142] BACK IN THE USSR *(Lennon–McCartney)*

McCartney double-tracked vocal, backing vocals, piano, lead
    guitar, bass, drums, handclaps, percussion; **Lennon** backing
    vocals, lead guitar, 6-string bass, drums, handclaps, percussion;
    Harrison backing vocals, lead guitar, bass, drums, handclaps,
    percussion
Recorded: 22nd–23rd August 1968, Abbey Road 2.
Producer: George Martin. Engineer: Ken Scott.
UK release: 22nd November 1968 (LP: *The Beatles*)
US release: 25th November 1968 (LP: *The Beatles*)

Inspired by 1968's pro-British industry campaign ('I'm Backing Britain'), this McCartney rocker was originally called 'I'm Backing the UK' before turning surrealistically into 'I'm Backing the USSR', and thence – via Chuck Berry's 1959 US hit 'Back in the USA' – arriving at its final title. Recorded as Soviet tanks rolled into Czechoslovakia, it was a rather tactless jest which, in America, prompted the John Birch Society to charge The Beatles with fomenting communism. (The song later percolated into the USSR on smuggled tapes and became a favourite among the group's Russian fans.)

The ill-feeling which had been brewing for several weeks (see [138]) finally erupted during the first of the two sessions for this number, with Starr 'leaving the group' after an argument with McCartney over the drum part. In Starr's absence, McCartney, Lennon, and Harrison had to pull themselves smartly together and the energy-level here is conspicuously higher than on most of their recent studio work. Layering the track on a basic take of drums by McCartney, lead guitar by Harrison, and bass by Lennon,[1] they constructed a thunderous wall of sound sprayed with jet-engine effects and falsetto backing vocals in the mould of full-tilt Beach Boys' records like 'Surfin' USA' and 'Fun Fun Fun'. Presumably because the tempo was too fast for his piano fingers, McCartney omitted the sharpened passing chord which rock-and-roll convention would normally demand in the final bar of each middle eight – a dislocation that, like so many of The Beatles' droll unorthodoxies, adds to the general aura of outrageous originality. Featuring McCartney's best vocal in his belting style since [64] DRIVE MY CAR, BACK IN THE USSR is the last of the band's great up-tempo rockers.

[143] DEAR PRUDENCE (Lennon–McCartney)

Lennon double-tracked vocal, backing vocal, guitar; **McCartney**
backing vocal, drums, bass, piano, flügelhorn, tambourine,
handclaps; **Harrison** backing vocal, lead guitar, handclaps; **Mal
Evans, Jackie Lomax, John McCartney** backing vocals,
handclaps
Recorded: 28th–30th August 1968, Trident Studios.
Producer: George Martin. Engineer: Barry Sheffield.
UK release: 22nd November 1968 (LP: *The Beatles*)
US release: 25th November 1968 (LP: *The Beatles*)

The circling four-chord sequence and plaintive pentatonic melody of DEAR PRUDENCE depicts the mental dilemma of its subject, Mia

---

[1] This was a Fender Bass VI, presented to The Beatles, along with a Rosewood Telecaster, in 1968. Lennon also used it on [140] ROCKY RACCOON and the film version of [164] LET IT BE; McCartney chose it for [136] WHILE MY GUITAR GENTLY WEEPS; and Harrison played it on [146] BIRTHDAY and [149] HONEY PIE. Another part of Fender's 1968 bequest, a Jazz Bass, was used by Harrison on some of the *Abbey Road* sessions (e.g., [175] GOLDEN SLUMBERS/[176] CARRY THAT WEIGHT).

Farrow's sister Prudence, who, made hypersensitive by too much meditation, found herself unable to leave her chalet in Rishikesh and had to be coaxed out by Lennon and Harrison. Founded on the finger-picking style[1] of many of The Beatles' songs written in India (see [128]), DEAR PRUDENCE uses a descending chromatic sequence akin to those of the verses of [103] LUCY IN THE SKY WITH DIAMONDS and [133] CRY BABY CRY, whose childhood resonances it shares. The lyric, Lennon's gentlest, works on similar nursery-rhyme principles.

Recorded, like [137] HEY JUDE, on the eight-track at Trident Studios, this was the second song the group taped in Starr's absence [142]. Filling in for him, McCartney is unsteady in the first half and his hi-hat work is stiff, but his continuous fill through the last verse/chorus brings the performance to a cathartic climax. The richest ingredient is Harrison's 'Indian' guitar, his first use of this once ubiquitous style since [121] THE INNER LIGHT, recorded six months earlier.

[144] GLASS ONION *(Lennon–McCartney)*

Lennon double-tracked vocal, acoustic guitar; **McCartney** bass,
   piano, recorder; **Harrison** lead guitar; **Starr**[2] drums,
   tambourine; **Henry Datyner, Eric Bowie, Norman
   Lederman, Ronald Thomas** violins; **John Underwood, Keith
   Cummings** violas; **Eldon Fox, Reginald Kilbey** cellos
Recorded: 11th–13th September, 10th October 1968, Abbey Road
   2.
Producers: Chris Thomas/George Martin. Engineer: Ken Scott.
UK release: 22nd November 1968 (LP: *The Beatles*)
US release: 25th November 1968 (LP: *The Beatles*)

It goes without saying that the late Sixties were drenched in mind-expanding drugs with all the extraneous 'creativity' this entailed. Wild rumours circulated like psychic epidemics: Dylan was in drag on the cover of *Bringing It All Back Home*, Warhol's peel-off banana on the sleeve of *The Velvet Underground and Nico* was impregnated with LSD, Jimi Hendrix was murdered by the Mafia, etc. The silliest of these pattern-seeking compulsions, the 'Paul is dead' hysteria, swelled into an

---

[1] As often in The Beatles' finger-picking songs, the D chord is germinal, but with the lower E string dropped to D. (Cf. [128].)
[2] Welcomed back with his drums wreathed in flowers, Starr returned on 5th September to work on the third version of [136] WHILE MY GUITAR GENTLY WEEPS and the remake of [134] HELTER SKELTER.

international folly which some diehards are loath to relinquish to this day.[1] That such credulity was dangerous became clear in August 1969 when the Manson Family crossed the interdisciplinary divide between textual analysis and mass-murder. Yet who had started the fashion for recording things backwards, leaving in mumbled off-mike obscurities, writing lyrics by throwing coins on the *I Ching*, and requesting LP covers with pictures of Aleister Crowley and Adolf Hitler on them?[2] Who set up chains of suggestive self-reference in their lyrics for the explicitly avowed fun of confusing people?[3]

Lennon's love of word games and louche sexual euphemisms was life-long, as was his running battle with those with a taste for over-interpretation.[4] Though there was little harm in it to begin with, there

---

[1] On 9th November 1966 Tara Browne [96] and McCartney went riding mopeds while stoned on cannabis, as a result of which the latter crashed, cutting his upper lip (an injury he hid by growing a moustache). Luridly reported – some versions claimed he'd been decapitated – this episode sparked a rumour that McCartney had died. (The contention was that he had been replaced by an actor, though who was supposed to be doing the singing and songwriting during The Beatles' last four years was never explained.) Partly because of the group's fondness for 'random', clues supporting this theory were discovered in abundance. For example, Lennon was thought, in the fade-out of [93] STRAWBERRY FIELDS FOREVER, to mutter 'I buried Paul', whereas (apropos of nothing) he really says 'Cranberry sauce'. His similarly meaningless mumble at the end of [153] I'M SO TIRED was interpreted as 'Paul is dead, man, miss him, miss him', while the line 'Bury my body' in the fade-out of [116] I AM THE WALRUS was inevitable grist to the rumour mill, despite having been written by Shakespeare. A dozen other song references were recruited to the myth while further 'clues' were discovered on The Beatles' LP covers, with *Sgt. Pepper* supplying a particularly rich fund of coincidences. There, McCartney (the only one holding a black instrument) wears a badge on his sleeve bearing the letters O.P.D., supposedly an abbreviation of 'officially pronounced dead' (in fact it stands for Ontario Police Department); he is likewise the only one facing away from the camera on some shots, while Peter Blake and Jann Haworth's cover shows an ominous hand above his head and The Beatles apparently clustered round a grave. The singer's black carnation in the [115] YOUR MOTHER SHOULD KNOW sequence of *Magical Mystery Tour* kept up a mad momentum brought to a climax by his barefoot appearance on the cover of *Abbey Road* and the adjacent number-plate 28 IF, supposedly signifying that he would have been 28 had he lived. (Actually he would have been – in fact, was – 27 at the time.)

[2] Hitler (Lennon's choice, needless to say) was left off the cover of *Sgt. Pepper* at the last minute.

[3] The 'promo' (video) for [120] HELLO, GOODBYE, made in November 1967, shows The Beatles ironically donning their Beatlemania 'Nehru jackets' and *Sgt. Pepper* costumes in an apparent attempt to debunk their own escalating mythology.

[4] He started leaving mistakes in his recorded lyrics as traps for such commentators in [53] YOU'VE GOT TO HIDE YOUR LOVE AWAY. On one take, he sang 'feeling two foot small' instead of 'two foot tall', then laughed and said 'Leave that in, the pseuds'll love it'.

was a double-standard at work here. (Obscurity was his sanctuary from the condescension of intellectuals, whose pretensions, which he hated, tended to mirror his own.) Later, though, his encounter with LSD and love-hate relationship with Dylan's surrealism impelled him to embrace creative confusion in a far more concerted way.

The essence of the confrontation between straight society and the counterculture was a clash between logical/literal and intuitive/lateral thinking. Central to hippie thought was the idea of disarming straight certainties by means of 'mind games' which paralleled the disorientating effects of psychedelic drugs. Many of The Beatles' records of 1966–70 embody such concepts, while most of those that don't were nonetheless shaped by them. The common factor was chance-determination, or 'random', as the group referred to it. Under the influence of LSD and avant-garde art, they came to accept accidental occurrences – and by extension the first things that entered their minds – as intrinsically valid, rather than, as they once had, working their inspirations and felicitous mistakes into something more disciplined. Listeners were left to generate their own connections and make their own sense of what they were hearing, thereby increasing the chances of dangerous misinterpretation along Mansonian lines.

This is not to damn creative randomness in itself. Few artists outside the canons of tradition have refused to improve their work merely because the way to do so struck them by accident. Yet to treat chance-determined productions as identical with material intentionally vested with meaning is to meddle in a relativism that can only escalate towards chaos – and chaos draws psychopaths. For many modern artists, 'aleatory' procedures (literally, those of the diceman) are so basic as to be beyond question, an assumption maintained by their audiences, which are usually small enough to prevent such phenomena spreading far enough to affect unstable minds.[1] In rock, the audience has no predictable bounds and stars have often found themselves harassed by demented individuals among the millions following their careers. (That this happens hardly at all nowadays is a perverse index of the vacuity of contemporary pop.) To the extent that they were invoked by the aleatory philosophy of derangement associated with the Sixties counterculture, obsessions such as those which beset Charles Manson, and later Lennon's assassin Mark Chapman, were inevitable. As prominent advocates of the free-associating state of mind, The Beatles attracted

---

[1] The effect is relative. The most famous artist of the Sixties, Andy Warhol, was shot by a deranged actress on 3rd June 1968 around the time The Beatles were recording the experimental [126] REVOLUTION 1.

more crackpot fixations than anyone apart from Dylan. While, at the time, they may have seemed enough like harmless fun for Lennon to make them the subject of the present sneeringly sarcastic song, in the end they returned to kill him.

The extent of the pattern of misleading self-quotations Lennon was disowning in this lyric is indicated by the fact that two of the five Beatles songs mentioned in it also contain references to other Beatles songs. (One, [122] LADY MADONNA, refers to [116] I AM THE WALRUS which in turn refers to [103] LUCY IN THE SKY WITH DIAMONDS.) A title-phrase its author had had in mind for some while, GLASS ONION had the right associations of transparency and endless layers of meaning, but didn't fit the metre of the chorus. This, though, failed to stop Lennon including it – indeed, the song features another phrase-in-search-of-a-lyric, 'the Cast Iron Shore', which he had long been looking for an excuse to use. (The reference, apt enough, is to the dismal waterfront between Aigburth and Garston on the north side of the Mersey where random rubbish from Liverpool's sewers washes up.)[1]

With its bluesily dissonant D sharp, the sour A minor melody of GLASS ONION eloquently voices its author's scorn, yet the song remains unlikeable. Whether or not Lennon was fed up with being a Beatle,[2] there was no excuse for berating those of their fans who had trustingly fallen for the group's multi-layered conceptual jokes. The string-section's bleary diminished chords at the end – doubtless meant to convey the dull-wittedness of the literal-minded – with hindsight seem to evoke a blurring of the boundary between playfulness and bad faith.[3] In the end, GLASS ONION says less about the credulity of pop fans than the self-regard of pop stars.

---

[1] For an explanation of the 'bent back tulips' of the first verse, see Miles, op. cit., p. 127.
[2] The line 'The Walrus was Paul' was his way of acknowledging McCartney's role in keeping The Beatles together between 1967 and 1968. McCartney believes it to be a reference to the fact that it was he who wore the walrus costume in the video for [116] I AM THE WALRUS (Miles, op. cit., p. 496).
[3] George Martin's arrangement replaced the original sound-effects ending (*Anthology 3*).

[145] I WILL (Lennon–McCartney)

McCartney vocal, acoustic guitars, 'vocal bass'; **Lennon** percussion;
   Starr cymbals, bongos, maracas
Recorded: 16th–17th September 1968, Abbey Road 2.
Producer: Chris Thomas. Engineer: Ken Scott.
UK release: 22nd November 1968 (LP: *The Beatles*)
US release: 25th November 1968 (LP: *The Beatles*)

I WILL anticipates the relaxed sentimentality of McCartney's first solo album and recalls the harmonic scheme of his early ballad [46] I'LL FOLLOW THE SUN. More straightforward, it soothes the listener with its simple verse/chorus melody and murmurous internal rhymes (close to muzak, were the craftsmanship not so cunning). Needing precisely the right performance from an acoustic set-up which exposed the slightest error, it required a gruelling sixty-seven takes. The apparent casualness of the result is a tribute to The Beatles' concentration. Few could have managed this feat without light relief and the session was regularly interrupted by ad-libs, including [U146] STEP INSIDE LOVE and two casual improvisations logged as [U147] LOS PARANOIAS and 'Can You Take Me Back?', the second of which ended up on the album as the sinister introduction to [127] REVOLUTION 9. Finishing the session with his recorder overdub on [144] GLASS ONION, McCartney returned the next day to add a sung bass part and soften his already dulcet lead vocal with ADT.

[U146] STEP INSIDE LOVE (Lennon–McCartney)

McCartney vocal, acoustic guitar; **Lennon** bongos; **Starr** claves(?)
Recorded: 16th September 1968, Abbey Road 2.
Producer: Chris Thomas. Engineer: Ken Scott.
UK release: 28th October 1996 (2-CD: *Anthology 3*)
US release: 28th October 1996 (2-CD: *Anthology 3*)

Casually busked between takes for [145] I WILL, this suave McCartney bossa nova was written for Cilla Black's first BBC TV series and, in her version, peaked at No. 9 in the UK chart on 10th April 1968. STEP INSIDE LOVE is one of its author's most urbane melodies, wending its typically scalar way through a six-key modulation with an intuitive sophistication neither Lennon nor Harrison could hope to match.

[U147] LOS PARANOIAS *(Lennon–McCartney–Harrison–Starr)*

McCartney vocal, acoustic guitar; Lennon bongos; Starr shaker
Recorded: 16th September 1968, Abbey Road 2.
Producer: Chris Thomas. Engineer: Ken Scott.
UK release: 28th October 1996 (2-CD: *Anthology 3*)
US release: 28th October 1996 (2-CD: *Anthology 3*)

After [U146] STEP INSIDE LOVE, *Anthology 3* shows McCartney covering himself with a joke as if anticipating a dig from Lennon – which duly comes in the form of the dry comment 'Los Paranoias'.[1] McCartney's chuckle is just exaggerated enough to let his partner know he was expecting the jibe, and his riposte – a smoothly ad-libbed jazz bossa nova – is impressively instant, as well as subtly pointed: 'Just enjoy us . . . harmonee-ee-y . . .' The subtext: Lennon, author of pop's most original songs, was nonetheless an inverted snob about music itself, distrusting the technical dexterity that came as second nature to his colleague. McCartney's love of harmony for its own sake seemed fatuous to Lennon, for whom musical decisions were always driven by emotional truth, never by beauty of form. In a moment of lighthearted studio banter, the fundamental – and deepening – difference between the two artists is exposed.

[146] BIRTHDAY *(Lennon–McCartney)*

McCartney vocal, piano; Lennon vocal, backing vocal, lead guitar;
  Harrison 6-string bass; Starr drums, tambourine; Patti
  Harrison, Yoko Ono backing vocals; All (plus Mal Evans)
  handclaps
Recorded: 18th September 1968, Abbey Road 2.
Producer: Chris Thomas. Engineer: Ken Scott.
UK release: 22nd November 1968 (LP: *The Beatles*)
US release: 25th November 1968 (LP: *The Beatles*)

The first British TV transmission of *The Girl Can't Help It* prompted The Beatles to arrange this session so as to let them slip out to McCartney's house partway through in order to watch it. In honour of the film's musical star Little Richard, McCartney wrote most of BIRTHDAY on the spot before the others arrived, bolting an A major

---

[1] A reference to the Trio Los Paraguayas, an imponderable favourite of BBC TV producers during the mid-Sixties.

blues to a C major boogie by means of a drum passage, a screaming crescendo on E major, and a brief Cream-style guitar/bass unison.[1] Like its lyric, this lay-out is a conceptual joke about arbitrariness and, like most such jokes, its archness quickly wears thin. Soullessly synthetic, BIRTHDAY decks its fabricated changes in a distorted production of compressed vocals and heavily filtered and flanged piano. (Compare this with the equally artificial but genuinely flamboyant [65] DAY TRIPPER.)

[147] PIGGIES *(Harrison)*

> Harrison vocal, guitar; Lennon tape loops; McCartney bass; Starr tambourine; Chris Thomas harpsichord; Henry Datyner, Eric Bowie, Norman Lederman, Ronald Thomas violins; John Underwood, Keith Cummings violas; Eldon Fox, Reginald Kilbey cellos
>
> Recorded: 19th–20th September 1968, Abbey Road Studios 1-2; 10th October 1968, Abbey Road 2.
>
> Producers: Chris Thomas/George Martin. Engineer: Ken Scott.
>
> UK release: 22nd November 1968 (LP: *The Beatles*)
>
> US release: 25th November 1968 (LP: *The Beatles*)

The misanthropy at the heart of so much spiritual piousness reveals itself in Harrison's bludgeoning satire on straight society. Begun in 1966, when American hippies chose to expand an insult aimed at the police to cover consumerism in general, PIGGIES was finished, with lyric assistance from Lennon and Harrison's mother Louise, two years later. Arriving in the USA in November 1968 – by which time Haight-Ashbury had degenerated into a ghetto and the counterculture was in violent confrontation with the establishment – the song's industrial-strength vitriol was guaranteed to fuel a bad atmosphere. Charles Manson's interpretation of it as an incitement to revolutionary mass-murder was, as Harrison's religious preceptors might have told him, implicit in the song's uncharitable karma.[2] During the first session in Studio 1, sitting beside George Martin's deputy Chris Thomas at a harpsichord which had been left after a classical recording, Harrison broke off to play another new song called [170] SOMETHING. 'That's great,' enthused Thomas, adding, pointedly: 'Why don't we do that

---

[1] McCartney recalls the song as '50-50 John and me' (Miles, op. cit., p. 496).

[2] The dead Leno LaBianca was left by the Manson family with a fork in his stomach and the legend 'Death to pigs' daubed in blood on a nearby wall – an apparent allusion to the last verse of PIGGIES.

instead?' Sadly Harrison ignored this advice and PIGGIES, an embarrassing blot on his discography, went ahead.[1]

[148] HAPPINESS IS A WARM GUN *(Lennon–McCartney)*

Lennon double-tracked vocal, backing vocal, lead guitar;
  McCartney backing vocal, bass; **Harrison** backing vocal, lead
  guitar; **Starr** drums, tambourine
Recorded: 23rd–25th September 1968, Abbey Road 2.
Producer: Chris Thomas. Engineer: Ken Scott.
UK release: 22nd November 1968 (LP: *The Beatles*)
US release: 25th November 1968 (LP: *The Beatles*)

The darkest song on *The Beatles*, HAPPINESS IS A WARM GUN is a
conflation of three or four separate fragments, the formal originality of
which may have owed something to the novel structures introduced by
The Incredible String Band in tracks like 'A Very Cellular Song' (on
their third album, *The Hangman's Beautiful Daughter*).[2] While the
lyric's obscurity is partly due to this, it was also deliberate. Former
Apple press officer Derek Taylor recalls that the first part was strung
together from phrases he and Lennon free-associated at random: the
lizard on the windowpane was a specific reminiscence of Los Angeles,
while the man in the crowd was allegedly a genuine character who
inserted small mirrors into the toe-caps of his boots so as to be able to
look up women's skirts at football matches. The title itself came from a
slogan of America's National Rifle Association, which Lennon saw in a
gun magazine. ('I thought, what a fantastic, insane thing to say. A warm
gun means you've just shot something.') From these and other clues,
including the fact that his passionate relationship with Yoko Ono was
then shading all his lyrics with erotic meaning,[3] the song would seem

---

[1] The guitar demo version on *Anthology 3* shows the song to have been written in
G, the A flat major final version on *The Beatles* presumably resulting from having
been varispeeded up a semitone.
[2] Like The Rolling Stones, Led Zeppelin, and other artists of the time, The
Beatles became fascinated by this multi-instrumental folk duo, whose second album
The 5000 Spirits or The Layers of the Onion emerged in 1967 as an acoustic equivalent
of *Sgt. Pepper*. Dismissed by most rock historians for the fey self-indulgence of their
later work, Mike Heron and Robin Williamson were, at the height of their creativity
(1966–8), among the most imaginative of British songwriters, as well as superb multi-
instrumentalists.
[3] The BBC banned the song for its sexual references. Mother Superior was one of
Lennon's names for Ono (see [125], [156]).

to concern sexual authenticity in a sordid world of unfeeling voyeurism and violence – though whether this is really so is hard to say, given its synthetic creation and Lennon's own contradictory statements about it. (Denying that it was about drugs, he described it as a 'sort of history of rock 'n' roll' which, while making some sense in musical terms, makes none at all as an account of the song's emotional burden.)

Musically, HAPPINESS IS A WARM GUN is in four sections: a folk-style finger-picked introduction switching from the disconsolate sadness of E minor to an angry A minor; an A Lydian section in 3/8 featuring bluesy phrase irregularities ('I need a fix'); a double-time continuation in the same tonality and in – more or less – rock style ('Mother Superior'); and a long C major conclusion using a standard Fifties doo-wop sequence.[1] The Beatles, all of whom especially liked this song, took fifteen hours and ninety-five takes to get it right, and even then had to edit two takes together (probably at 1:34).[2] This was hardly surprising, since HAPPINESS IS A WARM GUN is by far the most metrically irregular thing they ever recorded.[3] A further late change involved deleting a vocal in the instrumental bars of the second section. As with several other track-edits on Beatles recordings, the erasure was imperfect, leaving a trace of the original vocal (the word 'down' at 0:57).

Lennon rated this one of his best tracks and, while rationally it may not hang together, it packs a considerable punch, working on an emotionally allusive level few songwriters have been aware of, let alone succeeded at. The sound, the arrangement, and the performances (especially Lennon's vocal) all contribute to this effect; what's more they couldn't have done so unless the entire group had joined in piecing the whole thing together (so providing an exception to the view of *The Beatles* as a set of solo tracks on which each writer

---

[1] See [22], [50]. Just audible on the left channel are some doo-wop bass voices.

[2] The Esher demo of HAPPINESS IS A WARM GUN on *Anthology 3* (which omits the closing section in which the song's title appears) suggests that much of the 'rehearsal' spent on it during its recording was taken up with sorting Lennon's idiosyncratic structure into something intelligible to the rest of the group. (In the May 1968 sketch, he still had half the song to write – and some chords to *re*write!)

[3] Starting with four bars of common time, the first section changes key for an eight-and-three-quarter bar passage (1 x 4/4, 1 x 2/4, 6 x 4/4, 1 x 1/4, 1 x 4/4), before moving to the second section: twice round eleven bars in 3/8 (grouped as 3 + 4 + 4) with the extra complication of a rising two-bar bass phrase in canon with the vocal. After one tacit bar, the third section arrives: thrice round a highly unstable structure analysable as 1 x 6/8, 1 x 8/8, 1 x 4/8, 1 x 6/8, 1 x 8/8, 1 x 6/8. The closing section consists of four bars of 4/4, twelve of 3/8 (with the drums continuing in 4/4!), four of 4/4, an out-of-tempo pause on F minor, and a final five bars of 4/4.

employed his colleagues as session musicians). While the song could have been written by no one else, all four pitched for it: this is a *Beatles* performance.

In the end, the most purely Lennonian aspect of HAPPINESS IS A WARM GUN is its extreme ambiguity. From an initial mood of depression, it ascends through irony, self-destructive despair, and obscurely renewed energy to a finale that wrests exhausted fulfilment from anguish. Grippingly uneasy listening, the track's tense blend of sarcasm and sincerity stays unresolved until its final detumescent downbeat.

[149] HONEY PIE *(Lennon–McCartney)*

McCartney vocal, piano, lead guitar; Lennon lead guitar;
  Harrison 6-string bass; Starr drums; Dennis Walton, Ronald
  Chamberlain, Jim Chester, Rex Morris, Harry Klein
  saxophones; Raymond Newman, David Smith clarinets
Recorded: 1st–2nd, 4th October 1968, Trident Studios.
Producer: George Martin. Engineer: Barry Sheffield.
UK release: 22nd November 1968 (LP: *The Beatles*)
US release: 25th November 1968 (LP: *The Beatles*)

A consummate writing and performing pastiche from McCartney, this was later dismissed by Lennon as beyond redemption. Curious, then, that the slightly fluffed but stylistically authentic semi-acoustic guitar solo was played by him. HONEY PIE has a catchy tune, the correct period harmonic design, and all the proper passing chords.[1] George Martin's flapper dance-band arrangement is spot-on, as are McCartney's studied vocal mannerisms. All that prevents it from reviving the nostalgic charm of [94] WHEN I'M SIXTY-FOUR is its air of faintly smarmy pointlessness.

---

[1] Not all of these are present in the otherwise immaculately polished Esher demo, suggesting that George Martin lent a hand at the recording stage.

[150] SAVOY TRUFFLE *(Harrison)*

> Harrison double-tracked vocal, lead guitar; McCartney bass; Starr
> drums, tambourine; Chris Thomas organ, electric piano; Art
> Ellefson, Danny Moss, Derek Collins tenor saxes; Ronnie
> Ross, Harry Klein, Bernard George baritone saxes
> Recorded: 3rd, 5th October, Trident Studios; 11th, 14th October
> 1968, Abbey Road Studio 2.
> Producer: George Martin. Engineers: Barry Sheffield/Ken Scott.
> UK release: 22nd November 1968 (LP: *The Beatles*)
> US release: 25th November 1968 (LP: *The Beatles*)

As pointless as its predecessor, SAVOY TRUFFLE commemorates the habit
of Harrison's friend Eric Clapton of gorging himself on cheap
chocolates. Filling his lyric by listing most of the contents of a box of
Good News, Harrison got stuck for something to sing in the middle
eight, at which point Derek Taylor helpfully mentioned the title of a
contemporary film by his friend Alan Pariser, *You Are What You Eat.*
Little is known about the recording of this track which, like [149]
HONEY PIE and [151] MARTHA MY DEAR, was partly done at Trident
Studios [137]. With a sax section employing some of the stalwarts of
the contemporary British jazz scene, Chris Thomas's score strives to
make Harrison's mordant E minor sequence attractive, but has an uphill
fight against a particularly nasal vocal and a violently compressed
production.

[151] MARTHA MY DEAR *(Lennon–McCartney)*

McCartney double-tracked vocal, piano, bass, lead guitar, drums, handclaps; **Bernard Miller, Dennis McConnell, Lou Sofier, Les Maddox** violins; **Leo Birnbaum, Henry Myerscough** violas; **Reginald Kilbey, Frederick Alexander** cellos; **Leon Calvert, Stanley Reynolds, Ronnie Hughes** trumpets; **Leon Calvert** flügelhorn;[1] **Tony Tunstall** French horn; **Ted Barker** trombone; **Alf Reece** tuba
Recorded: 4th–5th October 1968, Trident Studios.
Producer: George Martin. Engineer: Barry Sheffield.
UK release: 22nd November 1968 (LP: *The Beatles*)
US release: 25th November 1968 (LP: *The Beatles*)

McCartney's most rhythmically unorthodox song, MARTHA MY DEAR was recorded ten days after a period of intense rehearsal work on Lennon's similarly irregular [148] HAPPINESS IS A WARM GUN. Since, like HAPPINESS, it includes an ascending bass phrase which temporarily expands the metre (fourth bar: 6/4), it's possible that McCartney, his musical funnybone tickled by his partner's eccentricities, here set out to create something equally tricky for his own amusement. As brilliantly fluent as Lennon's song is dark and crabbed, MARTHA MY DEAR is the most exuberant expression of its composer's jaunty personality since [95] PENNY LANE. Yet, while Penny Lane has a point of view, MARTHA MY DEAR is a part-technical *jeu d'esprit*[2] with a confused lyric in which its author's Old English sheepdog somehow gets muddled up in a recent love affair. Scintillatingly gifted as this song is, it's also virtually devoid of meaning.

The key of E flat major suggested a brass band and George Martin swiftly assembled one, the bulk of the recording being accomplished in a single brisk day's work. None of the other Beatles appears to have been involved – a tribute to McCartney's facile versatility and a measure, perhaps, of his colleagues' indifference to this breezy song.

---

[1] Counterpoint during the second middle sixteen in F. (The song actually has two different middle sections, the second effectively a fifteen-bar double-time extension of the first.)
[2] McCartney recalls the origin of the song as an 'exercise' for piano, designed to give him something more difficult to do (Miles, op. cit., p. 498).

[152] LONG, LONG, LONG *(Harrison)*

Harrison double-tracked vocal, acoustic guitars; **McCartney**
backing vocal, organ, bass; **Starr** drums; **Chris Thomas** piano
Recorded: 7th–9th October 1968, Abbey Road 2.
Producer: George Martin. Engineer: Ken Scott.
UK release: 22nd November 1968 (LP: *The Beatles*)
US release: 25th November 1968 (LP: *The Beatles*)

After the ponderous [136] WHILE MY GUITAR GENTLY WEEPS, the
nasty [147] PIGGIES, and the space-filling [150] SAVOY TRUFFLE, at last –
the real George. This touching token of exhausted, relieved reconciliation with God is Harrison's finest moment on *The Beatles*: simple,
direct, and, in its sighing, self-annihilating coda, devastatingly expressive. Based on the triple-time changes of Bob Dylan's 'Sad-Eyed Lady
of the Lowlands',[1] LONG, LONG, LONG rises from a whisper only in its
fourteen-bar middle section, where three bars of mechanically repeating boogie piano phrase depict the years wasted 'searching'. At the end,
the luckiest accident in any Beatles recording produced a striking
conclusion. As McCartney reached the final low inversion of C major
on the group's customised Hammond organ, the bottom note vibrated
a bottle of wine standing on the instrument's Leslie cabinet, creating an
eery rattle. Holding his chord as a bare fifth, McCartney turned it into a
spectral C minor suspended fourth, joined by Starr with a snare-roll and
Harrison with a disembodied wail. Together they sustained this for
thirty seconds before, with the organ and its accompanying rattle
fading, Harrison gave the harmony its final twist on his Gibson J200: a
skeletal G minor eleventh, closed out by the dying fall of Starr's drums.
With its simultaneous suggestion of a death, a new beginning, and an
enigmatic question, this minor version of the [31] A HARD DAY'S
NIGHT chord is, in its context, one of the most resonant in The Beatles'
discography.[2]

---

[1] Raised a minor third to fit Harrison's voice.
[2] The session for LONG, LONG, LONG was, appropriately, one of The Beatles' most
protracted. Starting with some tape-copying and mixing at 2.30pm on a Monday
afternoon, they recorded all evening and through the night, stopping at 7am on
Tuesday. Since they were in their customary rush to complete the album, they
returned nine hours later to finish the track. (The group recorded at Abbey Road
every day between 7th and 17th October, often starting in the late afternoon and
going through till breakfast.)

[153] I'M SO TIRED *(Lennon–McCartney)*

Lennon vocal, acoustic guitar, lead guitar, organ; **McCartney**
  harmony vocal, bass, electric piano; **Harrison** lead guitar; **Starr**
  drums
Recorded: 8th October 1968, Abbey Road 2.
Producer: George Martin. Engineer: Ken Scott.
UK release: 22nd November 1968 (LP: *The Beatles*)
US release: 25th November 1968 (LP: *The Beatles*)

Written in India while suffering from insomnia caused by too much
meditation and his anxiety about his marriage, Lennon's I'M SO TIRED
has the semitonal slouch and ambling tempo of [135] SEXY SADIE,
composed about the same time. Compared to [85] I'M ONLY SLEEPING,
it lacks poetic imagination, being impatient with its own inertia – a
mood which provokes one of its author's funniest lines (vis-à-vis the
discoverer of tobacco). This track was one of Lennon's favourites from
his own recordings, for the expressiveness of the sound in general and
his vocal in particular.

[154] THE CONTINUING STORY OF BUNGALOW BILL
(Lennon–McCartney)

Lennon vocal, acoustic guitar, organ; **McCartney** backing vocal,
  bass; **Harrison** backing vocal, acoustic guitar; **Starr** backing
  vocal, drums, tambourine; **Yoko Ono** vocal, backing vocal;
  Others (including Maureen Starkey) backing vocals; **Chris
  Thomas** Mellotron
Recorded: 8th October 1968, Abbey Road 2.
Producer: George Martin. Engineer: Ken Scott.
UK release: 22nd November 1968 (LP: *The Beatles*)
US release: 25th November 1968 (LP: *The Beatles*)

This lapse into tub-thumping banality was inspired by an American
visitor to the Rishikesh community who departed for a few weeks to
murder tigers before returning to resume his course of spiritual self-
improvement. In two disparate parts bluntly hammered together with
three clumping bass-drum beats, BUNGALOW BILL has a chorus half-
consciously borrowed from Ray Noble's Thirties standard 'Stay As
Sweet As You Are'.[1] Recorded with deliberately sloppy spontaneity

---

[1] On 6th June 1968, The Beatles gave a chaotic radio interview to the BBC's
Kenny Everett during which Starr burst into another Ray Noble song, 'Goodnight
Sweetheart'. Lennon's [130] GOOD NIGHT was recorded three weeks later.

in three takes, the track features backing vocals by almost everyone in Abbey Road at the time and some adroit mandolin and trombone impersonations by Chris Thomas on Mellotron.

[155] WHY DON'T WE DO IT IN THE ROAD?
(Lennon–McCartney)

McCartney vocals, acoustic guitar, piano, lead guitar, bass, handclaps; **Starr** drums, handclaps

Recorded: 9th October 1968, Abbey Road 1; 10th October 1968, Abbey Road 3.

Producer: Paul McCartney. Engineer: Ken Townsend.

UK release: 22nd November 1968 (LP: *The Beatles*)

US release: 25th November 1968 (LP: *The Beatles*)

In the scrambled final days of recording for *The Beatles*, McCartney slipped into Studio 1 while Lennon and Harrison were supervising mixes in Studio 2 and taped this raucously stylised D blues, asking Starr to drum on it. With its arch simplicity, confrontational vocal, and implicit allusion to countercultural street theatre, the track was Conceptual Art of precisely the kind Lennon liked[1] and twelve years later he still resented not having been asked to participate. (McCartney later mischievously hinted that it was tit-for-tat for being left out of [127] REVOLUTION 9.) Alluded to in Blake Edwards' film *10* as the epitome of adolescent anti-romance, WHY DON'T WE DO IT IN THE ROAD remains a minor relic of its long-gone let-it-all-hang-out era.

---

[1] McCartney described it at the time as 'a ricochet off John' and 'a very John song' (Davies, p. 468). He later recalled its origin in Rishikesh when he saw two monkeys casually copulating in the road (Miles, op. cit., p. 499).

[156] JULIA *(Lennon–McCartney)*

Lennon double-tracked vocal, double-tracked acoustic guitar
Recorded: 13th October 1968, Abbey Road 2.
Producer: George Martin. Engineer: Ken Scott.
UK release: 22nd November 1968 (LP: *The Beatles*)
US release: 25th November 1968 (LP: *The Beatles*)

The last of the sequence of folk-style finger-picking songs on *The Beatles* (see [128]), (and the last number to be recorded for the double-album as a whole, JULIA is psychologically one of Lennon's fulcrum pieces: a message to his dead mother telling her that, in 'ocean child' (the Japanese meaning of Yoko), he has finally found a love to replace her and that he can now relinquish his quasi-oedipal obsession (see [50]).

Born in 1914, Julia Stanley married Freddy Lennon in 1938, giving birth to John in 1940. When their marriage broke up two years later, John was adopted by Julia's sister Mimi and her husband George Smith, and he went to live with them at Mendips, their house in Menlove Avenue. Meanwhile, Julia set up home with John Dykins, by whom she had two illegitimate children. When he was six, John became the subject of a fraught tug-of-love between his parents, at the height of which he ran after Julia in the street sobbing 'Mummy, don't leave me'. After this, while continuing to live with George and Mimi, he saw his mother more frequently. Following the second crisis in his life (Uncle George's death in 1955), John and his mother grew closer. A free spirit, she was a laughing lover of life who positively encouraged the rebel in him. Siding with him and his friends against censorious adults, she followed the progress of The Quarry Men with genuine interest, teaching them tunes on her banjo. To John, Julia was a semi-dream-figure ('a young aunt or a big sister'): the only human being he had ever loved without reservation. Her death in a road accident outside Mendips on 15th July 1958 shattered him, and for the next two years he was consumed by 'a blind rage', drinking wildly and incessantly getting into fights. That his new friend Paul McCartney had also lost his mother in his teens brought them close despite their temperamental differences, while The Beatles gave Lennon a sanity-saving purpose. However, his relationships with women, who found themselves endlessly measured against the incomparable Julia, remained angry and often violent.[1]

---

[1] According to McCartney, Julia was 'a very beautiful woman, very good-looking, with long red hair . . . John absolutely adored her, and not just because she

JULIA, with which Yoko Ono helped,[1] expiates Lennon's tortured devotion to his mother. In the incantatory repeated notes of its intro, the song suggests an offering to an ancestral spirit: an attempt to break an obsession by commending the supplicant's new earthly love in the hope of a blessing. The heart of this ritual – the transfer of Lennon's love from Julia to Yoko – is its ten-bar middle where a quasi-oriental scale implies that the accompanying image ('Her hair of floating sky is shimmering') applies to both women: Julia in his boyhood memory, Yoko in his present and future thoughts. (Ono sent him many cryptic postcards while he was in India, one of which asserted that she was a cloud and that he should look for her in the sky.)[2]

Lennon's most childlike and self-revealing song, JULIA is almost too personal for public consumption. Nor did it succeed in laying his mother-fixation, as the exorcisms of 'Mother' and 'My Mummy's Dead' on his first solo album prove. To a great extent, Julia Lennon was her son's muse. Once he had rid his soul of grief for her, his creativity forfeited its pressure and, during his more reconciled final decade, his output lost most of the edge and forcefulness it displayed at its fundamentally unhappy zenith in the mid-Sixties.

With its thirty varied and variable tracks, *The Beatles* is a sprawling affair reflecting the group's post-Epstein indifference to corporate concerns. That it hangs together as well as it does is a tribute to the sequencing skills of Lennon, McCartney, and George Martin, who worked out the running order in a continuous 24-hour effort on 16th–17th October 1968 (The Beatles' longest single session). With its mood contrasts, cunning key-sequences, and clever *segues*, this 95-minute double-album is a masterpiece of programming. Mere expert presentation, however, cannot hide the fact that half the tracks on it are poor by earlier standards, or that many of its lyrics are little more than the lazy navel-gazing of pampered recluses.

Before the Leicester group Family issued their innovative debut

---

was his mum.'

[1] Her influence is detectable in the song's haiku-like images. (She may have suggested 'seashell eyes', taken from the then-fashionable Lebanese mystical poet Kahlil Gibran.)

[2] The Oedipal aspect of Lennon's love for Julia was replicated in his marriage to Ono (whom he called 'Mother Superior'), she being frequently cast in a maternal role, an arrangement in which each colluded.

album *Music in a Doll's House* in August 1968, The Beatles had been planning to call their new work *A Doll's House* (supposedly after Ibsen). The clash was unfortunate since this was an apt title for this musical attic of odds and ends, some charming, others sinister, many tinged with childhood memories, all absorbed in the interior worlds of their authors. There is a secret unease in this music, betraying the turmoil beneath the group's business-as-usual façade. Shadows lengthen over the album as it progresses: the slow afternoon of The Beatles' career. Sadly, none of this is captured in Richard Hamilton's modishly empty sleeve-design. One can only assume that this is because he wasn't able to hear the music before setting to work, since its crepuscular quality is so tangible. Certainly no other product of the noon-bright idiom of Sixties pop offers as many associations of guarded privacy and locked rooms, or concludes in such disturbing, dreamlike darkness.

[157] DIG A PONY *(Lennon–McCartney)*

Lennon vocal, lead guitar; **McCartney** harmony vocal, bass;
   Harrison lead guitar; **Starr** drums
Recorded: 22nd, 24th, 28th, 30th January, 5th February 1969,
   Apple Studios.
Producer: George Martin. Engineer: Glyn Johns.
UK release: 8th May 1970 (LP: *Let It Be*)
US release: 18th May 1970 (LP: *Let It Be*)

The ill-tempered and finally exhausting five months' work on *The Beatles* left the group in much the same mental limbo as had set in at the end of the *Sgt. Pepper* sessions the year before. Again McCartney took it upon himself to pull his colleagues together, this time suggesting that they reject the multi-layered artifice, parodies, and game-playing of their post-touring studio work and 'get back' to their roots as a live rock-and-roll band. Not that he meant returning to touring, a suggestion he knew Harrison would dismiss out of hand, but rather a filmed one-hour eight-song concert, to be staged at The Roundhouse in Camden, North London (see [U96], note).

   McCartney believed in live performance as a source of creative energy and missed the audience feedback he remembered from the group's early days. Because of this, some accounts unfairly represent him as boyishly badgering the others into something none of them wanted to do. Yet both Lennon and Harrison had recently enjoyed playing live – the former in The Rolling Stones' *Rock and Roll Circus*, the latter jamming with Californian musicians during a seven-week stay in Los Angeles – while Starr was amenable providing the project could be fitted round his forthcoming film-role in *The Magic Christian*. All, likewise, had enjoyed working on [148] HAPPINESS IS A WARM GUN, which, because of its difficulties, had forced them to revive their ensemble playing skills. Indeed, when it came to taping their next album, it was (according to George Martin) Lennon rather than McCartney who insisted that the live/no-overdub regime be religiously adhered to.

The Beatles, in short, set out on what became the 'Get Back' fiasco with enthusiasm and more than a hint of late Sixties megalomania, rejecting The Roundhouse in favour of a Tunisian amphitheatre, or even an Atlantic liner. (At this point, Lennon was heard to mutter 'I'm warming to doing it in an asylum'.) It was only when they convened at Twickenham Studios to hammer out their concert set that they realised they were deluding themselves.

Working on HAPPINESS IS A WARM GUN had been a special case – a stimulating challenge, but a tough one compared to idling by with edits and overdubs. Suddenly The Beatles found themselves faced with flogging through much the same process many times over. In effect, they had called their own bluff: this was too much like hard work for men with nothing to prove and no compelling financial reasons to put themselves through hoops.[1] Unfortunately the press had been notified and a film-crew hired in to shoot the proceedings. They *had* to do it – or at least pretend to. Their instinctive solution was to jam sporadically, sending the whole thing up, much as they did on loose nights in Abbey Road. This time, though, the meter was running: a film studio was rented and cameras were rolling. Driven by his ingrained work ethic and assumed burden of leadership, McCartney attempted to impose discipline on this devious disorder, but the others had had enough of his pedantic MD-ing and resented being drilled like schoolboys. (When he suggested that they were merely suffering from stage-fright, Lennon stared at him in stony disbelief.)

The truth was that they were adults and no longer adaptable to the teenage gang mentality demanded by a functional pop/rock group.

---

[1] Lennon announced in January 1969 that if Apple went on losing money at its present rate, he'd be bankrupt in six months. Yet while Apple was in a mess, it would have been impossible for a man with Lennon's mechanical royalties and performing rights to go bankrupt. Money was only an issue inasmuch as the group felt, justifiably, that they were owed a great deal more of it than they were getting – hence the recruitment of Allen Klein to sort out The Beatles affairs. (See Norman, p. 379 et seq.)

Harrison yearned to be third guitarist in an easygoing American band, Starr was looking forward to being an actor, and Lennon, who a few months earlier had been simultaneously attacked as a sell-out by the revolutionary Left and busted by the forces of the establishment for possession of drugs, wanted to break the mould completely and confront the world with *outré* cultural subversions in company with Yoko Ono. (Sitting inscrutably beside him throughout these dispiriting sessions, she contributed to their failure, something of which she seemed uncharacteristically oblivious.)

For a while they struggled on, trying out a variety of new material, including several songs which later turned up on solo albums.[1] At length, Harrison snapped – McCartney having tried once too often to get him to play his guitar solo *just so* – and walked out. (He went straight home and commemorated the fracas in 'Wah-Wah', later recorded for *All Things Must Pass*.) A few days later, Ono, squatting symbolically on Harrison's blue cushion, began to wail in her patent Banshee fashion, whereupon the others, admitting themselves beaten, joined in with a barrage of screaming feedback. The 'rehearsals' and their associated concert were forthwith abandoned.

Retreating a week later to the basement of the Apple office in Savile Row, the ill-tempered group discovered to their horror that self-styled electronics genius 'Magic Alex' Mardas, an eccentric befriended by Lennon during his LSD period, had installed a '72-track console' that turned out to consist of an antique oscilloscope held together by a few planks of wood. Imperturbably stepping in, 'Uncle George' Martin negotiated the loan of an eight-track from Abbey Road, and work commenced on what was now to be a new album: one recorded, The Beatles insisted (attempting to retain some saving shred of their original plan) 'honestly' – meaning without edits or overdubs. Since such a scheme would involve amassing dozens of takes of every song until usable ones occurred, and since every minute of the awful process was to be filmed, this was a recipe for lingering disaster. Wisely, George Martin delegated sessions to his assistant Glyn Johns, and found more congenial things to do elsewhere.

---

[1] [U168] ALL THINGS MUST PASS and 'Isn't It A Pity' (on Harrison's first solo album *All Things Must Pass*); 'Every Night', 'Maybe I'm Amazed', 'That Would Be Something' (on McCartney's first solo album *McCartney*); 'Back Seat Of My Car' (on McCartney's second solo album *Ram*); [U126] CHILD OF NATURE ('Jealous Guy') and 'Give Me Some Truth' (on Lennon's second solo album *Imagine*). Another track was a short jam noted as 'Suzy Parker', credited to Lennon–Starkey–Harrison–McCartney.

The first song rehearsed and played/recorded at Apple was Lennon's DIG A PONY (alias 'All I Want Is You'). Later described by its author as garbage, it went through various incarnations before being taped live during the short concert The Beatles gave on their office rooftop on Thursday 30th January 1969 – an event which stopped traffic in surrounding streets and ousted politics to make the lead story on lunchtime TV newscasts.[1] This appearance, arranged at short notice, was a way of fulfilling the group's original plans for a live concert without the stress of painstaking rehearsals and a proper performance. McCartney's brainwave, it obliged the group to straighten up, as a result of which DIG A PONY is a real ensemble performance (with, perhaps, some minor touching up in the studio afterwards). The comically lumbering unison 3/4 riff is undemanding but, considering The Beatles had by then been playing into a stiff winter breeze for thirty minutes, they get their fingers around it with surprising ease and even a hint of swing. Starr halts the count-in to blow his nose, McCartney misses his falsetto harmony on the second chorus, Lennon complains that his fingers are too cold to hold down the chords – but their enjoyment is obvious.[2]

The song itself is inconsequential fun with a lyric celebrating countercultural claims that society's old values and taboos were dead, that life was a game and art a free-for-all, and (especially) that words meant whatever the hell one wished them to. Suspect even in 1967, such whimsy was looking distinctly bedraggled by 1969, but enough people wanted it to be true to ensure that it survived in the minds of progressive educationalists for the next twenty years.

---

[1] Harrison: 'Nobody had ever done that, so it would be interesting to see what happened when we started playing up there, It was a nice little social study. We set up a camera in the Apple reception area, behind a window so nobody could see it, and we filmed people coming in. The police and everybody came in saying, "You can't do that! You've got to stop!" ' (*The Beatles Anthology*, p. 321).

[2] Glyn Johns has suggested (Carr, *The Beatles At The Movies*) that the picture of sullen disintegration painted by the *Let It Be* film is a misrepresentation based on director Michael Lindsay-Hogg's removal of footage giving a contrary impression. However, while The Beatles certainly perked up for the 'rooftop concert', neither Harrison, Starr, nor McCartney ('a horror story') have a good word to say about either the Twickenham or Apple interludes. Much of the ponderous false bonhomie of the group's banter on the surviving tapes of these sessions was clearly put on for the cameras. On the other hand, the exhilarating break-down take of [158] I'VE GOT A FEELING issued on *Anthology 3* proves that, at points during the ten days at Apple, the group's spirits and aspirations were genuinely high.

[158] I'VE GOT A FEELING (Lennon–McCartney)

McCartney vocal, bass; Lennon vocal, rhythm guitar; Harrison
  backing vocal, lead guitar; Starr drums; Billy Preston electric
  piano
Recorded: 22nd, 23rd, 24th, 27th–28th, 30th January, 5th February
  1969.
Producer: George Martin. Engineer: Glyn Johns.
UK release: 8th May 1970 (LP: *Let It Be*)
US release: 18th May 1970 (LP: *Let It Be*)

The first full fifty-fifty Lennon–McCartney collaboration since [96] A
DAY IN THE LIFE, I'VE GOT A FEELING fused two half-songs: (1) a
verse/chorus and ten-bar middle by McCartney concerning his fiancée
Linda Eastman; (2) a sort of 1968 yearbook by Lennon which, fitting
the same bluesy two-chord format, ended up sung simultaneously with
his partner's main line. (The diary style used here reflects both
McCartney's new absorption in his domestic life and Lennon's belief,
given ideological scaffolding by Ono, that all art is inescapably self-
referential.) Like its predecessor, this raunchy mid-tempo rocker was
recorded during the rooftop concert and, again, the performance is
robust and soulful. Part of this is due to the presence, on Hohner
electric piano, of Billy Preston, an Apple signing whom The Beatles
had met during their 1962 dates with Little Richard. Drafted in by
Harrison (who knew that having a gifted outsider on their sessions
would put his colleagues on their mettle), Preston plays discreetly in the
range of Lennon's rhythm guitar on the left channel.

[159] DON'T LET ME DOWN (Lennon–McCartney)

Lennon double-tracked vocal, rhythm guitar; McCartney harmony
  vocal, bass; Harrison lead guitar; Starr drums; Billy Preston
  electric piano
Recorded: 22nd, 28th, 30th January 1969.
Producer: George Martin. Engineer: Glyn Johns.
UK release: 11th April 1969 (B single/GET BACK)
US release: 5th May 1969 (B single/GET BACK)

Distantly derived from Dylan's 'I Shall Be Released' (as recorded by
The Band on their influential 1968 album *Music From Big Pink*), DON'T
LET ME DOWN thriftily shuffles three chords in such a way as to root
the music harmonically against the possibility of collapse admitted in

the chorus;[1] indeed, Lennon liked the rise-and-fall of this sequence so much that he also used it in [181] SUN KING.

Recorded, like [160] GET BACK, on 28th January (the 'rooftop' version of the 30th wasn't issued), DON'T LET ME DOWN is distinguished by a hoarsely passionate Lennon vocal, his melody carrying him symbolically close to the bottom of his voice via a bar which, equally symbolically, bursts out of 4/4 with an extra beat. As in the similarly paced [158] I'VE GOT A FEELING, the group's performance, both tight and fluid, benefits from the presence of Billy Preston, swinging off bluesy roulades and returning to earth on Harrison's calm, Leslie-toned recurring motif. Full of the bubbling octave-leaps which so irritated the older generation of British bassmen, McCartney's exuberant playing amounts to a running commentary on the song, shifting in the middle eight into syncopated counterpoint with Preston's piano while Starr plays the orthodox accents on his bass-drum, mixed left. (Starr's cymbal work is inventive throughout, especially his missed beats on the hi-hat in the final chorus.) With its deep, warm sound and maturely relaxed feeling, this track vies with [179] COME TOGETHER for consideration as the best of Lennon's late-style Beatles records.

[160] GET BACK (Lennon–McCartney)

> **McCartney** vocal, bass; **Lennon** harmony vocal, lead guitar; **Harrison** rhythm guitar; **Starr** drums; **Billy Preston** electric piano
>
> Recorded: 23rd, 27th–28th, 30th January, 5th February 1969, Apple Studios.
> Producer: George Martin. Engineer: Glyn Johns.
> UK release: 11th April 1969 (A single/DON'T LET ME DOWN)
> US release: 5th May 1969 (A single/DON'T LET ME DOWN)

McCartney's GET BACK, which in April became The Beatles' nineteenth British single, seems to have originated as a country blues in the style of Canned Heat's hits 'On The Road Again' and 'Going Up The Country'. (The musical links are tenuous, but McCartney liked both records and busked 'Going Up The Country' in the studio the night before starting work on GET BACK.) The title phrase, coined for the

---

[1] The 'love that has no past' of the lyric was Lennon's devotion to Yoko Ono, which (notionally) ended his mother-fixated early life (see [156]).

abortive concert project (see [157]), unfortunately became linked with a studio jam in which, over a vaguely Caribbean 12-bar, McCartney improvised a satirical pseudo-calypso about Enoch Powell's claim that immigration into the UK would cause a race war.[1] Preserved on bootlegs as 'Commonwealth Song', this squib had nothing to do with GET BACK itself, being merely part of the general self-conscious fooling about. (On one take, McCartney ad-libbed the entire lyric of GET BACK in Reeperbahn German.)[2]

Recorded on 27th January, the album version of the song lacks the polished mix and glamorous reverb of the single version, recorded on the 28th. It ends with an edit from the rooftop concert in which McCartney thanks Starr's wife Maureen for applauding, while the single, originally several minutes longer, simply fades out.[3] (Lennon claimed that every time McCartney sang the line 'Get back to where you once belonged' he looked meaningfully at Ono.) Made in the same afternoon session as its B-side [159] DON'T LET ME DOWN, the single version of GET BACK showcases The Beatles in smoothly grooving R&B mode, McCartney tossing off the lyric between infectious solos by Lennon and Preston. Deploying fewer chords than any Beatles single since [1] LOVE ME DO, its blend of grace, punch, and daftness charmed record buyers enough to shift four million copies worldwide.

---

[1] Powell's 'rivers of blood' speech was made in Birmingham on 20th April 1968 after 10,000 Asians had rushed to enter Britain in advance of the Commonwealth Immigration Bill. This openly racist declamation (which included a reference to 'wide-eyed grinning piccaninnies') coincided with the emergence of the neo-fascist National Front and an outbreak of 'Paki-bashing' in Luton, Leicester, and Bradford. The controversy became pointedly topical during the 'Get Back' sessions when, on 2nd January 1969, it was announced that Britain was to receive a substantial influx of Kenyan Asian refugees.

[2] The lyric of GET BACK – apparently concerning dope-smokers and transsexuals – evolved from random exchanges between McCartney and the others (*Rolling Stone*, 17th May 1969). The album version begins with McCartney murmuring 'Rosetta . . . Sweet Rosetta Martin' instead of 'Lauretta'. He may have been thinking of Earl Hines' 'Rosetta', a version of which he had produced (and played piano on) for fellow Liverpudlians The Fourmost in September 1968. The 'Jo Jo' of the song was probably suggested by Jo Jo Laine, wife of singer-songwriter Denny Laine of The Moody Blues who later joined McCartney in Wings. Tucson, Arizona, was where Linda McCartney studied at the state university following the break-up of her first marriage in 1965.

[3] The 'rooftop' version, the last song in The Beatles' final live appearance, was issued on *Anthology 3*.

[161] Two Of Us *(Lennon–McCartney)*

McCartney vocal, acoustic guitar; **Lennon** vocal, acoustic guitar;
  Harrison lead guitar; **Starr** drums
Recorded: 24th–25th, 31st January 1969, Apple Studios.
Producer: George Martin. Engineer: Glyn Johns.
UK release: 8th May 1970 (LP: *Let It Be*)
US release: 18th May 1970 (LP: *Let It Be*)

Two Of Us (or 'On Our Way Home' as it was called during recording) was, despite its early-sounding simplicity and Lennon's later claim of authorship, a new McCartney song. Supposedly about his relationship with Linda Eastman, the words of its jogging G major verse/chorus fit – they liked to drive out into the country and 'get lost' for a few hours – but, when the key jumps unexpectedly to wistful B flat for its six-bar middle, the lyric seems to be more to do with John and Paul than Paul and Linda. (The lines about chasing paper and getting nowhere are usually taken to refer to The Beatles' contractual troubles, which escalated into a full-blown lawsuit two days after the 'Get Back' sessions ended.) The close harmonies of Two Of Us reminded McCartney and Lennon of their teenage Everly Brothers impersonations and, during the second day's work on it, they broke off to sing 'Bye Bye Love'.

[U162] Teddy Boy *(McCartney)*

McCartney vocal, acoustic guitar; **Harrison** lead guitar; **Starr**
  drums
Recorded: 24th, 28th January 1969, Apple Studios.
Producer: None. Engineer: Glyn Johns.
UK release: 28th October 1996 (2-CD: *Anthology 3*)
US release: 28th October 1996 (2-CD: *Anthology 3*)

McCartney's attempts to proffer this annoyingly whimsical ditty – notable solely for its key change from D major to F sharp major – were sabotaged by Lennon's continuous burble of parody. It eventually surfaced on its author's first solo album (1970).

[161b] Maggie Mae *(trad. arr.*
Lennon–McCartney–Harrison–Starkey)

Lennon vocal, acoustic guitar; **McCartney** vocal, acoustic guitar;
  Harrison lead guitar; **Starr** drums
Recorded: 24th January 1969, Apple Studios.
Producer: None. Engineer: Glyn Johns.
UK release: 8th May 1970 (LP: *Let It Be*)
US release: 18th May 1970 (LP: *Let It Be*)

One of many ad-libs during the 'Get Back' sessions, this coarse
rendition of a ballad about a Liverpool prostitute (an old Beatles warm-
up) was taped during the first day's work on [161] Two Of Us – and,
for subversive reasons, added to the LP after the title track [164]. Other
non-originals tried at Apple during 22nd–31st January included 'Save
the Last Dance for Me' (The Drifters, 1960), 'Bye Bye Love' (see
[161]), [U164b] Rip It Up, [U164c] Shake Rattle And Roll, [44b]
Kansas City, 'Miss Ann' (Little Richard, 1957), 'Lawdy Miss Clawdy'
(Lloyd Price, 1952), [U164d] Blue Suede Shoes, [13b] You Really
Got A Hold On Me, 'Tracks Of My Tears' (Smokey Robinson and
the Miracles, 1965), 'The Walk' (Jimmy McCracklin, 1958), 'Not Fade
Away' (Buddy Holly, 1957/The Rolling Stones, 1964), [U166b]
Mailman Bring Me No More Blues (Buddy Holly, 1961), and [E6d]
Besame Mucho.

[162] Dig It *(Lennon–McCartney–Starkey–Harrison)*

Lennon vocal; **McCartney** piano; **Harrison** lead guitar; **Starr**
  drums; **Billy Preston** Hammond organ
Recorded: 24th, 26th January 1969, Apple Studios.
Producer: George Martin. Engineer: Glyn Johns.
UK release: 8th May 1970 (LP: *Let It Be*)
US release: 18th May 1970 (LP: *Let It Be*)

Featured on *Let It Be* as a group composition, Dig It is an excerpt from
a Lennon-led jam which originally ran for a vastly overprotracted
twelve minutes. Using a standard gospel three-chord sequence, it
catches him sardonically 'preaching' in nonsensical free association, but
the mood isn't happy enough to make it work. As with so much of the
ad-libbing during the 'Get Back' sessions (e.g., 'Commonwealth Song',
[160]), the joviality is forced and the atmosphere one of slapdash self-
congratulation. Concealing their unease by facetiously playing up for
the cameras, The Beatles did a lot of tiresome bantering during this
doomed enterprise but little substantial work.

[163] **FOR YOU BLUE** *(Harrison)*

Harrison vocal, acoustic guitar; **McCartney** piano; **Lennon** lap
  steel guitar; **Starr** drums
Recorded: 25th January 1969, Apple Studios.
Producer: George Martin. Engineer: Glyn Johns.
UK release: 8th May 1970 (LP: *Let It Be*)
US release: 18th May 1970 (LP: *Let It Be*)

Dedicated to Patti Harrison, this forgettable twelve-bar in D was taped
in six takes between work on [161] TWO OF US and [164] LET IT BE.
(Mississippi slide guitarist Elmore James, whom Harrison amusedly
invokes during Lennon's studious solo, revolutionised the Delta blues
style during the Fifties with numbers like 'Dust My Broom'.)

[164] **LET IT BE** *(Lennon–McCartney)*

McCartney vocal, backing vocal, piano, maracas; **Lennon** bass;
  Harrison backing vocal, lead guitar; **Starr** drums; **Billy Preston**
  organ, electric piano; **Uncredited** 2 trumpets, 2 trombones,
  tenor sax, cellos
Recorded: 25th–26th, 31st January 1969, Apple Studios; 30th April
  1969, 4th January 1970, Abbey Road 2.
Producers: George Martin/Chris Thomas. Engineers: Glyn Johns/
  Jeff Jarratt/Phil McDonald.
UK release: 6th March 1970 (A single/YOU KNOW MY NAME
  [LOOK UP THE NUMBER])
US release: 11th March 1970 (A single/YOU KNOW MY NAME
  [LOOK UP THE NUMBER])

Behind the motivator of The Beatles' erratic final years was a hurt and
worried man. McCartney threw everything into keeping the group
alive, but the price of his endless energy was a lack of instinct for when
to leave well alone. Half-afraid (as they all were) of Lennon's newly
revived sarcasm, he was alternately patronising and insensitive to
Harrison and Starr, finding it difficult to say anything to them that
didn't cause offence. During summer 1968, when sessions for *The
Beatles* were especially hostile, he would lie awake at night in a state of
insecurity very different from the light-toned charmer he liked to
present in public. In the end, he had an impressive dream in which his
dead mother Mary appeared to him and told him not to get so worked
up about things – to let them be. Like so many of his experiences, this
quickly turned itself into a song.

With its air of supernal consolation and universally understandable
lyric (naturally taken by many to refer to the Virgin Mary), LET IT BE
has achieved a popularity well out of proportion to its artistic weight.

Leaning further to rock than pop, its four-square gospel rhythm, religiose suspensions, and general harmonic monotony offer complacent uplift rather than revelation – [137] HEY JUDE without the musical and emotional release. Lennon made no secret of his aversion to the Catholic sanctimony he heard in this track and during the 31st January session cruelly asked McCartney 'Are we supposed to giggle during the solo?' (He was the moving force behind the mischievous sequencing of the *Let It Be* album, where the song is bracketed between him as a small boy piping 'Now we'd like to do Hark the Angels Come' and a ribald knees-up about a Lime Street whore [161b].)[1]

Harrison added a Leslie-toned guitar solo[2] to take 27 of LET IT BE on 30th April, after which, like most of the January 1969 material, it was left to accumulate dust for the rest of the year. Exhumed at the beginning of 1970, it was given a second, more organised solo with fuzz-tone, some high harmonised backing vocals by McCartney and Harrison, extra drums, maracas, and a George Martin score for brass and cellos. These extra instruments, virtually inaudible on the single version of the track, are mixed higher on the album, where Harrison's second solo is preferred.

[U164b] RIP IT UP *(Blackwell-Marascalco)/*
[U164c] SHAKE, RATTLE AND ROLL *(Calhoun)/*
[U164d] BLUE SUEDE SHOES *(Perkins)*

> **Lennon** vocal, guitar (?); **McCartney** vocal, piano; **Harrison** bass
>   (?); **Starr** drums; **Billy Preston** Hammond organ
> Recorded: 26th January 1969, Apple Studios.
> Producer: George Martin. Engineer: Glyn Johns.
> UK release: 28th October 1996 (2-CD: *Anthology 3*)
> US release: 28th October 1996 (2-CD: *Anthology 3*)

Rock-and-roll revival as displacement activity: a would-be-jolly medley jammed on autopilot in a directionless moment during the later stages of the 'Get Back' sessions. The original versions were respectively by Little Richard (1956), Bill Haley and 'his' Comets (1954), and Carl Perkins (1955).

---

[1] He believed the song to be an imitation of Simon and Garfunkel's gigantic hit 'Bridge Over Troubled Water', which it displaced from the American No. 1 position in April 1970. In fact, 'Bridge Over Troubled Water' was written a year *after* LET IT BE in summer 1969.

[2] This was played on the rosewood Telecaster presented to Harrison by Fender in 1968 and used by him throughout the filmed 'Get Back' sessions.

[165] THE LONG AND WINDING ROAD *(Lennon–McCartney)*

McCartney vocal, piano; **Lennon** bass; **Starr** drums; **Harrison**
 guitar; **Uncredited** 18 violins, 4 violas, four cellos, harp, 3
 trumpets, 3 trombones, 2 guitarists, 14 female voices
Recorded: 26th, 31st January 1969, 1st April 1970, Abbey Road 1.
Producers: George Martin/Phil Spector. Engineers: Glyn Johns/
 Peter Bown.
UK release: 8th May 1970 (LP: *Let It Be*)
US release: 18th May 1970 (LP: *Let It Be*)

Written on the same day as [164] LET IT BE,[1] THE LONG AND
WINDING ROAD was designed as a standard to be taken up by
mainstream balladeers.[2] (McCartney sent a demo of it to various
candidates, including Cilla Black and Tom Jones.) Sporadically tried out
at the Apple sessions, it was left undeveloped until Lennon invited Phil
Spector to salvage the January 1969 material a year later.[3] Spector has
been generally slammed for the way he treated certain tracks,
smothering them in orchestrations which obscure the group and
contradict the original concept of an 'honest' recording without
overdubs. In this case, while his solution is undeniably tasteless, he had
no choice but to cover the original tape with *something*, since it was
little more than a run-through with a good McCartney vocal.

Featuring only its author on piano and Lennon on bass, the basic
take of THE LONG AND WINDING ROAD is a demo, and a provisional
one at that.[4] In particular, it features some atrocious bass-playing by
Lennon, prodding clumsily around as if uncertain of the harmonies and
making many comical mistakes.[5] Whatever else one may say about his
production, Spector's feat in diverting attention from how badly played
the original track is can only be accounted a success. Yet his overdub
session, a stormy affair on 1st April 1970, took place in Abbey Road's
Studio 1 with McCartney, only minutes away, available to re-do the
bass part if asked. Why wasn't he?

In fact, neither McCartney nor George Martin knew that the 'Get
Back' tapes were being prepared for release, Lennon having taken it
upon himself to off-load the task to Spector after the latter had

---

[1] Leigh, p. 74.
[2] McCartney had Ray Charles in mind when he wrote it (Miles, op. cit., p. 539).
[3] McCartney now blames Allen Klein for this (*Mojo*, October 1996).
[4] Stripped of its orchestration, the original track can be heard on *Anthology 3*.
[5] Recurring wrong notes at 0:28, 2:10 and 3:07; mis-strikes at 2:39 and 2:52;
drop-outs at 2:59 and 3:14; a fumble at 0:19; a vague *glissando* at 1:03; a missed final
push at 3:26. (One can hear McCartney grin at his partner's incompetence at 1:59.)

impressed him with his production for the Plastic Ono Band's 'Instant Karma' on 27th January. The truth is that The Beatles' creative and financial wranglings had by then torn them apart and they hated each other. Lennon knew that if McCartney had realised THE LONG AND WINDING ROAD was being worked on, he would have stopped the whole *Let It Be* project – or at least taken over the session and produced the song his way (i.e., properly). Lennon's impatient indifference to the maintenance of The Beatles' production standards is, in this case, indefensible.[1] Shortly before his death in 1980, he accused McCartney of having treated Lennon songs with less care than his own – and certainly McCartney's improvisatory bass playing on his partner's tracks often contrasts with the careful lines created for his own material. Yet McCartney left no technical blemish on any Beatles tracks, whoever wrote them. By comparison, Lennon's crude bass playing on THE LONG AND WINDING ROAD, though largely accidental, amounts to sabotage when presented as finished work.

When McCartney heard Spector's patch-up job on his song, he was understandably livid, tried unsuccessfully to block it, and, having ensured that his solo album would be released ahead of it, promptly announced that he'd left the group. All this is customarily given as evidence of his high-handed egomania, yet while there was blame on his side, Lennon's behaviour over this track and the whole *Let It Be* affair was appalling. Even the gentlemanly George Martin was scathing about Richard Hewson's orchestration for THE LONG AND WINDING ROAD which, with its mushy wash of sound, flew in the face of the etched, incisive, and essentially anti-romantic idiom Martin had painstakingly created for The Beatles during the previous four years. Whether he could have rescued the original track (or would even have considered trying) is another question. Like the tinkling cymbals of Starr's overdub, Hewson's Mantovani strings and Home Service choir are there mainly to fool the listener's ear.

In the event, THE LONG AND WINDING ROAD was so touching in its fatalistic regret, and so perfect as a downbeat finale to The Beatles' career, that it couldn't fail, however badly dressed. Issued in America as the group's last single, it rose to No. 1 as a double A-side with

---

[1] He had, after all, been a prime supporter of the no-overdubs approach to the original sessions, telling George Martin – who had put so much effort into [93] STRAWBERRY FIELDS FOREVER and [116] I AM THE WALRUS – that he wanted none of his 'jiggery-pokery'.

Harrison's [163] FOR YOU BLUE.[1] ([186] I Me Mine would have been a more truthful choice.)

With its heartbreaking suspensions and yearning backward glances from the sad wisdom of the major key to the lost loves and illusions of the minor, THE LONG AND WINDING ROAD is one of the most beautiful things McCartney ever wrote. Its words, too, are among his most poignant, particularly the reproachful lines of the brief four-bar middle section. A shame Lennon didn't listen more generously.

[166] ONE AFTER 909 *(Lennon–McCartney)*

Lennon vocal, lead guitar; **McCartney** vocal, bass; **Harrison** rhythm guitar; **Starr** drums; **Billy Preston** electric piano
Recorded: 28th–30th January 1969, Apple Studios.
Producer: George Martin. Engineer: Glyn Johns.
UK release: 8th May 1970 (LP: *Let It Be*)
US release: 18th May 1970 (LP: *Let It Be*)

First tried out at the session for [10] FROM ME TO YOU on 5th March 1963 [U12], this rough-and-ready train-blues in B was written, largely by Lennon, at McCartney's house soon after their meeting at the Woolton garden fête in summer 1957. Rolled out again for the 'Get Back' project, it was stoked for a couple of days and let rip at the rooftop concert – a raggedly happy exercise in skiffle nostalgia with Harrison drolly mixing Carl Perkins and Eric Clapton.

[U166b] MAILMAN BRING ME NO MORE BLUES
(Roberts–Katz–Clayton)

Lennon vocal, guitar; **McCartney** vocal, bass; **Harrison** guitar; **Starr** drums
Recorded: 29th January 1969, Apple Studios.
Producer: George Martin. Engineer: Glyn Johns.
UK release: 28th October 1996 (2-CD: *Anthology 3*)
US release: 28th October 1996 (2-CD: *Anthology 3*)

Busked during the 'Get Back' sessions at Apple in January 1969, this Buddy Holly number had been in The Beatles' act between 1961 and 1962, having come to their attention as the B-side of [46d] WORDS OF LOVE, issued in 1957. As a sparse 12-bar with a rudimentary lyric,

---

[1] This was The Beatles' twentieth US No. 1 – more than any other act. (Elvis Presley had seventeen, The Supremes twelve.)

MAILMAN BRING ME NO MORE BLUES depends entirely on quality of performance. Holly's version, liberally infested with his trademark vocal hiccuping, is a faintly engaging pop throwaway. The Beatles' slower and sadder rendition is a frustratingly casual glimpse of something that might have been very effective had they been in a sufficiently creative mood to do a little work on it.

Playing his stripped Epiphone Casino (see note, p. 285), Lennon turns up the tremolo on a Fender Twin Reverb, creating a dusty, wavering, disconsolate sound. (Harrison may be playing through a Leslie, producing a similar timbre.) With Lennon's doleful vocal, the sound evokes a dowdy small-town melancholia which anticipates the mid-Western realism of Ry Cooder and J. J. Cale. Sadly this was a one-off, developed no further before The Beatles switched restlessly to a revamp of [E6d] BESAME MUCHO.

[167] I WANT YOU (SHE'S SO HEAVY) *(Lennon–McCartney)*

> **Lennon** vocal, harmony vocals, lead guitars, organ, Moog synthesiser; **Harrison** harmony vocals, lead guitars; **McCartney** harmony vocals, bass; **Starr** drums, congas; **Billy Preston** Hammond organ
> Recorded: 22nd February, Trident Studios; 18th, 20th April, 8th, 11th August 1969, Abbey Road 2/3.
> Producers: Glyn Johns/Chris Thomas/George Martin. Engineers: Barry Sheffield/Jeff Jarratt/Tony Clark/Geoff Emerick/Phil McDonald.
> UK release: 26th September 1969 (LP: *Abbey Road*)
> US release: 1st October 1969 (LP: *Abbey Road*)

The day after the rooftop concert, the group recorded three songs unsuited to recital in a moderate gale ([161], [164], [165]) before winding the project up in some relief. An ignominious failure which shook their faith in their collective judgement, it had pushed them to the verge of collapse.[1] Only isolated flashes of inspiration – the 28th January session for [159] DON'T LET ME DOWN and [160] GET BACK, the rooftop concert itself – had alleviated a miserable month; and worse was to come. Two days later, a fatal rift in the group's relationships opened when Lennon, Harrison, and Starr asked The Rolling Stones' American manager Allen Klein to take over The Beatles' affairs.

---

[1] The strain of their purist no-overdub policy showed on 31st January. At the end of a promising take of LET IT BE, Lennon joked 'OK, let's track it' (i.e., thicken the texture with overdubs) adding, sarcastically, 'You bounder, you cheat!'

McCartney, who favoured Linda Eastman's family firm of management consultants, immediately opened a court battle which long outlasted the remainder of The Beatles' career. While they tried to distance themselves from all this with Liverpudlian irony – at business meetings, the others took to asking McCartney's solicitor why he hadn't brought his bass guitar – the process gradually took its toll on their creativity. Yet they had been together too long and too closely to let it go that easily. Beneath their often viciously hurtful attacks on each other, The Beatles were still psychologically locked together at a deep level.[1] Things would have to get much nastier before they finally fell apart. Meanwhile, refusing to admit defeat by returning to EMI's orbit, yet unable to use Apple until Alex Mardas's mess had been cleaned up (see [157]), they reconvened at Trident on 22nd February to start work on what became their deceptively sunny swansong *Abbey Road*.

Among nine Beatles originals tried out but taken no further during the Apple sessions of 22nd–31st January[2] was the present brutally uncompromising Lennon creation – about as far from the plaintive, sentimental vein of McCartney's recent ballads as it was possible to get. With its bluesy A minor tune recalling Mel Tormé's 1962 hit 'Comin' Home Baby', I WANT YOU goes vocally even lower than Lennon's previous paean to Yoko Ono [159]: from a falsetto high C to a growling baritone A. Sharing more than an urge to plumb the depths, these songs are, in effect, two halves of a single statement: 'Don't let me down' because 'I want you'. Lennon's passion for Ono had shaken him to the core. His long dreamed-of erotic mother (see [156]) had finally arrived and the reality was almost too much for him. Sexually addicted to her, he was helplessly dependent, a predicament grindingly explicit in his chord sequence: the sickening plunge from E7 to B flat 7; the augmented A that drags his head up to make him go through it all again; the hammering flat ninth that collapses, spent, on the song's insatiable D minor arpeggio. Nightmarishly tormented, this is a musical

---

[1] Pride, too, played its part. When, during the 18th April session for I WANT YOU, engineer Jeff Jarratt asked Harrison to turn down a bit, the guitarist, who had twice 'left' the group in high dudgeon, replied icily: 'You don't talk to a Beatle like that.' Similarly, at the end of the take of [157] DIG A PONY issued on *Anthology 3*, an ironic voice from the control room congratulates the band on getting the end right, to which Lennon drily responds: 'Yer not talkin' to Ricky an' the Red Streaks, y'know'.

[2] The others: [1] LOVE ME DO, [122] LADY MADONNA, [171] OH! DARLING, [172] OCTOPUS'S GARDEN, [182] MEAN MR MUSTARD, [184] SHE CAME IN THROUGH THE BATHROOM WINDOW, [U162] TEDDY BOY (see McCartney's first solo album), and 'Isn't It A Pity' (see Harrison's *All Things Must Pass*).

tryst with a succubus. No wonder the lyric consists of the same phrase over and over again. Lennon is literally obsessed.

The surprising thing is that this song, the most emotionally extreme statement on any Beatles record, appealed strongly to all four of them. One might have expected Starr to enjoy it for its Latin groove and the switches of time-signature that place him in a crucial role. Harrison, too, would obviously have approved of the expressive chord sequence, so akin to his own tastes. (He worked closely with Lennon on the track, spending hours overdubbing the unison guitar riff and lending him the Moog synthesiser he'd brought back from California at the end of 1968.[1]) McCartney, on the other hand, scarcely seems the type to have revelled in what The Band's craftsmanlike Robbie Robertson dismissed in a contemporary *Rolling Stone* review as 'noisy shit'; yet his bass-playing is genuinely excited, and on one take during the first day's recording he actually took over the lead vocal.

Day two of work on I WANT YOU saw the surreptitious abandonment of the group's recently adopted regime of 'honest' recording (see [157]), a composite being edited together from the three best segments of thirty-five (!) takes from the first day. After that, the mixing and overdubbing process grew as tortuous as the song itself, taking longer than any other Beatles track (nearly six months). Was it worth it?

Out-and-out *rock* Beatles, this is the antithesis of their light pop touch and another of their attempts at the new heavy style (see [134]). Earnest in concept, it is, in the end, bathetic in effect, its fourth reprise of A minor offering only anti-climax, and the final fifteen repeats of its 12/8 arpeggio figure failing, at the cost of high tape-hiss and considerable tedium, to acquire the massiveness Lennon intended. While his simultaneous performance on voice and guitar has power and feeling, he fumbles too many notes to maintain the listener's belief. McCartney's pitching and yawing bass in the verse/chorus is appropriate, but his *glissandi* in the arpeggio section take the bottom out of the sound. All told, I WANT YOU is a bold lunge at something seriously adult which, perhaps doomed by its own desperation, doesn't come off.

---

[1] Lennon used the Moog's 'white noise' generator for the wind effects at the end of the track.

[U168] ALL THINGS MUST PASS *(Harrison)*

Harrison vocal, double-tracked electric guitar
Recorded: 25th February 1969, Abbey Road (studio unknown).
Producer: George Harrison. Engineer: Ken Scott.
UK release: 28th October 1996 (2-CD: *Anthology 3*)
US release: 28th October 1996 (2-CD: *Anthology 3*)

On his twenty-sixth birthday, George Harrison slipped into Abbey Road to tape this demo of what became the title track of his first solo album in 1970. He had spent part of the previous November at Big Pink, the Woodstock home studio where Dylan and The Band had based themselves since late 1966, and ALL THINGS MUST PASS shows a distinct influence from that quarter. The wisest song never recorded by The Beatles, it was (like 'Isn't It A Pity') put forward during the 'Get Back' sessions, but ignored.[1]

[168] THE BALLAD OF JOHN AND YOKO
(Lennon–McCartney)

Lennon vocal, lead guitars, acoustic guitar; **McCartney** harmony
 vocal, bass, drums, piano, maracas
Recorded: 14th April 1969, Abbey Road 3.
Producer: George Martin. Engineer: Geoff Emerick.
UK release: 30th May 1969 (B single/OLD BROWN SHOE)
US release: 4th June 1969 (B single/OLD BROWN SHOE)

Among Lennon's assortment of contradictions was a tension between self-absorption and sympathy for the underdog. Since this sympathy was based on a projection of the pessimistic side of his own self-image (John the orphan, the misfit, the reject), it might be seen as no different from his self-absorption; yet it *was* distinct in as much as it motivated some gentleness during times when distrust, aggression, and sarcasm were dominant. The softness cultivated in him by Yoko Ono had always been there, seeking expression; indeed, it was awoken before he met her by LSD. With its beatific impersonality, acid had a profound impact on the outlook of a generation, and Lennon, who took it in enormous quantities, was one of its most influential converts. Among other things, what the drug did for him was to elevate his psychologically conditioned sympathy for the underdog into a universal concern

---

[1] According to Mark Lewisohn (personal communication), 'Isn't It A Pity', which Harrison later recorded twice for *All Things Must Pass*, was also offered for *Revolver*.

for love and peace which, striking him with the force of conversion, quickly inflated into messianism (see [U126]).

Equally contradictory, Yoko Ono balanced a hard-headed, even heartless percipience with a fey narcissism which, held in check by her intellectual peers in the New York avant-garde scene, ran riot once liberated by Lennon's intuitive and untutored indiscipline. While exchanging comfort and confirmation, the pair brought out the worst in each other, he inadvertently diverting her from the sharp Oriental Dadaism of her early work into a fatuous fugue of legs, bottoms, and bags, she encouraging him to believe that orderly meaning was a male hang-up and that the secret of peace was to be sought in pure sensation and guiltless sex. Since she was his intellectual superior, most of the influence ran from her to him; and, since he was her artistic superior, this influence streamed straight into the public domain through his music. Their activities accordingly became unguardedly naive, their gesture of letting their pants down on the cover of *Two Virgins* showing how far intelligent people can infantilise themselves by pretending to believe what at heart they don't. Under the ostensibly selfless holy foolery they indulged in during 1968-70 was a core of exhibitionistic self-promotion. Behaving as if they had personally invented peace, they jetted round the world in first-class seats selling it at third-rate media-events. This was arrogant as well as silly, and the news media's derision, of which THE BALLAD OF JOHN AND YOKO self-righteously complains, was not only inevitable but, in the main, justified.

Of all the dangerous ideas Ono unloaded on her spouse around this time, the most damaging was her belief that all art is about the artist and no one else. Serving to confirm Lennon's self-absorption, this also torpedoed his universalism, and it was as a man struggling to resolve this exacerbation of his lifelong emotional contradictions that he reeled from heroin to Primal Therapy to Maoism and finally to drink during the next three years. Otherwise scathingly honest, he unwittingly put himself into a position in which he was obliged to defend things that, deep down, he cared nothing about. Uncompromising as ever, he threw himself into this trap with total commitment, not only refusing to draw a line between his public and private life but going out of his way to personalise everything that happened in his vicinity, a self-centredness which could hardly avoid occasionally degenerating into paranoia, as THE BALLAD OF JOHN AND YOKO demonstrates. Indeed, so outrageously egocentric is this song that it's difficult to know whether to deplore its vanity or admire its *chutzpah* in so candidly promoting Self to artistic central place.

Lennon's new autobiographical output soon grew too specific for inclusion in The Beatles' *oeuvre* and by summer 1969 he had done the decent thing and coined an extramural pseudonym: The Plastic Ono Band. Written before this, THE BALLAD OF JOHN AND YOKO fell to The Beatles to deal with and, with Starr booked on *The Magic Christian* and Harrison out of the country, it was down to McCartney to accommodate his partner's urgent need to express himself. Despite his wryness about Lennon's messianic excesses – asked for a sleevenote for *Two Virgins*, McCartney had obliged with 'When two great Saints meet, it is a humbling experience' – he did not hesitate to help, offering him the same unqualified support he had during Lennon's bad trip in 1967 (see note, p. 242) and even mucking in with the writing. Considering the bitterness of the 'Get Back' sessions eight weeks earlier and the fact that the two were now in legal dispute, this is remarkable; yet their friendship was still strong, albeit under strain.[1]

With Lennon's guitar phrases mocking his self-pity, this is a tolerably engaging rocker using a standard period riff, capped with a vintage Beatles sixth. Musically simple, it is enthusiastically played and, like its B-side [169], mixed with a big bass end. The mostly self-explanatory words[2] caused trouble in America where the reference to crucifixion prompted radio bans and an optimal chart position of 8. (Britain loyally sent the record to No. 1 for a fortnight.)

[169] OLD BROWN SHOE *(Harrison)*

Harrison vocal, guitars, organ; **McCartney** backing vocal, piano, bass; **Lennon** backing vocal; **Starr** drums
Recorded: 16th, 18th April 1969.
Producers: George Martin/Chris Thomas. Engineer: Jeff Jarratt.
UK release: 30th May 1969 (B single/THE BALLAD OF JOHN AND YOKO)
US release: 4th June 1969 (B single/THE BALLAD OF JOHN AND YOKO)

Demoed by Harrison at Abbey Road along with [U168] ALL THINGS MUST PASS and [170] SOMETHING on 25th February,[3] OLD BROWN

---

[1] Reconstructed from the multitrack, Lewisohn's account of the recording (*Sessions*, p. 173) paints a sunnier picture than does Hertsgaard (*A Day in the Life*, p. 293), who finds the off-mike banter between Lennon and McCartney 'forced, polite' and their attempts at humour 'subdued, even hollow'.
[2] The acorns in the fifth verse refer to the Lennons' 'plant an acorn for peace' campaign in which they posted acorns to all the world leaders they could think of. (See Chronology, 15th June 1968.)
[3] See *Anthology 3*.

SHOE opens with his sharpest lyric couplet and develops into one of his most forceful pieces. The hood-eyed spirit of Dylan presides over the song's dusty shuffle-beat[1] and ironic words, though the chord sequence, rising and falling from C to A minor via a supercharging A flat, is surprising and graphic in Harrison's patent style. A tightly-structured solo with an American flavour to its final bars is matched by a confident vocal, mixed too low. Featuring a powerful bass sound (created by Harrison tracking McCartney's line with his lead), this is an archetypal B-side from an era when B-sides were worth flipping a single for.

[170] SOMETHING *(Harrison)*

> **Harrison** double-tracked vocal, lead guitar, handclaps; **McCartney** backing vocals, bass, handclaps; **Lennon** guitar; **Starr** drums, handclaps; **Billy Preston** Hammond organ; **Uncredited** 12 violins, 4 violas, 4 cellos, 1 double-bass
> Recorded: 16th April, 2nd May 1969, Abbey Road 2; 5th May, Olympic Sound Studios; 11th, 16th July, Abbey Road 2; 15th August 1969, Abbey Road 1.
> Producers: George Martin/Chris Thomas. Engineers: Jeff Jarratt/ Glyn Johns/Phil McDonald/Geoff Emerick, Phil McDonald.
> UK release: 26th September 1969 (LP: *Abbey Road*)
> US release: 1st October 1969 (LP: *Abbey Road*)

Harrison and Apple publicist Derek Taylor had a standing joke. Whenever either of them had an idea, they would quip 'This could be the big one'. SOMETHING, written in mid-1968 on a piano in Abbey Road during a break from work on *The Beatles* [147], really did become the big one for Harrison. Hurried out as an unscheduled single, it sold only respectably, but it did its business as a vehicle for other artists, eventually acquiring more cover versions than any other Beatles number except [59] YESTERDAY. No less a luminary than Frank Sinatra described SOMETHING, somewhat extravagantly, as 'the greatest love song of the past fifty years'.

According to Harrison, the warmly yielding semitonal sigh of the verse/chorus, its words absent-mindedly taken from the title of a James Taylor song, came easily. The middle eight, on the other hand, had to wait till he found his way up to A major rather than back down to his initial C – and, by then, his lyric inspiration appears to have slackened.

---

[1] If the song was written on piano, it seems likely to have begun as an experiment in ska rhythm.

(This is the part of Sinatra's version where his maturity is incongruous with what are, in truth, callow sentiments.) Yet the song contains, in its second verse, its author's finest lines – at once deeper and more elegant than almost anything his colleagues ever wrote.

Made, after a false start on 16th April, in five widely separated sessions, SOMETHING was for some while nearly eight minutes long, owing to an extended instrumental appendage, later removed.[1] During this process there was plenty of time for second thoughts, and Starr and McCartney took the opportunity to add to or improve their parts. (Starr's is precisely right; McCartney's, while full of beautiful ideas, is too fussily extemporised.[2]) Harrison, meanwhile, fretted over his guitar solo, in the end redoing it during the session for the album's orchestral overdubs on 15th August, even then remaining unsatisfied with the result.[3] Conceded by Lennon to be the best song on *Abbey Road*, SOMETHING is the acme of Harrison's achievement as a writer. Lacking his usual bitter harmonies, it deploys a key-structure of classical grace and panoramic effect, supported by George Martin's sympathetic viola/cello countermelody and delicate pizzicato violins through the middle eight. If McCartney wasn't jealous, he should have been.

---

[1] Described by Mark Lewisohn as 'a long, repetitious and somewhat rambling, piano-led four-note instrumental fade-out', this passage – half of which was cut on 11th July, and the rest during one of the remaining sessions – was in fact an unrelated doodle led by Lennon on piano (not, as in *The Complete Beatles Recording Sessions*, Billy Preston, who was on Hammond organ). The musical substance was the four-chord riff of 'Remember', later recorded for *John Lennon/Plastic Ono Band*. Lennon began playing it after the final chord of SOMETHING, and the others uncertainly joined in, a bemused McCartney mainly on the keynote (E). Lennon's piano track for SOMETHING was wiped on 11th July.

[2] This is probably the bass part which caused a disgruntled Harrison some years later to remark that he'd rather have Willie Weeks play bass for him than Paul McCartney.

[3] Since he had played the same solo, note for note, on 5th May, the problem can only have been one of guitar sound.

[171] OH! DARLING *(Lennon–McCartney)*

McCartney vocal, backing vocals, bass, guitar; **Lennon** backing
  vocals, piano; **Harrison** backing vocals, guitar, synthesiser; **Starr**
  drums
Recorded: 20th April, Abbey Road 3; 26th April, Abbey Road 2;
  17th–18th, 22nd July, 11th August 1969, Abbey Road 3.
Producers: Chris Thomas/George Martin. Engineers: Jeff Jarratt/Phil
  McDonald.
UK release: 26th September 1969 (LP: *Abbey Road*)
US release: 1st October 1969 (LP: *Abbey Road*)

Tried out during the 'Get Back' sessions *(Anthology 3)*, OH! DARLING is
spoof doo-wop complete with clink-clink piano and Fifties saturation
echo on its middle eight. As such, it may have been prompted by Frank
Zappa's similar exercises in style on *Ruben and The Jets* (1968).[1]
Though the basic track – especially the lolloping drums – sounds like a
solo effort by McCartney, it appears to have been a genuine group
performance. Not having exercised his Little Richard screaming voice
for four years (see [58]), McCartney was careful to break himself in
gently, coming in for several mornings to do a loosener on the vocal
before he finally let rip. To judge from the punchy bass/bass-drum
synchronisation, he also redid his instrumental part, probably tracking it
in the style of [169] OLD BROWN SHOE. Connoisseurs of doo-wop
harmony vocals will enjoy the track's exquisite backing parts, sadly
underplayed in the mix.

---

[1] Despite Zappa's send-up of the *Sgt. Pepper* cover with The Mothers of
Invention's third album *We're Only In It For The Money*, both Lennon and
McCartney were established fans. McCartney once described *Sgt. Pepper* as 'our *Freak
Out!*', while Lennon leapt at the chance of performing with The Mothers in 1971
(*Some Time In New York City*, 1972).

[172] OCTOPUS'S GARDEN *(Starkey)*

Starr vocal, drums, percussion, effects; Harrison backing vocals,
  lead guitar, synthesiser; McCartney backing vocals, bass, piano;
  Lennon guitar
Recorded: 26th April, Abbey Road 2; 29th April, 17th–18th July
  1969, Abbey Road 3.
Producers: Chris Thomas/George Martin. Engineers: Jeff Jarratt/Phil
  McDonald.
UK release: 26th September 1969 (LP: *Abbey Road*)
US release: 1st October 1969 (LP: *Abbey Road*)

When Starr temporarily left The Beatles on 22nd August 1968 (see
[142]), he took his family on holiday to Sardinia where, chatting with a
fisherman, he was fascinated to learn that octopuses roam the seabed
picking up stones and shiny objects with which they build gardens.
After the stormy air of Abbey Road, the idea of living under the sea
must have held a certain attraction, and Starr forthwith set about
writing this, his second song. A commonplace tune in country and
western style, it was fondly welcomed back to Abbey Road along with
its author some days later, and worked on a little by Starr and Harrison
during the 'Get Back' sessions. With a spirited guitar solo and Starr's
usual vocal brand of forlorn good cheer, OCTOPUS'S GARDEN glides by
without drawing attention to itself – a poor man's [88] YELLOW
SUBMARINE.

[173] YOU NEVER GIVE ME YOUR MONEY
(Lennon–McCartney)

McCartney multitracked vocal, backing vocals, pianos, bass, guitars,
  wind-chimes, tape-loops; Lennon backing vocals, guitars;
  Harrison backing vocals, guitars; Starr drums, tambourine
Recorded: 6th May, Olympic Sound Studios; 1st July, Abbey Road
  2; 15th July, Abbey Road 3; 30th–31st July, Abbey Road 2; 5th
  August 1969, Abbey Road 3.
Producer: George Martin. Engineers: Glyn Johns/Phil McDonald,
  Geoff Emerick.
UK release: 26th September 1969 (LP: *Abbey Road*)
US release: 1st October 1969 (LP: *Abbey Road*)

McCartney's first post-'Get Back' composition reflects the upheavals of
February 1969. The Beatles' fall-out over money provided a metaphor
for their dissolving personal relationships, each harbouring an aggrieved
sense of being owed something he was no longer getting.[1] In

---

[1] McCartney has said (*Mojo*, October 1996; Miles, op. cit., p. 556) that he was

McCartney's case, the others' beef was that his middle-class reflex of adopting a diplomatic face served to repress his emotions, leaving him with little idea of how *they* felt. While there was justice in this, it was equally true that without his get-up-and-go, prolific ideas, and organisational gifts, The Beatles would have collapsed after *Sgt. Pepper* (possibly even before it). While McCartney was lecturing them about how to play their instruments, it was all too easy to forget that he had strong feelings for them and was vulnerable to their dry sniping. As a creative/commercial entity, The Beatles meant more to him than to Lennon and Harrison, who, tired of pop artifice, were inclining towards rock with its wider opportunities for self-expression (and self-indulgence). For McCartney, the group was a make-believe world in which he could be forever young. His colleagues, feeling too old for such frivolity, sourly declined to play shadows to his Peter Pan.

Acting as both The Beatles' musical director and a stand-in manager for them during their final three years, McCartney was deeply shaken when the others drafted in the streetfighting Allen Klein to claw their finances back into shape. Only 'Dear Friend', his song of shocked hurt at Lennon's venomous post-Beatles attacks on him, conveys a sadder reproach than the opening verses of YOU NEVER GIVE ME YOUR MONEY in which, a year ahead of Lennon, he acknowledges that the dream is over. To anyone who loves The Beatles, the bittersweet nostalgia of this music is hard to hear without a tear in the eye. Here, an entire era – the idealistic, innocent Sixties – is bravely bidden farewell.

Having regretted this loss, the song shows us what it was all about in a quick kaleidoscopic *resumé* of the group's ambiguous blend of sadness, subversive laughter, and resolute optimism. Everything hangs

---

thinking of Allen Klein rather than the other Beatles when he wrote this part of the lyric. This contradicts standard accounts of the period, when, disgruntled from the 'Get Back' debacle and locked in a complex business battle for NEMS, McCartney and his colleagues were on edgy terms. In order not to face this, he adopted a business-as-usual approach, working at Harrison's sessions with Jackie Lomax and attending mixes for the 'Get Back' material. In this way, he avoided confronting Allen Klein until 9th May when a session at Olympic dissolved into a squabble exacerbated by the arrival of Klein bearing an ultimatum on behalf of his company ABKCO. McCartney refused to play ball and the other Beatles left in a huff. This, though, can hardly have inspired the tender opening verses of YOU NEVER GIVE ME YOUR MONEY (not least because the song had been taped three days before and was clearly written some time earlier). McCartney's recollection of events thirty years later may be tinted by a desire to wish away bad memories of early 1969, when he was isolated within a group he loved and had fought hard for. (As with Lennon, his view of The Beatles can be self-exculpatingly selective. After all, it was not Lennon but McCartney who, seeking to renegotiate his EMI contract, first made an approach to Klein in November 1966.)

on the words 'nowhere to go', arrived at ruefully but instantly spun round and seen from the other side: as freedom, as opportunity. The Beatles' future may be gone, but McCartney is determined to salvage their spirit, and that of the Sixties, for *his* future. YOU NEVER GIVE ME YOUR MONEY marks the psychological opening of his solo career.

At this transitional moment, The Beatles' sense of occasion rallied for a final fling. If, as they must all have known, this was to be their last album together, they would do the appropriate Sixties thing and end in celebration rather than recrimination. Otherwise known as The Big One, the 'Long Medley' on what became Side 2 of *Abbey Road* was McCartney's idea,[1] but one readily accepted by the others – partly because it allowed them to use up a cluster of undeveloped snippets left over from *The Beatles*, but mainly because it would make for a spectacular finale[2] to their career together which, despite their differences, they still regarded with pride.

The first of the Side 2 numbers to be recorded, YOU NEVER GIVE ME YOUR MONEY was itself more of a suite than a song, perhaps taking its cue from Lennon's [148] HAPPINESS IS A WARM GUN. Like HAPPINESS, it was put together from several existing sections looking for a home, of which five can be discerned: (1) the poignant opening verse/chorus in A minor; (2) a double-time boogiewoogie passage in C ('Out of college . . .'); (3) a return to half-time with chiming Leslie-toned guitar from Harrison ('But oh that magic feeling . . .'); (4) a six-bar instrumental modulation to A major; and (5) the closing section ('One sweet dream . . .'), ending with a repeated arpeggiated progression possibly influenced by the similar figure in [167] I WANT YOU (SHE'S SO HEAVY).[3] Because the exact structure of the Long Medley

[1] Precedents for such a structure were plentiful, notably including The Who's nine-minute 'mini-opera' 'A Quick One While He's Away' (1966), The Mothers of Invention's *Absolutely Free* (1967), and The Jefferson Airplane's *After Bathing At Baxter's* (1968). McCartney himself cites Keith West's 'Excerpt from A Teenage Opera' (1968) as a model.

[2] The two sides of *Abbey Road* were, until the last minute (presumably at Lennon's insistence), programmed round the other way, with [167] I WANT YOU (SHE'S SO HEAVY) concluding the album.

[3] The Beatles seem to have had arpeggios on the brain around this time. See also the introductions to [158] I'VE GOT A FEELING and [181] SUN KING, the middle section of [177] HERE COMES THE SUN, [185] BECAUSE throughout, and Harrison's collaboration with Eric Clapton for Cream, 'Badge'. (One of McCartney's favourite ways of creating riffs and counter-melodies was by playing with arpeggios; for example, the counter-melody on [103] LUCY IN THE SKY WITH DIAMONDS. By the same token, many of his tunes appear to be derived, by way of brilliant little variations, from toying with scales.)

had yet to be worked out, the basic track of YOU NEVER GIVE ME YOUR MONEY, made in nine hours, came to a halt at 3:02 (where the guitar arpeggio changes tone and drop-out is detectable in the vocal track).[1] The rest was added later, McCartney bringing in his own tape-loops and wind-chimes for the cross-fade to [181] SUN KING.

Three days after the first session for this song, The Beatles were at Olympic supervising mixes from the 'Get Back' sessions when Allen Klein arrived and an argument broke out over business matters.[2] After the others had gone, McCartney stayed in the studio with American singer-guitarist Steve Miller, recording the suitably titled 'My Dark Hour', on which he played bass and drums and sang backing vocals. When Miller issued this as a single in the USA, McCartney was credited as Paul Ramon, his stage-name for The Silver Beatles' 1960 Scottish tour.[3]

[174] HER MAJESTY (Lennon–McCartney)

McCartney vocal, acoustic guitar
Recorded: 2nd July 1969, Abbey Road 2.
Producer: George Martin. Engineer: Phil McDonald.
UK release: 26th September 1969 (LP: *Abbey Road*)
US release: 1st October 1969 (LP: *Abbey Road*)

After the first session for [173] YOU NEVER GIVE ME YOUR MONEY, The Beatles took an eight-week summer break. McCartney was first back into Abbey Road on 2nd July, taping this party throwaway in the early afternoon before the others arrived. Reserved for inclusion in the Long Medley [173], it was initially placed between [182] MEAN MR MUSTARD and [183] POLYTHENE PAM but, after listening to the playback, McCartney rightly judged that it didn't fit and told second engineer John Kurlander to cut it out and throw it away. Kurlander, who had been instructed never to discard anything The Beatles recorded, instead edited it, for convenience's sake, to the end of the

---

[1] The original recording ran on into a loose jam, finally switching briefly into fast rock-and-roll 4/4.
[2] See note, p. 353–4.
[3] McCartney met Miller at the Monterey Festival in 1967. As a result, the latter brought his group to London in 1968 to record a *Sgt. Pepper*-like concept album, *Children Of The Future*, supervised by The Beatles' engineer on *Let It Be* and *Abbey Road*, Glyn Johns.

Medley, separating it from [180] THE END with twenty seconds of leader-tape. When McCartney heard this the following day, he liked the random effect and thus HER MAJESTY finished up at the end of *Abbey Road*, twenty seconds after the main album. (The crash at the beginning is the last chord of MEAN MR MUSTARD, an unexpected D major originally put in as a link to HER MAJESTY and snipped out of the 30th July rough mix.)

[175] GOLDEN SLUMBERS/
[176] CARRY THAT WEIGHT *(Lennon–McCartney)*

> **McCartney** double-tracked vocal, chorus vocal, piano, rhythm
> guitar; **Harrison** chorus vocal, bass, lead guitar; **Lennon** chorus
> vocal; **Starr** chorus vocal, drums; **Uncredited** 12 violins, 4
> violas, 4 cellos, 1 double-bass, 4 horns, 3 trumpets, 1 trombone,
> 1 bass trombone.
> Recorded: 2nd–4th, 30th–31st July, 15th August 1969, Abbey
> Road 2.
> Producer: George Martin. Engineers: Phil McDonald, Geoff
> Emerick.
> UK release: 26th September 1969 (LP: *Abbey Road*)
> US release: 1st October 1969 (LP: *Abbey Road*)

The heart of the Long Medley is the McCartney-composed sequence [175] GOLDEN SLUMBERS/[176] CARRY THAT WEIGHT, conceived and recorded as one piece. Picking up the mood of sad farewell established in the opening bars of [173] YOU NEVER GIVE ME YOUR MONEY, McCartney used the same chords (Am7–Dm–G7–C) for the similarly melancholy verse of GOLDEN SLUMBERS ('Once there was a way . . .'). The passionate *fortissimo* melody of the C major chorus sets a nursery-rhyme by one of Shakespeare's contemporaries, the playwright Thomas Dekker. Sitting at a piano at his father's house in Heswall, Cheshire, during the summer, McCartney found this verse[1] in a song-book belonging to his step-sister Ruth. Unable to read the sheet music (or so the story goes), he made up his own – yet the structure of GOLDEN SLUMBERS, and its family relationship to YOU NEVER GIVE ME YOUR MONEY, suggest that their composer was attempting something more complex and ambitious than merely improvising a tune at random.

This is certainly true of the continuation into CARRY THAT WEIGHT, where the rocking subdominant harmony of the preceding

---

[1] Golden slumbers kiss your eyes/Smiles awake you when you rise/Sleep pretty wantons, do not cry/And I will sing a lullaby.

chorus firms up on the tonic before moving into an orchestral recapitulation of YOU NEVER GIVE ME YOUR MONEY, followed by two restatements of that song's closing guitar arpeggios. The lyric of McCartney's second C major chorus, which, repeated, ends the sequence, looks ahead to The Beatles' post-Beatles careers. No matter what they do separately after this, he correctly guesses, it'll never match what they did together; the world will always hark back to their glory days as a foursome and they'll carry the weight of their achievement as The Beatles for the rest of their individual careers.[1] Otherwise absent from these tracks, Lennon[2] joins with McCartney, Harrison, and Starr in unison on this far-sighted chorus line.

[177] HERE COMES THE SUN *(Harrison)*

> **Harrison** vocal, backing vocal, acoustic guitar, harmonium, Moog synthesiser, handclaps; **McCartney** backing vocal, bass, handclaps; **Starr** drums, handclaps; **Uncredited** 4 violas, 4 cellos, 1 double-bass, 2 piccolos, 2 flutes, 2 alto flutes, 2 clarinets
> Recorded: 7th–8th July, Abbey Road 2; 16th July, 6th August, Abbey Road 3; 15th, 19th August 1969, Abbey Road 2.
> Producer: George Martin. Engineers: Phil McDonald, Geoff Emerick.
> UK release: 26th September 1969 (LP: *Abbey Road*)
> US release: 1st October 1969 (LP: *Abbey Road*)

Harrison shook off the cold of winter and the miserable 'Get Back' sessions with his second most popular tune. A consciously artless guitar-song, strummed as he sat in Eric Clapton's garden, 'sagging off' from the endless business meetings at Apple, HERE COMES THE SUN departs from its play-in-a-day simplicity only for the warmth of a major seventh on the second repeat of the title-phrase in each chorus. (The metrical irregularities of the chorus and middle derive largely from arpeggiated triads.) As with most of the songs on *Abbey Road*, it was, after its group-made basic track, looked after chiefly by its author. Apart from George Martin's unusual instrumentation (mixed too low to register much), the main colour comes from Harrison's rather wobbly Moog synthesiser, played on the slide-ribbon and overdubbed before the final mix on 19th August. Prettily atmospheric (and made wispier

---

[1] McCartney recalls the song as alluding merely to the 'weight' of the business hassles The Beatles were then going through with Allen Klein (Miles, op. cit., p. 557).

[2] He was hospitalised after a car accident in Golspie, Scotland, until 6th July.

with varispeed), the result is a little too *faux-naïf* to appeal to those lacking the requisite sweet tooth.

[178] MAXWELL'S SILVER HAMMER *(Lennon–McCartney)*

McCartney vocal, backing vocal, piano, guitars, Moog synthesiser; **Harrison** backing vocal, lead guitar; **Starr** backing vocal, drums; **Mal Evans** anvil; **George Martin** organ
Recorded: 9th–11th July, Abbey Road 2; 6th August 1969, Abbey Road 3.
Producer: George Martin. Engineer: Phil McDonald.
UK release: 26th September 1969 (LP: *Abbey Road*)
US release: 1st October 1969 (LP: *Abbey Road*)

If any single recording shows why The Beatles broke up, it is MAXWELL'S SILVER HAMMER. Compulsively fertile in melody and fascinated by music's formal beauties, McCartney could, when unrestrained by Lennon's cynicism, fatally neglect meaning and expression. This ghastly miscalculation – of which there are countless equivalents on his garrulous sequence of solo albums – represents by far his worst lapse of taste under the auspices of The Beatles. The cheery tale of a homicidal maniac, it was written towards the end of recording for *The Beatles* in October 1968 and tried out then (and later during the 'Get Back' sessions in January). According to Lennon, who despised the song, McCartney was convinced that, given the right production, it was a potential hit single, and so flogged it to death in the studio in a pedantic effort to perfect it. As he had with [131] OB-LA-DI, OB-LA-DA, he merely ended up driving his colleagues mad. Thus *Abbey Road* embraces both extremes of McCartney: the clear-minded, sensitive caretaker of The Beatles in [173] YOU NEVER GIVE ME YOUR MONEY and the Long Medley – and the immature egotist who frittered away the group's patience and solidarity on sniggering nonsense like this.[1]

---

[1] The song's allusion to 'pataphysical science' may have been suggested by The Soft Machine's 'Pataphysical Introduction', recorded on their second album at Olympic Studios during February–March 1969 while McCartney was there overseeing remixes of the 'Get Back' material. A spoof 'science of imaginary solutions', pataphysics was invented by the French absurdist Alfred Jarry (1873–1907), an icon of the mid-Sixties underground. A Pataphysical Society was founded in Jarry's honour in Paris and The Soft Machine's drummer Robert Wyatt was a member – as was Miles, who had introduced McCartney to Jarry's play *Ubu Roi* in the Royal Court production, starring Max Wall, in 1965.

[179] COME TOGETHER (Lennon–McCartney)

Lennon vocal, rhythm guitar, lead guitar, hand-claps; McCartney
   harmony vocal, bass, electric piano; Harrison guitar; Starr
   drums, maracas
Recorded: 21st–23rd July, Abbey Road 3; 25th, 29th, 30th July
   1969, Abbey Road 2.
Producer: George Martin. Engineers: Geoff Emerick/Phil
   McDonald.
UK release: 26th September 1969 (LP: *Abbey Road*)
US release: 1st October 1969 (LP: *Abbey Road*)

Lennon's return to Abbey Road on 9th July for the start of work on
[178] MAXWELL'S SILVER HAMMER represented his first contribution to
Abbey Road since a guitar part on [173] YOU NEVER GIVE ME YOUR
MONEY two months earlier. For the next fortnight he appears to have
done nothing more, having finished no new songs since [168] THE
BALLAD OF JOHN AND YOKO in April.[1] Instead, most of his energy
seems to have been devoted to importing a bed into the studio so that
his wife, more seriously injured than him in their Scottish car-crash at
the end of June, could survey proceedings and lend him moral support.
(She had a microphone suspended over her pillow so that she could
pipe up if she had anything to say.) Finally, he kick-started himself by
messing about with an old Chuck Berry number, 'You Can't Catch
Me', unwisely leaving part of Berry's lyric ('Here come old flat-top') in
the resulting song.[2]

   With its sex-political title, COME TOGETHER constitutes the last of
Lennon's espousals of the counterculture while still in the group.[3]
Exhortatory/pontifical in the style of his early post-Beatles songs,[4] it

[1] Apart from 'Give Peace A Chance', taped on 1st June at the Hotel Reine-
Elizabeth in Montreal and issued a month later as the debut of the Plastic Ono Band.
(Lennon credited 'Give Peace A Chance' to Lennon–McCartney in return for his
partner's help in recording THE BALLAD OF JOHN AND YOKO.)
[2] In 1973 Berry's publishers sued Lennon who settled out of court, agreeing to
record three of their songs (Berry's 'You Can't Catch Me' and [U13g] SWEET LITTLE
SIXTEEN, and Lee Dorsey's 'Ya Ya') on his *Rock 'n' Roll* LP.
[3] The phrase was coined by Timothy Leary as a campaign slogan for his planned
campaign against Ronald Reagan for the governorship of California in 1969. Leary
asked Lennon to write him a campaign song and, surprisingly, in view of the latter's
disenchantment with Leary's psychedelic proselytising, he agreed to try, this song
being the result. (Implacably opposed to LSD, Reagan saw to it that his challenger
was denied bail on a marijuana charge and kept in the Orange County Jail for the
duration of the election.)
[4] 'Give Peace A Chance', 'Power To The People', 'Imagine', 'Woman Is The
Nigger Of The World', 'Happy Christmas (War Is Over)', and so on.

pitches a stream of self-confessed 'gobbledygook' at the violent antagonisms of an unenlightened world, implying that the language deployed in such confrontations is a trap and a potential prison. Later taken up by separatist feminists (arguing that the trap and the prison were male creations), this idea was at the cutting edge of alternative politics in late 1969.

Nothing else on *Abbey Road* matches the *Zeitgeist*-catching impact of Lennon's cover-breaking announcement, after two verses of faintly menacing semi-nonsense: 'One thing I can tell you is you got to be free.' The freedom invoked here differs from previous revolutionary freedom in being a liberation from *all* forms and *all* norms, including left-wing ones. In COME TOGETHER, the personal preamble to [156] JULIA is propelled into the public sphere and elevated to the level of (anti-)ideology: a call to unchain the imagination and, by setting language free, loosen the rigidities of political and emotional entrenchment. As such, the song pursues a theme consistent in Lennon's work since [116] I AM THE WALRUS – one partly originating in his LSD-enhanced outsider mentality and partly imbibed from the prevailing countercultural atmosphere of anti-élitism as defined by pundits as diverse as Marshall McLuhan, Arthur Janov, R. D. Laing, and Herbert Marcuse. (See [125], [127], [129], [148], [158].)

The archetype of countercultural anti-politics as presented in COME TOGETHER was the head-gaming hippie sage: a bewildering guru/shaman modeled on Timothy Leary, Ken Kesey, Carlos Castaneda's fictional Don Juan, and 'trickster' figures like Mullah Nasruddin and the Zen masters of the Orient. An amalgam of these (with perhaps a dash of cartoonist Robert Crumb's lampoon Mr Natural), the character presented in Lennon's lyric has 'juju eyeball(s)' which suggest the cover of Dr John the Night Tripper's pseudo-voodoo album *Gris-Gris*, released in 1968 and a big hit in Britain's student/underground circles.[1] By verse three, Old Flat-top has metamorphosed into Lennon himself, with asides – 'sideboard(s)' – from Yoko Ono, a reference to her characteristic stance in their interviews. ('Spinal cracker' may refer

---

[1] Otherwise known as New Orleans session pianist Mac Rebennack, Dr John took his name from a dual allusion to his mentor Professor Longhair (Roy Byrd) and The Beatles' [65] DAY TRIPPER. The cover of *Gris-Gris* shows him superimposed on a nocturnal scene in the swamps of the Louisiana bayoux. In the title track, his juju/voodoo persona claims to 'fly through the smoke'. According to McCartney, Lennon asked him to make his electric piano 'very swampy and smoky' – cf. the final verse's associational link with 'muddy water' and 'mojo filter'. Bluesman Muddy Waters' most famous song was 'I Got My Mojo Working'. (A mojo is a voodoo charm – although, to addicts, it may also mean any narcotic; usually morphine.)

to the traditional practice of Japanese women of walking on their prone husband's backs to loosen muscular tension and keep the spine supple.)

Again suggesting the influence of Dr John (and, more distantly, that of The Band), the song, a D blues shifting to the relative minor for its chorus, adopts the then-new American 'laid-back' or 'spaced-out' style, in which a stoned laziness of beat and a generally low-profile approach offered a cool proletarian alternative to middle-class psychedelic artifice.[1] The associated drugs in this case were cocaine and heroin (and later the powerful tranquilisers known as quaaludes).[2] Implicit was a passive, observing state of mind perfectly caught in the cloudy white tone of Lennon's double-tracked guitar solo and McCartney's brilliantly idiomatic bass and piano, particularly in his wonderfully poised two-bar envoi to the solo. (Lennon, stingy with his praise, was rightly effusive about his partner's playing here.) A slightly murky mix completes this – for The Beatles – very unusual sound picture.[3]

Enthusiastically received in campus and underground circles, COME TOGETHER is *the* key song of the turn of the decade, isolating a pivotal moment when the free world's coming generation rejected established wisdom, knowledge, ethics, and behaviour for a drug-inspired relativism which has since undermined the intellectual foundations of Western culture.

---

[1] The song started out in faster tempo but was slowed down at the session, an adaption claimed by both Lennon and McCartney (*The Beatles Anthology*, p. 339).

[2] Depressed by their media vilification, Ono's miscarriage, and a doctor's (unwarranted) opinion that Lennon had made himself sterile by drug and alcohol abuse, the couple had recently become heroin addicts.

[3] Semi-audible, Lennon is whispering 'Shoot me' on the first beats of the first four bars. (Lewisohn, *Sessions*, p. 181.)

[180] THE END *(Lennon–McCartney)*

McCartney vocal, backing vocal, bass, piano, lead guitar; Lennon
backing vocal, lead guitar; Harrison backing vocal, rhythm and
lead guitar; Starr drums; Uncredited 12 violins, 4 violas, 4
cellos, 1 double-bass, 4 horns, 3 trumpets, 1 trombone, 1 bass
trombone.

Recorded: 23rd July, 5th August 1969, Abbey Road 3; 7th–8th
August 1969, Abbey Road 2; 15th August 1969, Abbey Road 1;
18th August 1969, Abbey Road 2.

Producer: George Martin. Engineers: Geoff Emerick, Phil
McDonald.

UK release: 26th September 1969 (LP: *Abbey Road*)
US release: 1st October 1969 (LP: *Abbey Road*)

The concluding section of the Long Medley builds the final A major of
[175] GOLDEN SLUMBERS/[176] CARRY THAT WEIGHT into a tough
rock-and-roll crescendo. Bridging to this, Starr takes a reluctant drum
solo – the only instance on a Beatles record of a drum-kit purpose-
recorded in stereo – before three two-bar guitar solos in rotating
sequence from McCartney, Harrison (sounding remarkably like Eric
Clapton), and Lennon. In conclusion, McCartney touches for the last
time on the poignant A minor of [173] YOU NEVER GIVE ME YOUR
MONEY for the famous line 'The love you take is equal to the love you
make', landing unexpectedly – if, in terms of the Medley's overall key-
structure, logically – on a sadly smiling C major.

Something odd happens hereabouts, as anyone trying to play along
with the record will discover. Following Lennon's last fuzz-toned
guitar snarl at 1:29, McCartney's piano enters slightly flat, whereupon
the remainder of the song is fractionally below concert pitch. Did the
overdub for the guitar solos put the track out of tune? If so, was the
final section, taped separately and overdubbed with the GOLDEN
SLUMBERS/CARRY THAT WEIGHT orchestra, varispeeded to cover this
up? That McCartney's piano from 1:29–1:43 had to be redone three
days later suggests as much.

[U181] COME AND GET IT (*McCartney*)

McCartney double-tracked vocal, piano, bass, drums, maracas
Recorded: 24th July 1969, Abbey Road 2.
Producer: Paul McCartney. Engineer: Phil McDonald
UK release: 28th October 1996 (2-CD: *Anthology 3*)
US release: 28th October 1996 (2-CD: *Anthology 3*)

An insight into the perpetual friction between McCartney and Harrison
can be had by contrasting this track, multi-instrumentally knocked off
in under an hour, with [U138] NOT GUILTY, which took four days and
over a hundred takes to come to nothing. McCartney's ability to see
perfect musical solutions immediately where the introspective Harrison
preferred to brood his way to a reasoned conclusion, must have caused
endless mutual annoyance – McCartney itching to perform the dazzling
guitar solo he'd dreamed up in the first few seconds, Harrison
stubbornly refusing to be hurried off his path of patient authenticity.

By far the best unreleased 'Beatles' song, COME AND GET IT is a
dexterous juxtaposition of regular crotchet common chords with an
irregular syncopated melody which shows how infuriatingly fluent and
casually inventive its composer could be.[1] Arriving an hour early for
an *Abbey Road* session (the first of three for [18] SUN KING/[182] MEAN
MR MUSTARD), he swiftly laid down a take of voice and piano,
following this with a tracked vocal and rhythm-section overdubs.
COME AND GET IT is usually said to have been conceived as a demo for
Apple signings Badfinger, whose almost identical version reached No. 4
in the UK charts six months later. Yet, according to McCartney, the
song was on offer for *Abbey Road*.[2] Lennon was in the control room
throughout and the fact that he didn't come out and add a harmony
vocal (the lack of which here makes Badfinger's version preferable),
suggests either that he was, at best, indifferent to the track or that there
were already enough McCartney songs in the can for the album.
Whether the latter's decision to give this obvious hit to someone other
than The Beatles was a loaded gesture remains unclear, although
McCartney has denied any hidden meaning in the song's title.[3]

---

[1] There is, in fact, an uncharacteristic mistake at 1:44 where McCartney goes
straight to E on bass against C major in the piano, instead of to G.
[2] *Mojo*, October 1996.
[3] Badfinger's version became the theme music for *The Magic Christian*, a film
scripted from a novel by Terry Southern, produced by Dennis O'Dell ([112] note),
and starring Peter Sellers and Ringo Starr. A satire on greed, it features a scene in
which people are invited to retrieve bank-notes deposited in a tank full of

[181] SUN KING/
[182] MEAN MR MUSTARD *(Lennon–McCartney)*

> **Lennon** multitracked vocal, lead guitar, maracas; **McCartney**
> harmony vocals, bass, harmonium, piano, tape-loops; **Harrison**
> lead guitar; **Starr** drums, bongos, tambourine; **George Martin**
> Lowery organ
> Recorded: 24th–25th July 1969, Abbey Road 2; 29th July 1969,
> Abbey Road 3.
> Producer: George Martin. Engineers: Geoff Emerick, Phil
> McDonald.
> UK release: 26th September 1969 (LP: *Abbey Road*)
> US release: 1st October 1969 (LP: *Abbey Road*)

Recorded in one sequence, these two Lennon scraps are at best half-
songs and would have been unusable without the excuse of the Long
Medley. A desultory mood-piece with a mock-Mediterranean postscript, SUN KING begins in yawning E major before languidly tipping
back its sombrero to hail the eponymous royal personage in C.[1] The
Beatles play this kitsch with a blend of stylishness (the main guitar
phrase, adapted from Fleetwood Mac's 1969 hit 'Albatross') and
tongue-in-cheek bad taste (a return of the brylcreemed night-club
organist from [38b] MR MOONLIGHT). Tracked in four- and five-part
harmony, Lennon bridges the gap between his keys with a Beach Boys
echo-fade G eleventh.

Lapsing back on E major, SUN KING *segues* from the sun-kissed
slumber of Torremolinos to the livelier and considerably more sordid
MEAN MR MUSTARD, a joke perpetrated in a fit of boredom during The
Beatles' spring 1968 sojourn at Rishikesh.[2] It comes as a shock, in the
bland sunshine of *Abbey Road*, to be confronted with this tongue-
poking throwback to *Sgt. Pepper*, complete with fairground waltz and
cartoon grotesquerie. Its melodic phrases spilling across bar-lines
delineated by McCartney's irascible fuzz-toned bass, MEAN MR
MUSTARD lasts barely a minute, before giving way to:

---

excrement. That this fits the title COME AND GET IT is apparently a coincidence.
[1] Lennon probably borrowed the title from Nancy Mitford's study of Louis XIV,
published in 1966.
[2] The Esher demo of May 1968 *(Anthology 3)* includes a vague chorus, not used in
the final recording. Since, at this stage, the song wasn't linked to [183] POLYTHENE
PAM, Mr Mustard's sister was named Shirley (possibly after Shirley Evans, the
accordionist in *Magical Mystery Tour*).

[183] POLYTHENE PAM/
[184] SHE CAME IN THROUGH THE BATHROOM
WINDOW *(Lennon–McCartney)*

Lennon double-tracked vocal, backing vocals, 12-string acoustic
    guitar; **McCartney** double-tracked vocal, backing vocals, bass,
    lead guitar, piano, electric piano; **Harrison** backing vocals, lead
    guitar; **Starr** drums, tambourine, maracas, cowbell
Recorded: 25th July 1969, Abbey Road 2; 28th July 1969, Abbey
    Road 3; 30th July 1969, Abbey Road 2.
Producer: George Martin. Engineers: Geoff Emerick, Phil
    McDonald.
UK release: 26th September 1969 (LP: *Abbey Road*)
US release: 1st October 1969 (LP: *Abbey Road*)

Recorded *en suite*, these half-songs – by Lennon and McCartney,
respectively – date, like their two predecessors, from 1968. Written in
Rishikesh, POLYTHENE PAM was held in reserve for *The Beatles* but
never used; SHE CAME IN THROUGH THE BATHROOM WINDOW was
allegedly composed in New York in mid-May[1] while the two chief
Beatles were there to announce the formation of Apple. Both were
rehearsed, without much enthusiasm, during the 'Get Back' sessions.

Maintaining the E major of [182] MEAN MR MUSTARD, POLYTHENE
PAM is a guitar song fanfared by massive chords on an acoustic 12-string
(probably cribbed from The Who's contemporary hit 'Pinball Wizard').
It concerns a real-life Liverpool 'judy' – Polythene Pat, one of The
Beatles' original Cavern fans.[2] Locally famed for her taste for
thermoplastic, she metamorphosed in Lennon's fantasy into Polythene
Pam, a ludicrously apparelled fetishist. Like the song's 'Yeah, yeah,
yeah' refrain, his thick Scouse accent harks back to the band's dirty days
in Merseyside divebars. Driven by heavy pseudo-samba percussion, the
track concludes by hustling down a five-step scalar staircase to the A
major basement of its successor.

To the extent that it means anything at all, SHE CAME IN THROUGH
THE BATHROOM WINDOW refers to some of the 'Apple scruffs' – the
female fans then given to standing guard outside Apple, Abbey Road,
and the group's homes – who climbed a ladder left in McCartney's

---

[1] 13th May 1968 (Fulpen, *The Beatles: An Illustrated Diary*). If this is true – the
source is Lennon's *Playboy* interview – it must mean that McCartney wrote the
music then, the lyric later. On the other hand, Lennon may simply have mixed up the
years up, much as he often mixed up Beatles LPs in retrospect.
[2] For more on Polythene Pat (Pat Dawson), see Turner, *A Hard Day's Write*, pp.
196–7. A different explanation is supplied in Miles, op. cit., pp. 556–7.

garden, got into his house through the bathroom window, and stole a precious photograph of his father.[1] To get this back, he had to negotiate with the girls outside. Unusual in placing only one verse/chorus before its middle eight, the song, accidentally or not, functions as a microcosm of the Long Medley's tonal axis of A major–minor and C major. With its suavely inventive running banter on guitar (presumably by McCartney), SHE CAME IN THROUGH THE BATHROOM WINDOW is irresistible pop/rock, poised on a walking bass which plays mischievous tricks against a powerful percussion track within a rhythmic feel and framework unique to this song.[2]

[185] BECAUSE *(Lennon–McCartney)*

> **Lennon** vocals, lead guitar; **McCartney** vocals, bass; **Harrison** vocals, Moog synthesiser; **George Martin** electric spinet
> Recorded: 1st, 4th August 1969, Abbey Road 2; 5th August 1969, Abbey Road 3.
> Producer: George Martin. Engineers: Geoff Emerick, Phil McDonald.
> UK release: 26th September 1969 (LP: *Abbey Road*)
> US release: 1st October 1969 (LP: *Abbey Road*)

The last song recorded for *Abbey Road* was Lennon's BECAUSE – a three-part harmony in C sharp minor inspired by hearing Yoko Ono play the *Adagio sostenuto* of Beethoven's Piano Sonata No. 14, Op. 27 No. 2 *(Moonlight)*.[3] Overdubbed twice, making nine voices in all, the

---

[1] The girls stole clothes and other photos, including slides of photos of McCartney taken during the 'Get Back' sessions by Linda Eastman. In order to recover his property, McCartney recruited some of these fans, claiming that the slides were needed for the *Let It Be* film. Salewicz (pp. 217–18) places this incident after McCartney's marriage to Linda Eastman on 12th March 1969, yet a demo of SHE CAME IN THROUGH THE BATHROOM WINDOW, complete with lyric, was taped nearly two months earlier.

[2] The version attempted at Apple on 22nd January 1969 *(Anthology 3)* treats the same material in a completely different way, slowing the song into a soulful Aretha Franklin groove and giving equal weight to the passing chord of F sharp minor which in the 'pop' version almost disappears. Supposing McCartney to have been trying to fit in with the R&B mood of the 'Get Back' project, he perhaps had in mind Dusty Springfield's contemporary Memphis-recorded hit 'Son Of A Preacher Man'. On the other hand, the song's uncharacteristically repetitious three-chord cycle suggests that it may have been written as a soul pastiche – which makes its *Abbey Road* transformation all the more remarkable.

[3] Lennon erroneously claimed that BECAUSE is based on playing Beethoven's chords in reverse. (For a discussion of the harmonic resemblances, see O'Grady, pp. 161–2.)

harmony is one of the most complex on any of the group's records and, even under the guidance of George Martin, took them some while to learn. Accompanied by continuous arpeggios on harpsichord (left), guitar (right), and synthesiser (centre), the chordal melody has an icy grandeur which fails to engage the emotions, instead floating on the lofty breeze of its high-flown word-play. Many have admired this song's mood of visionary detachment without taking account of the heroin then flowing coldly around its composer's body. Fifty days after finishing BECAUSE, he was back in the studio howling his addiction in 'Cold Turkey'.

Abbey Road is The Beatles' most technically accomplished album, its eight-track recordings filled with crystal-clear sounds, crisply EQ'd, if sometimes oddly mixed. The bass-end, which the group had been improving since 1966, is deep and rich, with Starr's kit captured more ringingly than ever. (His bass-drum, in particular, really socks home.) A sheen of spacious luxury is provided by the use of the Moog synthesiser[1] and Harrison's ubiquitous Leslie-toned guitar.[2] With George Martin back at the helm after the anarchic period of *The Beatles* and the chaos of the 'Get Back' sessions, the production is smooth and disciplined. The actual content, however, is erratic and often hollow. Now fondly recalled by McCartney, Starr, and Martin (although not by the reliably dry Harrison), *Abbey Road* was recorded in a peculiarly volatile atmosphere veering from friendly tolerance to childish violence. Lennon twice argued savagely with McCartney, at one point taking a less-than-peaceful swing at his wife Linda.[3] Another major

---

[1] This instrument, the first of its kind to be marketed commercially, was then very new, having previously been used on record mainly by Walter (later Wendy) Carlos, its co-developer with Dr Robert Moog. Harrison, who acquired his in California in November 1968, first used it on his album *Electronic Sounds*, issued by Apple's experimental label Zapple in May 1969. BECAUSE was the first Abbey Road track to be overdubbed with the Moog. Others were (in order): [178] MAXWELL'S SILVER HAMMER (played by McCartney), [167] I WANT YOU (played by Lennon), and [177] HERE COMES THE SUN (played by Harrison).

[2] [170], [171], [172], [173], [178], and various guitars during the 'Long Medley'. See also [169].

[3] McCartney's recollections of the *Abbey Road* sessions are beyond doubt to some extent rose-tinted. Even he admits that he was rebuked by Harrison and Starr for being too overbearing (*Musician*, October 1986). Gill Pritchard, then an Apple Scruff, recalls that, on one evening during the closing dates for *Abbey Road*, he 'came racing out of the front door of the studio in tears, went home and didn't come back.

schism flared when Ono took one of Harrison's chocolate digestives without asking him. For a while, Lennon wanted his songs on one side of the album and McCartney's on the other.[1]

The creative energy of The Beatles' earlier recordings was all but gone – over a third of the album's material was a year old[2] – and had it not been for McCartney's input as designer of the Long Medley (which Lennon disliked), *Abbey Road* would lack the semblance of unity and coherence that makes it appear better than it is.[3]

[186] I ME MINE *(Harrison)*

>**Harrison** vocal, harmony vocal, acoustic guitars, lead guitars;
>   **McCartney** harmony vocal, bass, Hammond organ, electric
>   piano; **Starr** drums; **Uncredited** 18 violins, 4 violas, 4 cellos, 1
>   harp, 3 trumpets, 3 trombones
>Recorded: 3rd January 1970, Abbey Road 2; 1st–2nd April 1970,
>   Abbey Road 1.
>Producers: George Martin/Phil Spector. Engineers: Phil McDonald/
>   Peter Bown.
>UK release: 8th May 1970 (LP: *Let It Be*)
>US release: 18th May 1970 (LP: *Let It Be*)

By a poetic stroke of fate, the last track to be recorded by The Beatles was this dry lament over divisive egotism, written by Harrison following a revelation of selflessness on LSD. After *Abbey Road*, the group was effectively dead: Lennon politically radicalised and aggrieved over the others' treatment of Ono; Harrison tired of McCartney's condescension and feeling betrayed and abandoned by Lennon; McCartney exhausted by the battle to keep The Beatles intact and soon

---

The next day he didn't turn up at all even though the studio was booked.' (*Mojo*, October 1996.) McCartney's failure to appear on this – or another? – occasion provoked a furious Lennon to hammer on his door and clamber over the garden wall for a shouting match with him, during which he smashed a picture he had given McCartney (the latter's favourite painting). (Salewicz, pp. 218–19.)

[1] Asked about [178] MAXWELL'S SILVER HAMMER only a month after finishing *Abbey Road*, Lennon replied 'That's McCartney, as you might know. We don't really write together any more.' In the same interview (*Mojo*, November 1995), he anticipated [170] SOMETHING and [179] COME TOGETHER being issued together as a single: 'So I can listen to (them) without having to listen to the rest of the album.'

[2] [170], [172], [178], [181], [182], [183], [184].

[3] At one stage, its working title was *Everest* (after engineer Geoff Emerick's favoured brand of cigarettes), but when it was suggested that the group fly to the Himalayas to shoot a cover, they discovered themselves prepared to go no further than just outside the studio – hence the cover and title.

to explode over what Lennon would do with [165] THE LONG AND WINDING ROAD; Starr bored with the bickering and bent on making an album of maudlin standards for his mother. The last time all four were in the studio together was for the final sequencing of *Abbey Road* on 20th August 1969. From then on, they concentrated on their own personal projects, for business reasons not announcing the group's break-up while behaving in every respect as if it had already happened.

Still to be disposed of was the 'no overdubs' material recorded at Apple in January 1969. Glyn Johns, The Beatles' elected producer for what was initially slated as the 'Get Back' project, took two shots at compiling a listenable LP out of it without compromising the principles on which it had foundered. Neither convinced the group and, lacking a solution, the project limped into 1970 – at which point, with the *Let It Be* film ready for release, something finally had to be done.

One of the first tasks was to make a proper recording of this song, which, in the film, Harrison is seen playing to Starr a day or two after writing it. With Lennon out of the country, it was up to the other three and they duly knocked off what was needed in a ten-hour session, producing a track of brusquely minimal length: 1:34. While the ferocity of the playing belies this, none of them were interested in treating the song as anything more than a filler. When Phil Spector came to it during his controversial remixes in March and April, he immediately doubled its length by copying the track from its first vocal entry and editing this on at 1:21.

I ME MINE juxtaposes a self-pitying Gallic waltz (complete with Piaf wobble) against a clamorous blues shuffle – suggesting that selfishness, personal or collective, subtle or crude, is always the same. Harrison's typically thoughtful lyric touches a nadir of worldly pessimism in the line 'Even those tears: I me mine'.[1]

On 10th April 1970, eight days after Phil Spector had dubbed a thirty-piece orchestra onto this track without telling its author, Paul McCartney announced that The Beatles no longer existed.

---

[1] For Harrison, the song was about 'the ego problem' – the soul's identification with the personal self to the exclusion of the universal Self, the 'I' that is God or Love (*The Beatles Anthology*, p. 319).

Part 4
Looking Back

Whatever happened to
The life we once knew?

Part 4

The Beatles' post-Beatles story is, on the whole, unedifying. All four recorded solo albums – around sixty to date[1] – but, in their various ways, none of them managed to sustain anything remotely approaching the quality of their work with The Beatles. Reflecting this dispiriting story, their relationships were for long periods distant and resentful. Lennon and McCartney spent the early 1970s in a state of prim estrangement, enlivened by digs at each other on their records; invited to join Harrison and Starr at the Concert for Bangladesh in New York in 1971, neither saw fit to comply. Starr managed to extract contributions from his colleagues for his 1973 album *Ringo*, but only separately. In the same year, Harrison summarised the group's fractious post-Beatles progress in 'Sue Me Sue You Blues' *(Living in the Material World)*.

Lennon's eighteen-month separation from Yoko Ono in 1973–4 supposedly included a few days of reminiscing with McCartney in Los

---

[1] Constraints of space, time, and interest prevent consideration of these albums. Lennon: *Unfinished Music No. 1*: Two Virgins (1968); *Unfinished Music No. 2*: Life With The Lions (1969); *The Wedding Album* (1969); *Live Peace In Toronto* (1969); *John Lennon/Plastic Ono Band* (1970); *Imagine* (1971); *Some Time In New York City* (1972); *Mind Games* (1973); *Walls And Bridges* (1974); *Rock 'n' Roll* (1975); *Double Fantasy* (1980); *Milk And Honey* (1984); *Menlove Avenue* (1986); *Live In New York City* [1972] (1988); McCartney: *McCartney* (1970); *Ram* (1971); *Wild Life* (1971); *Red Rose Speedway* (1973); *Band On The Run* (1973); *Venus And Mars* (1975); *Wings At The Speed Of Sound* (1976); *London Town* (1978); *Back To The Egg* (1979); *McCartney II* (1980); *Tug Of War* (1982); *Pipes Of Peace* (1983); *Give My Regards To Broad Street* (1984); *Press To Play* (1986); *Back In The USSR* (1987); *Flowers In The Dirt* (1989); *Tripping The Live Fantastic* (1990); *Unplugged* (1991); *Liverpool Oratorio* (1991); *Off The Ground* (1993); *Paul Is Live* (1993); *Flaming Pie* (1997); *Standing Stone* (1997); *Run Devil Run* (1999); *Working Classical* (1999); *Liverpool Sound Collage* (2000); *Driving Rain* (2001); Harrison: *Wonderwall* (1968); *Electronic Sounds* (1969); *All Things Must Pass* (1970); *The Concert For Bangla Desh* (1971); *Living In The Material World* (1973); *Dark Horse* (1974); *Extra Texture* (1975); *33 1/3* (1976); *George Harrison* (1979); *Somewhere In England* (1980); *Gone Troppo* (1982); *Cloud Nine* (1987); *The Traveling Wilburys* (1988); *Volume 3* (1990); *Live In Japan* (1992); Starr: *Sentimental Journey* (1970); *Beaucoups Of Blues* (1971); *Ringo* (1973); *Goodnight Vienna* (1974); *Blast From Your Past* (1975); *Rotogravure* (1975); *Ringo The 4th* (1977); *Bad Boy* (1978); *Stop And Smell The Roses* (1981); *Old Wave* (1983); *Time Takes Time* (1992).

Angeles[1] and by 1975 they were (independently) speculating about getting The Beatles together again. This, though, foundered on Harrison's indifference and relations cooled again, partly as a result of Lennon's return to Ono. When, in 1980, Lennon reactivated his career after five years as a 'house husband' bringing up his son Sean, his public attitude to McCartney was softer than it had been in 1970-1, though he spoke dismissively of the latter's hope of reviving their songwriting partnership. Meanwhile Harrison's autobiography *I, Me, Mine* appeared, barely mentioning Lennon (and thereby reportedly wounding him deeply). Even Lennon's death at the hands of a demented gunman did not physically reunite the remaining ex-Beatles. A sorrowful Harrison commemorated his friend with his song 'All Those Years Ago' in which he hoped to collaborate with McCartney and Starr. McCartney, though, had made his peace with Lennon before he was killed and felt no reason to co-operate with Harrison except at a distance. (Later that year, he and Harrison shelved their differences to attend Starr's marriage to actress Barbara Bach, but relations again deteriorated in 1985 when Harrison, Starr, and Ono took McCartney to court in a dispute over royalties.)

In the aftermath of Lennon's death, during which fans held memorial vigils all over the world, some commentators suggested that, with this event, the Sixties had finally ended.[2] More bathetically, the tragedy destroyed McCartney's dream of some day writing more songs with his old partner. Yet this was no nostalgic ambition. By the late Seventies, he had become aware that, while he could still sell millions of records, he was a shadow of the creative force he had been as one half of the Lennon–McCartney partnership. During the Eighties, he attempted collaborations with Eric Stewart, formerly of 10cc, and with Elvis Costello, but these were minnows compared to John Lennon and quite unable to inspire an artist who had punched the same creative

---

[1] According to McCartney, they jammed together at the Hit Factory studio during 1974, presumably during the sessions for Lennon's *Walls And Bridges*. Legend has it that May Pang, then Lennon's lover, has the results on tape.

[2] Others would say that 'the Sixties' ended with the legal dissolution of The Beatles on the last day of 1970, or perhaps with the shockingly sudden loss of Jimi Hendrix on 18th September 1970. (The present writer recalls learning of Hendrix's death that day from a news hoarding in London's Richmond Road. A bright summer afternoon, it seemed to cloud over at that moment.) A less sentimental judgement might choose 17th October 1973 when, in response to the Yom Kippur war, OPEC quadrupled the world price of oil, ending the relative affluence on which the preceding ten years of happy-go-lucky excess in the West had chiefly depended.

weight with him on WE CAN WORK IT OUT and A DAY IN THE LIFE. Neither Harrison nor Starr were, by then, pursuing their careers on anything more than a dilettante level. Operating on their own, the members of the most lavishly talented of pop groups quickly declined into something dismayingly like mediocrity. Why?

Age is part of it. Pop/rock is essentially young people's music and the eventual encroachment of home-making usually ensures that the gang-mentality of a group proves impossible to sustain beyond its members' late twenties. Something new has to take over: a switch to other pursuits – management, production, TV presentation, acting (in Harrison's case, gardening) – or solo careers based on more inward music befitting growing maturity, supposing this to be the case. When, in interviews between 1983 and 1996, McCartney looked back in amused disbelief at the sheer velocity of The Beatles' career, he voiced the perspective of a family man for whom such monomaniacal energy can only be the prerogative of wild youth. In the end, The Beatles quite simply had to grow up and settle down. While McCartney, Harrison, and Starr each ventured out on tour during the early Nineties, they were by then, as they would certainly have conceded if asked, long out of touch with the adolescent thrill-energy on which pop music relies.

If time simply caught up with The Beatles in personal terms, they also fell victims to time of a more universal kind. In their self-debunking, mostly inadvertent way, they made and changed history – yet history, indifferent as ever, simply moved on, leaving them behind. As the Seventies advanced, the apolitical Beatles came to seem irrelevant and by the Eighties they were regarded by the pop press as museum pieces. Only when a psychedelic revival occurred in pop culture during the late Eighties did The Beatles' records start to make emotional sense to their young descendants.

Time and place are integral to artistic creativity, and the extent to which The Beatles and the Sixties were symbiotic is difficult to exaggerate. Early in that decade, the group had mirrored their era of upward social mobility and technology-driven consumerism with infectious good-time music and carefree lyrics. They took the drugs of the time, alcohol and amphetamines, and cruised the surface, letting success propel them, content to leave the tiller to Brian Epstein. Then, late in 1964, they encountered marijuana, and their music became unsettled – needing something deeper and more original but uncertain of what this might be. Conditioned by their backgrounds and the presiding Sixties ethos of classlessness, they looked to their roots in lyrics about Liverpool and floated a 'comedy song' idea taken partly from music-hall and the Northern playhouse tradition – concepts later elaborated in *Sgt. Pepper*. Yet, instinctive as they were, The Beatles could not deduce the stylistic renaissance they knew they had to achieve. It was only when LSD arrived, bringing an 'alternative' outlook for which inner freedom was more important than material success, that the pieces fell into place and the group's new direction became clear.

Inspired by the advent of the counterculture and its view of the 'straight' society to which they had hitherto unwittingly belonged, The Beatles began making records that addressed their world instead of merely reflecting it. Often discussed as if it sprang out of thin air, the group's 'new sound' in *Revolver* was intrinsically linked to the onset of the second half of the Sixties, in which social aspiration gave way to the politico-spiritual idealism of the young. By the same token, once 'their' Sixties, an era of optimism and ambition, started to sour and sicken in 1968, so did The Beatles. Lennon's troubled [125/132] REVOLUTION opened the first crack in the band's façade. Cut off from their native historical background, they quickly began to lose their bearings.

Yet The Beatles were in no respect an ordinary phenomenon. Many have spoken of the charismatic atmosphere that switched on whenever all four were together – a group-mindedness which kept them united through a further eighteen months of in-fighting during which they recorded well over fifty more tracks and which continued, albeit less reliably than before, to function as the psychic antenna by which they maintained contact with the shifting currents of popular feeling at large. The sensitivity to cultural context which enabled The Beatles to remake their career in 1966 has been surpassed only by David Bowie in pop and, in their respective idioms (and, of course, over far longer stretches of time), by Stravinsky, Picasso, and Miles Davis. If, in 1969, the group's second attempt at transcending themselves ('Get Back') foundered on the sort of self-destructive shouting-matches solo artists are able to avoid, they nonetheless displayed at their peak a mutual understanding and collective intuition which kept them acutely in tune with each other and their time. The heart of The Beatles was an X-factor: a near-telepathic connectedness that provided home-from-home support, friendly competition, and the haven of a common outlook on life. This is what they missed in their solo careers, and what McCartney was wistfully hoping to contact again by resuscitating his partnership with Lennon.

More specifically, McCartney was seeking completion. While unique in functioning most of the time as two independent songwriters rather than as composer and lyricist, Lennon and McCartney formed a close partnership for most of the Sixties. If their characters and musical styles were fundamentally different, they were still sufficiently alike to allow seamless collaborations in many of their early records and remained perfectly complementary later on when they made songs out of unfinished pieces they each happened to have lying around. For the first two-thirds of The Beatles' career, they were genuinely tight, aware of how good they were and loyal in the face of the outside world. Lennon knew that while McCartney could be superficial, he was also the better musician and melodist and, when pushed, could rival and sometimes surpass him as an expressive writer. Conversely, McCartney's diplomatic charm and mainstream instincts worked as a brake on Lennon's anarchic disruptions and aggressive sarcasm. It was an ideal match. They laughed at the same things, thought at the same speed, respected each other's talent, and knew that their unspoken urge to best and surprise each other was crucial to the continuing vitality of their music.

Yet, in the end, the introspective Lennon needed McCartney less than McCartney needed him. Often portrayed as feathering his own nest in The Beatles, McCartney was far more committed to the group than his partner. There was a lot of pride at stake after their break-up and consequently much bad-mouthing, mostly from Lennon. Honest enough later to withdraw many of the vicious things he'd said about McCartney, he nevertheless remained too self-absorbed to admit that his post-Beatles music was missing anything, let alone that this absent element might perhaps be that friendly friction with his old colleague. McCartney, wounded by Lennon's attacks on him at the beginning of the Seventies, could have been excused for indulging in similar self-justifications. It's to his credit that he did not (at least at this stage) seek to promote his own view of their relationship, instead just getting on with his own career. Even more to his credit is that he finally came to face the obvious fact that Lennon and McCartney apart were less than half the songwriters they'd been together. What he did not seem to grasp was why their split was irreversible – that time, personal and universal, had overtaken them. Because of this, his itch to be creatively reunited with Lennon endured and, a quarter of a century later, was, in a curious way, fulfilled.

[187] FREE AS A BIRD (*Lennon*)

Lennon lead vocal, piano; McCartney lead vocal, harmony vocal,
  bass, acoustic guitar, piano, synthesiser (?); Harrison harmony
  vocal, electric slide guitar, acoustic guitar, ukelele (?); Starr
  drums, harmony vocal
Recorded: c. 1977, Dakota Apartments, New York; February,
  March 1994, Sussex, England.
Producers: John Lennon/Jeff Lynne/Paul McCartney/George
  Harrison/Richard Starkey. Engineer: Geoff Emerick.
UK release: 4th December 1995 (CD single: *Free As A Bird*)
US release: 4th December 1995 (CD single: *Free As A Bird*)

In 1994, McCartney went to New York to attend Lennon's
posthumous solo induction into the Rock 'n' Roll Hall of Fame.[1]
This was generous of him, since only shallow media bias can have
prevented him from being similarly honoured at the same time. The
general perception among rock critics was that Lennon had been the
prime force behind The Beatles and that his post-Beatles career had
displayed more rock-and-roll authenticity than that of his former
partner, regarded as a frothy lightweight who had frittered his populist
gifts away in trivial audience pandering.[2] Facing down this implicit
affront with his customary tactical grin, McCartney must have quietly
seethed during the ceremony, notwithstanding the fact that the
occasion allowed him to make his peace in person with Lennon's
widow Yoko Ono. Indeed, as prearranged, she had a present for him:
three Lennon demos which, McCartney hoped, might make the basis
of a 'virtual' Beatles reunion in the dimension of digital sound.

McCartney's reconciliation with Ono, which had been on the way
for two or three years, made up for times in the past when the Lennons
had loathed the McCartneys, and for Ono's decision, in tandem with
Harrison and Starr, to sue McCartney over disputed royalties in 1985.
In fact the lives of all the ex-Beatles had been one long dance of mutual
distrust, recrimination, and litigation. Because of this, McCartney's final
conceptual wheeze for The Beatles – *The Long And Winding Road*, a
100-minute collage of film-clips of their career assembled by Neil
Aspinall in 1969 – had gathered dust on Apple's shelves for twenty
years, stymied by legal squabbles and personal animosities between the
surviving participants. Only in 1989, when Apple won a reported £50

---

[1] The Beatles as an entity had been thus recognised seven years earlier.
[2] This bias is perpetuated in the jacket of Allan Kozinn's *The Beatles* (Phaidon,
1995), where Lennon's face fills the cover while McCartney is relegated to the back
and Harrison and Starr don't figure at all.

million settlement from EMI, did the log-jam loosen – whereupon Aspinall contacted McCartney, Harrison, Starr, and Ono, suggesting that the project be reactivated. Each gave cautious approval to what was now inaccurately referred to as an 'Anthology', and a director for the visual side of the project was appointed: Geoff Wonfor, creator of the influential Eighties live music TV show *The Tube*. Unsurprisingly, Harrison was the least enthusiastic participant,[1] though his attitude eased when he finally forced himself to sit down and watch the mass of footage of Beatlemania patiently accumulated by Aspinall. (Turning to Wonfor at one point, he grinned 'I want somebody like U2 to watch this. Then they'd see a band that was *really* famous.')[2] Equally unsurprisingly, McCartney was the hottest for the project, taking the lead in organising the audio side of it, which quickly assumed the form of three two-CD boxed sets. It was with this grandiose scheme in mind that he had asked Yoko Ono for anything by Lennon which hadn't already been officially recorded.

FREE AS A BIRD was the first of the three rough home demos which Ono gave the ex-Beatles: a song cassette-taped in the Lennons' New York apartment in 1977 for a vaguely envisaged musical about Lennon's life and times during the Sixties. Ever-nostalgic, McCartney was touched by what he heard and became determined to like it. Harrison was less impressed, remarking 'I sort of felt John was going off a little bit towards the end of his writing' – a realistic verdict sharply dismissed by McCartney as 'presumptuous'.[3] Before anything else could be decided, the mono cassette needed to be carefully cleaned up in a digital studio, synchronised to a sequencer using a time-stretch program to cure Lennon's typically unsteady tempo (thereby allowing the other Beatles to play in time with it) and, finally, transferred to multitrack. At Harrison's suggestion, this task was undertaken by Jeff Lynne at his Hollywood studio.[4] When George Martin politely turned down an invitation to produce on the grounds that his ears weren't what they used to be,[5] McCartney brought the tape to his

---

[1] Rumour has it that he got involved mainly because he needed money for a court case concerning his former company HandMade Films.

[2] U2 imitated The Beatles with their 'rooftop' video for 'Where The Streets Have No Name' in 1987.

[3] Interview with Jeff Giles in *Newsweek*, 23rd October 1995.

[4] Formerly of the sub-Beatles Electric Light Orchestra, Lynne co-produced Harrison's *Cloud Nine* in 1987 and formed The Traveling Wilburys with Harrison, Dylan, Roy Orbison, and Tom Petty in 1988.

[5] Oddly, Martin's hearing was good enough to 'produce and direct' the entire *Anthology* CD series.

Sussex studio and there, in February 1994, with Lynne in the producer's seat and their old engineer Geoff Emerick working the desk, the former Beatles set to work.

Deciding to tell themselves that Lennon had gone on holiday leaving them a half-complete song with a request to finish it, they managed to skirt round the eeriness of accompanying a disembodied vocal/piano track which sounded alarmingly as if filtering through from the next world. Some extra writing needed to be done before the recording could begin and this must have helped them get used to the strangeness of the situation. Finally they began to play, Starr using his old Ludwig kit, Harrison his psychedelically-sprayed Fender Stratocaster and a Martin D-28 acoustic, and McCartney his Wal Custom 5-string bass plus a Gibson Jumbo electro-acoustic.[1]

The lethargic downward drift of FREE AS A BIRD is based on the standard doo-wop four-chord cycle, with variations.[2] As with many later Lennon songs (e.g., 'Imagine', 'Mind Games'), the tempo is slow-medium, the metre and structure four-square regular. All that disturbs this tranquil sedateness is the yearning rise into C major in the last four of the verse/chorus's sixteen bars. The upward progression in a chromatically ambiguous A minor for the middle eight may seem striking in this sleepy context, but it's merely a variant of the same doo-wop cycle, subconsciously borrowed from the D minor verse of The Shangri-Las' kitsch 1964 classic 'Remember (Walking In The Sand)'.[3] The most effective moment arrives with a surprising modulation to C major for Harrison's slide guitar solo, the song temporarily taking flight as its title promises.[4] Apart from this, the effect is bland, Lynne having been obliged to mask the piano in Lennon's demo (taped in mono along with his voice) by soaking the track in a soggily un-Beatleish texture of Eighties synth 'pad' and massed acoustic guitars. Harrison's electric lead in the verses shows how FREE AS A BIRD might have been

---

[1] McCartney declined to play his famous Hofner 'violin bass' on either [187] or [188].

[2] See [22], note. The IV chord (D major) here becomes either the flat VI or its own minor.

[3] 'Whatever happened to/The boy that I once knew' becomes 'Whatever happened to/The life that we once knew'. Interviews and press reports are vague about this middle eight, some claiming that all that it needed was a lyric, others that Lennon had left gaps for a middle section which McCartney, who sings it, thus had to write from scratch. Neither alternative is reflected in the composer's credit, although the second option is strongly suggested by the ascending harmonic style, if nothing else.

[4] Here the effect is reinforced by McCartney going to the low C on his 5-string bass.

arranged for *Abbey Road*, while the George Formby ukelele (see [E5b]) at the end – presumably also played by him[1] – likewise transcends the lifelessness of song and sound.

Nothing better could have been done with Lennon's demo by anyone else, and as a soundtrack for Geoff Wonfor's adroitly nostalgia-exploiting video it works well enough. Ultimately, though, this is a dreary song, produced in a period of its writer's life when he was too content to care, or notice, whether his expression was banal or unfocused. FREE AS A BIRD stands no comparison with The Beatles' Sixties music.

[188] REAL LOVE *(Lennon)*

> **Lennon** double-tracked lead vocal, piano; **McCartney** lead vocal, backing vocal, electric bass, double bass, acoustic guitar, synth/organ (?), percussion; **Harrison** backing vocal, electric guitar, acoustic guitar, percussion; **Starr** drums, percussion; **Jeff Lynne**, backing vocal, guitar
>
> Recorded: c. 1979, Dakota Apartments, New York; February 1995, Sussex, England.
>
> Producers: John Lennon/Jeff Lynne/Paul McCartney/George Harrison/Richard Starkey. Engineers: Geoff Emerick, Jon Jacobs.
>
> UK release: 4th March 1996 (CD single: *Real Love*)
>
> US release: 4th March 1996 (CD single: *Real Love*)

For the second song, demoed in the same rough and ready way[2] and recorded a year after FREE AS A BIRD, McCartney changed to a Fender Jazz, tracking parts of his line on a double bass once owned by Elvis Presley's original bassist, Bill Black.[3] Like its predecessor, REAL LOVE uses a descending progression with a scheme employing the diminished and augmented chords typical of Lennon's later style, but this is evidence less of harmonic sophistication than of his lazy proclivity for finding sequences by moving his fingers as little as possible.[4]

---

[1] McCartney also plays the ukelele. Lennon, too, played one on [111] ALL TOGETHER NOW.

[2] Lennon had used a drum-machine on this occasion, so there was no need to apply time-stretch, but the track was much 'noisier' than FREE AS A BIRD and required considerably more EQ.

[3] Used on the session for 'Heartbreak Hotel' in 1956, this instrument was bought for McCartney by his wife Linda in 1975.

[4] As issued, the verse of REAL LOVE descends from (approximately) E major to G sharp major to C sharp minor 7 to B augmented by the simple means of holding the upper two notes of E major and moving the third finger down.

Essentially as tired as FREE AS A BIRD (it was varispeeded up about a tone to somewhere between D sharp and E to give it some zip), REAL LOVE appears to have had less time lavished on it and makes little impression. Unimpressed with the quality of these two 'reunion' tracks, Harrison declined to have anything to do with Lennon's third demo, which consequently remains in its original state and was not included on *Anthology 3*, as originally planned.[1]

Screened in autumn 1995 and issued in eight parts in October 1996, the video version of the *Anthology* project successfully evokes The Beatles' career, providing historic documentary footage cleverly put together. In some respects rather too expansive, in others a little too elliptical, the series nevertheless manages to present an outline of events which most will recognise as accurate, while at the same time summoning up a strong sense of the atmosphere of the time and offering much entertaining performance footage, some of which is genuinely impressive. The main flaw arises from the fact that the series was entirely controlled by Apple, and, more specifically, by McCartney, Harrison, Starr, and Ono. Notwithstanding the absence of an objective voice-over, which would have caused irreconcilable arguments, there's a Party Line tinge to the project – an 'official history' quality that obtrudes as a distinct smell of oil poured on troubled water, especially in the later episodes. The picture of the post-1967 Beatles is too nicely forgiving, too sentimentally nostalgic to fit the facts as recorded by independent observers at the time. Together, The Beatles could turn into a transcendent entity, impermeable to outsiders and borne along in its own bubble of private humour. When this entity was buoyant, the four could forget each other's faults and enjoy each other's company. However, when it began to deflate, tensions were exposed and tolerance became harder to sustain. In threes, they grew increasingly prickly; in pairs, they often didn't even like each other much. Despite the genial self-debunking of McCartney and Starr and the wry scepticism of Harrison, none of this is apparent in the *Anthology* video. Nor is there a single word from the female side of the story, ex-wives and lovers being ruled out by Ono's refusal to take part.

As for the material issued on compact disc since 1994 – eight full-

---

[1] Different sources refer to this song as 'Now And Then', 'Miss You', or 'Grow Old With Me'.

length CDs and three CD 'singles' – while initially interesting by virtue of being by The Beatles, little of it is worth a second listen, let alone the scores of millions of pounds it has cost the group's worldwide fans to acquire. Once the decision had been taken to attempt a ghost outline of The Beatles' career – putting in tracks at regular intervals to give the impression of a continuous documentary, rather than selecting the twenty or so unreleased songs and takes which would have sufficed to complete the group's story – padding became inevitable, and ever more blatantly resorted to as the *Anthology* series proceeded. Moreover, difficult or 'dangerous' options were ducked through committee compromises or individual vetoes. For instance, Harrison's dismissal of McCartney's bid to include [U96] CARNIVAL OF LIGHT on *Anthology 2* resulted in the largely pointless last-minute substitution of some straightforward backing tracks ([86] ELEANOR RIGBY, [105] WITHIN YOU WITHOUT YOU). Even more superfluous are most of the many near-identical 'alternative takes' from *The Beatles* and *Abbey Road* on *Anthology 3* puzzlingly selected instead of the original extended version of [125] REVOLUTION 1, one or two examples of the instrumental jams of 1968–9, and the long alternative takes of [134] HELTER SKELTER.[1] While most Beatles fans will be restless until they own these discs, they are unlikely to take them off their shelves very often.

If the money-spinning additions to the Parlophone/Apple discography during 1994–6 are hard to justify artistically, there is no doubt that The Beatles have, as a result of the business these have engendered, become an enormous media property again, thirty years after the events. While this was predictable, what is striking is the sheer intensity with which Nineties pop/rock now iconises The Beatles and the Sixties. Britpop groups play Beatles and Sixties records during recording sessions in order to prompt ideas and stimulate atmosphere. Modern versions of songs from the same era regularly top the UK singles charts, while a Beatles 'cover' is *de rigueur* for every local up-and-coming guitar-based group. Nor is this fascination superficial. The current pop generation in Britain understands its Sixties references in depth, pursuing its acquaintance with obscure artists and lesser-known B-sides of that period with a dedicated erudition akin to the Sixties hipsters' fanatical knowledge of blues and R&B.

---

[1] The edited excerpt from one of these provided on *Anthology 3* ludicrously fades just as the group is beginning to improvise.

Though some contemporary journalists affect to deplore it, such cross-decade interplay gives Nineties pop a sense of its roots, placing it in a historical tradition against which it can test its own ambitions. Moreover, this system of links with a classic foundation era is quite different from the postmodern attitude of recent years in which the past was treated as a shopping-mall from which one might pick themes and styles and slap them together with a hopefully knowing smirk. The extent to which today's stars are able to establish a productive relationship with the Sixties is potentially significant not only in terms of refreshing a machine-dominated and irony-paralysed popular art, but also for the possibility (however slim) of revitalising modern life in general through contact with the driving ambition and self-transcending idealism of what is now widely seen as this century's fulcrum era. Whether future generations can draw on the best of the Sixties so as to rebalance a culture badly knocked out of kilter by that decade's sheer charismatic energy is another question.

On a more mundane note, it should perhaps be pointed out, *pace* those pop commentators who are in it mainly for the clothes and the poses, that treating The Beatles as icons can only be fruitful for young pop musicians. Coining almost every trend which has succeeded them apart from musical mechanisation,[1] The Beatles, together and individually, amount to a veritable academy of pop cultural values and talents. The self-maintained high standards of the Lennon–McCartney partnership should remain a permanent inspiration and measure for all aspiring pop songwriters. Lennon's incessant quest for new, rule-breaking expression – since his heyday approached only by David Bowie – stands as a paradigm for innovation-hungry English pop. A clumsy guitarist, he probably had to grope around for the chords he needed while piecing his songs together,[2] yet his technical shortcomings were made irrelevant by – in fact to a very large extent actively fostered – the unique force of his imagination. Supreme as a melodist, McCartney will surely come to be seen as pop's finest multi-instrumentalist: one of its two or three most influential bass-players, a fluent pianist, an inventive drummer, and the performer of a handful of the genre's most striking guitar solos. Although a far less spontaneous player than McCartney, Harrison remains a role-model for student lead guitarists who will gain much from studying his function in The Beatles' 1963–6 output, carefully supporting Lennon and McCartney's parts with

---

[1] See below: Note to Chronology.

[2] Eg., the demo versions of [148] HAPPINESS IS A WARM GUN and [183] POLYTHENE PAM *(Anthology 3)* and the unissued demo of [U126] CHILD OF NATURE.

characterful lines and textural colourings without which the group's sound would have lacked an essential dimension. Less notable a contributor to The Beatles' song-book, he has one pop classic to his name, while most of his other songs display a quality rare in the culture of populism: thoughtfulness. As for Starr, long travestied as an amiable mediocrity riding The Beatles coat-tails, he is nothing less than the father of modern pop/rock drumming – the modest man who invented it. His faintly behind-the-beat style subtly propelled The Beatles, his tunings brought the bottom end into recorded drum-sound,[1] and his distinctly eccentric fills remain among the most memorable in pop music.

Warranted or not, the 1994–6 supplement to The Beatles' discography testifies in sales alone to the group's eminence in post-war popular culture. As expressive of England in the Sixties as the music of Britten in the Fifties, The Beatles made some of the world's best music during their era. This, though, is merely the judgement of our time – the way it appears to those who live in their immediate reverberation. It is harder to guess how they'll come to be seen by future generations (although that they *will* be seen is certain). For the First World, the 1960s were the key years of this century: a hectic transition from one of way of life to another. When Lennon remarked in 1966 that The Beatles had become 'more popular than Jesus', he put his finger on it. The Christian social values of the old culture were then giving way to a life dominated by technology-driven consumer materialism, an impatient expectation of instant gratification, and a self-before-others ethic that has since fragmented Western society. In their early records, The Beatles innocently embodied this; later on, they voiced the countercultural outlook which warned against it. As unwittingly unorthodox as it is cannily talented, their music captured an enduringly momentous and deeply ambiguous decade in sound. For this reason alone, their place in history is safe, although whether the 21st century will regard them askance as a result is impossible to predict.

---

[1] Aided, of course, by Geoff Emerick's revolutionary microphone set-ups and sound-production tricks.

NOTE TO CHRONOLOGY

The following pages provide an overview of trends and events in the Sixties correlated with significant dates in the career of The Beatles. (In the column devoted to the latter, entries consisting of record titles preceded by 'UK:' or 'US:' indicate release dates.) Apart from this, the main component is a monthly selection of records popular in the UK between 1960 and 1970. Since up to a hundred different singles register in any average month of Top 40s, these choices amount only to an impression of the music in vogue at a given time, though in all cases the top two or three singles are listed, and sometimes most of the Top 10. Less commercially successful but often more interesting or worthwhile Top 40 records make up the remainder.

Also included is a similar selection of albums. Readers will note that the number of these listed rises as the decade proceeds, doubling by its halfway point and tripling by its final two years. This reflects both record sales and a major structural change in the pop market which occurred around 1966–7: the birth of what later came to be called 'rock' – a heavily amplified, large venue, big money genre which shifted the creative centre of gravity from radio-orientated singles charts to live music and long-playing records. This growth in the album market coincided with an expansion of the audience for popular music and a corresponding increase in record company investment in artists and repertoire. More gold discs were awarded in the first half of 1968 than in any previous six-month period. In 1968, production of albums in the UK (49,184,000) for the first time exceeded that of singles (49,161,000). Overall sales were then at their highest since 1964, when singles accounted for three-quarters of the market.

Since the heyday of the late Sixties and early Seventies, sales in the singles market have fallen drastically. In 1993 it was possible to get a No. 1 with 20,000 sales per week, a figure which would barely have achieved a Top 50 placing in 1966. Between 1982 and 1992, annual singles sales fell by 25 million.[1] The reason for this is fairly obvious. In

---

[1] It has been said that the sales volumes of contemporary singles have, during the last few years, recovered to something like that of the Sixties. In fact, the 'millions' sometimes claimed by the singles artists of the Nineties are calculated by adding

whatever genre and of whatever artistic standard, the singles of the Sixties were as a rule more memorable, inventive, and affecting than those of today. Why this is so would take longer to cover than can be afforded here, yet one or two simple points are worth making.

In the Sixties, music was generally recorded live, its arrangements blocked out in advance. This method necessarily combined real urgency, a high level of empathic expertise from the players, and great ingenuity on the part of producers who had little scope for concealing errors under multiple overdubbing.[1] Because predesigned, the music's textures *breathed*, creating a space around the instruments and voices which, along with the ambience of valve amps and mixing desks, produced a vivid, atmospheric sound rarely captured in the clean digital recordings of today. Modern records, rather than embodying a *performance*, are usually built up as they go along using a layering principle which, apart from eliminating any possibility of a natural balance between instruments, leaves no pores through which the sound can respire. Moreover, most of today's sounds are synthetic, clogging frequencies and adding to the sense of aural asphyxiation. The result of all this has been the gradual replacement of expressive skills by technical ones – the decline of subtlety in songwriting and instrumental finesse mirrored by a monstrous efflorescence of boffin expertise in sound manufacture and studio-craft.

The driving force behind the modern recording ethos is automation – of signal-processing, sequencing, mixing, and instrument-linking (by MIDI, or Musical Instrument Digital Interface). These functions, while convenient, tend to distance artists from the integrity of the material they are building (as does the prolonged, additive nature of the whole recording procedure). It's hard to infuse real feeling into music so synthetically constructed, and correspondingly easy to lose a sense of proportion during a process less akin to traditional live recording than

---

together sales in all marketed forms, often including multiple 'remixes' issued simultaneously. The millions of 'album' CDs sold, however, are genuine.

[1] During most of the Sixties there was less reliance on EQ than has since become standard. Partly a question of lack of equipment in those days, it was, more centrally, because engineers then preferred to control sound through their knowledge of microphone-placing and echo-production. Signals in early Sixties recordings often went to tape with only levels modified *en route*, while compression and frequency modulation were used sparingly, particularly in black music (Motown's relatively hi-tech studio being a futuristic exception). The level of sonic artifice in The Beatles' 1966–9 records, facilitated without even the modest range of EQ devices then available in the most advanced US studios, was unprecedented and, with the exception of The Beach Boys' 1966–7 recordings, unparalleled.

to what's known in the cinema world as 'post-production'. In the absence of technical limits on dynamics and timbre, senses soon become sated and the law of diminishing returns ensures that the medium devours the message. There is a deadly parallel between the post-*Star Wars* genre of the 'special effects movie', with its bombastic premium on sensory impact, and the onset, in audio production, of the 'big drum sound' during the Eighties, when the faders on channels to drum microphones rose higher every year, habituating listeners to an ever-more gargantuan sound-image. Much the same has happened to the sound of the electric guitar, nowadays routinely smothered under a barrage of blazing distortion through which it can be difficult to identify the chords being played. This, in turn, has eliminated the need for anything more than a generalised strum technique, the instrumental craft-skills of yesteryear displaced by a detached knob-twiddling efficiency in the manipulation of samplers and effects units.

The most pervasive form of automation in pop during the last fifteen years has been the use of 'click-tracks' and drum-machines. Brought into disco music in the mid-Seventies, the drum-machine created new possibilities for rhythm cycles and sounds but at the same time it standardised the production of pop's dance-tempo 4/4, most obviously by reducing the bass-drum to regular crotchets. Admittedly, the rap and dance music created in the late Eighties and Nineties has displayed much rhythmic inventiveness within the confines of total mechanisation (rap, at its best, being a dazzling combination of street-doggerel and vocal drum-solo). Yet the effect of presetting rhythms by drum-machines, and later by drum-samplers slaved to sequencers, has been to elevate 'the groove' over every other musical priority. At its simplest this means that songs are now written from the rhythm track upwards, rather than from a melodic/harmonic idea, as was the case with almost all Sixties music apart from that of the futuristic inventor of 'funk', James Brown. Within such an ethos, melody is as likely to flourish as a rose in concrete, whilst sensitivity to harmonic nuance inevitably withers. The brutal thrills of today's gymnastic 'rave' music have an undeniable power, but this is bought at the expense of the subtlety of expression which created the desolate sigh (Am–Am6–Em) at the start of [148] HAPPINESS IS A WARM GUN, the fond wonder of the chromatic fall in the opening phrase of [170] SOMETHING, the sudden chill of F in G major in [96] A DAY IN THE LIFE ('I'd seen his *face* before'), and the simultaneously literal and metaphorical sense of the sun going behind a cloud as D major moves into D minor in [119] THE FOOL ON THE HILL.

Dominated by the synthetic slam of the sequenced off-beat –

crashing down tyrannically like some monstrous industrial time-keeping device – modern songs are regularised and formularised, their harmonic movements banal and predictable, their vocal lines devoid of independent melody and constructed from prefabricated melodic/lyric clichés bolted together as if by mechanics on an assembly-line. It may be unfair to compare the rapid rate of harmonic change in a song like [59] YESTERDAY with the sort of contemporary dance record that holds a single chord for five minutes, but the contrast is significant. Sixties music is generally two or three times more harmonically mobile than Eighties and Nineties music, and immeasurably freer and more alert in the relationship of its tunes to their accompanying chords. It goes without saying that, in terms of rhythmic variety, Sixties pop puts most of the music of succeeding decades to shame, The Beatles being a case-study in this respect. What is less obvious is that the absence of rhythmic mechanisation in Sixties music released the natural effervescence of the ensemble studio performance, as the subtle acceleration in tracks like [89] I WANT TO TELL YOU and [99] FIXING A HOLE demonstrates.

The differences between Sixties pop and what came after it are epitomised by the loss of one vital element: the unexpected. From functional drum-and-bass dance grooves to fulsome Heavy Metal ballads, the lack of melodic/harmonic surprise in Nineties music is numbing. Indeed, in terms of form, pop has almost come to a halt, displaying few originalities in structure, metre, or melody over the last ten years. By contrast, when Sixties listeners heard a new Beatles song – or good ones by Holland–Dozier–Holland, Jagger–Richard, Brian Wilson, Ray Davies, Bacharach–David, Syd Barrett, Smokey Robinson, Pete Townshend, etc., etc. – they never knew from bar to bar what was coming next. Sometimes this was because these songwriters were musically aware enough to make unusual moves on purpose, but mostly it reflected the quintessential quality of the Sixties: self-determined openness. Just as social and sexual restraints then fell into abeyance, the idea that there were orthodox compositional rules which had to be respected did not last long during that decade. Originality in popular culture then became – for a while – uniquely prized, creative unexpectedness stemming almost as much from attitude as from talent (although it would be altogether too 'Sixties' to claim that *anyone* could bring it off then, let alone now).

Lennon and McCartney generated many of their melodic and harmonic surprises by letting their fingers wander speculatively as they sang. A very simple instance of this occurs in the bridge of [13] I'LL GET YOU, where they shift unexpectedly to the minor dominant (A minor in D major). A musicologist might seize upon this unorthodoxy and spin a sophisticated theory to account for it, but the truth is simpler – and, for aspiring pop songwriters, more interesting. Lennon and McCartney chose this chord not to pique classical ears by creating modal instability in the melody line but because going to A major would have been too obvious and because A minor is a favourite guitarist's chord which, so far as they were concerned, forced an expressive flattening of the melody-line at that point. Almost everything they did as songwriters was done on instinct, controlled by a strong sense of line and very retentive ears. Self-trained by listening and trial-and-error rather than by sight-reading and rote-learning, their musical minds were clear and open and their memories alert enough to handle on-the-hoof changes in vocal harmonies between time-pressurised takes without the memory-aid of a score. That there are a few small harmony errors in their early records merely shows them to be a human; what is surprising, given their work-rate, is that there aren't three times as many. (There are more mistakes with lyrics in early Beatles records than with harmonies, and we must remember that the singers were also playing instruments – McCartney sometimes singing whilst simultaneously playing a bass line in quavers. And winking at the girls in the front row.)

No doubt there is scope for learned musicological analyses of The Beatles' many unorthodox musical traits, but these are unlikely to inspire much musical creativity, partly because alien to pop's intuitiveness but more basically because the dominance of harmonic, melodic, and rhythmic cliché during the last decade proves that originality in anything but the manipulation of effects technology is no longer appreciated, let alone missed. When listeners bemoan the dearth of 'good tunes' and send Robson and Jerome or The Fugees to the top of the charts, they register a protest-vote against the dim self-satisfaction of most of today's pop songwriters, who neither know they are failing to supply demand in this respect nor are equipped to remedy the failure were realisation suddenly to dawn. Few in any generation have the gift of writing great tunes or lasting songs, a fact which no amount of 'rock school' pedantry can alter. Yet there *are* clues to be found by thinking about music, and by listening to it with the closeness with which The Beatles absorbed the records that inspired them.

In polemicising against the decline of inspiration in pop since the Sixties,[1] Tony Parsons has spoken for a large constituency of older

---

[1] *Without Walls*, Channel 4, May 1993.

listeners who either grew up with Sixties music and have become steadily more disappointed by pop ever since, or of younger listeners who have since discovered the fresh excitement and imaginative freedom of Sixties pop via records. Because of this, Parsons has been attacked by the sociological sort of pop critic whose interest is less in music than in the style 'signifiers' manifested in each new pop microgeneration. A staple belief among such critics is that what changes in pop is not its objective level of 'soul' and inspiration but the subjective points of views of commentators as they get older and less involved with it. In the end, of course, such matters *are* subjective – yet the paucity of relativism will be clear to anyone with a modicum of musical instinct and an ounce of commonsense. For instance, Mark Edwards,[1] denying Parsons' claim that modern pop is declining into meaninglessness, observed that Parson's example – a 'techno' dance record in which the sampled phrase 'Gonna take you higher and higher' is looped and mechanically repeated over two incessantly reiterated chords – is no more meaningless than Little Richard's 'Awopbopaloomop' of 1956. While thoroughly contemporary, Edwards' quantitative and materialistic concept of meaning betrays an inability to distinguish between living expression and the creative equivalent of Frankenstein's monster. Meaning resides not in literal substance but in tone and expression, Little Richard's outburst being a spontaneous assertion of the soul's freedom from the constraints of form. Born of the moment, 'Tutti Frutti' embodies pop's essential instantaneity, something increasingly impossible to reproduce as time passes. (Nine-tenths of pop's decline is due to sheer staleness.) The phrase 'higher and higher', now reduced to a dead formula, has likewise been filtered down through several levels of dilution from its origin in Sly and the Family Stone's Sixties repertoire. Pressed into service in countless modern dance records – literally so in that it is a sample activated by one finger casually jabbing a computer keyboard – it has become gutted of the significance it originally had in 1969, when it was chanted by Sly Stone and his group to the mass white audience of Woodstock. Then it signified transcendence: a music capable of addressing the body and the soul at once, dissolving sexual, social, and racial barriers. Twenty years later, this mantric incantation had become mechanical mass-production, its overtones of meaning reduced to a crudely erotic sound accessory.

There is a great deal more to be said about the catastrophic decline of pop (and rock criticism) – but not here. All that matters is that, when

[1] *Sunday Times*, 9th May 1993.

examining the following Chronology of Sixties pop, readers are aware that they are looking at something on a higher scale of achievement than today's – music which no contemporary artist can claim to match in feeling, variety, formal invention, and sheer out-of-the-blue inspiration. That the same can be said of other musical forms – most obviously classical and jazz – confirms that something in the soul of Western culture began to die during the late Sixties. Arguably pop music, as measured by the singles charts, peaked in 1966, thereafter beginning a shallow decline in overall quality which was already steepening by 1970. While some may date this tail-off to a little later, only the soulless or tone-deaf will refuse to admit any decline at all. Those with ears to hear, let them hear.

Chronology:
The Sixties

1960 THE BEATLES	UK POP	CURRENT AFFAIRS	CULTURE
January The Quarry Men – reduced to Lennon, McCartney, and Harrison after failing fortunes in 1959 – are joined by Stuart Sutcliffe on bass. No engagements.	**45s:** Michael Holliday *Starry-Eyed;* Anthony Newley *Why;* Craig Douglas *Pretty Blue Eyes;* Bobby Darin *La Mer,* Cliff Richard & The Shadows *Voice in the Wilderness;* Freddy Cannon *Way Down Yonder in New Orleans;* Platters *Harbour Lights.* **LPs:** Soundtrack *South Pacific,* Buddy Holly *Buddy Holly Story;* Cliff Richard *Cliff Sings.*	10 Nasser lays foundation stone for Aswan Dam. 20 British government announces curbs on the sale of 'pep pills' (amphetamines). 21 De Gaulle dismisses General Massu to defuse French settlers revolt in Algeria.	**Cinema** Reisz *Saturday Night and Sunday Morning;* Wayne *The Alamo;* Sturges *The Magnificent Seven;* Hitchcock *Psycho;* Wilder *The Apartment;* Fellini *La Dolce Vita;* Antonioni *L'Avventura; La Notte;* Malle *Zazie dans le Métro.* d. Clark Gable, Mack Sennett.
February No engagements. 25 Harrison is 17.	Everly Brothers leave Cadence for Warner Brothers. Eddie Cochran and Gene Vincent start UK tour. **45s:** Newley *Why;* Darin *La Mer,* Cliff Richard & The Shadows *Voice in the Wilderness;* Cannon *Way Down Yonder in New Orleans;* Johnny Preston *Running Bear.* **LPs:** Soundtrack *South Pacific,* Holly *Buddy Holly Story;* Richard *Cliff Sings.*	3 Macmillan's 'wind of change' speech in South Africa. 4 Dr Barbara Moore reaches Land's End after 1,000-mile walk from John O'Groats. 7 Discovery of the Dead Sea scrolls. 10 Castro jails political opponents. 22 Plans for the building of joint Anglo-French supersonic airliner (Concorde) are announced.	**Jazz** Coleman *Free Jazz;* Coltrane *Giant Steps; My Favourite Things;* Davis *Sketches Of Spain;* Gil Evans *Out Of The Cool;* Mingus *At Antibes;* Taylor *The World Of Cecil Taylor,* Dolphy *Outward Bound;* Brubeck *Time Out.* d. Oscar Pettiford.
March The Quarry Men change their name to The Beatals. No engagements.	Presley leaves the US army. Everly Brothers begin UK tour with Duane Eddy. **45s:** Adam Faith *Poor Me;* Preston *Running Bear,* Lonnie Donegan *My Old Man's a Dustman;* Percy Faith *Theme from A Summer Place;* Max Bygraves *Fings Ain't What They Used To Be;* Marv Johnson *You Got What It Takes.* **LPs:** Soundtrack *South Pacific,* Holly *Buddy Holly Story;* Freddy Cannon *Explosive;* Richard *Cliff Sings.*	1 Agadir earthquake: 5,000 dead. 1 Protest against segregation in Montgomery, Alabama. 14 Plan for a Thames flood-barrier. 15 Eisenhower advises bi-racial talks on segregation. 21 Sharpeville massacre: 56 black South Africans killed by police in the Transvaal. 29 Britain and America agree plan for a nuclear test-ban. 30 State of emergency in South Africa.	**Classical** Britten *A Midsummer Night's Dream;* Walton *Symphony No. 2;* Shostakovich *Quartet No. 8;* Rautavaara *Symphony No. 3;* Bernstein *Symphonic Dances from West Side Story;* Stockhausen *Carré;* Kontakte;* Penderecki *Threnody For The Victims Of Hiroshima;* Nono *Intolleranza 1960;* Messiaen *Chronochromie.* d. Ernst von Dohnányi, Edwin Fischer, Dimitri Mitropoulos, Joessi Bjoerling.

			Fiction
April 23–4 Lennon and McCartney appear at The Fox and Hounds, Caversham, as The Nerk Twins.	**16** Eddie Cochran killed in a car-crash on the way to Heathrow airport. **23** *Wham!*, Jack Good's new pop programme for ABC. **45s:** Donegan *My Old Man's a Dustman*; Preston *Running Bear*; Newley *Do You Mind?*; Jimmy Jones *Handy Man*; Percy Faith *Theme from A Summer Place*; Bygraves *Fings Ain't What They Used To Be*; Johnny & The Hurricanes *Beatnik Fly*. **LPs:** Soundtrack *South Pacific*; Holly *Buddy Holly Story*; Duane Eddy *The Twang's the Thang*; Cannon *Explosive*; Richard *Cliff Sings*.	**7** Race riots in Durban. **9** Verwoerd shot in attempted assassination. **13** British government cancels Blue Streak missile. **19** East Germans flee agricultural collectivisation to West Germany. **25** Ten black Americans shot by Mississippi police during protest on segregated beach.	Updike *Rabbit, Run*; Lee *To Kill A Mockingbird*; Barth *The Sot-Weed Factor*, Powell *Casanova's Chinese Restaurant*; Sillitoe *The Loneliness of the Long Distance Runner*; Durrell *Clea*; Amis *Take A Girl Like You*; Fleming *For Your Eyes Only*; Moore *The Luck of Ginger Coffey*; Spark *The Ballad of Peckham Rye*. Nobel: St-John Perse d. Albert Camus, Nevil Shute. **Poetry** Auden *Homage to Clio*; Durrell *Collected Poems*; Pound *Thrones*; Betjeman *Summoned By Bells*; Hughes *Lupercal*; Plath *The Colossus*; Ginsberg *Kaddish*. d. Boris Pasternak, Jules Supervielle, Pierre Reverdy.
May Allan Williams becomes the group's agent and part-time manager. They recruit drummer Tommy Moore and change their name to The Silver Beetles. **5** Failing an audition to back Bill Fury, they impress Fury's manager Larry Parnes enough to be booked to back Johnny Gentle. **14** Gig in Seaforth as The Silver Beats. **20–28** Tour of Scotland as The Silver Beetles, supporting Johnny Gentle. **30** First gig at Allan Williams' Liverpool club The Jacaranda.	American DJ Alan Freed indicted in New York on payola charge. Cavern drops 'jazz only' policy. **45s:** Everly Brothers *Cathy's Clown*; Newley *Do You Mind*; Johnny & The Hurricanes *Beatnik Fly*; Duane Eddy *Shazam!*; Eddie Cochran *Three Steps to Heaven*; Johnny Preston *Cradle of Love*; Adam Faith *Someone Else's Baby*. **LPs:** Soundtrack *South Pacific*; Holly *Buddy Holly Story*; Eddy *The Twang's the Thang*; Cannon *Explosive*; Richard *Cliff Sings*.	**5** U-2 spy-plane scandal. **6** Princess Margaret marries society photographer Anthony Armstrong-Jones (Lord Snowdon). **9** South Africa's policy of apartheid provokes a 'major showdown' at the Commonwealth Conference in London. **11** Eisenhower refuses to apologise to USSR for the U-2 episode. **16** Unopposed second reading of parliamentary bill to curb Teddy Boys. **23** Israelis seize Nazi war-criminal Adolf Eichmann in Argentina.	

1960 THE BEATLES	UK POP	CURRENT AFFAIRS	CULTURE
June Eleven performances around Liverpool as The Silver Beetles. 13 Tommy Moore quits the group. 18 McCartney is 18.	**45s:** Everly Brothers *Cathy's Clown*; Cochran *Three Steps To Heaven*; Preston *Cradle Of Love*; Eddy *Shazam!*; Jimmy Jones *Good Timin'*; Adam Faith *When Johnny Comes Marching Home*; Tommy Steele *What A Mouth*. **LPs:** Soundtrack *South Pacific*; Elvis Presley *Elvis is Back*; Holly *Buddy Holly Story*; Eddy *The Twang's the Thang*; *Cannon Explosive*.	2 British planners publish scheme to restrict the uncontrolled spread of high-rise buildings. 20 Floyd Patterson defeats Ingmar Johansson in world heavyweight boxing championship. 21 Patrice Lumumba first premier of newly-independent Congo. 22 Sino-Soviet Communist split becomes official. 23 Eleven die in blaze at Henderson's department store, Liverpool. 26 Madagascar independent.	**Stage** Lionel Bart's *Oliver!* signals revival of British musical. Peter Hall and Peggy Ashcroft form Royal Shakespeare Company. Zeffirelli directs *Romeo and Juliet* at The Old Vic. *Beyond the Fringe* opens at the Edinburgh Festival, before moving to the Lyceum. Ionesco *Rhinoceros*; Wesker *I'm Talking About Jerusalem*; Bolt *A Man for All Seasons*; Pinter *The Caretaker*; Rattigan *Ross*; Newley–Bricusse *Stop the World, I Want To Get Off*. d. Oscar Hammerstein II. **Non-fiction** Laing *The Divided Self*; Maxwell *Ring of Bright Water*; Ayer *Logical Positivism*; Packard *The Waste Makers*; Thompson (ed) *Out of Apathy*; Goodman *Growing Up Absurd*.
July Now The Silver Beatles, they do six more performances in Liverpool (including one backing a stripper named Janice). Lennon leaves Liverpool College of Art. 2 Johnny Gentle joins the group for a few numbers at the Jacaranda Club. 7 Starr is 20. 9–23 Drummer Norman Chapman joins (and leaves) the group. 24 Allan Williams invites Hamburg club-owner Bruno Koschmider to hear The Silver Beatles at The Two I's in Soho.	**45s:** Jones *Good Timin'*; Johnny & The Hurricanes *Down Yonder*; Cliff Richard *Please Don't Tease*; Johnny Kidd & The Pirates *Shakin' All Over*; Duane Eddy *Because They're Young*; Elvis Presley *Mess of Blues*; Steele *What a Mouth*. **LPs:** Presley *Elvis is Back*; Everly Brothers *It's Everly Time*; Holly *Buddy Holly Story*; Eddy *The Twang's the Thang*; Peggy Lee *Latin A La Lee*.	6 Princess Margaret marries Anthony Armstrong-Jones. 11 Katanga revolt in Congo. 12 Khrushchev supports Cuba in attempt to oust American forces from Guantanamo naval base. 12 French Congo, Chad, Central African Republic independent. 13 Kennedy wins the Democratic nomination. 15 UN sends troops to Congo. 21 58-year-old Francis Chichester sets new record for a solo crossing of the Atlantic.	

August
Pete Best is recruited on drums. 17–October 3 They are booked by Koschmider to play forty-eight nights at the Indra Club, Hamburg – for which they change their name to The Beatles.

September
The Beatles continue at the Indra Club, living in squalor and playing seven nights a week (six hours per night at weekends) to raucous audiences of sailors, criminals, and prostitutes – experience which soon builds them into 'a charismatic powerhouse' (Best).

October 4–November 30
Banned from the Indra Club for being too loud, they are moved to The Kaiserkeller, playing a further fifty-eight nights in tandem with Rory Storm and The Hurricanes (drummer: Ringo Starr).
9 Lennon is 20.
15 Lennon, McCartney, Harrison, and Starr cut some records (including a version of Gershwin's Summertime) at a small studio in Hamburg.
16 Koschmider signs The Beatles for another two and a half months.

45s: Richard Please Don't Tease; Presley Mess of Blues; Eddy Hyland Itsy Bitsy Teeny Weeny Yellow Polka Dot Bikini; Shadows Apache; Everly Brothers When Will I Be Loved. **LPs:** Presley Elvis is Back; Everly Brothers It's Everly Time; Holly Buddy Holly Story; Eddy The Twang's the Thang; Peggy Lee Latin A La Lee.

Trad jazz craze sweeps UK: Acker Bilk, Kenny Ball, Chris Barber. The Shadows tour UK. Oriole acquires UK rights to Tamla Motown label. **45s:** Shadows Apache; Richard Please Don't Tease; Presley Mess of Blues; Eddy Because They're Young; Ricky Valance Tell Laura I Love Her, Roy Orbison Only the Lonely. **LPs:** Presley Elvis is Back; Everly Brothers It's Everly Time, Holly Buddy Holly Story; Eddy The Twang's the Thang.

45s: Valance Tell Laura I Love Her; Orbison Only the Lonely; Cliff Richard Nine Times out of Ten; Everly Brothers Lucille; Adam Faith How About That; Sam Cooke Chain Gang; Johnny & The Hurricanes Rockin' Goose; Ventures Walk Don't Run. **LPs:** Soundtrack South Pacific; Presley Elvis is Back; Eddie Cochran Memorial Album; Everly Brothers It's Everly Time; Cliff Richard Me and My Shadows.

7 Castro nationalises American-owned property.
16 Martial law in Congo.
16 Cyprus achieves independence.
19 Penguin Books prosecuted for intended publication of Lady Chatterley's Lover.
31 East Germany closes its border with West Germany.

14 Mobutu deposes Lumumba.
26 Kennedy and Nixon in key TV election debate. Nixon, revealed in close-up to have a 'five o'clock shadow' and to be sweating under the studio lights, is deemed by TV audience to have 'lost' the debate. Radio listeners declare it a draw.
30 Brigitte Bardot attempts suicide.

1 Nigeria independent.
3 Labour Party Conference in chaos over CND move to ban the bomb.
12 Khrushchev bangs his shoe on his desk at the United Nations.
20 Trial of Penguin Books for planning to publish Lady Chatterley's Lover. Judge asks jury: 'Is it a book you would wish your wife or servant to read?'
22 Professional debut of Cassius Clay (Mohammed Ali).
26 South Vietnamese army skirmishes with Viet Cong.

Science fiction
Sturgeon Venus Plus X; Dick Dr Futurity; Pohl Drunkard's Walk; Amis New Maps of Hell. Hugo: Robert Heinlein Starship Troopers.

Fashion
Fifties couture (Balenciaga, Chanel) holds sway. Marc Bohan takes over at Dior. Street fashion: casual existentialist Left Bank (France) and Beatnik (USA, UK). Tight sweaters and jeans, stiletto heels.

TV/Media
Evelyn Waugh interviewed on Face to Face. The Strange World of Gurney Slade (starring Anthony Newley). First episodes of Maigret, Danger Man, Candid Camera, Spycatcher, 77 Sunset Strip. News Chronicle and The Star close down. First issue of New Left Review. d. Gilbert Harding.

398

1960 THE BEATLES	UK POP	CURRENT AFFAIRS	CULTURE
November The Beatles continue at the Kaiserkeller. In their spare time, they jam with Tony Sheridan and The Jets at the Top Ten. 21 Harrison deported for being underage. 29 McCartney and Best jailed briefly for arson before being deported.	**45s:** Elvis Presley *It's Now or Never*, Bassey *As Long As He Needs Me*; Orbison *Only the Lonely*; Johnny & The Hurricanes *Rockin' Goose*; Johnny Burnette *Dreamin'*; Drifters *Save the Last Dance for Me*. **LPs:** Soundtrack *South Pacific*; Holly *Buddy Holly Story Vol. 2*; Presley *Elvis is Back*; Everly Brothers *Fabulous Style*; Cochran *Memorial Album*.	2 Jury clears *Lady Chatterley's Lover* of obscenity. 9 Kennedy elected President of the USA by tight margin over Nixon. 10 Penguin sells 200,000 copies of *Lady Chatterley's Lover* in one day. 23 Viscount Stansgate renounces his title, becoming Tony Benn.	**Visual arts** Picasso exhibition in London. Yves Klein uses nudes as brushes in Paris 'happening'. Frank Stella: shaped canvases. Jean Tinguely: self-destructive kinetic sculpture. First use of term 'postmodernism'.
December 1–10 The group straggles back to the UK, virtually penniless. Stuart Sutcliffe stays in Hamburg with Astrid Kirchherr. 17 The Casbah (first date after Hamburg). Chas Newby joins on bass. 27 Famous gig at the Litherland Ballroom establishes The Beatles as Liverpool's most exciting group. Promoter Brian Kelly books them for thirty-six dances (for £6–£8 each). 31 The Casbah. Chas Newby leaves to go to college. McCartney takes over bass.	Adam Faith appears on *Face to Face*. **45s:** Presley *It's Now or Never*; Cliff Richard *I Love You*; Drifters *Save the Last Dance for Me*; Anthony Newley *Strawberry Fair*; Johnny Tillotson *Poetry in Motion*; Roy Orbison *Blue Angel*. **LPs:** Elvis Presley *GI Blues*; Holly *Buddy Holly Story Vol. 2*; Everly Brothers *Fabulous Style*; Cochran *Memorial Album*; Richard *Me and My Shadows*.	2 Lumumba arrested. 13 French extremists riot in Algeria. 31 End of National Service in Britain. Young men no longer have to enlist in the armed services for three years, as was the case 1939–60.	**Science** Microwave laser developed. Mossbauer Effect (gamma rays). Nobel: Burnet and Medawar (acquired immunity).

1961 THE BEATLES	UK POP	CURRENT AFFAIRS	CULTURE
January Nineteen performances in Liverpool.	Frank Sinatra founds Reprise label. Jackie Wilson shot and seriously wounded in New York. **45s:** Tillotson *Poetry in Motion*; Elvis Presley *Are You Lonesome Tonight*; Cliff Richard *I Love You*; Drifters *Save the Last Dance for Me*; Ventures *Perfidia*; Bobby Vee *Rubber Ball*; Johnny Horton *North to Alaska*; Johnny Burnette *You're Sixteen*; Orbison *Blue Angel*. **LPs:** Presley *GI Blues*; Holly *Buddy Holly Story Vol. 2*; Cliff Richard *Me and My Shadows*.	3 USA breaks diplomatic relations with Cuba. 8 Special Branch breaks Kroger–Lonsdale spy-ring. 17 Lumumba killed 'while escaping'. 22 Lumumba's supporters rampage in Stanleyville. 30 Contraceptive pill goes on sale in Britain.	**Cinema** Furie *The Young Ones*; Dearden *Victim*; Richardson *A Taste of Honey*; Wise *West Side Story*; Rossen *The Hustler*; Edwards *Breakfast At Tiffany's*; Corman *The Pit and the Pendulum*; Resnais *Last Year in Marienbad*; Buñuel *Viridiana*. d. Gary Cooper, Charles Coburn, George S. Kaufman, Ernest Thesiger, Joan Davis.
February In demand, The Beatles need transport between their gigs. Neil Aspinall becomes their roadie. Thirty-seven performances in Liverpool. 9 Beatles' debut at the Cavern Club. 25 Harrison is 18.	Presley makes first live appearance since 1957 (Memphis). Tamla Records has first million-seller: *Shop Around* by Smokey Robinson and The Miracles. **45s:** Presley *Are You Lonesome Tonight*; Petula Clark *Sailor*; Vee *Rubber Ball*; Burnette *You're Sixteen*; Shadows *FBI*; Everly Brothers *Ebony Eyes/Walk Right Back*; Gary U. S. Bonds *New Orleans*. **LPs:** Presley *GI Blues*; Connie Francis *Greatest Hits*; Cliff Richard *Me and My Shadows*.	3 UN troops fight pro-Lumumba forces in Congo. 8 BBC drops radio programme *Children's Hour* on the grounds that television has diminished its audience.	**Jazz** Coltrane *Africa/Brass*; Davis *At Carnegie Hall*; *Some Day My Prince Will Come*; Getz *Focus*; Bill Evans *Sunday Night At The Village Vanguard*; Dolphy *Far Cry*; *At The Five Spot*; Mingus *Oh Yeah*; Kirk *We Free Kings*; Russell *Ezz-Thetics*; Lacy *Evidence*; Nelson *Blues And The Abstract Truth*. d. Booker Little.

1961 THE BEATLES	UK POP	CURRENT AFFAIRS	CULTURE
March Thirty-three performances in Liverpool.	Presley to concentrate on films. **45s:** Everly Brothers *Ebony Eyes/Walk Right Back*; Elvis Presley *Wooden Heart*; Shirelles *Will You Still Love Me Tomorrow*; Neil Sedaka *Calendar Girl*; Brenda Lee *Let's Jump the Broomstick*; Allisons *Are You Sure*; Matt Monro *My Kind of Girl*; Cliff Richard *Theme for A Dream*; Adam Faith *Who Am I?* **LPs:** Presley *GI Blues*; Everly Brothers *A Date With the Everly Brothers*; Cliff Richard *Me and My Shadows*.	1 Kennedy forms Peace Corps of international volunteers. 15 Against background of continued international condemnation of apartheid, South Africa announces its intention of leaving the Commonwealth.	**Classical** Debut of cellist Jacqueline du Pré. Joan Sutherland scores hit in *Lucia di Lammermoor* at La Scala, Milan. Britten *War Requiem*; Tippett *King Priam*; Shostakovich *Symphony No. 12*; Carter *Double Concerto*; Lutosławski *Venetian Games*; Ligeti *Atmosphères*; Maw *Scenes and Arias*; Arnold *Symphony No. 5*. d. Sir Thomas Beecham.
April 1–July 1 Ninety-two nights at the Top Ten Club, Hamburg (negotiated by the group).	**45s:** Presley *Wooden Heart*; Allisons *Are You Sure*; Bobby Darin *Lazy River*, Monro *My Kind of Girl*, Ferrante & Teicher *Theme from Exodus*; Connie Francis *Where the Boys Are*. **LPs:** Presley *GI Blues*; Duane Eddy *Million Dollars' Worth of Twang*; Everly Brothers *A Date With the Everly Brothers*; Cliff Richard *Listen to Cliff*.	7 UN censures South Africa for racism. 12 Yuri Gagarin is first man in space. 18 Spy George Blake arrested. 19 Bay of Pigs fiasco (failed US-sponsored invasion of Cuba). 20 Portuguese colonists massacred in Angola. 24 De Gaulle battles attempted coup by Algerian army officers. 26 Tshombe arrested in Congo. 28 Britain applies to join the Common Market.	**Fiction** Henry Miller's *Tropic of Cancer* (1934) published in USA. Heller *Catch-22*; Kerouac *On the Road*; Baldwin *Nobody Knows My Name*, Burroughs *The Soft Machine*, Salinger *Franny and Zooey*; Hughes *The Fox in the Attic*; White *Riders in the Chariot*; Naipaul *A House for Mr Biswas*; Greene *A Burnt-out Case*; Spark *The Prime of Miss Jean Brodie*; Murdoch *A Severed Head*; Wilson *The Old Men At the Zoo*; Waugh *Unconditional Surrender*, Fleming *Thunderball*; Robbins *The Carpetbaggers*. d. Ernest Hemingway, Dashiell Hammett, Louis-Ferdinand Céline, James Thurber.

May The Beatles continue at the Top Ten Club.	**45s:** Marcels *Blue Moon*; Temperance Seven *You're Driving Me Crazy*; Floyd Cramer *On the Rebound*; Del Shannon *Runaway*; Shadows *Frightened City*; Helen Shapiro *Don't Treat Me Like A Child*; Bobby Vee *More Than I Can Say*. **LPs:** Presley *GI Blues*; Presley *His Hand in Mine*; Duane Eddy *Million Dollars' Worth of Twang*; Everly Brothers *A Date With the Everly Brothers*; Cliff Richard *Listen to Cliff.*	**1** Betting and Gaming Act leads to rapid growth of highstreet betting shops in UK. Disused churches converted to bingo halls. **8** George Blake jailed for 42 years for espionage. **14, 25** White racists attack 'freedom riders' in Birmingham, Alabama. **31** South Africa leaves the Commonwealth.	**Poetry** Gunn *My Sad Captains*; Masefield *Bluebells*; Nash *Collected Verses.* d. Blaise Cendrars.
June **18** McCartney is 19. **22–23(?)** They record in Hamburg as The Beat Brothers backing Tony Sheridan, produced by Bert Kaempfert.	**45s:** Presley *Surrender*; Shannon *Runaway*; Shadows *Frightened City*; Vee *More Than I Can Say*; Clarence 'Frogman' Henry *But I Do*; Lonnie Donegan *Have a Drink on Me*; Ricky Nelson *Hello Mary Lou*; Jerry Lee Lewis *What'd I Say*; Roy Orbison *Running Scared*. **LPs:** Presley *GI Blues*; Presley *His Hand in Mine*; Eddy *Million Dollars' Worth of Twang*; Everly Brothers *A Date With the Everly Brothers*; Richard *Listen to Cliff.*	**25** Iraq lays claim to Kuwait. **28** Judge declares a ballot of members of the Electrical Trades Union rigged by communists.	**Stage** Sensation of the year: Jonathan Miller, Alan Bennett, Peter Cook and Dudley Moore in satirical hit *Beyond the Fringe* (see 1960). Rudolf Nureyev defects. Anouilh *Becket*; Osborne *Luther*; Beckett *Happy Days*; Pinter *The Collection*; Whiting *The Devils.* d. George Formby.
July **3** Return to Liverpool. Twenty-five appearances. **6** First edition of *Mersey Beat* (including Lennon's 'Being A Short Diversion On The Dubious Origins Of The Beatles'). **7** Starr is 21.	The Twist is latest 'craze' in USA. **45s:** Shannon *Runaway*; Everly Brothers *Temptation*; Nelson *Hello Mary Lou*; Cliff Richard *A Girl Like You*; Billy Fury *Halfway to Paradise*; Buddy Holly *Baby I Don't Care*. **LPs:** Soundtrack *South Pacific*; Presley *GI Blues*; Presley *His Hand in Mine*; Eddy *Million Dollars' Worth of Twang*; Richard *Listen to Cliff.*	**1** British troops defend Kuwait against possible Iraqi attack. **5** French troops kill 80 Arabs during demonstration in Algiers. **17** East Germans refugees race to enter West Berlin.	**Non-fiction** Williams *The Long Revolution*; Van der Post *The Heart of the Hunter*; Freud *Letters 1873–1939*; Sartre *Critique of Dialectical Reason*; Russell *Has Man A Future?* d. Carl Gustav Jung.

1961 THE BEATLES	UK POP	CURRENT AFFAIRS	CULTURE
August Thirty-four appearances in Liverpool.	Newcomer Bob Dylan causes excitement in N.Y. folk clubs. **45s:** Eden Kane *Well I Ask You*; Helen Shapiro *You Don't Know*; John Leyton *Johnny Remember Me*; Petula Clark *Romeo*; Holly *Baby I Don't Care*; Temperance Seven *Pasadena*. **LPs:** TV Cast *The Black and White Minstrel Show*; Presley *GI Blues*; Presley *His Hand in Mine*; Eddy *Million Dollars' Worth of Twang*, Richard *Listen to Cliff*.	**10** Britain applies for membership of the Common Market (EEC). **13** East Germany closes Berlin border. **17** John Osborne's letter 'Damn you, England' published in *Tribune*. **20–31** The Berlin Wall is built.	**Science fiction** Heinlein *Stranger in a Strange Land*; Aldiss *The Primal Urge*. Hugo: Walter M. Miller *A Canticle for Leibowitz*.
September Thirty-one appearances in Liverpool.	Dylan signed to Columbia by John Hammond. Tony Meehan leaves Shadows. **45s:** Leyton *Johnny Remember Me*; Shirley Bassey *Reach for the Stars*/*Climb Every Mountain*; Gary U. S. Bonds *Quarter to Three*; Shapiro *You Don't Know*; Shadows *Kon-Tiki*; Sam Cooke *Cupid*; Presley *Wild in the Country*/*I Feel So Bad*. **LPs:** Soundtrack *South Pacific*; Shadows *The Shadows*, Presley *GI Blues*; Presley *His Hand in Mine*, Richard *Listen to Cliff*.	**3** UK and US call for nuclear atmospheric test-ban. **12** Bertrand Russell and Arnold Wesker jailed for inciting a breach of the peace at a CND protest. **17** Violence at 'ban-the-bomb' (CND) demonstration in Trafalgar Square. **18** UN Secretary General Dag Hammarskjold dies in air-crash.	**Fashion** André Courrèges opens Paris house. *Elle* features designs by Emmanuelle Khahn.
October Nineteen appearances in Liverpool. **9** Lennon is 21. **1–14** Lennon and McCartney holiday in Paris, hanging out in left bank cafés. **19** The Beatles and Gerry and The Pacemakers play together as The Beat-Makers at Litherland Town Hall.	Dick James launches publishing business. **45s:** Shadows *Kon-Tiki*; Highwaymen *Michael*; Helen Shapiro *Walking Back to Happiness*; Leyton *Johnny Remember Me*; Connie Francis *Together*, Del Shannon *Hats off to Larry*. **LPs:** Shadows *The Shadows*; Cliff Richard *21 Today*; Billy Fury *Halfway to Paradise*; Presley *GI Blues*; Presley *His Hand in Mine*.	**11** UN censures South Africa for racism (again). **17** Khrushchev expels Albania from Soviet bloc. **20** Algerians protest against curfew in Paris. **25** Allied and Soviet tanks confront each other at Berlin border.	**TV/Media** BBC Shakespeare history cycle, *An Age of Kings*. Tony Hancock stars in solo TV show. First episodes of *Coronation Street*, *The Avengers*, *The Morecambe and Wise Show*. BBC drops Children's Hour. Marvel Age of Comics begins with *Fantastic Four*.

			Visual arts
November Thirty-four appearances in Liverpool. 9 Brian Epstein attends a lunchtime performance by The Beatles at The Cavern.	Berry Gordy forms Motown label. **45s:** Presley *His Latest Flame*; Shapiro *Walking Back to Happiness*; John Leyton *Wild Wind*; Ray Charles *Hit the Road Jack*; Dion *Runaround Sue*; Cliff Richard *When the Girl in Your Arms*; Dave Brubeck *Take Five*; Jimmy Dean *Big Bad John*; Andy Williams *Moon River*, Shadows *The Savage*. **LPs:** Richard *21 Today*; Presley *Something for Everybody*; Buddy Holly *That'll Be the Day*; Shadows *The Shadows*; Presley *GI Blues*; Fury *Halfway to Paradise*.	3 U Thant becomes Secretary General of United Nations. 11 Height of de-Stalinisation at the 22nd Parry Congress in Moscow. 14 US increases 'military advisers' in South Vietnam.	Exhibition of British Pop Art: in London: David Hockney, Allen Jones, Patrick Caulfield, R. B. Kitaj. 'The Art of Assemblage' at N.Y. Museum of Modern Art. George Maciunas coins Fluxus. d. Augustus John, Grandma Moses.
			Science Crick and Brenner's work with DNA. d. Erwin Schrödinger.
December Twenty-five appearances in Liverpool, one in Aldershot, one in London. 3 Epstein offers to manage the group. 6 The Beatles ask Epstein to manage them. Epstein prepares a contract. 10 The group agrees Epstein's contract. 13 Epstein arranges for a Decca A&R man to hear The Beatles at The Cavern.	15 Cliff Richard and Shadows: *The Young Ones* (film). **45s:** Frankie Vaughan *Tower of Strength*; Presley *His Latest Flame*; Williams *Moon River*, Bobby Vee *Take Good Care of My Baby*; Dean *Big Bad John*; Kenny Ball *Midnight in Moscow*; Sandy Nelson *Let There Be Drums*; Dion *Runaround Sue*. **LPs:** Presley *Blue Hawaii*; Cliff Richard *The Young Ones*; Shadows *The Shadows*; Holly *That'll Be the Day*.	4 Contraceptive pills become available on the NHS. 15 Adolf Eichmann sentenced to death for ordering the killing of millions of Jews in World War II. 21 End of rebellion in Katanga.	

404

1962 THE BEATLES	UK POP	CURRENT AFFAIRS	CULTURE
January Thirty-one appearances in Liverpool. **1** Audition for Decca in London. Nervous and forced to use unfamiliar equipment, The Beatles record fifteen songs, but fail to make an impression. **24** They sign with Epstein. A week later Decca turns them down.	The Twist (see July 1961) hits UK. **45s:** Williams *Moon River*; Cliff Richard *The Young Ones*; Ball *Midnight in Moscow*; Nelson *Let There Be Drums*; Acker Bilk *Stranger on the Shore*; Billy Fury *I'd Never Find Another You*; Neil Sedaka *Happy Birthday Sweet Sixteen*; Chubby Checker *The Twist*; Tokens *The Lion Sleeps Tonight*. **LPs:** Richard *The Young Ones*; Presley *Blue Hawaii*; Shadows *The Shadows*; Holly *That'll Be the Day*.	**4** Kennedy increases military aid to South Vietnam. **24** De Gaulle orders crackdown on OAS terrorists.	**Cinema** Schlesinger *A Kind of Loving*; Forbes *The L-Shaped Room*; Young *Dr No*; Lean *Lawrence of Arabia*; Frankenheimer *The Manchurian Candidate*; Kubrick *Lolita*; Aldrich *Whatever Happened to Baby Jane?*; Buñuel *The Exterminating Angel*; Antonioni *L'Eclisse*; Truffaut *Jules et Jim*; Various *Boccaccio '70*. d. Charles Laughton, Marilyn Monroe, Michael Curtiz, Tod Browning.
February Thirty-four appearances in Liverpool, one in Manchester. **10** Furious Epstein breaks off relations with Decca: 'You must be out of your minds. These boys are going to explode. I am completely confident that one day they will be bigger than Elvis Presley!' **13** Epstein arranges meeting with George Martin at Parlophone. **25** Harrison is 19.	**45s:** Richard *The Young Ones*; Checker *Let's Twist Again*; Eden Kane *Forget Me Not*; Sedaka *Happy Birthday Sweet Sixteen*; Bilk *Stranger on the Shore*; Presley *Rock-a-hula Baby/Can't Help Falling in Love With You*; Bobby Vee *Run To Him*; Everly Brothers *Cryin' in the Rain*. **LPs:** Richard *The Young Ones*; Presley *Blue Hawaii*; Shadows *The Shadows*.	**3** Kennedy embargoes Cuban exports. **8** Police and left-wingers clash in Paris over OAS campaign. **17** James Hanratty found guilty of A6 murder. **20** Six British anti-nuclear protestors jailed. **25** Bertrand Russell attacks the imprisonment of anti-nuclear protestors.	**Jazz** Coltrane *Live At The Village Vanguard*; Rollins *The Bridge*; Our *Man In Jazz*; Ellington *Money Jungle*; Bill Evans *How My Heart Sings!*; Monk: *Monk's Dream*; Russell *The Outer View*; Taylor *Nefertiti*; MJQ *Lonely Woman*; Getz/Byrd *Jazz Samba*; Smith *Walk On The Wild Side*.

March		15 Liberal candidate Eric Lubbock overturns huge Conservative majority in Orpington by-election. 26 French army launches counter-offensive against OAS in Algeria.	**Classical** Britten's *War Requiem* (1961) the success of the year. Shostakovich *Symphony No. 13*; Stravinsky *The Flood*; Maxwell Davies *Fantasia On An In Nomine Of John Taverner*; Henze *Symphony No. 5*; Sallinen *Mauermusik*; Cage *0:00*; *Imaginary Landscape V*; Ligeti *Symphonic Poem For 100 Metronomes*. d. John Ireland, Hanns Eisler, Jacques Ibert, Kirsten Flagstad, Alfred Cortot, Bruno Walter, Fritz Kreisler.
Thirty-six appearances in Liverpool, one in Stroud. One radio broadcast for BBC Manchester.	Dylan's debut album released. **45s:** Presley *Rock-a-hula Baby/Can't Help Falling in Love With You*; Shadows *Wonderful Land*; Helen Shapiro *Tell Me What He Said*; Karl Denver *Wimoweh*; Richard *The Young Ones*; Checker *Let's Twist Again*; Dion *The Wanderer*. **LPs:** Presley *Blue Hawaii*; Richard *The Young Ones*; Shadows *The Shadows*; Helen Shapiro *Tops With Me*; Bobby Vee *Take Good Care of My Baby*.		
April		4 Hanratty hanged for A6 murder. He protests his innocence to the last. 20 General Salan, head of OAS, arrested in Algiers. 24 USA resumes atmospheric nuclear tests. 30 Peter Cook funds new satirical magazine *Private Eye*.	**Fiction** Kesey *One Flew Over the Cuckoo's Nest*; Kerouac *The Subterraneans*; Baldwin *Another Country*; Burroughs *The Ticket That Exploded*; Braine *Life At the Top*; Burgess *A Clockwork Orange*; Lessing *The Golden Notebook*; Murdoch *An Unofficial Rose*; Isherwood *Down There on a Visit*; Powell *The Kindly Ones*; Solzhenitsyn *One Day in the Life of Ivan Denisovich*. Nobel: John Steinbeck. d. William Faulkner, Herman Hesse, Vita Sackville-West, Karen Blixen.
Eleven appearances in Liverpool. 10 Death of Stuart Sutcliffe. 13–May 31 Forty-eight nights at the Star-Club, Hamburg. Epstein negotiates with Parlophone.	**45s:** Shadows *Wonderful Land*; Roy Orbison *Dream Baby*; Presley *Rock-a-hula Baby/Can't Help Falling in Love With You*; Bruce Channel *Hey Baby*; Sam Cooke *Twistin' the Night Away*; Dion *The Wanderer*; Del Shannon *Hey Little Girl*; B. Bumble & The Stingers *Nut Rocker*; Jimmy Justice *When My Little Girl is Smiling*. **LPs:** Presley *Blue Hawaii*; Richard *The Young Ones*; Shadows *The Shadows*; Shapiro *Tops With Me*; Vee *Take Good Care of My Baby*.		

1962 THE BEATLES	UK POP	CURRENT AFFAIRS	CULTURE
May They continue their Hamburg season. 9 Epstein secures a recording contract with Parlophone.	**45s:** Shadows *Wonderful Land*; B. Bumble & The Stingers *Nut Rocker*; Presley *Good Luck Charm*; Channel *Hey Baby*; Cooke *Twistin' the Night Away*; Brenda Lee *Speak To Me Pretty*; Ketty Lester *Love Letters*; Orbison *Dream Baby*; Justice *When My Little Girl is Smiling*; Cliff Richard *I'm Looking Out the Window/Do You Want To Dance*. **LPs:** Presley *Blue Hawaii*; Richard *The Young Ones*; Shadows *The Shadows*; Shapiro *Tops With Me*.	10 Kennedy sends marines to defend Laos against Communist incursion. 10 Conservatives lose heavily in council elections. 23 OAS leader General Salan sentenced to life imprisonment. 31 Eichmann hanged in Israel.	**Poetry** Barker *The View from A Blind I*; Ashbery *The Tennis Court Oath*; Creeley *For You*; Day Lewis *The Gate*; Enright *Addictions*; Fuller *Collected Poems*. d. Richard Aldington, e. e. cummings.
June Twenty-five appearances in Liverpool. One radio broadcast for BBC Manchester. 2 The Beatles return to Liverpool. 4 They sign to EMI. 6 The EMI 'audition': they record demos of *Besame Mucho*, *Love Me Do*, *P.S. I Love You*, and *Ask Me Why*. 18 McCartney is 20.	**45s:** Presley *Good Luck Charm*; Cliff Richard *I'm Looking Out the Window/Do You Want To Dance*; Mike Sarne *Come Outside*; Joe Brown *Picture of You*; Brian Hyland *Ginny Come Lately*; Jimmie Rodgers *English Country Garden*; Duane Eddy *Deep in the Heart of Texas*; Shirelles *Soldier Boy*. **LPs:** Presley *Blue Hawaii*; Soundtrack *West Side Story*; Richard *The Young Ones*; The Shadows *The Shadows*.	17 OAS terror campaign ends. 17 Brazil wins the World Cup.	**Stage** Paul Scofield in Peter Brook's RSC *King Lear*. Vanessa Redgrave as Rosalind in *As You Like It*. Nureyev and Fonteyn in *Le Corsaire* at Covent Garden. Albee *Who's Afraid of Virginia Woolf*; Loesser/Burroughs *How to Succeed in Business Without Really Trying*; Wesker *Chips With Everything*; Osborne *Under Plain Cover*.

			Non-fiction
July Thirty-seven appearances, mostly in Liverpool. **7** Starr is 22.	The Rolling Stones debut at The Marquee. **45s:** Same *Come Outside*; Brown *Picture of You*; Charles *I Can't Stop Loving You*; Hyland *Ginny Come Lately*; Frank Ifield *I Remember You*; Pat Boone *Speedy Gonzales*; Brenda Lee *Here Comes That Feeling.* **LPs:** Presley *Pot Luck*; Soundtrack *West Side Story*; Presley *Blue Hawaii*; Richard *The Young Ones*; Shadows *The Shadows.*	**1** Rwanda and Burundi independent. **3** Algeria independent. **10** Martin Luther King jailed for leading an illegal march in Albany, Georgia. **11** Telstar satellite allows live cross-Atlantic TV link. **13** Harold Macmillan sacks a third of his cabinet after by-election losses indicate unpopularity of government pay restraint policy. **31** Mosleyite fascists parade in East End of London.	Lévi-Strauss *The Savage Mind*; Marcuse *Eros and Civilisation*; McLuhan *The Gutenberg Galaxy*; Auden *The Dyer's Hand*; Sampson *Anatomy of Britain.* d. G. M. Trevelyan.
August Thirty-four appearances, mostly in Liverpool. **16** Pete Best is sacked. **18** Ringo Starr joins the group. **22** Granada TV (Manchester) films The Beatles at The Cavern. **23** Lennon marries his long-term girlfriend from art-school, Cynthia Powell.	**45s:** Ifield *I Remember You*; Boone *Speedy Gonzales*; Ray Charles *I Can't Stop Loving You*; Shadows *Guitar Tango*; Bobby Darin *Things*; Brian Hyland *Sealed With A Kiss*; Nat King Cole *Let There Be Love*; Billy Fury *Once Upon A Dream*; Neil Sedaka *Breaking Up Is Hard To Do*; Bobby Vinton *Roses Are Red.* **LPs:** Presley *Pot Luck*; Soundtrack *West Side Story*; Richard *The Young Ones*; Duane Eddy *Twistin' and Twangin'*; Ray Charles *Modern Sounds in Country & Western.*	**8** US Nazi George Lincoln Rockwell expelled from Britain. **10** Martin Luther King released from jail in Georgia. **13–20** West Berliners riot at the Wall **22** OAS gunmen attempt to assassinate De Gaulle.	**Science fiction** Aldiss *Hothouse*; Ballard *The Drowned World*; Blish *A Life for the Stars*; Bradbury *Something Wicked This Way Comes.* Hugo: Robert Heinlein *Stranger in a Strange Land.*

1962 THE BEATLES	UK POP	CURRENT AFFAIRS	CULTURE
September Thirty-three appearances, mostly in Liverpool. **4, 11** Recording *Love Me Do*.	**45s:** Presley *She's Not You*; Tornados *Telstar*; Ifield *I Remember You*; Cliff Richard *It'll Be Me*; Sedaka *Breaking Up Is Hard To Do*; Little Eva *The Locomotion*; Tommy Roe *Sheila*; Holly *Reminiscing*; Jerry Lee Lewis *Sweet Little Sixteen*. **LPs:** Soundtrack *West Side Story*; Presley *Pot Luck*; Cliff Richard *32 Minutes and 17 Seconds*; Kenny Ball, Chris Barber, Acker Bilk *Best Of*; Charles *Modern Sounds in Country & Western*; Eddy *Twistin' and Twangin'*.	**2** Fascist marches provoke street battles in London's East End. **4** Kennedy vows to counter Cuban aggression. **13** Spy William Vassall arrested. **24** Congress grants Kennedy power to call up reservists against Cuba. **25** Sonny Liston defeats Floyd Patterson to become heavyweight champion. **30–1st October** Whites riot as black student James Meredith enrolls at University of Mississipi.	**Fashion:** Yves Saint Laurent opens his own couture house in Paris. Elie and Jacqueline Jacobson open *Dorothée Bis* chain in France and America: young girl styles for adult women.
October Twenty-three appearances, mostly in Liverpool. Two TV engagements (Granada, Manchester), three radio broadcasts. **5** UK: *Love Me Do*. **9** Lennon is 22.	Little Richard and Sam Cooke tour UK. BBC bans 'offensive' *Monster Mash* by Boris Pickett & the Crypt-Kickers. **45s:** Tornados *Telstar*; Little Eva *The Locomotion*; Roe *Sheila*; Carole King *It Might As Well Rain Until September*; Shirley Bassey *What Now My Love*; Nat King Cole *Ramblin' Rose*; Mark Wynter *Venus in Blue Jeans*; Chris Montez *Let's Dance*; Del Shannon *Swiss Maid*; Susan Maughan *Bobby's Girl*; Richard *32 Minutes and 17 Seconds*; Soundtrack *West Side Story*; Ball, Barber, Bilk *Best Of*; Charles *Modern Sounds in Country & Western*; Lonnie Donegan *Golden Age*; Eddy *Twistin' and Twangin'*.	**15** Amnesty International founded. **22** Kennedy blockades Cuba; spy Vassall jailed for eighteen years. **28** Khrushchev backs down over Cuban missile crisis.	**TV/Media** *Z-Cars* brings authenticity to a genre previously typified by comfortable *Dixon of Dock Green*. First episodes of *Crossroads*, *Steptoe and Son*, *Doctor Finlay's Casebook*, *The Saint*. Ken Russell: *Elgar*. First *Sunday Times* colour supplement. First issue of *Gay News*.

November 1-14 The Beatles share the bill with Little Richard at the Star-Club, Hamburg. They meet Billy Preston, who is playing in Richard's backing group. Seventeen UK performances, mostly in Liverpool. Two radio broadcasts. **26** Recording *Please Please Me*.	**45s:** Tornados *Telstar*; Frank Ifield *Lovesick Blues*; Montez *Let's Dance*; Little Eva *The Locomotion*; Wynter *Venus in Blue Jeans*; Shannon *Swiss Maid*; Maughan *Bobby's Girl*; Marty Robbins *Devil Woman*; Duane Eddy *Guitar Man*; Four Seasons *Sherry*; Rolf Harris *Sun Arise*; Beatles *Love Me Do*. **LPs:** Soundtrack *West Side Story*; Shadows *Out of the Shadows*; Richard *32 Minutes and 17 Seconds*; Ball, Barber, Bilk *Best Of*; Charles *Modern Sounds in Country & Western*; Lonnie Donegan *Golden Age*.	**2** Soviet missile bases in Cuba are destroyed. **2** Greville Wynne arrested in Budapest. **7** African National Congress leader Nelson Mandela jailed. **16-21** Chinese troops invade India. **24** First edition of BBC TV's live satire programme *That Was The Week That Was*.	**Visual arts** National Gallery buys Leonardo da Vinci cartoon for £800,000. Andy Warhol, Roy Lichtenstein, Claes Oldenburg exhibit in New York ('The New Realists'). Pop Art makes covers of *Time*, *Life*, *Newsweek*. Sir Basil Spence: Coventry Cathedral. d. Franz Kline.
December Twenty performances, three TV engagements. **18-31** Final thirteen nights at the Star-Club, Hamburg.	Tamla Motown Rock & Roll Show: Christmas residence at the Apollo. **45s:** Presley *Return To Sender*; Ifield *Lovesick Blues*; Harris *Sun Arise*; Maughan *Bobby's Girl*; Four Seasons *Sherry*; Cliff Richard *The Next Time*; Shadows *Dance On*; Eddy *Guitar Man*; Stan Getz/Charlie Byrd *Desafinado*; Ray Charles *Your Cheating Heart*; Beatles *Love Me Do*; Crystals *He's A Rebel*. **LPs:** Mitchell Minstrels *Onstage*; Shadows *Out of the Shadows*; Richard *32 Minutes and 17 Seconds*; Presley *Rock'n'Roll No. 2*; Soundtrack *West Side Story*; Ball, Barber, Bilk *Best Of*; Lonnie Donegan *Golden Age*.	**21** Britain buys Polaris from USA. **25-30** Revolt in Katanga province.	**Science** Thalidomide scandal. UK government backs fluoridisation. Royal College of Physicians report on Smoking and Health. d. Niels Bohr.

1963 THE BEATLES	UK POP	CURRENT AFFAIRS	CULTURE
January Twenty-four performances, three TV engagements, five radio broadcasts. **11** UK: *Please Please Me*. **19** National television debut on ITV's *Thank Your Lucky Stars*.	Dylan's first visit to Britain. **10** Cliff Richard & the Shadows: *Summer Holiday* (film). **45s**: Cliff Richard *The Next Time/ Bachelor Boy*; Presley *Return To Sender*, Shadows *Dance On*; Ifield *Lovesick Blues*; Eddy *Guitar Man*; Mel Tormé *Coming Home Baby*; Mark Wynter *Go Away Little Girl*; Tijuana Brass *Lonely Bull*; Jet Harris & Tony Meehan *Diamonds*; Del Shannon *Little Town Flirt*; Four Seasons *Big Girls Don't Cry*. **LPs**: Soundtrack *West Side Story*; Richard & The Shadows *Summer Holiday*; Presley *Rock'n'Roll No. 2*; *Girls! Girls! Girls!*; Shadows *Out of the Shadows*.	**2** Viet Cong shoot down five US helicopters in Mekong Delta. **9** President Tshombe of Katanga arrested by UN troops. **14** De Gaulle rebuffs Britain's attempt to enter the Common Market. **15** Katanga rebellion ends. **18** Death of Labour Party leader Hugh Gaitskell.	**Cinema** Richardson *The Loneliness of the Long Distance Runner*; Tom Jones; Anderson *This Sporting Life*; Schlesinger *Billy Liar*, Yates *Summer Holiday*; Young *From Russia With Love*, Hitchcock *The Birds*; Kubrick *Dr Strangelove*; Fuller *Shock Corridor*, Edwards *The Pink Panther*, Mankiewicz *Cleopatra*; Bergman *The Silence*; Fellini *Eight and a Half*. d. Adolphe Menjou, Dick Powell.
February On tour with Helen Shapiro. Thirty performances, one TV engagement, one radio broadcast. **2** First date of Helen Shapiro tour. **11** Recording *Please Please Me* (LP). **22** Formation of Northern Songs. **25** US: *Please Please Me* (first release).- Harrison is 20.	Dick James and Lennon-McCartney form Northern Songs. **45s**: Jet Harris & Tony Meehan *Diamonds*; Frank Ifield *The Wayward Wind*; Beatles *Please Please Me*; Richard *The Next Time/Bachelor Boy*; Shannon *Little Town Flirt*; Bobby Vee *The Night Has a Thousand Eyes*; Four Seasons *Big Girls Don't Cry*; Brenda Lee *All Alone Am I*; Paul & Paula *Hey Paul*; Cliff Richard *Summer Holiday*; Acker Bilk *A Taste of Honey*. **LPs**: Richard & The Shadows *Summer Holiday*; Soundtrack *West Side Story*; Presley *Girls! Girls! Girls!*; Shadows *Out of the Shadows*; Ifield *I'll Remember You*.	**8** Army coup in Iraq. **9** Rebel leader Joshua Nkomo arrested in Rhodesia. **14** Harold Wilson becomes leader of the Labour Party. **14** First kidney transplant (at Leeds General Hospital).	**Jazz** Davis *At Antibes*; *Seven Steps To Heaven*; Mingus *The Black Saint And The Sinner Lady*, Mingus *Mingus Mingus Mingus*; Ellington *Afro Bossa*; Bill Evans *Conversations With Myself*. Monk *Criss Cross*; Shepp *New York Contemporary Five*; Hill *Black Fire*; Bley *Footloose*; MJQ *The Sheriff*; Santamaria *Watermelon Man*; Brubeck *At Carnegie Hall*. d. Dinah Washington, Ike Quebec.

			Classical
March On tour with Chris Montez and Tommy Roe. Twenty-seven performances, one TV engagement, four radio broadcasts. 2 *Please Please Me* tops the British charts. 5 Recording *From Me To You*. 22 UK: *Please Please Me* (LP).	5 Patsy Cline dies in an air-crash. **45s:** Ifield *The Wayward Wind*; Richard *Summer Holiday*; Beatles *Please Me*; Vee *The Night Has a Thousand Eyes*; Joe Brown *That's What Love Will Do*; Paul & Paula *Hey Paul*; Shadows *Foot Tapper*; Bachelors *Charmaine*; Ned Miller *From a Jack to a King*; Springfields *Island of Dreams*; Billie Davis *Tell Him*. **LPs:** Richard & The Shadows *Summer Holiday*; Frank Ifield *I'll Remember You*; Soundtrack *West Side Story*; Presley *Girls! Girls! Girls!*; Shadows *Out of the Shadows*.	3 Spy Kim Philby defects to USSR. 15 War minister John Profumo offers to resign. 22 Profumo denies 'impropriety' with 'model' Christine Keeler. 27 Beeching abolishes many branch lines in British railways reform.	Tippett *Concerto For Orchestra*; Panufnik *Sinfonia Sacra*; Berio *Sequenza II*; Messiaen *Sept Haï-Kai*; Walton *Variations On A Theme Of Hindemith*; Crumb *Night Music I*; Penderecki *Stabat Mater*. d. Francis Poulenc, Paul Hindemith, Ferenc Fricsay.
April Twenty performances, four TV engagements, six radio broadcasts. 4 They play Stowe public school. 8 Birth of Lennon's son Julian. 11 UK: *From Me To You*. 18 They take part in a concert at the Albert Hall. McCartney meets Jane Asher. 21 *NME* Poll-Winners Concert at Wembley (audience: 10,000). 27–May 9 McCartney, Harrison, Starr, and their partners holiday in Tenerife. Lennon and Epstein holiday in Spain.	12 Dylan gives first major solo concert in New York. Pye acquires UK rights to Chess Records. 28 Andrew Loog Oldham signs The Rolling Stones at recommendation of George Harrison. **45s:** Richard *Summer Holiday*; Gerry & The Pacemakers *How Do You Do It?*; Miller *From a Jack to a King*; Ronnie Carroll *Say Wonderful Things*; Buddy Holly *Brown-eyed Handsome Man*; Cascades *Rhythm of the Rain*; Little Eva *Let's Turkey Trot*; Roy Orbison *In Dreams*; Beatles *From Me To You*; Four Seasons *Walk Like A Man*. **LPs:** Richard & The Shadows *Summer Holiday*; Buddy Holly *Reminiscing*; Soundtrack *West Side Story*; Presley *Girls! Girls! Girls!*; Beatles *Please Please Me*; Shadows *Out of the Shadows*.	1 First issue of underground magazine *OZ* in Australia. 12 Martin Luther King arrested for leading civil rights march in Birmingham, Alabama. 15 50,000 anti-nuclear protestors march in London. 17 Special Branch arrest 'Spies for Peace' (CND activists). 24 Mandy Rice Davies arrested.	**Fiction** Solzhenitsyn's *One Day in the Life of Ivan Denisovich* (1962) reaches the West in translation. McCarthy *The Group*; Updike *The Centaur*; Grass *Dog Years*; Donleavy *A Singular Man*; Malamud *Idiots First*; Pynchon *V*; Burroughs *Dead Fingers Talk*; Plath *The Bell Jar*; Amis *One Fat Englishman*; Spark *The Girls of Slender Means*; Bates *Oh! To Be in England*; Le Carré *The Spy Who Came in from The Cold*; Fleming *On Her Majesty's Secret Service*. d. Jean Cocteau, Aldous Huxley, John Cowper Powys, C. S. Lewis.

1963 THE BEATLES	UK POP	CURRENT AFFAIRS	CULTURE
May On tour with Roy Orbison. Seventeen performances, two TV engagements, three radio broadcasts. 2 *From Me To You* tops the UK chart (seven weeks). 4 *Please Please Me* tops the UK LP charts. 24 BBC give the group their own radio show: *Pop Go The Beatles*. 27 US: *From Me To You*.	Dylan, Joan Baez, Pete Seeger, and Peter, Paul, & Mary at first Monterey Folk Festival. 12 Dylan banned from performing *Talking John Birch Society Blues* on The Ed Sullivan Show. **45s:** Beatles *From Me To You*; Gerry & The Pacemakers *How Do You Do It?*; Andy Williams *Can't Get Used To Losing You*; Orbison *In Dreams*; Jet Harris & Tony Meehan *Scarlett O'Hara*; Chiffons *He's So Fine*, Wink Martindale *Deck of Cards*; Chantays *Pipeline*; Billy J Kramer & The Dakotas *Do You Want To Know A Secret?* **LPs:** Beatles *Please Please Me*; Richard & The Shadows *Summer Holiday*; Soundtrack *West Side Story*; Shannon *Hats Off to Del Shannon*; Holly *Reminiscing*; Presley *It Happened At the World's Fair*.	5 5,000 arrested on civil rights march in Alabama. 11 Greville Wynne jailed for eight years for spying in Moscow. Oleg Penkovsky sentenced to death. 18 Kennedy sends federal troops to quell race riots in southern states. 27 Jomo Kenyatta elected prime minister of Kenya. 28 Drs Alpert and Leary sacked from Harvard for experimenting on their students with LSD.	**Poetry** Penguin: *The Beat Poets* (Ginsberg, Corso, Ferlinghetti). Ginsberg *Reality Sandwiches*; Frost *In the Clearing*; Thomas *The Bread of Truth*. d. Robert Frost, William Carlos Williams, Louis MacNeice, Tristan Tzara, Sylvia Plath.
June Continuing tour with Roy Orbison. Twenty-one performances, two TV engagements, five radio broadcasts. 18 McCartney is 21. 21 National newspapers carry reports of Lennon beating up Cavern M.C. Bob Wooler at McCartney's 21st birthday party. (Wooler had insinuated that Lennon had slept with Epstein during their holiday in April/May.) 22 Lennon appears on *Juke Box Jury*. 23 ITV's *Thank Your Lucky Stars* celebrates the 'Mersey Beat' boom.	**45s:** Beatles *From Me To You*; Billy J Kramer & The Dakotas *Do You Want To Know A Secret?*; Gerry & The Pacemakers *I Like It*; Ray Charles *Take These Chains From My Heart*; Freddie & The Dreamers *If You Gotta Make A Fool of Somebody*; Shadows *Atlantis*. **LPs:** Beatles *Please Please Me*; Shadows *Greatest Hits*; Richard & The Shadows *Summer Holiday*; Presley *It Happened At the World's Fair*; Soundtrack *West Side Story*; Shannon *Hats Off to Del Shannon*; Billy Fury *Billy*; Roy Orbison *Lonely and Blue*; Berry *Chuck Berry*.	1 Governor George Wallace refuses to open University of Alabama to black students. 5 Profumo admits he lied to House of Commons (March) and resigns. 11 Kennedy orders National Guards to protect two black students enrolling at University of Alabama. 15 Riots in American south after shooting of civil rights leader Medgar Evers. 26 Kennedy makes Berlin speech.	**Stage** First performance of National Theatre: *Hamlet*, starring Peter O'Toole, directed by Laurence Olivier. Joan Littlewood's production of *Oh What A Lovely War* at Stratford East. Sir Frederick Ashton takes over Royal Ballet from Dame Ninette de Valois. *My Fair Lady* closes after six-year run in Drury Lane. Arden *The Workhouse Donkey*; Pinter *The Dwarfs*; *The Lover*. d. Clifford Odets, John Whiting, Edith Piaf, Max Miller.

			Non-fiction
July Ten performances, ten radio broadcasts. 1 Recording *She Loves You*. 7 Starr is 23. 18 Recording *With The Beatles*. 22 US: *Introducing The Beatles*. 30 Recording *With The Beatles*.	EMI launches Stateside label. **45s:** Gerry & The Pacemakers *I Like It*; Frank Ifield *Confessin'*; Presley *Devil In Disguise*; Holly *Bo Diddley*; Jim Reeves *Welcome To My World*; Crystals *Da Doo Ron Ron*; Lesley Gore *It's My Party*; Searchers *Sweets For My Sweet*; Roy Orbison *Falling*; Brian Poole & The Tremeloes *Twist and Shout*; Surfaris *Wipe Out*. **LPs:** Beatles *Please Please Me*; Shadows *Greatest Hits*; Richard & The Shadows *Summer Holiday*; Presley *It Happened At the World's Fair*, Shannon *Hats Off to Del Shannon*; Fury *Billy*; Roy Orbison *Crying*.	22 Trial of Dr Stephen Ward begins. 22 Independent enquiry into the rents rackets of Peter Rachman. 29 Kim Philby granted Soviet citizenship. 31 Stephen Ward takes overdose.	Shanks *The Stagnant Society*; Mitford *The American Way of Death*; Lorenz *On Aggression*; Arendt *Eichmann in Jerusalem*; Bishop of Woolwich *Honest to God*; Baldwin *The Fire Next Time*, Carson *Silent Spring*.
			Science fiction Dick *The Game-Players of Titan*; Vonnegut *Cat's Cradle*; Simak *Way Station*; Vance *The Dragon Masters*. Hugo: Philip K. Dick *The Man in the High Castle*.
August Thirteen performances, three TV engagements, two radio broadcasts. 3 Final gig (of 274) at The Cavern. 23 UK: *She Loves You*. 27-30 Filming for Don Haworth's BBC TV documentary *The Mersey Sound*.	Everly Brothers tour UK with Bo Diddley and Rolling Stones. **45s:** Presley *Devil In Disguise*; Searchers *Sweets For My Sweet*; Ifield *Confessin'*; Crystals *Da Doo Ron Ron*; Billy J Kramer & The Dakotas *Bad To Me*; Brian Poole & The Tremeloes *Twist and Shout*; Freddie & The Dreamers *I'm Telling You Now*; Surfaris *Wipe Out*. **LPs:** Beatles *Please Please Me*; Shadows *Greatest Hits*; Richard & The Shadows *Summer Holiday*; Shannon *Hats Off to Del Shannon*; Searchers *Meet The Searchers*; Holly *Reminising*; Berry *Chuck Berry*; Fury *Billy*; Presley *It Happened At the World's Fair*.	3 Ward dies. 8 Tripartite nuclear test-ban treaty signed in Moscow. 8 Great Train Robbery. 18 James Meredith becomes first black student at University of Mississippi. 28 200,000 march for civil rights in Washington. Martin Luther King gives 'I have a dream' speech.	

1963 THE BEATLES	UK POP	CURRENT AFFAIRS	CULTURE
September Eight performances, one TV engagement, six radio broadcasts. **11–12** Recording *With The Beatles*. **12** *She Loves You* tops the UK chart (four weeks). **16** US: *She Loves You*. **16–October 2** Lennon, his wife Cynthia, and Epstein holiday in Paris. Starr and McCartney go to Greece, Harrison to USA.	Little Richard joins Everly Brothers' UK tour. **45s:** Billy J Kramer & The Dakotas *Bad To Me*; The Beatles *She Loves You*; Richard *It's All in the Game*; Johnny Kidd & The Pirates *I'll Never Get Over You*; Trini Lopez *If I Had A Hammer*, Roy Orbison *Blue Bayou*; Rolling Stones *Come On*. **LPs:** Beatles *Please Please Me*; Richard *Cliff's Hit Album*; Shadows *Greatest Hits*; Searchers *Meet The Searchers*; Ball *Kenny Ball's Greatest Hits*; Frank Ifield *Born Free*.	**2** Wallace seals off Tuskegee High School to halt integration. **5** Christine Keeler arrested. **10** Kennedy assumes control of Alabama National Guard. **15** Bombing of black church service in Birmingham, Alabama. **26** Denning report blames Macmillan cabinet over Profumo scandal. **30** Mass arrest of black civil rights protestors in Alabama.	**Fashion** Mod style in Britain: mohair suits, Cuban heels, Lambrettas, anoraks ('parkas'). Pierre Cardin: 'Clothes are a form of protest.' Beatles adopt Cardin's collarless jackets; Emmanuelle Khanh creates *Ye Ye* style (after *She Loves You*). Mary Quant starts Ginger Group to mass-produce her styles. US designer Geoffrey Beene founds own label: simple dresses, T-shirts.
October Eleven performances, five TV engagements, four radio broadcasts. **3** Recording *With The Beatles*. **9** Lennon is 23. **13** *Sunday Night at the London Palladium* – official beginning of 'Beatlemania'. **17** Recording *I Want To Hold Your Hand*; *With The Beatles*. **23** Recording *With The Beatles*. **24–31** To Sweden – first foreign tour. Hysterical fans welcome the group back at Heathrow.	**45s:** The Beatles *She Loves You*; Brian Poole & The Tremeloes *Do You Love Me?*; Gerry & The Pacemakers *You'll Never Walk Alone*, Crystals *Then He Kissed Me*; Orbison *Blue Bayou*; Lopez *If I Had A Hammer*, Shirley Bassey *I Who Have Nothing*; Fourmost *Hello Little Girl*; Rolling Stones *Come On*. **LPs:** Beatles *Please Please Me*; Searchers *Meet The Searchers*; Ifield *Born Free*, Gerry & The Pacemakers *How Do You Like It?*; Cliff Richard *When in Spain*; Shadows *Greatest Hits*; Diddley Bo Diddley; Chuck Berry *On Stage*.	**1** Harold Wilson promises 'white heat' of technological revolution under a Labour government. **6** Crowds pelt fascist leader Colin Jordan with eggs at his wedding. **10** Macmillan resigns. **18** Lord Home takes over, mysteriously preferred to Rab Butler as prime minister. Macleod and Powell refuse to serve under him. **23** Home renounces his title.	**TV/Media** *Ready, Steady, Go!* goes on air (August). First episodes of *Dr Who, Naked City, World In Action.* Newspaper printers strike in New York.

November Twenty-six performances, eleven TV engagements, three radio broadcasts. **1–December 13** UK tour. Beatlemania now in full cry. Foreign news teams film some dates. **4** Royal Command Performance at Prince of Wales Theatre, London. Lennon suggests those in the richer seats rattle their jewellery (expletive deleted). **22** UK: *With The Beatles*. **28** *She Loves You* returns to the top of the UK chart (two weeks). **29** UK: *I Want To Hold Your Hand*	Dylan and Peter, Paul, & Mary create 'folk boom'. **45s:** Gerry & The Pacemakers *You'll Never Walk Alone*; The Beatles *She Loves You*; Searchers *Sugar and Spice*; Ronettes *Be My Baby*; Orbison *Blue Bayou*; Peter Paul & Mary *Blowin' in the Wind*; Chuck Berry *Let It Rock*. **LPs:** Beatles *Please Please Me*; Searchers *Meet The Searchers*; *Sugar and Spice*; Gerry & The Pacemakers *How Do You Like It?*; Freddie & The Dreamers *Freddie and The Dreamers*; Shannon *Little Town Flirt*; Shadows *Greatest Hits*.	**2** Diem overthrown in South Vietnam. **8** Home elected to House of Commons in hasty by-election. **13** BBC governors decide to take controversial *That Was The Week That Was* off the air early. **22** President Kennedy assassinated in Dallas, Texas. Vice President Lyndon Johnson sworn in. **24** Jack Ruby shoots Lee Harvey Oswald on live TV broadcast. **29** Warren Commission is set up.	**Visual arts** Goya Exhibition at the Royal Academy. Art Nouveau revival. New York Gallery of Modern Art opens. Major Pop Art exhibition at the Guggenheim (Andy Warhol, Robert Rauschenberg, Jasper Johns). Warhol founds The Factory. Duchamp retrospective in California. Soviet authorities repress Russian abstract artists. d. Georges Braque, Sir David Low.
December Twenty-one performances, four TV engagements, four radio broadcasts. **7** Group take over *Juke Box Jury*. **12** *I Want To Hold Your Hand* tops the UK chart (five weeks). **24–January 11** The Beatles' Christmas Show at the Finsbury Park Astoria, London. **26** US: *I Want To Hold Your Hand*. **27** *The Times* calls Lennon and McCartney 'the outstanding English composers of 1963'.	Sonny Boy Williamson records live with Yardbirds at The Marquee. **45s:** The Beatles *She Loves You*; The Beatles *I Want To Hold Your Hand*; Freddie and The Dreamers *You Were Made For Me*; Dave Clark Five *Glad All Over*, Rolling Stones *I Wanna Be Your Man*; Hollies *Stay*; Gene Pitney *24 Hours From Tulsa*; Kathy Kirby *Secret Love*. **LPs:** Beatles *With The Beatles*; *Please Please Me*; Gerry & The Pacemakers *How Do You Like It?*; Soundtrack *West Side Story*; Orbison *In Dreams*; Freddie & The Dreamers *Freddie and The Dreamers*; Searchers *Sugar and Spice*.	**6** Christine Keeler jailed for nine months. **12** Kenya independent. **28** Under establishment pressure, hugely popular *That Was The Week That Was* is pulled from BBC TV schedules 13 weeks before end of its current run (officially because 1964 will be an election year).	**Science** Friction welding. Hodgkin and Eccles' work on the transmission of nerve impulses. Measles vaccine. Quasars discovered.

416

1964 THE BEATLES	UK POP	CURRENT AFFAIRS	CULTURE
January Twenty-six performances, one TV engagement, five radio broadcasts. 12 Second engagement on *Sunday Night At The London Palladium*. 16–**February** 4 Lukewarm season at the Paris Olympia. French press hostile. 20 US: *Meet The Beatles!* 29 Recording *Can't Buy Me Love* in Paris. 30 US: *Please Please Me* (2nd release).	Rolling Stones and Ronettes tour UK. BBC TV launches *Top of the Pops*. Pye signs The Kinks. 7 UK R&B harmonica player Cyril Davies dies. **45s**: The Beatles *I Want To Hold Your Hand*; Dave Clark Five *Glad All Over*, Searchers *Needles and Pins*; Pitney *24 Hours From Tulsa*; Swinging Blue Jeans *Hippy Hippy Shake*; Dusty Springfield *I Only Want To Be With You*; Ronettes *Baby I Love You*; Manfred Mann *5 4 3 2 1*. **LPs**: Beatles *With The Beatles*, *Please Please Me*; Presley *Fun in Acapulco*; Gerry & The Pacemakers *How Do You Like It?*; Freddie & The Dreamers *Freddie and The Dreamers*; Soundtrack *West Side Story*; Berry *More Chuck Berry*.	1 Archbishop Makarios breaks international treaties on Cyprus. 3 Right-wing Republican Barry Goldwater announces his Presidential candidacy. 29 Military coup in South Vietnam.	**Cinema** Lester *A Hard Day's Night*; Hamilton *Goldfinger*, Clayton *The Pumpkin Eater*; Endfield *Zulu*; Cukor *My Fair Lady*; Huston *Night of the Iguana*; Frankenheimer *Seven Days in May*; Corman *The Masque of the Red Death*; Antonioni *The Red Desert*; Dymytryk *The Carpetbaggers*; Leone *A Fistful of Dollars*. d. Ben Hecht, Peter Lorre, Alan Ladd, Harpo Marx, Eddie Cantor, Sir Cedric Hardwicke.
February Two performances, six TV engagements, three radio broadcasts. 1 *I Want To Hold Your Hand* tops the US singles chart (seven weeks). 5 They return to the UK from France. 7 To America. Hysterical crowds hail the group on their arrival at Kennedy Airport. 9 *The Ed Sullivan Show* – historic live TV performance to an estimated audience of 73 million (a record). 12 The Beatles play Carnegie Hall. 16 Second live performance on *The Ed Sullivan Show*. 22 They return to UK. 25 Harrison is 21. 25–27 Recording *A Hard Day's*	Georgie Fame and The Blue Flames record live at The Flamingo. Bluebeat label forms to distribute Jamaican ska records in UK. **45s**: Searchers *Needles and Pins*; Bachelors *Diane*; Cilla Black *Anyone Who Had A Heart*; Gerry & The Pacemakers *I'm The One*; Manfred Mann *5 4 3 2 1*; Ronettes *Baby I Love You*; Dave Clark Five *Bits and Pieces*. **LPs**: Beatles *With The Beatles*; *Please Please Me*; Soundtrack *West Side Story*; Gerry & The Pacemakers *How Do You Like It?*; Searchers *Meet the Searchers*; Hollies *Stay with The Hollies*.	10 John Cleland's *Fanny Hill* (1750) ruled obscene. 12 Hostilities break out between Greek and Turkish Cypriots. 19 1,500 British troops sent to Cyprus. 25 Cassius Clay takes world heavyweight championship from Sonny Liston.	**Jazz** Coltrane *A Love Supreme*; Gil Evans *Individualism*; Dolphy *Out To Lunch!*; Ayler *Spirits*; Mingus *Town Hall Concert*; Kirk *I Talk With The Spirits*; Hill *Point Of Departure*, Shepp *Four For Trane*; Monk *Blue Monk*; Getz Getz/Gilberto; Smith *The Cat*; Morgan *The Sidewinder*. d. Jack Teagarden, Meade Lux Lewis, Don Redman, Eric Dolphy.

	45s / LPs	**News**	**Classical / Fiction**
March No performances (due to filming), five TV engagements, seven radio broadcasts. **1** Recording *Long Tall Sally*, *A Hard Day's Night* (LP). **2** US: *Twist and Shout* (single). Harrison meets Patti Boyd. **2–31** Filming *A Hard Day's Night* in and around London. **16** US: *Can't Buy Me Love*. **20** UK: *Can't Buy Me Love*. **21** *She Loves You* tops the US chart (two weeks). **23** US: *Do You Want To Know A Secret*. Lennon's first book, *In His Own Write*, is published.	**45s:** Black *Anyone Who Had A Heart*; Billy J Kramer *Little Children*; Dave Clark Five *Bits and Pieces*; Rolling Stones *Not Fade Away*; Hollies *Just One Look*; Major Lance *Um Um Um Um Um Um*; Jim Reeves *I Love You Because*. **LPs:** Beatles *With The Beatles*; *Please Please Me*; Soundtrack *West Side Story*; Hollies *Stay with The Hollies*; Gerry & The Pacemakers *How Do You Like It?*; Shadows *Greatest Hits*; Searchers *Sugar and Spice*.	**4** UN forces to Cyprus. **8** Malcolm X leaves Black Muslims. **12** Teamster boss Jimmy Hoffa jailed for eight years for jury-fixing. **28** 'Pirate' Radio Caroline begins pop transmissions from ship in North Sea. **30** Mods and Rockers battle in Clacton.	**Classical** Deryck Cooke's performing edition of Mahler's *Symphony No. 10*. Messiaen *Et Expecto resurrectionem mortuorum*; Britten *Curlew River*; *Cello Suite No. 1*; Shostakovich *Quartets Nos. 9 and 10*; Stravinsky *Variations*; Berio *Folk Songs*; Copland *Music For A Great City*; Maxwell Davies *Second Fantasia*; Stockhausen *Momente*; *Mixtur*; Crumb *Night Music II*; Birtwistle *Three Movements With Fanfares*; Riley *In C*. d. Mark Blitzstein.
April Two performances, seven TV engagements, two radio broadcasts. **2** *Can't Buy Me Love* tops the UK chart (three weeks). **4** *Can't Buy Me Love* tops the US chart (five weeks). The Beatles hold the top five positions in the American chart plus eleven other places in the Top 100. **1–24** More filming on *A Hard Day's Night*. **10** US: *The Beatles' Second Album*. **16** Recording *A Hard Day's Night* (single). **23** Foyle's holds a literary luncheon in honour of Lennon. **27** US: *Love Me Do*.	**45s:** Beatles *Can't Buy Me Love*; Peter & Gordon *World Without Love*; Billy J Kramer *Little Children*; Bachelors *I Believe*; Hollies *Just One Look*; Rolling Stones *Not Fade Away*; Searchers *Don't Throw Your Love Away*; Millie *My Boy Lollipop*; Dionne Warwick *Walk On By*. **LPs:** Beatles *With The Beatles*; *Please Please Me*; Rolling Stones *The Rolling Stones*; Hollies *Stay with The Hollies*; Soundtrack *West Side Story*; Shadows *Greatest Hits*.	**3** Khrushchev attacks Chinese Communist Party in Budapest. **13** Ian Smith becomes prime minister of Rhodesia. **15** Ronald Biggs guilty of taking part in Great Train Robbery. **21** BBC-2 goes on air. **22** Spy Greville Wynne swapped for Gordon Lonsdale at Berlin checkpoint.	**Fiction** Bellow *Herzog*; Vidal *Julian*; Southern *Candy*; Beckett *How It Is*; Golding *The Spire*; Powell *The Valley of Bones*; Burroughs *Nova Express*; Donleavy *Meet My Maker The Mad Molecule*; Isherwood *A Single Man*; Snow *Corridors of Power*; Murdoch *The Italian Girl*; Lessing *African Stories*; Fleming *You Only Live Twice*. d. T. H. White, Naomi Mitchison, Ian Fleming, Grace Metallious.

1964 THE BEATLES	UK POP	CURRENT AFFAIRS	CULTURE
May One performance, one radio broadcast. 2-27 On holiday. 30 *Love Me Do* tops the US chart (one week).	Rolling Stones deliberately court 'bad' publicity. **45s:** Peter & Gordon *World Without Love*; Searchers *Don't Throw Your Love Away*; Four Pennies *Juliet*; Cilla Black *You're My World*; Millie *My Boy Lollipop*; Gerry & The Pacemakers *Don't Let The Sun Catch You Crying*; Warwick *Walk On By*; Roy Orbison *It's Over*; Chuck Berry *No Particular Place To Go*. **LPs:** Rolling Stones *The Rolling Stones*; Beatles *With The Beatles*; Dave Clark Five *Session*; Shadows *Dance with The Shadows*; Hollies *Stay with The Hollies*; Searchers *It's The Searchers*; Soundtrack *West Side Story*.	3 Extra British troops to Aden. 12 'Pirate' Radio Atlanta starts broadcasting from North Sea. 18 Mods and Rockers clash in Brighton, Margate, Southend, Clacton, and Bournemouth. 28 Indian premier Jawaharlal Nehru dies.	**Poetry** Larkin *The Whitsun Weddings*; Berryman *77 Dream Songs*; Lowell *For the Union Dead*; Graves *Man Does, Woman Is*; Jennings *Recoveries*. d. Edith Sitwell, Samuil Marshak.
June Seventeen performances, two TV engagements, three radio broadcasts. 1-2 Recording *A Hard Day's Night* (LP). 18 McCartney is 22. 19 UK: *Long Tall Sally* (EP). 26 US: *A Hard Day's Night* (LP). 4-30 Tour of Denmark, Holland, Hong Kong, Australia, New Zealand (ill Starr temporarily replaced by Jimmy Nicol).	**45s:** Black *You're My World*; Orbison *It's Over*; Mary Wells *My Guy*; Swinging Blue Jeans *You're No Good*; Hollies *Here I Go Again*; Bachelors *Ramona*; Louis Armstrong *Hello Dolly*; Berry *No Particular Place To Go*; Lulu & The Luvvers *Shout*; Little Richard *Bama Lama Bama Loo*. **LPs:** Rolling Stones *The Rolling Stones*; Beatles *With The Beatles*; Searchers *It's The Searchers*; Berry *His Latest and Greatest*; Dave Clark Five *Session*; Buddy Holly *Showcase*; Shadows *Dance with The Shadows*; Bob Dylan *Freewheelin''*.	2 PLO founded in Jerusalem. 3 Martial law in South Korea. 9 Lord Beaverbrook dies. 11 Martin Luther King jailed for civil rights action in Florida. 14 Nelson Mandela sentenced to life-imprisonment for treason. 16 Comedian Lenny Bruce tried for obscenity in New York. 23 Three civil rights activists go missing after arrest in Mississippi. President Johnson orders massive search for them. 26 Civil rights leaders urge Johnson to take control in Mississippi.	**Stage** Shakespeare Quatercentenary at Stratford-on-Avon. Olivier plays *Othello* at the National. Peter Hall and John Barton produce 12-hour *Wars of the Roses* (the Aldwych). Windmill Theatre closes. Osborne *Inadmissible Evidence*; Pinter *The Homecoming*; Weiss *Marat-Sade*; Miller *After the Fall*; Schaffer *The Royal Hunt of the Sun*; Orton *Entertaining Mr Sloane*; Arden *Armstrong's Last Goodnight*; Bock *Fiddler on the Roof*; Herman *Hello Dolly*. d. Sean O'Casey, Brendan Behan, Cole Porter, Phyllis Dixey.

			Non-fiction
July Five performances, eight TV engagements, four radio broadcasts. **6** Premiere of *A Hard Day's Night* (film) in London. **7** Starr is 24. **10** UK: *A Hard Day's Night* (single and LP). Liverpool holds a civic reception for the group. **13** US: *A Hard Day's Night*. **20** US: *I'll Cry Instead; And I Love Her; Something New* (LP). **23** *A Hard Day's Night* tops the UK singles chart (three weeks). **28** McCartney and Lennon receive electric shocks from unearthed microphones during a performance in Sweden.	The High Numbers, soon to be The Who, release debut single. **25** Rolling Stones provoke riot at Empress Ballroom, Blackpool. **31** Jim Reeves killed in air-crash. **45s:** Orbison *It's Over*, Animals *House of the Rising Sun*; Rolling Stones *It's All Over Now*; Beatles *A Hard Day's Night*; P. J. Proby *Hold Me*; Dusty Springfield *I Just Don't Know What To Do With Myself*; Manfred Mann *Do Wah Diddy Diddy*; Nashville Teens *Tobacco Road*. **LPs:** Beatles *A Hard Day's Night*; Rolling Stones *The Rolling Stones*; Searchers *It's The Searchers*; Cliff Richard & The Shadows *Wonderful Life*; Presley *Kissin' Cousins*; Holly *Showcase*; Shadows *Dance with The Shadows*; Orbison *In Dreams*; Dylan *Freewheelin''*.	**2** Johnson signs Civil Rights Act, ending racial discrimination. **2** Pirate radios Caroline and Atlanta amalgamate. **12** Viet Cong inflict major defeat on South Vietnam government forces. **15** Republicans nominate right-winger Barry Goldwater. **27** US to send 5,000 'military advisers' to South Vietnam. **27** Race riots in Rochester, N.Y. **28** Malcolm X founds Organisation for Afro-American Unity. **28** Sir Winston Churchill leaves House of Commons, aged 89.	McLuhan *Understanding Media*; Leary *The Psychedelic Experience*; Marcuse *One Dimensional Man*; Berne *Games People Play*; Koestler *The Act of Creation*; Fromm *The Heart of Man*; Martin Luther King *Why We Can't Wait*; Hemingway *A Moveable Feast* (posthumous).
August Fourteen performances, one TV engagement, two radio broadcasts. **1** *A Hard Day's Night* tops the US chart (two weeks). **11, 14** Recording *Beatles For Sale*. **19–September 20** first American Tour' (see above, February 7–22). **23** They play Hollywood Bowl in Los Angeles. Recorded and issued in 1977. (See also 1965: 30 August). **24** US: *Matchbox*.	Rolling Stones headline Richmond Jazz & Blues Festival. **45s:** Beatles *A Hard Day's Night*; Manfred Mann *Do Wah Diddy Diddy*; Barron Knights *Call Up The Groups*; Rolling Stones *It's All Over Now*; Honeycombs *Have I the Right?*; Nashville Teens *Tobacco Road*; Kinks *You Really Got Me*; Beach Boys *I Get Around*; Marianne Faithfull *As Tears Go By*; Dave Berry *The Crying Game*; Zombies *She's Not There*; Dionne Warwick *You'll Never Get To Heaven*. **LPs:** Beatles *A Hard Day's Night*; Rolling Stones *The Rolling Stones*; Richard & The Shadows *Wonderful Life*; Presley *Kissin' Cousins*; Jim Reeves *Moonlight and Roses; A Touch of Velvet*; Dylan *The Times They Are A-Changin'*; Joan Baez *In Concert Vol. 2*.	**2** USS *Maddox* fired on in Gulf of Tonkin. **5** Johnson orders retaliatory strikes against North Vietnam. **2** Police quell clashes between Mods and Rockers in Hastings. **4** Bodies of three missing civil rights workers (June) found. **10** Turkey and Greece accept UN ceasefire over Cyprus. **18** South Africa banned from the Olympics.	**Science fiction** Ballard *The Terminal Beach*; Aldiss *The Dark Light Years; Greybeard*; Dick *Clans of the Alphane Moon*; Leiber *The Wanderer*; Blish *Dr Mirabilis*. Hugo: Clifford D. Simak *Way Station*.

1964 THE BEATLES	UK POP	CURRENT AFFAIRS	CULTURE
September Continuing American tour. Twenty-one performances, one TV engagement. **11** Group refuses to play Gator Bowl, Jacksonville, Florida, without guaranteed unsegregated audience. **29–30** Recording *Beatles For Sale*.	**45s:** Honeycombs *Have I the Right?*; Kinks *You Really Got Me*; Herman's Hermits *I'm Into Something Good*; Reeves *I Won't Forget You*; Faithfull *As Tears Go By*; Four Seasons *Rag Doll*; Zombies *She's Not There*; Berry *The Crying Game*; Supremes *Where Did Our Love Go*; Roy Orbison *Oh Pretty Woman*; Animals *I'm Crying*. **LPs:** Beatles *A Hard Day's Night*; Rolling Stones *The Rolling Stones*; Reeves *Moonlight and Rose*; Manfred Mann *Five Faces*; Richard & The Shadows *Wonderful Life*; The Bachelors *16 Great Songs*.	**3** State of emergency in Malaysia. **15** Home calls general election. **27** Warren Commission report rules out conspiracy in Kennedy assassination. **28** Survey shows Radio Caroline has more listeners than the BBC.	**Fashion** Mary Quant and Jean Muir declare Paris styles out of date, advocate inexpensive bold designs, short skirts for younger women. Boutique scene. John Stephens' Mod mens'-wear (Carnaby Street). John Bates (designer for Emma Peel/Diana Rigg in *The Avengers*) founds Varnon to market catsuits and pantsuits. Cardin unveils 'space-age' collection. Rudi Gernreich starts sports-wear label. Beehive hair-styles in vogue. Topless dresses worn in London.
October Thirty-six performances, five TV engagements. **6, 8** Recording *Beatles For Sale*. **9** Lennon is 24. **9–November 10th** The Beatles tour the UK. **18, 26** Recording *Beatles For Sale*.	Rolling Stones cause hysteria on Ed Sullivan Show. Musicians' Union bans tours of South Africa. **45s:** Herman's Hermits *I'm Into Something Good*; Orbison *Oh Pretty Woman*; Shaw *Always Something There To Remind Me*; Searchers *When You Walk In The Room*; Supremes *Where Did Our Love Go*; Animals *I'm Crying*; Cliff Bennett & The Rebel Rousers *One Way Love*; Shangri-Las *Remember (Walking in the Sand)*; Ronettes *Do I Love You*; Rockin' Berries *He's In Town*. **LPs:** Beatles *A Hard Day's Night*; Rolling Stones *The Rolling Stones*; Manfred Mann *Five Faces*; Reeves *Moonlight and Rose*; Kinks *The Kinks*; Richard & The Shadows *Wonderful Life*; Roy Orbison *In Dreams*.	**2** Two charged with killing three civil rights workers in Mississippi. (See June.) **15** Khrushchev ousted. Brezhnev takes over. **15** China explodes her first atomic bomb. **16** Labour wins general election.	**TV/Media** BBC-2 launched. BBC TV series *The Great War*. First episode of *The Man from UNCLE*. *The Sun* replaces *The Daily Herald*. No Pulitzers for fiction, music, or drama this year. First issues of *Telegraph Weekend Magazine*, *Observer Colour Magazine*, *The Psychedelic Review*. d. Gracie Allen.

November

Continuing UK tour. Eighteen performances, six TV engagements, three radio broadcasts.
23 US: *I Feel Fine*.
27 UK: *I Feel Fine*.

45s: Sandie Shaw *Always Something There To Remind Me*; Orbison *Oh Pretty Woman*; Supremes *Baby Love*, Kinks *All Day and All of the Night*; Wayne Fontana & The Mindbenders *Um Um Um Um Um Um*; Pretty Things *Don't Bring Me Down*; Martha & The Vandellas *Dancing in the Street*; Rolling Stones *Little Red Rooster*. **LPs:** The Beatles *A Hard Day's Night*; Rolling Stones *The Rolling Stones*; Manfred Mann *Five Faces*; Kinks *The Kinks*; Animals *The Animals*; Hollies *Hollies In The Hollies Style*; Dylan *Freewheelin'*; *Another Side*; Fame *Fame At Last*; Orbison *In Dreams*.

1 Viet Cong attack US airbase at Bien Hoa.
3 Lyndon Johnson re-elected.
19 South Vietnam opens major offensive against Viet Cong.

Visual arts
National Gallery buys Cézanne's *Les Grandes Baigneuses*. Vatican sends Michelangelo's *Pietà* to New York World's Fair. Marc Chagall's ceiling of the Paris Opera. 'Art of a Decade' at the Tate. 'New Generation' at the Whitechapel. Biennale Prize: Robert Rauschenberg.
d. Alexander Archipenko, Clive Bell.

December

Sixteen performances, one TV engagement.
4 UK: *Beatles For Sale*.
10 *I Feel Fine* tops the UK chart (five weeks).
15 US: *Beatles '65*.
24–January 16 The Beatles' Christmas Show at the Hammersmith Odeon, London.
26 *I Feel Fine* tops the US chart (three weeks).

Brian Wilson stops touring with Beach Boys to concentrate on writing and production. Smokey Robinson & The Miracles perform on *Ready, Steady, Go!* 10 Sam Cooke shot dead at Los Angeles motel. **45s:** Rolling Stones *Little Red Rooster*; Beatles *I Feel Fine*; Gene Pitney *I'm Gonna Be Strong*; Petula Clark *Downtown*; Dusty Springfield *Losing You*; Val Doonican *Walk Tall*; Georgie Fame *Yeh Yeh*. **LPs:** Beatles *Beatles For Sale*; *A Hard Day's Night*; Rolling Stones *The Rolling Stones*; Kinks *The Kinks*; Animals *The Animals*; Dylan *Another Side*; Orbison *Oh Pretty Woman*; Reeves *Moonlight and Roses*; Val Doonican *Lucky 13 Shades*.

10 Martin Luther King gets Nobel Peace Prize.
12 Jomo Kenyatta becomes President of Kenya.
21 Last execution in UK takes place.

Science
'Brain-drain' of UK scientists and engineers to USA. Hoyle's theory of strong and weak gravitation. Omega-minus particle discovered.
d. J. B. S. Haldane, Norbert Wiener, Rachel Carson.

1965 THE BEATLES	UK POP	CURRENT AFFAIRS	CULTURE
January Continuing Christmas Show. Twenty-eight performances. After this, Lennon and his wife Cynthia go on skiing trip to St Moritz with George Martin and his wife. McCartney and Jane Asher holiday in Tunisia. 9 Lennon reads his poetry on *Not Only . . . But Also* (BBC-2).	US Labor Department refuses visas for British groups. **45s:** Beatles *I Feel Fine*; Fame *Yeh Yeh*; Moody Blues *Go Now*; Twinkle *Terry*; Sandie Shaw *Girl Don't Come*; Sounds Orchestral *Cast Your Fate To The Winds*; Them *Baby Please Don't Go*; P. J. Proby *Somewhere*; Gerry & The Pacemakers *Ferry Cross The Mersey*; Righteous Brothers *You've Lost That Lovin' Feelin'*. **LPs:** Beatles *Beatles For Sale*; Rolling Stones *The Rolling Stones No. 2*; Doonican *Lucky 13 Shades*; Dylan *Another Side*; Kinks *The Kinks*; Orbison *Oh Pretty Woman*; Supremes *Meet The Supremes*.	1 Stanley Matthews becomes first footballer to be knighted. 7 Kray Brothers arrested. 12 Indonesia leaves the UN. 25 Death of Sir Winston Churchill, aged 90. 27 Thousands file past Churchill's coffin in Westminster Hall. 30 Churchill buried at Blenheim.	**Cinema** Lester *The Knack*, *Help!*; Furie *The Ipcress File*; Schlesinger *Darling*; Boorman *Catch Us If You Can*; Lean *Dr Zhivago*; Wise *Sound of Music*; Donner *What's New Pussycat?*; Leone *For a Few Dollars More*; Malle *Viva Maria*; Fellini *Juliet of the Spirits*; Godard *Alphaville*; Polanski *Repulsion*; Pontecorvo *The Battle of Algiers*. d. Stan Laurel, Clara Bow, Dorothy Dandridge, Jeanette MacDonald, Judy Holliday, David O. Selznick.
February No performances or engagements. 11 Starr marries Maureen Cox. 15 US: *Eight Days A Week*. Recording *Ticket To Ride*, *Help!* (LP) 16–20 Recording *Help!* (LP) 18 Northern Songs becomes a public company. 25 Harrison is 22. 23–28 Filming *Help!* in the Bahamas.	**45s:** Righteous Brothers *You've Lost That Lovin' Feelin'*; Kinks *Tired of Waiting for You*; Del Shannon *Keep Searchin'*; Them *Baby Please Don't Go*; Shangri-Las *Leader of the Pack*; Animals *Don't Let Me Be Misunderstood*; Ivy League *Funny How Love Can Be*; Seekers *I'll Never Find Another Game of Love*; Tom Jones *It's Not Unusual*. **LPs:** Rolling Stones *The Rolling Stones No. 2*; Beatles *Beatles For Sale*; Reeves *Best Of*; Dylan *Another Side*, Animals *The Animals*; Kinks *The Kinks*.	1 Martin Luther King arrested on civil rights protest in Selma, Alabama. 5 TV cigarette advertising banned in UK. 11 US warplanes bomb North Vietnam. 21 Malcolm X assassinated in New York.	**Jazz** Ellington: first Sacred Concert. Ornette Coleman Trio tours Europe. Coltrane *Ascension*; *Kulu Se Mama*; Coleman *At The Golden Circle*; Davis *E.S.P.*; Ayler *Spirits Rejoice*; Kirk *Rip, Rig And Panic*; Taylor *Conquistador*; Sun Ra *Heliocentric Worlds*; Rollins *On Impulse!*; Shepp *New Thing At Newport*; Bley *Closer*; Shorter *The All-Seeing Eye*; Young *Unity*; Hancock *Maiden Voyage*; Hutcherson *Dialogue*; Brand *Anatomy Of A South African Village*. d. Nat King Cole, Sonny Boy Williamson.

			Classical / Fiction
March 1-9 Filming *Help!* in the Bahamas. 14-20 Filming *Help!* in Austria. 24-31 Filming *Help!* at Twickenham. 22 US: *The Early Beatles.* 28 Final appearance on ITV's *Thank Your Lucky Stars.* 30 Recording *Help!* (LP).	1 The Cavern closes. **45s:** Seekers *I'll Never Find Another You;* Jones *It's Not Unusual;* Rolling Stones *The Last Time;* Ivy League *Funny How Love Can Be;* Dobie Gray *The In Crowd;* Herman's Hermits *Silhouettes;* Pretty Things *Honey I Need;* Goldie & The Gingerbreads *Can't You Hear My Heart Beat;* Unit 4 Plus 2 *Concrete and Clay;* The Who *I Can't Explain;* Donovan *Catch The Wind.* **LPs:** Rolling Stones *The Rolling Stones No. 2;* Beatles *Beatles For Sale;* Kinks *Kinda Kinks;* Dylan *Another Side; Freewheelin';* Pretty Things *The Pretty Things.*	9 Kray Brothers trial begins. 10 Civil rights protest in Selma, Alabama, banned. Further protests follow. 28 Martin Luther King leads 25,000 civil rights marchers in Montgomery, Alabama.	**Classical** Royal Opera House production of Schoenberg's *Moses und Aron.* Britten *Songs and Proverbs of William Blake;* Maxwell Davies *Revelation And Fall;* Bernstein *Chichester Psalms;* Birtwistle *Tragoedia;* Berio *Laborintus II; Sequenza III;* Ligeti *Requiem;* Henze *The Bassarids;* Crumb *Madrigals;* Boulez *Pli Selon Pli;* Zimmerman *The Soldiers;* Reich *It's Gonna Rain.* d. Edgard Varèse. **Fiction** Mailer *An American Dream;* Spark *The Mandelbaum Gate;* Greene *The Comedians;* Robbe-Grillet *La maison de rendezvous;* Lessing *Landlocked;* Le Carré *The Looking-Glass War.* Nobel: Mikhail Sholokhov. d. Somerset Maugham.
April One performance, five TV engagements, three radio broadcasts. 1-14 Filming *Help!* at Twickenham. 9 UK: *Ticket To Ride.* 13 *Eight Days A Week* tops the US chart (two weeks). Recording *Help!* (single). 14 McCartney buys house in St John's Wood, London. 19 US: *Ticket To Ride.* 20-30 Filming *Help!* at Twickenham. 22 *Ticket To Ride* tops the UK chart (three weeks).	**45s:** Rolling Stones *The Last Time;* Unit 4 Plus 2 *Concrete and Clay;* Cliff Richard *The Minute You're Gone;* Beatles *Ticket To Ride;* Yardbirds *For Your Love;* Donovan *Catch The Wind;* Them *Here Comes the Night;* Supremes *Stop in the Name of Love;* The Who *I Can't Explain;* Animals *Bring It On Home To Me;* Martha & The Vandellas *Nowhere To Run;* Roger Miller *King of the Road;* Bob Dylan *The Times They Are A-Changin'.* **LPs:** Rolling Stones *The Rolling Stones No. 2;* Beatles *Beatles For Sale;* Dylan *Freewheelin'; The Times They are a-Changin';* Kinks *Kinda Kinks;* Pretty Things *The Pretty Things;* Soundtrack *Sound of Music.*	2 US increases financial and military aid to South Vietnam. 6 Kray Brothers cleared of charges of running a protection racket. 18 Police arrest Mods and Rockers in Brighton. 27 Anti-Vietnam demonstrations in Paris. 30 Right-wing junta seizes power in Dominican Republic.	

1965 THE BEATLES	UK POP	CURRENT AFFAIRS	CULTURE
May One TV engagement, one radio broadcast. **3–11** UK location filming for *Help!* **10** Recording *Help!* (LP). **22** *Ticket To Ride* tops the US chart (one week). **26** Last BBC radio performance.	Dylan tours UK (filmed by D. A. Pennebaker for *Don't Look Back*). Alan Price leaves the Animals. **45s:** Beatles *Ticket To Ride*; Miller *King of the Road*; Jackie Trent *Where Are You Now*; Sandie Shaw *Long Live Love*; Peter & Gordon *True Love Ways*; Bob Dylan *Subterranean Homesick Blues*; Shirley Ellis *The Clapping Song*; Manfred Mann *Oh No Not My Baby*; Cilla Black *I've Been Wrong Before*. **LPs:** Beatles *Beatles For Sale*; Bob Dylan *Bringing It All Back Home*; *Freewheelin'*; *The Times They are a-Changin'*; Soundtrack *Sound of Music*; *Mary Poppins*; Rolling Stones *The Rolling Stones No. 2*.	**7** White nationalist Rhodesian Front party wins election. **28** State of emergency declared in parts of Rhodesia.	**Poetry** Wholly Communion: day-long recital of Beat poetry at the Albert Hall (June). Plath *Ariel* (posthumous); Day Lewis *The Room*; Fuller *Buff*; Gascoyne *Collected Poems*; Graves *Collected Poems*; Raine *The Hollow Hill*. d. T. S. Eliot, Jacques Audiberti.
June Thirteen performances, two TV engagements, eight radio broadcasts. **12** The Queen awards The Beatles MBEs. Some award-holders send their medals back in protest. **14** US: *Beatles VI*. **14, 15, 17** Recording *Help!* (LP). **18** McCartney is 23. **24** Lennon's second book *A Spaniard In The Works* is published. **20–July 3** Tour of France, Italy, and Spain.	**45s:** Shaw *Long Live Love*; Presley *Crying in the Chapel*; Hollies *I'm Alive*; Seekers *World of Our Own*; Ellis *The Clapping Song*; Burt Bacharach *Trains and Boats and Planes*; Kinks *Set Me Free*; Walker Brothers *Love Her*; The Who *Anyway Anyhow Anywhere*; Yardbirds *Heart Full of Soul*; Sir Douglas Quintet *She's About A Mover*; Dixie Cups *Iko Iko*; Byrds *Mr Tambourine Man*. **LPs:** Dylan *Bringing It All Back Home*; Soundtrack *Sound of Music*; Bacharach *Hit Maker*; Donovan *What's Bin Did*; Beatles *Beatles For Sale*; Soundtrack *Mary Poppins*; Animals *Animal Tracks*; Baez *Joan Baez 5*.	**16** De Gaulle condemns US intervention in Latin America and South-East Asia. **29** US troops go on first offensive against Viet Cong east of Saigon.	**Stage** Maria Callas's final performance (as Tosca). Rudolf Nureyev and Margot Fonteyn star in Kenneth Macmillan's production of Prokofiev's *Romeo and Juliet*. Spike Milligan in *Son Of Oblomov*. Bruce Lacey's *An Evening of British Rubbish*. Osborne *A Patriot for Me*; Naughton *Spring and Port Wine*; Marcus *The Killing of Sister George*; Baldwin *The Amen Corner*.

July Two performances, one TV engagement, two radio broadcasts. **7** Starr is 25. **19** US: *Help!* **23** UK: *Help!*	**45s:** Presley *Crying in the Chapel*; Hollies *I'm Alive*; Byrds *Mr Tambourine Man*; Yardbirds *Heart Full of Soul*; Fortunes *You've Got Your Troubles*; Dusty Springfield *In the Middle of Nowhere*; Animals *We Gotta Get Out of This Place*; Sam the Sham & The Pharaohs *Woolly Bully*; Four Tops *I Can't Help Myself*; The Who *Anyway Anyhow Anywhere*; Donovan *Colours*. **LPs:** Dylan *Bringing It All Back Home*; Soundtrack *Sound of Music*; Baez *Joan Baez 5*; Soundtrack *Mary Poppins*; Shadows *The Sound of The Shadows*; Seekers *A World of Our Own*.	**4** Martin Luther King calls for end to Vietnam war. **27** Edward Heath becomes Tory leader. **28** Johnson sends 50,000 more troops to Vietnam.	**Non-fiction** Robbe-Grillet *Towards a New Novel*; Woolf *The Kandy-Kolored Tangerine-Flake Streamline Baby*. d. Martin Buber, Paul Tillich, Albert Schweitzer.
August Sixteen performances, three TV engagements, two radio broadcasts. **5** *Help!* tops the UK chart (three weeks). **6** UK: *Help!* (LP). **13** US: *Help!* (LP). **14–31** Second American Tour. **15** Shea Stadium. 55,600 attend. **27** Beatles meet Elvis Presley in Los Angeles. **29** Film *Help!* opens in London. **29–30** Hollywood Bowl. Recorded and issued in 1977. (See 1964: 23 August.)	George Martin forms Associated Independent Records (AIR). **45s:** Beatles *Help!*; Sonny & Cher *I Got You Babe*; Fortunes *You've Got Your Troubles*; Animals *We Gotta Get Out of This Place*; Jonathan King *Everyone's Gone To The Moon*; Sam the Sham & The Pharaohs *Woolly Bully*; Byrds *All I Really Want To Do*; Kinks *See My Friend*. **LPs:** Beatles *Help!*; Soundtrack *Sound of Music*; *Mary Poppins*; Baez *Joan Baez 5*; Dylan *Bringing It All Back Home*; Byrds *Mr Tambourine Man*; Moody Blues *The Magnificent Moodies*; Andy Williams *Almost There*; Dave Clark Five *Catch Us If You Can*.	Ken Kesey and the Merry Pranksters take LSD. **12** Britain appoints first woman judge. **18** Photographer David Bailey marries film actress Catherine Deneuve. **11–15** Race riots in Watts, Los Angeles. **25** India and Pakistan clash over Kashmir.	**Science fiction** Michael Moorcock's first Jerry Cornelius stories published in *New Worlds*. Herbert *Dune*; Dick *The Three Stigmata of Palmer Eldritch*; Pohl *A Plague of Pythons*; Aldiss *The Saliva Tree*; Ballard *The Drought*; Disch *The Genocides*; Ellison *Paingod*. Hugo: Fritz Leiber *The Wanderer*. Nebula: Frank Herbert *Dune*.

1965 THE BEATLES	UK POP	CURRENT AFFAIRS	CULTURE
September No engagements. 4 *Help!* tops the US chart (three weeks). 13 US: *Yesterday.* Zak Starkey born. 26 The Beatles receive their MBEs at Buckingham Palace.	**45s:** Sonny & Cher *I Got You Babe*; Rolling Stones *Satisfaction*; Walker Brothers *Make It Easy On Yourself*; Ken Dodd *Tears*; Beatles *Help!*; Dylan *Like A Rolling Stone*; Jones *What's New Pussycat*; Barry McGuire *Eve of Destruction*; Righteous Brothers *Unchained Melody*; McCoys *Hang On Sloopy*; Beach Boys *California Girls*; Hollies *Look Through Any Window*; Manfred Mann *If You Gotta Go Go Now*; Honeycombs *That's the Way*. **LPs:** Beatles *Help!*; Soundtrack *Sound of Music*; *Mary Poppins*; Baez *Joan Baez5*; Dylan *Bringing It All Back Home*; Byrds *Mr Tambourine Man*; Orbison *There Is Only One Roy Orbison*; Presley *Flaming Star and Summer Kisses*.	8 India invades Pakistan. 13 Pakistani planes bomb Bombay. 20 UN orders ceasefire in Kashmir conflict. 22 Pakistan bombs Amritsar.	**Fashion** Explosion of boutiques (street style); 'youthquake' rocks fashion world. John Stephens' Carnaby Street empire. Mary Quant defines Mod girl look: Op Art mini-dresses, PVC 'kinky' boots, coloured tights, soft bras, cropped hair (Vidal Sassoon). Models: Jean Shrimpton, Penelope Tree, Twiggy. Similar look in France (Courrèges) and USA (Anne Fogarty, Geoffrey Beene). Paco Rabanne produces dresses in industrial materials: metal, plastic. USA: Betsey Johnson design-edits *Mademoiselle* (gangster-stripe pant suits, plastic dresses with stick-on-yourself stars). November: British Customs reclassifies miniskirts from child's-length hems to adult-wear in order to tax them. d. Helena Rubinstein.

			TV/Media
October	**45s:** Dodd *Tears*; Manfred Mann *If You Gotta Go Go Now*; Andy Williams *Almost There*; McGuire *Eve of Destruction*; McCoys *Hang On Sloopy*; Dusty Springfield *Some Of Your Lovin'*; Wilson Pickett *In the Midnight Hour*; Yardbirds *Evil Hearted You/Still I'm Sad*; Chris Andrews *Yesterday Man*; Hedgehoppers Anonymous *It's Good News Week*. **LPs:** Beatles *Help!*; Soundtrack *Sound of Music*; Rolling Stones *Out of Our Heads*; Dylan *Highway 61 Revisited*; Sonny and Cher *Look At Us*; Soundtrack *Mary Poppins*; Williams *Almost There*; Manfred Mann *Mann Made*; Hollies *Hollies*.	28 Ian Brady and Myra Hindley arrested for the 'Moors murders'. 29 Wilson flies to Rhodesia to dissuade Smith from declaring UDI.	Mary Whitehouse founds National Viewers' and Listeners' Association. First UK transmission of *Peyton Place*. First episodes of *Going for a Song, Call My Bluff, Stingray, Jackanory*. First issue of *Penthouse*. d. Richard Dimbleby, Ed Murrow, Spike Jones.
9 *Yesterday* tops the US chart (four weeks). Lennon is 25. **12–13, 16, 18, 20–22, 23, 29** Recording *Rubber Soul*.			
			Visual arts
November	**45s:** Rolling Stones *Get Off Of My Cloud*; Seekers *The Carnival Is Over*; Andrews *Yesterday Man*; The Who *My Generation*; Barry *1-2-3*; Yardbirds *Evil Hearted You/Still I'm Sad*; Animals *It's My Life*; Everly Brothers *Love Is Strange*; Toys *A Lover's Concerto*; James Brown *Papa's Got A Brand New Bag*; Dylan *Positively 4th Street*. **LPs:** Soundtrack *Sound of Music*; Rolling Stones *Out of Our Heads*; Beatles *Help!*; Soundtrack *Mary Poppins*; Dylan *Highway 61 Revisited*; Dusty Springfield *Everything's Coming Up Dusty*; Sonny and Cher *Look At Us*.	9 Power-cut blacks out New York. 11 Rhodesia declares UDI. 13 Kenneth Tynan says 'fuck' on television. 16 Britain enforces economic sanctions on Rhodesia.	Rembrandt's *Titus* sold at Christie's for £800,000. Moore: *Lincoln Centre Reclining Figure*. Giacometti exhibition (London). Picasso: *Self Portrait*. Op Art in vogue: Bridget Riley, Victor Vasarely. 'The Responsive Eye' at the N.Y. Museum of Modern Art. Artistic 'minimalism'. d. Le Corbusier.
One TV engagement, three radio broadcasts. **3–4, 6, 8–11, 15** Recording *Rubber Soul*. 23 Filming promo-clips (videos).			

1965 THE BEATLES	UK POP	CURRENT AFFAIRS	CULTURE
December Last UK tour. Eighteen performances. 3 UK: *We Can Work It Out/Day Tripper; Rubber Soul.* 6 US: *We Can Work It Out/Day Tripper; Rubber Soul.* 16 *We Can Work It Out/Day Tripper* tops the UK chart (five weeks).	**45s:** Seekers *The Carnival Is Over;* Beatles *We Can Work It Out/Day Tripper;* Cliff Richard *Wind Me Up;* Ken Dodd *The River;* Walker Brothers *My Ship Is Coming In;* The Who *My Generation;* Barry 1-2-3; Four Seasons *Let's Hang On;* Fontella Bass *Rescue Me;* Kinks *Till the End of the Day;* Spencer Davis Group *Keep On Running.* **LPs:** Beatles *Rubber Soul;* Soundtrack *Sound of Music; Mary Poppins;* Beatles *Help!;* Rolling Stones *Out of Our Heads;* Who *My Generation;* Walker Brothers *Take It Easy;* Kinks *Kinks Kontroversy;* Baez *Farewell Angelina.*	17 Britain calls for oil embargo on Rhodesia. 24 Christmas truce in Vietnam.	**Science.** First commercial communications satellite, Early Bird.

429

1966 THE BEATLES	UK POP	CURRENT AFFAIRS	Culture
January No engagements. **5** Studio overdubs for *The Beatles At Shea Stadium*. **8** *We Can Work It Out* tops US chart (three weeks). **21** Harrison marries Pattie Boyd. McCartney attends. (Other Beatles are on holiday.)	Tamla Motown outsells all other American labels in singles market. **45s:** Beatles *We Can Work It Out/Day Tripper*; Spencer Davis Group *Keep On Running*; Overlanders *Michelle*; Cliff Richard *Wind Me Up*; Walker Brothers *My Ship Is Coming In*; Four Seasons *Let's Hang On*; Bass Rescue Me; Len Barry *1-2-3*; The Who *My Generation*; Kinks *Till the End of the Day*; Crispian St Peters *You Were On My Mind*; Herman's Hermits *A Must To Avoid*. **LPs:** Beatles *Rubber Soul*; Soundtrack *Sound of Music*; *Mary Poppins*; Who *My Generation*; Dodd *Tears*; Rolling Stones *Out of Our Heads*; Walker Brothers *Take It Easy*; Spencer Davis Group *1st*.	**1** The Psychedelic Shop opens on Haight Street, San Francisco. **8** US ground troops attack the Iron Triangle northwest of Saigon. **15** Trips Festival, San Francisco: foundation of American hippie movement. **16** Military coup in Nigeria. **17** American B-52 bomber crashes in sea near Spain with H-bomb on board. **19** Indira Gandhi becomes prime minister of India.	**Cinema** Gilbert *Alfie*; Antonioni *Blow Up*; Losey *Modesty Blaise*; Reisz *Morgan – a Suitable Case for Treatment*; Narizzano *Georgy Girl*; Zinnemann *A Man for All Seasons*; Ritt *The Spy Who Came in from The Cold*; Nichols *Who's Afraid of Virginia Woolf*; Welles *Chimes at Midnight*; Penn *The Chase*; Frankenheimer *Seconds*; Lelouch *A Man and A Woman*; Truffaut *Fahrenheit 451*; Leone *The Good, the Bad, and the Ugly*; Menzel *Closely Observed Trains*; Bergman *Persona*; Polanski *Cul de Sac*; Warhol *Chelsea Girls*. d. Buster Keaton, Montgomery Clift, Walt Disney, Nancy Carroll, Robert Rossen, Hedda Hopper.

1966 THE BEATLES	UK POP	CURRENT AFFAIRS	CULTURE
February No engagements. The Harrisons honeymoon in Barbados. The Lennons and the Starrs are on holiday. **21** US: *Nowhere Man.* **25** Harrison is 23. **28** The Cavern closes.	The Who move from Brunswick to Reaction. **45s:** Overlanders *Michelle;* Nancy Sinatra *These Boots Were Made For Walking;* Spencer Davis Group *Keep On Running;* Herb Alpert and the Tijuana Brass *Spanish Flea;* St Peters *You Were On My Mind;* Mindbenders *Groovy Kind of Love;* Rolling Stones *Nineteenth Nervous Breakdown;* Len Barry *Like A Baby;* Otis Redding *My Girl;* Dusty Springfield *Little By Little;* Beach Boys *Barbara Ann;* Lee Dorsey *Get Out of My Life Woman;* Stevie Wonder *Uptight.* **LPs:** Beatles *Rubber Soul;* Spencer Davis Group *2nd;* Soundtrack *Sound of Music; Mary Poppins;* Who *My Generation;* Sinatra *A Man and His Music;* Beach Boys *Party!;* Walker Brothers *Take It Easy;* Redding *Otis Blue.*	**8** Freddie Laker sets up independent airline. **14** US H-bomb found on seabed off Spain (January). **24** Military coup topples Nkrumah in Ghana.	**Jazz** Coltrane *Live at The Village Vanguard Again;* Davis *Miles Smiles;* Ellington *Far East Suite;* Taylor Unit *Structures;* Bley *Ramblin';* Cherry *Complete Communion;* Monk *Straight, No Chaser,* Lloyd *Dream Weaver, Forest Flower,* AMM *AMMMusic.* d. Bud Powell, George Lewis, Red Nichols.

March

No engagements. McCartney and Asher holiday in Switzerland.

4 London *Evening Standard* publishes Maureen Cleave's interview with Lennon in which he remarks that The Beatles are more popular than Jesus.

20 World Cup stolen in London.
23 First meeting of Archbishop of Canterbury and Pope in 400 years.
27 World Cup recovered.

45s: Nancy Sinatra *These Boots Were Made For Walking*; Walker Brothers *The Sun Ain't Gonna Shine Any More*; Rolling Stones *Nineteenth Nervous Breakdown*; Mindbenders *Groovy Kind of Love*; Beach Boys *Barbara Ann*; Small Faces *Sha La La La Lee*; Hollies *I Can't Let Go*; Yardbirds *Shapes of Things*; Kinks *Dedicated Follower of Fashion*; Lou Christie *Lightning Strikes*; Mitch Ryder and The Detroit Wheels *Jenny Take A Ride*; Wonder *Uptight*; The Who *Substitute*; Brown *I Got You*; Bob Lind *Elusive Butterfly*; Spencer Davis Group *Somebody Help Me*; Wilson Pickett *634-5789*; Gene Pitney *Backstage*. **LPs:** Soundtrack *Sound of Music*; Beatles *Rubber Soul*; Beach Boys *Party!*; Spencer Davis Group *2nd*; Redding *Otis Blue*; Walker Brothers *Take It Easy*; Soundtrack *Mary Poppins*.

Classical

Metropolitan Opera House opens in New York.

Stravinsky *Requiem Canticles*; Shostakovich *Cello Concerto No. 2*; *Quartet No. 11*; Britten *The Burning Fiery Furnace*; Maw *Sinfonia*; Penderecki *St Luke Passion*; Bussotti *La Passion Selon Sade*; Ligeti *Lux Aeterna*; Stockhausen *Telemusik*; Pärt *Symphony No. 2*; Tavener *The Whale*; Carter *Piano Concerto*; Berio *Sequenza IV*; Partch *Delusion Of The Fury*; Riley *Dorian Reeds*; Reich *Come Out*.

d. Herman Scherchen.

1966 THE BEATLES	UK POP	CURRENT AFFAIRS	CULTURE
April 6–8, 11, 13–14, 16–17, 19–22, 26–29 Recording *Revolver*.	**45s:** Walker Brothers *The Sun Ain't Gonna Shine Any More*; Spencer Davis Group *Somebody Help Me*; Dusty Springfield *You Don't Have To Say You Love Me*; Hollies *I Can't Let Go*; Kinks *Dedicated Follower of Fashion*; Lind *Elusive Butterfly*; Yardbirds *Shapes of Things*; Cilla Black *Alfie*; Alan Price Set *I Put A Spell On You*; Dave Dee Dozy Beaky Mick and Tich *Hold Tight*; The Who *Substitute*; Cher *Bang Bang*; Manfred Mann *Pretty Flamingo*; Norma Tanega *Walking My Cat Named Dog*. **LPs:** Soundtrack *Sound of Music*, Rolling Stones *Aftermath*; Beatles *Rubber Soul*; Walker Brothers *Take It Easy*; Byrds *Turn, Turn, Turn*; Simon and Garfunkel *Sounds of Silence*; Mantovani *Mantovani Magic*.	1 Labour wins majority of 96 in general election. 5 Oil discovered in the North Sea. 7 US H-bomb recovered from sea off Spain. (See February.) 8 Illegitimate births have doubled in UK since 1956. 15 Cover story in *Time* proclaims 'Swinging London', the 'City of the Decade'.	**Fiction** Soviet authorities jail Yuli Daniel and Andrei Sinyavsky. White *The Solid Mandala*; Burgess *Inside Mr Enderby*; Murdoch *The Time of the Angels*; Malamud *The Fixer*; Pynchon *The Crying of Lot 49*; Burroughs *Junkie*; Barth *Giles Goat-Boy*; Rhys *Wide Sargasso Sea*; Scott *The Jewel in the Crown*; Susann *Valley of the Dolls*. d. Evelyn Waugh, C. S. Forester, Flann O'Brien, Georges Duhamel, Margery Allingham.

May
1 Last UK concert: *NME* Poll-Winners Concert at Wembley.
5–6, 9, 16, 18, 19 Recording *Revolver*.
19–20 Filming promos for *Paperback Writer* and *Rain*.
26 Recording *Revolver*.
27 D. A. Pennebaker films Lennon and Dylan together in London. Lennon and Harrison attend Dylan's second Albert Hall concert.
30 US: *Paperback Writer*.

20 Pete Townshend and Keith Moon in onstage fracas. Moon threatens to leave Who. 267 Dylan appears at the Albert Hall with The Hawks (aka The Band).
45s: Manfred Mann *Pretty Flamingo*; Rolling Stones *Paint It Black*; Lovin' Spoonful *Daydream*; Cher *Bang Bang*; Springfield *You Don't Have To Say You Love Me*; Beach Boys *Sloop John B*; Crispian St Peters *Pied Piper*; Simon and Garfunkel *Homeward Bound*; Alan Price Set *I Put A Spell On You*; Roy C *Shotgun Wedding*; Merseys *Sorrow*; Troggs *Wild Thing*; Mamas and Papas *Monday Monday*; *California Dreamin'*. **LPs:** Rolling Stones *Aftermath*; Soundtrack *Sound of Music*; Small Faces *Small Faces*; Beatles *Rubber Soul*; Beach Boys *Today*; Lovin' Spoonful *Daydream*; Black *Cilla Sings a Rainbow*; Animals *Most of the Animals*.

2 Chairman Mao (through speech by Chou En-lai) proclaims Cultural Revolution: strategy to regain control of Chinese Communist Party by inciting young Red Guards to purge 'revisionists' and 'bourgeois reactionaries'.
6 Brady and Hindley jailed for life for the 'Moors murders'.
15 8,000 Vietnam protestors encircle the Pentagon in effort to 'levitate' it.
16 British Seamen's Union goes on strike.

Poetry
Barker *Dreams of A Summer Night*; Ashbery *Rivers and Mountains*; Bunting *Briggflatts*; Plomer *Taste and Remember*, Gunn *Positives*; Yevtushenko *Poetry* (translated). d. Anna Akhmatova, André Breton, Hans Arp, Delmore Schwartz.

434

1966 THE BEATLES	UK POP	CURRENT AFFAIRS	CULTURE
June 7 performances, 2 TV engagements. 1–3, 6, 8–9 Recording *Revolver.* 10 UK: *Paperback Writer.* 14 Recording *Revolver.* 15 Capitol withdraws the 'butcher' cover to *Yesterday' ... and Today.* 16–17 Recording *Revolver.* 17 McCartney buys a farm on the Mull of Kintyre, his birthday present to himself. 18 McCartney is 24. 20 US: *Yesterday ... and Today* (with different cover). See 15. 21 Recording *Revolver.* 23 *Paperback Writer* tops the UK chart (two weeks). 23–July 4 Tour of West Germany, Japan, and The Philippines. 25 *Paperback Writer* tops US chart (two weeks). 26 Concert in Hamburg. Lennon and McCartney revisit old haunts.	**45s:** Sinatra *Strangers in the Night;* Beatles *Paperback Writer;* Rolling Stones *Paint It Black;* Troggs *Wild Thing;* Merseys *Sorrow;* Mamas and Papas *Monday Monday;* Dylan *Rainy Day Women Nos. 12 and 35;* Percy Sledge *When A Man Loves A Woman;* Roy C *Shotgun Wedding;* Animals *Don't Bring Me Down;* Beach Boys *Sloop John B;* Byrds *Eight Miles High;* Yardbirds *Over Under Sideways Down;* Ike and Tina Turner *River Deep and Mountain High;* Kinks *Sunny Afternoon;* Simon and Garfunkel *I Am A Rock;* Chiffons *Sweet Talkin' Guy;* Four Seasons *Opus 17;* Georgie Fame *Get Away.* **LPs:** Rolling Stones *Aftermath;* Soundtrack *Sound of Music;* Small Faces *Small Faces;* Georgie Fame *Sweet Things;* Animals *Animalisms;* Beatles *Rubber Soul;* Black Cilla *Sings a Rainbow.*	7 James Meredith shot during civil rights march in Mississippi. 7 Ronald Reagan wins Republican nomination for governship of California. 10 Mary Quant awarded OBE. 20 Harold Wilson attacks 'Communist subversion' allegedly behind the strike by the National Union of Seamen (see May 16). 25 James Meredith rejoins civil rights march in Mississippi. 30 US planes bomb Hanoi and Haiphong.	**Stage** Peter Brook stages anti-war play *US* at RSC. Lord Chamberlain bans Edward Bond's *Saved.* Robert Rauschenberg and John Cage: 'happening' in New York. The People Show is founded. Albee *A Delicate Balance;* Orton *Loot;* Dyer *Staircase;* Shaffer *Black Comedy;* Leigh *Man of La Mancha;* Lane *On A Clear Day You Can See Forever.* d. Erwin Piscator, Edward Craig, Sophie Tucker, Lenny Bruce.

July			Non-fiction
Six performances, two TV engagements. 5 Riot in Manila after The Beatles are reported to have snubbed Imelda Marcos. 7 Starr is 26. 29 Lennon's *Evening Standard* interview (see March) reprinted in the USA.	29 Dylan has motorcycle accident; begins year of retreat at Woodstock. **45s:** Kinks *Sunny Afternoon*; Fame *Get Away*; Chris Farlowe and The Thunderbirds *Out Of Time*; Beatles *Paperback Writer*; Sinatra *Strangers in the Night*; Ike and Tina Turner *River Deep and Mountain High*; Sledge *When A Man Loves A Woman*; Los Bravos *Black Is Black*; Gene Pitney *Nobody Needs Your Love*; Hollies *Bus Stop*; Dusty Springfield *Going Back*; James Brown *It's A Man's Man's Man's World*; Troggs *With A Girl Like You*; Chris Montez *The More I See You*; Lovin' Spoonful *Summer In The City*; Alan Price Set *Hi Lili Hi Lo*. **LPs:** Soundtrack *Sound of Music*; Rolling Stones *Aftermath*; Beach Boys *Pet Sounds*; *Summer Days and Summer Nights*; Mamas and Papas *The Mamas and the Papas*; Fame *Sweet Things*; Yardbirds *Yardbirds*.	3 Thirty-one arrested during anti-Vietnam protest in front of US embassy in Grosvenor Square. 20 Prime Minister Harold Wilson announces a freeze on pay and dividends. 30 US planes bomb the demilitarised zone (between North and South Vietnam). 30 England beat West Germany 4–2 to win the World Cup. 31 Race riots in New York, Chicago and Cleveland.	Capote *In Cold Blood*; Mitford *The Sun King*; Brown *Love's Body*; Leary *Psychedelic Prayers after the Tao Te Ching*; Mao *Quotations from Chairman Mao (The Little Red Book)*. d. Sir Ernest Gowers.

1966 THE BEATLES	UK POP	CURRENT AFFAIRS	CULTURE
August Twenty-one performances, two radio broadcasts. **1–12** Christian protests against Lennon's 'blasphemy' spread throughout the American Bible Belt. Records and books are banned and burned. **5** UK: *Eleanor Rigby/Yellow Submarine; Revolver.* **8** US: *Eleanor Rigby/Yellow Submarine; Revolver.* **18** *Eleanor Rigby/Yellow Submarine* tops the UK chart (four weeks). **12–31** Third and last American tour begins with Lennon publicly apologising for his remark about Jesus. **29** Final concert at Candlestick Park, San Francisco. Sick of touring, The Beatles cease live performances.	**45s:** Troggs *With A Girl Like You;* Beatles *Eleanor Rigby/Yellow Submarine,* Los Bravos *Black Is Black;* Beach Boys *God Only Knows;* Lovin' Spoonful *Summer In The City;* Napoleon XIV *They're Coming To Take Me Away;* Small Faces *All or Nothing;* Alan Price Set *Hi Lili Hi La;* Dylan *I Want You;* Temptations *Ain't Too Proud To Beg;* Four Tops *Loving You Is Sweeter Than Ever,* Robert Parker *Barefootin';* Manfred Mann *Just Like A Woman.* **LPs:** Beatles *Revolver,* Soundtrack *Sound of Music,* Beach Boys *Pet Sounds;* Summer Days and Summer Nights; Rolling Stones *Aftermath;* Dylan *Blonde on Blonde;* John Mayall and Eric Clapton *Bluesbreakers;* Troggs *From Nowhere;* Yardbirds *Yardbirds.*	**1** General Gowon seizes power in Nigeria. **1** Charles Whitman massacres twelve with a rifle from the tower of Texas University, Austin (subject later turned into song by David Bowie: *Running Gun Blues*). **11** End of war between Indonesia and Malaysia.	**Science fiction** Ballard *The Crystal World;* Dick *Now Wait For Last Year;* Delany *Babel-17;* *Empire Star;* Zelazny *This Immortal;* Herbert *The Eyes of Heisenberg;* Ellison *'Repent, Harlequin!' Said the Ticktockman.* Hugo: Frank Herbert *Dune.* Nebulas: Daniel Keyes *Flowers for Algernon;* Samuel R. Delany *Babel-17.*

September
Lennon appears in *How I Won The War*, filmed in West Germany and Spain. Harrison goes to India to study sitar with Ravi Shankar. McCartney and Starr take time off.

Pete Quaife leaves Kinks. **45s:** Beatles *Eleanor Rigby/Yellow Submarine*; Small Faces *All or Nothing*; Jim Reeves *Distant Drums*; Beach Boys *God Only Knows*; Lee Dorsey *Working in a Coal Mine*; Junior Walker and The All-Stars *How Sweet It Is*; Percy Sledge *Warm and Tender Love*; The Who *I'm A Boy*; Roy Orbison *Too Soon To Know*; Supremes *You Can't Hurry Love*; Cliff Bennett and The Rebel Rousers *Got To Get You Into My Life*; Otis Redding *I Can't Turn You Loose*; Wilson Pickett *Land of a Thousand Dances*; New Vaudeville Band *Winchester Cathedral*; Georgie Fame *Sunny*. **LPs:** Beatles *Revolver*; Soundtrack *Sound of Music*; Beach Boys *Pet Sounds*; Walker Brothers *Portrait*; Spencer Davis Group *Autumn '66*; Dylan *Blonde on Blonde*; John Mayall and Eric Clapton *Bluesbreakers*; Kinks *Well Respected Kinks*.

13 Vorster becomes prime minister of South Africa.

Fashion
'Swinging London' is the fashion capital of the world: Carnaby Street (John Stephens' men's styles), King's Road (Mary Quant, Ossie Clark), Kensington Church Street (Barbara Hulanicki's *Biba*). Antonioni sets *Blow Up* in the London fashion scene (with cameo appearance by The Yardbirds). Ray Davies satirises the 'Carnabetian Army' in 'Dedicated Follower Of Fashion'. Paris: British Op Art used by Courrèges, Ungaro. Black and white check mini-dresses. Saint Laurent opens ready-to-wear *Rive Gauche* chain. Rabanne starts own label. d. Elizabeth Arden.

1966 THE BEATLES	UK POP	CURRENT AFFAIRS	CULTURE
October Lennon filming, Harrison in India. Starr holidays in Spain. **9** Lennon is 26.	Denny Laine leaves Moody Blues. **45s:** Reeves *Distant Drums*; Four Tops *Reach Out I'll Be There*; The Who *I'm A Boy*; Small Faces *All or Nothing*; Rolling Stones *Have You Seen Your Mother Baby Standing In The Shadow*; Spencer Davis Group *When I Come Home*, New Vaudeville Band *Winchester Cathedral*; Supremes *You Can't Hurry Love*; Troggs *I Can't Control Myself*; Hollies *Stop Stop Stop*; Herman's Hermits *No Milk Today*; Sandpipers *Guantanamera*; Temptations *Beauty Is Only Skin Deep*. **LPs:** Soundtrack *Sound of Music*, Beatles *Revolver*, Walker Brothers *Portrait*; Beach Boys *Pet Sounds*; Fame *Sound Venture*; Spencer Davis Group *Autumn '66*; Kinks *Well Respected Kinks*; Byrds *5th Dimension*.	**3** Outbreak of Nigerian civil war. **7** LSD outlawed in California. **10** *International Times* launched in London. **15** Black Panther Party founded in Oakland. **21** Aberfan slag heap disaster. **22** Spy George Blake escapes from Brixton prison.	**TV/Media** Jeremy Sandford's *Cathy Come Home*, directed by Ken Loach and Tony Garnett. Peter Watkins *The War Game* is banned by BBC. Johnny Speight's *Till Death Us Do Part* begins. First episodes of *Batman*, *The Likely Lads*, *The Frost Report*, *Softly Softly*, *The Monkees*, *It's A Knockout*. *The Times* prints news on the front page for the first time. *New York Herald Tribune* closes. First issue of *Mayfair*.

			Visual arts
November McCartney begins the soundtrack for *The Family Way*. **9** McCartney crashes his moped while biking with Tara Browne. A rumour spreads that he was decapitated (origin of the 'Paul is dead' myth). Lennon meets Yoko Ono at her exhibition *Unfinished Paintings and Objects* at the Indica Gallery. **15** Epstein denies press reports that The Beatles have broken up. **24, 28–29** Recording *Strawberry Fields Forever*.	Pete Quaife rejoins Kinks. **45s:** Four Tops *Reach Out I'll Be There*; Beach Boys *Good Vibrations*; Hollies *Stop Stop Stop*; Troggs *I Can't Control Myself*; Lee Dorsey *Holy Cow*; Cat Stevens *I Love My Dog*; Manfred Mann *Semi-Detached Suburban Mr James*; Spencer Davis Group *Gimme Some Loving*; Ike and Tina Turner *A Love Like Yours*; Easybeats *Friday On My Mind*; Tom Jones *Green Green Grass of Home*; Jimmy Ruffin *What Becomes of the Broken-Hearted*. **LPs:** Beach Boys *Best Of*; Rolling Stones *High Tide and Green Grass*; Reeves *Distant Drums*; Manfred Mann *As Is*; Dusty Springfield *Golden Hits*.	Sunset Strip Riots: 'hippies' and liberal celebrities confront LA police over local curfew (enforced to allow high-rise developments). **1** Viet Cong shell Saigon. **8** Reagan elected governor of California. **9** Floods ruin artworks in Florence.	Abu Simbel temples moved to avoid flooding caused by Aswan Dam. Van Gogh's *Portrait of Mlle Ravoux* sold at Christie's for £160,000. Royal Academy mixes abstraction and tradition at summer exhibition. Whitney Museum opens. Centre Point built. Ed Kienholz: *Back Seat Dodge '38*. Robert Venturi *Complexity and Contradiction in Architecture*. d. Alberto Giacometti, Maxfield Parrish, Carlo Carrà, Hans Hofmann, Vicky (Victor Weisz). **Science** Bakey's work on artificial hearts. Fermi Prize: Otto Hahn, Lise Meitner, Fritz Strassmann.
December **6, 8–9** Recording *Sgt. Pepper*. **9** UK: *A Collection of Beatles Oldies*. **15** Recording *Sgt. Pepper*. **18** Death of Tara Browne. **20–21** Recording *Sgt. Pepper*. **26** Lennon appears on *Not Only ... But Also*. (See January 9, 1965.) **29–30** Recording *Sgt. Pepper*.	Scott Engel of Walker Brothers enters a monastery. *NME* starts publishing the Top 15 albums. **45s:** Jones *Green Green Grass of Home*; Beach Boys *Good Vibrations*; Spencer Davis Group *Gimme Some Loving*; Ruffin *What Becomes of the Broken-Hearted*; Dorsey *Holy Cow*; Supremes *You Keep Me Hangin' On*; The Who *Happy Jack*; Donovan *Sunshine Superman*; Easybeats *Friday On My Mind*; Kinks *Dead End Street*; ? and The Mysterians *96 Tears*. **LPs:** Soundtrack *Sound of Music*; Beach Boys *Best Of*; Beatles *A Collection of Beatles Oldies*; Who *A Quick One*; Cream *Fresh Cream*; Rolling Stones *High Tide and Green Grass*; Reeves *Distant Drums*.	**3** After six months of severe deflation, the British Labour government announces large increases in regional investment grants. **6** Ian Smith rejects Wilson's proposals for ending the dispute over majority rule in Rhodesia. **22** Rhodesia leaves the Commonwealth. **23** Countercultural UFO club opens in London.	

440

1967 THE BEATLES	UK POP	CURRENT AFFAIRS	CULTURE
January **4–6, 9–10, 12, 17, 19–20,** Recording *Sgt. Pepper*. **30** Lennon and McCartney go to Saville Theatre to hear The Who and The Jimi Hendrix Experience. **30–31** Filming promo for *Strawberry Fields Forever/Penny Lane*.	**45s:** Jones *Green Green Grass of Home;* Monkees *I'm A Believer;* Seekers *Morningtown Ride;* Donovan *Sunshine Superman;* Kinks *Dead End Street;* Move *Night of Fear;* The Who *Happy Jack;* Four Tops *Standing in the Shadows of Love;* Cat Stevens *Matthew and Son;* Cream *I Feel Free;* Jimi Hendrix Experience *Hey Joe;* Temptations *Losing You;* Wilson Pickett *Mustang Sally.* **LPs:** Soundtrack *Sound of Music;* Beach Boys *Best Of;* Monkees *The Monkees;* Seekers *Come the Day;* Cream *Fresh Cream;* Beatles *A Collection of Beatles Oldies;* Reeves *Distant Drums;* Who *A Quick One;* Rolling Stones *Between the Buttons.*	**4** Donald Campbell dies in Bluebird on Coniston Water. **9** Rebellion against Mao in Shanghai. **14** First Human Be-In at Golden Gate Park, San Francisco. **18** Jeremy Thorpe becomes leader of the Liberal Party. **31** Students break into a meeting to demand resignation of LSE head Walter Adams (a Rhodesian). A porter dies during the uproar.	**Cinema** Donner *Here We Go Round the Mulberry Bush;* Schlesinger *Far From the Madding Crowd;* Losey *Accident;* Fisher *The Devil Rides Out;* Russell *Billion Dollar Brain;* Boorman *Point Blank;* Penn *Bonnie and Clyde;* Jewison *In the Heat of the Night;* Nichols *The Graduate;* Rosenberg *Cool Hand Luke;* Corman *The Trip;* Brooks *The Producers;* Buñuel *Belle de Jour;* Vadim *Barbarella;* Sjoman *I Am Curious Yellow;* Bergman *The Hour of the Wolf;* Widerberg *Elvira Madigan;* Godard *Weekend.* d. G. W. Pabst, Spencer Tracy, Nelson Eddy, Anthony Mann, Vivien Leigh, Martine Carol, Bert Lahr, Paul Muni, Claude Rains, Anton Walbrook, Basil Rathbone, Jayne Mansfield.

February
1–3, 5 Recording Sgt. Pepper.
7 Filming promo for Penny Lane.
8–10, 13–14, 16–17 Recording Sgt. Pepper.
13 US: Strawberry Fields Forever/Penny Lane.
17 UK: Strawberry Fields Forever/Penny Lane.
20–24 Recording Sgt. Pepper.
25 Harrison is 24.
28 Recording Sgt. Pepper.

3 Producer Joe Meek commits suicide (on the eighth anniversary of Buddy Holly's death). 5 Rolling Stones' Let's Spend the Night Together banned from Eamonn Andrews' TV show. 45s: Monkees I'm A Believer, Petula Clark This Is My Song; Stevens Matthew and Son; Move Night of Fear, Rolling Stones Let's Spend the Night Together; Jimi Hendrix Experience Hey Joe; Spencer Davis Group, I'm A Man; Marvin Gaye and Kim Weston It Takes Two; Royal Guardsmen Snoopy vs. The Red Baron; Lovin' Spoonful Nashville Cats; Engelbert Humperdinck Release Me. LPs: Monkees The Monkees; Soundtrack Sound of Music; Rolling Stones Between the Buttons; Beach Boys Best Of; Who A Quick One; Cream Fresh Cream; Four Tops Live; Reeves Distant Drums.

3 Emil Savundra in 'trial by television' interview with David Frost.
5 Somoza elected President of Nicaragua.
12 Drug Squad 'busts' Rolling Stone Keith Richards.
14 A hundred Labour MPs vote to condemn renewed US bombing in Vietnam.
25 Gallup poll shows Labour holds an 11% lead over the Conservatives.
26 American troops attack Ho Chi Minh trail on Cambodian border.

Jazz
Coltrane Interstellar Space; Kirk The Inflated Tear, Davis Nefertiti; Shepp Mama Too Tight; Ayler In Greenwich Village; Getz Sweet Rain; Burton A Genuine Tong Funeral; Shorter Schizophrenia.
d. John Coltrane, Billy Strayhorn, Henry 'Red' Allen, Stuff Smith, Rex Stewart, Muggsy Spanier, Elmo Hope, Paul Whiteman.

Classical
Stockhausen Hymnen; Prozession; Nono Per Bastiana Tai-Yang Cheng; Berio Sequenza V, VI; Shostakovich Violin Concerto No. 2; Lutoslawski Symphony No. 2; Britten Cello Suite No. 2; Arnold Symphony No. 6; Crumb Echoes of Time and The River; Reich Piano Phase; Bolcom Black Host; Cardew Treatise; Foss Baroque Variations; Ligeti Lontano; Takemitsu November Steps; Panufnik Katyn Epitaph.
d. Zoltan Kodaly, Franz Waxman, Sir Malcolm Sargent.

March
2–16 Engelbert Humperdinck's Release Me prevents Strawberry Fields Forever/Penny Lane from topping the UK chart.
1–3, 6–7, 9 Recording Sgt. Pepper.
11 Beatles receive three Grammy Awards (for Michelle, Eleanor Rigby, Revolver).
13, 15, 17 Recording Sgt. Pepper.
18 Penny Lane tops US chart (one week).
20–23, 28–31 Recording Sgt. Pepper.
30 Derek Taylor flies back from California to become The Beatles' publicist.

Warner-Reprise signs Jimi Hendrix for over fifty thousand dollars. 45s: Humperdinck Release Me; Beatles Strawberry Fields Forever/Penny Lane; Donovan Mellow Yellow; Seekers Georgy Girl; Vince Hill Edelweiss; Supremes Love Is Here And Now You're Gone; Sonny and Cher The Beat Goes On; Alan Price Set Simon Smith and The Amazing Dancing Bear; Eddie Floyd Knock On Wood; Prince Buster Al Capone. LPs: Monkees The Monkees; Soundtrack Sound of Music; Rolling Stones Between the Buttons; Beach Boys Best Of; Four Tops Live; Geno Washington Hand Clappin' Foot Stompin' Funky Butt Live.

9 Police raid International Times.
13 LSE students stage all-night 'sit-in'.
14 German manufacturers of thalidomide on trial in Aachen.
19 Tanker Torrey Canyon runs aground off Cornwall.
24 Oil from Torrey Canyon washes ashore.
30 RAF planes bomb Torrey Canyon to disperse and burn leaking oil.

1967 THE BEATLES	UK POP	CURRENT AFFAIRS	CULTURE
April 1, 3 Recording *Sgt. Pepper*. 3–12 McCartney flies to California and Colorado. 10 McCartney visits The Beatles' rivals The Beach Boys in their Los Angeles studio, warning Brian Wilson to 'hurry up' with his 'reply' to *Revolver*. 11 McCartney sketches out the plan for *Magical Mystery Tour*. 20–21 Recording *Sgt. Pepper*. 25–27 Recording *Magical Mystery Tour*.	**45s:** Humperdinck *Release Me*; Frank and Nancy Sinatra *Somethin' Stupid*; Sandie Shaw *Puppet On A String*; Alan Price Set *Simon Smith and The Amazing Dancing Bear*; Manfred Mann *Ha! Ha! Said The Clown*; Move *I Can Hear The Grass Grow*; Jimi Hendrix Experience *Purple Haze*; Four Tops *Bernadette*; Pink Floyd *Arnold Layne*; Martha and The Vandellas *Jimmy Mack*; Sam and Dave *Soothe Me*; Monkees *A Little Bit You A Little Bit Me*; Turtles *Happy Together*. **LPs:** Monkees *The Monkees*; *More of The Monkees*; Soundtrack *Sound of Music*; Beach Boys *Best Of*; Four Tops *Live*; Walker Brothers *Images*; Cat Stevens *Matthew and Son*; John Mayall *A Hard Road*.	3 *Last Exit To Brooklyn* on trial for obscenity in London. 15 400,000 protest against Vietnam War outside the UN in New York. 21 Military coup in Greece. 28 Muhammad Ali stripped of his world title for refusing the draft. 29 '14-hour Technicolour Dream' at Alexandra Palace, London. 30 Detroit Love-In ends in police riot.	**Fiction** Isherwood *A Meeting by the River*; Golding *The Pyramid*; Wilson *No Laughing Matter*; Vidal *Washington, D.C.*; Naipaul *The Mimic Men*; Levin *Rosemary's Baby*. d. Dorothy Parker, Carson McCullers, Alice B. Toklas, Ilya Ehrenburg, Marcel Aymé.
May 3, 9 Recording *Magical Mystery Tour*. 11–12, 17 Recording. 20 BBC bans *A Day In The Life* for its 'drug references'. 25, 31 Recording.	Scott Engel leaves Walker Brothers. **45s:** Shaw *Puppet On A String*; Tremeloes *Silence Is Golden*; Mamas and Papas *Dedicated To The One I Love*; The Who *Pictures of Lily*; Jeff Beck *Hi-Ho Silver Lining*; Bee Gees *New York Mining Disaster 1941*; Beach Boys *Then I Kissed Her*; Arthur Conley *Sweet Soul Music*; Jimi Hendrix Experience *The Wind Cries Mary*; Kinks *Waterloo Sunset*; P. P. Arnold *The First Cut Is The Deepest*. **LPs:** Soundtrack *Sound of Music*; Monkees *More of The Monkees*; Jimi Hendrix Experience *Are You Experienced*; Tom Jones *Green Green Grass*; Beach Boys *Best Of*; Walker Brothers *Images*; Byrds *Younger Than Yesterday*.	10 Rolling Stones Mick Jagger and Keith Richards in court on drugs charges. Brian Jones arrested. 21 Peace Rally against Vietnam in Trafalgar Square. 30 Biafra secedes from Nigeria.	**Poetry** Penguin: *The Liverpool Scene* (Henri, McGough, Patten). Auden *About the House*; *Collected Shorter Poems*; Lowell *Near the Ocean*; Hughes *Wodwo*; Jennings *Collected Poems*. d. John Masefield, Carl Sandburg, Patrick Kavanagh, Siegfried Sassoon, Langston Hughes.

			Stage
June 1 UK: *Sgt. Pepper's Lonely Hearts Club Band*. Recording (improvisations). 2 US: *Sgt. Pepper's Lonely Hearts Club Band*. Recording. 7–9 Recording *You Know My Name (Look Up The Number)*. 14 Recording *All You Need Is Love*. 16 McCartney admits taking LSD. 18 McCartney is 25. 19, 23–26 Recording *All You Need Is Love*. 25 Appearance on BBC's *Our World* global TV broadcast. (Estimated audience: 400 million.)	16–18 Monterey Pop Festival: Jimi Hendrix, Who, Otis Redding, Byrds, Mamas and Papas, Ravi Shankar, Big Brother and the Holding Company, Jefferson Airplane. **45s:** Tremeloes *Silence Is Golden*; Procol Harum *A Whiter Shade Of Pale*; Kinks *Waterloo Sunset*; Jimi Hendrix Experience *The Wind Cries Mary*; Supremes *The Happening*; Engelbert Humperdinck *There Goes My Everything*; New Vaudeville Band *Finchley Central*; Hollies *Carrie-Anne*; Conley *Sweet Soul Music*; Cream *Strange Brew*; Otis Redding *Shake*. **LPs:** Beatles *Sgt. Pepper's Lonely Hearts Club Band*; Soundtrack *Sound of Music*; Jimi Hendrix Experience *Are You Experienced*; Monkees *More of The Monkees*; London Cast *Fiddler on the Roof*.	1 English counterculture leader John ('Hoppy') Hopkins jailed for 9 months on drug charges. 3 Race riots in Boston. 5–10 Israel defeats Arab coalition in 'Six Day War'. 25 Muhammad Ali sentenced to 5 years in jail for refusing the draft. 29 Mick Jagger and Keith Richards jailed on drugs charges. 29 Founding of Release organisation to provide legal aid to those 'busted' for drugs.	National Theatre's all-male *As You Like It*. Stoppard *Rosencrantz and Guildenstern Are Dead*; Shaw *The Man in the Glass Booth*; Hochhuth *The Soldiers*; Feiffer *Little Murders*; Terson *Zigger Zagger*. **Non-fiction** McLuhan *The Medium Is The Message*; Laing *The Politics of Experience*; Galbraith *The New Industrial State*; Barthes *Writing Degree Zero*; Koestler *The Ghost in the Machine*; Fanon *The Wretched of the Earth*; Debord *Society of the Spectacle*; Steiner *Language and Silence*; Morris *The Naked Ape*; Mailer *Why Are We in Vietnam?* d. André Maurois, Isaac Deutscher.
July No engagements. The Beatles go on a cruise holiday together in the Aegean. 7 UK: *All You Need Is Love*. Starr is 27. 17 US: *All You Need Is Love*. 19 *All You Need Is Love* tops the UK chart (three weeks).	The Who release single *Under My Thumb/ The Last Time* in support of Mick Jagger and Keith Richard (see Current Affairs). **45s:** Procol Harum *A Whiter Shade Of Pale*; Beatles *All You Need Is Love*; Monkees *Alternate Title*; Turtles *She'd Rather Be With Me*; Hollies *Carrie-Anne*; Young Rascals *Groovin'*; Traffic *Paper Sun*; Pink Floyd *See Emily Play*; Scott McKenzie *San Francisco*; Gladys Knight and The Pips *Take Me In Your Arms And Love Me*; Vicki Carr *It Must Be Him*; Aretha Franklin *Respect*; Desmond Dekker *007*. **LPs:** Beatles *Sgt. Pepper's Lonely Hearts Club Band*; Soundtrack *Sound of Music*; Monkees *Headquarters*; *More of The Monkees*; Jimi Hendrix Experience *Are You Experienced*; Beach Boys *Best Of*; Mamas and Papas *Deliver*.	1 *Times* editorial protests against jailing of Jagger and Richards: 'Who Breaks a Butterfly on a Wheel?' 7 Nigerian troops invade Biafra. 11–15 Newark race riots. 16 'Legalise Pot' rally in Hyde Park. 23 Los Angeles Love-In. 23–7 Detroit race riots. Paratroops restore order. 24 Celebrities sign pro-cannabis advertisement in London *Times*. 27 Homosexuality legalised in UK. 31 Mick Jagger wins appeal against jail sentence.	

444

1967 THE BEATLES	UK POP	CURRENT AFFAIRS	CULTURE
August 1–9 Harrison and his wife Patti visit California. 8 Harrison visits Haight-Ashbury in San Francisco. 19 *All You Need Is Love* tops US chart (one week). Jason Starkey born. 22–23 Recording *Magical Mystery Tour*. 25 Group travels to Bangor, Wales, with Maharishi Mahesh Yogi. 27 Brian Epstein is found dead from an overdose of tranquillisers at his flat in Belgravia, London.	Jimi Hendrix Experience dropped from Monkees' US tour for being 'too erotic'. **45s:** Beatles *All You Need Is Love*; McKenzie *San Francisco*; Dave Davies *Death Of A Clown*; Stevie Wonder *I Was Made To Love Her*; Mamas and Papas *Creeque Alley*; Otis Redding and Carla Thomas *Tramp*; Amen Corner *Gin House Blues*; Pink Floyd *See Emily Play*; Mann Singers *Up Up And Away*; Alan Price Set *The House That Jack Built*; Small Faces *Itchycoo Park*. **LPs:** Beatles *Sgt. Pepper's Lonely Hearts Club Band*; Soundtrack *Sound of Music*; Monkees *Headquarters*; Pink Floyd *Piper At the Gates of Dawn*; Jimi Hendrix Experience *Are You Experienced*; Beach Boys *Best Of*.	9 Playwright Joe Orton murdered by his lover Kenneth Halliwell. 14 British offshore 'pirate' radio stations close. 25–7 Hippies gather for 'Festival of the Flower Children' at Woburn Abbey.	**Science fiction** Dick *Counter-Clock World*; Delany *The Einstein Intersection*; Zelazny *Lord of Light*; Ballard *The Disaster Area*; Silverberg *Thorns*; Disch *Echo Round His Bones*; Ellison *I Have No Mouth And I Must Scream*; *Dangerous Visions*. Hugo: Robert Heinlein *The Moon Is A Harsh Mistress*. Nebula: Samuel R. Delany *The Einstein Intersection*.
September 5–8 Recording *Magical Mystery Tour*. 11–15 Filming *Magical Mystery Tour* in Hampshire and the West Country. 16 Recording *Magical Mystery Tour*. 18–25 Filming *Magical Mystery Tour* in London and Kent. 25–26, 27–29 Recording *Magical Mystery Tour*. 30 Lennon and Harrison appear on ITV's *The Frost Programme*.	23 Mothers of Invention play the Albert Hall. **45s:** Engelbert Humperdinck *The Last Waltz*; Tom Jones *I'll Never Fall In Love Again*; Keith West *Excerpt from A Teenage Opera*; Rolling Stones *We Love You*; Small Faces *Itchycoo Park*; Monkees *Pleasant Valley Sunday*; Beach Boys *Heroes and Villains*; Jimi Hendrix Experience *The Burning of the Midnight Lamp*; Tremeloes *Even the Bad Times Are Good*; Move *Flowers in the Rain*; Traffic *Hole in My Shoe*; Supremes *Reflections*; Bee Gees *Massachusetts*. **LPs:** Beatles *Sgt. Pepper's Lonely Hearts Club Band*; Soundtrack *Sound of Music*; Scott Walker *Scott*; Pink Floyd *Piper At the Gates of Dawn*; Beach Boys *Best Of*; Monkees *Headquarters*; Soundtrack *Dr Zhivago*.	3 Sweden switches to driving on the right.	**Fashion** Hippie street fashions are picked up in designer 'ethnic' collections (Pucci, Fiorucci): Nehru jackets, rajah coats, djellabas, silk scarves, bracelets, jewellry. Psychedelic clothes by The Fool. 'Space age' styles (influenced by *Barbarella*): Rabanne, Khanh, Rosier (plastic/metal/leather mini-dresses, culottes, squared-off fluorescent wigs). *Sgt. Pepper* inspires 'military' look (Lord John, I Was Lord Kitchener's Valet, etc).

445

October		Worst monthly UK trade deficit in history.	TV/Media

October
1 Filming *Magical Mystery Tour* in Kent.
2, 6 Recording *Magical Mystery Tour*.
9 Lennon is 27.
12 Recording *Magical Mystery Tour*.
17 Memorial service for Brian Epstein at the New London Synagogue.
18 *How I Won The War* opens in London.
19, 20, 25 Recording *Magical Mystery Tour*, *Hello, Goodbye*.
29–31 Filming *Magical Mystery Tour* in London and Nice.

2 The Grateful Dead busted at their San Francisco mansion. 9 First edition of *Rolling Stone*. **45s:** Humperdinck *The Last Waltz*; Bee Gees *Massachusetts*; Move *Flowers in the Rain*; Traffic *Hole in My Shoe*; Box Tops *The Letter*, Bobbie Gentry *Ode to Billy Joe*; Procol Harum *Homburg*; Foundations *Baby Now That I've Found You*; Herd *From the Underworld*. **LPs:** Beatles *Sgt. Pepper's Lonely Hearts Club Band*; Soundtrack *Sound of Music*, Beach Boys *Best Of Vol. 2*; Soundtrack *Dr Zhivago*; Donovan *Universal Soldier*, Scott Walker *Scott*; John Mayall *Crusade*; Incredible String Band *The 5000 Spirits*.

Worst monthly UK trade deficit in history.
4 Nigerian army captures Biafran capital Enugu.
6 'Death of Hippie' ceremony in Haight-Ashbury, San Francisco.
9 Death of Che Guevara.
16 Joan Baez arrested at anti-war demonstration in California.
21 Vietnam protest outside the Pentagon. Norman Mailer arrested.
30 Rolling Stone Brian Jones charged with possessing drugs.

TV/Media
Patrick McGoohan in *The Prisoner*. BBC's *The Forsyte Saga* (January–July). *The First Programme*. The Smothers Brothers' *Comedy Hour*. BBC drops old Light and Third Programme and Home Service for Radios 1-4. *Zap Comix*.

November
2 Recording *Magical Mystery Tour*.
10 Filming promo for *Hello, Goodbye*.
24 UK: *Hello, Goodbye*.
27 US: *Hello, Goodbye*; *Magical Mystery Tour*. (BBC places unofficial radio ban on *I Am The Walrus*.)
November–December Harrison records *Wonderwall* in London.

45s: Bee Gees *Massachusetts*; Foundations *Baby Now That I've Found You*; Long John Baldry *Let the Heart Aches Begin*; Dave Dee Dozy Beaky Mick and Tich *Zabadak*; Kinks *Autumn Almanac*; Eric Burdon *San Franciscan Nights*; The Who *I Can See For Miles*; Sam and Dave *Soul Man*. **LPs:** Soundtrack *Sound of Music*; Beatles *Sgt. Pepper's Lonely Hearts Club Band*; Various *Motown Chartbusters*; Cream *Disraeli Gears*; Beach Boys *Best Of Vol. 2*; *Smiley Smile*; Donovan *Universal Soldier*.

Founding of 'Yippies' (Youth International Party).
4–6 Anti-draft demonstrations in New York.
18 Prime Minister Harold Wilson capitulates to market pressure and devalues the pound by 14.3%.
23 *Last Exit To Brooklyn* found obscene.
27 De Gaulle vetoes British entry to Common Market.

Visual arts
Picasso, Ingres, Tutenkhamen exhibitions in Paris. Monet's *La Terasse à St.-Adresse* sold at Christie's for £588,000. Francis Bacon exhibition in London. Conceptual Art is new buzzword. The Los Angeles 'Look'.
d. René Magritte, Edward Hopper, Ad Reinhardt.

1967 THE BEATLES	UK POP	CURRENT AFFAIRS	CULTURE
December 4 Opening of the Apple Boutique in Baker Street. 6 *Hello, Goodbye* tops the UK chart (seven weeks). 7–16 Starr appears in *Candy*. 8 UK: *Magical Mystery Tour* (2-EP). 26 BBC screens *Magical Mystery Tour*. The critics pan it. 27 *Magical Mystery Tour* EP is No. 2 in the UK chart (three weeks). 30 *Hello Goodbye* tops the US chart (three weeks).	10 Otis Redding killed in air-crash. **45s:** Beatles *Hello, Goodbye*; Gene Pitney *Something's Gotten Hold Of My Heart*; Bee Gees *World*; Monkees *Daydream Believer*; Traffic *Here We Go Round the Mulberry Bush*; Scaffold *Thank U Very Much*; Beatles *Magical Mystery Tour* (EP); Four Tops *Walk Away Renee*; Chris Farlowe *Handbags and Gladrags*. **LPs:** Soundtrack *Sound of Music*, Beatles *Sgt. Pepper's Lonely Hearts Club Band*; Val Doonican *Rocks, But Gently*; Rolling Stones *Their Satanic Majesties Request*; Jimi Hendrix Experience *Axis: Bold As Love*; Various Motown *Chartbusters*; Cream *Disraeli Gears*.	9 Ceausescu becomes premier of Romania. 11 First supersonic airliner, Anglo-French co-project Concorde. 12 Brian Jones put on probation for drug possession. 26 North Vietnam attacks Laos. 30 Ho Chi Minh sends New Year greeting to US anti-war protestors.	**Science** First heart-transplant by Christian Barnard in South Africa. Laser surgery. Seven new mesons are discovered. Synthetic DNA. Cryosurgery. d. Robert Oppenheimer, Robert J. Van de Graaff.

1968 THE BEATLES	UK POP	CURRENT AFFAIRS	CULTURE
January 7–12 Harrison records *Wonderwall* in Bombay.	Syd Barrett leaves Pink Floyd. **45s:** Beatles *Hello, Goodbye*; Georgie Fame *Ballad of Bonnie and Clyde*; Love Affair *Everlasting Love*; Beatles *Magical Mystery Tour* (EP); Four Tops *Walk Away Renee*; Sam and Dave *Soul Man*; Moody Blues *Nights in White Satin*; Monkees *Daydream Believer*, and The Miracles *I Second That Emotion*; Manfred Mann *The Mighty Quinn*. **LPs:** Beatles *Sgt. Pepper's Lonely Hearts Club Band*; Doonican *Rocks, But Gently*; Soundtrack *Sound of Music*; Rolling Stones *Their Satanic Majesties Request*; Four Tops *Reach Out*; Jimi Hendrix Experience *Axis: Bold As Love*; Traffic *Mr Fantasy*; Monkees *Pisces, Aquarius, Capricorn, and Jones Ltd.*	5 Alexander Dubcek takes over as head of state in Czechoslovakia. 5 Dr Benjamin Spock indicted for encouraging evasion of Vietnam draft. 31 Viet Cong launch Tet Offensive.	**Cinema** Anderson *If . . .* ; Lester *How I Won the War*, Finney *Charlie Bubbles*; Reed *Oliver!*; Yates *Bullitt*; Richardson *The Charge of the Light Brigade*; Schaffner *Planet of the Apes*; Polanski *Rosemary's Baby*; Jewison *The Thomas Crown Affair*; Perry *The Swimmer*; Marquand *Candy*; Rafaelson *Head*; Pasolini *Theorem*; Costa-Gavros *Z*. d. Carl Dreyer, Tallulah Bankhead, Franchot Tone, Anthony Asquith, Kay Francis, Virginia Maskell.
February 3–4, 6, 8 Recording *Lady Madonna, Across The Universe*. 11 Recording *Hey Bulldog*. 15–19 The group and their wives fly to Rishikesh to meditate with the Maharishi. 25 Harrison is 25.	**45s:** Love Affair *Everlasting Love*; Manfred Mann *The Mighty Quinn*; Esther and Abi Ofarim *Cinderella Rockefella*; John Fred and the Playboy Band *Judy in Disguise*; Amen Corner *Bend Me Shape Me*; Beach Boys *Darlin'*; Status Quo *Pictures of Matchstick Men*; Bee Gees *Words*; Move *Fire Brigade*; Martha and The Vandellas *Honeychile*; Don Partridge *Rosie*. **LPs:** Supremes *Greatest Hits*; Soundtrack *Sound of Music*; Four Tops *Greatest Hits*; Reach Out; Beatles *Sgt. Pepper's Lonely Hearts Club Band*; Who *The Who Sell Out*; Jimi Hendrix Experience *Axis: Bold As Love*; Redding *Otis Blue*; Monkees *Pisces, Aquarius, Capricorn, and Jones Ltd*; Love *Forever Changes*.	Tet Offensive continues. TV images of violence and atrocities bring war home to USA and Europe. Domestic protests rise. 24 American and South Vietnamese forces recapture provincial capital Hue from Viet Cong.	**Jazz** Ellington: Second Sacred Concert. Davis *Miles In The Sky; Filles De Kilimanjaro*; Sanders *Tauhid*; Tyner *Expansions*; Bill Evans *Live At Montreux*; Kirk *Volunteered Slavery*; Ayler *Love Cry*; Hutcherson *Total Eclipse*; Hancock *Speak Like A Child*; Corea *Now He Sings, Now He Sobs*; Coryell *Coryell*; Lady *Coryell*; Jazz Composers Orchestra *Communications*. d. George Lewis, Wes Montgomery.

1968 THE BEATLES	UK POP	CURRENT AFFAIRS	CULTURE
March No engagements. Group remains in Rishikesh (except for Starr, who quits around 1st, and McCartney, who leaves in mid-March). **15** UK: *Lady Madonna*. **18** US: *Lady Madonna*. **27** *Lady Madonna* tops the UK chart (two weeks). It only makes No. 4 in the USA.	**45s:** Esther and Abi Ofarim *Cinderella Rockefella*; Dave Dee Dozy Beaky Mick and Tich *Legend of Xanadu*; Beatles *Lady Madonna*; Partridge *Rosie*; Otis Redding *Dock of the Bay*; Donovan *Jennifer Juniper*; Move *Fire Brigade*; Showstoppers *Ain't Nothin' But A House Party*; Reparata and The Delrons *Captain of Your Ship*; Tom Jones *Delilah*; Cilla Black *Step Inside Love*; Sam and Dave *I Thank You*. **LPs:** Supremes *Greatest Hits*; Dylan *John Wesley Harding*; Four Tops *Greatest Hits*; Bee Gees *Horizontal*; Soundtrack *Sound of Music*; Redding *History of Otis Redding*, *Otis Blue*; Fleetwood Mac *Fleetwood Mac*; Beatles *Sgt. Pepper's Lonely Hearts Club Band*.	**8–12** Anti-Communist riots in Poland. **16** My Lai massacre. **17** Anti-Vietnam War protest in London turns into battle with police outside US embassy in Grosvenor Square. **31** Lyndon Johnson announces he will not seek re-election.	**Classical** Colin Davis succeeds Georg Solti at the Royal Opera House. Berio *Sinfonia*; Stockhausen *Stimmung*; Shostakovich *Quartet No. 12*; *Violin Sonata*; Henze *The Raft Of The Medusa*; Birtwistle *Punch And Judy*; Britten *The Prodigal Son*; Dallapiccola *Ulisse*; Lutoslawski *Livre Pour Orchestre*; Riley *Poppy Nogood And The Phantom Band*. d. Charles Munch, Tullio Serafin.
April No engagements. Lennon and Harrison return, disillusioned, from Rishikesh.	Zoot Money disbands Dantalion's Chariot. **45s:** Beatles *Lady Madonna*; Cliff Richard *Congratulations*; Louis Armstrong *What A Wonderful World/Cabaret*; Jones *Delilah*; Redding *Dock of the Bay*; Black *Step Inside Love*; Reparata and The Delrons *Captain of Your Ship*; Showstoppers *Ain't Nothin' But A House Party*; Jeff Beck *Love Is Blue*; Honeybus *I Can't Let Maggie Go*; 1910 Fruitgum Company *Simon Says*; Small Faces *Lazy Sunday*; The Supremes *Forever Came Today*. **LPs:** Dylan *John Wesley Harding*; Various *This Is Soul*; Redding *History of Otis Redding*; Soundtrack *Sound of Music*; Supremes *Greatest Hits*; Incredible String Band *The Hangman's Beautiful Daughter*; Fleetwood Mac *Fleetwood Mac*; Four Tops *Greatest Hits*; Beach Boys *Wild Honey*; Scott Walker *Scott 2*; Move *The Move*.	**4** Martin Luther King assassinated in Memphis. **11** Black communities across USA riot after Dr King's funeral. **12–15** Students riot in West Germany after attempted murder of their leader 'Red Rudi' Dutschke. **21** French students occupy campus at Nanterre. **21** Enoch Powell makes 'rivers of blood' speech in Birmingham, predicting future race war in UK. 971. **26** Drug Squad seizes LSD valued at £1.5 million in London.	**Fiction** Amis *I Want It Now*; Braine *The Crying Game*; Updike *Couples*; Vidal *Myra Breckinridge*; Rolfe *Hadrian VII*; Powell *The Military Philosophers*; Solzhenitsyn *The First Circle*; Cancer Ward*; Baldwin *Tell Me How Long The Train's Been Gone*. d. Max Brod, Upton Sinclair, John Steinbeck, Mervyn Peake, Richmal Crompton, Enid Blyton.

May
15 Lennon and McCartney announce the formation of Apple Corps in New York.
18 Lennon convenes group meeting at Apple to inform the others that he is Jesus.
19 Lennon and Yoko Ono unite, recording Two Virgins.
30-31 Recording The Beatles.

June
4-6, 10-11 Recording The Beatles.
15 Lennon and Ono plant acorns 'for peace' in the grounds of Coventry Cathedral.
18 Theatrical adaption of Lennon's In His Own Write opens in London. First public appearance together of Lennon and Ono.
18 McCartney is 26.
21 Apple buys an office in Savile Row.
20-21, 26-28 Recording The Beatles.

Eric Clapton guests with Mothers of Invention in LA. 45s: Armstrong What A Wonderful World/Cabaret; Union Gap Young Girl; 1910 Fruitgum Company Simon Says; Small Faces Lazy Sunday; Bobby Goldsboro Honey; Julie Driscoll and Brian Auger This Wheel's On Fire; Engelbert Humperdinck A Man Without Love; Dionne Warwick Do You Know the Way to San Jose; Beach Boys Friends. LPs: Various This Is Soul; Dylan John Wesley Harding; Walker Scott 2; Redding History of Otis Redding; Jimi Hendrix Experience Smash Hits; Soundtrack Sound of Music; Incredible String Band The Hangman's Beautiful Daughter; Supremes Greatest Hits; Fleetwood Mac Fleetwood Mac; Byrds The Notorious Byrd Brothers.

11 Roof of Olympic Studios catches fire as Rolling Stones record Sympathy for the Devil. 45s: Union Gap Young Girl; Rolling Stones Jumping Jack Flash; Donovan Hurdy Gurdy Man; Julie Driscoll and Brian Auger This Wheel's On Fire; Goldsboro Honey; Manfred Mann My Name Is Jack; Equals Baby Come Back; O. C. Smith Son of Hickory Holler's Tramp. LPs: Various This Is Soul; Walker Scott 2; Dylan John Wesley Harding; Andy Williams Love Andy; Small Faces Ogden's Nut Gone Flake; Redding Dock of the Bay; Soundtrack Sound of Music; Jimi Hendrix Experience Smash Hits; Fleetwood Mac Fleetwood Mac; Incredible String Band The Hangman's Beautiful Daughter, Donovan A Gift from a Flower to a Garden.

5-7 French students riot. Sorbonne closed. Heavy street fighting in Paris's Latin Quarter: a thousand injured.
9 Soviet armies mass on Czech borders.
16 Ronan Point flats collapse.
21 French workers call general strike in support of students. France comes to standstill
24 French policeman killed during student riots in Lyons.
30 De Gaulle announces strong measures against rioters, dissolves the National Assembly, and calls elections.
30 Students at Hornsey College of Art declare 'state of anarchy'.

3 Andy Warhol shot by Valerie Solanas in New York.
5 Bobby Kennedy assassinated in Los Angeles.
12 De Gaulle bans theatre demonstrations.
30 French elections take place amid new riots. Gaullists returned with landslide; Communists defeated.

Poetry
C. Day Lewis becomes Poet Laureate. Auden Collected Longer Poems; Berryman His Toy, His Dream, His Rest; Bunting Collected Poems; Fuller New Poems.
d. Salvatore Quasimodo, Gunnar Ekelöf, Sir Herbert Read.

Stage
'Tribal Love-Rock' musical Hair is the year's sensation. Abolition of Lord Chamberlain ends theatre censorship in Britain.
Osborne The Hotel in Amsterdam; Nichols A Day in the Death of Joe Egg; Bennett Forty Years On; Simon Plaza Suite; Sackler The Great White Hope.
d. Sir Donald Wolfit.

450

1968 THE BEATLES	UK POP	CURRENT AFFAIRS	CULTURE
July **1** Lennon's art exhibition *You Are Here* opens at the Robert Fraser Gallery. **1–5** Recording *The Beatles.* **7** Starr is 28. **8–12, 15–16** Recording *The Beatles.* **17** *Yellow Submarine* film opens in London. **18–19, 22–25** Recording *The Beatles.* **28** 'The Mad Day Out': the group visits various North London locations to have promotional photographs taken of them by, among others, Don McCullin. **29–August 2** Recording *Hey Jude.* **31** Apple Boutique closes.	Mick Jagger films with Donald Cammell and Nicolas Roeg in *Performance*. **45s:** Equals *Baby Come Back*; Des O'Connor *I Pretend*; Tommy James and The Shondells *Mony Mony*; Smith *Son of Hickory Holler's Tramp*; Manfred Mann *My Name Is Jack*; Cupid's Inspiration *Yesterday Has Gone*; Ohio Express *Yummy Yummy Yummy*; Richard Harris *MacArthur Park*; Crazy World of Arthur Brown *Fire*; The Nice *America*; Simon and Garfunkel *Mrs Robinson*. **LPs:** Small Faces *Ogden's Nut Gone Flake*; Various *This Is Soul*; Soundtrack *Sound of Music*; Dylan John Wesley Harding; Crazy World of Arthur Brown *Crazy World*; Brian Auger/Julie Driscoll *Open*; Fleetwood Mac *Fleetwood Mac*; Mayall *Bare Wires*; Pink Floyd *A Saucerful of Secrets*; Monkees *The Birds, The Bees, and The Monkees*; Mothers of Invention *We're Only In It For The Money*; Tyrannosaurus Rex *My People Were Fair.*	**10** Dr Spock jailed for advocating draft-dodging. **22** Dubcek summoned to Moscow and shouted at by Brezhnev. **31** Hubert Selby Jnr's *Last Exit to Brooklyn* acquitted of obscenity at Old Bailey. (See November 1967.)	**Non-fiction** Mailer *The Armies of the Night*; Cleaver *Soul On Ice*; Nuttall *Bomb Culture*; Marcuse *Psychoanalysis and Politics*; Woolf *The Electric Kool-Aid Acid Test*; Castaneda *The Teachings of Don Juan: A Yaqui Way of Knowledge.* **d.** Helen Keller, Harold Nicolson, Leonard Woolf, Konstantin Paustovsky.

			Science fiction
August 7–9, 12–16, 20–23, 28–29 Recording *The Beatles*. 22 Cynthia Lennon sues her husband for divorce, citing adultery with Yoko Ono. 26 US: *Hey Jude*. 30 UK: *Hey Jude*.	**45s:** Tommy James and The Shondells *Mony Mony*; Crazy World of Arthur Brown *Fire*; Beach Boys *Do It Again*, Simon and Garfunkel *Mrs Robinson*; Herb Alpert *This Guy's In Love With You*, Kinks *Days*; Dusty Springfield *I Close My Eyes and Count To Ten*; Bee Gees *I've Gotta Get A Message To You*; Fleetwood Mac *Need Your Love So Bad*; Sly and The Family Stone *Dance to the Music*. **LPs:** Simon and Garfunkel *Bookends*; Tom Jones *Delilah*; Crazy World of Arthur Brown *Crazy World*; Mayall *Bare Wires*; Cream *Wheels of Fire*; Pink Floyd *A Saucerful of Secrets*; Various *This Is Soul*; Small Faces *Ogden's Nut Gone Flake*; Jimi Hendrix Experience *Smash Hits*; Hollies *Greatest Hits*; Canned Heat *Boogie*.	**12** Race riot in Watts, Los Angeles. **21–23** Warsaw Pact forces invade Czechoslovakia. Communists impose return to totalitarianism. **29** Mayor Daley's police 'run wild' at Chicago Democratic Convention: hundreds injured.	Dick Do *Androids Dream of Electric Sheep?*; Sladek *The Reproductive System*; Herbert *The Santaroga Barrier*, Brunner *Stand on Zanzibar*; Blish *Black Easter*, Silverberg *Hawksbill Station*; Aldiss *Report on Probability A*; Disch *Camp Concentration*; Moorcock *The Final Programme*. Hugo: Roger Zelazny *Lord of Light*. Nebula: Alexei Panshin *Rite of Passage*.
September 3 Recording *The Beatles*. 4 Filming promo for *Hey Jude*. 5–6 Recording *The Beatles*. 11 *Hey Jude* tops the UK chart (two weeks). 9–13, 16–20, 23–26 Recording *The Beatles*. 28 *Hey Jude* tops the US chart (nine weeks – biggest selling American single). 30 Hunter Davies's *The Beatles* is published.	**45s:** Bee Gees *I've Gotta Get A Message To You*; Beatles *Hey Jude*; Mary Hopkin *Those Were The Days*; Aretha Franklin *I Say A Little Prayer*, Canned Heat *On the Road Again*; Otis Redding *Hard To Handle*; Mama Cass *Dream A Little Dream Of Me*; Mason Williams *Classical Gas*. **LPs:** Simon and Garfunkel *Bookends*; Hollies *Greatest Hits*; Jones *Delilah*; Cream *Wheels of Fire*; Fleetwood Mac *Mr Wonderful*; Moody Blues *In Search of the Lost Chord*; Canned Heat *Boogie*; Mayall *Bare Wires*; Family *Music in A Doll's House*; Soundtrack *Sound of Music*; Doors *Waiting for the Sun*; Franklin *Aretha Now*.	Repression in Czechoslovakia; thousands arrested. **26** Theatre censorship abolished in UK. **27** Cast of musical *Hair* appears naked onstage in London.	**Fashion** Ethnic look from Morocco, Turkey, Kashmir: kaftans, silks, beads, fringe dresses and jackets, sandals. Regency dandy look for pop stars: filled shirts, satin trousers. Very long hair-styles. Betsey Johnson: cowhide mini-dresses. St Laurent: safari jacket. Courrèges: plastic dresses with punched holes. Rudi Gernreich: see-through blouses and dresses. Calvin Klein sets up sportswear label. Ralph Lauren: Polo line. Thea Porter's N.Y. shop. Balenciaga retires.

1968 THE BEATLES	UK POP	CURRENT AFFAIRS	CULTURE
October 1–5, 7–11, 13–14 Recording *The Beatles.* 9 Lennon is 28. 16 Harrison goes to Los Angeles to produce Jackie Lomax's album. 16–17 Sequencing *The Beatles.* 18 Lennon and Ono raided by drug squad at Starr's flat in Montagu Square. Film *How I Won The War* opens.	20 Yardbirds evolve into Led Zeppelin. **45s:** Hopkin *Those Were The Days*; Union Gap *Lady Willpower*, Jose Feliciano *Light My Fire*; Tyrannosaurus Rex *One Inch Rock*; Williams *Classical Gas*; Doors *Hello I Love You*; Joe Cocker *With A Little Help From My Friends*; Hugo Montenegro *The Good, the Bad, and the Ugly*; The Band *The Weight*, Cream *Sunshine of Your Love*. **LPs:** Hollies *Greatest Hits*; Seekers *At the Talk of the Town*; Simon and Garfunkel *Bookends*; Cream *Wheels of Fire*; Bee Gees *Idea*; Soundtrack *Sound of Music*, Traffic *Traffic*, Jethro Tull *This Was*; Franklin *Aretha Now*; Doors *Waiting for the Sun*; Canned Heat *Boogie*.	6 RUC attacks Catholic civil rights demonstrators in Londonderry. 12–27 Mexico Olympics. Black athletes give 'black power' salutes. 18 First abortion clinic opens in UK. 27 Vietnam protest in London. 28 Thousands protest in Prague against Soviet occupation.	**TV/Media** First episodes of *Dad's Army*, *Please Sir*, *The Forsyte Saga*, *Whicker's World*. Nigel Kneale's *The Year of the Sex Olympics*. First issues of listings magazine *Time Out* and *19* (magazine for young women). d. Bud Flanagan, Tony Hancock.
November No engagements. Marxist magazine *Black Dwarf* attacks Lennon for advocating a pacifist line in *Revolution.* 1 UK: *Wonderwall.* 8 John and Cynthia Lennon divorce. 11 US: *Two Virgins.* 15 Harrison appears on *The Smothers Brothers Comedy Hour.* 21 Ono miscarries. 22 UK: *The Beatles.* 25 US: *The Beatles.* 28 Lennon and Ono are fined £150 for possessing cannabis. (Scandal over album cover which shows Lennon and Ono frontally naked.)	26 Cream play farewell concert at the Albert Hall. **45s:** Cocker *With A Little Help From My Friends*; Montenegro *The Good, the Bad, and the Ugly*; Barry Ryan *Eloise*; Isley Brothers *This Old Heart of Mine*; Jimi Hendrix Experience *All Along the Watchtower*, The Who *Magic Bus*; Marvin Gaye and Tammi Terrell *You're All I Need To Get By*; Johnny Johnson and The Bandwagon *Breaking Down the Walls of Heartache*; Scaffold *Lily the Pink*; Turtles *Elenore*. **LPs:** Hollies *Greatest Hits*; Beatles *The Beatles*; Jimi Hendrix Experience *Electric Ladyland*; Simon and Garfunkel *Bookends*; Soundtrack *Sound of Music, The Good, The Bad, and The Ugly; The Graduate*; Bee Gees *Idea*; Jethro Tull *This Was*.	1 Johnson orders cessation of bombing in North Vietnam. 6 Richard Nixon elected. 7 Anti-Soviet riot in Prague. 17 Czech students occupy Prague university in protest against the Soviet occupation.	**Visual arts** Buckminster Fuller receives gold medal of RIBA. Dada/Surrealist exhibition at New York Museum of Modern Art. Warhol's first London show. Hepworth retrospective at the Tate. d. Marcel Duchamp, Kees Van Dongen, John Heartfield, Lucio Fontana.

December
No engagements.
10-11 Lennon and Ono take part in The Rolling Stones' Rock and Roll Circus.
18 Lennon and Ono 'appear' inside a white bag at a happening in the Albert Hall.

Graham Nash leaves Hollies. 10-11 Rolling Stones film TV extravaganza, Rock and Roll Circus, at Wembley. (Screened 1996.) 45s: Montenegro The Good, the Bad, and the Ugly; Scaffold Lily the Pink; Nina Simone Ain't Got No—I Got Life; Foundations Build Me Up Buttercup; Bonzo Dog Doo-Dah Band I'm the Urban Spaceman; Jeannie C. Riley Harper Valley PTA; Love Sculpture Sabre Dance; Fleetwood Mac Albatross; William Bell and Judy Clay Private Number. LPs: Beatles The Beatles; Seekers Best Of; Rolling Stones Beggars Banquet; Jimi Hendrix Experience Electric Ladyland; Val Doonican World Of; Hollies Greatest Hits; Soundtrack Sound of Music; The Graduate.

5 Student sit-in protest in Bristol.
27 American astronauts of Apollo 8 mission orbit the Moon.

Science
Discovery of pulsars. Max Perutz: structure of the haemoglobin molecule.
Watson The Double Helix.
d. Lise Meitner, Otto Hahn, Charles Mayo, Yuri Gagarin.

1969 THE BEATLES	UK POP	CURRENT AFFAIRS	CULTURE
January Lennon replies to *Black Dwarf* (November 1968), defending his position as expressed in *Revolution*. **2** Filming starts on rehearsals in Twickenham (later included in *Let It Be*). **3** *Two Virgins* confiscated by the New Jersey police on the grounds of obscenity. **10** Major argument during session at Twickenham. Harrison walks out. **15** Filming at Twickenham abandoned. Beatles decide to record an album at Apple instead. **17** US: *Yellow Submarine* (LP). **22–29** Recording *Let It Be* (LP). **30** 'Rooftop concert' at Apple in Savile Row, London. **31** Recording *Let It Be* (LP).	Atlantic achieves 23 gold records in one year. **45s:** Marmalade *Ob-la-di Ob-la-da*; Scaffold *Lily the Pink*; Fleetwood Mac *Albatross*; Foundations *Build Me Up Buttercup*; Bonzo Dog Doo-Dah Band *I'm the Urban Spaceman*; Dusty Springfield *Son of a Preacher Man*; Stevie Wonder *For Once in My Life*; William Bell and Judy Clay *Private Number*; Edwin Starr S.O.S.; Move *Blackberry Way*; Canned Heat *Going Up the Country*; Martha and the Vandellas *Dancing in the Street*. **LPs:** Beatles *The Beatles*; Seekers *Best Of*; Rolling Stones *Beggars Banquet*; Soundtrack *The Graduate*; Tom Jones *Help Yourself*; Jimi Hendrix Experience *Electric Ladyland*; Ross, Supremes, Temptations *Diana Ross and The Supremes Join The Temptations*; Hollies *Greatest Hits*; Cohen *Songs*.	**1** Kenya revokes Asian trading licences; 15,000 to emigrate to UK. **3** Catholics riot in Londonderry. **12** Police fight with anti-racist demonstrators in London. **19** Student Jan Palach immolates himself in Prague in protest against Soviet occupation. **21** Jan Palach dies. **24** Students in demonstration at LSE. **26** Students protest Jan Palach's death in Wenceslas Square. **27** 1,000 students 'sit in' at LSE. **30** Student leaders banned from entering LSE.	**Cinema** Schlesinger *Midnight Cowboy*; Hill *Butch Cassidy and the Sundance Kid*; Peckinpah *The Wild Bunch*; Penn *Alice's Restaurant*; Hopper *Easy Rider*; Lester *The Bed Sitting Room*; Kazan *The Arrangement*; Wexler *Medium Cool*; Kubrick *2001: A Space Odyssey*; Antonioni *Zabriskie Point*; Fellini *Satyricon*; Leone *Once Upon a Time in the West*; Bertolucci *The Conformist*; Widerberg *Ådalen 31*. d. Josef Von Sternberg, Judy Garland, Boris Karloff, Robert Taylor, Thelma Ritter, Miles Malleson.

February 3 Lennon, Harrison, and Starr invite American businessman Allen Klein to sort out the group's chaotic affairs. McCartney objects to Klein and appoints Eastman and Eastman as general counsels. A fatal fracture in The Beatles' relationship results. 3–May 2 Starr appears in *The Magic Christian*. 22, 25 Recording *Abbey Road*. 25 Harrison is 26.	**45s:** Move *Blackberry Way*; Amen Corner *Half As Nice*; Peter Sarstedt *Where Do You Go To My Lovely*; Fleetwood Mac *Albatross*; *Wonder For Once in My Life*; Nina Simone *To Love Somebody*; Supremes/Temptations *I'm Gonna Make You Love Me*; Sam and Dave *Soul Sister Brown Sugar*; Glen Campbell *Wichita Lineman*; Tymes *People*. **LPs:** Ross, Supremes, Temptations *Diana Ross and The Supremes Join The Temptations*; Beatles *The Beatles*; *Yellow Submarine*; Seekers *Best Of*; Soundtrack *The Graduate*; *Sound of Music*; London Cast *Hair*; Rolling Stones *Beggars Banquet*; Bonzo Dog Doodah Band *Doughnut in Granny's Greenhouse*.	3 Yasser Arafat becomes head of Palestine Liberation Organisation. 3 LSE closed down.	**Jazz** Davis *In A Silent Way*; Sanders *The Creator Has A Master Plan*; Ayler *Music Is The Healing Force Of The Universe*; Art Ensemble of Chicago *People In Sorrow*; Brand *African Piano*; McLaughlin *Extrapolation*; Westbrook *Marching Song*. d. Coleman Hawkins, Pee Wee Russell
March 2 Lennon and Ono perform at a jazz avant-garde concert with John Tchicai in the Lady Mitchell Hall in Cambridge. 12 McCartney marries Linda Eastman. 13 The drug squad raids the Harrisons' house. 20 Lennon and Ono marry in Gibraltar. 25–31 Lennon and Ono hold their 'bed-in' at the Amsterdam Hilton.	1 Jim Morrison arrested in Miami for exposing himself during Doors concert. **45s:** Sarstedt *Where Do You Go To My Lovely*; Marvin Gaye *I Heard It Through the Grapevine*; Cilla Black *Surround Yourself With Sorrow*; Campbell *Wichita Lineman*; Dean Martin *Gentle On My Mind*; Engelbert Humperdinck *The Way It Used To Be*; Hollies *Sorry Suzanne*; Joe South *Games People Play*. **LPs:** Ross, Supremes, Temptations *Diana Ross and The Supremes Join The Temptations*; Cream *Goodbye*; Beatles *The Beatles*; *Yellow Submarine*; Seekers *Best Of*; London Cast *Hair*; Soundtrack *The Graduate*; *Sound of Music*; Ten Years After *Stonedhenge*; Beach Boys *20/20*.	2 Chinese and Russian troops in border clash. 2 First flight of Concorde. 5 Kray Twins jailed for life at the Old Bailey. 10 James Earl Ray jailed for 99 years for assassinating Martin Luther King. 17 Golda Meir becomes premier of Israel. 29 Chinese and Russian troops clash over island in Ussuri River.	**Classical** Formation of Scratch Orchestra. Messiaen *La Transfiguration de Notre Seigneur Jésus-Christ*; *Méditations sur le mystère de la Sainte Trinité*; Shostakovich *Symphony No. 14*; Berio *Sequenza VII*; Gubaidulina *Rubaiyat*; Cage *HPSCHD*; *Cheap Imitation*; Kagel *Repertoire*; Penderecki *The Devils of Loudun*; Bussotti *Rara Requiem*; Maxwell Davies *Eight Songs For A Mad King*; *Vesalii Icones*; Tavener *Celtic Requiem*; Sallinen *Quartet No. 3*; Panufnik *Universal Prayer*; Riley *A Rainbow In Curved Air*. d. Ernest Ansermet, Wilhelm Backhaus.

1969 THE BEATLES	UK POP	CURRENT AFFAIRS	CULTURE
April 11 UK: *Get Back*. 14 Recording *The Ballad of John and Yoko*. 16, 18, 20 Recording *Abbey Road*. 21 Lennon and Ono form Bag Productions. 22 Lennon and Ono record *The Wedding Album*. 23 *Get Back* tops the UK chart (3 weeks) singles chart (seven weeks). 25–27, 29–30 Recording *Abbey Road*.	**45s:** Gaye *I Heard It Through the Grapevine*; Desmond Dekker *The Israelites*; Beatles *Get Back*; Martin Gentle *On My Mind*; South *Games People Play*; Noel Harrison *Windmills of Your Mind*; Lulu *Boom Bang-a-Bang*; Beach Boys *I Can Hear Music*; The Who *Pinball Wizard*; Temptations *Get Ready*; Bob and Earl *Harlem Shuffle*; Stevie Wonder *I Don't Know Why*; Mary Hopkin *Goodbye*; Cream *Badge*; Fleetwood Mac *Man of the World*; Isley Brothers *Behind a Painted Smile*; Clodagh Rodgers *Come Back and Shake Me*. **LPs:** Cream *Goodbye*; Seekers *Best Of*; Beatles *The Beatles*; R.oss, Supremes, Temptations *Diana Ross and The Supremes Join The Temptations*; Walker Scott 3; Beach Boys 20/20; Led Zeppelin *Led Zeppelin*; Soundtrack *Sound of Music*; *Oliver!*; Moody Blues *On the Threshold of a Dream*; *Family Family Entertainment*.	1 France withdraws from NATO. 17 Husak replaces Dubcek in Czechoslovakia. 19 Student leader Daniel Cohn-Bendit deported from France to Germany. 24 Major anti-war protest in New York. 28 De Gaulle resigns, defeated in constitutional referendum.	**Fiction** P. H. Newby wins first Booker Prize. Roth *Portnoy's Complaint*; Puzo *The Godfather*; Malamud *Pictures of Fidelman*; Greene *Travels With My Aunt*; Donleavy *The Beastly Beatitudes of Balthazar B*; Lessing *The Four-Gated City*; Nabokov *Ada*. Nobel: Samuel Beckett. d. Jack Kerouac, Ivy Compton-Burnett, Stephen Potter, B. Traven.

May
2 UK: *Electronic Sound*. Recording *Abbey Road*.
4 Lennon and Ono buy Tittenhurst Park.
5 Recording *Abbey Road*.
5 US: *Get Back*.
6 Recording *Abbey Road*.
8 Lennon, Harrison, and Starr sign a management contract with Klein.
9 UK: *Life With The Lions*.
16 Lennon's visa application for the USA is refused on the grounds of his drug conviction (November 28, 1968).
24 *Get Back* tops the US chart (five weeks).
25-June 2 Lennon and Ono fly to Canada for various 'bed-ins' for peace. Lennon urges students at 'People's Park' in Berkeley not to provoke the police.
26 US: *Life With The Lions*.
30 UK: *The Ballad of John and Yoko*.

6 Blind Faith 'supergroup' formed. 12 Fairport Convention in M1 car-crash. Drummer Martin Lamble and designer Jeannie Franklin killed. **45s:** Beatles *Get Back*; Hopkin *Goodbye*; Rodgers *Come Back and Shake Me*; The Who *Pinball Wizard*; Harrison *Windmills of Your Mind*; Sinatra *My Way*; Herman's Hermits *My Sentimental Friend*; Isley Brothers *Behind a Painted Smile*; Simon and Garfunkel *The Boxer*; Tommy Roe *Dizzy*; Fleetwood Mac *Man of the World*; Bob and Earl *Harlem Shuffle*; Fifth Dimension *Aquarius/Let the Sunshine In*; Edwin Hawkins Singers *Oh Happy Day*. **LPs:** Moody Blues *On the Threshold of a Dream*; Dylan *Nashville Skyline*; Cream *Goodbye*; Seekers *Best Of*; Led Zeppelin *Led Zeppelin*; Hollies *Hollies sing Dylan*; Walker *Scott 3*; Presley *NBC TV Special*; Cohen *Songs from a Room*; The Who *Tommy*.

2 New York campuses closed after student rioting.
2 Major Soviet clampdown in Czechoslovakia.
3 Jimi Hendrix arrested in Toronto for possession of heroin.
18-26 Apollo 10 mission orbits the moon.

Poetry
Berryman *Complete Dream Songs*.

458

1969 THE BEATLES	UK POP	CURRENT AFFAIRS	CULTURE
June 1 Lennon records *Give Peace A Chance* in Montreal. (Soon after returning to UK, Lennon and Ono move into Tittenhurst Park, Ascot, and begin sniffing heroin.) 4 US: *The Ballad of John and Yoko.* 11 *The Ballad of John and Yoko* tops the UK chart (three weeks). 18 McCartney is 27.	*NME* starts publishing the Top 20 albums. **45s:** Roe *Dizzy*; Beatles *Ballad of John and Yoko*; Beatles *Get Back*; Edwin Hawkins Singers *Oh Happy Day*; Fleetwood Mac *Man of the World*; Booker T and The MGs *Time Is Tight*; Jackie Wilson *Higher and Higher*; Smokey Robinson and The Miracles *The Tracks of My Tears*; Jethro Tull *Living in the Past*; Elvis Presley *In the Ghetto*; Beach Boys *Breakaway*; Thunderclap Newman *Something in the Air*; Creedence Clearwater Revival *Proud Mary.* **LPs:** Dylan *Nashville Skyline*; Moody Blues *On the Threshold of a Dream*; Sinatra *My Way*; Soundtrack *2001: A Space Odyssey*; *Oliver!*; London Cast *Hair*; Who *Tommy*; Cream *Goodbye*; Cohen *Songs from a Room*; Seekers *Best of*; Tyrannosaurus Rex *Unicorn.*	8 Spain closes land border with Gibraltar. 15 Georges Pompidou elected President of France.	**Stage** Barry Humphries' first one-man show at the Fortune Theatre. Orton *What the Butler Saw*; Various *Oh! Calcutta!*; Nichols *The National Health*; Storey *The Contractor.* d. Frank Loesser, Irene Castle.

July			**Non-fiction**
1–4 Recording *Abbey Road*. Lennon absent due to car-crash in Scotland. 4 UK/US: *Give Peace A Chance*. 7 Starr is 29. 7–11, 15–18, 21–25, 28–31 Recording *Abbey Road*.	Noel Redding leaves Jimi Hendrix Experience. Neil Young joins Crosby, Stills, and Nash. Newport Jazz Festival features rock for the first time. 2 Brian Jones drowns in his swimming pool. 5 Rolling Stones give free concert in Hyde Park. 250,000 attend. **45s:** Thunderclap Newman *Something in the Air*; Rolling Stones *Honky Tonk Women*; Presley *In the Ghetto*; Beatles *Ballad of John and Yoko*; Amen Corner *Hello Susie*; Billy Preston *That's the Way God Planned It*; Plastic Ono Band *Give Peace A Chance*; Desmond Dekker *It Mek*; Stevie Wonder *My Cherie Amour*; Donovan and Jeff Beck *Barabajagal*. **LPs:** Jones *This is Tom Jones*; Sinatra *My Way*; Dylan *Nashville Skyline*; Presley *Flaming Star*, Reeves *According to my Heart*; Moody Blues *On the Threshold of a Dream*; Soundtrack *2001: A Space Odyssey*; *Oliver!*; Cohen *Songs from a Room*; London Cast *Hair*, Pink Floyd *More*; Procol Harum *A Salty Dog*.	20 Mary Jo Kopechne drowns in Senator Edward Kennedy's car at Chappaquiddick bridge. 21 Neil Armstrong and Buzz Aldrin land on the moon.	Mailer *Miami and the Siege of Chicago*; Roszak *The Making of a Counter Culture*; Marcuse *An Essay on Liberation*; Greene *Collected Essays*; Booker *The Neophiliacs*. d. Karl Jaspers, Theodor Adorno, Sir Osbert Sitwell.

1969 THE BEATLES	UK POP	CURRENT AFFAIRS	CULTURE
August **1, 4–8, 11, 15, 18–20, 25** Recording *Abbey Road*.	**14–31** Woodstock festival: The Who, Jimi Hendrix, The Band, Grateful Dead, Jefferson Airplane, Santana, Sly and the Family Stone, Crosby, Stills, Nash, and Young, Richie Havens, etc. 400,000 attend. **26–31** Isle of Wight festival: Dylan, The Band, The Who. 200,000 attend. **45s:** Rolling Stones *Honky Tonk Women*; Zager and Evans *In the Year 2525*; Plastic Ono Band *Give Peace A Chance*; Wonder *My Cherie Amour*, Joe Dolan *Make Me an Island*; Clodagh Rodgers *Goodnight Midnight*; Move *Curly*. **LPs:** Jethro Tull *Stand Up*; Presley *Flaming Star, From Elvis in Memphis*; Dylan *Nashville Skyline*; Jones *This Is Tom Jones*; Soundtrack *2001: A Space Odyssey; Oliver!*; Fairport Convention *Unhalfbricking*; London Cast *Hair*; Blodwyn Pig *Ahead Rings Out*.	**9** Manson 'family' murders Sharon Tate and four friends in Los Angeles. **16** British troops begin patrolling Catholic areas of Belfast. **21** Soviet tanks enter Prague to quell anniversary protests over invasion. **28** British troops erect the 'peace wall' between Protestant and Catholic communities in Belfast.	**Science fiction** Vonnegut *Slaughterhouse Five*; Dick *Ubik*; Ellison *A Boy and His Dog*; Le Guin *The Left Hand of Darkness*; Herbert *Dune Messiah*; Moorcock *A Cure for Cancer*, Silverberg *Nightwings*; Aldiss *Barefoot in the Head*; Spinrad *Bug Jack Barron*; Zelazny *Creatures of Light and Darkness*. Hugo: John Brunner *Stand on Zanzibar*. Nebula: Ursula K. Le Guin *The Left Hand of Darkness*.

			Fashion
September 13 The Plastic Ono Band performs in Toronto. 25 Lennon records *Cold Turkey*. 26 UK: *Abbey Road*. 28 Lennon records *Cold Turkey*.	24 Deep Purple and the RPO under Malcolm Arnold: Concerto for Group and Orchestra at the Albert Hall. **45s:** Zager and Evans *In the Year 2525*; Creedence Clearwater Revival *Bad Moon Rising*; Bee Gees *Don't Forget to Remember*; Jane Birkin and Serge Gainsbourg *Je t'aime . . . Moi non plus*; Humble Pie *Natural Born Bugie*; Marvin Gaye *Too Busy Thinking About My Baby*; Bobbie Gentry *I'll Never Fall In Love Again*; Bob Dylan *Lay Lady Lay*. **LPs:** Jethro Tull *Stand Up*; Johnny Cash *At San Quentin*; Blind Faith *Blind Faith*; Nice *Nice*; Rolling Stones *Through the Past Darkly*; Soundrack *2001: A Space Odyssey*; Dylan *Nashville Skyline*; London Cast *Hair*; Fleetwood Mac *The Pious Bird of Ill Omen*; Fairport Convention *Unhalfbricking*; CSN *Crosby, Stills & Nash*.	1 Gaddafi mounts coup in Libya. 3 Death of Ho Chi Minh. 5 First colour TV transmissions in UK. 21 Police storm 144 Piccadilly to evict 250 hippie squatters.	Triumph of 'anti-fashion': no uniform theme in collections. Midi and maxi skirts. St Laurent: pant-suits. Afro hairstyles for white women. Betsey Johnson opens New York boutique. Biba moves to Kensington High Street. Rei Kawakubo: *Comme des Garons*.
October 1 US: *Abbey Road*. 3, 5 Lennon records *Cold Turkey*. 9 Lennon is 29. 12 Ono miscarries again (see November 21, 1968). 20 US: *The Wedding Album*. 31 UK: *Come Together/Something*.	Christine Perfect leaves Chicken Shack. **45s:** Creedence Clearwater Revival *Bad Moon Rising*; Birkin and Gainsbourg *Je t'aime . . . Moi non plus*; Gentry *I'll Never Fall In Love Again*; Archies *Sugar Sugar*; Johnny Cash *A Boy Named Sue*; Dylan *Lay Lady Lay*; David Bowie *Space Oddity*; Fleetwood Mac *Oh Well*; Lou Christie *I'm Gonna Make You Mine*; Hollies *He Ain't Heavy He's My Brother*; Nilsson *Everybody's Talking*. **LPs:** Beatles *Abbey Road*; Cash *At San Quentin*; Rolling Stones *Through the Past Darkly*; Blind Faith *Blind Faith*; Jethro Tull *Stand Up*; Dylan *Nashville Skyline*; Ten Years After *Sssh*; Fleetwood Mac *Then Play On*; Jack Bruce *Songs for a Tailor*; Jeff Beck Group *Beck-Ola*.	Trial of the 'Chicago Eight'. Weathermen mount violent Days of Rage protest. 5 First edition of *Monty Python's Flying Circus*. 15 Vietnam 'Moratorium' in USA. 15 Rupert Murdoch buys *The Sun*. 17 Divorce Reform Bill in UK. 21 Willi Brandt becomes German chancellor.	**TV/Media** Colour television arrives in Britain. First episodes of *Callan*, *Star Trek*, *Nationwide*, *On the Buses*. Kenneth Clark's *Civilization*. (Also *Monty Python's Flying Circus* – see October.) Drama: *A Family at War*, *The Six Wives of Henry VIII*. d. Eric Portman, Kenneth Horne, Billy Cotton, Robert Pitman.

462

1969 THE BEATLES	UK POP	CURRENT AFFAIRS	CULTURE
November Starr begins recording *Sentimental Journey*. 6 US: *Come Together/Something*. 7 UK: *The Wedding Album*. 22 *Come Together/Something* peaks at No. 4 in the UK chart. 25 Lennon returns his MBE in protest against Biafra, Vietnam, and '*Cold Turkey* slipping down the chart'. 29 *Come Together/Something* tops the US chart (one week).	**45s:** Archies *Sugar Sugar*; Christie *I'm Gonna Make You Mine*; Hollies *He Ain't Heavy He's My Brother*; Fleetwood Mac *Oh Well*; Upsetters *Return of Django*; Bowie *Space Oddity*; Beatles *Something*; Plastic Ono Band *Cold Turkey*; Tremeloes *Number One*; Jimmy Cliff *Wonderful World Beautiful People*; Joe Cocker *Delta Lady*; Stevie Wonder *Yester-me Yester-you Yesterday*; Junior Walker *What Does It Take*; Kenny Rogers *Ruby Don't Take Your Love To Town*. **LPs:** Beatles *Abbey Road*; Cash *At San Quentin*; Various *Motown Chartbusters Vol. 3*; Led Zeppelin *II*; King Crimson *In the Court of the Crimson King*; Ten Years After *Sssh*; Fleetwood Mac *Then Play On*; Bruce *Songs for a Tailor*, Pink Floyd *Ummagumma*; Rolling Stones *Through the Past Darkly*.	1–6 Sex Fair in Copenhagen. 5, 15 Anti-apartheid protestors fight with police over South African rugby tour of Britain. 14–24 Apollo 12 moon mission. 24 Lt William Calley charged with ordering massacre at My Lai (March 1968). 27 The Rolling Stones play Madison Square Gardens.	**Visual arts** Self-portrait by Rembrandt sold at Christie's for 1.25m dollars. Judy Chicago founds Feminist Art Program. Process Art. *Art-Language* begins publication. d. Walter Gropius, Mies van der Rohe, Ben Shahn.
December No engagements. McCartney begins recording *McCartney* at home. 11–14 Lennon and Ono mount a protest campaign over the conviction of 'A6 murderer' James Hanratty. 12 UK/US: *Live Peace in Toronto*. 16 Lennon and Ono put up posters in eleven cities worldwide: 'War Is Over – If You Want It. Happy Christmas from John and Yoko.'	6 Rolling Stones' disastrous free concert at Altamont: Hell's Angels run riot, killing a member of the audience, Meredith Hunter. **45s:** Archies *Sugar Sugar*, Rolf Harris *Two Little Boys*; Wonder *Yester-me Yester-you Yesterday*; Rogers *Ruby Don't Take Your Love To Town*; Blue Mink *Melting Pot*; Presley *Suspicious Minds*; Beatles *Something*. **LPs:** Beatles *Abbey Road*; Cash *At San Quentin*; Various *Motown Chartbusters Vol. 3*; Rolling Stones *Let It Bleed*; Tom Jones *Live in Las Vegas*; Led Zeppelin *II*; Pink Floyd *Ummagumma*; Moody Blues *To Our Children's Children's Children*; Cream *Best Of*.	2 A hundred arrested during anti-apartheid protests against Springboks. 12 Terrorist bombings in Italy. 13 US Supreme Court orders the end of segregation in the South. 18 Death penalty abolished in UK. 24 Manson gang arrested and charged with murder. (See August.)	**Science** Cambridge: first 'test-tube baby'. Dorothy Hodgkin: structure of insulin. USA bans DDT, phases out cyclamates and restricts use of monosodium glutamate. UN report: *Problems of the Human Environment*.

1970 THE BEATLES	UK POP	CURRENT AFFAIRS	CULTURE
January **3–8** Recording *Let It Be* (LP). **16** Police raid an exhibition of lithographs by Lennon in Bond Street. **27** Lennon records *Instant Karma!*	Diana Ross leaves Supremes. Bonzo Dog Doodah Band break up. **45s:** Harris *Two Little Boys*; Edison Lighthouse *Love Grows*; Rogers *Ruby Don't Take Your Love To Town*; Blue Mink *Melting Pot*; Cufflinks *Tracy*; Badfinger *Come and Get It*; Arrival *Friends*; Peter, Paul and Mary *Leavin' on a Jet Plane*; Marmalade *Reflections of My Life*. **LPs:** Beatles *Abbey Road*; Various *Motown Chartbusters Vol. 3*; Rolling Stones *Let It Bleed*; Jones *Live in Las Vegas*; Led Zeppelin II; Moody Blues *To Our Children's Children's Children*; Cash *At San Quentin*; Pentangle *Basket of Light*; Fairport Convention *Liege and Lief*; Soundtrack *Easy Rider*, Chicago *Chicago Transit Authority*.	**1** Age of majority in UK reduced from 21 to 18. **12** Biafra capitulates to Nigeria. **16** Col. Gaddafi becomes premier of Libya. **25** Violent anti-war protest in Whitehall. **26** Mick Jagger fined £200 for possession of cannabis.	**Cinema** Roeg/Cammell *Performance*; Losey *The Go-Between*; Russell *The Devils*; Altman *M*A*S*H*; Nichols *Catch 22*; McGrath *The Magic Christian*; Penn *Little Big Man*; Nelson *Soldier Blue*; Petri *Investigation of a Citizen Above Suspicion*; Meyer *Beyond the Valley of the Dolls*; Hiller *Love Story*; Warhol *Trash*. d. Frances Farmer, Alfred Newman.
February **Starr records** *Sentimental Journey*. Lennon and Ono get involved with Michael X's Black House project, the anti-*apartheid* movement, and the Campaign for Nuclear Disarmament. **6** UK: *Instant Karma*. **25** Lennon summonsed for the 'indecent exhibition' of his lithographs (January). **25** Harrison is 27. **26** US: *Hey Jude* (LP).	The Who record live at Leeds University. **45s:** Edison Lighthouse *Love Grows*; Peter, Paul and Mary *Leavin' on a Jet Plane*; Canned Heat *Let's Work Together*; Jethro Tull *Witch's Promise*; Badfinger *Come and Get It*; Venus *Shocking Blue*; Chicago *I'm A Man*; Jackson Five *I Want You Back*; Lee Marvin *Wand'rin' Star*; Plastic Ono Band *Instant Karma*; Sasha Distel *Raindrops Keep Falling On My Head*. **LPs:** Led Zeppelin II; Various *Motown Chartbusters Vol. 3*; Simon and Garfunkel *Bridge Over Troubled Water*, Beatles *Abbey Road*; Rolling Stones *Let It Bleed*; Family *A Song for Me*; Soundtrack *Easy Rider*; Paint Your Wagon; Pentangle *Basket of Light*; Chicago *Chicago Transit Authority*; Creedence Clearwater *Green River*, Band *The Band*.	**3** Andy Warhol's film *Flesh* seized by police at Open Space theatre, London. **9** Equal pay for women becomes law in UK.	**Jazz** Davis *Bitches Brew*; *Jack Johnson*; Hancock *Fat Albert Rotunda*; Kirk *Rahsaan Rahsaan*; Haden *Liberation Music Orchestra*. d. Johnny Hodges, Albert Ayler.

1970 THE BEATLES	UK POP	CURRENT AFFAIRS	CULTURE
March 6 UK: *Let It Be* (single). 11 US: *Let It Be* (single). 14 *Let It Be* enters at No. 2 in the UK chart – but fails to make No. 1. 22 McCartney records *Maybe I'm Amazed*. 23–27 Phil Spector remixes *Let It Be*. 27 UK: *Sentimental Journey*.	16 Death of Tammi Terrell. **45s:** Marvin *Wand'rin'* Star', Simon and Garfunkel *Bridge Over Troubled Water*; Jackson Five *I Want You Back*; Beatles *Let It Be*; Plastic Ono Band *Instant Karma*; Steam *Na Na Hey Hey Kiss Him Goodbye*; Bob and Marcia *Young, Gifted and Black*; Andy Williams *Can't Help Falling in Love*; Rare Bird *Sympathy*. **LPs:** Simon and Garfunkel *Bridge Over Troubled Water*; Soundtrack *Paint Your Wagon*; *Easy Rider*; Led Zeppelin II; Various *Motown Chartbusters Vol. 3*; Beatles *Abbey Road*; Zappa *Hot Rats*; *Canned Heat Cookbook*; Tyrannosaurus Rex *A Beard of Stars*; Jefferson Airplane *Volunteers*.	1 B-52s bomb Ho Chi Minh trail. 3 US police intervene to stop whites attacking 'bussed' black children. 5 Nuclear Non-Proliferation Treaty. 17 *New English Bible* published. 18 Sihanouk ousted in Cambodia. 29 Troops seal off Bogside area of Londonderry after clashes with Catholic rioters.	**Classical** First American performance of Shostakovich's *Symphony No. 13*. Shostakovich *Quartet No. 13*; Cardew *The Great Learning*; Henze *El Cimarrón*; Maxwell Davies *Taverner*; Maw *The Rising Of The Moon*; Bolcom *Piano Rags*; Cage *Solos*; Crumb *Black Angels*; Reich *Phase Patterns*. d. Sir John Barbirolli, George Szell.
April 1–2 Phil Spector remixes *Let It Be*. 1–27 Lennon's lithograph trial. Jury finds in favour of the defendants. 10 McCartney announces the break-up of The Beatles. 11 *Let It Be* tops the US chart (two weeks). 17 UK: *McCartney*. 20 US: *McCartney*. 28 Lennon and Ono fly to California for Primal Therapy with Dr Arthur Janov.	**45s:** Simon and Garfunkel *Bridge Over Troubled Water*, Dana *All Kinds of Everything*; Mary Hopkin *Knock Knock Who's There*; Williams *Can't Help Falling in Love*; Bob and Marcia *Young, Gifted and Black*; Norman Greenbaum *Spirit in the Sky*; Pipkins *Gimme Dat Ding*. **LPs:** Simon and Garfunkel *Bridge Over Troubled Water*; Soundtrack *Easy Rider*; *Paint Your Wagon*; Andy Williams *Greatest Hits*; Led Zeppelin II; Black Sabbath *Black Sabbath*; Various *Fill Your Head With Rock*; Chicago *Chicago*; McCartney *McCartney*; Creedence Clearwater Revival *Willy and the Poor Boys*; Doors *Morrison Hotel*; Mothers of Invention *Burnt Weenie Sandwich*; Morrison *Moondance*.	13–17 Abortive Apollo 13 moon mission manages to get back to Earth. 29 Student unrest begins at Kent State University, Ohio. 30 US troops attack Viet Cong bases in Cambodia.	**Fiction** Bellow *Mr Sammler's Planet*; Updike *Bech: A Book*; Murdoch *A Fairly Honourable Defeat*. Nobel: Alexander Solzhenitsyn. d. John Dos Passos, E. M. Forster, Francois Mauriac, John O'Hara, Erich Maria Remarque, Yukio Mishima, Erle Stanley Gardner.

May
8 UK: *Let It Be* (LP).
11 US: *The Long and Winding Road.*
13 World premiere of *Let It Be* film in New York. No Beatles attend.
18 US: *Let It Be* (LP).

45s: Greenbaum *Spirit in the Sky;* England World Cup Squad *Back Home;* Dana *All Kinds of Everything;* Simon and Garfunkel *Bridge Over Troubled Water;* Stevie Wonder *Never Had a Dream Come True;* Frijid Pink *House of the Rising Sun;* Move *Brontosaurus;* The Band *Rag Mama Rag;* Christie *Yellow River;* Moody Blues *Question;* Supremes *Up the Ladder to the Roof;* Jackson Five *ABC.* **LPs:** Simon and Garfunkel *Bridge Over Troubled Water,* McCartney *McCartney;* Beatles *Let It Be;* Soundtrack *Easy Rider,* Williams *Greatest Hits;* Jethro Tull *Benefit;* Black Sabbath *Black Sabbath;* Clearwater Revival *Willy and the Poor Boys;* Various *Fill Your Head With Rock;* Led Zeppelin II; King Crimson *In the Wake of Poseidon.*

4 Four students shot dead by National Guard during riots at Kent State University.
5 Furore in USA over invasion of Cambodia.
28 Maoist students riot in Paris.

Poetry
Auden *City Without Walls;* Lowell *Notebook;* Meredith *Earth Walk.* d. Nelly Sachs.

1970 THE BEATLES	UK POP	CURRENT AFFAIRS	CULTURE
June 13 *The Long and Winding Road* tops the US chart (two weeks). 18 McCartney is 28.	Emerson, Lake and Palmer form. 7 The Who perform *Tommy* at the Metropolitan Opera House. **45s:** Christie *Yellow River*; Mungo Jerry *In the Summertime*; England World Cup Squad *Back Home*; Moody Blues *Question*; Tom Jones *Daughter of Darkness*; Ray Stevens *Everything is Beautiful*; Mr Bloe *Groovin' with Mr Bloe*; Jackson Five *ABC*; Beach Boys *Cottonfields*; Marvin Gaye *Abraham, Martin and John*; Fleetwood Mac *The Green Manalishi*; Arrival *I Will Survive*; Free *All Right Now*. **LPs:** Beatles *Let It Be*; Simon and Garfunkel *Bridge Over Troubled Water*; McCartney *McCartney*; Who *Live At Leeds*; CSNY *Deja-Vu*; Soundtrack *Easy Rider*; Jethro Tull *Benefit*; King Crimson *In the Wake of Poseidon*; Led Zeppelin *II*; Ten Years After *Cricklewood Green*; Elton John *Elton John*; Mitchell *Ladies of the Canyon*.	8 Obscene Publications Squad 'busts' OZ for its Schoolkids issue. 19 Conservatives defeat Labour in general election. Edward Heath becomes prime minister.	**Stage** Kenneth MacMillan takes over the Royal Ballet from Sir Frederick Ashton. Natalia Makarova defects from Kirov Ballet in London. Hampton *The Philanthropist*; Mercer Flint; A. Schaffer *Sleuth*; P. Schaffer *The Battle of Shrivings*; Storey *Home*; Simon *Last of the Red Hot Lovers*; Bolt *Vivat! Vivat Regina!*; Mortimer *A Voyage Round My Father*, Sondheim *Company*.

467

July
7 Starr is 30.

3-5 Atlanta Festival: Jimi Hendrix, Johnny Winter, B.B. King, etc. 200,000 attend. **18** Pink Floyd give free concert in Hyde Park. **45s:** Mungo Jerry *In the Summertime*; Free *All Right Now*; Mr Bloe *Groovin' with Mr Bloe*; Gerry Monroe *Sally*; Beach Boys *Cottonfields*; Creedence Clearwater Revival *Up Around the Bend*; Nicky Thomas *Love of the Common People*; Kinks *Lola*; Four Tops *It's All in the Game*; Hodegs *Neanderthal Man*; Shirley Bassey *Something*; Joni Mitchell *Big Yellow Taxi*; Stevie Wonder *Signed Sealed and Delivered*. **LPs:** Simon and Garfunkel *Bridge Over Troubled Water*, Beatles *Let It Be*; Dylan *Self Portrait*; Soundtrack *Easy Rider*, Free *Fire and Water*, McCartney *McCartney*; Deep Purple *In Rock*; Who *Live At Leeds*; Cream *Live*; CSNY *Déjà-Vu*; Nice *Five Bridges*; Jimi Hendrix Experience *Band of Gypsies*; Soft Machine *Third*.

3 Violent Catholic demonstrations in Belfast.
16 National dock strike in UK.
18 *Oh! Calcutta!* opens at the Round House.

Non-fiction
Neville *Play Power*; Greer *The Female Eunuch*; Woolf *Radical Chic & Mau-Mauing the Flak Catchers*; Janov *The Primal Scream*; Laing *Knots*; Klibansky *Contemporary Philosophy*.
d. Bertrand Russell.

1970 THE BEATLES	UK POP	CURRENT AFFAIRS	CULTURE
August	Christine Perfect joins Fleetwood Mac. **26-30** Isle of Wight Festival: Jimi Hendrix, Who, Doors, ELP, Procul Harum, Family, Sly and the Family Stone, Miles Davis, Joni Mitchell, etc. 600,000 attend. **45s:** Presley *The Wonder of You; Free All Right Now;* Kinks *Lola;* Hotlegs *Neanderthal Man;* Bassey *Something;* Mitchell *Big Yellow Taxi;* Wonder *Signed Sealed and Delivered;* Smokey Robinson and The Miracles *Tears of a Clown;* Marmalade *Rainbow;* Jackson Five *The Love You Save;* Jimmy Ruffin *I'll Say Forever My Love.* **LPs:** Beatles *Let It Be;* Simon and Garfunkel *Bridge Over Troubled Water;* Dylan *Self Portrait; Free Fire and Water;* Deep Purple *In Rock;* Led Zeppelin II; Moody Blues *A Question of Balance;* Presley *Onstage February 1970; Soundtrack Paint Your Wagon;* Traffic *John Barleycorn Must Die;* Blood Sweat and Tears *BS&T.*	**2** First use of rubber bullets in Ulster. **9** Race riot in Notting Hill.	**Science fiction** Niven *Ringworld;* Silverberg *Tower of Glass;* Dick *A Maze of Death;* Sladek *The Müller-Fokker Effect;* Aldiss *The Moment of Eclipse,* Ballard *The Atrocity Exhibition;* Russ *And Chaos Died.* Hugo: Ursula K. Le Guin *The Left Hand of Darkness.* Nebula: Larry Niven *Ringworld.*

September
25 UK: *Beaucoups of Blues.*
28 US: *Sentimental Journey; Beaucoups of Blues.*

Presley tours USA.
Holland-Dozier-Holland found Invictus.
18 Jimi Hendrix dies of drug overdose in London. **45s:** Presley *The Wonder of You*; Smokey Robinson and The Miracles *Tears of a Clown*; Freda Payne *Band of Gold*; Three Dog Night *Mama Told Me Not To Come*; Chairmen of the Board *Give Me Just A Little More Time*; Bread *Make It With You*; Jimmy Cliff *Wild World*; Desmond Dekker *You Can Get It If You Really Want*; Deep Purple *Black Night.* **LPs:** Moody Blues *A Question of Balance*; Simon and Garfunkel *Bridge Over Troubled Water*; Beatles *Let It Be*; Presley *Onstage February 1970*; Rolling Stones *Get Your Ya-Yas Out*; Creedence Clearwater Revival *Cosmo's Factory*; Led Zeppelin *II*; Clapton *Eric Clapton*; *Free Fire and Water*; Deep Purple *In Rock*; Black Sabbath *Paranoid*; Soundtrack *Paint Your Wagon.*

4 Salvador Allende elected President of Chile.
6-12 Palestinian terrorists seize and blow up three airliners.
27 Jordan evicts the PLO ('Black September').
28 Ohio students burn their draft cards in protest against campus killings (May).

Fashion
Japan: launch of *An An.* Kenzo opens *Jungle Jap.* Henri Bendel of New York incorporates boutiques (Thea Porter, Sonia Rykiel) into large store. Corduroy jeans, skin-tight sweaters, bandanas in vogue.

1970 THE BEATLES	UK POP	CURRENT AFFAIRS	CULTURE
October 9 Lennon is 30.	4 Janis Joplin dies of drug overdose in Los Angeles. **45s:** Payne *Band of Gold*; Matthews Southern Comfort *Woodstock*; Dekker *You Can Get It If You Really Want*; Bobby Bloom *Montego Bay*; Poppy Family *Which Way You Goin' Billy?*; Black Sabbath *Paranoid*; Carpenters *Close To You*; Ross *Ain't No Mountain High Enough*; Aretha Franklin *Don't Play That Song*; Temptations *Ball of Confusion*. **LPs:** Simon and Garfunkel *Bridge Over Troubled Water*, Black Sabbath *Paranoid*; Moody Blues *A Question of Balance*; Rolling Stones *Get Your Ya-Yas Out*; Led Zeppelin III; Creedence Clearwater Revival *Cosmo's Factory*; Pink Floyd *Atom Heart Mother*; Melanie *Candles in the Rain*; Cocker *Mad Dogs and Englishmen*; Band *Stage Fright*; Deep Purple *In Rock*; Grateful Dead *Workingman's Dead*; Mott the Hoople *Mad Shadows*.	5 Anwar Sadat becomes president of Egypt.	**TV/Media** BBC: *Doomwatch* eco-disaster series. *A Man Called Ironside, Take Three Girls.*

November
27 US: *All Things Must Pass.*
30 UK: *All Things Must Pass.*

NME starts publishing the Top 30 albums.
45s: Matthews Southern Comfort *Woodstock*; Jimi Hendrix Experience *Voodoo Chile*; Dave Edmunds *I Hear You Knocking*; Clarence Carter *Patches*; Edwin Starr *War*; Don Fardon *Indian Reservation*; Christie *San Bernardino*; Melanie *Ruby Tuesday*; T. Rex *Ride a White Swan*; Presley *I've Lost You*; Rattles *The Witch.*
LPs: Led Zeppelin *Led Zeppelin III*; Various Motown *Chartbusters Vol. 4*; Black Sabbath *Paranoid*; Simon and Garfunkel *Bridge Over Troubled Water*; Melanie *Candles in the Rain*; Rolling Stones *Get Your Ya-Yas Out*; Pink Floyd *Atom Heart Mother*; Deep Purple *In Rock*; Young *After the Goldrush*; Dylan *New Morning.*

20 150,000 drowned by tidal wave in East Pakistan.
20 Feminists disrupt Miss World contest in London.
26 More working days lost through strikes in UK than any year since 1926.
27 Gay Liberation Front holds first demonstration in London.

Visual arts
Matisse exhibition in Paris.
Velázquez's *Portrait of Juan de Pareja* sold at Christie's for 5.5m dollars.
Performance Art. Fashion Aesthetic.
Conceptual Art now dominant.
d. Mark Rothko.

1970 THE BEATLES	UK POP	CURRENT AFFAIRS	CULTURE
December 8 Lennon interviewed at length by *Rolling Stone*'s Jann Wenner. 11 UK/US: *Plastic Ono Band*. 31 McCartney institutes proceedings in High Court to dissolve The Beatles' partnership. Official end of The Beatles' career together.	Jim Morrison leaves The Doors. (Dies of drug overdose July 1971.) 6 Rolling Stones' Altamont documentary *Gimme Shelter*. **45s:** Edmunds *I Hear You Knocking*; Jimi Hendrix Experience *Voodoo Chile*; Neil Diamond *Cracklin' Rosie*; T. Rex *Ride a White Swan*; Glen Campbell *It's Only Make Believe*, McGuiness–Flint *When I'm Dead and Gone*; Gilbert O'Sullivan *Nothing Rhymed*. **LPs:** Led Zeppelin *Led Zeppelin III*; Various *Motown Chartbusters Vol. 4*; Simon and Garfunkel *Bridge Over Troubled Water*; Dylan *New Morning*; Andy Williams *Greatest Hits*; Emerson, Lake, and Palmer *ELP*; Deep Purple *In Rock*; Santana *Abraxas*; Taylor *Sweet Baby James*; Pink Floyd *Atom Heart Mother*, Young *After the Goldrush*; Melanie *Candles in the Rain*; Young *After the Goldrush*; Harrison *All Things Must Pass*.	**16–20** Anti-Communist riots in Gdansk. **17** *Pravda* attacks Solzhenitsyn. **20** Polish uprising suppressed. Gomulka resigns; replaced by Gierek.	**Science** First use of atom-powered heart pacemakers. Gene synthesis. Intel patents the microprocessor. d. Hans Kronberger.

RECOMMENDED FURTHER READING

Despite its hostile portrait of McCartney, Philip Norman's *Shout!* remains the sharpest account of The Beatles' career. For balance, supplement it with Barry Miles's definitive *Paul McCartney: Many Years From Now*, one of the best books on The Beatles and full of prime McCartney reminiscences. Hunter Davies's 1968 study is racily informative and contains valuable reportage on The Beatles' writing methods. The two-volume biography of Lennon by Ray Coleman is reliably complete, if a little dogged. Pete Shotton's book is a revealingly affectionate portrait of his boyhood friend and an hilarious antidote to Coleman's solemnity, while Lennon's interviews with *Rolling Stone* (Wenner) and *Playboy* (Sheff and Golson) afford vital glimpses into his turbulent mind. A wealth of reminiscences about the group can be found in Spencer Leigh's *Speaking Words Of Wisdom*. For The Beatles in 1967, see Derek Taylor's warm and evocative *It Was Twenty Years Ago Today*.

Mark Lewisohn's *The Complete Beatles Recording Sessions* is an indispensable day-by-day account of the making of The Beatles' records. For those uninterested in technical details, his *The Complete Beatles Chronicle* combines the gist of *Recording Sessions* with the data on their performing career previously published in his *The Beatles Live!* (1986), thereby qualifying it as the standard Beatles reference book.

SELECT BIBLIOGRAPHY

The Beatles

The Beatles. *The Beatles Anthology*. Cassell, 2000.

–. *The Beatles Complete*. (Records transcribed by Tetsuya Fujita, Yuji Hagino, Hajime Kubo, and Goro Sato.) Hal Leonard, 1993.

Babiuk, Andy. *Beatles Gear: All The Fab Four's Instruments, From Stage To Studio*. Backbeat, 2001.

Berkenstadt, Jim and Belmo. *Black Market Beatles*. Collector's Guide, 1996.

Best, Pete and Patrick Doncaster. *Beatle! The Pete Best Story*. Plexus, 1985.

Braun, Michael. *Love Me Do: The Beatles' Progress*. Penguin, 1964.

Bresler, Fenton. *Who Killed John Lennon?* St Martin's, 1989.

Brown, Peter and Steven Gaines. *The Love You Make: An Insider's Story of The Beatles*. Macmillan, 1983.

Campbell, Colin and Allan Murphy. *Things We Said Today: The Complete Lyrics and a Concordance to The Beatles' Songs 1962–1970*. Pierian, 1980.

Carr, Roy and Tony Tyler. *The Beatles: An Illustrated Record*. Triune, 1978.

Coleman, Ray. *John Winston Lennon. Volume 1: 1940–1966*. Sidgwick & Jackson, 1984.

– *John Ono Lennon. Volume 2: 1967–1980*. Sidgwick & Jackson, 1984.

Cooke, Deryck. 'The Lennon–McCartney songs.' *The Listener*, 1st February 1968.

Davies, Hunter. *The Beatles*. Cape, 1985. 2nd edition.

DeWitt, Howard. *Paul McCartney: From Liverpool To Let It Be*. Horizon, 1992.

DiLello, Richard. *The Longest Cocktail Party: An Insider's View of The Beatles*. Pierian, 1983.

Dowlding, William J. *Beatlesongs*. Fireside, 1989.

Epstein, Brian with Derek Taylor. *A Cellarful of Noise*. Souvenir, 1964.

Evans, Mike. *The Art of The Beatles*. Anthony Blond, 1984.

Gambaccini, Paul. *Paul McCartney in His Own Words*. Flash, 1976.

Giuliano, Geoffrey. *Dark Horse: The Secret Life of George Harrison*. Bloomsbury, 1989.

– *Blackbird: The Unauthorised Biography of Paul McCartney*. Smith Gryphon, 1991.

Goldman, Albert. *The Lives of John Lennon*. Morrow, 1988.

Harrison, George with Derek Taylor. *I, Me, Mine*. Simon & Schuster, 1980.

Harry, Bill. *Mersey Beat: The Beginnings of The Beatles*. Omnibus, 1977.

– *The Beatles Who's Who*. Aurum, 1982.

Hertsgaard, Mark. *A Day in the Life: The Music and Artistry of The Beatles*. Delacorte, 1995.

Inglis, Ian (ed.). *The Beatles, Popular Music, and Society*. Palgrave Macmillan, 2000.

Kelly, Michael Bryan. *The Beatle Myth: The British Invasion of American Popular Music, 1956–1969*. McFarland, 1991.

Leigh, Spencer. *Speaking Words of Wisdom: Reflections on The Beatles*. Cavern City Tours, 1991.

Lennon, Cynthia. *A Twist of Lennon*. Allen, 1978.

Lennon, John. 'A Very Open Letter to John Hoyland from John Lennon.' *Black Dwarf*, January 10th 1969.

– *Skywriting by Word of Mouth*. Harper & Row, 1986.

Lewisohn, Mark. *The Complete Beatles Recording Sessions*. Hamlyn/EMI, 1988.
– *The Complete Beatles Chronicle*. Pyramid, 1992.
Martin, George with Jeremy Hornsby. *All You Needs Is Ears*. St Martin, 1979.
Martin, George with William Pearson. *Summer of Love: The Making of Sgt. Pepper*. Macmillan, 1994.
McCabe, Peter and Schonfield, Robert D. *Apple to the Core: The Unmaking of The Beatles*. Brian & O'Keefe, 1972.
McKeen, William. *The Beatles: A Bio-Bibliography*. Greenwood, 1989.
Mellers, Wilfrid. *Twilight of the Gods: The Beatles in Retrospect*. Faber, 1973.
Miles, Barry. *Paul McCartney: Many Years From Now*. Secker & Warburg, 1997.
Neises, Charles P. *The Beatles Reader: A Selection of Contemporary Views, News, and Reviews of The Beatles in Their Heyday*. Pierian, 1984.
Norman, Philip. *Shout! The Beatles in Their Generation*. Elm Tree, 1982.
O'Grady, Terence P. *The Beatles: A Musical Evolution*. Twayne, 1983.
Pedler, Dominic. *The Songwriting Secrets of The Beatles*. Omnibus, 2002.
Riley, Tim. *Tell Me Why: A Beatles Commentary*. Bodley Head, 1988.
Robertson, John. *The Art and Music of John Lennon*. Omnibus, 1990.
Rorem, Ned. 'The music of The Beatles.' *New York Review of Books*, 18th January 1968.
Russell, Jeff. *The Beatles: Album File and Complete Discography*. Blandford, 1989.
Salewicz, Chris. *McCartney*. St Martin's Press, 1986.
Sheff, David. and G. Barry Golson *The Playboy Interviews with John Lennon and Yoko Ono*. Playboy Press, 1981.
Shotton, Pete with Nicholas Schaffner. *John Lennon in My Life*. Coronet, 1984.
Somach, Denny and Kathleen Somach. *Ticket to Ride*. Macdonald, 1989.
Sulpy, Doug. *Drugs, Divorce, and a Slipping Image: The Unauthorized Story of the Beatles' 'Get Back' Sessions*. The 910, 1994.
Taylor, Alistair. *Yesterday: The Beatles Remembered*. Sidgwick & Jackson, 1988.
Taylor, Derek. *It Was Twenty Years Ago Today*. Bantam, 1987.
Terry, Carol. *Here, There, and Everywhere: The Beatles First International Bibliography*. Pierian, 1990.
Turner, Steve. *A Hard Day's Write*. Little, Brown, 1994.
Wenner, Jann. *Lennon Remembers: The Rolling Stone Interviews*. Penguin, 1973.
Wiener, Jon. *Come Together: John Lennon in His Time*. Faber, 1984.

The Sixties

Aitken, Jonathan. *The Young Meteors*. Secker & Warburg, 1967.
Allsop, Kenneth. *The Angry Decade: A Survey of the Cultural Revolt of the Nineteen-Fifties*. Goodchild, 1958.
Alpert, Richard. *Be Here Now*. Lama Foundation, 1971.
Anthony, Gene. *The Summer of Love*. Celestial Books, 1980.
Bailey, David. *Goodbye Baby and Amen: A Saraband for the Sixties*. Collins, 1969.
Barker, Paul (ed.). *Arts in Society*. Fontana, 1977.
Beer, Samuel H. *Britain Against Itself: The Political Contradictions of Collectivism*. Faber, 1982.
Booker, Christopher. *The Neophiliacs: A Study of the Revolution in English Life in the Fifties and Sixties*. Collins, 1969.
Brustein, Robert. *Revolution as Theatre*. Liveright, 1971.
Bugliosi, Vincent and Curt Gentry. *The Manson Murders: An Investigation into Motive*. Bodley Head, 1974.
Carr, Gordon. *The Angry Brigade*. Gollancz, 1975.

Caute, David. *Sixty-Eight; The Year of the Barricades*. Hamilton, 1988.

Cleaver, Eldridge. *Soul on Ice*. Cape, 1969.

Cook, Bruce. *The Beat Generation*. Scribner's, 1971.

Cook, Fred J. *The Nightmare Decade*. Random House, 1971.

Cooper, David (ed.). *The Dialectics of Liberation*. Penguin, 1968.

Crouch, Colin. *The Students' Revolt*. Bodley Head, 1970.

Crow, Thomas. *The Rise of the Sixties. American and European Art in the Era of Dissent: 1955–69*. Everyman Art Library, 1996.

Dickstein, Morris. *Gates of Eden: American Culture in the Sixties*. Basic, 1977.

Eisen, Jonathan (ed.). *The Age of Rock*. Random House, 1969.

– *The Age of Rock, Volume Two*. Random House, 1970.

Fisera, Vladimir (ed.). *Writing on the Wall: May 1968 – A Documentary Anthology*. Allison & Busby, 1978.

Fong-Torres, Ben (ed.). *The Rolling Stone Rock 'n' Roll Reader*. Bantam, 1974.

George, Nelson. *Where Did Our Love Go? The Rise and Fall of the Motown Sound*. St Martin's Press, 1987.

Gleason, Ralph J. *The Jefferson Airplane and the San Francisco Sound*. Ballantine, 1969.

Glessing, Robert J. *The Underground Press in America*. Indiana University Press, 1971.

Goldie, Grace Wyndham. *Facing the Nation: Television and Politics 1936–1976*. Bodley Head, 1977.

Goodman, Paul. *New Reformation*. Random House, 1970.

Green, Jonathon. *Days In The Life: Voices from the English Underground 1961–1971*. Heinemann, 1988.

Greenland, Colin. *The Entropy Exhibition: Michael Moorcock and the British New Wave in Science Fiction*. Routledge & Kegan Paul, 1983.

Greer, Germaine. *The Female Eunuch*. MacGibbon & Kee, 1970.

Guralnick, Peter. *Sweet Soul Music: Rhythm and Blues and the Southern Dream of Freedom*. Harper & Row, 1986.

Henri, Adrian. *Environments and Happenings*. Thames & Hudson, 1974.

Hewison, Robert. *Too Much: Art and Society in the Sixties, 1960–75*. Methuen, 1986.

Hoffman, Nicholas von. *We Are the People Our Parents Warned Us Against*. Quadrangle, 1968.

Hoffmann, Abbie. *Revolution for the Hell of It*. Dial, 1968.

– *Woodstock Nation*. Vintage, 1969.

Hollingshead, Michael. *The Man Who Turned On The World*. Blond & Briggs, 1973.

Holloway, David (ed.). *The Sixties: A Chronicle of a Decade*. Simon & Schuster, 1992.

Huxley, Aldous. *The Doors of Perception*. Chatto, 1954.

Jackson, George. *Soledad Brother*. Penguin, 1971.

Jacobs, Paul and Saul Landau (ed.). *The New Radicals*. Penguin, 1967.

Laing, R. D. *The Politics of Experience and The Bird of Paradise*. Penguin, 1966.

Leary, Timothy. *The Politics of Ecstasy*. Paladin, 1970.

Leary, Timothy, Ralph Metzner, and Richard Alpert. *The Psychedelic Experience*. University Books, 1964.

Leech, Kenneth. *Youthquake: The Growth of a Counter-Culture Through Two Decades*. Sheldon, 1973.

Lewis, Roger. *Outlaws of America: the Underground Press and its Context*. Pelican, 1972.

Lippard, Lucy. *Pop Art*. Thames & Hudson, 1970.

Mailer, Norman. *Armies of the Night*. Penguin, 1968.

– *Miami and the Siege of Chicago*. Penguin, 1969.

Mairowitz, David Zane. *The Radical Soap Opera*. Wildwood, 1974.

Malcolm X. *The Autobiography of Malcolm X*. Penguin, 1968.

Marcus, Greil. *Mystery Train: Images of America in Rock 'n' Roll Music*. Dutton, 1982.

Marowitz, Charles. *Confessions of a Counterfeit Critic: A London Theatre Notebook 1958–1971*. Methuen, 1973.

McLuhan, Marshall. *Understanding Media*. Routledge & Kegan Paul, 1964.

Melly, George. *Revolt into Style*. Allen Lane, 1970.

Mitford, Jessica. *The Trial of Dr Spock*. Macdonald, 1969.

Morgan, Robin (ed.). *Sisterhood is Powerful*. Vintage, 1970.

Neville, Richard. *Play Power*. Paladin, 1971.

– *Hippie Hippie Shake: the dreams, the trips, the trials, the love-ins, the screw ups . . . the Sixties*. Bloomsbury, 1995.

Nuttall, Jeff. *Bomb Culture*. MacGibbon & Kee, 1968.

Palmer, Tony. *The Trials of OZ*. Blond & Briggs, 1971.

Perry, Helen. *The Human Be-In*. Allen Lane, 1968.

Poirier, Richard. *The Performing Self*. Oxford University Press, 1971.

Raskin, Jonah. *For The Hell Of It: The Life and Times of Abbie Hoffman*. University of California, 1995.

Reich, Charles. *The Greening of America*. Random House, 1970.

Roszak, Theodore. *The Making of a Counter-Culture*. Faber, 1970.

Rubin, Jerry. *Do It!* Simon & Schuster, 1970.

Sanders, Ed. *Trips: Rock Life in the Sixties*. Scribner's, 1973.

Savage, Jon. *The Kinks: The Official Biography*. Faber & Faber, 1984.

Seale, Bobby. *Seize the Time: The Story of the Black Panther Party and Huey P. Newton*. Hutchinson, 1970.

Searle, John. *The Campus War*. Penguin, 1969.

Shea, Robert and Robert Anton Wilson. *Illuminatus*. Dell, 1975. 3 volumes.

Stanshill, Peter and David Mairowitz. *BAMN (By Any Means Necessary): Outlaw Manifestos and Ephemera 1965–1970*. Penguin, 1971.

Stevens, Jay. *Storming Heaven: LSD and the American Dream*. Heinemann, 1988.

Sutherland, John. *Offensive Literature: Decensorship in Britain 1960–1982*. Junction, 1982.

Taylor, Derek. *As Time Goes By: Living in the Sixties*. Davis-Poynter, 1973.

Tyler, Tony. *I Hate Rock-and-Roll*. Vermilion, 1984.

Weeks, Jeffrey. *Sex, Politics, and Society*. Longmans, 1981.

Wheen, Francis. *The Sixties: A Fresh Look at the Decade of Change*. Century, 1982.

Widgery, Charles. *The Left in Britain, 1956–1968*. Penguin, 1976.

Willis, Paul E. *Profane Culture*. Routledge & Kegan Paul, 1978.

GLOSSARY

A capella. Unaccompanied. Lit. 'chapel-style', meaning 'voices only'.

Accelerando. Gradually increasing in speed (tempo). The opposite of *ritardando*.

Aeolian. See Modes.

ADT. Artificial double-tracking. Now standard in all studios, ADT was developed by EMI engineer Ken Townsend. It consists of taking the signal from the sync head of the multitrack, recording it to a variably-oscillated loop, and sending it back to the multitrack about a fifth of a second out of phase. (Known as 'flanging' after a joke between George Martin and John Lennon. See Lewisohn, *Sessions*, p. 70.)

Amp. Amplifier. Unit for increasing current, voltage, or output. The basic technical ingredient in rock-and-roll music.

Arpeggio. The notes of a chord played in succession as a fan-like spread rather than as single sound, as if on a harp. (Italian *arpeggiare* = to play the harp.)

Augmented (chord). Chord in which the fifth (or seventh, or ninth, etc.) is raised (augmented) by a semitone.

Back beats. In pop, the stressed second and fourth beats of a bar in common time.

Backline. A pop act's own amps, speaker-amps, and speakers. (Sometimes the term is used to include the road support crew.) See PA.

Bar. The basic metrical unit, divided into beats. Each bar is separated from the next by a bar line. In America, the bar line is called a bar, and a bar is called a measure.

Barrelhouse. Bar-room style. In Twenties Texas, a bar consisted of a plank nailed across two barrels.

Bass-drum. Largest drum in the pop/jazz drum-kit, played with a pedal (right foot). In modern dance music known as the 'kick'.

Beat music. Name applied by the UK press to the group-dominated pop of the mid-Sixties.

Bitonal. Music employing two keys at once.

Block harmony. Harmony in three or more parts of parallel motion without anticipations or retardations.

Boogiewoogie. Early blues piano style in which the left hand continuously plays a rising and falling ('rolling') figure in quavers. Outstanding boogiewoogie pianists were Jimmy Yancey, Meade Lux Lewis, Albert Ammons, and Pete Johnson.

Bouncing down. Mixing process in which the contents of two tracks are recorded as a mix of both to a third in order to clear the original tracks for further recording. (The more channels/tracks on a mixing desk, the less need for bouncing down.)

Bridge. A transitional passage between verse and chorus, 'bridging' the gap between their keys if these are different. Rarely longer than four bars. See also Song structure.

Cadence. Melodic or harmonic progression associated with the ending of a phrase, section, or composition.

Call-and-response. Repeated exchanges between soloist(s) and a choir or group, often exhortatory and usually climactic. With its origins in work-song and field hollers, call-and-response is a standard feature of gospel music and, as such, entered pop through doo-wop and R&B. Distantly related to 'responses' in Anglican church music.

Capo, capoed. *Capotasto* or *capodastro*. Lit. 'Head of the touch.' Originally, the frets of a stringed instrument. In pop, a capo is a movable *barre* used to raise the tuning of a guitar by semitonal increments. It is held in place across the strings by an elasticated strap around the neck of the instrument ('capoed').

Celesta A 19th-century keyboard with hammers which strike steel plates placed over wooden resonators, producing an ethereal sound (as in Tchaikovsky's *Dance of the Sugar Plum Fairy*).

Cha-cha. A mambo, featuring a prominent guiro part, which became a staple ingredient of ballroom dancing in the late Fifties.

Changes. Successions, or 'sequences', of chords.

Chart. Session slang for a written arrangement.

Chocalho. Tubular wooden shaker filled with small stones, used in Latin music.

Chord. The simultaneous sounding of at least three notes. See also Changes.

Chorus. In pop, the section of the song including the title phrase and the main musical 'hook'. While this rule is rarely broken in modern pop, the music of the Sixties was much freer in form and there are many exceptions in The Beatles' repertoire. The discipline of the two-minute track sometimes led Lennon and McCartney to collapse verse and chorus into a 'verse/chorus', or to telescope the chorus into a single line. In America, influenced by jazz usage, the verse is called the chorus, the chorus being referred to as the refrain.

Chorusing. Slightly desynchronised multiplication of a signal on one track, thereby producing a 'chorused' sound. Usually obtained with a special effect unit.

Chromatic. Chromatic notes are those not included in the diatonic scale. The chromatic scale consists of twelve successive semitones (sharps ascending, flats descending).

Claves. A pair of rounded hardwood sticks struck together in Latin music.

Clavichord. Early keyboard instrument in which the strings are fretted by brass wedges.

Clean up (track). During pop recording, drop-ins (or punch-ins) are used to correct mistakes – a process during which the producer or engineer must simultaneously encourage the performer and make sure that he or she matches the quality of the existing recording as precisely as possible. This allows no time for the elimination of small cueing errors, overhanging notes, and general off-mike noises, which have to be 'cleaned up' (erased) during interludes set aside for bouncing down.

Click-track. A track set aside for the recording of a regular beat intended as a guide for voices or instruments to be added subsequently. The studio equivalent of a metronome, the click-track is usually generated from a drum-machine (nowadays controlled by a sequencer) and is generally used where a recording is to be built up in layers from scratch rather than added to an already-recorded rhythm track. Also called a clock-track.

Close harmony. Harmony in which the notes of the chords lie close together.

Coda. A closing section, following the final chorus, sometimes taking the form of a fade-out. Most fade-outs consist of repetitions of the chorus. See Song structure.

Comping. To ac*compan*y with simple rhythmic chording.

Compression. Reduction of the overall dynamics generated by a voice or instrument. Originally a recording procedure, it became (as 'compressors') part of the range of signal-distortion effects available for live amplified performance.

Conga. Tall, narrow, barrel-shaped, low-toned drum used in Latin music. Used in pairs.

Country and Western. Folk music of the

white rural South and mid-West of America.

Cover. *vb.* To record a song previously recorded by another artist. Hence 'cover version'.

Crash cymbal. Cymbal with extra-deep or extra-bright timbre and long decay used for accents. In a standard drum-kit, placed midway between the hi-hat and the ride cymbal.

Damper, damping. A unit or process by which a signal is attentuated (reduced in force).

Delay. Artificial echo(es) of an original signal, controllable in spacing and duration via a delay unit or time processor. Very short delays are used in chorusing units.

Demo. Demonstration recording. A rough sketch of a final recording, done either on a domestic portastudio or in a commercial demo studio.

DI. See Direct injection.

Diatonic. The major and minor scales in the Western classical system, consisting of fixed stepwise relationships of tones and semitones arranged in octaves.

Dilruba Long-necked Indian instrument with three or four main strings and some sympathetic strings, played with a bow.

Diminished (chord). Chord in which the fifth (or seventh, or ninth, etc.) is reduced (diminished) by a semitone.

Direct injection, DI-ing. Recording an electric instrument by plugging it directly into the mixing desk rather than miking it through a speaker.

Distortion unit. All amplification entails distortion of the acoustic signal, but in pop distortion is often maximised by overloading the signal so as to achieve varieties of linear (frequency) and non-linear (overtone) distortion. There are scores of pedal-operated distortion units, each devoted to a particular effect. In The Beatles' day, the main distortion units were the fuzz-box and the wah-wah.

Dominant. The fifth degree of the diatonic scale; the triad on the fifth (V) degree.

Doo-wop. *A capella* street-corner harmony style developed in New York around 1950. With instrumental backing, doo-wop became commercial during the Fifties with records by acts like The Clovers ('Your Cash Ain't Nothin' But Trash', 'Love Potion No. 9'), The Chords ('Sh-boom'), The Flamingos ('I Only Have Eyes For You'), The Penguins ('Earth Angel'), The Platters ('Only You', 'The Great Pretender', 'Smoke Gets In Your Eyes', 'Harbour Lights'), The Marcels ('Blue Moon'), Gene Chandler ('Duke of Earl'), and The Drifters *(passim)*.

Dorian. See Modes.

Double-track ('track'). To duplicate an already recorded performance on another channel (track). The effect depends on the natural differences between each track, although these must be minimised by the performer. Often singers 'track' (double-track) their voices to hide what they believe to be weaknesses.

Drone. Sustained bass note. Ubiquitous in synthesiser music (particularly film and TV soundtracks). See also Pedal.

Dropping-in. To switch from playback to record without stopping the tape. Allows a performer to cue in to (a) repair a mistake, (b) continue recording at a point where an earlier take broke down, or (c) 'track' an existing part recorded on another channel. See also Punch-in.

Dropping-out. The opposite of dropping-in.

Drop-out. Short hiatus on a magnetic tape, due either to dirt on the recording head, 'clipping' (amp overloading), or incompetent tape-operation.

Dry. Recorded or mixed with little or no echo or reverb. (Opposite of 'wet').

Engineer. Head of the technical side of recording and first lieutenant to the producer (q.v.). If the producer leans more to the musical side (i.e., plays an instrument and writes arrangements), an engineer must translate his creative requests into technical realities. Many producers are ex-engineers and like to run their sessions 'hands on', controlling all aspects of the mixing desk. In this case the engineer becomes a *de facto* tape-op (q.v.).

EQ. Equalise. An equaliser is a unit which controls the frequency range of an amplifier. Since pop/rock mixing largely depends on balancing sounds against each other by isolating their frequencies, 'EQ-ing' is synonymous with final mixing or balancing.

Fader. Slide control on a mixing desk for adjusting volume.

Feedback. The return of a fraction of the output signal from one stage of a circuit or amplifier to the input of the same or of a preceding stage. Uncontrolled, this consists of a piercing howl. In the hands of an expert, it can be the basis of a sound or style.

Filter, filtering. A unit or process by which some frequency-responses or timbres of a signal are weakened or cut off.

Flam. Two sticks striking a drum at almost the same instant, yet heard separately.

Flanger, flanging. A unit or process by which a signal is processed via two different conveyance routes, so putting the 'shadow' signal slightly out of time and producing phase modulation ('phasing'). Commonly achieved by using a tape-loop. (See also ADT.)

Full close. A perfect cadence, i.e., the chord of the dominant followed by that of the tonic.

Gate, gate pulse. An electrical signal used to trigger or control the passage of other signals in a circuit. Commonly a control current used for 'limiting' snare sounds (switching in when triggered by the signal from the snare itself). Hence a 'gated' snare.

Gig. An engagement for a musical act (or the place at which the performance takes place). The origin of this word, first bandied about by jazz bands in the Twenties, is unknown, although it may derive from a 19th-century usage meaning 'fun (a bit of)'.

Glissando. Scalar runs made by dragging the finger across adjacent notes or by sliding up or down an uncalibrated instrument. (Fake Italian from French *glisser* = to slide.)

Glockenspiel. Instrument consisting of small bells or metal bars struck with a hammer, or by levers manipulated from a keyboard. (German = 'bell play'.)

Grace-notes. Ornaments to the melody, indicated on a score in small notation.

Groove. The rhythmic 'feel' of a piece of music. Originally a soul music term, the groove became a focus for white pop and rock during the late Seventies with the introduction of drum machines on which it was possible to programme rhythm cycles in fine detail. High-end sequencers offer algorithmic modules in which 'grooves' (essentially intuitive constructions) may be logically analysed and varied in unpredictable ways.

Guiro. Wooden pipe or gourd with a serrated surface, rubbed with a stick to produce a rhythmical rasping sound. (Latin-American.)

Harmonium. A domestic portable reed-organ, operated by bellows worked by treadles.

Hi-hat. Pair of facing horizontal cymbals, pedal-operated by the left foot and played closed, half-closed, or open, with a drum stick (right hand).

Home triad. Triad on the tonic. The chord on the key-note of a song.

Hook. Sixties term for a feature of a song, arrangement, or production which catches the attention, remains in the mind, and is hence liable to be hummed or whistled.

Interval. The 'distance' (difference in pitch) between two notes.

Latin. Latin-American. Musical styles from South America (chiefly Brazil) or the Spanish Caribbean (Cuba, Puerto Rico).

Leakage. Sounds recorded at the same time on different channels which, whether through neglect or design, are audible on tracks other than their own.

Legato. With the notes smoothly linked. (Italian = tied.) Opposite of *staccato*.

Leslie cabinet. Rotating speaker system employing the Döppler Effect. See also [60].

Limiter, limiting. A unit or process by which the peaks of a signal are flattened, producing a compacted sound. See also Compression.

Loop, tape-loop. A tape edited back onto itself in a circle and played endlessly, creating a looping signal.

Jew's harp. Small iron frame with metal vibrating strip, played with one end in the mouth while twanging the vibrating strip and shaping the mouth to change the harmonics.

Maraca. Latin percussion instrument made from the dried shell of a gourd with beans or beads inside to produce a rattling sound. Introduced to pop by Mick Jagger.

Master. The final two-track stereo mix, produced from the multitrack for commercial release in the form of a record, tape, or disc. In recent years, it has become the custom for several alternative masters, or 'remixes', to be issued from one multitrack tape.

Melisma. In singing, the ornamental (or functional) prolongation of one syllable over a number of notes. A standard feature of gospel music, *ad libitum* ornamental melismatic singing entered pop in the Sixties mainly through the records of Aretha Franklin, a mistress of the idiom. A more mannered, florid style was introduced in the Seventies by Chaka Khan. Modern black singing (e.g., Whitney Houston) is incessantly melismatic.

Mellotron. Cabinet containing a bank of tape-loops of wind, string, and brass tones played by a keyboard, each key triggering a tape of one pre-recorded note in a particular timbre. Invented by a Birmingham firm in 1963, it was used by local group The Moody Blues and later, and most famously, by King Crimson on the title track of their album *In the Court of the Crimson King*. John Lennon claimed to own the first Mellotron ever sold.

Middle eight. Jazz term, referring to the contrasting third quarter of a thirty-two bar chorus. In pop, it refers to a section, usually in the relative major or minor key, contrasting with the verse–bridge––chorus structure. The introductions to many pop songs consist of instrumental versions of their middle eights. The Beatles' middle sections became more irregular as they progressed, rarely consisting of the orthodox eight bars. See also Song structure.

MIDI. Musical Instrument Digital Interface. Studio system for 'chaining' (linking) instruments, sequencers, and effects units.

Mix. (1) *n*. The balance of sounds recorded on a multitrack at any stage of the recording. The 'final mix' is the balance as chosen for recording to the two-track. (See Master.) (2) *vb*. The process of balancing existing signals or of recording two tracks together onto a spare track in such a way as to combine their signals into a third one. See also Bouncing down.

Mixolydian. See Modes.

Modes. Scales on the natural notes, used in Gregorian chant, folk music, and some jazz. There are seven: the Ionian (tonic C; the C major scale), the Dorian (tonic D), Phrygian (tonic E), Lydian (tonic F), Mixolydian (tonic G), Aeolian (tonic A; the natural minor scale), and the rare Locrian (tonic B). Since the differences between the modes is not limited to pitch but determined by the order in which their tones and semitones fall, they are transposable (for example, 'in' C, the Dorian produces flat E and B, while the Lydian gives F sharp). Many folk-tunes are modal, e.g., 'Scarborough Fair' (Dorian). The Mixolydian's bluesy tint accounts for its appeal to Lennon.

Motivic. Of or pertaining to a musical motive or *motif*.

Multitrack. (1) The main tape-deck in a recording studio, linked to a mixing desk and providing anything from four to sixty-four channels (tracks) of recordable sound. (2) The multitrack tape from which the two-track stereo 'master' (q.v.) is produced.

Obbligato. A fundamental (obligatory) instrumental part, usually continuous and of an unusual or otherwise prominent nature. The opposite of an *ad libitum* or optional part.

Octave. Intervals between notes of the same name but twice the frequency, arranged at distances of eight notes in the diatonic scale.

Off-beats. Usually synonymous with 'back beats'; sometimes refers to the quavers between the 'on' (1 and 3) and the 'off' (2 and 4) beats in a bar of 4/4.

Oscillation. Periodic wave movement measured in frequency (cycles per second).

Overdubbing. To add sounds to sounds already recorded. See also Track.

PA. Public Address; power amplification. Sound system used for live performances, consisting of a network of mikes and DI boxes connected by multicore cables to an 'out-front' mixing desk. The signals from an act's backline (q.v.) are mixed, processed, and either 'folded back' to them through on-stage monitors, or sent via 'power amplifiers' to the main banks of loudspeakers.

Pad. Studio term for a track of sustained chords (played on an organ or organ-like instrument, such as a synthesiser) used to establish the harmonic lay-out of a song at an early stage of recording. Thereafter the pad is usually erased to make way for an arrangement structured around the gaps and accents in a guide vocal. (Eg., [78].)

Pakavaj. Loglike double-headed drum used in North Indian music. Equivalent of South Indian *mridangam*.

Pedal, pedal point. A bass note sustained

below changing harmonies. Refers to the pedals used in church organs.

Pentatonic. Five-note scale often found in folk music and in Oriental classical music. (Eg., [19], [67], [188].)

Perfect pitch. The ability to identify pitches by ear alone. Also called absolute hearing.

Picardy third (Tierce de Picardie). Major third used to finish a piece otherwise in a minor key, thereby giving the impression of an optimistic, resolute, or 'solved' conclusion.

Polychord. Two or more chords sounded simultaneously. A local instance of polytonality (music using more than one key at once).

Popping. One of several sorts of 'proximity effect' incurred by speaking or singing too close to a microphone.

Press roll (closed roll). A fast double-beat (daddy-mammy) roll on the snare.

Producer. The recording studio's equivalent of a film director (incorporating aspects of a film producer). In general, the producer oversees sessions, supervising the hiring of equipment and outside players, and seeing that this process stays more or less within its allotted time and budget. In detail, he or she controls the processes of arranging and recording, the planning of the track-sheets, the selection and modification of the sounds, and the main stages of the mixing. Some producers rely on their engineers to take care of the technical side of studio work, concentrating on the music. As the link between the artist's conception and its realisation, much of a good producer's skill is psychological.

Punch-in. A brief, inch-perfect version of dropping-in (q.v.), followed almost instantly by a 'punch-out' – a hazardous procedure, risking the erasure of something on tape which one wishes to keep. Used for correcting ('patching') tiny mistakes in an otherwise flawless performance.

Push, pushed beat. A note or accent anticipating the first beat of the bar by a quaver or semiquaver. A form of syncopation common in R&B, soul, and disco music.

R&B. Rhythm-and-blues. Strictly speaking, a Forties fusion of swing jazz and novelty-blues introduced by the 'jump bands' of Louis Jordan ('G.I. Jive', 'Reet Petite', etc.), Jimmy Forrest ('Night Train'), Earl Bostic ('Flamingo', 'Temptation'), Jack McVea ('Open the Door, Richard'), Bill Doggett ('Honky Tonk'), etc. Honking tenor sax, lead electric guitar, and racy vocals came to the fore around 1950. Cross-bred with country-and-western and rockabilly for white consumption, R&B turned into rock-and-roll around 1955. Thereafter the term was used increasingly loosely.

Reverb. Reflective sound; room ambience. A generalised form of echo. These days there are scores of different effects units each devoted to producing many varieties of reverb.

Ride cymbal. Main drum-kit cymbal, sharing time-keeping function with the hi-hat. Played with the right hand, sometimes on the bell (central area with ringing tone).

Riff. Simple phrase repeated with a strong or syncopated rhythm, usually played in unison, and often following blues changes.

Rim-shot. Snare-drum stroke in which the stick hits the rim of the drum (or the rim and the head at the same time).

Ritard, ritardando. (Italian *ritardare* = to slow down.) A gradual reduction of speed.

Sampler. Device for recording digital 'samples' of sounds for editing into tones or loops to be played back by a synthesiser.

Santoor. Arab-Persian dulcimer also played in Hindustani classical music.

Sarod. North Indian lute of Persian origin with four strings and up to a dozen sympathetic strings.

Saturation. In-put distortion due to over-amplification (setting the level too high for the amp).

Scalar. Of a scale.

Scale. A stepwise series of ascending or descending notes from which the key or mode of a piece of music may be established. (From Italian *scala* = staircase.)

Segue. (Italian = follows.) Uninterrupted transition from one piece of music or record to another.

Sequencer. Hardware unit or computer software programme which can record the characteristics of a musical performance played to it, via MIDI, from an instrument. Nowadays, most multitrack recordings are controlled, edited, and to a great extent generated by sequencers.

Shaker. Any shaken percussion instrument.

Shake. Trill (17th century).

Shehnai. Harsh-sounding Moslem/Hindu oboe, as played by Bismillah Khan.

Shuffle, shuffle-beat. Bipartite division of the blues-rock metre triplet style (notated as a dotted quaver tied to a semiquaver).

Sitar. Long-necked, guitar-like Indian instrument with movable frets, three to seven strings, and ten or more sympathetic strings which the player plucks.

Ska. Sixties fusion of *mento* (Jamaican calypso) and R&B (with particular reference to Fats Domino). Precursor of reggae.

Skiffle. A light blend of R&B, folk, and trad jazz which, during the Fifties, served as a poor man's rock-and-roll for those who couldn't afford the proper instruments and amps. Originally a synonym for the American 'jug band' or 'washboard rhythm' style.

Snare drum. Side drum. Small flat drum with skein of wires (the 'snare') stretched under the lower resonance skin. Played mainly with the left-hand drum-stick in off beats.

Song structure. The classic pop song structure is: introduction–verse–bridge–chorus–verse–bridge–chorus–middle eight–instrumental verse–middle eight–verse–bridge–chorus–coda. However, variations on this pattern, particularly during the Sixties, have been equally prevalent. A common departure is to begin, ear-catchingly, with the chorus before jumping back to the verse. (American musicians, following jazz usage, call the verse the chorus, and the chorus the refrain.)

Staccato. Detached. Notes played sharply and singly. Opposite of *legato*.

Stop-time. In jazz, refers to choruses in which only the first chord of each change is played, *staccato*, as the accompaniment to a solo. In pop, refers to similar discontinuities, tacit bars, out-of-tempo pauses, etc.

Subdominant. The fourth degree of the diatonic scale; the triad on the fourth (IV) degree.

Submediant. The sixth degree of the diatonic scale; the triad on the sixth (VI) degree.

Supertonic. The second degree of the diatonic scale; the triad on the second (II) degree.

Suspension. Note in a chord which is held over, or played slightly late, so as to create a discord implying a resolving note or chord to follow.

Syncopation. Starting a note on a normally unaccented part of the bar and sustaining it into the normally accented part, so as give the effect of shifting the accent.

Tabla. Pair of skin-covered copper drums used in North Indian music, of which the left-hand (bass, or *bonya*) head is larger than the other (tenor) head.

Tambura. Long-necked fretless lute with four wire strings plucked by the fingers, used to provide a drone accompaniment in Indian music.

Tamla Motown. Two Detroit record labels, Tamla and Motown, launched in 1960 by Berry Gordy Jr., and marketed as one label in Britain and Europe. As a musical style, it was influenced by gospel and doo-wop with a particularly heavy off-beat (emphasised so as to appeal to white audiences). Commercially the most successful black label, Tamla Motown represents the acme of black pop, its success built on a roster of songwriting talents which included many of its major performing artists (e.g., Smokey Robinson, Marvin Gaye, Stevie Wonder).

Tape-op. Tea boy. Also: apprentice/assistant to the engineer (q.v.), responsible for mechanical tasks like threading tapes, preparing mikes and MIDI set-ups, running errands, and (occasionally) operating the tape-transport controls during recording.

Tessitura. (Italian = texture.) The part of a 'range' of a voice or instrument containing most of the notes to be performed. Thus the range of a piece may be high in terms of the voice or instrument, but the *tessitura* low or medium.

Timbre. Characteristic sound quality of a voice, instrument, or sample.

Timpani. Kettle drum(s).

Tom-toms ('toms'). The drums pitched between the snare and the bass-drum in the standard drum-kit. One or more small tom-toms are mounted on the bass-drum, one or more large or 'floor' tom-toms are free-standing to the drummer's right.

Tonic ('root'; key-note). The first degree of the diatonic scale; the triad on the first (I) degree.

Transpose. To raise or lower the key of a piece.

Track. (1) *n*. A recorded song. (2) *n*. One of the paths along the recording surface of the tape on a multitrack recorder, corresponding to an in-put channel on the mixing desk. (3) *vb*. To double-track (q.v.) a part already recorded on another channel/track.

Tremolo. (Italian = trembling.) Rapid reiteration of one note or oscillation between two notes. (Cf. vibrato.)

Triad. Three-note chord consisting of the root, third, and fifth.

Triplet. Three notes grouped in the space of two.

Trochee. (Verse.) Metrical foot consisting of a long followed by a short syllable. Opposite of *iamb*.

Vamp. To improvise an accompaniment.

Varispeed. Varying the capstan speed of the multitrack, or the metronome rate of a sequencer, to globally slow/quicken the tempo (thereby lowering/raising the key).

Verse. The main section of the song apart from the chorus. See Song structure.

Verse/chorus. See Chorus.

Vibrato. (Italian = 'vibrated'.) Rapid undulation of pitch by controlled vibration to give extra glamour of tone. (Cf. tremolo.)

VU meter. Volume Unit meter. A meter indicating volume by means of a needle swinging across a semicircular scale of measurement.

Wah-wah. Filter-effect unit in which the cut-off frequency is altered using a pedal, giving the characteristic underwater sound suggested by its name. The first significant use of the wah-wah was by Eric Clapton on Cream's *Tales of Brave Ulysses* (1967).

Walking bass. Regularly-spaced rising and falling bass-line, as in boogiewoogie but in crotchets.

White Noise. A random and dense accumulation of high frequency signals.

COMPACT DISCOGRAPHY

Alternative versions of tracks issued as part of the original Sixties discography are indicated with an asterisk; additional alternative versions are indicated with further asterisks. The letters/numbers applied to tracks issued in the 1994–6 supplementary discography indicate their chronological place within the original Sixties sequence.[1]

Please Please Me (CDP 746435-2) 1963
[6] I Saw Her Standing There; [8] Misery; [9b] Anna (Go To Him); [9d] Chains; [9c] Boys; [4] Ask Me Why; [3] Please Please Me ■ [1] Love Me Do; [2] P.S. I Love You; [9e] Baby It's You; [7] Do You Want To Know A Secret; [6b] A Taste Of Honey; [5] There's A Place; [9f] Twist And Shout

With The Beatles (CDP 746436-2) 1963
[14] It Won't Be Long; [18] All I've Got To Do; [15] All My Loving; [20] Don't Bother Me; [17] Little Child; [13e] Till There Was You; [13f] Please Mister Postman ■ [14b] Roll Over Beethoven; [9] Hold Me Tight; [13b] You Really Got A Hold On Me; [16] I Wanna Be Your Man; [13d] Devil In Her Heart; [19] Not A Second Time; [13c] Money

A Hard Day's Night (CDP 746437-2) 1964
[31] A Hard Day's Night; [26] I Should Have Known Better; [28] If I Fell; [29] I'm Happy Just To Dance With You; [25] And I Love Her; [27] Tell Me Why; [23] Can't Buy Me Love ■ [34] Any Time At All; [32] I'll Cry Instead; [35] Things We Said Today; [36] When I Get Home; [24] You Can't Do That; [33] I'll Be Back

Beatles For Sale (CDP 746438-2) 1964
[42] No Reply; [38] I'm A Loser; [37] Baby's In Black; [46c] Rock And Roll Music; [46] I'll Follow The Sun; [38b] Mr Moonlight; [44b] Kansas City/Hey, Hey, Hey, Hey ■ [43] Eight Days A Week; [46d] Words Of Love; [46e] Honey Don't; [39] Every Little Thing; [40] I Don't Want To Spoil The Party; [41] What You're Doing; [46b] Everybody's Trying To Be My Baby

Help! (CDP 746439-2) 1965
[56] Help!; [51] The Night Before; [53] You've Got To Hide Your Love Away; [49] I Need You; [48] Another Girl; [55] You're Going To Lose That Girl; [47] Ticket To Ride ■ [60b] Act Naturally; [60] It's Only Love; [52] You Like Me Too Much; [54] Tell Me What You See; [57] I've Just Seen A Face; [59] Yesterday; [56b] Dizzy Miss Lizzy

---

[1] See p.41: Note on the cataloguing system.

Rubber Soul (CDP 746440-2) 1965

[64] Drive My Car; [63] Norwegian Wood (This Bird Has Flown); [75] You Won't See Me; [69] Nowhere Man; [73] Think For Yourself; [74] The Word; [71] Michelle ■ [72] What Goes On; [76] Girl; [70] I'm Looking Through You; [67] In My Life; [61] Wait; [66] If I Needed Someone; [62] Run For Your Life

Revolver (CDP 746441-2) 1966

[84] Taxman; [86] Eleanor Rigby; [85] I'm Only Sleeping; [79] Love You To; [91] Here, There And Everywhere; [88] Yellow Submarine; [92] She Said She Said ■ [90] Good Day Sunshine; [83] And Your Bird Can Sing; [87] For No One; [82] Doctor Robert; [89] I Want To Tell You; [78] Got To Get You Into My Life; [77] Tomorrow Never Knows

Sgt. Pepper's Lonely Hearts Club Band (CDP 746442-2) 1967

[97] Sgt Pepper's Lonely Hearts Club Band; [107] With A Little Help From My Friends; [103] Lucy In The Sky With Diamonds; [104] Getting Better; [99] Fixing A Hole; [106] She's Leaving Home; [101] Being For The Benefit Of Mr Kite! ■ [105] Within You Without You; [94] When I'm Sixty-Four; [102] Lovely Rita; [98] Good Morning, Good Morning; [108] Sgt Pepper's Lonely Hearts Club Band (Reprise); [96] A Day In The Life

Magical Mystery Tour (CDP 748062-2) 1967

[109] Magical Mystery Tour; [117] The Fool On The Hill; [119] Flying; [118] Blue Jay Way; [115] Your Mother Should Know; [116] I Am The Walrus ■ [120] Hello Goodbye; [93] Strawberry Fields Forever; [95] Penny Lane; [110] Baby You're A Rich Man; [114] All You Need Is Love

The Beatles (CDP 7464443-2, 2 discs) 1968 ['The White Album']

[142] Back In The USSR; [143] Dear Prudence; [144] Glass Onion; [131] Ob-La-Di, Ob-La-Da; [141] Wild Honey Pie; [154] The Continuing Story Of Bungalow Bill; [136] While My Guitar Gently Weeps; [148] Happiness Is A Warm Gun ■ [151] Martha My Dear; [153] I'm So Tired; [128] Blackbird; [147] Piggies; [140] Rocky Raccoon; [126] Don't Pass Me By; [155] Why Don't We Do It In The Road?; [145] I Will; [156] Julia ■ [146] Birthday; [139] Yer Blues; [138] Mother Nature's Son; [129] Everybody's Got Something To Hide Except Me And My Monkey; [135] Sexy Sadie; [134] Helter Skelter; (152] Long, Long, Long ■ [125] Revolution 1; [149] Honey Pie; [150] Savoy Truffle; [133] Cry Baby Cry; [127] Revolution 9; [130] Good Night

Yellow Submarine (CDP 746445-2) 1969

[88] Yellow Submarine; [100] Only A Northern Song; [111] All Together Now; [124] Hey Bulldog; [113] It's All Too Much; [114] All You Need Is Love ■ Orchestral soundtrack by George Martin

Abbey Road (CDP 746446-2) 1969

[179] Come Together; [170] Something; [178] Maxwell's Silver Hammer; [166] Oh! Darling; [172] Octopus's Garden; [168] I Want You (She's So Heavy) ■

[177] Here Comes The Sun; [185] Because; [173] You Never Give Me Your Money; [181] Sun King; [182] Mean Mr Mustard; [183] Polythene Pam; [184] She Came In Through The Bathroom Window; [175] Golden Slumbers; [176] Carry That Weight; [180] The End; [174] Her Majesty

Let It Be (CDP 7464447-2) 1970

[161] Two Of Us; [157] Dig A Pony; [123] Across The Universe; [186] I Me Mine; [162] Dig It; [164] Let It Be; [161b] Maggie Mae ■ [158] I've Got A Feeling; [167] One After 909; [165] The Long And Winding Road; [163] For You Blue; [160] Get Back

Past Masters • Volume One (CDP 790043-2) 1988

[1] Love Me Do; [10] From Me To You; [11] Thank You Girl; [12] She Loves You; [13] I'll Get You; [21] I Want To Hold Your Hand; [22] This Boy; [21] Komm, Gib Mir Deine Hand; [12] Sie Liebt Dich; [29b] Long Tall Sally; [30] I Call Your Name; [32b] Slow Down; [31b] Matchbox; [45] I Feel Fine; [44] She's A Woman; [56c] Bad Boy; [50] Yes It Is; [58] I'm Down

Past Masters • Volume Two (CDP 790044-2) 1988

[65] Day Tripper; [68] We Can Work It Out; [80] Paperback Writer; [81] Rain; [122] Lady Madonna; [121] The Inner Light; [137] Hey Jude; [132] Revolution; [160] Get Back; [159] Don't Let Me Down; [171] The Ballad Of John And Yoko; [169] Old Brown Shoe; [123] Across The Universe; [164] Let It Be; [112] You Know My Name (Look Up The Number)

The Beatles 1962-66 (CDPCSP 717-2, 2 discs) 1993 ['The Red Album']

[1] Love Me Do; [3] Please Please Me; [10] From Me To You; [12] She Loves You; [21] I Want To Hold Your Hand; [15] All My Loving; [23] Can't Buy Me Love; [31] A Hard Day's Night; [25] And I Love Her; [43] Eight Days A Week; [45] I Feel Fine; [47] Ticket To Ride; [59] Yesterday ■ [56] Help!; [53] You've Got To Hide Your Love Away; [68] We Can Work It Out; [65] Day Tripper; [64] Drive My Car; [63] Norwegian Wood (This Bird Has Flown); [69] Nowhere Man; [71] Michelle; [67] In My Life; [76] Girl; [80] Paperback Writer; [86] Eleanor Rigby; [88] Yellow Submarine

The Beatles 1967-70 (CDPCSP 718-2, 2 discs) 1993 ['The Blue Album']

[93] Strawberry Fields Forever; [95] Penny Lane; [97] Sgt. Pepper's Lonely Hearts Club Band; [107] With A Little Help From My Friends; [103] Lucy In The Sky With Diamonds; [96] A Day In The Life; [114] All You Need Is Love; [116] I Am The Walrus; [120] Hello, Goodbye; [117] The Fool On The Hill; [109] Magical Mystery Tour; [122] Lady Madonna; [137] Hey Jude; [132] Revolution ■ [142] Back In The USSR; [136] While My Guitar Gently Weeps; [131] Ob-La-Di, Ob-La-Da; [160] Get Back; [159] Don't Let Me Down; [171] The Ballad Of John And Yoko; [169] Old Brown Shoe; [177] Here Comes The Sun; [179] Come Together; [170] Something; [172] Octopus's Garden; [164] Let It Be; [123] Across The Universe; [165] The Long And Winding Road

The Beatles Live At The BBC (831796-2, 2 discs) 1994

[10*] FROM US TO YOU; [U13p] I GOT A WOMAN; [U15e] TOO MUCH MONKEY BUSINESS; [U4b] KEEP YOUR HANDS OFF MY BABY; [U13] I'LL BE ON MY WAY; [U11b] YOUNG BLOOD; [U15d] A SHOT OF RHYTHM AND BLUES; [U11c] SURE TO FALL (IN LOVE WITH YOU); [U11e] SOME OTHER GUY; [11*] THANK YOU GIRL; [9e*] BABY IT'S YOU; [U13b] THAT'S ALL RIGHT (MAMA); [U13c] CAROL; [U13d] SOLDIER OF LOVE; [U13f] CLARABELLA; [U13k] I'M GONNA SIT RIGHT DOWN AND CRY (OVER YOU); [U13m][1] CRYING, WAITING, HOPING; [13b*] YOU REALLY GOT A HOLD ON ME; [U13n] TO KNOW HER IS TO LOVE HER; [6b*] A TASTE OF HONEY; [29b*] LONG TALL SALLY; [6*] I SAW HER STANDING THERE; [U13o] THE HONEYMOON SONG; [U22c] JOHNNY B GOODE; [U13s][2] MEMPHIS, TENNESSEE; [U15f] LUCILLE; [23*] CAN'T BUY ME LOVE; [13e*] TILL THERE WAS YOU ■ [31*] A HARD DAY'S NIGHT; [16*] I WANNA BE YOUR MAN; [14b*] ROLL OVER BEETHOVEN; [15*] ALL MY LOVING; [35*] THINGS WE SAID TODAY; [44*] SHE'S A WOMAN; [U13g] SWEET LITTLE SIXTEEN; [U13i] LONESOME TEARS IN MY EYES; [U13h] NOTHIN' SHAKIN; [U13t][3] THE HIPPY HIPPY SHAKE; [U13q] GLAD ALL OVER; [U13r] I JUST DON'T UNDERSTAND; [U13j] SO HOW COME (NO ONE LOVES ME); [45*] I FEEL FINE; [38*] I'M A LOSER; [46b*] EVERYBODY'S TRYING TO BE MY BABY; [46c*] ROCK AND ROLL MUSIC; [47*] TICKET TO RIDE; [56b*] DIZZY MISS LIZZY; [44b*] KANSAS CITY/HEY, HEY, HEY, HEY; [31b*] MATCHBOX; [U31c] I FORGOT TO REMEMBER TO FORGET; [U11d] I GOT TO FIND MY BABY; [U15b] OOH! MY SOUL; [U15c] DON'T EVER CHANGE; [32b*] SLOW DOWN; [46e*] HONEY DON'T; [1*] LOVE ME DO

Baby It's You (CDR 6406, CD-single) 1995

[9e*] BABY IT'S YOU; [46*] I'LL FOLLOW THE SUN; [13d*] DEVIL IN HER HEART; [9c*] BOYS

Anthology 1 (834445-2, 2 discs) 1995

[187] FREE AS A BIRD; [E1b] THAT'LL BE THE DAY; [E1] IN SPITE OF ALL THE DANGER; [E1c] HALLELUJAH, I LOVE HER SO; [E2] YOU'LL BE MINE; [E3] CAYENNE; [E3b] MY BONNIE; [E3c] AIN'T SHE SWEET; [E4] CRY FOR A SHADOW; [E6c] SEARCHIN'; [E6b] THREE COOL CATS; [E5b] THE SHEIK OF ARABY; [E5] LIKE DREAMERS DO; [E6] HELLO LITTLE GIRL; [E6d] BESAME MUCHO; [E7] LOVE ME DO;[4] [E7b] HOW DO YOU DO IT?; [3*] PLEASE PLEASE ME; [U12] ONE AFTER 909; [U13e] LEND ME YOUR COMB; [13*] I'LL GET YOU; [6**] I SAW HER STANDING THERE; [10**] FROM

---

[1] As a result of their release on *Live At The BBC*, sixteen hitherto unissued non-originals now come between [13] I'LL GET YOU (made on 1st July 1963) and [13b] YOU REALLY GOT A HOLD ON ME (begun on 18th July 1963). These are catalogued as [U13b]–[U13r]. Strictly speaking, CRYING, WAITING, HOPING should be [U13l] but, since this might be read as [U131], it is listed instead as [U13m].

[2] MEMPHIS, TENNESSEE was recorded a day after [13b] YOU REALLY GOT A HOLD ON ME, and logically should appear as [U13c]. However, [U13c] is already allotted to CAROL (see previous note). Rather than begin again with another system which might solve this uninteresting problem (suggestions will be ignored), I've included MEMPHIS, TENNESSEE in the [U13b]–[U13r] sequence. – I. M.

[3] Owing to the problem referred to in the preceding note, this track, which should have been listed as [U13f] (allotted to CLARABELLA), is treated instead as part of the [U13b]–[U13r] sequence.

[4] Audition version.

ME TO YOU; [13c*] MONEY; [13b**] YOU REALLY GOT A HOLD ON ME; [14b**]
ROLL OVER BEETHOVEN ■ [12*] SHE LOVES YOU; [13e**] TILL THERE WAS YOU; [9f*]
TWIST AND SHOUT; [22**] THIS BOY; [21*] I WANT TO HOLD YOUR HAND; [U22b]
MOONLIGHT BAY; [23**] CAN'T BUY ME LOVE; [15**] ALL MY LOVING; [24*] YOU
CAN'T DO THAT; [25*] AND I LOVE HER; [31**] A HARD DAY'S NIGHT; [16**] I
WANNA BE YOUR MAN; [29b**] LONG TALL SALLY; [9c**] BOYS; [U31b] SHOUT;
[33*] I'LL BE BACK; [U37] YOU KNOW WHAT TO DO; [42*] NO REPLY; [38b**] MR
MOONLIGHT; [U38c] LEAVE MY KITTEN ALONE; [42**] NO REPLY; [43*] EIGHT DAYS
A WEEK; [44b**] KANSAS CITY/HEY, HEY, HEY, HEY

Free As A Bird (882587-2, CD-single) 1995

[187] FREE AS A BIRD; [6***] I SAW HER STANDING THERE; [22*] THIS BOY; [U121]
CHRISTMAS TIME (IS HERE AGAIN)

Real Love (882646-2, CD-single) 1996

[188] REAL LOVE; [37*] BABY'S IN BLACK; [88*] YELLOW SUBMARINE; [91*] HERE, THERE
AND EVERYWHERE

Anthology 2 (834448-2, 2 discs) 1996

[188] REAL LOVE; [50*] YES IT IS; [58*] I'M DOWN; [53*] YOU'VE GOT TO HIDE YOUR
LOVE AWAY; [U54] IF YOU'VE GOT TROUBLE; [U56] THAT MEANS A LOT; [59*]
YESTERDAY; [60*] IT'S ONLY LOVE; [45**] I FEEL FINE; [47*] TICKET TO RIDE; [59**]
YESTERDAY; [56*] HELP!; [46b**] EVERYBODY'S TRYING TO BE MY BABY; [63*]
NORWEGIAN WOOD (THIS BIRD HAS FLOWN); [70*] I'M LOOKING THROUGH YOU;
[U73] 12-BAR ORIGINAL; [77*] TOMORROW NEVER KNOWS; [78*] GOT TO GET YOU
INTO MY LIFE; [83*] AND YOUR BIRD CAN SING; [84*] TAXMAN; [86*] ELEANOR
RIGBY; [85*] I'M ONLY SLEEPING; [46c**] ROCK AND ROLL MUSIC; [44**] SHE'S A
WOMAN ■ [93*] STRAWBERRY FIELDS FOREVER; [93**] STRAWBERRY FIELDS FOREVER;
[93***] STRAWBERRY FIELDS FOREVER; [95*] PENNY LANE; [96*] A DAY IN THE LIFE;
[98*] GOOD MORNING GOOD MORNING; [100*] ONLY A NORTHERN SONG; [101*]
BEING FOR THE BENEFIT OF MR KITE!; [103*] LUCY IN THE SKY WITH DIAMONDS;
[105*] WITHIN YOU WITHOUT YOU; [108*] SGT. PEPPER'S LONELY HEARTS CLUB
BAND (REPRISE); [112*] YOU KNOW MY NAME (LOOK UP THE NUMBER); [116*] I AM
THE WALRUS; [117*] THE FOOL ON THE HILL; [115*] YOUR MOTHER SHOULD KNOW;
[117**] THE FOOL ON THE HILL; [120*] HELLO, GOODBYE; [122*] LADY MADONNA;
[123*] ACROSS THE UNIVERSE

Anthology 3 (834451-2, 2 discs) 1996

'A BEGINNING'; [148*] HAPPINESS IS A WARM GUN; [134*] HELTER SKELTER; [182*]
MEAN MR MUSTARD; [183*] POLYTHENE PAM; [144*] GLASS ONION; [U125] JUNK;
[147*] PIGGIES; [149*] HONEY PIE; [126*] DON'T PASS ME BY; [131*] OB-LA-DI, OB-
LA-DA; [130*] GOOD NIGHT; [133*] CRY BABY CRY; [128*] BLACKBIRD; [135*] SEXY
SADIE; [136*] WHILE MY GUITAR GENTLY WEEPS; [137*] HEY JUDE; [U138] NOT
GUILTY; [138*] MOTHER NATURE'S SON; [144**] GLASS ONION; [140*] ROCKY
RACCOON; [U141*] WHAT'S THE NEW MARY JANE; [U146] STEP INSIDE LOVE; [U147]
LOS PARANOIAS; [153*] I'M SO TIRED; [145*] I WILL; [155*] WHY DON'T WE DO IT
IN THE ROAD?; [156*] JULIA ■ [158*] I'VE GOT A FEELING; [184*] SHE CAME IN
THROUGH THE BATHROOM WINDOW; [157*] DIG A PONY; [161*] TWO OF US; [163*]
FOR YOU BLUE; [U162] TEDDY BOY; [U164b] RIP IT UP; [U164c] SHAKE, RATTLE

AND ROLL; [U164d] BLUE SUEDE SHOES; [165★] THE LONG AND WINDING ROAD; [166★] OH! DARLING; [U168] ALL THINGS MUST PASS; [U166b] MAILMAN BRING ME NO MORE BLUES; [160★] GET BACK; [169★] OLD BROWN SHOE; [172★] OCTOPUS'S GARDEN; [178★] MAXWELL'S SILVER HAMMER; [170★] SOMETHING; [179★] COME TOGETHER; [U181] COME AND GET IT; [U181b] AIN'T SHE SWEET;[1] [185★] BECAUSE; [164★] LET IT BE; [186★] I ME MINE; [180★] THE END

---

[1] A different arrangement from [E3c].

INDEX OF SONGS AND KEYS

Figures in **bold** refer to main treatments

INDEX TO MAIN TEXT